American History:
A Survey

Volume II: Since 1865

Richard N. Current

University of North Carolina at Greensboro

T. Harry Williams

Louisiana State University

Frank Freidel

Harvard University

*New pictorial essays on "The Course of American Art"
by Gerald Bernstein, Brandeis University*

Fourth Edition

American History

A Survey

Volume II: Since 1865

ALFRED · A · KNOPF

New York

To the Memory of William Best Hesseltine

(1902 – 1963)

THIS IS A BORZOI BOOK   PUBLISHED BY ALFRED A. KNOPF, INC.

Fourth Edition
98765432
Copyright © 1959, 1961, 1964, 1966, 1971, 1975 by Richard N. Current, T. Harry
Williams, Frank Freidel

Library of Congress Cataloging in Publication Data

Current, Richard Nelson.
  American history: a survey.

  Based on A history of the United States, by
T. H. Williams, R. N. Current, and F. Freidel.
  Includes bibliographical references.
  1. United States – History. I. Williams, Thomas
Harry, 1909 –   joint author. II. Freidel, Frank
Burt, joint author. III. Williams, Thomas Harry,
1909 –   A history of the United States. IV. Title.
[E178.1.C93   1975b]   973   74-19278
ISBN 0-394-31864-1 (v. I)
ISBN 0-394-31865 -x (v. II)

MANUFACTURED IN THE UNITED STATES OF AMERICA

**Published 1961, reprinted five times   Second edition, 1966; reprinted
three times   Third edition, 1971; reprinted four times
Fourth edition, 1975**

Cartographic consultants:

David Ward
Randall Sale
University of Wisconsin

Douglas McManis
Columbia University

Cartographic additions and revisions:

Jean Paul Tremblay

Cover art by Gerald McConnell

Preface

Editor's note: In order to provide an alternative format for those who find it inconvenient to use the one-volume hardcover edition of American History: A Survey, *Fourth Edition, the same text is also being made available in this two-volume paperbound edition. Except for the addition of separate indexes for each volume, the contents of this edition are exactly the same as those of the one-volume hardcover edition. Also, Chapter 16, "Reconstructing the Nation," has been included both at the end of Volume I and at the beginning of Volume II, so that the semester or quarter break can be conveniently made at either 1865 or 1877. The* Instructor's Manual *that accompanies the one-volume edition applies equally well to this edition.*

During the four years since the previous edition of this book appeared, a good deal of new history has been made—new history both in the sense of actual events and in the sense of scholarly writings. In revising the book, we have extended our account to include recent events, and we have made numerous changes throughout in order to reflect developments in historical scholarship. In particular, we have given increased attention to the role of minorities and of women in American history.

We have revised not only the text itself but also the special features. We have replaced a number of the "boxes" containing excerpts from historical records of various kinds and thus introducing the student to aspects of the past as it was experienced by people of the time. We have incorporated some of the latest views in our historiographical essays, "Where Historians Disagree," which acquaint the student with some of the continuing conflicts of interpretation among historians. To this series we have added an essay, "Why Historians Disagree," to suggest reasons for and limits to the differences in interpretation. Gerald Bernstein, an expert in art history, has provided a completely new series of pictorial essays on "The Course of American Art." These inserts, with pictures in full color and with a running commentary, provide a synopsis of trends in art and architecture.

In the text proper, over half of the illustrations have been freshly chosen for this edition. Several new maps have been drawn, and some of the others have been redrawn in the interest of clarity and informativeness. A few of the charts and graphs are new. Bibliographies and appendices have been brought up to date.

In the work of revision we have had the benefit of editorial expertise provided by Alfred A. Knopf, Incorporated. We wish particularly to thank Helen D. Litton, who as project editor of this edition has had a truly creative part in its production. We have been immeasurably aided by historical scholars, experts in their respective fields, who have examined and criticized parts of our earlier editions. For the sake of objectivity, some of these scholars have made their critiques without our being informed of their names. Since it is impossible to identify all the critics, we have decided to identify none of them, but we cannot forgo this opportunity to extend to all of them our most sincere thanks. We have been greatly helped also by users of the text, students as well as instructors, who have sent us criticisms and corrections. To these sharp-eyed and well informed readers, too, we wish to express our profound gratitude. We shall continue to be grateful for suggestions regarding corrections or other improvements to be made in future reprintings and revisions.

R.N.C.
T.H.W.
F.F.

Contents

THE COURSE OF AMERICAN ART

WHERE HISTORIANS DISAGREE

Illustrations

Maps

Charts

American History:
A Survey

Volume II: Since 1865

Reconstructing the Nation

Sixteen

When Americans of a later generation looked back on the 1860s and 1870s, it seemed to many of them that there had been a sharp break between the Civil War and the ensuing period of Reconstruction. The war itself, for all its suffering and sacrifice, was remembered on the whole as an ennobling experience, one of high purpose and gallantry on both sides. The postwar years, by contrast, appeared to have been a time of low, unscrupulous politics, a time when vengeful men among the victors disgraced the country while unnecessarily delaying a real, heartfelt reunion of the North and the South.

That view contains elements of historical reality, but it misses an essential truth about the troubled postwar period. The struggle over Reconstruction was, in part, a continuation of the Civil War. It was a struggle, as the war had been, that involved (among other things) the question of both state rights and human rights. The victory for Union and emancipation had not been completely won at Appomattox. In the postwar years an effort was made to confirm the supremacy of the national government over the Southern states and to assure the benefits of freedom to the millions of emancipated slaves. This effort, provoking resistance as it did, had the effect of keeping the country psychologically divided.

Politicians on both sides added to the divisive effect by playing upon the hatreds left over from the war. Republicans implied that all Democrats, Northern as well as Southern, had been traitors. "Every man that shot Union soldiers was a Democrat," a typical Republican orator declaimed. "The man that assassinated Abraham Lincoln was a Democrat." This technique of reviving wartime emotions in order to win postwar elections came to be known, among Democrats, as "waving the bloody shirt." But in the South the Democrats waved a bloody shirt of their own. They denounced their opponents, black and

"Worse than Slavery"
During Reconstruction the blacks of the South suffered at the hands of white supremacists, as depicted in this 1874 wood engraving by Thomas Nast. The greatest American political cartoonist of the nineteenth century, Bavarian-born Nast made the elephant and donkey the symbols respectively of the Republican and Democratic parties. (Library of Congress)

417

white, as desecrators of the Confederate cause. The Ku Klux Klan, an anti-Republican terrorist group, pretended that its members were ghosts of the Confederate army.

The struggle over Reconstruction ended in the Compromise of 1877. This arrangement, a combination of "reunion and reaction," brought the sections together at the expense of the Negro. The federal government gave up the attempt to enforce the Negro's rights and left the Southern states in the hands of the Democrats. Yet two great charters of human liberty still stood as documents of the Reconstruction era—the Fourteenth and Fifteenth amendments to the federal Constitution—which had been intended to assure citizenship and the suffrage to the former slaves. For the time being, these documents were disregarded, but a day was to come, several decades later, when they would provide the legal basis for a renewed drive to bring true freedom and equality to all Americans.

The Problem of Peacemaking

The Constitution provides for peacemaking at the end of a foreign war. The President, with the advice and consent of the Senate, ratifies a treaty of peace. But the Constitution naturally makes no provision for ending a civil war. And Lincoln could not negotiate a treaty with Confederate leaders, for that would mean recognizing the legal existence of the Confederacy. Yet, once the armies had stopped fighting, a peace arrangement somehow had to be made.

RECONSTRUCTION: THE ISSUES

The word "Reconstruction," as contemporaries used it, referred to the process by which peace was to be made, that is, the process by which the states of the defeated Confederacy were to be brought back to their former places in the Union. One possibility would be to grant easy terms, permitting the states to return promptly and with little internal change except for the elimination of slavery. Another possibility would be to make a harsh peace, delaying the readmission of the states until they had been reconstructed in such a way as to reduce the power of the rebel leaders.

A quick and easy restoration of the Union would be to the advantage of the former Confederates and the Democratic party North and South. Ironically, the abolition of slavery would increase the power of the Southern states in national politics. In the past, under the "three-fifths clause" of the Constitution, only three-fifths of the slaves had been counted in determining a state's representation in Congress and its electoral votes in presidential elections. In the future, *all* the former slaves would be counted, whether or not they themselves were given political rights. A state such as South Carolina, where about half of the population was black, would have its congressional representation increased, for example, by approximately 20 percent. With this added strength the Southern Democrats could rejoin the Northern Democrats and get control of both Congress and the presidency.

The consequences of an easy peace, by the same token, could be disastrous for the Republican party. The Republicans had gained control of the federal government in 1860–1861 only because of the split in the Democratic party and the secession of the Southern states. Once these had been restored and the Democratic party had been reunited, the Republicans would face the uncomfortable prospect of being reduced to a minority group once again. The outlook was disturbing also for Northern businessmen who during the war had obtained favors from the federal government—a high tariff, railroad subsidies, the national banking system—which might be ended once the Democrats were back in power.

For the Negroes emerging from slavery, a quick restoration of the Southern states would be catastrophic. The master class, which had dominated the state governments before and during the war, would continue to do so. The Negroes then could expect to be kept in a position that, at best, would be somewhere between slavery and freedom.

Thus the issues of Reconstruction were very similar to those of the war itself. So far as the Southern leaders were concerned, the war had been fought for the independence of the South and for the preservation of slavery (in 1861 the Confederate Vice President, Alexander H. Stephens, had frankly proclaimed that slavery was the "cornerstone" of the Confederacy). After the war these leaders hoped to maintain a considerable degree of Southern autonomy through the assertion of state rights, and they hoped to retain much of the essence of slavery by finding some substitute for it. If they should have their way in Reconstruction, the "lost cause" they had fought for would not be completely lost.

The issues were often obscured and complicated by the emotionalism of the controversy over Reconstruction. On both sides people approached the question in a spirit of hatred left over from the four years of bloodshed. In the North there was the memory of sacrifice, suffering, and personal loss; in the South there was even more of that, plus the added bitterness of defeat. In the North there was a widespread feeling that Southerners ought to be required to acknowledge their defeat by some gesture of submission, and that at least a few of them ought to be punished for their guilt in bringing on the war and also for the atrocities which, according to Northern wartime propaganda, they had committed in the course of it. Moreover, there was a general conviction that the former slaves ought to be protected in their freedom and assured of justice. And there was a growing belief that Reconstruction offered a heaven-sent opportunity to recast the South in the image of the North—to take that supposedly backward, feudal, undemocratic section and civilize and modernize it.

The Reconstruction question was further complicated by disputes over the respective roles that the President and Congress were to play. Presumably, the task should have been one for the executive and the legislative branches, the two acting in cooperation. As it happened, however, the President and the congressional majority differed on the policy to be followed. Hence arose the issue of presidential as opposed to congressional powers.

Even among the majority in Congress—the Republicans—there was disagreement as to the kind of peace that should be imposed upon the South. The same factions of the party (the Conservatives and the Radicals) that had clashed on wartime emancipation now confronted each other on the issue of Reconstruction. The Conservatives advocated a mild peace and the rapid restoration of the defeated states to the Union; beyond insisting that the South accept the abolition of slavery, they would not interfere with race relations or attempt to alter the social system of the South. The Radicals, directed by leaders like Thaddeus Stevens of Pennsylvania and Charles Sumner of Massachusetts, stood for a hard peace; they urged that the civil and military chieftains of the late Confederacy be subjected to severe punishment, that large numbers of Southern whites be disfranchised, and that the property of rich Southerners who had aided the Confederacy be confiscated and distributed among the freedmen. From the first, some Radicals favored granting suffrage to the former slaves, as a matter of right or as a means of creating a Republican electorate in the South. Other Radicals agreed with them, but hesitated to state a position for fear of public opinion— not all Northern states permitted Negroes to vote.

Between the Radicals and the Conservatives stood a faction of uncommitted Republicans who may be termed the Moderates. They would go further than the Conservatives in demanding concessions of the South, particularly in regard to rights for Negroes, but they rejected the punitive goals of the Radicals. As the Reconstruction controversy developed, the pressure of events would inexorably force the Moderates into the Radical camp.

The various proponents of a Reconstruction policy, following an honored American tradition, attempted to buttress their position with constitutional sanction. The Conservatives, claiming that secession was illegal, contended that the seceded states had never legally been out of the Union, were still in it, and had all the rights of states. The Radicals, the uncompromising nationalists of the war, now insisted that the Southern states had in fact withdrawn from the nation and had therefore forfeited their rights as states. Sumner argued that by seceding they had committed "state suicide," and Stevens bluntly referred to them as "conquered provinces." On the other hand, Southerners who had fought to uphold the right of secession now demanded all the privileges they had previously enjoyed in the Union they had tried to dissolve.

LINCOLN'S PLAN

The process of Reconstruction was put into motion while the war was still going on, and the first plan was presented by President Lincoln. He believed there were a considerable number of actual or potential Unionists in the South. These people, most of them former Whigs, could possibly be encouraged to rejoin the old Whigs of the North and thus strengthen the Republican party, once the Union had been restored. More immediately, these men could serve as the nucleus for setting up new and loyal states in the South and thereby hastening reunion. All along, Lincoln was concerned with principle as well as politics: the principle of the inviolability of the Union. He wanted to restore the American experiment in democracy as soon as possible. Consequently, he proposed an easy mode of Reconstruction. He would subordinate to his larger goal such questions as punishment of the defeated side or determination of the status of the freedmen. The question of whether the defeated states were in or out of the Union he dismissed as a "merely pernicious abstraction." They were only out of their proper, practical relationship to the Union, he said, and they should be restored to that relationship as soon as possible.

Specifically, Lincoln's plan, which he announced to the public in a proclamation of December 1863, offered a general amnesty to all who would take an oath pledging future loyalty to the government. Temporarily excluded from the right to swear the oath were high civil and military officials of the Confederacy. Whenever in any state 10 percent of the number of voters in 1860 took the oath, they could proceed to set up a state government. The oath required acceptance of the wartime acts and proclamations of Congress and the President concerning slavery. This was the only provision in the plan that imposed on the South a condition for readmission and the only part of the plan that dealt with national supervision of race relations. Instead of demanding outright abolition (the Thirteenth Amendment had not yet been passed, and the postwar effect of the Emancipation Proclamation was uncertain, since it was a war measure), Lincoln told Southern leaders that he hoped they would provide for permanent freedom. He also urged them to give the ballot to at least a few Negroes—to those who were educated, owned property, and had served in the Union army. In three Southern states—Louisiana, Arkansas, and Tennessee—loyal governments were reestablished under the Lincoln formula in 1864.

The Radical Republicans were angered and astonished at the mildness of Lincoln's program, and they were able to induce Congress to repudiate his governments. Representatives from the Lincoln states were not admitted to Congress, and the electoral vote of those states was not counted in the election of 1864. In defeating Lincoln's plan, the Radicals were aided by a number of Moderate Republicans who thought that the President's scheme did not provide adequate protection for the freedmen. The Radicals could not stop, however, with a rejection of Lincoln's plan. The requirements of politics dictated that they produce a plan of their own. But at the moment the Radicals had not thought the Reconstruction problem through. They were not agreed as to how "hard" a peace they should enforce on the South, and they were not certain that Northern opinion would support the ideas of their more extreme leaders.

Under pressure, they prepared and passed (in July 1864) the Wade-Davis Bill, which may be considered the first Radical plan of Reconstruction. By its provisions, the President was to appoint for each conquered state a provisional governor who would take a census of all adult white males. If a majority of those enrolled—instead of Lincoln's 10 percent—swore an oath of allegiance, the governor was to call an election for a state constitutional convention. The privilege of voting for delegates to this meeting was limited to those who could swear that they had never borne arms against the United States, the so-called iron-clad oath. The convention was required to put provisions into the new constitution abolishing slavery, disfranchising Confederate civil and military leaders, and repudiating the Confederate and state war debts. After these conditions had been met, Congress would readmit the state to the Union. The Wade-Davis Bill was more drastic in almost every respect than the Lincoln plan, and it assumed that the seceded states were out of the Union and hence under the dictation of Congress. But the bill, like the President's proposal, left up to the states the question of political rights for Negroes.

The Wade-Davis Bill was passed a few days before Congress adjourned, which enabled Lincoln to dispose of it with a pocket veto. His action enraged the authors of the measure, Benjamin F. Wade and Henry Winter Davis, who issued a blistering denunciation of the veto, the Wade-Davis Manifesto, warning the President not to interfere with the powers of Congress to control Reconstruction. Lincoln could not ignore the bitterness and the strength of the Radical opposition. Practical as always, he realized that he would have to accept some of the objections of the Radicals. He began to move toward a new approach to Reconstruction, possibly one that included greater national supervision of the freedmen.

What plan he would have come up with nobody can say. On April 14, 1865, a crazed actor, John Wilkes Booth, under the delusion that he was helping the South, shot the President in a Washington theater. Lincoln died early the following morning, and because of the circumstances of his death—the heroic leader, the Great Emancipator struck down in the hour of victory by an assassin—he achieved immediate martyrdom. In the wild excitement of the hour, it was widely assumed that Booth had been instigated to his mad act by men in the South, and the Radicals played on this theme with reckless charges implicating high Confederates. Ironically, Lincoln's death helped to kill his policy of a generous peace.

JOHNSON AND "RESTORATION"

The conservative leadership in the controversy over Reconstruction fell upon Lincoln's successor, Andrew Johnson. Of all the men who accidentally inherited the presidency, Johnson was undoubtedly the most unfortunate. A Southerner and former slaveholder, he became President as a bloody war against the South was drawing to a close. A Democrat before he had been placed on the Union ticket with Lincoln in 1864, he became the head of a Republican administration at a time when partisan passions, held in some restraint during the war, were about to rule the government. As if these handicaps of background were not enough, Johnson was intemperate in language and tactless in manner, and he lacked Lincoln's skill in handling people. Unlike Lincoln, he was theoretical rather than practical, dogmatic rather than pragmatic. In dealing with Reconstruction, he stood righteously by the Constitution,

even though that document obviously did not envision the unprecedented constitutional situation that existed after the war.

Johnson revealed his plan of Reconstruction—or "Restoration," as he preferred to call it—soon after he took office, and he proceeded to execute it during the summer of 1865 when Congress was not in session. He applied it to the eight states of the late Confederacy that had not come under the Lincoln plan; he recognized as legal organizations the Lincoln governments in Louisiana, Arkansas, Tennessee, and Virginia.

In some ways Johnson's scheme resembled Lincoln's; in others it was similar to the Wade-Davis Bill. Like his predecessor, Johnson assumed that the seceded states were still in the Union, and, also like Lincoln, he an-

Andrew Johnson
Born in North Carolina, Johnson moved to Tennessee as a young man and worked as a tailor before going into politics. He had a dark complexion and piercing black eyes. A powerful orator on the stump, he easily lost his temper when heckled and used crude and intemperate language. Sincerely devoted to his principles, he was sometimes too theoretical in upholding them. (Library of Congress)

nounced his design in a proclamation of amnesty that extended pardon for past conduct to all who would take an oath of allegiance. Denied the privilege of taking the oath until they received individual pardons from the President were high-ranking Confederate officials and also men with land worth $20,000 or more; Johnson excluded a larger number of leaders than Lincoln had. For each state the President appointed a provisional governor who was to invite the qualified voters to elect delegates to a constitutional convention. Johnson did not specify that a minimum number of voters had to take the oath, as had the Lincoln and Wade-Davis proposals, but the implication was plain that he would require a majority. As conditions of readmittance, the state had to revoke the ordinance of secession, abolish slavery and ratify the Thirteenth Amendment, and repudiate the Confederate and state war debts – essentially the same stipulations that had been laid down in the Wade-Davis Bill. The final procedure before restoration was for a state to elect a state government and send representatives to Congress.

By the end of 1865 the states affected by Johnson's plan had complied with its requirements. Indeed, if the Lincoln governments are included, all of the seceded states had been reconstructed and were ready to resume their places in the Union – if Congress chose to recognize them when it met in December 1865. Recognition of the Johnson governments was exactly what the Radicals were determined to prevent. And many people in the North agreed with them that Reconstruction was being rushed too fast and was being accomplished too easily.

Northerners were disturbed by the seeming reluctance of some members of the Southern conventions to abolish slavery and by the refusal of all the conventions to grant suffrage to even a few Negroes. They were astounded that states claiming to be "loyal" should elect as state officials and representatives to Congress prominent leaders of the recent Confederacy. Particularly hard to understand was Georgia's choice of Alexander H. Stephens, former Vice President of the Confederacy, as a United States senator.

Radical Reconstruction

When Congress met in December 1865, it denied admission to the senators and representatives from the states that President Andrew Johnson had "restored." The Radical leaders explained that the Southerners should be excluded until Congress knew more about conditions in the South. Congress must first be assured that the former Confederates had accepted the results of the war and that Southern Negroes and loyal whites were safe. Accordingly, Congress set up the Joint Committee on Reconstruction to investigate opinions in the South and to advise Congress in laying down a Reconstruction policy.

CONGRESS TAKES OVER

During the next few months the Radicals, though disagreeing among themselves, advanced toward a more severe program than their first plan, the Wade-Davis Bill of 1864, which left to the states the question of what rights the freed slaves should have. The Radicals gained the support of moderate Republicans because of Johnson's intransigent attitude. Johnson insisted that Congress had no right even to consider a policy for the South until his own plan had been accepted and the Southern congressmen and senators had been admitted.

Northern opinion was aroused by the so-called Black Codes, which the Southern legislatures adopted during the sessions of 1865–1866. These measures were the South's solution for the problem of the free Negro laborer, and they were also the South's substitute for slavery as a white supremacy device. Economically, the codes were intended to regulate the labor of a race that, in the opinion of the whites, would not work except under some kind of compulsion. Although the economic provisions varied in stringency from state to state, they all authorized local officials to apprehend unemployed Negroes, fine them for vagrancy, and hire them out to private employers to satisfy the fine. Some of the codes tried to force Negroes to work on the plantations by forbidding

The Black Code of Louisiana

The sections in the Black Codes regulating Negro labor angered Northern opinion and turned many people in favor of Radical Reconstruction. The Louisiana Code had this to say:

Sec. 1. Be it enacted by the Senate and House of Representatives of the State of Louisiana in general assembly convened, That all persons employed as laborers in agricultural pursuits shall be required, during the first ten days of the month of January of each year, to make contracts for labor for the then ensuing year, or for the year next ensuing the termination of their present contracts. All contracts for labor for agricultural purposes shall be made in writing, signed by the employer, and shall be made in the presence of a Justice of the Peace and two disinterested witnesses, in whose presence the contract shall be read to the laborer, and when assented to and signed by the latter, shall be considered as binding for the time prescribed. . . .

Sec. 2. Every laborer shall have full and perfect liberty to choose his employer, but, when once chosen, he shall not be allowed to leave his place of employment until the fulfillment of his contract . . . and if they do so leave, without cause or permission, they shall forfeit all wages earned to the time of abandonment. . . .

---

them to own or lease farms or to take other jobs except as domestic servants. Socially, the codes were designed to govern relations between the races and to invest the Negroes with a legal although subordinate status. The acts conferred certain civil rights upon blacks, but they also placed special restrictions on Negroes that did not apply to whites. To the South, the Black Codes were a realistic approach to a great social problem. To the North, they seemed to herald a return to slavery.

An appropriate agency for offsetting the Black Codes was the Freedmen's Bureau, but its scheduled year of existence was about to end. It had been losing some of its original functions. With the passing of the immediate postwar emergency, there was decreasing need for the bureau's relief activities. And President Johnson had been pardoning so many former rebels – thus restoring to them their confiscated plantations – that there was less and less land available for resettling former slaves.

In February 1866 Congress passed a bill to prolong the life of the bureau and to widen its powers by authorizing special courts for settling labor disputes. Thus the bureau could set aside work agreements that might be forced upon Negroes under the Black Codes. Johnson vetoed the bill, denouncing it as unconstitutional.

In April Congress again struck at the Black Codes by passing the Civil Rights Bill, which made United States citizens of Negroes and

empowered the federal government to intervene in state affairs when necessary for protecting the rights of citizens. Johnson vetoed this bill, too. With Moderates and Radicals acting together, Congress had the necessary two-thirds majority, and it promptly overrode the veto. Then, despite another veto, Congress repassed the Freedmen's Bureau Bill.

Emboldened by their evident support in Congress, the Radicals now struck again, and harder. The Joint Committee on Reconstruction submitted to Congress in April 1866 a proposed amendment to the Constitution, the Fourteenth, which constituted the second Radical plan of Reconstruction.

The Fourteenth Amendment, which was adopted by Congress and sent to the states for approval in the early summer, is so important, both in its immediate bearing upon Reconstruction and in its future influence upon federal-state relationships, as to deserve particular analysis.

Section 1 declared that all persons born or naturalized in the United States were citizens of the United States and of the state of their residence. This clause, which set up for the first time a national definition of citizenship, was followed by a statement that no state could abridge the rights of citizens of the United States or deprive any person of life, liberty, or property without due process of law or deny to any person within its jurisdiction the equal protection of the laws.

Section 2 provided that if a state denied the suffrage to any of its adult male inhabitants, its representation in the House of Representatives and the electoral college should suffer a proportionate reduction. This clause was intended to be a corrective to the curious effect of emancipation upon the basis of representation, by which every Southern state stood to increase its influence in the national government.

Section 3 disqualified from any state or federal office persons who had previously taken an oath to support the Constitution and later had aided the Confederacy — until Congress by a two-thirds vote of each house should remove their disability.

The Southern legislatures knew that if they ratified the amendment their states would be readmitted and Reconstruction probably would be ended. But they could not bring themselves to approve the measure, mainly because of Section 3, which put a stigma on their late leaders. Johnson himself advised Southerners to defeat the amendment. Only Tennessee, of the former Confederate states, ratified it, thus winning readmittance. The other ten, joined by Kentucky and Delaware, voted it down.

The amendment thus failed to receive the required approval of three-fourths of the states and was defeated — but only temporarily. When the time was more propitious, the Radicals would bring it up again. Meanwhile, its rejection by the South strengthened the Radical cause. To many people in the North, the amendment had seemed to be a reasonable and moderate proposal.

Public acceptance of the Radical program was strikingly manifested in the elections of 1866. This was essentially a contest for popular support between Johnson and the Radicals. The Radicals could point to recent events in the South — bloody race riots in which Negroes were the victims — as further evidence of the inadequacy of Johnson's policy. Johnson harmed his own cause by the intemperate, brawling speeches he made on a stumping tour from Washington to Chicago and back. The voters returned to Congress an overwhelming majority of Republicans, most of them of the Radical variety. In the Senate the line-up of the parties was 42 Republicans to 11 Democrats; in the House, 143 Republicans to 49 Democrats. Now the Republicans could enact any kind of

Reconstruction plan they could themselves agree on. Confidently they looked forward to the struggle with Johnson that would ensue when Congress assembled in December 1866 — and to their final victory over the President.

THE CONGRESSIONAL PLAN

After compromising differences among themselves and with the Moderates, the Radicals formulated their third plan of Reconstruction in three bills that passed Congress in the early months of 1867. All three were vetoed by Johnson and repassed. As these Reconstruction Acts were really parts of one piece, their provisions may be studied as a unit.

This plan was based squarely on the principle that the seceded states had lost their political identity. The Lincoln-Johnson governments were declared to have no legal standing, and the ten seceded states (Tennessee was now out of the Reconstruction process) were combined into five military districts. Each district was to be put in the charge of a military commander, supported by troops, who was to prepare his provinces for readmission as states. To this end, he was to have made a registration of voters, which was to include all adult Negro males and white males who were not disqualified for participation in rebellion. The whites who were excluded were those coming under the disability of the Fourteenth Amendment; but each voter had to swear a complicated loyalty oath, and the registrars were empowered to reject white men on the suspicion that they were not acting in good faith.

After the registration was completed in each province, the commanding general was to call on the voters to elect a convention to prepare a new state constitution that had to provide for Negro suffrage. If this document were ratified by the voters, elections for a state government could be held. Finally, if Congress approved the constitution, if the state legislature ratified the Fourteenth Amendment, and if this amendment were adopted by the required number of states and became a part of the Constitution — then the state was to be restored to the Union.

By 1868 six of the former Confederate states — Arkansas, North Carolina, South Carolina, Louisiana, Alabama, and Florida — had

The Nature of Reconstruction

Historical writing on Reconstruction, even more controversial than that on the Civil War, similarly reflects the patterns of thought that have prevailed from time to time. The first professional historian of Reconstruction, William A. Dunning, who taught at Columbia University from the 1880s to the 1920s, carried on his work during a period when scholars generally held that certain racial and ethnic groups were inherently superior to others. Dunning assumed that Negroes were inferior and hence unfit to receive the vote. Many of his students wrote books dealing with Reconstruction in particular states, and he himself provided a general account, *Reconstruction, Political and Economic* (1907), which for many years was accepted as authoritative. According to Dunning and the members of the "Dunning school," the Republicans imposed their Radical program upon the South mainly to keep their party in power. (Some later writers, notably Howard K. Beale, added an economic motive—to protect Northern business interests.) Under the Radical plan, the Southern states suffered the agonies of "bayonet rule" and "Negro rule," when with army support the blacks and their unscrupulous white accomplices plundered the people in an unbelievable orgy of corruption, ruinous taxation, and astronomical increases in the public debt.

The first historian seriously to challenge the Dunning interpretation was the Negro scholar William E. B. Du Bois. In an article in the *American Historical Review* (1910) Du Bois pointed out that the misdeeds of the Reconstruction state governments had been exaggerated and their achievements overlooked. These governments were expensive, he explained, because they undertook to provide public education and other public services on a scale never before attempted in the South. In a long book, *Black Reconstruction* (1935), Du Bois described Reconstruction politics in the Southern states as an effort on the part of the masses, black and white, to create a true democratic society. Writing under the influence of Marxism, he assumed a class consciousness for which few other historians could find much evidence.

By the 1940s the attitudes toward race, on the part of scholars at least, had drastically changed. Since that time a new generation of historians has arisen—among them C. Vann Woodward, John Hope Franklin, Eric McKitrick, and John and La Wanda Cox—who assume that the freedmen of the 1860s and 1870s, despite the handicaps of their previous servitude, were by nature quite capable of participating in self-government. According to the new historians, the Radical Republicans were motivated less by partisan or economic interests than by a determination to guarantee basic rights to the former slaves and thus to secure the war aims of reunion and freedom. There was little if anything in the South that could properly be called either military rule or Negro rule, and the Negro, carpetbagger, and scalawag politicians were at least as honest and capable as others of their time. The mistake in Reconstruction was not the attempt to confer civil and political rights upon blacks, but the failure to provide an adequate economic and educational basis and sufficient governmental protection for the assurance of those rights. The recent views are ably synthesized in Kenneth M. Stampp, *The Era of Reconstruction* (1965).

complied with the process of restoration outlined in the Reconstruction Acts and were readmitted to the Union. Delaying tactics by the whites held up the return of Mississippi, Virginia, Georgia, and Texas until 1870. These four laggard states had to meet an additional requirement, which with the existing requirements constituted the fourth and final congressional plan of Reconstruction. They had to ratify another constitutional amendment, the Fifteenth, which forbade the states and the federal government to deny the suffrage to any citizen on account of "race, color, or previous condition of servitude."

The great majority of the Northern states still denied the suffrage to Negroes at the time when the Reconstruction Acts granted it to Negroes in the Southern states. Recent attempts to give the vote to Northern blacks by amending the state constitutions had met with practically no success. Hence an amendment to the federal Constitution seemed necessary. Its sponsors were motivated by both idealistic and practical considerations. They would be consistent in extending to the Negro in the North a right they had already given to him elsewhere. At the same time they would be putting into the Constitution, where it would be safe from congressional repeal, the basis of Republican strength in the South. They were also concerned with the party's future in the North. A warning of trouble ahead had appeared in the state elections of 1867 in Pennsylvania, Ohio, and Indiana, all of which went Democratic that year. "We must establish the doctrine of national jurisdiction over all the states in state matters of the franchise," the Radical leader Thaddeus Stevens now concluded. "We must thus bridle Pennsylvania, Ohio, Indiana et cetera, or the South *being in,* we shall drift into Democracy." In several of the Northern states the Negro vote, though small, would be large enough to decide close elections in favor of the Republicans.

A number of the Northern and border states refused to approve the Fifteenth Amendment, and it was adopted only with the support of the four Southern states that had to ratify it in order to be readmitted to the Union. In the case of both the Fourteenth and Fifteenth amendments, the Southern states were deemed capable of ratifying even while they were not otherwise recognized as states and had no representation in Congress.

CONGRESSIONAL SUPREMACY

The Radicals thought of themselves as architects of a revolution, and they did not intend to let either the executive or the judiciary get in their way. They were prepared, if necessary, to establish a kind of congressional dictatorship.

To curb the President, and also to facilitate Radical administration of the acts of 1867, Congress passed two remarkable laws. One, the Tenure of Office Act (1867), forbade the President to remove civil officials, including members of his cabinet, without the consent of the Senate. Its principal purpose was to protect the job of Secretary of War Edwin M. Stanton, who was cooperating with the Radicals. The other law, the Command of the Army Act (1867), prohibited the President from issuing military orders except through the commanding general of the army (General Grant), whose headquarters were to be in Washington and who could not be relieved or assigned elsewhere without the consent of the Senate.

The Supreme Court, under Chief Justice Salmon P. Chase, declared in *Ex parte Milligan* (1866) that military tribunals were unconstitutional in places where civil courts were functioning. Although the decision was applied to a case originating in the war, it seemed to threaten the system of military government that the Radicals were planning for the South. Radical anger at the Court was instant and intense. In Congress proposals were made to require a two-thirds majority of the justices for overruling a law of Congress, to deny the Court jurisdiction in Reconstruction cases, to reduce its membership to three, and even to abolish it. The judges apparently took the hint. When the state of Mississippi in 1867 asked for an injunction restraining Johnson from enforcing the Reconstruction Acts, the Court refused to accept jurisdiction (*Mississippi* v. *Johnson*). But the next year the Court agreed to hear arguments, on a writ of habeas corpus, in a case involving military courts in Mississippi (*Ex parte McCardle*) and by implication involving the legality of the Reconstruction Acts. The Radicals rushed through Congress a law denying the Court appellate jurisdiction in cases concerning habeas corpus. The Court bowed by refusing to hear the case. It bowed again in *Texas* v. *White* (1869), in which Chase, while accepting the Lincoln-Johnson theory that the seceded states were still in the Union, conceded that Congress possessed the power to determine permanent conditions of Reconstruction.

Although the Supreme Court evaded the Reconstruction issue, it was not an ineffective agency during this period. In the entire history of the country before 1864 the Court had declared only two acts of Congress unconstitutional. During Chase's tenure (1864–1873), it voided ten of them.

The most aggressive move of the legislative against another branch of the government occurred when the Radicals attempted to remove the President from office. They wanted to get rid of him because of his opposition to their Reconstruction program. Early in 1867 they began searching for evidence that Johnson had committed crimes or misdemeanors in office, the only legal grounds for impeachment, but they could find nothing upon which to base charges. Then he gave them a plausible reason

for action by deliberately violating the Tenure of Office Act. He suspended Secretary of War Stanton, who had worked with the Radicals against Johnson, and named General Grant as his successor. Johnson hoped in this manner to secure a Court test case of the tenure law, which he believed to be unconstitutional. But when the Senate refused to concur in the suspension, Grant relinquished the office to Stanton. Johnson then dismissed Stanton.

In the House of Representatives the elated Radicals framed and presented to the Senate eleven charges against the President. The first nine accusations dealt with the violation of the Tenure of Office Act. The tenth and eleventh charged Johnson with making speeches calculated to bring Congress into disrespect and of not faithfully enforcing the various Reconstruction Acts. In the trial before the Senate (March 25 to May 26, 1868) Johnson's lawyers main-

The Impeachment of Andrew Johnson

In this print the Senate is voting on the charges against the President. Chief Justice Chase, the presiding officer, stands at the right. At the left Senator Ross of Kansas announces he votes "Not Guilty." From Frank Leslie's Illustrated Newspaper *(1868).*

tained that he was justified in technically violating a law in order to force a test case and that the measure did not apply to Stanton anyway: it gave tenure to cabinet members for the term of the President by whom they had been appointed, and Stanton had been appointed by Lincoln. The House managers of the impeachment stressed the theme that Johnson had opposed the will of Congress. They implied that in doing so he was guilty of crimes and misdemeanors. They brought terrific pressure upon all the Republican senators, but seven Republicans joined the twelve Democrats to vote for acquittal. On three of the charges the vote was identical, 35 to 19, one short of the required two-thirds majority. Thereupon the Radicals called off the proceedings.

THE RECONSTRUCTED STATES

In the ten states of the South that were reorganized under the congressional plan, approximately one-fourth of the white men were at first excluded from voting or holding office. The voter registration of 1867 enrolled a total of 703,000 black and 627,000 white voters. The Negro voters constituted a majority in half of the states—Alabama, Florida, South Carolina, Mississippi, and Louisiana—though only in the last three of these states did the blacks outnumber the whites in the population as a whole. However, once new constitutions had been made and new governments launched, most of these permitted nearly all whites to vote (though for several years the Fourteenth Amendment continued to keep the leading ex-Confederates from holding office). This meant that in most of the Southern states the Republicans could maintain control only with the support of a great many Southern whites.

These Southern white Republicans, whom their opponents derisively called "scalawags," consisted in part of former Whigs who, after the breakup of the Whig organization in the 1850s, had acted with the Southern Democrats but had never felt completely at home with them. Some of the scalawag leaders were wealthy (or once wealthy) planters or businessmen. James L. Alcorn, for example, had been one of the largest slaveholders in Mississippi, a Whig leader of the state, and an opponent of secession. Such men, having long controlled the Negroes as slaves, expected to control them also as vot-

ers. Many other Southern whites who joined the Republican party were farmers living in areas where slavery had been unimportant or nonexistent. These men, many of whom had been wartime Unionists, favored the Republican program of internal improvements, which would help them get their crops to market.

White men from the North also served as Republican leaders in the South. Opponents of Reconstruction referred to them as "carpetbaggers," thus giving the impression that they were penniless adventurers who had arrived with all their possessions in a carpetbag (a then common kind of valise covered with carpeting material) in order to take advantage of the Negro vote for their own power and profit. In fact, the majority of the so-called carpetbaggers were veterans of the Union army who had looked upon the South as a new frontier, more promising than the West, and at the war's end had settled in it as hopeful planters or business or professional men. They had brought with them money to invest, but many of them lost it because of their own inexperience and the hostility of their Southern white neighbors.

The most numerous Republicans in the South were the freedmen, the vast majority of whom had no formal education and no previous experience in the management of affairs. Among the Negro leaders, however, were well-educated, highly intelligent, and even brilliant men, most of whom had never been slaves and many of whom had been brought up in the North or abroad. The blacks quickly became politically self-conscious. In various states they held their own "colored conventions," the one in Alabama announcing (1867): "We claim exactly *the same rights, privileges and immunities as are enjoyed by white men*—we ask nothing more and will be content with nothing less." Negroes were organized, often with the assistance of Freedmen's Bureau agents and other Northern whites, in chapters of the Union League, which had been founded originally as a Republican electioneering agency in the North during the war. At secret night meetings, with mysterious ritual, the new members of the Union League in the South received instruction in political rights and political techniques. Another organization that gave unity and self-confidence to black people was the Negro church. Once they were emancipated, they had begun to withdraw from the white churches and form their own. "The colored preachers are *the great power* in controlling and uniting the colored vote," a carpetbagger observed in 1868.

Negroes served as delegates to the conventions that, under the congressional plan, drew up new state constitutions in the South. Then, in the reconstructed states, Negroes were elected to public offices of practically every kind. All together (between 1869 and 1901) twenty of them were sent to the House of Representatives in Washington. Two went to the United States Senate, both of them from Mississippi. Hiram R. Revels—an ordained minister of the African Methodist Episcopal Church and a former North Carolina free Negro who had been educated at Knox College in Illinois—took the Senate seat (1870) that Jefferson Davis once had occupied. Blanche K. Bruce, who had escaped from slavery in Virginia and studied in the North, was made a senator in 1874 (he was the only Negro to be elected to a full term in the Senate until the election of Edward Brooke, of Massachusetts, in 1966).

Yet no such thing as "Negro rule" ever existed in any of the states. No Negro was elected governor, though Lieutenant-Governor P. B. S Pinchback briefly occupied the governor's chair in Louisiana. Negroes never controlled any of the state legislatures, though they held a majority in the lower house of South Carolina In the South as a whole the number of Negro officeholders was less than proportionate to the number of Negroes in the population. Nor did the state governments show much if any favoritism toward blacks as a group. Constitutions or statutes prohibited, on paper,

Hiram R. Revels
Revels was one of the few Negroes to attain high office during Reconstruction, acting as United States Senator from Mississippi from 1870–1871. Born in North Carolina of free parents, Revels became a Methodist minister and during the Civil War served as an army chaplain in Mississippi. Returning to the state after the war, he resumed his ministerial duties but entered politics. He was a moderate Republican and in 1875 joined with the Democrats to overthrow the Republican state regime. For years he was president of Alcorn College, a Negro institution. (Library of Congress)

discrimination on the basis of color, but segregation remained the common practice. Only in New Orleans were there, for a time, a few integrated schools.

The record of the Reconstruction governments is many-sided. As some of the leaders in the convention that framed the new state constitutions were Northerners, they put into these documents the most advanced provisions in those of the most progressive Northern states – provisions embodying the latest advances in local government, judicial organization, public finance, and poor relief. Generally, these changes had the effect of modernizing Southern state government and placing it in step with governmental trends in the rest of the country. But some of the provisions, which looked excellent on paper, were not suited to the peculiar environment of the rural South.

The financial program of the Republican governments was a compound of blatant corruption and well-designed, if sometimes impractical, social legislation. The corruption and extravagance are familiar aspects of the Reconstruction story. State budgets expanded to hitherto unknown totals, and state debts soared to previously undreamed of heights. In South Carolina, for example, the public debt increased from $7 million to $29 million in eight years.

In large measure, the corruption in the South was a phase of a national phenomenon, with the same social force – an expanding capitalism eager to secure quick results – acting as the corrupting agent. Included in the spending programs of the Reconstruction governments were subsidies for railroads and other internal improvements, some of which materialized and some of which did not – because the promoters and the politicians pocketed the subsidies. That much of the alleged corruption was a product of deep forces in contemporary society is demonstrated by the continuance of dishonesty in state government after Republican rule was overthrown.

The state expenditures of the Reconstruction years seem huge only in comparison with the niggardly budgets of the conservative governments of the prewar era; they do not appear large when measured against the sums appropriated by later legislatures. The reconstructed governments represented the poor Negroes, and these people had a concept, albeit a vague one, of what today would be called the welfare state. They demanded public education, public-works programs, poor relief, and other services that cost money. If there were thieving and foolish spending there were also positive and permanent accomplishments, particularly in education. One example is offered by South Carolina, which in 1860 had only 20,000 children in public schools; by 1873 some 50,000 white and 70,000 Negro students were enrolled.

The Grant Administration

The voters looked trustingly to General Ulysses S. Grant, the conquering hero of the war, to guide them through the troubled postwar years. He was President during a time (1869–1877) that would have taxed the abilities of a master of statecraft. Only a superb politician with profound spiritual insight – some rare leader like Lincoln – could have held the presidency at that time and escaped with an unblemished reputation. Grant, for all his fine qualities, proved to be no such political leader.

A SOLDIER PRESIDENT

At the end of the war both parties had angled to make Grant their candidate, and he could have had the nomination of either party. As he watched the congressional Radicals triumph over President Johnson, he concluded that the Radical Reconstruction policy expressed the real wishes of the people. He was receptive when the Radical leaders approached him with offers of the Republican nomination.

The Republicans placed candidate Grant on an ambiguous platform. They endorsed Radical Reconstruction and Negro suffrage for the South, but declared that in the North the question of Negro voting should be determined by each state. (Thus during the campaign the Republicans opposed the suffrage amendment, the Fifteenth, which they were to pass soon after the election.) Reflecting the influence of business, the platform called for the payment of the national debt in "the spirit of the laws" under which it had been contracted, which

U. S. G. AS A RAG-PICKER.

U. S. G.—*"Why, here is Zach Chandler thrown out of the Senate Chamber as rubbish! But he may be worth something to me. I must pick him up and fling him into my basket."*

"U. S. G. as a Rag-Picker"

One of the complaints of the anti-Grant, Liberal Republicans was the President's use of the spoils system. In this cartoon from Leslie's Illustrated Newspaper, *Grant is pictured as a rag-picker, or junkman, because of his having retrieved Zachariah Chandler and made him Secretary of the Interior. Chandler, Republican boss of Michigan, had been defeated for reelection to the Senate in 1874. (Culver)*

meant in gold instead of greenbacks; on the tariff issue, the platform was discreetly silent. Obviously the Republicans meant to make Reconstruction the big issue while subordinating economic questions that might divide the party.

Unwisely the Democrats decided to meet the Republican challenge. Their platform also emphasized Reconstruction, denouncing in extravagant terms the Radical program and demanding restoration of "home rule" in the South. Thus the Democrats chose to fight the campaign on an issue that was related to the war and its emotions—an issue that enabled their opponents to associate them with rebellion. They did, however, attempt to inject a new question of an economic nature into the contest. In 1868 approximately $356 million of the Civil War greenbacks were in circulation, and Middle Western Democrats, led by George Pendleton of Ohio, wanted to keep the paper currency and use it when legally possible to pay off the national debt. Behind this so-called Ohio idea was the larger question of retaining the greenbacks as a permanent part of the money supply. This proposal appealed to the debtor farmers of the West and also to many hard-pressed businessmen of the East. The Westerners succeeded in writing the Ohio idea into the platform, but the party nominated Horatio Seymour of New York, a gold or "sound money" man, who repudiated the currency plank.

After a bitter campaign revolving around Reconstruction and Seymour's war record as governor of New York (he had been a Peace Democrat), Grant carried twenty-six states and Seymour only eight. But Grant got only 3,012,000 popular votes to Seymour's 2,703,000, a scant majority of 310,000, and this majority was due to Negro votes in the reconstructed states of the South.

Ulysses S. Grant was the second professional soldier to be elected to the presidency (Zachary Taylor having been the first), and the last to be chosen until Dwight D. Eisenhower was selected in 1952. After graduating from West Point with no particular distinction, Grant had entered the regular army, from which after years of service he resigned under something of a cloud. In civilian life he undertook several dismal ventures that barely yielded him a living. His career before 1861 could be characterized as forty years of failure. Then came the Civil War, and Grant found at last the one setting, the one vocation for which he was supremely equipped—war.

His political naïveté as President was displayed in many of his appointments. For the important office of secretary of state he chose an old friend, the former Illinois Congressman Elihu B. Washburne. By agreement, Washburne was to hold the position only a week before resigning to become minister to France, the purpose being to enable him to brag in Par-

is that he had headed the foreign office. After offering the appointment to another man, who declined it on the grounds of expense, Grant named Hamilton Fish of New York. Like other Americans of the time, Grant inordinately admired millionaires, and he appointed A. T. Stewart, a wealthy merchant, secretary of the treasury. Stewart, however, was ineligible because of a law barring from the office any person in "trade or commerce."

In choosing his official family, Grant proceeded as if he were creating a military staff. He sent several appointments to the Senate for confirmation without asking the recipients if they would serve; they first heard the news in the papers. Fish, who had been out of politics for twenty years, wired Grant that he could not accept, but his name was already being acted on in the Senate and he was persuaded to let it go through. During his two administrations, Grant named a total of twenty-five men to the cabinet. Most of his later appointments went to men who were, at best, average, and some to men who were incompetent or corrupt, or both. Increasingly, in dispensing cabinet and executive patronage, Grant came to rely on the machine leaders in the party, on the groups most ardently devoted to the spoils system.

SUCCESSES IN FOREIGN AFFAIRS

In foreign affairs the Grant administration achieved its most brilliant successes, as the Johnson administration also had done. These were the accomplishments of two outstanding secretaries of state: William H. Seward (1861–1869) and Hamilton Fish (1869–1877).

An ardent expansionist and advocate of a vigorous foreign policy, Seward acted with as much daring as the demands of Reconstruction politics and the Republican hatred of President Johnson would permit. By exercising firm but patient pressure, he persuaded Napoleon III of France to abandon his Mexican empire, which was established during the war when the United States was in no position to protest. Napoleon withdrew his troops in 1867, his puppet Emperor Maximilian was executed by the Mexicans, and the validity of the Monroe Doctrine was strikingly reaffirmed.

When Russia let it be known that she would like to sell Alaska to the United States, the two nations long having been on friendly terms, Seward readily agreed to pay the asking price of $7.2 million. Only by strenuous efforts was he able to induce the Senate to ratify the treaty and the House to appropriate the money (1867–1868). Critics jeered that the secretary had bought a useless frozen wasteland – "Seward's Icebox" and "Walrussia" were some of the terms employed to describe it – but Alaska, a center for the fishing industry in the North Pacific and potentially rich in such resources as gold, was a distinct bargain. Seward was not content with expansion in continental

Hamilton Fish

Fish, a member of a distinguished New York family, had been out of politics for years when Grant offered him the position of Secretary of State. Accepting it reluctantly, he served for both of Grant's terms, and left a record of solid accomplishments. Fish represented the older tradition of cultivated gentlemen in politics. This sketch, almost a caricature, exaggerates some of his features but still conveys his aura of dignity. (Culver)

North America. In 1867 he engineered the annexation of the tiny Midway Islands west of Hawaii.

In contrast with its sometimes shambling course in domestic politics, the performance of the Grant administration in the area of foreign affairs was generally decisive and firm, yet showing a wise moderation. For this, Secretary Fish, to whom President Grant gave almost a free hand, deserves the major credit. A number of delicate and potentially dangerous situations confronted Fish from the beginning, but the most serious one arose out of strained relations with Great Britain.

The United States had a burning grievance against England which had originated during the Civil War. At that time the British government, according to the American interpretation, had violated the laws of neutrality by permitting Confederate cruisers, the *Alabama* and others, to be built and armed in English shipyards and let loose to prey on Northern commerce. American demands that England pay for the damages committed by these vessels became known as the "Alabama claims." Although the British government realized its diplomatic error in condoning construction of the cruisers (in a future war American-built *Alabamas* might operate against Britain), it at first hesitated to submit the issue to arbitration.

Other differences clouded Anglo-American relations. England contended that the United States should compensate British subjects who had suffered property losses in the way of cotton and ships during the war. The ancient controversy of the North Atlantic fisheries and American rights off Canadian shores had flared up again. Another dispute involved the location of the boundary between the United States and British Columbia in Puget Sound. And finally there were the Fenians – the Irish-American crusaders who thought they could free Ireland of British rule by conquering Canada. Several times during the Johnson-Grant period Fenian "armies" harassed the Canadian border. Although the American government tried to restrain these outbreaks, it refused British suggestions that it should pay for the damages committed by the Fenians.

Seward tried earnestly to settle the Alabama claims before leaving office. The American minister to England, Reverdy Johnson, negotiated an agreement, the Johnson-Clarendon Convention (1869), providing that all claims on both sides since 1853 be submitted to arbitration. The pact was distasteful to Americans because it embraced so many issues and contained no expression of British regret for the escape of the *Alabama*. Coming before the Senate immediately after Grant took office, it was rejected 54 to 1. The debate featured a speech by Charles Sumner, chairman of the Committee on Foreign Relations, denouncing Britain for her course in the Civil War and arguing that her conduct had prolonged the war by two years. Therefore, said Sumner, England owed the United States for "direct damages" committed by the cruisers and "indirect damages" for the cost of the war for two years – which would have reached the staggering total of some $2 billion. Americans who supported Sumner's position, and they were undoubtedly a majority, professed themselves willing to accept the cession of Canada as a substitute for a cash payment.

England naturally would have nothing to do with any arrangement involving indirect claims, and settlement of the problem was temporarily stalled. Secretary Fish, however, continued to work for a solution, and finally in 1871 the two countries agreed to the Treaty of Washington, one of the great landmarks in international pacification, providing for arbitration of the cruiser issue and other pending controversies. The Alabama claims were to be laid before a five-member tribunal appointed by the governments of the United States, England, Italy, Switzerland, and Brazil. In the covenant Britain expressed regret for the escape of the *Alabama* and agreed to a set of rules governing neutral obligations that virtually gave the British case away. In effect, this meant that the tribunal would have only to fix the sum to be paid by Britain. Convening at Geneva in Switzerland, the arbitrators awarded $15.5 million to the United States.

The other disputes covered by the treaty were compromised just as pacifically. The question of the Puget Sound boundary was submitted to the German Emperor, who ruled in favor of the United States title to the contested San Juan Islands. An arbitration commission awarded nearly $2 million to England for damages suffered by her citizens during the Civil War. Because the treaty had extended American fishing privileges, England claimed a payment for the concessions, and a special commission, after some wrangling, decided in 1877 that the United States should compensate Britain with $5.5 million. If the value of the arbitrations were computed in money, which of course it really could not be, the United States thus netted approximately $8 million from the awards. The real and enduring significance of the procedure was that again the two countries – as they had been doing since 1818 – adjusted serious differences without resorting to force.

THE LIBERALS DEFECT

Through both his foreign and his domestic policies, President Grant antagonized and alienated a number of prominent Republicans, among them the famous Radical, Charles Sumner. Senator Sumner's extravagant demand for damages from Great Britain embarrassed Secretary Fish in the latter's diplomacy. Still worse, from the President's point of view, Sumner blocked a treaty for the annexation of Santo Domingo, a project in which Grant took a deep personal interest – indeed, it was a kind of monomania with him. The angry President got revenge by inducing his Senate friends to remove Sumner from the chairmanship of the Committee on Foreign Relations.

Sumner and other Republican leaders joined with civil-service reformers to criticize Grant for his use of the spoils system, his reliance on ruthless machine politicians. Scholarly journalists like E. L. Godkin of the *Nation* and George William Curtis of *Harper's Weekly* were arguing that the government ought to base its appointments not on services to the party but on fitness for office as determined by competitive examinations, as the British government already was doing. Grant yielded to the extent of recommending the establishment of a Civil Service Commission, which Congress authorized in 1871, to devise a system of hiring based on merit. This agency, under the headship of Curtis, proposed a set of rules that seemed to meet Grant's approval. But Grant was not really much interested in reform, and even if he had been he could not have persuaded his followers to accept a new system that would undermine the very basis of party loyalty – the patronage. Congress, by neglecting to renew the commission's appropriation, soon ended its existence.

FRANK LESLIE'S ILLUSTRATED NEWSPAPER.

A REMARKABLE SACRIFICE.

U. S. G.—"*I don't want to go to Washington; I want to go to the races with Tom Murphy.*"
R. C——G.—"*Oh, but you must make a sacrifice now, and after election you can go to as many races as you like.*"

Grant Wants to Go to the Horse Races

This print depicts a widely held impression of Grant. Because the President admired fine horses, it was believed that he liked racing and gambling. Grant, shown here as an obvious weakling, is saying that he does not want to go to the White House but to the races. Two party bosses, Roscoe C. Conkling and Oliver P. Morton, are forcing him to shoulder his political responsibilities. From Frank Leslie's Illustrated Newspaper *(1872).*

Republican critics of the President also denounced him for his support of Radical Reconstruction. He continued to station federal troops in the South, and on numerous occasions he sent them to the support of Negro-and-carpetbag governments that were on the point of collapsing. To growing numbers in the North this seemed like dangerous militarism, and they were more and more disgusted by the stories of governmental corruption and extravagance that came up from the South. Some Republicans were beginning to suspect that there was corruption not only in the Southern state governments but also in the federal government itself. Still others criticized Grant because he had declined to speak out in favor of a reduction of the tariff. The high wartime duties remained substantially unchanged even though the wartime justification for them was past.

Thus, before the end of Grant's first term, members of his own party had begun to oppose him for a variety of reasons—his foreign policies, his use of the patronage, his resort to military force in the South, his high-tariff stand, and his suspected taint of corruption—all of which added up to what the critics called "Grantism." In 1872, hoping to prevent Grant's reelection, his opponents bolted the party. Referring to themselves as Liberal Republicans, they proceeded to set up their own organization for running presidential and vice-presidential candidates.

The greatest weakness of the Liberal movement lay in its diversity and disunity. This was cruelly exposed when the Liberals held their national convention and began to consider a platform. They were able to agree on resolutions that approved of civil-service reform and endorsed the basic policy of Reconstruction, but called for universal amnesty (with the restoration of full political rights to former Confederates) and the withdrawal of troops from the South. When the tariff question came up, however, the convention found itself hopelessly divided. The delegates finally compromised on an evasive plank referring the issue to the people and Congress. This evasion lessened the Liberals' chances of gaining Democratic endorsement and Southern support. They compounded their blunder in choosing a nominee. Passing over Charles Francis Adams and other able and available men, they named Horace Greeley, veteran editor and publisher of the New York *Tribune*.

Greeley over a course of thirty years had stated his position on practically every issue before the country. He had been a Whig and a Republican, a proponent of antislavery and a high tariff, an economic and political national-

ist. Impulsive and erratic, he had crusaded for most of the fads that had at one time or another intrigued popular attention—spiritualism, vegetarianism, and others—and he cultivated an idiosyncratic dress and manner. With his record and personality, he was hardly the strongest candidate the Liberals could have put forward to attract the Democratic, Southern, and independent vote. The Democratic convention, seeing in his candidacy the only chance to unseat the Republicans, endorsed him with no great enthusiasm. Despite his recent attacks on Radical Reconstruction, many Southerners, remembering Greeley's own Radical past, prepared to stay at home on Election Day. The Republicans, with Grant as their standard-bearer and a platform justifying Reconstruction and calling for a high tariff, moved into the campaign with confidence.

To everybody's surprise, Greeley turned out to be a vigorous and hard-hitting campaigner. Breaking with precedent, he stumped the country advocating the Liberal cause. But the factors surrounding his candidacy made the odds against him impossible. In November Grant polled 286 electoral votes and 3,597,000 popular votes to Greeley's 62 and 2,834,000. The optimistic editor carried only two Southern and four border states. Three weeks later Greeley, apparently crushed by his defeat, died.

During the campaign the first of a series of political scandals had come to light. Although the wrongdoing had occurred before Grant took office, it involved his party and the onus for it fell on his administration. This scandal originated with the Crédit Mobilier construction company that helped build the Union Pacific Railroad. In reality, the Crédit Mobilier was controlled by a few Union Pacific stockholders who awarded huge and fraudulent contracts to the construction company, thus milking the Union Pacific, a company of which they owned a minor share, of money which in part came from government subsidies. To avert a congressional inquiry into the deal, the directors, using Oakes Ames, a Massachusetts representative, as their agent, sold at a discount (in effect gave) Crédit Mobilier stock to key members of Congress. A congressional investigation was held, and it revealed that some high-placed Republicans had accepted stock, including Schuyler Colfax, now Grant's Vice President.

One dreary episode followed another in Grant's second term. Benjamin H. Bristow, Grant's third secretary of the treasury, discovered that some of his officials and a group of distillers operating as a "Whiskey Ring" were cheating the government out of taxes by means of false reports. Among the prominent Republicans involved was the President's private secretary, Orville E. Babcock. Grant defended Babcock, appointed him to another office, and eased Bristow out of the cabinet. A House investigation revealed that William W. Belknap, secretary of war, had accepted bribes to retain an Indian-post trader in office. Belknap resigned with Grant's blessing before the Senate could act on impeachment charges brought by the House. Lesser scandals involved the Navy Department, which was suspected of selling business to contractors, and the Treasury, where John D. Sanborn, a special agent appointed to handle overdue taxes, collected $427,000 and retained a 50-percent commission for himself and the Republican bigwigs who had placed him in the job. Not to be left out of the picture, Congress passed an act doubling the annual salary of the President from $25,000 to $50,000 (the first increase since George Washington's time), and raising the salaries of members of Congress from $5,000 to $7,500 a year. The increases were justifiable, but the country was enraged to learn that its representatives had also voted themselves two years of back pay. Bowing before a storm of denunciation, the next Congress hastened to repeal the so-called "Salary Grab."

THE GREENBACK QUESTION

Meanwhile the Grant administration along with the country as a whole had suffered another blow when the Panic of 1873 struck. It was touched off by the failure of a leading investment banking firm, Jay Cooke and Company, the "financier of the Civil War," which had done well in the handling of government war bonds but had sunk excessive amounts in postwar railroad building. Depressions had come before with almost rhythmic regularity—in 1819, 1837, and 1857—but this was the worst one yet. It lasted four years, during which unemployment rose to 3 million, and agricultural prices fell so far that thousands of farmers, unable to meet mortgage payments, went more deeply into debt or lost their farms.

Debtors hoped the government would follow an inflationary, easy-money policy, which would have made it easier for them to pay their debts and would have helped to stimulate recovery from the depression. But President Grant and most Republicans preferred what they called a "sound" currency, which was to the advantage of the banks, moneylenders, and other creditors.

The money question, after figuring in the election of 1868, had confronted Grant and the Republicans in Congress from the beginning of his administration. The question was twofold: How should interest and principal of the war bonds be paid, and what should be the permanent place of the greenbacks in the national currency? Supporters of the Ohio idea, representing debtor interests, argued that the bonds had been purchased in greenbacks of depreciated value and should, unless stipulated otherwise by law, be redeemed in the same currency. The President favored payment in gold, and the Republican Congress moved speedily to promise redemption in "coin or its equivalent" and to enact a refunding act providing for long-term refinancing of the debt (1869–1870).

Approximately $450 million in greenbacks had been issued during the Civil War, and $400 million of them were still in circulation at the end of the conflict. In the Johnson administration, Congress had authorized the Treasury to reduce their quantity, but the protests of farmers and some business groups had halted further action. When Grant entered the White House, the greenback circulation was some $356 million, and the gold value of a greenback dollar was 73 cents.

Before Congress could make any disposition of the problem, the Supreme Court intervened with a decision concerning the legality of the greenbacks as legal tender. In *Hepburn* v. *Griswold* (1870), Chief Justice Chase, speaking for a divided 4-to-3 Court, declared that greenbacks were not legal tender for debts contracted prior to their issuance. This pronouncement angered agrarians and alarmed businessmen who had incurred obligations that they would now have to pay with a more valuable dollar. Demands for a reversal of the Court's decision were insistent. It so happened that Congress was about to raise the number of justices (recently reduced to seven) back to nine, and Grant appointed two men who were known to oppose the decision. It was charged that he had ascertained their opinions and was in effect packing the Court, but no proof of this exists. The government did, however, move immediately for a rehearing, and in *Knox* v. *Lee* (1871) the Court by a 5-to-4 vote reversed the previous decision.

With the legality of greenbacks established, the Treasury, as a relief measure after the Panic of 1873, increased the amount in circulation. For the same reason Congress, in the following year, voted to raise the total to $400 million. Grant, responding to pressures from the financial interests, vetoed the measure. In 1875 the Republican Congress enacted the Resumption Act, providing that after January 1, 1879, the government would exchange gold dollars for greenbacks and directing the government to acquire a gold reserve for redemption purposes. The law had its intended result: with the specie value of greenbacks assured, they were equal in worth to gold. The interests of the creditor classes were adequately protected, but at the same time, the debtor groups could take some comfort in the retention of the greenbacks. (Subsequently, in 1878, Congress decided that some $346 million of greenbacks should form a permanent part of the money supply.) Not all the agrarian-debtor groups accepted resumption as a satisfactory conclusion. Some dissident elements created the National Greenback party in 1875, which was active in the next three presidential elections. It failed, however, to attract wide support. After 1879 those interests favoring inflation would turn to forms of currency other than paper.

A Return to White Supremacy

The period of Republican control in the South varied from state to state. In a few states the Democrats (or Conservatives) got into power as soon or almost as soon as restoration occurred. The longest that Republican rule lasted in any of the states was about ten years. It was ended in Virginia, North Carolina, and Georgia in 1870; in Texas in 1873; in Alabama and Arkansas in 1874; in Mississippi in 1875; and in South Carolina, Louisiana, and Florida in 1877.

SOUTHERN REPUBLICANS LOSE

In the states where the whites constituted a majority—the upper South states—overthrow of Republican control was a relatively simple matter. The whites had only to organize and win the elections. Their success was facilitated by the early restoration of the suffrage to those whites who had been deprived of it by national or state action. Presidential and congressional pardons returned the privilege to numerous individuals, and in 1872 Congress, responding to public demands to forgive the penalties of the war, enacted the Amnesty Act, which restored political rights to 150,000 ex-Confederates and left only 500 excluded from political life.

In other states, where the Negroes were in the majority or the population difference be-

The Ku Klux Klan: A Southern View
This Klan broadside depicts the organization as most Southerners saw it. The figure with the flag and sword epitomizes white culture and has overthrown the Negro enemy. Note the incendiary torch in the hand of the Negro and the broken chains symbolizing his former slave status. (Rutherford B. Hayes Library)

tween the races was small, the whites resorted to intimidation and violence. Frankly terroristic were the secret societies that appeared in many parts of the South—the Ku Klux Klan, the Knights of the White Camellia, and others—which attempted to frighten or physically prevent Negroes from voting. Although the societies were effective, their influence has been exaggerated by writers intrigued by their romantic hooded and robed apparel and their elaborate ritual. Moving quickly to stamp out these societies, Congress passed two Force Acts (1870–1871) and the Ku Klux Klan Act (1871) which authorized the President to use military force and martial law in areas where the orders were active.

More potent than the secret orders were the open semimilitary organizations that operated under such names as Rifle clubs, Red Shirts, and White Leagues. After the first such society was founded in Mississippi, the idea spread to other states, and the procedure employed by the clubs was called the Mississippi Plan. Briefly stated, the plan called for the whites in each community to organize and arm, and to be prepared, if necessary, to resort to force to win elections. But the heart of the scheme was in the phrase "drawing the color

The Ku Klux Klan: A Northern View

This drawing in a Northern illustrated paper shows a group of Klansmen about to murder a carpetbagger whom they have abducted. (Library of Congress)

line." By one method or another, legal or illegal, every white man was to be forced to join
the Democratic party or leave the community.
By similar methods, every Negro male was to
be excluded from political action; in a few
states he was permitted to vote—if he voted
Democratic.

Perhaps an even stronger influence than
the techniques practiced by the armed bands
was the simple and unromantic weapon of economic pressure. The war had freed the Negro,
but he was still a laborer—a hired worker or a
tenant—dependent upon the whites for his livelihood. The whites readily discovered that this
dependence placed the Negro in their power.
Planters refused to rent land to Republican
Negroes, storekeepers refused to extend them
credit, employers refused to give them work.
Economic pressure was a force that the Negro
could not fight. If the Radicals, in bringing the
Negro to political power, had accomplished a
revolution, it was a superficial one. They failed
to provide the Negro with economic power, as
they might have done by giving him possession
of confiscated land. Hence, his political rights
had no lasting basis.

Certainly the Negro's political position was
hopeless without the continued backing of the
Republican party and the federal government.
But he was losing the support of people in the
North, even of many humanitarian reformers
who had worked for emancipation and Negro
rights. After the adoption of the Fifteenth
Amendment (1870), most of the reformers convinced themselves that their long campaign in
his behalf at last was over, that with the vote he
ought to be able to take care of himself. Republican disillusionment with the corruption and
disorders in the Southern states helped to
bring about the party split of 1872, which in
turn weakened the Republicans in the South
still further. They beheld the discouraging
spectacle of former Radical leaders like
Charles Sumner and Horace Greeley now calling themselves Liberals, cooperating with the
Democrats, and outdoing even them in denunciations of what they viewed as Negro-and-
carpetbag misgovernment. Most of the white
Republicans of the South, including some of
those who had come from the North, joined the
Liberal movement and went over to the Democrats. Friction between the remaining carpetbaggers and the black Republicans grew be-

cause of a well-justified feeling on the part of
the blacks that they were not receiving a fair
share of the power and the jobs.

When the depression came in 1873, the
hard times aggravated political discontent both
North and South. In the congressional elections
of 1874 the Democrats gained a majority of the
seats in the national House of Representatives.
After 1875, when the new House met, the Republicans no longer controlled the whole Congress, as they had done since the beginning of
the war. And President Grant, in view of the
changing temper of the North, no longer was
willing to use military force to save from violent
overthrow the Republican regimes that were
still standing in the South. In 1875, when
the Mississippi governor, Adelbert Ames
(originally from Maine), appealed to Washington for troops to protect the Negroes from the
terrorism of the Democrats, he received in reply a telegram that quoted Grant as saying:
"The whole public are tired out with these
annual autumnal outbreaks in the South, and
the great majority are now ready to condemn
any interference on the part of the government."

After the Democrats had taken Mississippi,
only three states were left in the hands of the
Republicans—South Carolina, Louisiana, and
Florida. In the elections of 1876, again using
terrorist tactics, the Democrats claimed victory
in all three. But the Republicans maintained
that they themselves had won, and they were
able to continue holding office because federal
troops happened to be on the scene. If the
troops should be withdrawn, the last of the
Republican regimes would fall. The future was
to depend on the settlement of the presidential
election of 1876, which was disputed in consequence of the electoral disputes in the South.

THE COMPROMISE OF 1877

Ulysses S. Grant was eager to run for another
term in 1876, and his friends among the Republican bosses tried to secure the nomination for
him. But the majority of the Republican leaders
ruled Grant out. Impressed by the recent upsurge of Democratic strength, which had delivered the House of Representatives and a number of state governments to the opposition party, and fearful of the third-term issue, they

Ingersoll's Speech Nominating Blaine [1876]

At the Republican convention in 1876 Robert G. Ingersoll nominated Blaine in a speech typical of the extravagant rhetoric of the time. Like all Republican orators, Ingersoll seized the opportunity to recall the emotions of the Civil War and to equate Democrats with traitors. After this speech Blaine was known to his admirers as "the plumed knight":

This is a grand year—a year filled with recollections of the Revolution; filled with the proud and tender memories of the past; with sacred legends of liberty; a year in which the sons of freedom will drink from the fountains of enthusiasm; a year in which the people call for a man who has preserved in Congress what our soldiers won upon the field; a year in which they call for the man who has torn from the throat of treason the tongue of slander—for the man who has snatched the mask of Democracy from the hideous face of rebellion; for this man who, like an intellectual athlete, has stood in the arena of debate and challenged all comers, and who is still a total stranger to defeat. Like an armed warrior, like a plumed knight, James G. Blaine marched down the halls of the American Congress and threw his shining lance full and fair against the brazen foreheads of the defamers of his country and the maligners of her honor.

---

searched for a candidate who was not associated with the scandals of the past eight years and who could entice the Liberals back into the fold and unite the party until after the election.

Senator James G. Blaine of Maine offered himself, but he had recently been involved in an allegedly crooked railroad deal. In a remarkable display of oratory and effrontery, Blaine defended himself against the charge of corruption by reading to Congress some private letters that were supposed to incriminate him. Actually, he had carefully selected innocent portions of the correspondence, and many people were unconvinced. The so-called Mulligan letters hurt his chances in 1876 and would impede his career in the future.

The Republican convention passed over Blaine and other hopefuls and named as the standard-bearer Rutherford B. Hayes, a former Union army officer and congressman, three times governor of Ohio, and a champion of civil-service reform. The platform included the usual endorsements of Reconstruction and Republican economic legislation.

No personal rivalries divided the Democrats. Only one aspirant commanded serious attention, and with him as their candidate the Democrats were confident of returning to power. The bearer of the party's hopes was Governor Samuel J. Tilden of New York, whose name had become synonymous with governmental reform. A corporation lawyer and a millionaire, Tilden had long been a power in the Democratic organization of his state, but he had not hesitated to turn against Tammany's corrupt Tweed Ring and aid in its overthrow. His fight against Tweed brought him national fame and the governorship, in which position he increased his reputation for honest administration. The Democratic platform contained some general references to the tariff and currency problems, but its emphasis was upon reform in government. It called for an end to Reconstruction and the establishment of civil service, and declared that the primary issue of the campaign was the ejection of rascals from government and the installation in their place of "honest men."

Despite the fury of the charges flung at each other by the parties in the canvass, there were almost no differences of principle between the candidates. Hayes was on record as favoring withdrawal of troops from the South, he advocated civil service, and his record for probity was equal to Tilden's. Although the New York governor, reflecting Eastern importing interests, was amenable to some kind of tariff reduction, on other economic issues he was at least as conservative as his rival. He was a gold or "sound money" man, and he believed that government had no business interfering with economic processes. He looked on himself as a modern counterpart of Thomas Jefferson.

The November election revealed an apparent Democratic victory. In addition to the South, Tilden carried several large Northern states, and his popular vote was 4,300,000 to 4,036,000 for Hayes. But the situation was complicated by the disputed returns from Louisiana, South Carolina, and Florida, whose total electoral vote was 19. Both parties claimed to have won these states, and double sets of returns were presented to Congress. Adding to the confusion was a contested vote in Oregon, where one of the three successful Republican electors was declared ineligible because he held a federal office. The Democrats contended that the place should go to the highest Democratic elector, but the Republicans insisted that according to state law the remaining electors were to fill the vacancy. The dual and disputed returns threw the outcome of the election into doubt. As tension and excitement gripped the country, two clear facts emerged from the welter of conflicting claims. Tilden had for certain 184 electoral votes, only one short of the majority. The 20 votes in controversy would determine who would be President, and Hayes needed all of them to secure the prize.

With suprise and consternation, the nation now learned that no measure or method existed to determine the validity of disputed returns. The Constitution stated: "The President of the Senate shall, in the presence of the Senate and House of Representatives, open all the certificates and the votes shall then be counted." The question was, how and by whom? The Senate was Republican and so, of course, was its president, and the House was Democratic. Constitutional ambiguity and congressional division rendered a fair and satisfactory solution of the crisis impossible. If the president of the Senate counted the votes, Hayes would be the victor. If the Senate and House judged the returns separately, they would reach opposite decisions and checkmate each other. And if the houses voted jointly, the Democrats, with a numerical majority, would decide the result. Resort to any one of these lines of action promised to divide the country and possibly result in chaos.

Not until the last days of January 1877 did Congress act to break the deadlock. Then it created a special Electoral Commission to pass on all the disputed votes. The commission was to be composed of five senators, five representatives, and five justices of the Supreme Court. Because of the party line-up, the congressional delegation would consist of five Republicans and five Democrats. The creating law named four of the judicial commissioners, two Republicans and two Democrats. The four were to select their fifth colleague, and it was understood that they would choose David Davis, an independent Republican, thus ensuring that the deciding vote would be wielded by a relatively unbiased judge. But at this stage Davis was elected to the Senate from Illinois and suddenly resigned his seat. His place on the commission fell to a Republican. Sitting throughout February, the commission by a partisan vote of 8 to 7 decided every disputed vote for Hayes. Congress accepted the final verdict of the agency on March 2, only two days before the inauguration of the new President.

Ratification of the commission's findings was not accomplished, however, without some complicated compromising among the politicians. Behind the dealing, and partially directing it, were certain powerful economic forces with a stake in the outcome. A decision by the commission was not final until approved by Congress, and the Democrats could have prevented action by filibustering. The success of a filibuster, however, depended on concert between Northern and Southern Democrats, and this the Republicans disrupted by offering the Southerners sufficient inducement to accept the commission's findings. According to the traditional account, certain Republicans and Southern Democrats met at Washington's Wormley Hotel, and the Republicans pledged that Hayes, after becoming President, would withdraw the troops from the South. As withdrawal would mean the downfall of the last carpetbag governments, the Southerners, convinced they were getting as much from Hayes as they could get from Tilden, abandoned the filibuster.

Actually, the story behind the "Compromise of 1877" is somewhat more complex. Hayes was on record before the election as favoring withdrawal of the troops, and in any event the Democrats in the House could have forced withdrawal simply by cutting out appropriations for the army in the Reconstruction process. The real agreement, the one that brought the Southern Democrats over, was reached before the Wormley meeting. As the price for their cooperation the Southern Democrats (among them some old Whigs) exacted from the Republicans the following pledges: the appointment of at least one Southerner to the Hayes cabinet, control of federal patronage in their sections, generous internal improvements, national aid for the Texas and Pacific Railroad, and, finally, withdrawal of the troops. The Conservatives who were running the redeemed Southern states were primarily interested in economics—in industrializing the South—and they believed that the Republican program of federal aid to business would be more beneficial for their region than the archaic state-rights policy of the Democrats.

DISCRIMINATION MADE LEGAL

In his inaugural address Hayes stressed the Southern problem. While he took care to say that the rights of the Negroes must be preserved, he announced that the most pressing need of the South was the restoration of "wise, honest, and peaceful local self-government"— which meant that he was going to withdraw the troops and let the whites take over control of the state governments. Hayes laid down this policy knowing that his action would lend weight to current charges that he was paying off the South for acquiescing in his election and would strengthen those critics who referred to him as "his Fraudulency."

The President hoped to build up a "new Republican" party in the South composed of whatever conservative white groups could be weaned away from the Democrats and committed to some acceptance of Negro rights. But his efforts, which included a tour of Southern cities, failed to produce any positive results. Although many Southern leaders sympathized with the economic credo of the Republicans, they could not advise their people to support the party that had imposed Reconstruction. Nor were Southerners pleased by Hayes' bestowal of offices on carpetbaggers who now had to leave the section or by his vetoes of Democratic attempts to repeal the Force Acts. The "solid South" had come into existence, and there was nothing Hayes or any Republican could do to crack it.

The withdrawal of the troops was a symbol that the national government was giving up its attempt to control Southern politics and to determine the place of the Negro in Southern society. The surrender, it is to be noted, was made by the Republicans. They could yield with good grace because after 1877 they had no particular need for the support of the reconstructed South. The economic legislation of the war and postwar years was safe from repeal; industry was securely entrenched in the national economy; and Republican dominance could be maintained without Southern votes.

Another symbol of retreat was furnished by the Supreme Court, which in a series of decisions emasculated the Fourteenth and Fifteenth amendments of much of their significance. In the Civil Rights Cases (1883) the Court took the position that the Fourteenth Amendment prohibited states from discriminating against people on account of color but did not restrict private individuals or organizations. That is, railroads, hotels, theaters, and the like could legally practice segregation. Eventually the Court validated state legislation that discriminated against Negroes. In *Plessy* v. *Ferguson* (1896), a case involving a law that required separate seating arrangements for the races on railroads, the Court held that separate accomodations did not deprive the Negro of equal rights if the accommodations were equal. And in *Cumming* v. *County Board of Education* (1899) the Court held that laws establishing separate schools for whites and Negroes were valid if the facilities were equal for both.

The men who came to power in the South after 1877 were not in the old agrarian planter tradition. Known as "Bourbons" or "Redeemers," they were industrialists or would-be industrialists. They preached the industrialization of the South through the importation of Northern capital, a policy of low taxes to attract business, and a political alliance with the Northeast instead of with the South's traditional ally, the West. Controlling state governments through the medium of the Democratic party, which as a result of Reconstruction was the only party in the section, they practiced a program marked by economy in government, reduced taxes, and few social services. They did not attempt to abolish Negro suffrage but instead used the Negro vote to maintain white power, as men of their class had tried to use it

The Plight of the Negro [1880]

Frederick Douglass, famous as an escaped slave who had become an abolitionist orator, remained the outstanding spokesman for black Americans after the Civil War. On August 1, 1880, he said in a speech to a great convention of blacks in Elmira, New York:

We have laid the heavy hand of the constitution upon the matchless meanness of caste, as well as upon the hell-black crime of slavery. We have declared before all the world that there shall be no denial of rights on account of race, color, or previous condition of servitude. The advantage gained in this respect is immense.

It is a great thing to have the supreme law of the land on the side of justice and liberty. It is the line up to which the nation is destined to march—the law to which the nation's life must ultimately conform. It is a great principle, up to which we may educate the people, and to this extent its value exceeds all speech.

But today, in most of the Southern States, the fourteenth and fifteenth amendments are virtually nullified.

The rights which they were intended to guarantee are denied and held in contempt. The citizenship granted in the fourteenth amendment is practically a mockery, and the right to vote, provided for in the fifteenth amendment, is literally stamped out in face of government. The old master class is today triumphant, and the newly-enfranchised class in a condition but little above that in which they were found before the rebellion.

during Reconstruction. Negroes continued to vote after the return of white supremacy, but in reduced numbers. In some states they were prevented from voting by an implied threat of force; in others, their influence was nullified by tricky devices—tissue ballots and a complicated arrangement of ballot boxes—that disqualified their votes. But in many areas the black vote was a purchased and directed vote, paid for by the Bourbons and used by them to beat down attempts of the farmers to take over control of the Democratic party.

Not until the 1890s did the Southern states pass laws to disfranchise the Negroes, and the impetus for the attempt was furnished by the white farmers. The farmers demanded disfranchisement because they were opposed for racial reasons to Negro voting and because they objected to the Negro vote being employed against them. The rich whites acquiesced, partly out of a desire to placate the white masses and partly because in the agrarian unrest that characterized the nineties the farmers in some states had sought to get the Negro vote on their side. The threat of competition for the Negro vote frightened all whites, and there was a general feeling that the time had come to close ranks if white supremacy was to be maintained.

In devising laws to disfranchise the Negroes, the Southern states had to take care to evade the intent of the Fifteenth Amendment. That measure did not confer suffrage upon the Negroes but merely prohibited states from denying it because of color. The Southern problem, then, was to exclude Negroes from the franchise without seeming to base the exclusion on race. Two devices were widely employed before 1900. One was the poll tax or some form of property qualification. The other was the literacy and understanding test, which required a voter to demonstrate an ability to read and to interpret the Constitution. The reasoning behind the latter law was that local registrars could administer an impossible reading test to Negroes or rule that their interpretation of the Constitution was inadequate. Both of these devices could be used, and were used, to deny the franchise to poor white men, who protested against tests being applied to them. So, many states passed so-called grandfather laws, which permitted men who could not meet the literacy and property qualifications to be admitted to the suffrage if their ancestors had voted before 1867 or some date before Reconstruction began.

The Supreme Court proved as compliant in ruling on the disfranchising laws as it was in dealing with the civil-rights cases. Although the Court eventually voided the grandfather laws, it validated the literacy tests (*Williams* v. *Mississippi*, 1898) and manifested a general willingness to let the Southern states define suffrage standards — provided the evasions of the Fifteenth Amendment were not too glaring.

One Negro leader believed that his race would have to acquire economic independence before it could ask for complete social acceptance. This was Booker T. Washington, who became the head of the Tuskegee Institute in Alabama, an industrial school for Negroes, and eventually the spokesman for a large segment of his people. Washington feared that in what he called "the great leap from slavery to freedom" the Negroes had forgotten that they would have to live by the work of their hands. Therefore, he preached that education for Negroes should stress industrial and practical aspects rather than classical matters. Eventually, Washington evolved a whole new concept of race relations. He set it forth in a speech at Atlanta in 1895. Known as the Atlanta Compromise, it proposed that for the time the Negro eschew agitation for social equality and devote his efforts to achieving economic security. Upper-class whites approved Washington's philosophy and supported his endeavors, as did some wealthy whites in the North. Most Negroes also accepted the Atlanta strategy, but some were soon to reject it as too passive.

As the turn of the century approached, Southern whites seemed to have won a complete victory over the outside influences that had sought to disturb their way of life, and Reconstruction seemed to these people like a bad dream receding into the past. But the deep and turbulent forces generated in the years between 1865 and 1877 were only temporarily exhausted. They would appear again as Americans continued to search for solutions to the problems left by the Civil War and its troubled aftermath.

THE "NEW SOUTH"

With relative rapidity, the South recovered from the effects of war and restored its economic life. Since it was an agricultural society, its productive powers rested on the basis of land, and the land had survived the war. The chief problem was to get the plantations and farms under cultivation again. Work began at once (crops were harvested in 1865), and progress was steady. By 1879 the cotton crop exceeded that of 1860, part of the increase resulting from the opening of new growing areas west of the Mississippi, in Texas and Arkansas.

The rehabilitation of the South's economy was accomplished with relatively few changes in its agriculture. There was something of a shift in the distribution of land ownership, resulting in an increase in the number of small holders. In the economic travail following the war, many planters were unable to hold on to their property and were forced to offer their

---

Plessy v. Ferguson [1896]

In this famous case the Supreme Court held that enforced separate facilities for Negroes did not imply that Negro people were inferior and did not violate the Fourteenth Amendment:

The object of the amendment was undoubtedly to enforce the absolute equality of the two races before the law, but in the nature of things it could not have been intended to abolish distinctions based upon color, or to enforce social, as distinguished from political, equality, or a commingling of the two races upon terms unsatisfactory to either. Laws permitting, and even requiring their separation in places where they are liable to be brought into contact do not necessarily imply the inferiority of either race to the other, and have been generally, if not universally, recognized as within the competency of the state legislatures in the exercise of their police power. The most common instance of this is connected with the establishment of separate schools for white and colored children, which have been held to be a valid exercise of the legislative power even by courts of states where the political rights of the colored race have been longest and most earnestly enforced. . . .

land for sale at low prices. In many cases the purchasers were white yeomen. According to the census, the number of farms in Mississippi increased from 43,000 in 1860 to 68,000 by 1870; in South Carolina from 33,000 to 52,000; and in Louisiana from 17,000 to 28,000. Actually, these figures are somewhat deceptive because some of the farms listed were under ten or twenty acres in area and were really units in a plantation, worked by tenants who were sometimes white but usually Negro.

The plantation system was modified, but it did not disappear. In the ownership of the system, however, an important change took place. The old planter (or the old type of planter who lived on the plantation) tended to disappear. More and more, the large land units were owned and administered by merchants, banks, and corporations—or by planters who lived in towns or cities where they could devote themselves to business as well as agriculture.

During the Reconstruction period, perhaps a third or more of the farmers in the South were tenants; by 1900 the figure had increased to 70 percent. Several factors accounted for the trend toward tenancy. The Negroes, when they became freedmen, had, of course, no property. They were forced, as a simple matter of survival, to become laborers or tenants, and most of them were unable to accumulate enough resources to rise above this status. As late as 1890 there were only 121,000 Negro landowners in the South. Probably the strongest influence promoting tenancy among both races was the lack of an adequate credit system, with a resulting scarcity of money. The National Bank System was slow to establish itself in the Southern states, and state banks were slow to recover from the effects of the war. Landlords did not have enough cash to hire laborers to work their land, and laborers could not secure loans to buy land or even raise sufficient currency to rent land on a cash basis.

Out of this situation developed an economic arrangement peculiar to the South, the sharecrop and crop-lien system, in which produce and labor took the place of money. There were share tenants and sharecroppers, and there was a difference between the two groups. The share tenants, most of whom were whites, worked strips of land on a large unit and paid as rent to the landlord one-fourth to one-third of their crop; they provided their own tools, seed, stock, and other supplies. The sharecroppers, most of whom were Negroes, provided nothing but their own labor. For the average cropper, the landlord would furnish all the previously mentioned materials, and a horse or mule and a house as well. In addition, until the crop was harvested he would arrange credit facilities for the cropper and his family at a local country store owned by himself or a merchant. The cropper, for his part, agreed to consign from one-third to one-half of his crop to the landlord. Moreover, the storekeeper, the source of credit, protected his interest by taking a mortgage or lien on the tenant's share of the crop. (As time passed, the landlord and the merchant tended to become one person, and the planter-storekeeper became a major figure in the Southern credit complex.)

The lien system was a necessary credit device in the postwar years; but when it was continued and expanded after that period, it had a harmful influence upon Southern agriculture. The merchant or landlord pressed the cropper to produce a single money crop, cotton, to the neglect of diversified farming and scientific farming methods. More serious were the social results of the system. The typical sharecropper was an unlettered person who did not know how to handle his own money carefully and who did not understand the mechanics of credit. Frequently, after harvesting his crop, he found himself owing money to the storekeeper and hence forced to pledge his labor to the same source for another year. Not only did the lien system prevent tenants from rising to the owning class, but it also operated to bind them to particular pieces of land, to create a state of peonage. The Negro sharecropper was not a slave, but he was not completely free.

The Reconstruction period witnessed a restoration of Southern industrial facilities damaged or destroyed during the war, as well as some promising beginnings in new industrial activities. Most of the rehabilitation and expansion was financed with local, Southern capital, which was subscribed by the people of a town who wanted to improve their community by locating a factory in it. The only Southern enterprise that attracted Northern and European investors was the railroad. With outside aid, the war-weakened rail system was soon put in running order again, and by 1873 over 4,000 miles of new track had been constructed. Modest but noteworthy progress was recorded in tobacco manufacturing, in the lumber industry, and in iron making.

The most substantial growth occurred in textiles, which had a prewar basis to build on. Southern leaders during Reconstruction preached the economic advantage of building cotton mills where the raw material was produced, and the Southern people took this logic to heart. Practically all the mills that began to appear in Southern towns were financed by local investors. By 1880 the South could boast of 161 textile factories housing 524,000 spindles and employing 16,000 workers.

But the great industrial development of the section, the development that created the "New South," would not come until later. And even that forward economic surge would not greatly change the nature of Southern life, would not make the South very "new." As late as 1910 only 15 percent of all the people in the region were connected with manufacturing. For many years the South would remain, as it was in the Reconstruction era, a rural and a traditional land.

Selected Readings

Reconstruction: General Accounts
W. A. Dunning, *Reconstruction, Political and Economic, 1865–1877** (1907); W. E. B. Du Bois, *Black Reconstruction** (1935); J. S. Allen, *Reconstruction: The Battle for Democracy, 1865–1876** (1937); E. M. Coulter, *The South During Reconstruction, 1865–1877* (1947); J. H. Franklin, *Reconstruction After the Civil War** (1962); W. R. Brock, *An American Crisis** (1963); K. M. Stampp, *The Era of Reconstruction** (1965).

Reconstruction: Special Studies
J. E. Sefton, *The United States Army and Reconstruction* (1967); S. I. Kutler, *Judicial Power and Reconstruction Politics* (1968); H. M. Hyman, *A More Perfect Union: The Impact of the Civil War and Reconstruction on the Constitution* (1973); M. L. Benedict, *The Impeachment and Trial of Andrew Johnson** (1972); M. E. Mantell, *Johnson, Grant and the Politics of Reconstruction* (1973); A. W. Trelease, *White Terror: The Ku Klux Conspiracy and Southern Reconstruction* (1971); R. N. Current, *Three Carpetbag Governors* (1967); R. O. Curry, ed., *Radicalism, Racism, and Party: The Border States During Reconstruction* (1972); H. L. Trefousse, *The Radical Republicans* (1969); David Donald, *Charles Sumner and the Rights of Man* (1970); Joseph Logsdon, *Horace White, Nineteenth Century Liberal* (1972); E. N. Paolino, *The Foundations of Empire: William Henry Seward and U.S. Foreign Policy* (1973).

Grant and the Republicans
L. D. White, *The Republican Era** (1958); M. R. Dearing, *Veterans in Politics* (1952); C. H. Coleman, *The Election of 1868* (1933); W. B. Hesseltine, *U. S. Grant, Politician* (1935); Allan Nevins, *Hamilton Fish: The Inner History of the Grant Administration* (1936); Goldwin Smith, *The Treaty of Washington, 1871* (1941); Sumner Welles, *Naboth's Vineyard* (2 vols., 1928), on the U.S. and Santo Domingo; A. B. Callow, Jr., *The Tweed Ring* (1966); E. D. Ross, *The Liberal Republican Movement* (1919); C. M. Fuess, *Carl Schurz, Reformer* (1932); Ari Hogenboom, *Outlawing the Spoils* (1961); R. P. Sharkey, *Money, Class,* and Party* (1959); Irwin Unger, *The Greenback Era* (1964); W. T. K. Nugent, *Money and American Society, 1865–1880* (1968).

The Democratic Opposition
Stewart Mitchell, *Horatio Seymour* (1938); A. C. Flick, *Samuel Jones Tilden* (1939); Irving Katz, *August Belmont: A Political Biography* (1968); K. I. Polakoff, *The Politics of Inertia: The Election of 1876 and the End of Reconstruction* (1973).

The New South
C. V. Woodward, *Origins of the New South, 1877–1913** (1951) and *Reunion and Reaction: The Compromise of 1877 and the End of Reconstruction** (1951); V. P. De Santis, *Republicans Face the Southern Question: The New Departure Years, 1877–1897* (1959); S. P. Hirshson, *Farewell to the Bloody Shirt: Northern Republicans and the Southern Negro, 1877–1893* (1962); Harry Barnard, *Rutherford B. Hayes and His America* (1964); R. B. Nixon, *Henry W. Grady, Spokesman of the New South* (1943); Broadus Mitchell, *The Rise of Cotton Mills in the South* (1921); P. H. Buck, *The Road to Reunion, 1865–1900** (1937).

The Negro After 1865
William Gillette, *The Right to Vote: Politics and the Passage of the Fifteenth Amendment** (1967); R. W. Logan, *The Negro in American Life and Thought: The Nadir, 1877–1901* (1954); Paul Lewinson, *Race, Class, and Party: A History of Negro Suffrage and White Politics in the South** (1932); August Meier, *Negro Thought in America, 1880–1915** (1963); B. T. Washington, *Up from Slavery** (1901); S. R. Spencer, Jr., *Booker T. Washington and the Negro's Place in American Life** (1955); L. R. Harlan, *Booker T. Washington: The Making of a Black Leader, 1856–1901* (1973); C. V. Woodward, *The Strange Career of Jim Crow** (1966); V. L. Wharton, *The Negro in Mississippi, 1865–1900** (1947); G. B. Tindall, *South Carolina Negroes, 1877–1900** (1952); J. R. Williamson, *After Slavery: The Negro in South Carolina During Reconstruction* (1966).

*Titles available in paperback.

Industrialization and Urbanization

Seventeen

"With a stride that astonished statisticians, the conquering hosts of business enterprise swept over the continent; twenty-five years after the death of Lincoln, America had become, in the quantity and value of her products, the first manufacturing nation of the world," the historians Charles and Mary Beard have written. "What England had accomplished in a hundred years, the United States had achieved in half the time."

This rise to industrial supremacy during the last decades of the nineteenth century was due to a combination of factors. The United States was not necessarily superior in every one of them but certainly had an advantage in respect to all of them taken together.

First, this nation had an abundance of basic raw materials and sources of energy: coal, iron and other ores, timber, petroleum, water power. Second, there was a large and growing supply of willing labor, consisting in the main of American farmers and European peasants who flocked from the countryside of two continents to the rising industrial centers of the United States. Third, Americans had inherited a good deal of technological ingenuity — the "Yankee inventiveness" that had become a mark of the American character — which was capable of devising or adapting the necessary machines. Fourth, a number of remarkable business organizers, "captains of industry," had the skill to bring together raw materials, workers, and machines, to use them efficiently in the processes of production, and to distribute the resulting goods profitably in the national market. Fifth, this market itself, which was being enlarged by the growth of population and the extension of the rail network, made possible the mass consumption that is a prerequisite to mass production. Finally, the federal government, while refraining from interference with business enterprise, encouraged and assisted it by turning over public resources for private exploitation, by giving tariff protection against foreign competition, by setting up a

---

Tenement Street
The teeming life of a tenement district and something of its squalor are suggested in this view of Mulberry Street in New York City. (Library of Congress)

helpful banking and monetary system, and by providing direct subsidies of land and money.

In the United States, large-scale industry had received a start before the Civil War. The war, while temporarily setting back some industrial activities, stimulated others and — most important — removed the Southern planters as a political obstacle to governmental policies favoring Northern capitalists. The rate of industrial growth increased so rapidly in the postwar decades that these came to constitute a new age of industrialization. It was also an age of urbanization, in which cities assumed greater and greater importance. The tremendous increase in the output of goods — and the multiplication of conveniences that city life afforded — made possible a higher and higher average level of living. But all the people did not share equally in the benefits of the industrial system. There were gross inequalities, and these provoked severe criticisms of the system and led to determined and sometimes violent attempts to bring about a redistribution of income.

The Rise of Big Business

Between 1865 and 1900 American business moved in the direction of monopoly. Fewer and fewer firms produced more and more of the nation's goods. Small corporations were merged to create large ones. These often were brought together to form still larger combinations: *pools*, the members of which agreed to avoid competition and divide profits; *trusts*, in which a board of trustees controlled several corporations; or *holding companies*, which held stock in other companies and thus directed them. Regardless of their specific nature, the various combinations were popularly known as "trusts." By 1900 there were more than 300 of these trusts, and the largest ones, comprising fewer than 2 percent of the manufacturing firms, turned out almost 50 percent of all the manufactured goods in the country.

SOME BASIC INVENTIONS

This economic transformation was accompanied by a flood of inventions and technological innovations. In the entire history of the country up to 1860 only 36,000 patents had been granted, but for the period from 1860 to 1890 the figure was 440,000.

Many of the postwar inventions and discoveries were in the field of communication. In 1866 Cyrus W. Field succeeded in his project of laying a transatlantic cable to Europe. During the next decade Alexander Graham Bell developed the first practicable telephone, and by the 1890s the American Telephone and Telegraph Company, which handled his interests, had installed nearly half a million instruments in American cities. Other inventions that speeded the pace of business organization were the typewriter (by Christopher L. Sholes in 1868), the cash register (by James Ritty in 1879), and the calculating or adding machine (by William S. Burroughs in 1891).

Undoubtedly the technological innovation that had the most revolutionary effect upon industry and upon lives of the urban masses in the industrial centers was the introduction in the 1870s of electricity as a source of light and power. Among the several men who pioneered in developing a commercially practical dynamo were Charles F. Brush, who devised the arc lamp for street illumination, and Thomas A. Edison, who invented, among many other electrical contrivances, the incandescent lamp, which could be used for both street and home lighting. Edison and others designed improved generators and built central power plants to furnish electricity to office buildings, factories, and dwellings. Before the turn of the century 2,774 power stations were in operation, and some 2 million electric lights were in use in the country. Already electric power was being employed in street railway systems and in electric elevators in urban skyscrapers, as well as for driving the machines of factories. The electric power industry was dominated by two large corporations: the General Electric Company, which took over the Edison interests, and the Westinghouse Electric and Manufacturing Company.

railroad employer, the head of the Pennsylvania Railroad. Soon Carnegie had built up his company to a place of dominance in the industry.

His methods were those commonly employed by other great consolidationists of the times. He obtained rebates from railroads on his shipments, so that he could cut his costs and hence his prices, and he bought out rival concerns that could not meet his competition. In collaboration with his ablest associate, Henry Clay Frick, he set up a policy of integration designed to control the processing of steel from mine to market. His company operated a fleet of ore ships on the Great Lakes, acquired railroads and coal mines, and leased part of the Mesabi range.

The machines of the Age of Steel could not run without lubrication, and so another vast enterprise came into being in the postwar era, the petroleum industry. For years before the Civil War the existence of petroleum had been known, particularly in western Pennsylvania where it often seeped to the surface of streams and springs. No one was quite sure what it was or what to do with it. Some enterprising individuals peddled it in bottles as a patent medicine. The first person to glimpse its commercial possibilities as an illuminant was George H. Bissell, who sent a sample of oil to Professor Benjamin Silliman of Yale for analysis. Silliman reported in 1855 that the substance could be used for lighting purposes, and that it would also yield such products as paraffin, naphtha, and lubricating oil. Bissell then raised enough money to begin drilling operations, and in 1859 Edwin L. Drake, employed by Bissell, put down the first oil well near Titusville, Pennsylvania. Labeled "Drake's folly" by the skeptical, it was soon producing oil at the rate of 500 barrels a month.

It also started an oil rush, as promoters searched for and found other fields, not only in Pennsylvania but in Ohio and West Virginia as well. By the 1870s nearly 40 million barrels of petroleum had been produced, oil had advanced to fourth place among the nation's exports, and the annual production was approaching 20 million barrels. Because relatively little capital was required for a man to make a start in the oil business, either as a producer or a refiner, competition at first ran wild. Refineries, which were even more profitable than wells, dotted the Pennsylvania-Ohio region, with Pittsburgh and Cleveland constituting the two principal refining centers. Then the greatest consolidationist of the time stepped into the picture to bring order to the industry.

John D. Rockefeller was a successful businessman at an age when most boys of today would be in college. When only nineteen, he became a partner in a produce commission company in Cleveland that took solid profits selling goods to the government during the Civil War. Far sighted, highly acquisitive, and possessing abundant talents for organization, he decided that his economic future lay with oil. He also concluded that Cleveland, connected by rail and water with the Eastern and Western markets, was destined to surpass Pittsburgh, which had access only to the East through the Pennsylvania Railroad, as the oil-refining center of the country. At the end of the war he and Sidney Andrews, a Cleveland refiner, launched their own business. From the beginning Rockefeller sought to eliminate the competition and the small-scale companies that in his opinion were ruining the petroleum industry. He and Andrews enlarged their operations, took in H. M. Flagler and S. V. Harkness as allies, and proceeded methodically to buy out other refineries. In 1870 the associates formed the Standard Oil Company of Ohio, which in a few years had acquired twenty of the twenty-five refineries in Cleveland, in addition to plants in Pittsburgh, Philadelphia, New York, and Baltimore.

In its rise to dominance Standard Oil employed the familiar consolidating devices of the period, plus a few which were its own invention. The company emphasized efficient and economic operation, research, and sound financial practices. At Rockefeller's insistence, a large cash reserve was maintained to avoid reliance on banks and to purchase competitors. The company obtained rebates from railroads, and even, for a brief time, forced three of the Eastern roads to pay rebates to it on oil shipped by competing companies. Rockefeller waged price wars to drive competitors out of business and, always victorious, took over the defeated concerns.

Like Carnegie in steel, Rockefeller set up an integrated system of production. He built his own terminal warehouses and barrel factories and a network of pipelines that gave him control over most of the facilities for transporting petroleum. Standard also owned its own marketing organization, thus escaping commissions to middlemen. For sales purposes the United States was divided into districts, each of which was administered by a company executive who was assisted by a corps of agents. The salesmen were under orders to sell Standard products by almost any method, and almost always they succeeded. When the Standard Oil Trust was formed in 1882, it was only a formal recognition of the near monopoly that Rockefeller and his associates had already established.

OTHER INDUSTRIES

Three developments brought significant changes to the meat-packing business. They were the appearance of the range-cattle industry in Texas and the Great Plains, the extension of railroad lines across the Mississippi into the plains country, and the introduction of the refrigerated freight car. Chicago, situated close to the cattle supply of the trans-Mississippi area and the hog supply of the Middle West, and elaborately connected by railroads with both the producing areas and the urban markets, became the undisputed capital of the meat-packing industry. Imaginative and aggressive leaders, the counterparts of Rockefeller and Carnegie, appeared to form the inevitable combinations: Philip D. Armour, Nelson Morris, and Gustavus F. Swift. Swift sponsored the most important technological development in the industry, the refrigerator car cooled by artificial ice.

Like the meat business, flour milling was originally a localized enterprise, carried on in thousands of small mills in all parts of the country. And like meat packing, the milling industry moved west to be nearer the source of the wheat supply, adopted new technological processes, and originated large-scale organizations which turned out standardized products. By the close of the Civil War the center of wheat production had shifted to the upper Mississippi Valley, and Minneapolis, Minnesota, became the center of the milling industry. The leading millers were Cadwallader C. Washburn, Charles A. Pillsbury, and George M. Christian, the last of whom eventually merged his interests with Washburn. Two manufactur-

ing methods introduced from Europe resulted in a greatly improved product. The first, called the "middlings-purifier" or "gradual-reduction" process, preserved a higher content of gluten in finished flour than previously had been the case. The second was a process of passing wheat slowly through chilled iron rollers to achieve a flour of superior quality and unusual whiteness. By 1880 flour milling had become one of the country's largest businesses and was supplying its product to European as well as to American markets.

Many other industries, some of them antedating the war and some emerging after it, also underwent the common process of expansion and concentration. The coal industry, which supplied the bulk of the fuel used by the nation's industries, increased its output from approximately 20 million tons in 1860 to 270 million by 1900. In 1890 a near monopoly was created in tobacco manufacturing when James B. Duke fused five large corporations into the American Tobacco Company.

The prepared-foods business, concentrating on the canning of vegetables, became a major industry and in the process helped to alter the eating habits of the American people. A leader in this industry was Gail Borden. Born in rural New York, Borden had less than two years of formal schooling. After a business career in Texas, he interested himself in the possibilities of concentrated foods. He developed a process for condensing milk by evaporation and set up his first large condensary in New York State in 1861. His condensed milk was used by the Northern armies in the Civil War and thus became known to the general public. After the war he founded the town of Borden in Texas and established a plant there for concentrating fruit juices, cocoa, tea, and coffee.

Industries of a prewar origin that continued to experience growth after 1865 were boots and shoes, ready-made clothing, textiles, firearms, distilled liquors, and agricultural machinery.

RAILROAD EXPANSION

In 1860 the railroads constituted the biggest business and the most important single economic interest in the United States. Their total mileage was approximately 30,000, and in rolling stock they counted 100,000 freight and passenger cars and 1,000 locomotives. Every decade the trackage figure increased: 52,000 miles in 1870, 93,000 in 1880, 163,000 in 1890, and 193,000 in 1900. The railroads made it possible for industry to secure its raw materials from a national producing area and to distribute its products in a national market.

Accompanying the expansion of railroad facilities was a host of technological improvements that made rail travel and transportation more efficient, convenient, and safe. Among the innovations were steel rails, heavier locomotives and cars, a uniform gauge (4 feet, 8½ inches), and wider roadbeds. Perhaps the most important invention affecting railroads was the Westinghouse air brake, developed by George Westinghouse in 1869. In 1874 interlocking block signals were introduced from England. George Pullman had produced in 1864 the first sleeping car, and within a few years dining, parlor, and drawing-room cars appeared.

The major Eastern railroads were the New York Central, the Pennsylvania, the Erie, and the Baltimore and Ohio. By 1874 all of them had consolidated lesser lines into their systems and established connections with the Western market at Chicago. The creator of the New York Central system was Cornelius Vanderbilt, a salty, colorful character who had previously operated a steamship line and was endearingly known as "Commodore." A ruthless competitor but a sound railroad man, Vanderbilt improved facilities on the Central and bought up smaller roads to complete his empire. Second only to the Central in facilities was the Pennsylvania Railroad, whose original route ran between Philadelphia and Pittsburgh. Under the leadership of J. Edgar Thompson, the Pennsylvania established connections with Chicago, St. Louis, Baltimore, and Richmond, and in 1899, by tunneling under the Hudson River, entered New York City to compete directly with the Central. The Erie, chartered in the 1850s to link New York City and Lake Erie, in the postwar years stretched its connections to Cleveland, Cincinnati, and St. Louis. Unfortunately for the Erie, it was controlled during the seventies by Daniel Drew, Jay Gould, and James Fisk, three of the most unscrupulous speculators of the era, who were more interested in milking it of profits than in making it into a railroad. The

Baltimore and Ohio had built lines from Baltimore as far as Wheeling on the Ohio River before the Civil War. After the war John W. Garrett, its president, extended its lines to Chicago, Cincinnati, St. Louis, and Philadelphia; it was not able, however, to obtain access to New York.

In the South the first railroad activity in the years immediately after 1865 was the rehabilitation of facilities damaged in the war. Then an outburst of construction, financed by Northern and European capital, got under way, and by 1890 the South had increased its trackage from 9,000 to 50,000 miles. In 1893 the Southern Railway was organized, with lines extending from Washington to New Orleans and connecting with the Middle West at St. Louis and Cincinnati. Chief rival to the Southern was the Atlantic Coast Line Railroad, which consolidated dozens of small roads to monopolize transportation from Richmond to Florida. The third big system in the South, the Illinois Central, was really a Middle Western road with a Southern terminal. Shortly before the Civil War it had built as far as Cairo, Illinois, at the confluence of the Ohio and the Mississippi. In the postwar era the Central achieved its original purpose of reaching the Gulf of Mexico. By gobbling up smaller lines in the South, it increased its trackage from approximately 1,000 to 9,000 miles, reached New Orleans on the Gulf, and eventually touched the Atlantic at Savannah, Georgia.

From 1865 to 1873 there was more railroad construction in the Mississippi Valley than in any other part of the country. The Chicago and Northwestern stretched its lines to Omaha; the Chicago, Burlington and Quincy drove through to Kearney, Nebraska; the Missouri Pacific built from Kansas City to St. Louis; and the Kansas Pacific moved from Kansas City to Denver and then on to Cheyenne in Wyoming Territory.

THE TRANSCONTINENTAL LINES

Of all the stupendous railroad projects of the era between 1865 and 1900, none so gripped the popular imagination as the great "transcontinental" lines. An act of Congress passed in 1862 and amended in 1864 chartered two railroad corporations, the Union Pacific and the Central

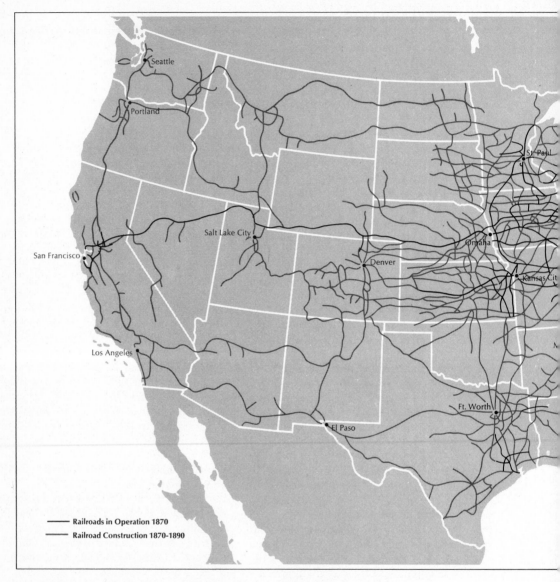

Railroads in Operation   1870; Railroad Construction   1870–1890

Railroads in Operation 1870
Railroad Construction 1870-1890

Pacific. The Union Pacific was to build westward from Omaha, Nebraska, and the Central Pacific eastward from Sacramento, California, until they met.

To provide the financial aid deemed necessary to initiate the roads, Congress donated a right of way across the public domain and offered the companies special benefits: for each mile of track a company laid, it would receive twenty square miles of land in alternate sec-

tions along the right of way and a thirty-year loan of $16,000, $32,000, or $48,000, depending on whether the construction was in plains, foothill, or mountain country.

Because of a scarcity of labor, the Union Pacific resorted to hiring thousands of Irish immigrants, while the Central Pacific imported several thousand Chinese workers. The builders had to cross deserts, penetrate mountain ranges, and fight off Indians. In the spring of

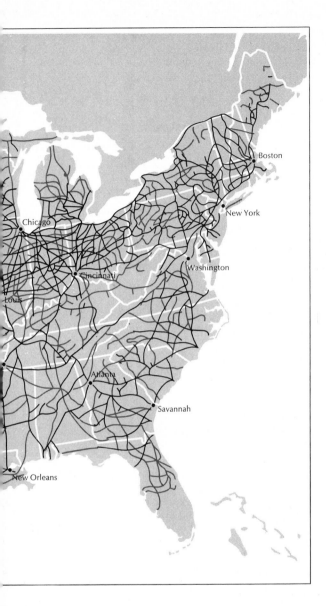

Portland, Oregon; (4) the Atchison, Topeka, and Santa Fe, running from Atchison, Kansas, to San Diego, California; and (5) the Great Northern, stretching from Duluth and St. Paul to Seattle and Tacoma, Washington. All except the Great Northern were built with some form of assistance from the national government or from state governments.

State governments put up an estimated $228 million to entice promoters into their boundaries, and in addition placed their credit at the disposal of railroads, subscribed to stock, and donated 50 million acres of land. The federal government granted over 130 million acres and provided over $60 million in loans to various Western roads. In a number of cases, the aid supplied by the government more than paid for the cost of construction. It was small wonder that many people regarded the railroads, although operated by private enterprise, as essentially public projects.

As the network of rails covered the country, it became evident that the railroad industry was being overbuilt and overextended; many railroad corporations, including some of the largest ones, were overexpanded, overcapitalized, and afflicted with impossible debt burdens. Moreover, many roads were looted and wrecked by their own directors or subjected to harassing competition by speculators like Jay Gould. In some areas of the country certain railroads enjoyed monopolies, but wherever competition existed it was savage and sustained. Competing roads fought ferocious rate wars and struggled for business by offering rebates to big shippers. The inevitable effects of overexpansion, fraudulent management, and cutthroat competition were apparent in the depression of the seventies, when 450 roads went into bankruptcy. Twenty years later, in the hard times of the nineties, 318 companies controlling 67,000 miles fell into the hands of receivers.

After the economic crisis of 1893 railroad capitalists moved to curb competition by creating larger systems. Reorganizing the railroads required huge sums of cash and credit, which could be supplied only by the big New York investment banking houses. The investment bankers, led by J. P. Morgan, were eager to finance consolidation in order to stop the railroads, with their wild financing and frenzied speculating, from ruining the investment busi-

1869, engines of the two lines met at Promontory Point in Utah Territory, and the nation was linked by rail from the Atlantic to the Pacific.

By the end of the century five transcontinental systems were in operation: (1) the Union Pacific–Central Pacific, joining Omaha to Sacramento and San Francisco; (2) the Southern Pacific, extending from San Francisco to St. Louis and New Orleans; (3) the Northern Pacific, linking St. Paul and Minneapolis to

ness. But the bankers, as the price for their aid, insisted on being given a voice in the management of the roads, a condition which the railroad promoters had to accept. By the end of the century a few major railroad systems controlled over half the mileage in the country, and these systems were wholly or partially controlled by two banking houses.

Growth of Cities

Society was being transformed along with the economy: a rural nation was being reshaped in an urban mold as cities grew with the growth of industry. The urban areas were the seats of the developing economic system, the places where most of the factories and corporate offices were located. Cities had existed from colonial times, of course, but now they assumed a new character, size, and significance.

The movement to cities was a contemporary phenomenon of much of the Western world. From countries—or parts of countries—that were industrializing slowly if at all, people moved to other countries—or to other parts of their own country—that were industrializing rapidly. Rural folk from both America and Europe made their way to the business and industrial centers of the United States.

THE CITY'S LURE

"We cannot all live in cities, yet nearly all seem determined to do so," Horace Greeley wrote soon after the Civil War. " 'Hot and cold water,' baker's bread, gas, the theatre, and the streetcars . . . indicate the tendency of modern taste." The city lured people because of its many conveniences, among them the telephone and the electric light, which it enjoyed for years before such things reached the village or the farm. It drew people because of its institutions of entertainment and culture, not only its theaters and other amusements but also its libraries and museums, its superior colleges and schools. It attracted people because, above all, it offered opportunities for employment at higher pay than the countryside afforded. The lure of the city persisted even though many who came were disappointed and urban life acquired some very unpleasant characteristics.

In the half century from 1860 to 1910 the rural population almost doubled, but the urban population increased seven times. In 1860 ap-

proximately one-sixth of the people lived in towns of 8,000 or larger; by 1900, one-third of the people. The number of cities with more than 50,000 inhabitants was 16 in 1860 and 109 in 1910. The population of the New York urban area (the city and its environs) grew from less than 1 million in 1860 to more than 3 million in 1900. Even more spectacular was the growth of Chicago, which had 100,000 inhabitants in 1860 and more than a million at the end of the century. Towns and cities were getting bigger and more numerous in all sections of the country. And this vast industrial-urban complex that was taking shape was linked in all its parts by rapid railroad transportation and instantaneous telegraphic communication.

While the cities gained, some rural parts of the country were actually losing population (as had happened to a much smaller extent in the early nineteenth century). During the 1880s, for instance, the number of inhabitants was decreasing in two-fifths of Pennsylvania's total area, three-fifths of Connecticut's, more than half of Ohio's and Illinois', and five-sixths of New York's. People seldom moved directly to a city from the farms. As the historian A. M. Schlesinger has observed, "the tendency was to move from the countryside to the nearest hamlet, from the hamlet to the town, and from the town to the city." So for a time the country town retained some importance as a market and a cultural center, but more and more the city overshadowed it. The city was the ultimate goal of restless farm and village folk. They and the immigrants, most of whom also came from rural areas, made up the great majority of urban dwellers.

THE NEWER IMMIGRANTS

Between 1860 and 1900 the total population of the United States more than doubled, rising from about 31 million to almost 76 million. Im-

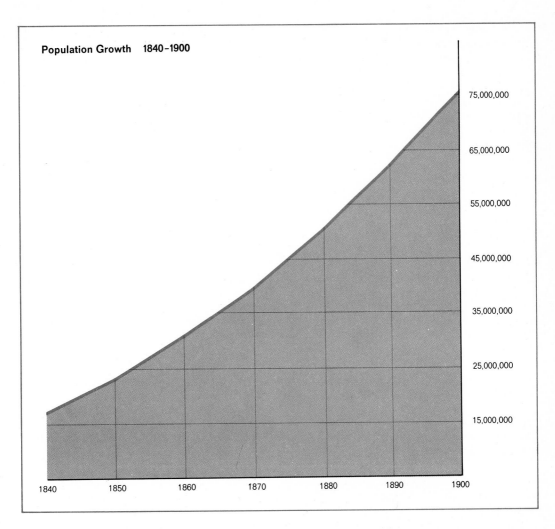

Population Growth   1840–1900

75,000,000

65,000,000

55,000,000

45,000,000

35,000,000

25,000,000

15,000,000

1840   1850   1860   1870   1880   1890   1900

The total population of the country increased significantly every decade between 1840 and 1900. At the close of the century the number of Americans was over four times the figure in 1840 and over twice that at the beginning of the Civil War.

migration accounted for a substantial portion of the increase; in this forty-year period some 14 million aliens entered the country. This was almost three times the 5 million who had come in the four decades preceding 1860, but in relation to the total population the immigrant tide was no greater after the Civil War than before. The percentage of foreign-born was about the same. In 1880 the ethnic composition of the population was substantially what it had been fifty years before. Up to that year the great majority of the immigrants had originated in the countries of Western and Northern Europe: England, Ireland, Germany, and the Scandinavian countries.

But in the eighties the immigrant stream began to flow from another source – Southern and Eastern Europe. By the 1890s about fifty-two in one hundred immigrants were coming from this part of the world (in the 1860s it had been fewer than two in one hundred). Among the new ethnic stocks were Austrians, Hungarians, Bohemians, Poles, Serbs, Italians, Russians, and Jews from Poland and Russia.

The Mixed Crowd [1890]

In his famous book *How the Other Half Lives* (1890) the Danish-born newspaper reporter Jacob A. Riis had this to say about what he called "The Mixed Crowd" as it developed in New York City during the 1880s:

When once I asked the agent of a notorious Fourth Ward alley how many people might be living in it I was told: one hundred and forty families, one hundred Irish, thirty-eight Italian, and two that spoke the German tongue. Barring the agent herself, there was not a native-born individual in the court. The answer was characteristic of the cosmopolitan character of lower New York, very nearly so of the whole of it, wherever it runs to alleys and courts. One may find for the asking an Italian, a German, a French, African, Spanish, Bohemian, Russian, Scandinavian, Jewish, and Chinese colony. Even the Arab, who peddles "holy earth" from the Battery as a direct importation from Jerusalem, has his exclusive preserves at the lower end of Washington Street. The one thing you shall vainly ask for in the chief city of America is a distinctively American community. There is none; certainly not among the tenements. . . .

The once unwelcome Irishman has been followed in his turn by the Italian, the Russian Jew, and the Chinaman, and has himself taken a hand at opposition, quite as bitter and quite as ineffectual, against these later hordes. Wherever these have gone they have crowded him out, possessing the block, the street, the ward with their denser swarms. . . .

A map of the city, colored to designate nationalities, would show more stripes than the skin of a zebra, and more colors than any rainbow.

These people came for essentially the same reasons as earlier immigrants: the desire to escape unfavorable economic and political conditions at home. Now railroads, in order to dispose of landholdings, painted an alluring picture of America in advertisements. Industrial employers demanded cheap labor and until 1885 could import workers under the labor contract law, paying for their passage in advance and deducting the amount later from their wages. After the repeal of the law, employers continued to encourage the immigration of unskilled laborers, often with the assistance of foreign-born labor brokers such as the Greek and Italian *padrones* who provided work gangs of their fellow nationals.

Of the earlier immigrants only the Irish had tended to congregate in the Eastern cities. Most of the Germans went West to become farmers, while those that had a proclivity for urban life settled in such Middle Western centers as Milwaukee, St. Louis, and Cincinnati. Nearly all of the Scandinavians took up land in the Middle West or the Great Plains. Those earlier arrivals who became urban dwellers were, with exception of the Irish, businessmen,

professional men, or skilled laborers; and the Irish, who at first were unskilled laborers, rapidly achieved economic independence and raised their social status. In direct contrast, the later immigrants flocked in preponderant numbers to the industrial cities and became unskilled laborers. They did not have the capital to begin farming operations in the West. They had to have immediate employment, and this was offered them by the meat packers, railroads, coal producers, and steel manufacturers, hungry for cheap labor. Besides, in a strange land the newcomers felt the need of that association with their fellows that only city life could give.

The later immigrants provoked fear and resentment among native Americans, as many of the earlier arrivals had done. The newcomers were in overwhelming numbers Catholics in a predominantly Protestant country, and their influx called into existence a short-lived nativist organization, the American Protective Association, which was vaguely but bitterly antialien and anti-Catholic. Some people reacted against the immigrants out of plain prejudice, while others honestly wondered if they could be absorbed into national life. Laborers, fighting to raise their incomes and improve their working conditions, were incensed by the willingness of the immigrants to accept lower wages and to take over jobs of strikers.

With the mounting of the alien tide, the first demands for immigration restrictions rose in the land. Congress acted in 1882 to exclude the Chinese. In the same year it passed a general immigration law denying entry to certain undesirables—convicts, paupers, idiots—and placed a tax of 50 cents on every person admitted. Later legislation of the nineties enlarged the proscriptive list and increased the tax. These measures reflected a rising fear that continuing unlimited immigration would exhaust the resources of the nation and endanger its social institutions. They kept out only a small number of aliens, however, and were far from fulfilling the purposes of the extreme exclusionists. The latter group worked for a literacy test, a device intended to exclude immigrants from Eastern and Southern Europe. Congress passed a literacy law in 1897, but President Grover Cleveland vetoed it. Powerful business interests, the employers of cheap labor, continued to oppose restrictions.

THE URBAN SCENE

The city was a place of unbelievable contrasts, with the most palatial homes and the most wretched hovels, the greatest of conveniences and the worst of problems—misgovernment, poverty, overcrowding, traffic jams, filth, epidemics, and conflagrations. The basic trouble was that the city was growing too fast for planning and building to keep pace. "The problem in America," as one municipal reformer said, "has been to make a great city in a few years out of nothing."

Most city people rented the places they lived in. Landowners, to maximize the rent, encouraged as many as possible to crowd into a given space. New York was not only the largest but also the most congested city. On Manhattan Island, by 1894, the average population density had reached 143 per acre, as compared with 127 for Paris and 101 for Berlin. More than a million poor New Yorkers were jammed in tenements. (Originally the word *tenement* meant simply a multiple-family rented build-

ing; eventually the term was applied only to slum dwellings.) When the first tenement was put up (in 1850), it was hailed as a great improvement in housing for the poor. "It is built with the design of supplying the laboring people with cheap lodgings," a local newspaper commented, "and will have many advantages over the cellars and other miserable abodes, which too many are forced to inhabit." But tenements themselves became miserable abodes, three to five stories high, with many windowless rooms, little or no provision for plumbing or for central heating, and perhaps a row of privies in the basement. A New York state law of 1879 required a window in every bedroom of tenements built thereafter. Still, in 1890, the Danish immigrant and New York newspaper reporter Jacob Riis found deplorable conditions, which he described in his book *How the Other Half Lives*. A typical building was sunless and practically airless and "poisoned" by "summer stenches." "The hall is dark and you might stumble over the children pitching pennies back there."

Some of the wealthy lived in downtown mansions. Many of the rich or the reasonably well-to-do tried to combine the advantages of city and country living by moving to the city's outskirts. In the 1870s Chicago boasted of nearly one hundred residential suburbs connected with the city by railroad and offering the joys of "pure air, peacefulness, quietude, and natural scenery." The growth of the city and its suburbs—and indeed the maintenance of the very life of the city—depended on improvements in urban transportation.

Old city streets were in many cases too narrow for the heavy traffic that was beginning to move over them. A few were paved with cobblestones, but most of them lacked a hard surface and were filled alternately with mud and dust. In the last decades of the century, more and more streets were paved, usually with wooden blocks, bricks, or asphalt, but paving could not even keep up with the laying out of new thoroughfares. By 1890 Chicago had surfaced only about 600 of more than 2,000 miles of streets.

Up and down the streets of every city a variety of horse-drawn vehicles clattered—wagons and drays, hacks and omnibuses, and private carriages of many kinds—littering the ground with horse droppings that attracted

Street Scene, New York City
*By 1895, horse-drawn streetcars had given way to electric trolleys, and
steam-powered elevated trains to electrified lines. Cabs and other vehicles
continued to be pulled by horses. From a drawing, "The Bowery at Night," by
W. Louis Sonntag, Jr. (Museum of the City of New York)*

flies in summer. The great cities of the time
could hardly have existed without the horse,
and many of them were nearly paralyzed when
an epidemic of the epizootic, a horse disease,
swept through the Northeast and the Midwest
in the 1870s. In normal times the vehicles could
scarcely move at the busiest hours of the day.
As early as the 1850s New York visitors had
been amazed by the frequency with which the
"whole traffic of the city" came to a "deadlock."

Already streetcars drawn by horses were
operating on rails laid down in many city
s. eets; by 1866 New York had 16 lines using
800 cars and nearly 8,000 horses. Passengers
found the horsecars smoother and a little faster

than omnibuses, but not fast enough. In 1870
New York opened its first elevated railway,
with cars pulled by steam locomotives, which
were noisy and often scattered hot ashes on
pedestrians below. New York, Chicago, San
Francisco, and other cities experimented with
cable cars, which were towed by an endless
cable that moved underground and was pow-
ered by a stationary steam engine. A better
solution came with the development of the
electrified railway, which first appeared in
Richmond, Virginia, in 1888, when 40 trolley
cars began to run over a 12-mile line. Trolley
systems spread rapidly, and by 1895 they were
operating in 850 towns and cities, with a total of
10,000 miles of track. Interurban lines were

beginning to be extended through the country-side. In 1897, putting streetcars below ground, Boston opened the first American subway, a mile and a half long.

The horsecar and then the trolley enabled cities to expand and suburbs to grow. As a rule, cities spread fastest along the radiating lines of transportation, in a kind of star-shaped pattern. They grew upward as well as outward. The technique of constructing skyscrapers, with cast-iron and then steel frames, was first perfected in Chicago, where a ten-story office building rose in 1884. By that time the electric elevator was replacing the steam-powered hoist and making possible safe and rapid vertical movement. As tall buildings became more numerous, traffic congestion increased on city streets.

Chicago had been forced to rebuild after a conflagration in 1871, and Boston suffered a disastrous fire the same year. While more fire-proof structures were appearing, wooden buildings continued to predominate in every city, and these were always in danger of going up in flames. To meet the hazard, volunteer fire fighters were beginning to give way to professional fire departments.

An even greater hazard was disease, especially in the slums, whence it often spread to the better areas of a city. Even though the germ theory was known to public-health experts, few people appreciated the relationship of sewage disposal and water contamination to such epidemic diseases as typhoid fever and cholera. To the end of the nineteenth century, most city dwellers relied on private vaults and cesspools for the disposal of human wastes. The water closet (flush toilet) had been perfected in the 1870s, and a number of cities had begun to extend their sewerage systems, but these seldom kept up with population growth. Besides, the sewer commonly emptied into an open ditch within the city limits or into a stream nearby, from which the city itself or some other city derived its drinking water. Philadelphia, for example, polluted its own water supply by pouring raw sewage into the Delaware River. By 1900 a few cities had fairly adequate sewage disposal, regular garbage collections, and water-purification systems.

Urbanization brought more than new conveniences and new insecurities. "The complex interrelationship of life in the modern city called for unprecedented precision," as the historian Oscar Handlin has written. "The arrival of all those integers who worked together, from whatever part of the city they inhabited, had to be coordinated to the moment. There was no natural span for such labor; arbitrary beginnings and ends had to be set and adhered to. The dictatorship of the clock and the schedule became absolute." Thus the modern city brought a new concept of time, which to rural Americans had been a matter of human whims and natural phenomena such as sunrises and sunsets. Rural Americans, still the great majority, had an ambivalent attitude toward the city. While a place of strong allure, it was also to them a place of poverty and sin, and of foreigners with their strange customs. However country people felt toward it, the city imposed its ways upon them as well as its own inhabitants. More and more, it set the pattern for American character and culture.

BOSS RULE

The new immigrants, like the old ones, came with high hopes to what they expected to be a land of opportunity. In New York harbor, where most of them arrived, they received a symbolic welcome from the Statue of Liberty after it was erected in 1886 as a gift from the people of France. The welcome was later to be spelled out in these words of Emma Lazarus, inscribed on the statue's base:

> *Give me your tired, your poor,*
> *Your huddled masses yearning to*
>   *breathe free. . . .*

After landing, however, most of the newcomers faced frustration and bewilderment. Unused to city life, unable to speak English, scorned by native Americans and by rival immigrant groups as well, desperate for jobs, people of the various nationalities remained as "huddled masses" in the wretchedness of their separate ghettoes.

Needy families, both native and foreign-born, could look to private charitable societies for assistance, but generally these were run by middle-class humanitarians who insisted on middle-class standards of morality. Such societies operated on the belief that poverty was more commonly due to laziness and vice than to misfortune. After careful investigation they confined their help to the "deserving poor." In 1879, a year after its founding in London, the Salvation Army began its work in American cities, but at first it concentrated on religious revivals rather than on the relief of the homeless and hungry. Not till many years later was the government—local, state, or federal—to assume much responsibility for welfare work.

For most of the urban poor, especially the foreign-born and their families, the main welfare agency was the political machine, headed by a boss, who himself was typically of foreign birth or parentage, most commonly Irish. To maintain his power, the boss needed votes, and in exchange for these he offered favors of various kinds. He provided the poor with occasional relief, such as a basket of groceries or a bag of coal. He stepped in to save from jail those arrested for petty crimes. When he could, he found work for the unemployed. Most important, he rewarded his followers with political jobs, with opportunities to rise in the party organization.

The boss made money for himself and financed his machine through corruption. He awarded contracts for the construction of streets, sewers, public buildings, and other projects at prices well above the real cost, then divided the extra money with the contractors. He also sold franchises for the operation of public utilities such as street railways, waterworks, and electric light and power systems. Since many of the wealthiest and most prominent citizens profited from their dealings with him, he had strong support among the rich as well as the poor.

Boss rule was made possible if not inevitable by the weakness of city government. Within the government, no single official was given decisive power or responsibility. Power was divided among a number of officeholders—the mayor, the aldermen, and others—and was limited by the state legislature, which had the ultimate authority over municipal affairs. Centralizing power in his own hands, the boss together with his machine formed a sort of "invisible government" that made up for the inadequacy of the regular government. He might or might not hold an official position himself. Through his organization, upon which the politicians of his party depended for election, he controlled a majority of those who were in office.

From time to time middle-class reformers along with disgruntled politicians might manage to overthrow a boss, as they did with William M. Tweed of New York City's notorious "Tweed Ring" in 1871. Yet the system of boss rule continued to flourish, in New York and in other large cities, because the conditions that produced it remained essentially unchanged.

Capitalism and Its Critics

With the rise of big business, a varied rationale was developed to justify its methods and its consequences. There also appeared a variety of criticisms. Still, the philosophy of business prevailed not only among the captains of industry themselves but also among the majority of the American people.

SELF-MADE MEN

The economic revolution raised up a new ruling class in America. The industrialists and the investment bankers now sat in the seats of power formerly held by Southern planters and Northeastern merchants, by members of the old aristocracy of inherited wealth and the old middle class, by politicians and statesmen of the antebellum Webster-Clay model.

Before the Civil War there had been few millionaires in America; by 1892 there were more than 4,000 of them. Most of the new business tycoons had begun their careers from comfortable and privileged positions in the economic scale. But some—enough to invest the entire group with the aura of the American success story—had emerged from obscurity to riches. Andrew Carnegie had worked as a bobbin boy in a Pittsburgh cotton mill, James J. Hill had been a frontier clerk, John D. Rockefeller had started out as a clerk in a Cleveland commission house, and E. H. Harriman had begun as a broker's office boy. Regardless of economic background, the new millionaires were—or considered themselves to be—self-made men.

Many had gotten ahead through a ruthless disregard for the public welfare. Their attitude was epitomized by Commodore Vanderbilt's belligerent question: "Can't I do what I want with my own?" and by the much quoted statement of his son William: "The public be damned." Once, when the Commodore's lawyers warned him that a move he contemplated was illegal, he bellowed: "What do I care about the law? Hain't I got the power?" Men like Vanderbilt had the power, indeed. Through their financial contributions to politicians and to parties, by gifts of stock and outright bribes to political personages, they generally managed to get what they wanted from the national and the state governments. It was said that Standard Oil did everything to the Ohio legisla-

ture except to refine it. On one occasion a member of the Pennsylvania legislature was reported to have said: "Mr. Speaker, I move we adjourn unless the Pennsylvania Railroad has some more business for us to transact."

Wholesale bribery was a weapon in the notorious "Erie war" fought by Commodore Vanderbilt against Jay Gould and Jim Fisk for control of the Erie Railroad. Vanderbilt attempted to take over the Erie by buying stock, a move which his antagonists blocked by the simple expedient of printing more stock than he could purchase. When a bill to legalize the issue of the new stock was introduced in the New York legislature, Gould was present with $500,000, and also on hand was a Vanderbilt agent. Exactly how much money was paid out by both parties before the Commodore admitted defeat is not known. The market price of

The Modern Robber Barons

In this cartoon the millionaires of business are likened to the "robber barons" of the Middle Ages. As the serfs brought tribute to the feudal lords, so farmers, laborers, and small businessmen had to pay tribute in the form of wages and interest to the masters of the trusts. The term "robber baron" as a descriptive tag for the big businessmen of the period became popular and even passed into historical usage. From Puck *(1889).*

legislators during the fight was $15,000 a head. One influential and imaginative leader collected $75,000 from Vanderbilt and $100,000 from Gould.

Before passing judgment on the relation of business to government, however, it should be noted that in many cases the politicians deliberately created situations where they had to be bought — in effect, they blackmailed businessmen. And whatever indictments may be brought against the lords of business, these men were emphatically products of their environment; even the most crude and crass of their activities reflected prevailing mores in American society. The big corporations did a quick, if sometimes wasteful and ruthless, job of developing the country's potential economic resources. And the businessmen who headed the corporations ran various risks in whatever they did — the risk of overexpansion, the risk of unscrupulous competition. Not every businessman became a Rockefeller or a Gould.

Even the most ruthless of the tycoons were builders rather than wreckers. They were building, perhaps without realizing what they were doing, the basis of a great economic society. By integrating operations and cutting costs, they were, says Frederick Lewis Allen, opening the way to economical mass production: "In the process of playing remunerative games with the tokens that represented capital, the bankers and the steel men had introduced into America something new: twentieth-century industry, undisciplined still, but full of promise."

SURVIVAL OF THE FITTEST

Most tycoons believed that they had attained their wealth by exercising the old American and Protestant virtues of hard work, acquisitiveness, and thrift. They had gotten where they were because they deserved it; people who were not so fortunate were lazy, unintelligent, or profligate. In some way it was all connected with the moral law and with divine will. "God gave me my money," explained John D. Rockefeller.

To many businessmen, the formula of social Darwinism seemed to explain both their own success and the nature of the society in which they operated. Social Darwinism was Charles Darwin's law of evolution applied to social organization. As expounded by the Englishman Herbert Spencer, it taught that struggle was a normal human activity, especially in economic life. The weak went down, the strong endured and became stronger, and society was benefited because the unfit were eliminated and the fit survived.

Men who had risen to dominance by crushing their competitors were intrigued and comforted by a doctrine that justified any method that succeeded, and they proclaimed that wealth was a reward of competence. Carnegie, who made himself the leading disciple of Spencer in the United States, contended that the natural law of competition was responsible for the great material growth of the country: "It is here; we can not evade it; no substitutes for it have been found; and while the law may be sometimes hard on the individual, it is best for the race, because it insures the survival of the fittest in every department."

According to social Darwinism, all attempts by labor to raise its wages by forming unions and all endeavors by government to regulate economic activities would fail, because economic life was controlled by a natural law, the law of competition. This coincided with another supposed "law" that seemed to justify business practices and business dominance: the law of supply and demand as defined by Adam Smith and the classical economists. According to them, the economic system was like a great and delicate machine functioning by natural and automatic rules. The greatest among these rules, the law of supply and demand, determined all economic values — prices, wages, rents, interest rates — at a level that was just to all concerned. Supply and demand worked because man was essentially an economic creature who understood and followed his own interests, and because he operated in a free market where competition was open to all.

Businessmen mouthed the clichés of classical economics even though the combinations they were creating were undermining the foundations of the free competitive market and modifying, if not destroying, the validity of the law of supply and demand. Samuel C. T. Dodd, the lawyer who devised the trust organization for Standard Oil, spoke glowingly of the unrestrained right of competition and the unrestrained right of combination. What would happen to competition if combination triumphed, Dodd did not explain.

Leaders of Big Business

Reflecting the division of public opinion, contemporary writings about late nineteenth-century business leaders usually were either flattering or denunciatory. In the "muckraking" years of the early twentieth century, denunciation came to predominate. Thus Ida M. Tarbell, *The History of the Standard Oil Company* (1904), presented John D. Rockefeller as a predatory character who drove smaller oilmen out of business by unscrupulous means. Gustavus Myers, *The History of the Great American Fortunes* (1907), undertook to show that other successful businessmen had also amassed their wealth by crushing competitors and corrupting politicians, not by practicing the old-fashioned American virtues of honesty, thrift, and hard work.

The treatment of these businessmen became more favorable during the prosperous 1920s. In *The Rise of American Civilization* (1927) Charles and Mary Beard described them as "captains of industry" who contributed to industrial development through their remarkable powers of organization. During the depression of the 1930s, however, the pioneers of big business again fell into disrepute. Matthew Josephson gave them a name that most historians accepted in his popular book *The Robber Barons* (1934). Josephson compared them to feudal lords who got rich by preying on legitimate commerce.

Allan Nevins challenged the Josephson view in *John D. Rockefeller: The Heroic Age of American Enterprise,* which was originally published in 1940 and republished with revisions and elaborations in 1953. Nevins depicted Rockefeller as an industrial statesman who brought order and efficiency to the oil business. The Nevins interpretation reflected the changed attitude that came with World War II and the cold war, when it seemed to many Americans that the industrial greatness of the United States made possible a successful effort to save the world from totalitarianism.

Meanwhile, from the 1920s on, historians at the Harvard Business School and elsewhere were writing business history without moral judgments. These "entrepreneurial historians," among them Kenneth W. Porter and Thomas C. Cochran, were primarily interested in techniques of management, in the kinds of decision-making that had led particular companies to success or to failure. Such writers looked for object lessons in the past that might be of value to business managers in the present.

Tempering the principle of the survival of the fittest was the "gospel of wealth." If rich men held economic power, they also had responsibilities to exercise their power with Christian magnanimity. If God gave the tycoons their money, as John D. Rockefeller believed, it behooved them to use the money for social purposes.

Carnegie himself elaborated on the idea in his book *The Gospel of Wealth* (1901). The man of wealth, he wrote, ought to consider all revenues in excess of his own needs as "trust funds" that he should administer for the good of the community, "thus becoming the mere trustee and agent for his poorer brethren." Carnegie did not believe in giving directly to the poor, for he feared that such charity would have a pauperizing effect. He preferred to contribute to institutions, notably libraries, that presumably would help the poor to help themselves. He and other men of wealth devoted part of their fortunes to philanthropic works.

The notion of private wealth as a public blessing was spread by numerous popularizers. One of the most persistent was Russell H. Conwell, a Baptist minister, who delivered one lecture on the subject, *Acres of Diamonds*, over 6,000 times. "We ought to get rich if we can by honorable and Christian methods," cried Conwell (who got rich by lecturing), "and those are the only methods that sweep us quickly toward the goal of riches."

Conwell was a champion of another concept that was becoming a part of the American myth: the success story, the notion that any poor boy who was industrious and thrifty could succeed in business. Most of the millionaires in the country, Conwell claimed, had begun on the lowest rung of the economic ladder. Another promoter of the success story was Horatio Alger, a New York minister who wrote over a hundred novels of which, all together, more than 20 million copies were sold. These books rejoiced in such titles as *Andy Grant's Pluck, Tom the Bootblack,* and *Sink or Swim.* In every volume a poor boy from a small town went to the big city to seek his fortune, and by work, perseverance, and luck he became rich.

DOUBT AND DISSENT

Most people, poor as well as rich, accepted the rationalizations that were made by and for big business, but there were many who listened to voices of doubt and dissent. Thoughtful Americans did not agree among themselves on the lessons to be derived from Darwin's theory of evolution.

It was, perhaps, characteristic of optimistic Americans to combine the Darwinian method with the older idea of progress and come up with a hopeful prognostication. Such an analysis was attempted by Lewis H. Morgan, a pioneer anthropologist, in his *Ancient Society* (1878), in which he traced human development from its first simple beginnings to the complex but beneficent industrial order of the nineteenth century. The works of men like Morgan stressed that change was gradual and cumulative in character and that present society was safely linked with the past. Although such writers foresaw a hopeful future, they rejected the concept of unlimited progress that had marked earlier American thought. They also departed from former notions in insisting that change was evolutionary instead of revolutionary and that American development was a phase of a larger European or world scheme and not a unique experiment in a specially favored land. Opposing directions taken by American Darwinians are illustrated by the writings of two pioneers in sociology: William Graham Sumner and Lester F. Ward.

Sumner, a scholar with a tough mind and a sharp tongue, elaborated his theories in lectures at Yale, in magazine articles, and finally in a famous book, *Folkways* (1906). In contradiction to earlier thinkers who had held that man was a free agent actuated by rational powers, Sumner contended that the human mind was molded by circumstances beyond its control and that men's activities consisted of routine behavior determined by mechanistic forces. In short, man had no innate ideas and no power to reform his environment. His freedom was limited to certain narrow areas in which tradition permitted him to operate. But within these areas, Sumner insisted, man must have absolute freedom to struggle, to compete, to gratify his instinct for self-interest. The struggle for survival should be allowed to work itself out, and should not be delimited by laws or the state. Sumner's devotion to the principle of the survival of the fittest caused him to be known as the foremost champion of social Darwinism. Yet his insistence on the freedom to compete caused him to oppose protective tariffs and thus made him a critic of business policy. Essentially, he was trying to preserve the older America of truly free enterprise by employing the new insights of Darwinism.

Standing in direct opposition to Sumner was Lester Ward, though he was just as much a Darwinian as the Yale sage. Ward expressed his concepts in a number of notable books, beginning with *Dynamic Sociology* (1883). He argued that various forces altered the Darwinian process when applied to complex societies. Desire became subordinate to and controlled by intelligence. Mind thus became the master of nature, and man became capable of devising instruments to direct and improve his evolutionary future. The chief goal of modern society, Ward said, was the greatest good of all its members, and the best instrument to attain the goal was government. In contrast to Sumner, who believed that state intervention to remodel the environment was futile, Ward thought that a positive, planning government was man's only hope.

There came to be widespread acceptance of the principle that institutions should meet social needs and thus be "functional." Even in the churches there was an effort to accommodate functional concepts. Noted ministers and theologians like Washington Gladden, Walter Rauschenbusch, and Shailer Mathews proclaimed that religion had to concern itself with the material conditions in which Christ's children lived, and these men advocated such causes as industrial peace, better working conditions, slum clearance, and temperance.

SOCIALISTS AND SINGLE-TAXERS

While some Americans questioned the beneficence of capitalism, others proposed more or less drastic changes in the system, and at least a few thought it should be thrown out entirely.

Americans were less inclined than Europeans to adopt extremely radical programs such as the "scientific socialism" of Karl Marx (whose *Capital,* the first volume of which appeared in 1867, was one of the most influential books ever written) or the violent anarchism of Mikhail Bakunin. But Marxism and Anarchism had some following in America, especially among recent immigrants.

The Socialist Labor party, founded in the seventies, fell under the leadership of Daniel De Leon, an immigrant from the West Indies;

other party chiefs hailed from Eastern Europe. Although De Leon aroused something of a following in the industrial cities, the party never succeeded in polling over 82,000 votes. De Leon's somewhat theoretical and dogmatic approach pleased intellectuals but evoked no warmth among workers and seemed ill-suited to the American scene. A right-wing faction of the party sensed the fault in its approach and, seeking a more American approach, split away in 1900 to form the Socialist party.

Native radicals, with less extreme programs, gained a wider following. One of the most influential was Henry George. His angrily eloquent *Progress and Poverty*, published in 1879, was an immediate success; reprinted in successive editions, it became one of the ten best-selling nonfiction works in American publishing history. George addressed himself to the question of why poverty existed amidst the wealth created by modern industry. "This association of poverty with progress is the great enigma of our times," he wrote. "So long as all the increased wealth which modern progress brings goes but to build up great fortunes, to increase luxury and make sharper the contrast between the House of Have and the House of Want, progress is not real and cannot be permanent."

George blamed all this on monopoly, and he proposed a remedy, a "single tax" on the "unearned increment" in the value of land. An increase in the value of land resulted from the growth of society around it. Hence, George argued, the private owner had not earned the increment, and the community should receive it. A tax taking the whole of this increase would supposedly destroy monopolies, distribute wealth more equally, and eliminate poverty. Single-tax societies sprang up in many cities, and in 1886 George, backed by labor and the Socialists, narrowly missed being elected mayor of New York.

Rivaling George in popularity was Edward Bellamy, whose *Looking Backward*, published in 1888, became a best seller within a few years and eventually topped the million mark. Bellamy's book was a novel, a romance of a socialist utopia. It described the experiences of a young Bostonian who in 1887 went into a hypnotic sleep from which he awakened in the year 2000. He found a new social order, based on collective ownership of property, where want, politics, and vice were unknown, and where people were incredibly happy. All this had come about through a peaceful and evolutionary process: trusts had gone on combining with one another until they formed one big trust, and the government had taken this over. Shortly, over 160 "Nationalist Clubs" sprang up to propagate Bellamy's ideas, and the author devoted the remainder of his life to championing his brand of socialism.

Thirty-eight similar novels appeared in the nineties, though none of them approached Bellamy's in success. It is not to be thought that the hundreds of thousands of Americans who read Bellamy and the other utopian authors wished to see a socialist system established in the United States. Nor were they merely seeking

in literary fantasies an escape from the real problems of their times. The great majority were intrigued by the descriptions of societies that were prosperous and stable because government played a large role, and in their own troubled society they saw the need, not for a collective state, but for a larger place for government.

More realistic was the philosophy in Henry Demarest Lloyd's *Wealth Against Commonwealth*. Published in 1894, this book was a tremendous, although not always accurate, attack on the Standard Oil trust and the methods by which it had risen to dominance. Lloyd advocated strict governmental regulation of such monopolies.

Industrial Conflict

Very few industrial workers or labor leaders in late nineteenth-century America aimed to overthrow capitalism itself. What most of them wanted was a larger share of its benefits. Their efforts to get a larger share led to industrial conflicts that were often bitter and sometimes bloody.

LABOR ORGANIZES

As business became big, consolidated, and national, inevitably labor attempted to create its own organizations that would match the power of capital. The economic revolution changed the worker from an artisan who owned his own tools to a factory laborer who operated machines owned by his employer; it placed his wages, his tenure, his working environment at the pleasure of an impersonal corporation too powerful for the individual worker to bargain with. Between 1865 and 1897 – a period of falling prices and a consequent decline in the cost of living – real wages increased, except for those workers who lost their jobs because of technological or cyclical unemployment. Nevertheless, at the turn of the century the income of the average worker was pitifully small: $400 – $500 a year. Students of the standard of living estimated that, to maintain a decent level of comfort, a yearly income of $600 was the absolute minimum. According to one survey, 10

million Americans lived in poverty. The average workday in 1900 was ten hours, for a six-day week. Because employers paid little attention to safety devices or programs, the accident rate was appalling: 1 in every 26 railroad workers was injured, 1 in every 399 killed per year.

Against such conditions, labor fought back by forming unions to bargain collectively with employers. During the Civil War, twenty craft unions were formed, and by 1870 the industrial states counted thirty such organizations, nearly every one of which represented skilled workers. The first attempt to federate separate unions into a single national organization came in 1866, when, under the leadership of William H. Sylvis, the National Labor Union was founded. Claiming a membership of 640,000, it was a polyglot association that included, in addition to a number of unions, a variety of reform groups having little direct relationship with labor. After the Panic of 1873 the National Labor Union disintegrated and disappeared.

The trade unions experienced stormy times during the hard years of the 1870s. Their bargaining power weakened by depression conditions, they faced antagonistic employers eager to destroy them, and a hostile public that rejected labor's claim to job security. Several of the disputes with capital were unusually bitter and were marked by violence, some of it labor's fault and some not, but for all of which labor received the blame. Startling to most

Americans was the exposure of the activities of the "Molly Maguires" in the anthracite coal region of Pennsylvania. A terrorist group, the "Mollies" operated within the Ancient Order of Hibernians (that is, Irishmen) and intimidated the coal operators with such direct methods as murder. But excitement over this was nothing compared to the near hysteria that gripped the country during the railroad strikes of 1877. The trouble started when the principal Eastern railroads announced a 10-percent slash in wages. Immediately railroad workers, whether organized or not, went out on strike. Rail service was disrupted from Baltimore to St. Louis, equipment was destroyed, and rioting mobs roamed the streets of Pittsburgh and other cities.

The strikes were America's first big labor conflict and a flaming illustration of a new reality in the American economic system: with business becoming nationalized, disputes between labor and capital could no longer be localized but would affect the entire nation. State militia were employed against the strikers, and finally, and significantly, federal troops were called on to suppress the disorders. The power of the various railroad unions was seriously sapped by the failure of the strikes, and the prestige of unions in other industries was weakened by similar setbacks.

THE KNIGHTS AND THE AFL

Meanwhile, another national labor organization appeared on the scene, the Noble Order of the Knights of Labor, founded in 1869 under the leadership of Uriah S. Stephens. Instead of attempting to federate unions, as the National Labor Union had done, the Knights organized their association on the basis of the individual. Membership was open to all who "toiled," and the definition of a toiler was extremely liberal: the only excluded groups were lawyers, bankers, liquor dealers, and professional gamblers. The amorphous masses of members were arranged in local "assemblies" that might consist of the workers in a particular trade or a local union or simply all the members of the Knights in a city or district. Presiding laxly over the entire order was an agency known as the general assembly. Much of the program of the Knights was as vague as the organization. Although they championed an eight-hour day and the

abolition of child labor, the leaders were more interested in the long-range reform of the economy than in the immediate objectives of wages and hours which appealed to the trade unions.

Under the leadership of Terence V. Powderly, the order entered upon a spectacular period of expansion that culminated in 1886 with the total membership reaching 700,000. Important factors contributing to the increase in numerical strength were a business recession in 1884 that threw many workers out of jobs, and a renewal of industrial strife that impelled unorganized laborers as well as some trade unions to affiliate with the Knights. Not only was the membership enlarged, but the order now included many militant elements that could not always be controlled by the moderate leadership. Against Powderly's wishes, local unions or assemblies associated with the Knights proceeded to inaugurate a series of strikes. In 1885 striking railway workers forced the Missouri Pacific, a link in the Gould system, to restore wage cuts and recognize their union. Although this victory redounded to the credit of the Knights, it was an ephemeral triumph. In the following year a strike on another Gould road, the Texas and Pacific, was crushed and the power of the unions in the Gould system was broken. By 1890 the membership of the Knights had shrunk to 100,000, and within a few years the order would be a thing of the past.

Even before the Knights had entered on their period of decline, a rival organization, based on an entirely different organizational concept, had appeared. In 1881 representatives of a number of craft unions formed the Federation of Organized Trade and Labor Unions of the United States and Canada. Five years later this body took the name which it has borne ever since, the American Federation of Labor (AFL). Under the direction of its president and guiding spirit, Samuel Gompers, the Federation soon became the most important labor group in the country. As its name implies, it was a federation or association of national trade unions, each of which enjoyed essential autonomy within the larger organization. Rejecting completely the idea of individual membership and the corollary of one big union for everybody, the Federation was built on the principle of the organization of skilled workers into craft unions.

The Haymarket Tragedy
This is a contemporary artist's conception of the bomb exploding among the police.
(Library of Congress)

The program of the Federation differed as markedly from that of the Knights as did its organizational arrangements. Gompers and his associates accepted the basic concepts of capitalism; their purpose was to secure for labor a greater share of capitalism's material rewards. Repudiating all notions of fundamental alteration of the existing system or long-range reform measures or a separate labor party, the AFL concentrated on labor's immediate objectives: wages, hours, and working conditions. While it hoped to attain its ends by collective bargaining, the Federation was ready to employ the strike if necessary.

As one of its first objectives, the Federation called for a national eight-hour day, to be attained by May 1, 1886, and to be obtained, if necessary, by a general strike. On the target day, strikes and demonstrations for a shorter workday took place all over the country. Although the national officers of the Knights had refused to cooperate in the movement, some local units joined in the demonstrations. So did a few unions that were dominated by anarchists — European radicals who wanted to destroy "class government" by terroristic methods — and that were affiliated with the so-called Black International. The most sensational demonstrations occurred in Chicago, which was a labor stronghold and an anarchist center.

At the time, a strike was in progress at the McCormick Harvester Company; and when the police harassed the strikers, labor and anarchist leaders called a protest meeting at the Haymarket Square. During the meeting, the police appeared and commanded those present to disperse. Someone — his identity was never determined — threw a bomb that resulted in the death of seven policemen and injury to sixty-seven others. The police, who on the previous day had killed four strikers, fired into the crowd and killed four more people. The score was about even. News of the Haymarket affair struck cold fear into Chicago and the business community of the nation. Blinded by hysteria, conservative, property-conscious Americans demanded a victim or victims—to demonstrate to labor that it must cease its course of violence. Chicago officials finally rounded up eight anarchists and charged them with the murder of the policemen on the grounds that they had incited the individual who hurled the bomb. In one of the most injudicious trials in the record of American juridical history, all were found guilty. One was sentenced to prison and seven to death. Of the seven, one cheated his sentence by committing suicide, four were executed, and two had their penalty commuted to life imprisonment.

Although some of the blame for the Haymarket tragedy was unloaded on the AFL, at least as much fell on the Knights, who had had almost nothing to do with the May demonstrations. In the public mind the Knights were dominated by anarchists and Socialists. The Knights never managed to free themselves from the stigma of radicalism as the AFL did.

THE HOMESTEAD STRIKE

Some of the most violent strikes in American labor history occurred in the nineties. Two of the strikes, the one at the Homestead plant of the Carnegie Steel Company in Pennsylvania

The Homestead Riot

The scene at the Homestead plant of the Carnegie Steel Company in Pennsylvania after the Pinkerton strikebreakers had surrendered to the striking employees. Drawing by W. P. Snyder in Harper's Weekly, *July 16, 1892. (Library of Congress)*

and the one against the Pullman Palace Car Company in the Chicago area, took place in companies controlled by men who prided themselves on being among the most advanced of American employers: Andrew Carnegie, who had written magazine articles defending the rights of labor, and George M. Pullman, who had built a "model town" to house his employees.

The Amalgamated Association of Iron and Steel Workers, which was affiliated with the American Federation of Labor, was the most powerful trade union in the country. It had never been able, however, to organize all the plants of the Carnegie Steel Company, the largest corporation in the industry; of the three major steel mills in the Carnegie system, the union was a force only in one, the Homestead plant. In 1892, when the strike occurred, Carnegie was in Scotland, visiting at a castle that he maintained as a gesture of ancestral pride, and the direction of the company was in the hands of Henry Clay Frick, manager of Homestead and chairman of the Carnegie firm. Carnegie was, nevertheless, responsible for the company's course. Despite his earlier fine words about labor, he had decided with Frick before leaving to operate Homestead on a non-union basis, even if this meant precipitating a clash with the union.

The trouble began when the management announced a new wage scale that would have meant cuts for a small minority of the workers. Frick abruptly shut down the plant, and asked the Pinkerton Detective Agency to furnish 300 guards to enable the company to resume operations on its own terms. (The Pinkerton Agency was really a strikebreaking concern.)

The hated Pinkertons, whose mere presence was enough to incite the workers to violence, approached the plant on barges in an adjacent river. Warned of their coming, the strikers met them at the docks with guns and dynamite, and a pitched battle ensued on July 6, 1892. After several hours of fighting, which brought death to three guards and ten strikers and severe injuries to many participants on both sides, the Pinkertons surrendered and were escorted roughly out of town. The company and local law officials then asked for militia protection from the Pennsylvania governor, who responded by sending the entire National Guard contingent, some 8,000 troops, to Homestead. Public opinion, at first sympathetic to the strikers, turned against them when an anarchist made an attempt to assassinate Frick. Slowly workers drifted back to their jobs.

THE PULLMAN STRIKE

A dispute of greater magnitude and equal bitterness, although involving less loss of life, was the Pullman strike in 1894. The Pullman Palace Car Company leased sleeping and parlor cars to most of the nation's railroads. At its plant near Chicago it manufactured and repaired cars. The company had built the 600-acre town of Pullman, containing dwellings that were rented to the employees. George M. Pullman, inventor of the sleeping car and owner of the company, liked to exhibit his town as a model solution of the industrial problem and to refer to the workers as his "children."

Nearly all of the workers were members of a union, a very militant one, the American Railway Union. This had recently been organized by Eugene V. Debs, a labor leader formerly active in the Railroad Brotherhoods. Becoming disgusted with the Brotherhoods' lack of interest in the lot of the unskilled workers, he had formed his own union, which soon attained a membership of 150,000, mainly in the Middle West.

The strike at Pullman began when the company during the winter of 1893–1894 slashed wages by an average of 25 percent. With revenues reduced by depression conditions, there was some reason for the company's action, but the cut was drastic, and several workers who served on a committee to protest to the management were discharged. At the same time, Pullman refused to reduce rentals in the model town, even though the charges were 20 to 25 percent higher than for comparable accommodations in surrounding areas. The strikers appealed to the Railway Union for support, and that organization voted to refuse to handle Pullman cars and equipment.

The General Managers' Association, representing twenty-four Chicago railroads, prepared to fight the boycott. Switchmen who refused to handle Pullman cars were summarily discharged. Whenever this happened, the union instructed its members to quit work. Within a few days thousands of railroad workers in twenty-seven states and territories were

Contrasting Opinions on the Pullman Strike [1894]

Eugene Debs issued this appeal for support of the boycott of Pullman cars:

To the Railway Employes of America: The struggle with the Pullman Company has developed into a contest between the producing classes and the money power of the country. We stand upon the ground that the workingmen are entitled to a just proportion of the proceeds of their labor. This the Pullman Company denied them. Reductions had been made from time to time until the employees earned barely sufficient wages to live, not enough to prevent them from sinking deeper and deeper into Pullman's debt, thereby mortgaging their bodies and souls, as well as their children's, to that heartless corporation.

One editor thus denounced the boycott:

The brigand who demands ransom for his prisoner, with mutilation or death as the alternative; the police captain who sells for money his power to arrest the dealers in vice and crime; the newsmonger who gathers scandal in order that he may be paid for suppressing it—these are the types of blackmailers whom all the world loathes. The boycott ordered by the railway union is morally no better than any of these acts. It is an attempt at blackmail on the largest scale.

---

on strike, and transportation from Chicago to the Pacific coast was paralyzed.

Ordinarily, state governors responded readily to appeals from strike-threatened business, but the governor of Illinois was different. John P. Altgeld had pardoned the Haymarket anarchists remaining in prison. Business was not likely to appeal to such an executive for aid, and Altgeld was not the man to employ militia to smash a strike.

By-passing Altgeld, the railroad operators besought the national government to send regular army troops to Illinois. At the same time federal postal officials and marshals were bombarding Washington with information that the strike was preventing the movement of mail on the trains. President Cleveland was inclined to gratify the companies, and so was his Attorney General, Richard Olney, a former railroad lawyer and a bitter foe of labor. Cleveland and Olney decided that the government could employ the army to keep the mails moving, and in July 1894 the President, over Altgeld's protest, ordered 2,000 troops to the Chicago area.

At Olney's suggestion, government lawyers obtained from a federal court an order restraining Debs and other union officials from interfering with the interstate transportation of the mails. This "blanket injunction" was so broad in scope that it practically forbade Debs and his associates to continue the strike. They ignored the injunction and were arrested, tried for contempt of court (without a jury trial), and sentenced to six months in prison. With federal troops protecting the hiring of new workers and with the union leaders in a federal jail, the strike quickly collapsed.

It left a bitter heritage. Labor was convinced that the government was not a neutral arbiter representing the common interest, but a supporter of one side alone. Debs emerged from prison a martyr in the eyes of workingmen, a convert to Marxian socialism, and a dedicated enemy of capital.

Despite all the organizations that were formed and all the strikes and demonstrations that were so hopefully launched, labor accomplished relatively little for its cause in the years between 1865 and 1900. Its leaders could point to a few legislative victories: the abolition by Congress in 1885 of the Contract Labor law; the establishment by Congress in 1868 of an eight-hour day on public works and in 1892 of the same work period for government employees; and a host of state laws governing hours of labor and safety standards, most of which were not enforced. But an overwhelming majority of employers still regarded labor as a force to be disregarded when possible and to be crushed when practicable, and the American public in overwhelming numbers considered unions to be alien and dangerous elements in the national economy.

Labor's greatest weakness was that only a small part of its vast strength was organized.

The AFL with its half million members, and the Railroad Brotherhoods (engineers, conductors, firemen, trainmen) represented the skilled workers, but the mass of laborers were not enrolled in any union. All told, only 868,500 workers were union members at the turn of the century. Big Business was firmly entrenched; Big Labor awaited the future.

Selected Readings

General Accounts
I. M. Tarbell, *The Nationalizing of Business, 1878–1898* (1936); S. P. Hays, *The Response to Industrialism, 1885–1914** (1957); E. C. Kirkland, *Industry Comes of Age: Business, Labor, and Public Policy, 1860–1897* (1961); Rendig Fels, *American Business Cycles, 1865–1897* (1959).

Inventions and Industries
Roger Burlingame, *Engines of Democracy: Inventions and Society in Mature America* (1940); Matthew Josephson, *Edison** (1959); R. N. Current, *The Typewriter and the Men Who Made It* (1954); H. C. Passer, *The Electrical Manufacturers, 1875–1900* (1953); R. A. Clemens, *The American Livestock and Meat Industry* (1932); C. B. Kuhlmann, *The Development of the Flour-Milling Industry in the United States* (1929).

The Railroads
G. R. Taylor and I. D. Neu, *The American Railroad Network, 1861–1900* (1956); E. G. Campbell, *The Reorganization of the American Railroad System, 1893–1900* (1938); J. F. Stover, *Railroads of the South, 1865–1900* (1955); R. E. Overton, *Burlington West: A Colonization History of the Burlington Railroad* (1941) and *Gulf to Rockies* (1953); James McCague, *Moguls and Iron Men* (1964), on the transcontinental lines.

Business Leaders
Matthew Josephson, *The Robber Barons** (1934); T. C. Cochran, *Railroad Leaders, 1845–1900* (1953); Allan Nevins, *Study in Power: John D. Rockefeller* (2 vols., 1953); B. J. Hendrick, *Andrew Carnegie* (2 vols., 1932); J. F. Wall, *Andrew Carnegie* (1971).

Capitalism, Pro and Con
E. C. Kirkland, *Dream and Thought in the Business Community, 1860–1900** (1956); Sidney Fine, *Laissez Faire and the General Welfare State: A Study of Conflict in American Thought, 1865–1901** (1956); Richard Hofstadter, *Social Darwinism in American Thought** (1944); I. G. Wyllie, *The Self-Made Man in America** (1954); A. E. Morgan, *Edward Bellamy* (1944); C. A. Barker, *Henry George* (1955); Samuel Churgerman, *Lester F. Ward, the American Aristotle* (1939); C. M. Destler, *Henry Demarest Lloyd and the Empire of Reform* (1963); H. H. Quint, *The Forging of American Socialism* (1953).

Immigration and Poverty
Oscar Handlin, *The Uprooted* (1951); John Higham, *Strangers in the Land* (1955); Barbara Solomon, *Ancestors and Immigrants** (1956); M. A. Jones, *American Immigration** (1960); R. H. Bremner, *From the Depths: The Discovery of Poverty in the United States* (1956); Jacob Riis, *How the Other Half Lives** (1890); C. D. Long, *Wages and Earnings in the United States, 1860–1890* (1960).

The Labor Movement
Henry Pelling, *American Labor** (1960); N. J. Ware, *The Labor Movement in the United States, 1860–1893** (1929); Philip Taft, *The A. F. of L. in the Time of Gompers* (1957); Bernard Mandel, *Samuel Gompers* (1963); S. B. Kaufman, *Samuel Gompers and the Origins of the American Federation of Labor* (1973); R. V. Bruce, *1877: Year of Violence* (1959); Henry David, *History of the Haymarket Affair* (1936); A. L. Lindsay, *The Pullman Strike** (1942); Harry Barnard, *"Eagle Forgotten": The Life of John Peter Altgeld** (1938); Ray Ginger, *Altgeld's America—Lincoln Ideal Versus Changing Realities** (1958).

Urban Development
A. M. Schlesinger, *The Rise of the City, 1878–1898* (1933); Blake McKelvey, *The Urbanization of America, 1860–1915* (1963); C. M. Green, *The Rise of Urban America* (1965); C. N. Glaab and A. T. Brown, *A His-*

*tory of Urban America** (1967); S. B. Warner, Jr., *Streetcar Suburbs: The Process of Growth in Boston, 1870–1900** (1962) and *The Urban Wilderness: A History of the American City** (1973); Stephan Thernstrom, *The Other Bostonians: Poverty and Progress in the American Metropolis, 1880–1970* (1973); David Ward, *Cities and Immigrants: A Geography of Change in Nineteenth Century America* (1971); C. W. Patton, *The Battle for Municipal Reform: Mobilization and Attack, 1875–1900* (1940).

*Titles available in paperback.

The End of the Old Frontier

Eighteen

The census report for 1890 noted that the unsettled area of the West had been "so broken into by isolated bodies of settlement" that a continuous frontier line could no longer be drawn. Three years later a young historian from the University of Wisconsin, Frederick Jackson Turner, startled the American Historical Association with a memorable paper, "The Significance of the Frontier in American History." The roots of the national character, Turner asserted, lay not so much in the East or in Europe as in the West. As he saw it, "the existence of an area of free land, its continuous recession, and the advance of settlement westward, explain American development." This experience, by stimulating individualism, nationalism, and democracy, had made Americans the distinctive people that they were. "Now," Turner concluded ominously, "four centuries from the discovery of America, at the end of a hundred years of life under the Constitution, the frontier has gone, and with its going has closed the first period of American history."

The foreboding of Professor Turner was, in one respect, a bit premature. A vast public domain still existed in 1890, and during the forty years thereafter the government was to give away many more acres than it had given as homesteads before that time. Nevertheless, most of the best farming land had already been taken up. Gone was the chance of acquiring a farm for little or nothing, of cultivating it at a relatively low cost, of selling it at a profit and moving on west to start all over again.

In the passing of the frontier, perhaps the greatest loss to the American people was a psychological one. So long as the country had remained open at one end, there had seemed to be constantly revitalizing opportunities in American life. Now there was a vague, premonitory sense of being hemmed in. The psychological loss was all the greater because of what Henry Nash Smith in *Virgin Land* (1950) has called the

Railroad Construction in the West
Railroads preceded settlement on much of the last frontier. Here workers are setting new speed records as they lay track across the bare plains from Minot, Dakota Territory, to Helena, Montana Territory, in 1887. This stretch later became part of the Great Northern Railway. (Burlington Northern photo)

"myth of the garden," the once widely held belief (to be found in many poems, novels, and other writings) that the West was a kind of potential Garden of Eden where life could be begun anew and all the ideals of democracy realized. The setting for utopia, once the New World as a whole, had shrunk to the West of the United States. To some extent Professor Turner himself reflected the myth in his "frontier interpretation" of American history.

Actually, long before 1890, the city had come to replace the "virgin land" as the symbol of opportunity in America. The great folk movement of the time was from the country to the city, not the other way around. But American values had long been shaped by the rural background in which most of the people were brought up. Only slowly and with considerable stress did these values change in response to the more and more pervasive influence of the urban environment. Change they nevertheless did, and in the last decades of the nineteenth century the culture of the city came to predominate in American civilization.

The Last West

In 1860 the frontier line, the western rim of settlement, conformed roughly to the western boundaries of the tier of states immediately beyond the Mississippi—Minnesota, Iowa, Missouri, Arkansas—jutting outward to include the eastern parts of Nebraska and Kansas and cutting across central Texas. West of this line was a huge expanse inhabited by roving Indians and wild animals, and peopled only thinly by whites until the settled districts of California and Oregon on the Pacific coast were reached. Within the confines of this vast West are three distinct natural, or physiographic, regions: the Great Plains, the Rocky Mountains, and the Basin and Plateau region between the Rockies on the east and the Sierra Nevada–Cascade mountain chain on the west.

DELAYED SETTLEMENT

When the westward-pushing pioneers entered upon the Great Plains, they saw a strange and even alien environment, utterly different from the fertile prairie lands behind them or the wooded areas of the Ohio Valley and the East. The physical features that in combination distinguish the Great Plains from earlier frontiers are a level surface, a dearth of timber, and a deficiency in rainfall. Early explorers had dubbed this region "the Great American Desert," and in the 1840s settlers had hastened through it on their way to California and Oregon. Its forbidding reputation was largely responsible for the curious fact that the frontier, after crossing the Mississippi, had jumped 1,500 miles to the Pacific coast.

By the 1860s, however, people had begun to head for the unsettled parts of the West. They were attracted by gold and silver deposits, by the short-grass pasture for cattle and sheep, and finally by the plains' sod and the mountain meadowland that seemed suitable for farming or ranching.

Settlement was encouraged by the great transcontinental railroad lines. These roads and their feeders moved settlers and supplies into the vast interior spaces and furnished access to outside markets; they provided what the region could not have had without them—the basis for a permanent population and a durable economy. In addition, they directly excited migration by disposing of their lands to settlers. All told, in national and state land grants, the railroads owned over 183 million acres. Although some companies attempted to reserve their lands or sell them at fancy prices, most of the lines realized that an increased population meant larger freight and passenger revenues. Consequently, they offered land for as little as $2.50 an acre, advertised the glories of the West in the East and in Europe, and transported prospective buyers at reduced rates.

Settlement was also encouraged by the land policy of the federal government, though

III. AFTER THE CIVIL WAR:
Academic Tradition and Its Challenger

Plate 1: Albert Bierstadt, THE ROCKY MOUNTAINS *(The Metropolitan Museum of Art, Rogers Fund, 1907)*

The post-Civil War period was characterized by a tremendous growth of industry, bringing with it a class of wealthy businessmen who turned to works of art to reflect both their nationalistic pride and their newfound status. Although American artists continued to look to European models for inspiration, in landscape painting the wonders of the newly explored far West generated an intense interest. With the same reverent feeling for the land that had earlier inspired the Hudson River painters, artists of the so-called Rocky Mountain School created grandiose panoramas of the Western wilderness, emphasizing the rugged terrain and unlimited horizons.

The most popular of these painters was Albert Bierstadt, born in Germany but brought to Massachusetts as a child. Bierstadt went to Europe for his training at the Düsseldorf Academy, but on his return to

America in 1857 he joined an expedition mapping an overland route across the Rocky Mountains to the Pacific Ocean. His firsthand observations of nature on this trip and many others are evident in the minute attention to topographical detail and the expressive textural quality to be found in Bierstadt's work. His paintings became increasingly popular and brought unprecedented prices from wealthy middle-class collectors. Although Bierstadt's huge canvases, such as "The Rocky Mountains," 1863 *(Plate 1)*, were painted inside the artist's studio, they were based on sketches made on location and provided an accurate if melodramatic sense of the expanding American frontier.

The large canvases of the Rocky Mountain School found adequate wall space in the high ceilinged rooms of the Victorian period. The family portrait painted by Eastman Johnson in 1871 for the prominent New York

Plate 2: Eastman Johnson, THE HATCH FAMILY *(The Metropolitan Museum of Art, Gift of Frederic H. Hatch, 1926)*

stockbroker A. S. Hatch *(Plate 2)* shows a gilt-framed landscape panorama among the ornate furnishings and heavy wine-colored drapery of the drawing room.

Johnson, like Bierstadt, had acquired his technical facility at the Düsseldorf Academy, and his skill is evident in the informal arrangement of the large group of family members. In addition, his careful recording of specific detail in furniture and clothing provides an accurate picture of an upper-middle-class American home and family in the 1870s.

Although Americans traveled to other European academies for their artistic education, the Ecole des Beaux Arts in Paris remained throughout the nineteenth century by far the most important center of formal training. Augustus Saint-Gaudens, after his return from Parisian study in 1875, became the dominant figure in American sculpture during the last quarter of the century. He rejected the neoclassicism that had previously influenced American sculptors, such as Greenough, in favor of a greater naturalism that included more textured surfaces and

more realistic poses. Saint-Gaudens's innovations in the design of commemorative statuary are exemplified by his Sherman Monument in New York's Central Park, 1903 *(Plate 3)*. Unlike Greenough's stiffly posturing George Washington, Sherman is seated on horseback, and the rhythmically flowing robes of the winged allegorical figure beside him contribute to the general feeling of movement. Again in contrast to the Greenough, the sturdy, sculpturally conceived pedestal makes the whole statue appropriate for its outdoor setting.

Philadelphian Thomas Eakins also studied in Paris, where he learned the value of close observation and the precise technique which would characterize his painting throughout his long career.

Eakins's love for sports and the out-of-doors were combined in his 1871 painting of his boyhood friend Max Schmitt *(Plate 4)*. The artist's psychological insight, which is most evident in his portrayal of individual character, along with his life-long interest in anatomy and the scientific laws of perspective, enabled him to develop an objective style

Plate 3: Augustus Saint-Gaudens, SHERMAN MEMORIAL *(Photo by Sandak)*

Plate 4: Thomas Eakins, MAX SCHMITT IN A SINGLE SCULL
(The Metropolitan Museum of Art, Alfred N. Punnett Fund and gift of George D. Pratt, 1934; Photo by Sandak)

devoid of the sentimentality common to the period. In this remarkable portrait, the clarity of the composition and the brilliant technical handling of the light reinforce the honesty of the artist's perception.

Before the founding of the first architectural school in America after the Civil War, an individual interested in a career as a professional architect had two roads open to him. He might apprentice himself to an established architect and, after long years of diligent work, strike out on his own. Or he could sail to Europe, enroll at the Ecole des Beaux Arts in Paris and, after completing the course of study, return to America with the academic stamp of approval.

One of the first Americans to study architecture at the Ecole in Paris was Henry Hobson Richardson. He returned to Boston in 1865 and began his practice modestly in domestic design. But in 1872 he entered and won the competition for Trinity Church, Boston *(Plate 6)*. Richardson followed accepted nineteenth-century practice by cloaking his building in a style borrowed from the past, in this case the massive French Romanesque. The building, constructed between 1873 and 1877, features such medieval elements as arched portals, a central tower, turrets, and pinnacles. But despite its borrowings from the past, Trinity Church was no mere copy of an historic building; it was an original conception based on the needs of its congregation and the irregular site chosen for its location.

The success of Richardson's choice of the Romanesque had a profound impact on American architecture for the next quarter-century. Many designers began to utilize the dramatic masses and textural surfaces associated with the style in all types of structures, from libraries to railroad stations.

Equally influential was the interior of Trinity Church. Under the direction of the American artist John La Farge, the walls were covered with brightly painted murals. La Farge was also responsible for many of the stained-glass windows that grace the church. He had studied the medieval stained-glass technique while a student in France in

1856, and he developed a personal style characterized by the use of richly colored glass and of larger stained-glass sections that reduced the amount of metal framework required. His "Welcome" Window, 1909 *(Plate 5)* is characteristic of La Farge's stained-glass technique.

While many American artists continued to make their pilgrimage to Europe, others found inspiration closer to home. Boston-born painter Winslow Homer rejected the cold precision of French academic art in favor of a greater naturalism. Beginning his career as a free-lance illustrator for *Harper's Weekly*, Homer first came to public notice for his keenly observed illustrations of Civil War subjects. His later work, although continuing in the naturalistic tradition, showed figures on a more monumental scale and expressed a deep concern for humanity.

The conflict between man and nature was a common theme in Homer's painting. In his "Huntsman and Dogs," 1891 *(Plate 7)*, the figure of the young hunter stands silhouetted against the cloud-filled sky as his dogs circle around him. The deerskin and

Plate 5: John La Farge, WELCOME WINDOW *(The Metropolitan Museum of Art, Gift of Susan Dwight Bliss, 1944; Photo by Sandak)*

Plate 6: Henry Hobson Richardson, TRINITY CHURCH, BOSTON, MASSACHUSETTS *(Photo by Sandak)*

Plate 7: Winslow Homer, HUNTSMAN AND DOGS *(Philadelphia Museum of Art: The William L. Elkins Collection)*

felled tree stump symbolize man's triumph over the wilderness.

Although most Americans who traveled to Paris studied at the Ecole des Beaux Arts, some were more sympathetic with the new avant-garde French painting. The Impressionists, who had challenged the Academy in the 1870s with freer brushwork and greater interest in naturalistic conditions of light, inspired a number of American artists, including John Singer Sargent. In one of his most famous portraits, "The Daughters of Edward D. Boit," 1882 *(Plate 8)*, Sargent places his subjects in an interior of strongly contrasting lights and darks. The informal composition gives a feeling of spontaneity, as though the four young girls were surprised in a moment of play.

Like two of his notable contemporaries, James McNeill Whistler and Mary Cassatt, Sargent became an expatriate, choosing to live and work in Europe because he felt that the center of artistic life was still to be found there rather than in this country.

In architecture, the last years of the nineteenth century were characterized by an increased interest in eclectic design. French chateaux and Italian Renaissance palaces

began to rise on the Cliff Walk of Newport, Rhode Island as the summer "cottages" of the new millionaires. Paris-trained Richard Morris Hunt was the most sought-after architect of this exuberant and often extravagant pursuit of elegance. In his design for the Vanderbilts' "Marble House," 1892 *(Plate 9)*, Hunt achieved a lavish display of grandeur by his use of expensive imported materials and unrestrained ornamental decoration.

Another architect who studied in Paris was Louis Sullivan; but Sullivan rejected the academic precepts of eclectism in favor of an architecture based on experimentation and innovation. Sullivan's major contribution was in his design of the skyscraper, which he conceived of as a "proud and soaring thing." The skyscraper had been made possible by the newly developed technology of steel frame construction and the invention of the elevator; the increased price of land was creating a need for taller buildings. Sullivan executed a number of important tall buildings in cities from Chicago, where he began his career, to New York. In Buffalo he designed the Prudential Building, 1895 *(Plate 10)*, in which he stressed the height of the structure by

Plate 8: John Singer Sargent, THE DAUGHTERS OF EDWARD D. BOIT *(Courtesy Museum of Fine Arts, Boston)*

Plate 9: Richard Morris Hunt, MARBLE HOUSE:
DINING ROOM (The Preservation Society of Newport County Photo)

accenting the vertical supports from the base
to the cornice. Although Sullivan continued to
use ornamental motifs on his buildings, they
were not derived from historical sources but
were products of his own imagination.

Although the influence of the academic
tradition continued into the twentieth
century, many American artists began to
reject the fashionable Beaux Arts style.
Following the lead of such innovative
designers as Sullivan, they sought to create
an art more expressive of the realities of an
increasingly industrial and urban America.

Plate 10: Louis Sullivan,
PRUDENTIAL BUILDING,
BUFFALO, NEW YORK
(Photo by Sandak)

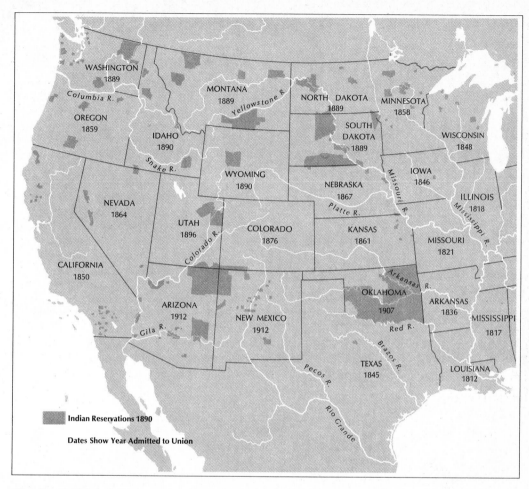

WASHINGTON
1889

Columbia R.

OREGON
1859

IDAHO
1890

MONTANA
1889

Yellowstone R.

NORTH DAKOTA
1889

MINNESOTA
1858

Snake R.

WYOMING
1890

SOUTH
DAKOTA
1889

WISCONSIN
1848

NEVADA
1864

UTAH
1896

Colorado R.

COLORADO
1876

NEBRASKA
1867

Platte R.

IOWA
1846

Missouri R.

ILLINOIS
1818

Mississippi R.

KANSAS
1861

MISSOURI
1821

CALIFORNIA
1850

Arkansas R.

ARIZONA
1912

Gila R.

NEW MEXICO
1912

OKLAHOMA
1907

Red R.

ARKANSAS
1836

MISSISSIPPI
1817

Pecos R.

TEXAS
1845

Brazos R.

LOUISIANA
1812

Rio Grande

Indian Reservations 1890

Dates Show Year Admitted to Union

The Last Frontier

this had less effect than had been intended. According to the Homestead Act of 1862, for a small fee a settler could obtain a plot of 160 acres if he occupied and improved it for five years. (A similar acreage could be secured, ordinarily for $1.25 per acre, by the terms of the Preemption Act of 1841.) A good deal of idealism had gone into the framing of the Homestead Act. It was intended to be a democratic measure, the bestowal of a free farm on any American who needed one, a form of government relief to raise the living standards of the masses. But in practice the act proved a disappointment. Some 400,000 homesteaders became landowners, but a much larger number abandoned the attempt to stake out a farm on the windswept plains.

The Homestead Act was defective. It assumed that mere possession of land was enough to sustain farm life, but this ignored the increasing mechanization of agriculture and the rising costs of operation. Even worse, it was based on Eastern agricultural experiences that were inapplicable to the region west of the Mississippi. A unit of 160 acres was too small for the grazing and grain farming that came to be carried on in the Great Plains.

Responding to Western pressures, Congress acted to increase allotments. The Timber Culture Act (1873) permitted a homesteader to

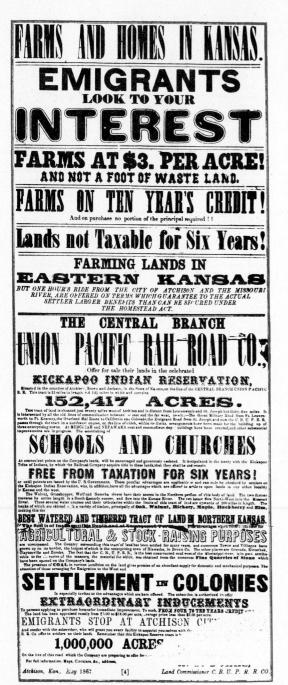

Railroad Land Promotion
Railroads were eager to hasten the settlement of the West. They stood to profit from the transportation of migrants, the sale of land to them, and the freight business from settled farmers. This 1867 poster of the Union Pacific is fairly typical of Western railroad advertisements from the 1860s to the 1890s. (Union Pacific Railroad Museum Collection)

receive a grant of 160 additional acres if he planted on it 40 acres of trees. The Desert Land Act (1877) provided that a claimant could buy 640 acres at $1.25 an acre provided he irrigated part of his holding within three years. The Timber and Stone Act (1878), presumably applying to nonarable land, authorized sales of quarter sections at $2.50 an acre.

Through the operation of the various laws, it was possible for an individual to acquire at little cost 1,280 acres. Some enterprising persons got much more. Fraud ran rampant in the administration of the acts. Lumber, mining, and cattle companies, by employing "dummy" registrants and using other tricky devices, grasped millions of acres of the public domain.

Settlement was made possible by the readiness of the federal government to police the vast and desolate region and to subdue the red men who resisted the white advance.

Political organization followed on the heels of settlement. After the admission of Kansas as a state in 1861, the remaining territories of Washington, New Mexico, Utah, and Nebraska were divided into smaller and more convenient units. By the close of the sixties territorial governments were in operation in the new provinces of Nevada, Colorado, Dakota, Arizona, Idaho, Montana, and Wyoming. Statehood rapidly followed. Nevada became a state in 1864, Nebraska in 1867, and Colorado, attracting attention as the centennial state, in 1876. In 1889 the "omnibus states," North and South Dakota, Montana, and Washington, won admission; Wyoming and Idaho entered the next year. Utah was denied statehood until its Mormon leaders convinced the government in 1896 that polygamy had been abandoned. At the turn of the century only three territories remained outside the fold: Arizona and New Mexico, excluded because of their scanty population and wrong politics (they were predominantly Democratic) and their refusal to accept admission as a single state, and Oklahoma, which was opened to white settlement and granted territorial status in 1889–1890.

THE MINERS ARRIVE

The first colonists of the last frontier were miners, and the first part of the area to be settled was the mineral-rich region of mountains and plateaus. The life span of the mining frontier was brief. It burst into being around 1860, flourished brilliantly until the 1890s, and then abruptly declined.

News of a gold or silver strike would start a stampede reminiscent of the California gold rush of 1849. Settlement usually followed a pattern of successive stages: (1) individual prospectors exploited the first ores with pan and placer mining; (2) after the shallower deposits were depleted, corporations moved in to engage in lode or quartz mining; (3) commercial mining either disappeared eventually or continued on a restricted basis, and ranchers and farmers appeared on the scene to establish a more permanent economy.

The first great strikes occurred just before the Civil War. In 1858 gold was discovered in the Pike's Peak district of what would soon be the territory of Colorado, and the following year a mob of 50,000 prospectors stormed in from California and the Mississippi Valley and the East. Denver and other mining camps blossomed into "cities" overnight. Almost as rapid-

A Sod House on the Plains
Many settlers on the treeless Great Plains lived their first years in sod houses. They made these by cutting strips of the tough turf into pieces and laying them on top of one another to form walls. In some cases they first excavated and then erected the walls around the partial dugout. This photograph shows a combined dugout and sod house under construction in Nebraska in 1892. The wagon is bringing a fresh load of turf. (Solomon D. Butcher Collection, The Nebraska State Historical Society)

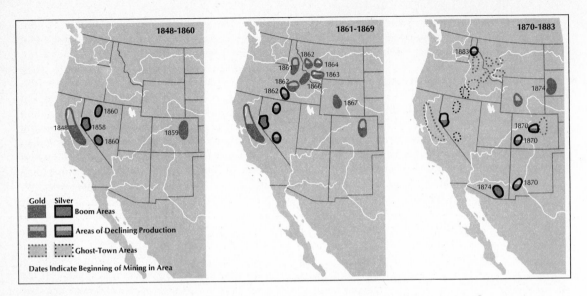

Gold	Silver	
		Boom Areas
		Areas of Declining Production
		Ghost-Town Areas

Dates Indicate Beginning of Mining in Area

Mining Towns

ly as it developed, the boom ended. Eventually corporations, notably the Guggenheim interests, revived some of the glories and profits of the gold boom, and the discovery of silver near Leadville supplied a new source of mineral wealth.

While the Colorado rush of 1859 was in progress, news of another strike drew miners to Nevada, then a part of Utah Territory. Gold had been found in the Washoe district, but the most valuable ore in the great Comstock Lode and other veins was silver. The first prospectors to reach the Washoe fields came from California (here the frontier movement was from west to east), and from the beginning Californians dominated the settlement and development of Nevada. In a remote desert without railroad transportation, the territory produced no supplies of its own, and everything, from food and machinery to whiskey and prostitutes, had to be freighted in from California to Virginia City, Carson City, and other roaring camp towns. When the placer deposits ran out, California capital bought the claims of the pioneer prospectors and installed quartz mining. For a brief span the outside owners reaped tremendous profits; from 1860 to 1880 the Nevada lodes yielded bullion worth $306 million.

No new discoveries agitated the mining frontier until 1874, when gold was found in the Black Hills of southwestern Dakota Territory. Prospectors swarmed into the area, which was then and for years later served only by stagecoach transportation. Deadwood burst into life as a center of supplies and sin for other camps. For a short time the boom flared, and then came the inevitable fading of resources. Corporations took over from the miners, and one gigantic company, the Homestake, came to dominate the fields. The population declined, and the Dakotas, like other boom areas of the mineral empire, waited for the approach of the agricultural frontier.

Life in the camp towns of the mineral empire had a hectic tempo and a gaudy flavor not to be found in any other part of the last frontier. The speculative spirit, a mood of incredible optimism, a get-rich-quick philosophy gripped everybody and dominated every phase of community activity. The conditions of mine life—the presence of precious minerals, the vagueness of claim boundaries, the cargoes of gold being shipped out—tempted outlaws and "bad men," operating as individuals or gangs, to ply their trade. When the situation became intolerable in a community, those members interested in order set up their own law and enforced it through a vigilance committee, an agency used earlier in California. Sometimes criminals themselves secured control of the committee and sometimes the vigilantes continued to operate as private "law" enforcers after the creation of regular governments.

THE DAY OF THE COWBOY

The open range — that is, the unclaimed grass-lands of the public domain — provided a huge area on the Great Plains where cattlemen could graze their herds free of charge and un-restricted by the boundaries that would have existed in a farming economy. The railroads gave the range-cattle industry access to mar-kets and thus brought it into being; then they destroyed it by bringing the farmers' frontier to the plains.

In ancestry the cattle industry was Mexi-can and Texan. Long before the Americans invaded the Southwest, Mexican ranchers and vaqueros had developed the techniques and tools employed later by the cattlemen and cowboys of the Great Plains: branding (a de-vice known in all frontier areas where stock was common), roundups, roping, and the equipment of the herder — his lariat, saddle, leather chaps, and spurs. All these things and others were taken over by the Americans in Texas and by them transmitted to the northern-most ranges of the cattle kingdom. Also in Texas were found the largest herds of cattle in the country, the animals descended from im-ported Spanish stock — the famous wiry, hardy longhorns — and allowed to run wild or semi-wild. Here too were the horses that enabled the caretakers of the herds to control them — the small, muscular broncos or mustangs — sprung from blooded progenitors brought in by the Spanish and ideally adapted to the require-ments of the cow country.

At the end of the Civil War an estimated 5 million cattle roamed the Texas ranges, and Northern markets were offering fat prices for steers in any condition. Early in 1866 some

Cowboys Branding Calves

To identify his own herd (which mingled with other herds on the open range) each cattleman had his calves branded with his distinctive mark of ownership. At the spring roundup, cowboys caught the calves, "wrassled" them to the ground, and applied searing hot branding irons. (Western History Research Center, University of Wyoming)

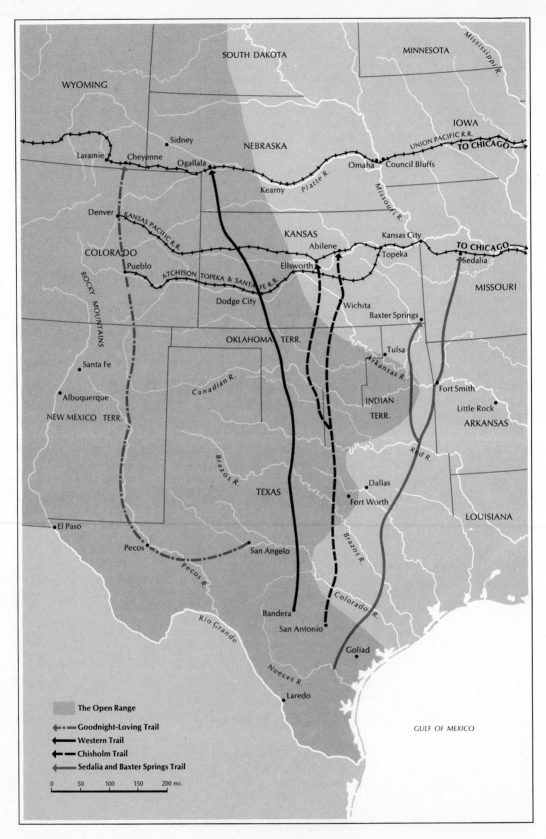

The Cattle Kingdom

Texas cattlemen started their combined herds, some 260,000 head, north for Sedalia, Missouri, on the Missouri Pacific Railroad. Traveling over rough country and beset by outlaws, Indians, and property-conscious farmers, the caravan suffered heavy losses, and only a fraction of the animals were delivered to the railroad. But a great experiment had been successfully tested—cattle could be driven to distant markets and pastured along the trail and would gain weight during the journey. The first of the "long drives" prepared the way for the cattle kingdom.

With the precedent established, the next step was to find an easier route leading through more accessible country. Special market facilities were provided at Abilene, Kansas, on the Kansas Pacific Railroad, and for years this town reigned as the railhead of the cattle kingdom. Between 1867 and 1871, 1,460,000 cattle were moved up the Chisholm Trail to Abilene, a town that when filled with rampaging cowboys at the end of a drive rivaled the mining towns in robust wickedness. But as the farming frontier pushed farther west in Kansas and as the supply of animals increased, the cattlemen had to develop other market outlets and trails. Railroad towns that flourished after Abilene were Dodge City and Wichita in Kansas, Ogallala and Sidney in Nebraska, Cheyenne and Laramie in Wyoming, and Miles City and Glendive in Montana.

From first to last, a long drive was a spectacular episode. It began with the spring, or calf, roundup. The cattlemen of a district met with their cowboys at a specified place to round up the stock of the owners from the open range. As the cattle were driven in, the calves were branded with the marks of their mothers. Stray calves with no identifying symbols, "mavericks," were divided on a pro-rata basis. Then the cows and calves were turned loose to pasture, while the yearling steers were readied for the drive to the north. The combined herds, usually numbering from 2,000 to 5,000 head, moved out, attended by the cowboys of each outfit.

Among the cowboys the majority (in the early years) were veterans of the Confederate army. Outnumbering all the rest—white Northerners, Mexicans, and other foreigners—were the Negroes, who usually were assigned the humbler jobs on the trail crew, such as those of wrangler or cook. (In the Wild West black men played a role not only as cowboys but also as explorers, trappers, miners, outlaws, and cavalrymen.) The cowboy was glorified as a Nordic superman in Owen Wister's novel *The Virginian* (1902) and in countless later "Westerns" that followed the Wister pattern. Actually the life of the cowboy, whatever his color, was dull, dirty, and rather brutish. He was at best only a hired hand who made little money and kept still less. The big profits went to his employer, the cattleman.

All cattlemen had to have a permanent base from which to operate, and so the ranch emerged. A ranch consisted of the employer's dwelling, quarters for employees, and a tract of grazing land. It might be fenced in or open, owned or leased or held by some quasi-legal claim, but it was definite and durable. Possession of a ranch meant unquestioned access to precious water. As farmers and sheepmen encroached on the open plains, the ranch began to replace the range.

There had always been an element of risk and speculation in the open-range cattle business. At any time the "Texas fever," transmitted by a parasite carried by ticks, might decimate a herd. Rustlers and Indians frequently drove off large numbers of animals. Sheepmen from California and Oregon brought their flocks onto the range to compete for grass and force cattle out (cattle will not graze after sheep); bitter "wars" followed between cattlemen and sheepherders in which men and stock were killed and equipment destroyed. Farmers, "nesters," threw fences around their claims, blocking trails and breaking up the open range. More wars were fought bringing losses to both sides.

Accounts of the lofty profits to be made in the cattle business—it was said that an investment of $5,000 would return $45,000 in four years—tempted Eastern, English, and Scottish capital to the plains. Increasingly the structure of the cattle economy became corporate in form; in one year twenty corporations with a combined capital of $12 million were chartered in Wyoming. The inevitable result of this frenzied extension was that the ranges, already severed and shrunk by the railroads and the farmers, were overstocked. There was not enough grass to support the crowding herds or sustain the long drives. Overstocking tumbled prices downward, and then nature intervened with a destructive finishing blow. Two severe winters, in 1885–1886 and 1886–1887, with a searing summer between them, stung and scorched the plains. Hundreds of thousands of cattle died, streams and grass dried up, princely ranches and costly investments disappeared in a season.

The open-range industry never recovered; the long drive disappeared for good. But the cattle ranches – with fenced-in grazing land and stocks of hay for winter feed – survived and grew and prospered, eventually producing more beef than ever.

The Dispersal of the Tribes

When the miners and cowmen sifted into the last frontier, they came face to face with its Indian inhabitants, and they had to advance against more determined and sustained resistance than whites had met anywhere else in the sweep across the continent. In the end the invaders triumphed. The Indian tribes were broken and their members were forced to adapt themselves to an approximation of the white man's culture.

THE PLAINS INDIANS

On the rolling, semiarid, treeless plains, the Indians followed a nomadic life. Riding their small but powerful horses, which were descendants of Spanish stock, the tribes roamed the spacious expanses of the grasslands. Permanent abodes were rare; when a band halted, tepees carried on the journey were quickly pitched as temporary dwellings.

The magnet that drew the wanderers and guided their routes was the buffalo, or bison. This huge grazing animal provided the economic basis for the plains Indians' way of life. Its flesh was their principal source of food, and the skin supplied materials for clothing, shoes, tepees, blankets, robes, and utensils. To the Indians, the buffalo was, as someone had said, "a galloping department store." They trailed the herds, estimated to number at least 15 million head in 1865, all over the plains.

The plains Indians were almost uniformly martial, proud, and aggressive. Mounted on their horses, they were a formidable foe, whether armed with bow, spear, or rifle. They possessed a mobility enjoyed by no previous Indians, and students of war have ranked them among the best light cavalry in military history.

It was the traditional policy of the federal government to regard the tribes as independent nations (but also as wards of the Great White Father in Washington) and to negotiate agreements with them in the shape of treaties that were solemnly ratified by the Senate. This concept of Indian sovereignty was responsible for the attempt of the government before 1860 to erect a permanent frontier between whites and red men, to reserve the region west of the bend of the Missouri as permanent Indian country. But by the sixties the related principles of tribal independence and a perpetual line of division were breaking down before harsh realities. Administration of Indian matters was divided between the Bureau of Indian Affairs, located in the Department of the Interior, and the army. The bureau was vested with general powers to supervise the disposition of Indian lands, disburse annuities, and, through its agents in Western posts, distribute needed supplies. From top to bottom, the personnel was shot through with the spoils system. Although some agents were conscientious and able men, more were dishonest and incompetent.

The army came into the picture only when trouble developed – when bands of Indians attacked homes or stagecoach lines or when a tribe went on the warpath. In short, its principal function was to punish, not to police. The army of the frontier was an effective fighting body, and it was led by some able officers. Still, in its "wars" with the Indians the army frequently experienced rugged going. The mobile plains tribesmen were fully a match for cavalrymen armed with carbines. But soon the superior technology of the whites shifted the balance. The Colt repeating revolver gave the army increased fire power, the railroads facilitated quick troop concentrations, and the telegraph reported almost immediately the movements of hostile bands. Even so, the business of suppressing Indians was frightfully expensive.

The Slaughter of the Buffalo

*This sketch, sardonically entitled "Sport on the Plains," shows the way in which
the buffalo was often hunted. A wealthy hunter has employed a guide and a driver
and carriage to take him out to get a trophy. (Culver)*

Three wars in the sixties cost the government
$100 million, and one official estimated that the
cost per Indian killed was $1,000.

The subjection of the fierce plains Indians
was accomplished by economic as well as orthodox warfare—by the slaughter of the buffalo herds that supported their way of life. After
the Civil War the demand for buffalo hides
became a national phenomenon. It was partly
based on economics—a commercial demand
for the hides developing in the East; and it was
partly a fad—suddenly everyone east of the
Missouri seemed to require a buffalo robe from
the romantic West. Gangs of professional
hunters swarmed over the plains to shoot the
huge animals, divided by the Union Pacific
Railroad into southern and northern herds.
Some hunters killed merely for the sport of the
chase, though the lumbering victims did not
present much of a challenge. The southern
herd was virtually exterminated by 1875, and
within a few years the smaller northern herd

met the same fate. Fewer than a thousand of
the magnificent beasts survived. The army and
the Indian agents condoned and even encouraged the killing. With the buffalo went the Indians' source of food and supplies and their will
and ability to resist the white advance.

THE WARRIORS' LAST STAND

There was almost incessant Indian fighting on
the frontier from the sixties to the eighties. During the Civil War the eastern Sioux in Minnesota, cramped on an inadequate reserve and
exploited by agents, suddenly took to the warpath. Led by Little Crow, they killed over 700
whites before being subdued by a force of regulars and militia. Thirty-eight of the Indians
were hanged, and the tribe was exiled to the
Dakotas.

At the same time trouble flared in Colorado, where the Arapaho and Cheyenne had

Apache Warrior
*Geronimo (left, mounted) was not a chief, but he assumed the leadership of one of
the Apache bands when, in 1876, the United States government attempted to confine
the Apaches on a reservation in Arizona. He established a base in the mountains
of Mexico, and from there he led his warriors on raids across the border to
terrorize the American countryside. He kept this up for more than ten years.
(Culver Pictures)*

been restricted to the Sand Creek reserve.
Bands of braves attacked stagecoach lines and
settlements, provoking a concentration of territorial militia and threats from the army. The
governor urged all friendly Indians to congregate at army posts before retribution fell on the
hostiles. One Arapaho and Cheyenne band
under Black Kettle came into Fort Lyon on
Sand Creek and encamped nearby. Although
some braves just off the warpath were undoubtedly members of the party, Black Kettle understood he was under official protection. Nevertheless, Colonel J. M. Chivington, apparently
encouraged by the army commander of the
district, led a militia force to the unsuspecting
camp and massacred a disputed (but large)
number of men, women, and children. The

government then forced the Arapaho and
Cheyenne to accept an even less desirable
reservation, but the Senate neglected to ratify
the treaty.

At the end of the war against the southern
rebels, wars against the western Indians flared
up on several fronts. The most serious and sustained conflict was in Montana, where the
army attempted to build a road, the Bozeman
Trail, from Fort Laramie, Wyoming, to the mining centers. The western Sioux resented this
intrusion into the heart of their buffalo range,
and led by one of their great chiefs, Red Cloud,
they so harried the soldiers and the construction party that the road could not be completed.

Meanwhile, Congress, shocked by the
Chivington massacre and the continued hostili-

ties, appointed a committee to investigate the situation on the scene, and after studying its report created an Indian Peace Commission, composed of soldiers and civilians, to recommend a permanent Indian policy. The commission called the southern tribes to council at Medicine Lodge Creek in 1867, and the following year it met with the northern tribes at Fort Laramie. At Medicine Lodge the Arapaho and Cheyenne and other tribes agreed to accept reserves in the Indian Territory. At Laramie the Sioux accepted a reserve in southwestern Dakota, with rights to hunt as far as the Big Horn Mountains in Wyoming; they insisted, however, that the government abandon the Bozeman road, marking probably the only instance in which whites formally yielded to Indians. The minor plains tribes and the mountain

tribes consented to smaller reserves. For its part, the government pledged annuity payments and regular supplies. Some of the Arapaho and Cheyenne had another bad experience before being finally settled on their reserve. Black Kettle, who had escaped the Chivington massacre, and his Cheyennes, some of whom had taken the warpath, were caught on the Washita River, near the Texas border, by Colonel George A. Custer, and the chief was killed and his people slaughtered.

After 1870 the broad outlines of a new Indian policy began to take shape. The tribes were now concentrated in two large reserves, one in Dakota and the other in the Indian Territory. Thus restricted, they found their powers to wage war severely limited. An advisory civilian Board of Indian Commissioners counseled the

---

A White Defender of the Indians

Among the few voices raised to defend the Indians and criticize the government's policy toward them was that of Helen Hunt Jackson, a writer who lived in Colorado Springs, Colorado. She presented her views in *A Century of Dishonor* (1881):

There is not among these three hundred bands of Indians [in the United States] one which has not suffered cruelly at the hands either of the Government or of white settlers. The poorer, the more insignificant, the more helpless the band, the more certain the cruelty and outrage to which they have been subjected. This is especially true of the bands on the Pacific slope. These Indians found themselves of a sudden surrounded by and caught up in the great influx of gold-seeking settlers, as helpless creatures on a shore are caught up in a tidal wave. There was not time for the Government to make treaties; not even time for communities to make laws. The tale of the wrongs, the oppressions, the murders of the Pacific-slope Indians in the last thirty years would be a volume by itself, and is too monstrous to be believed.

It makes little difference, however, where one opens the record of the history of the Indians; every page and every year has its dark stain. The story of one tribe is the story of all, varied only by differences of time and place; but neither time nor place makes any difference in the main facts. Colorado is as greedy and unjust in 1880 as was Georgia in 1830, and Ohio in 1795; and the United States Government breaks promises now as deftly as then, and with added ingenuity from long practice.

One of its strongest supports in so doing is the wide-spread sentiment among the people of dislike to the Indian, of impatience with his presence as a "barrier to civilization," and distrust of it as a possible danger. The old tales of the frontier life, with its horrors of Indian warfare, have gradually, by two or three generations' telling, produced in the average mind something like an hereditary instinct of unquestioning and unreasoning aversion which it is almost impossible to dislodge or soften.

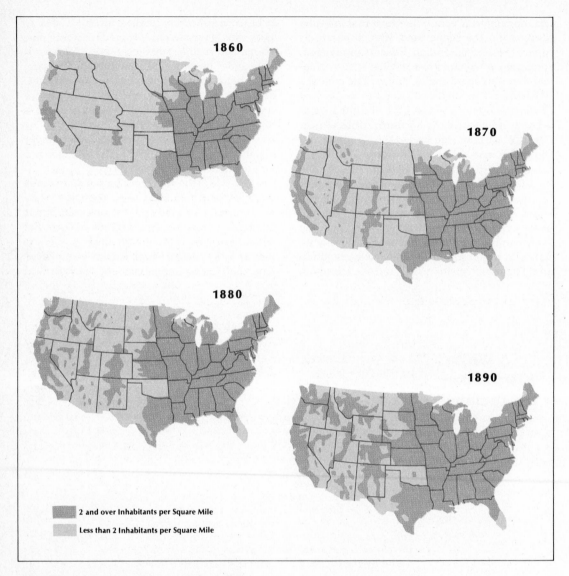

The Receding Frontier, 1860–1890

The term "frontier" refers to the line—and also to the area bordering the line—that divides the settled part of the country (population two or more per square mile) from the unsettled part (population less than two per square mile).

government to continue the reservation program and to break down the tribal structure with a view to assimilating the Indians to white culture. Congress responded in 1871 by abolishing the practice of treating the tribes as sovereignties, a step calculated to undermine the collective nature of Indian life.

But Indian resistance was far from ended. A source of potential conflict smouldered on the northern plains, where the Sioux roamed from Dakota to Wyoming. It burst into flame in 1875 when many of the tribesmen, angered by the dealings of crooked agents and alarmed by the entrance of miners into the Black Hills, suddenly left the reserve. Commanded to return, they gathered in Montana under Crazy Horse, probably the greatest leader of the plains Indians, and Sitting Bull. Three army columns were sent to round them up. With the expedition as colonel of the famous Seventh Cavalry was the colorful and controversial George A. Custer, golden-haired romantic and alleged glory seeker. At the Battle of the Little Bighorn (1876) the Indians surprised Custer with part of his regiment and killed every man. Custer has been accused of rashness, but he seems to have ridden into something that no white man would have believed possible. On this occasion the chiefs had concentrated at least 2,500 warriors, perhaps 4,000, the largest Indian army ever assembled at one time in the United States.

But the Indians did not have the political organization or the commissary to keep their troops united. Soon they drifted off in bands to elude pursuit or search for food, and the army ran them down singly and returned them to Dakota. The power of the Sioux was now broken. The proud leaders, Crazy Horse and Sitting Bull, accepted defeat and the monotony of agency existence, and both were later killed by reservation police after being tricked or taunted into a last pathetic show of resistance.

In 1877 one of the most dramatic episodes in Indian history occurred in Idaho. Here the Nez Percé, a small and relatively pacific and civilized tribe, refused to accept a smaller reservation and were, in effect, forced into resistance. When troops converged on them, their able leader, Chief Joseph, attempted to conduct the band to Canada. A remarkable chase ensued. Joseph moved with 200 warriors and 350 women, children, and old people. Pursued by four columns, he covered 1,321 miles in seventy-five days, but was caught just short of the Canadian border. Like so many other crushed tribes, the Nez Percé were shipped to the Indian Territory.

The last Indians to maintain organized resistance against the whites were the Apaches, who fought intermittently from the sixties to the late eighties. The two ablest chiefs of this fierce tribe were Mangas Colorados and Cochise. Mangas was murdered during the Civil War, and in 1872 Cochise agreed to peace and a reservation for his followers. But one leader, Geronimo, continued to carry on the fight. When he was finally captured in 1886, formal warfare between Indians and whites may be said to have ended.

A final, tragic encounter in 1890 was hardly a battle. As the Indians saw their culture and their glories fading, they turned to an emotional religion which emphasized the coming of a Messiah and featured the "ghost dance," which inspired visions. Agents on the Sioux reservation, fearing the frenzy might turn into an outbreak, called for troops, and some of the Indians fled to the Badlands. The soldiers caught and tried to disarm them, at Wounded Knee. In the shooting that followed, about 40 of the soldiers were killed and more than 200 of the Indians, including women and children.

In 1887 Congress had finally moved to destroy the tribal structure that was the cornerstone of Indian culture. Although the motivation was partially a humanitarian impulse to help the Indian, the action was frankly designed to force him to become a landowner and farmer, to abandon his collective society and culture, to become, in short, a white man. The Dawes Severalty Act provided for the gradual abrogation of tribal ownership of land and the allotment of tracts to individual owners: 160 acres to the head of a family, 80 acres to a single adult or orphan, 40 acres to each dependent child. Adult owners were accorded the status of citizenship but, unlike other citizens, they could not alienate their property for twenty-five years. The act was hardly a success. The Indians were not ready for a wrenching change from a collective society to individualism. Congress attempted to facilitate the transition with the Burke Act of 1906. Citizenship was deferred until after the completion of the twenty-five-year period contemplated in the Dawes Act, but Indians who proved their adaptability could secure both citizenship and land ownership in a shorter period. Full rights of citizenship were conferred on all Indians in 1924. Even then many resisted white ways, and in the 1930s the government would make a notable attempt to restore some of the institutions of tribal culture.

Decline of the Farmer

The development of an industrial and urban civilization would have been impossible without a great increase in the productivity of agriculture. Yet on the whole the nation's farmers, while producing more than ever, were getting less and less in both pecuniary and psychological reward for their effort. Those who tried farming on the last frontier soon discovered that the West no longer provided much of a way out for them.

FARMING ON THE PLAINS

Some farmers had drifted into the Great Plains during its first stages of development, following the miners and cattlemen, but the great rush of settlement came in the late seventies. In the next decade the relentless advance of the farming frontier would gradually convert the plains country to an agricultural economy. The surge of migration came at a time when for years in succession the rainfall was well above the average. People scoffed at the idea that the plains were the Great American Desert, and they looked forward to an indefinite era of prosperity. They scoffed too at the old cowmen who warned that the light soil of the plains should not be deprived of its protecting turf by cultivation.

But even under the most favorable conditions, farming on the plains presented problems not encountered in any previous region.

Threshing Wheat on the Great Plains

This print of a Dakota field shows the magnitude of operations on a large landed unit and gives an idea of the high cost of farming on the plains. Here several steam-driven machines are in use. The average farmer could not afford even one thresher. In some areas owners of the machines went from farm to farm with hired crews during the harvest season. According to Raymond M. Wik in Steam Power on the American Farm, *the total horsepower of these engines increased from 1,200,000 in 1880 to 3,600,000 by 1910. (The Bettmann Archive)*

First and most critical was the problem of fencing. The farmer had to enclose his land, if for no other reason than to protect it from the herds of the cattlemen. But the traditional wood or stone fences were impossible on the plains. The cost of importing the material was prohibitive, and besides, such barriers were ineffective against range cattle. In the mid-seventies two Illinois farmers, Joseph H. Glidden and I. L. Ellwood, solved this problem by developing and putting on the market barbed wire. Produced in mass quantities — 40,000 tons a year — it sold cheaply, became standard equipment on the plains, and revolutionized fencing practices all over the country.

The second problem, present even when the rainfall was above average, was water. It became particularly acute after 1887, when a series of dry seasons began. One expedient resorted to was the use of deep wells and steel windmills, which assured a steady water supply for stock. Another was dry farming — a system of tillage designed to conserve moisture in the soil by covering it with a dust blanket — and the utilization of drought-enduring crops. In many areas of the plains, agriculture could not exist without irrigation. Large-scale irrigation, the only practicable kind, would have to be planned and supported by the government. The national government tried to hand the issue to the states, turning over to them in the Carey Act (1894) several million acres of public land to be reclaimed. The states made little progress, largely because the problems of reclamation cut across state boundaries.

Farming on the plains was always expensive and often risky. The uncertainty of rainfall and the danger of grasshopper plagues and tornadoes made every farm year a speculative experiment. Costs of operation ran high, partly because many supplies had to be imported into the region from distant points, but mainly because of the nature of plains farming. In all the farm areas of the country, machines were playing a larger part in the agricultural process, and they were especially vital on the plains, where grain farming was conducted on large land units.

The last West was not, as has so often been claimed, a refuge for the urban poor or a safety valve for proletarian unrest. The people who settled this area were mostly farmers, and they came from farms in the Middle West, the East, or Europe. In the booming eighties, with land values rising, credit was easy, and the farmers confidently expected to retire their obligations. With the advent of the arid years of the late eighties, the prospect changed with grim suddenness. There followed a reversal of the frontier movement, as many settlers retreated from the Great Plains. Those who remained gave an unintentional boost to the overproduction that caused farm prices to fall (wheat, which had sold for $1.60 a bushel at the end of the Civil War, dropped to 49 cents in the 1890s) and added to the distress of farmers elsewhere in the country.

CHANGES IN AGRICULTURE

Americans had always liked to talk about the wonderful life of the farmer. According to the popular myth, he was a sturdy yeoman, a simple, honest, happy man who dwelt close to nature and embodied all the virtues. Producing most of the things he and his family required, he was independent, subsisting on his own labor, depending not on the marketplace, and owing no man. The myth may have had some basis in Jefferson's time, but its reality was being destroyed by one of the great agricultural changes of the nineteenth century, the shift from subsistence, or self-sufficient, farming to commercial farming.

In commercial husbandry, the farmer specialized in a cash crop, sold it in a national or world market, ceased making his household supplies and bought them at the town or village store. This kind of farming, when it was successful, raised the farmer's living standards. But now he was dependent on other people and on impersonal factors he could not control: bankers and interest rates, railroads and freight rates, national and European depressions, world supply and demand. In short, he had become a businessman — but with a difference. Unlike the capitalists of the industrial order, he could not regulate his production or influence the prices of what he sold.

Machines came to the aid of the farmer as to the manufacturer. The mechanization of agriculture had accelerated during the Civil War, when the government called thousands of laborers into military service and forced farmers to employ labor-saving devices. For example, approximately 100,000 reapers were in use at the beginning of the war but 250,000 at its close.

In the years after 1860 a host of new machines—and improved models of old ones—were unveiled. Among these were the chilled steel plow, perfected by James Oliver; the sulky, or riding, plow; the disc and gang plows; various improvements of the reaper, notably the twine binder, introduced by John F. Appleby, which cut and bound grain; the grain drill, the seed planter, the corn binder, the corn lister, the potato planter, the cream separator, and the poultry incubator. The effect of the machines on production and labor was revolutionary.

Before 1900 farmers were generally hostile to the theories and teachings of scientific agriculture, to what they scornfully termed "book learning." In 1887 Congress passed the Hatch Act, providing for a system of agricultural experiment stations; this was the only major agricultural legislation passed by Congress between 1865 and 1900. But farmers generally spurned the new information because they felt no need for its aid and could see no benefits for themselves in its lessons. American agriculture before 1900 was, as it always had been, extensive and wasteful.

The period between 1865 and 1900 witnessed a tremendous expansion of agricultural facilities, not only in the United States but all over the world: in Brazil and the Argentine in South America, in Canada, in Australia and New Zealand, and in Russia. World production increased at the same time that modern means of communication and transportation—the telephone, telegraph, cable, steam navigation, railroads—were welding the producing nations into one international market. The American commercial farmer, always augmenting his production, produced more than the domestic market could absorb and disposed of his surplus in the world market. Cotton farmers depended on export sales for 70 percent of their annual income, and wheat farmers for 30 to 40 percent; other producers relied on a smaller percentage—it might be 10 to 25—but it was large enough to make the difference between a year of profit and one of loss.

In the forty years after 1860 huge new areas of land were put under cultivation in America, machines became standard equipment on most farms, land values boomed, and produc-tion soared to ever higher levels. But while costs of operation increased, prices dropped after 1870. Meanwhile, though the proportion of people living on farms declined in relation to the total population, farm population increased by absolute standards. From 1860 to 1910 the number of farm families rose from 1.5 million to over 6 million. In 1860 agriculture represented 50 percent of the total wealth of the country, in the early 1900s only 20 percent. The farmer received 30 percent of the national income in 1860 and 18 percent in 1910. By the decade of the nineties, 27 percent of the owned farms in the country were under mortgages, and by 1910, 33 percent. In 1880, 25 percent of all farms were operated by tenants; in 1910, 37 percent. The agrarian scene as it presented itself in the 1890s hardly realized Jefferson's dream of sturdy and independent yeomen owning the land they tilled.

THE FARMERS' GRIEVANCES

The farmers were painfully aware that something was wrong. They did not recognize—and it would have been strange if they had recognized—the intricate implications of national and world overproduction. Instead, they concentrated their attention and anger on more immediate and easily understood problems, problems that were in truth real and important to them, such as freight rates, interest charges, and an adequate currency.

The farmers' first and most burning grievance was that against the railroads. In all sections, and especially in the states west of the Mississippi, farmers depended on the railroads to carry crops to the markets. In many cases the roads charged higher rates for farm than for other shipments and higher rates in the South and West than in the Northeast. Freight rates sometimes consumed so much of the current price that farmers refused to ship their crops and either let them rot or used them as fuel. Railroads controlled elevator and warehouse facilities in buying centers and charged arbitrary storage rates.

In the farmers' list of villains the sources that controlled credit—banks, loan companies, insurance corporations—ranked second to the railroads. Commercial farming was by its nature expensive, and ambitious producers needed credit to purchase machines or enlarge holdings. Though eager to advance loans during the boom period of rising land values, the lenders insisted on high interest rates. The farmers were in no position to resist, and in the West and the South they had to submit to charges running from 10 to 25 percent. Usually they borrowed money when it was cheap, or abundant, and then had to retire their debts when money had become dear, or scarce. According to one estimate, 1,200 bushels of grain would buy a $1,000 mortgage in the 1860s; twenty years later it took 2,300 bushels to repay the mortgage. With good reason, the farmers fought for an increase in the volume of currency.

A third grievance of the farmer concerned prices, both the prices he received for his products and the prices he paid for goods he bought. He disposed of his products as an individual in competition with countless other individuals in this and other countries. He possessed little or no advance information on the state of the market and probable price changes; he did not have storage facilities to hold his crop for a favorable price; and he was powerless to regulate his production. Instead of changing his marketing procedures, the farmer blamed his woes on personal villains—grain speculators in distant cities, international bankers, or regional and local middlemen. These operators, he became convinced (sometimes with justice), were combining to fix prices so as to benefit themselves while hurting him.

The farmer was also convinced that there was something of a conspiracy against him in the prices of the goods he purchased. He sold his crops in a competitive market but bought in a domestic market protected by tariffs and dominated by trusts and corporations. According to government reports, over one hundred articles purchased by farmers—farm machinery, tools, sewing machines, blankets, staple foods, clothing, plowshares, and others—were protected. On these necessary items the tariff added from 33 to 60 percent to the purchase price.

Last on the agrarian catalog of grievances was a vague yet tremendous resentment. In part, this was an outgrowth of the isolation of farm life before the days of paved roads, automobiles, telephones, and radios. Farm families in some parts of the country, particularly in the prairie and plains region where large farms were scattered over vast areas, were virtually cut off from the outside world and from other human companionship during the winter months or protracted spells of bad weather. This enforced seclusion was only partially alleviated when the national government established rural free delivery of mail in 1896. The drabness and the dullness of farm existence, the lack of adequate educational, recreational, and medical facilities, and the absence of community culture and action—these things helped to account for the tremendous migration of young people from the farms to the cities. The farmer, once eulogized as the surest support of American democracy, was now ridiculed as a "hayseed." He was losing status, and he knew it.

Knowledge for a New Society

While the farmer's ways declined in prestige, the urban environment increasingly made its influence felt upon the mind of the entire nation, despite the persistence of stereotypes from the rural past. The city's influence was spread through the educational system, which was being broadened and extended, and through the publishing industry, which centered in New York and reached out for a wider and wider readership.

THE PRAGMATIC APPROACH

Along with the economic and social changes of the time, there was a change in the philosophical assumptions of thinking Americans. This came about largely in response to the doctrine of evolution—the thesis that all living things had evolved from earlier forms and that the various species had resulted from a process of natural selection.

Christian Science

One of the new religions that came into being in the 1870s was Christian Science, founded by a woman, Mary Baker G. Eddy. She explained the essence of her belief as follows:

> The Scriptures name God as good, and the Saxon term for God is also good. From this premise comes the logical conclusion that God is naturally and divinely infinite good. How, then, can this conclusion change, or be changed, to mean that good is evil, or the creator of evil? What can there be besides infinity? Nothing! Therefore the Science of good calls evil nothing. In divine Science the terms God and good, as Spirit, are synonymous. That God, good, creates evil, or aught that can result in evil,—or that Spirit creates its opposite, named matter,—are conclusions that destroy their premise and prove themselves invalid. Here is where Christian Science sticks to its text, and other systems of religion abandon their own logic. Here also is found the pith of the basal statement, the cardinal point in Christian Science, that matter and evil (including all inharmony, sin, disease, death) are unreal.

Here was a doctrine that challenged almost every tenet of the American faith. If Darwin and the scientists were right, man was not endowed with a higher nature, but was only a biological organism, another form of animal life—the highest form, it was true, but still like the other animals that had had their day in past ages. Instead of history's being the working out of a divine plan, it was a random process dominated by the fiercest or luckiest competitors.

All over the United States Darwinism became a subject of popular interest and an issue of debate. By 1900 the evolutionists had carried the day, except in the South and parts of the rural Midwest. Many Protestant ministers, especially those in urban centers, had managed a reconciliation between religion and science. Particularly in the cities and larger towns, more and more people accepted the basic principles of evolution. Science was enshrined in the university and college curriculums.

Out of the controversy over Darwinism there arose finally a new philosophy which was peculiarly American and peculiarly suited to America's changing material civilization. The name of the philosophy was pragmatism, and its principal formulators were Charles Peirce and William James in the period before 1900, and John Dewey later.

Pragmatism is difficult to define, partly because its advocates differed as to its meaning, but mainly because it avoided absolutes and dealt with relative standards. According to the pragmatists, who accepted the idea of organic evolution, the validity of human institutions and actions should be determined by their consequences. If the ends of an institution or the techniques of a group did not satisfy social needs, then a change was in order. In blunt terms, the pragmatists applied their one standard: Does it work? They subjected truth to the same test. There were no final truths or answers, they contended, but a series of truths for each generation and each society. Truth, like institutions, had to be validated by consequences. Said James: "The ultimate test for us of what a truth means is the conduct it dictates or inspires."

TOWARD UNIVERSAL SCHOOLING

Mary Antin, a Russian girl who came as an immigrant to the United States, had heard that in America everything was free. Best of all: "Education was free. That subject my father had written about repeatedly, as comprising his chief hope for us children, the essence of American opportunity, the treasure that no thief could touch, not even misfortune or poverty." Education in America after the Civil War was indeed free or in the process of becoming so—free, public, and almost universal.

In 1860 there were only 100 public high schools in the country, but by 1900 the number had reached 6,000; their total enrollment, however, was not more than 200,000. The most spectacular expansion occurred at the elementary or grade school level. Below the elementary level appeared the kindergartens, the first of which was established in St. Louis in 1873. By 1900 compulsory school attendance laws were in effect, although not always enforced, in thirty-one states and territories. In the expansion of school facilities, the Northeast led, the Middle West followed, and the South trailed behind.

Most of the elementary schools and many of the high schools in all sections were, by modern standards, small, inadequate, and unattractive. Dominating the curriculum were the traditional three Rs—reading, writing, and arithmetic—with history and a few other subjects holding a secondary place. Also traditional were the textbooks used, among them the Webster Spellers and the McGuffey Readers.

Teaching was not yet regarded as a profession. In 1900 the average annual salary was a mere $325, less than the average wage of unskilled workers. Thousands of teachers, with only a high school or elementary education, knew little more than their pupils. Nevertheless, real progress was achieved in establishing the idea that teaching was a profession and education a science. In 1865 there were only twelve teacher-training institutions, or normal schools, as they were called, in the country. By 1900 every state supported at least one such school, and in some of the leading universities, Chicago, Harvard, Columbia, Stanford, and others, schools of education had been set up. The states created boards or commissions of education to raise standards, and in 1867 the national government manifested its interest by establishing the office of Commissioner of Education to collect and disseminate educational information. By the turn of the century one in every five of the elementary teachers was a graduate of a professional school.

In the 1880s a number of innovations in educational methods began to make their influence felt. New, more up-to-date textbooks were introduced, and the curriculum was expanded to include more science and practical or vocational courses. At the same time German educational doctrines, stressing the neces-sity of arousing the student's desire to learn, stirred the attention of American educators. Among those impressed by the German theories was John Dewey, one of the pragmatic philosophers and a member of the faculty of the school of education of the University of Chicago. In lectures and essays in the 1890s, Dewey proposed that education should be considered as a part of the social process, that its purpose should be to prepare students to live in modern society, and that pupils should learn by doing instead of by the traditional rote or drill method. His program of progressive education had its greatest impact after 1900.

EXPANDING HIGHER EDUCATION

Powerfully stimulating the expansion of higher learning were huge new financial resources made available by the national government and private benefactors. The national government, by the Morrill Land Grant Act of the Civil War period, donated land to states for the establishment of colleges to teach, among other subjects, agriculture and mechanical arts. After 1865, particularly in the West and the South, states began to exploit the possibilities of the act to strengthen existing institutions or to found new ones. In some cases the proceeds went to a single state university with an agricultural and mechanical division, and in other cases to a separate college for the practical arts. In all, sixty-nine "land grant" institutions came into existence, among them the universities of Wisconsin, California, Minnesota, and Illinois.

Supplementing the resources of the government were the millions of dollars contributed by business and financial tycoons, who endowed private institutions. The motives of the magnates were various: they were influenced by the gospel of wealth; they thought that education would blunt class differences; they realized that the demands of an industrial society called for specialized knowledge—or they were simply vain. Men like Rockefeller and Carnegie gave generously to such schools as Harvard, Chicago, Northwestern, Syracuse, Yale, and Columbia. Other philanthropists founded new universities and thereby perpetuated their family names—Vanderbilt, Johns Hopkins, Cornell, Tulane, and Stanford.

Booker T. Washington on Negro Education [1895]

Washington rose from slavery to the leadership of his people. Founding Tuskegee Institute in Alabama, he advocated that the Negro improve his economic status before reaching for political rights. To that end Washington, in a speech in 1895, advocated a vocational type of education, which prompted some Negroes to accuse him of subordinating the race's struggle for equal rights:

Our greatest danger is that in the great leap from slavery to freedom we may overlook the fact that the masses of us are to live by the productions of our hands, and fail to keep in mind that we shall prosper in proportion as we learn to dignify and glorify common labour and put brains and skill into the common occupations of life; shall prosper in proportion as we learn to draw the line between the superficial and the substantial, the ornamental gewgaws of life and the useful. No race can prosper till it learns that there is as much dignity in tilling a field as in writing a poem. It is at the bottom of life we must begin, and not at the top. Nor should we permit our grievances to overshadow our opportunities.

Taking over as president of Harvard in 1869 at the age of thirty-five, Charles W. Eliot pioneered a break with the traditional curriculum. The usual course of studies at American universities emphasized classical and humanistic courses: ancient languages, mathematics, ethics, and rhetoric; and each institution prescribed a rigid program of required courses. Under Eliot's leadership, Harvard dropped most of its required courses in favor of an elective system and increased its course offerings to stress the physical and social sciences, the fine arts, and modern languages. Soon other institutions in all sections of the country were following Harvard's lead.

Eliot also renovated the Harvard medical and law schools, raising the requirements and lengthening the residence period, and again the Harvard model affected other schools. Improved technical training in other professions accompanied the advances in medicine and law. Both state and private universities hastened to establish schools of architecture, engineering, education, journalism, and business. The leading center for graduate study, based on the German system with the Ph.D. degree as its highest award, was the Johns Hopkins University (founded in 1876). In 1875 there were only 399 graduate students in the United States, but by 1900 the number had risen to more than 5,000.

Two groups in American society—women and Negroes—did not receive the full benefits of higher education. Before the Civil War, girls had been generally admitted on an equal basis to elementary and secondary schools, but the doors of most colleges were closed to them. A few private colleges for women had been founded, and a very few schools (three, to be exact) admitted girls to study with boys. After the war a number of additional women's colleges came into existence, generally as the result of donations from philanthropists: Vassar, Wellesley, Smith, Bryn Mawr, and Goucher. In addition, some the largest private universities established on their campuses separate colleges for women. But the greatest educational opportunities for women opened in the Middle West, where the state universities began to admit women along with men.

Negroes reaped the fewest advantages from the educational renaissance. In the South, and also in most parts of the North, they attended segregated elementary and secondary schools that were nearly always poorer than the white schools. Negroes desiring a higher education were almost universally barred from white institutions and had to attend one of the colleges established for their race by Northern philanthropy: Howard University, in Washington; Fisk University, in Nashville; Straight University, in New Orleans; or Shaw University, in Raleigh. Some Negro leaders were disturbed by the tendency of their people to seek a "classical" education that did not fit them for the economic position they occupied in the South. For the transitional period after emancipation, these leaders believed, an industrial education, stressing vocational training and the dignity of labor, was preferable. The result of their thinking was the establishment, with aid from private sources, of the Hampton Normal and Industrial Institute in Virginia and the Tuskegee Institute in Alabama, the latter presided over by Booker T. Washington, the most influential Negro leader of his times.

Many adults sought learning through agencies other than colleges. Summer after summer, thousands flocked to the Chautauqua Institution in western New York to hear lectures on a variety of subjects. Chautauqua offered a concentrated short course for teachers and others in residence; it also provided extension courses and a four-year home reading program for nonresident clients. In addition Chautauqua companies toured rural America bringing music and lectures to people who received no other exposure to such culture.

Public libraries appeared in increasing numbers, especially in the cities and larger towns. Andrew Carnegie gave $45 million of his steel fortune for the construction of public libraries, wisely stipulating that communities taking his money had to maintain the institutions. Through the benefactions of men like Carnegie and through public support, over 9,000 free libraries had come into being by 1900.

THE PUBLISHING BUSINESS

Newspapers and magazines provided the reading matter for most Americans. During the period 1870–1910 the circulation of daily newspapers had a nearly ninefold increase (from less than 3 million to more than 24 million), which was over three times as great as the increase in population.

Meanwhile, journalism changed in various ways: (1) Newspapers became predominantly news organs, while editorial opinion and the editorial page declined in importance. (2) The nature of news changed. Politics received less attention, and there was an increasing emphasis on what was called the "human-interest" story. (3) Journalism became a recognized and respected profession. Salaries of reporters doubled. Able and educated men were attracted to the profession, and schools of journalism

were begun on university campuses. (4) With the passing of personal journalism, newspapers became corporations, impersonal business organizations similar to those emerging in industry, their worth often reckoned in millions of dollars. At the same time, they tended to become standardized. The press services furnished the same news to all their subscribing papers, and syndicates came into existence to provide their customers with identical features, columns, editorials, and pictures. By the turn of the century there were several newspaper chains, harbingers of a development that would become stronger in the future. Thus the newspapers conformed to and reinforced the trend toward uniformity that characterized American society as a whole. (5) There was a distinct improvement in the physical appearance of newspapers. The traditional pages of poorly and closely printed columns, each with its own headlines, disappeared; in their place came something resembling the modern paper, complete with varied make-up, pictures, cartoons, and imaginative advertising.

For almost twenty years after the Civil War, the principal magazines in the country were monthlies and weeklies that reached only a limited number of readers. Essentially, they were literary journals run by literary men. They were always genteel and in good (but often dull) taste; they sold for 35 cents a copy (a high price for those times); and the circulation of the largest did not exceed 130,000. The leading monthlies were *Harper's Magazine* and the *Atlantic Monthly*, both of which antedated the war, *Scribner's Monthly*, which was founded in 1870 and became the *Century* in 1881, and *Scribner's Magazine*, established in 1887. Somewhat similar were the weeklies: the *Nation*, the *Independent*, and *Harper's Weekly*, all published in New York.

During the decade of the eighties, a new type of magazine appeared—the popular magazine, designed to appeal to the masses and to achieve a mass circulation. One of the important pioneers of the popular journal was Edward W. Bok, who took over the *Ladies' Home Journal* in 1889 and, by employing writers who produced material to appeal to female readers, built the circulation of the magazine to over 700,000. Following Bok was Frank A. Munsey, the greatest of the popular publishers, who utilized the techniques of mass production and technology—cheap but attractive printing, low prices, and lavish advertising—to make *Munsey's Magazine* one of the most widely read organs in the country. The older *Saturday Evening Post* adopted many of the new methods and, by catering to the standards of the middle class, it led all other journals in circulation. Popular magazines, priced at 5 to 15 cents, had circulations of up to a million.

Book publishing became a business, and, in line with the trend in industry, a big business. The corporation replaced the individual publisher, and publishing became more impersonal and increasingly commercial. For approximately twenty years after the war most publishing houses, of whom the American Publishing Company of Hartford, Connecticut, was a leading example, sold books only by subscription. But gradually this type of organization was supplanted by the large firm that sold its products to book stores and reached the public through advertising techniques. By 1900 most of the big publishing houses were centered in New York City, the recognized publishing capital of the country and also the largest literary market. The passage by Congress in 1891 of an International Copyright Law prevented American publishers from pirating foreign books without payment (and also prevented foreign pirating of American books). The result was that publishers had to rely more on American authors and pay them better.

Culture in the Gilded Age

In a novel, *The Gilded Age* (1873), Mark Twain and Charles Dudley Warner satirized the men and manners of industrial society and thus provided a name that is sometimes applied to the last decades of the nineteenth century. The novel deals with greedy men and their get-rich-quick schemes. It suggests that American life, though showy on the surface, was essentially acquisitive and corrupt. Its authors thus reflected the economic and social changes of the time. Different writers responded to these changes in a variety of ways. Some faced up to the realities of the industrializing and urbanizing trend; others sought a vicarious escape for themselves and for their readers.

REFLECTIONS IN LITERATURE

Though New York City was the publishing center, the production of literature—the actual writing—was done all over the country. A literary renaissance began in the West and the South as well as the East. Writers in each section, describing their home scenes in local-color stories, found a national market for their wares.

Writers of the local-color school thought of themselves as realists. Rebelling against the sentimentality of the tear-jerking popular novelists like Mary Jane Holmes (whose thirty-nine novels sold more than 2 million copies), they insisted on careful reporting, real people and real plots, and an honest rendition of such things as dialect, dress, food, and manners. Usually, however, they were content with an accurate surface description that did not come to grips with fundamental problems, and on occasion some of them wrote sentimental nonsense.

In New England, Sarah Orne Jewett and Mary E. Wilkins Freeman portrayed the disappearing social order of their section: its rural scenes and ways, its isolated farms, and its decaying seaport towns. Of the two, Miss Jewett was the finer artist; her *The Country of the Pointed Firs* (1896) was far above the reportorial level of the average local-color author. In the South, George Washington Cable affectionately described the antebellum Creole life of Louisiana but was so outspoken on the race question that he had to take refuge in the North. Most famous of the Southern writers was Joel Chandler Harris, who recorded Georgia folk tales and Negro life in *Uncle Remus* (1880). Thomas Nelson Page extolled in fiction the old Virginia aristocracy. In the Middle West, Edward Eggleston presented an honest account of early Indiana life in *The Hoosier Schoolmaster* (1871), and James Whitcomb Riley gave a folksy view of contemporary Indiana life in his popular verse. In the Far West, Bret Harte

Mark Twain with His Friends
The author sat regally at the head of the table at a dinner given him on his seventieth birthday in the famous and garish Delmonico's restaurant in New York City. (Library of Congress)

wrote sentimental stories of the mining frontier. Mark Twain, while living in California, burst into national prominence with a humorous sketch, "The Celebrated Frog of Calaveras County," and he portrayed aspects of the last frontier in *Roughing It* (1872).

Mark Twain (born Samuel Clemens) began his career on a newspaper, and he long considered himself to be a journalist. The public long insisted on regarding him as merely a humorist, but he was probably the greatest American novelist in the era between 1865 and 1900. His first important success, *The Innocents Abroad* (1869), a tale of American tourists in Europe, was a loud and scornful laugh at Old World decay and hypocrisy — and also at American worship of European institutions. His literary fame, however, rests primarily on *The Adventures of Tom Sawyer* (1876) and *The Adventures of Huckleberry Finn* (1885), sensi-

tive and sympathetic accounts of life in rural mid-America.

Not all the writers were concerned with depicting departing cultures. Some viewed with misgiving the culture of their own times, and deplored its materialism and economic inequalities. Gradually there developed a literature of protest, expressed chiefly in the medium of the problem novel. The dissenters attacked their targets from many and varied angles. A few, like Henry Adams in *Democracy* (1880) and John Hay in *The Breadwinners* (1884), spoke for the old aristocracy, the former ruling class; in criticizing the crassness of the new rich, they merely expressed the resentment of their group at being dethroned. No novelist of stature voiced the aspirations of labor, although Stephen Crane in *Maggie: A Girl of the Streets* (1893) described slum conditions and urban poverty with somber realism. For rural America and its small towns, Hamlin Garland and Edgar W. Howe grimly performed a similar descriptive job. Garland, smashing the traditional idyllic picture of pastoral culture, exposed in *Main-Travelled Roads* (1891) the ugliness, isolation, and drudgery of farm life, and Howe in *The Story of a Country Town* (1883) starkly painted the narrow, provincial nature of the American village.

A few literary critics of the American scene retreated from its vigor and materialism and found refuge in Europe. Preeminent among them was Henry James, who studied and described his country from England. In such novels as *The American* (1876), *An International Episode* (1878), and *Daisy Miller* (1879), he detailed the impact of Europe's ancient culture upon visiting Americans. In his coldly realistic volumes, the Americans are usually frustrated or defeated by Europe, but nearly always they appear more virile than the civilization they cannot understand. During his later years, James confessed he wished he had remained in America.

The greatest realistic novelist of the period, ranking second only to Twain in the hierarchy of letters, was William Dean Howells. His realism was confined to the common and the average; shunning the abnormal, he was the most painstaking literary historian of what was normal in the America of his age. In *The Rise of Silas Lapham* (1884), he portrayed shrewdly and in not completely flattering terms the psychology of the self-made businessman. His later novels, written during the social upheaval and labor strife of the nineties, dealt with social problems and social injustices.

ART AND ARCHITECTURE

American attitudes toward the arts in the Gilded Age paralleled those manifested toward literature. Popular tastes, largely determined by the middle class, admired paintings that told a conventional story, pointed a moral, or photographically reproduced familiar people and scenes. The artists whose works were most widely viewed were the illustrators for the popular magazines and the weeklies.

But Americans also had opportunities to see the best painting and sculpture of Europe's past. The newly rich business magnates set out with vigorous determination to patronize art and artists and to acquire, as part of their process of acquiring culture, the finest collections their money would buy. They purchased, regardless of cost, many of the art treasures of Europe, which possessed, their agents taught them, the only art worthy of the name, and installed them in their palace homes. Sometimes they did more—they established public art galleries or museums of fine arts, and eventually nearly all of the private collections found their way into public depositories. At the close of the Civil War not a single American city could boast of a good art gallery, but by 1900 there was a gallery or museum of at least adequate status in every metropolitan center. Thousands of Americans could and did see the best paintings and sculpture of Europe's past.

In the years after the Civil War most American painters received their training in Europe. Some remained there as expatriates (like the writer Henry James), among them James McNeill Whistler and John Singer Sargent. Whistler, who is often ranked as the greatest genius in the history of American art, was equally proficient in several media—oil, watercolor, etching—and with several themes—portraits and his so-called nocturnes, impressionistic sketches of moonlight on water and other scenes. He was one of the first to appreciate the beauty of Japanese color prints and to introduce Oriental concepts into Western art. Equally versatile but not as talented was Sargent, who built his international reputation on his portraits.

Breaking away from European influences was a small group of artists, of whom the ablest were John La Farge, Winslow Homer, and Thomas Eakins. La Farge's experiments with light and color anticipated the Impressionists. He worked with both landscapes and portraits, was our first important muralist, and probably is still America's most distinguished stained-glass artist. Homer, who began as a magazine illustrator, was vigorously and almost blatantly American. All of his powerful and rugged paintings dealt with native scenes and people; his best pictures were of the sea and maritime life on the New England coast.

American sculpture in the years immediately following the Civil War was dominated by Italian influences and the neoclassical tradition. When American sculptors made statues of

American leaders, they produced figures that resembled Roman senators and indeed were often clothed in flowing robes or togas. But gradually France supplanted Italy as an influence, and American sculptors, many of whom were trained in Paris, began to work out an art form distinctively American. One of the first to break from the Italian tradition was John Quincy Adams Ward with his statues of Indians and Negroes. Another was Daniel Chester French, who produced a number of realistic statues of great Americans, the most famous being the imposing Lincoln in the Lincoln Memorial at Washington. Incomparably the greatest American sculptor of the period was Augustus Saint-Gaudens, an Irish shoemaker's son who did more than any native artist to free American sculpture from its European bonds. His statues of Generals Grant and Sherman and of Admiral Farragut and, above all, his Lincoln in Lincoln Park, Chicago, were authentically American and impressively beautiful.

Before the Civil War the dominant influence in American architecture had been the classic Greek. Public buildings and dwellings throughout the country copied the lines of ancient Greek edifices. By 1860, however, the so-called Greek revival had spent its force, and another style, also a revival, had appeared. It became the rage of the Gilded Age. This was Gothic or, more accurately, an American version of the Gothic, with generous borrowings from other styles and some original native techniques added.

One of the first Americans to break with the Gothic tradition was Richard Morris Hunt, who designed dozens of homes for the business tycoons and became known as the architect of fashionable society. Although his houses were as large and elaborate as the Gothic edifices, they sprang from a different influence and reproduced a different mood—the light and lavish spirit of the French Renaissance. French chateaux and townhouses by Hunt dotted the rural resort areas of the East and its cities. Another rebel against the Gothic was Henry Hobson Richardson, the best-known architect of the period, who attempted to adapt the Romanesque form of France and Spain to the American scene. His public buildings, of which his churches are the most famous, and his houses were marked by solid but often graceful arches, heavy, short pillars, and simple carving; in

their low-lying strength they resembled nothing so much as forts. Still another dissenting note was sounded by C. F. McKim, of the New York firm of McKim, Mead, and White, who endeavored to revive the Renaissance style by fitting it to American needs.

These men, however large their talents, were essentially imitative and derivative. They copied and adapted European forms, and their designs had little relevance to the facts of American life and little utility for the needs of the American scene, especially for the growing urban centers. Both the virtues and the faults of American architecture were demonstrated at the Chicago World's Fair of 1893. Most of the buildings shown were in the classical style; although they possessed a certain stately beauty, they revealed fully the unimaginative character of American architecture and the strength of the European bonds holding it. But there also emerged from the Fair an authentic genius, the first great original American architect— Louis Sullivan. Sullivan, who designed the Transportation Building for the Fair, denounced the work done there by most of his colleagues as mere copies rather than creations, "a naked exhibition of charlatanry . . . conjoined with expert salesmanship of the materials of decay."

NEW USES OF LEISURE

Many Americans, especially those of the urban middle and professional classes, found that they had more leisure at their command, and they had incomes sufficient to gratify their demands for pleasure. Even the workers had more free time, and they too sought satisfactory forms of recreation. The late nineteenth century witnessed the rise of organized spectator sports, the presentation of athletic events as entertainment for large audiences, and the organization of sports as a business.

Most popular of all the organized sports and well on its way to becoming the national game was baseball. Its origins probably stretched back to 1839, when Abner Doubleday, a civil engineering student, laid out a diamond-shaped field at Cooperstown, New York, and attempted to standardize the rules governing the playing of such games as town ball and four old cat, the ancestors of baseball. By the

An Early Football Game

*Here, in an 1899 contest between Cornell and Rochester, the ball is being put into
play by a "scrum," similar to that of rugby. The ball was placed on the ground,
and a circle of players tried to kick it out to their respective teammates. The
"father of American football," one-time Yale star Walter Camp, led in modernizing
the game. He persuaded the rulemakers to reduce the number of players to eleven
on each side, to permit the offensive team to put the ball into play from a line of
scrimmage, with a quarterback, and to require the team to advance the ball five
yards in three plays (and then, later, ten yards in four plays) or give it up to the
opposing team. Camp also helped to eliminate excessive roughness from what had
been a remarkably brutal sport. He selected the first "All-American" eleven.
(Library of Congress)*

end of the Civil War, interest in the game had
grown rapidly. Over 200 teams or clubs existed,
some of which toured the country playing rivals; they belonged to a national association of
"Baseball Players" that had proclaimed a set of
standard rules. These teams were amateurs or
semiprofessionals, but as the game waxed in
popularity, it offered opportunities for profit,
and the first professional team, the Cincinnati
Red Stockings, appeared in 1869. Other cities
soon fielded professional teams, and in 1876 the
present National League was organized, chiefly by Albert Spalding. Soon a rival league appeared, the American Association. Competition
between the two was intense, and in 1883 they
played a postseason contest, the first "world's
series." The American Association eventually
collapsed, but in 1900 the American League
was organized.

The second most popular game, football,
arose in the colleges and universities. At first
football had been played by rival student

groups at the same school. Then in 1869 occurred the first intercollegiate game in this country, between Princeton and Rutgers, with twenty-five men on each side. Soon other Eastern schools fielded teams, organized a conference, the American Intercollegiate Football Association, and attempted to standardize the rules.

As football grew in popularity, it spread to other sections, notably to the Middle Western state universities, soon destined to overthrow the Eastern schools as the powers of the game. It also began to exhibit those taints of professionalism that have marked it ever since. Some schools employed as players "ringers," tramp athletes who were not even registered as students. In an effort to eliminate such abuses, Amos A. Stagg, athletic director and coach at the University of Chicago, led in forming the Western Conference, or Big Ten, in 1896.

A game that would eventually become one of the great spectator sports, basketball, was invented in 1891 at Springfield, Massachusetts, by Dr. James A. Naismith. It is the only major sport that is completely American in origin.

Boxing did not become a respectable sport until the 1880s. Before that time prize fights were illegal in practically every state, and bouts had to be conducted in isolated places beyond the reach of law officials. The existing rules were few and encouraged brutality. Contestants fought without gloves; a round ended when one man was knocked down; and a fight continued until one of the participants was unwilling or unable to go on. In the 1870s the Marquis-of-Queensberry rules were introduced in England and later in the United States. By these regulations, fighters were required to wear padded gloves, a round was limited to three minutes, and certain rough practices and types of blows were ruled out. The first American boxer to adopt the new rules was John L. Sullivan, who had become heavyweight champion of the world in 1882. Although Sullivan occasionally returned to bare-knuckle fighting, he invested the sport with a respectability it had never known. It was raised to a higher plane by James J. Corbett, "Gentleman Jim," who dethroned Sullivan in 1892. Five years later Corbett dropped the title to Bob Fitzsimmons, who in turn was knocked out by James J. Jeffries in 1899.

Before 1900 golf and tennis were almost completely participant rather than spectator sports. The first modern golf course in the United States was laid out at Yonkers, New York, in 1888, and the first golf tournament in the country was played at Newport, Rhode Island, six years later. The only courses were at exclusive private clubs, and until after 1900 the game was restricted to the rich. Much the same was true of tennis, first played at Eastern resorts frequented by the wealthy. The United States Lawn Tennis Association was organized in 1881 to standardize the rules and encourage the game, and in 1897 American tennis players engaged an English team in the first international match.

In the small towns and villages of rural America, recreation continued to follow more traditional patterns. People came together for entertainment at county fairs, political rallies, and court sessions. Always a big event in a rural community was the arrival of a Chautauqua company with its tent and array of lecturers, musicians, and other luminaries. Even more colorful was the circus with its display of exotic wonders, amazing to rural people who had never traveled far from their birthplace. To send a circus across the country was expensive, and many smaller companies could not stand the cost. By 1900 the circus industry was dominated by two large firms, Barnum and Bailey, and Ringling Brothers.

The nineties saw the birth of the bicycle craze. Bicycling was both a recreation and, for many people in urban areas, a convenient method of transportation. The bicycle in the 1880s, with a high wheel in front, often pitched the rider over the handlebars for a "header" in the dirt. It was too dangerous for practically everyone except the most daring young men. The "safety" bicycle of the 1890s, with two wheels of equal size and with pneumatic tires, invited riders of both sexes and all ages. By 1900 an estimated 10 million Americans, mostly adults, were riding bicycles. While it lasted, the mania had some influence on American life. It brought into being a new industry for the manufacture of the vehicles. The cyclists, organized in the League of American Wheelmen, spurred local governments to improve highways. And cycling changed clothing styles as many young women put on blouses and moderate-length skirts in place of the former dragging street dresses, which got in the rider's way.

The bicycle prepared the way for the coming of the automobile. The two-wheeler not only brought some good roads for the first cars to run on; it also provided essential components of the early models, such as tubular steel, wire wheels, pneumatic tires, and the chain-and-sprocket drive. Many of the pioneers among American automobile builders, such as Henry Ford, once had been bicycle mechanics.

Selected Readings

Frontier Interpretations and Miscellany
F. J. Turner, *The Frontier in American History** (1920); R. A. Billington, *Frederick Jackson Turner* (1973); H. N. Smith, *Virgin Land: The American West as Symbol and Myth** (1950); W. P. Webb, *The Great Plains** (1931); J. C. Malin, *The Grassland of North America* (1947); H. R. Lamar, *The Far Southwest, 1846–1912* (1966); R. M. Robbins, *Our Landed Heritage: The Public Domain, 1776–1936** (1942); E. S. Pomeroy, *The Territories and the United States, 1864–1890* (1947); Wayne Gard, *The Great Buffalo Hunt* (1959).

Mining
W. S. Greever, *The Bonanza West: The Story of the Western Mining Rushes, 1848–1900* (1963); R. W. Paul, *Mining Frontiers of the Far West, 1848–1880* (1963); C. H. Shinn, *Mining Camps: A Study in American Frontier Government** (1885); Wayne Gard, *Frontier Justice* (1949).

Cattle and Sheep Raising
E. S. Osgood, *The Day of the Cattleman** (1929); E. E. Dale, *The Range Cattle Industry* (1930); Lewis Atherton, *The Cattle Kings* (1961); J. B. Frantz and J. E. Choate, Jr., *The American Cowboy: The Myth and the Reality* (1955); Philip Durham and E. L. Jones, *The Negro Cowboy* (1965); E. N. Wentworth, *Shepherd's Empire* (1945).

Farming
F. A. Shannon, *The Farmer's Last Frontier, 1860–1897* (1945); G. C. Fite, *The Farmer's Frontier, 1865–1900* (1966); Everett Dick, *The Sod-House Frontier, 1854–1890* (1937).

The Indians
F. G. Roe, *The Indian and the Horse* (1955); H. H. Jackson, *A Century of Dishonor** (1881); L. G. Priest, *Uncle Sam's Stepchildren: The Reformation of the United States Indian Policy, 1865–1887* (1942); H. E. Fritz, *The Movement for Indian Assimilation, 1860–1890* (1963); C. M. Oehler, *The Great Sioux Uprising* (1959); Robert Utley, *Last Days of the Sioux Nation** (1963); J. C. Olson, *Red Cloud and the Sioux Problem* (1965); Stanley Vestal, *Warpath and Council Fire* (1948) and *Sitting Bull* (1957); F. F. Van de Water, *Glory Hunter* (1934), on Custer; Jay Monaghan, *Custer* (1959); Stan Hoig, *The Sand Creek Massacre* (1961); O. B. Faulk, *The Geronimo Campaign* (1969); R. K. Andrist, *The Long Death: The Last Days of the Plains Indians* (1964); Dee A. Brown, *Bury My Heart at Wounded Knee: An Indian History of the American West* (1971); M. D. Beal, *"I Will Fight No More"* (1963), on Chief Joseph.

Education
Frederick Rudolph, *The American College and University: A History** (1962); L. R. Veysey, *The Emergence of the American University* (1965); Richard Hofstadter and Walter Metzger, *The Development of Academic Freedom in the United States* (1955); L. A. Cremin, *The Transformation of the School: Progressivism in American Education, 1876–1957** (1961); L. R. Harlan, *Booker T. Washington: The Making of a Black Leader, 1856–1901* (1972).

Religion
C. H. Hopkins, *The Rise of the Social Gospel in American Protestantism, 1865–1915* (1940); A. I. Abell, *The Urban Impact on American Protestantism, 1865–1900* (1943); H. F. May, *Protestant Churches and Industrial America* (1949).

Literature
Van Wyck Brooks, *New England: Indian Summer, 1865–1915** (1940); Larzer Ziff, *The American 1890's: Life and Times of a Lost Generation* (1966); Everett Carter, *Howells and the Age of Realism* (1954); Bernard De Voto, *Mark Twain's America** (1932); Justin Kaplan, *Mr. Clemens and Mark Twain* (1966); Elizabeth Stevenson, *Henry Adams** (1955); R. B. Perry, *The Thought and Character of William James* (2 vols., 1935); F. O. Matthiessen, *The James Family* (1947); Stow Persons, *The Decline of American Gentility* (1973).

Architecture

W. A. Starrett, *Skyscrapers and the Men Who Built Them* (1928); John Szarkowski, *The Idea of Louis Sullivan* (1957).

Popular Culture

Ray Ginger, *The Age of Excess: The United States from 1877 to 1914* (1965); R. O. and Victoria Case, *We Called It Culture: The Story of Chautauqua* (1958); J. D. Hart, *The Popular Book** (1950); F. L. Mott, *A History of American Magazines*, vol. 3, *1865–1885* (1938), and vol. 4, *1885–1905* (1957); D. C. Seitz, *Joseph Pulitzer* (1924); J. K. Winkler, *W. R. Hearst* (1928); F. R. Dulles, *America Learns to Play* (1940); J. A. Krout, *Annals of American Sport* (1924).

*Titles available in paperback.

The Swell of Agrarian Protest

Nineteen

In the 1880s the major parties in the United States were like two bottles that had different labels but otherwise were identical—and both were empty. So it seemed to the Englishman James Bryce, the most perspicacious of all foreign commentators on American institutions next to the Frenchman Alexis de Tocqueville. "Tenets and policies, points of political doctrine and points of political practice, have all but vanished," Bryce wrote in *The American Commonwealth* (1888). "All has been lost, except office or the hope of it."

In American society there were serious problems arising out of the development of big business and monopoly, the organization of labor and the resulting industrial conflict, the decline of agricultural prices and the worsening position of the farmer, and the defects in the economic system that caused it to collapse every twenty years or so (in 1873 and again in 1893). But the leaders of the major parties evaded these problems as best they could.

Politics was more highly professionalized than ever, and the politicians played it like a game that had little to do with economic and social realities. With the politicians the object was to win power and jobs. In many cities or entire states a political boss headed a machine (organization) that operated as an "invisible government" controlling the official government of the city or state. The machine bought votes and sold governmental favors. The national parties looked to the boss and the machine to provide the votes with which to win elections.

The parties depended for support not only on the patronage of government but also on contributions from business. It took the assassination of a President to shock the politicians into accepting a partial reform of the spoils system. After that, the parties had to depend more and more on corporation gifts. The president of the sugar trust testified before a congressional investigating committee that during the 1892 campaign

---

"Division of Labor"
The farmer turns the grindstone of "war taxes" while the monopolist sharpens the ax of "high protection." The feeling that big business—with the aid of government taxes and tariffs—exploited the common people led to late-nineteenth-century protests such as Populism. From Puck, *February 1, 1888. (Culver Pictures)*

his company had contributed money to both the Republicans and the Democrats. "The American Sugar Refining Company has no politics of any kind," he concluded. "Only the politics of business?" he was asked. "Only the politics of business," he replied.

Already, in the early 1890s, a tide of protest was swelling and dashing against the politics of business. It was headed by discontented farmers, but it included other dissatisfied groups whose numbers were increased by the onset of the depression. It encountered the forces of conservatism and partially recoiled before them but recovered to reach a roaring climax in the election of 1896. Thereafter the protest movement receded, as the economic system demonstrated its capacity to enlarge the general well-being, and the political system showed its ability to absorb dissenters into the traditional two parties. Meanwhile, the protesters had displayed a moral fervor and a class bitterness that frightened and appalled the more secure and sober elements of society. "It was a fanaticism like the crusades," wrote the Kansas editor William Allen White.

The Politics of Complacency

It has sometimes been thought that political parties ought to define and discuss issues as sharply as do debating clubs. But the major parties in the United States have seldom divided on fundamental principles except in times of crisis (as during the 1850s and the 1890s). More commonly the parties have been concerned with confusing issues rather than clarifying them, with harmonizing interests rather than antagonizing them. The politics of the years from 1877 to 1888 illustrate in extreme form this function of the parties.

REPUBLICANS AND DEMOCRATS

Republicanism was almost a religion in the North. The Republican party, the Grand Old Party of Abraham Lincoln and the boys in blue, had saved the Union and freed the slaves. In election after election, long after Appomattox, Republican campaigners continued to recall the war record of their own party and attack the opposition as the party of treason and slavery. Related to this, as another reminder of the war, was the practice, every four years (except in 1884), of nominating as the Republican presidential candidate a veteran officer of the Union army.

Flights of campaign oratory thinly masked the economic composition and goals of the dominant party. Even more powerful in the party's councils than in the prewar era was the business element, composed of manufacturers, bankers, investors, and government bondholders—more powerful because business was forging ahead of agriculture in the indices of national wealth and because industry was reaching out into every area and raising up champions in the West and South, which had been solidly agricultural. But still influential in the party was the farming wing, particularly because the farmers had more votes than businessmen. Other important elements of the party were the veterans of the Union armies, numbering perhaps a million and organized in potent pressure groups such as the Grand Army of the Republic, which found the Republicans cordial to the idea of soldier pensions, and which served as an auxiliary of the party.

In its economic composition the Democratic organization was, much as it had been in Jackson's time, largely a party of farmers and laborers—of small property holders. But it was a party without clear direction or goals, and here probably is the principal reason for its minority condition. The important Eastern wing, representing importing interests, was willing to accept the traditional Democratic low-tariff policy, but on other issues, and particularly on the question of a "sound" currency, it was as conservative as the Republicans. Any Democratic move to challenge the Republicans on economic issues was certain to scare off the Easterners. Even on the tariff, the Democrats

The Stalwart Boss of the Republicans
Handsome Roscoe Conkling, senator from New York, led the Stalwart faction of the Republicans. Blaine, who despised him, described Conkling as a "majestic, supereminent, overpowering, turkey-gobbler strut." In this cartoon Conkling is casting covetous eyes at the Republican presidential nomination for 1880, represented by the eagle. The smaller bird looking doubtfully at the boss is the independent vote. From Harper's Weekly *(1879).*

failed to demonstrate unity or take a firm position. As industry moved into the West and South, islands of protection appeared in these once free-trade regions to divide a once cohesive public opinion. In many elections the Democrats adopted an ambiguous tariff plank that hardly differed from that of their opponents, causing wags to quip that the party of Jefferson and Jackson stood for "a protective tariff for revenue only." In short, the party failed to devise a program that distinguished it from the Republicans, failed to offer a set of issues to those groups who were alarmed by the rise of big business, failed, above all, to be a party of opposition. It was a "me too" party asking for votes on the grounds that it could do what the Republicans were doing—only better and with less corruption.

Although the Republicans in a general sense represented the upper- and middle-income groups and the Democrats the average and lower groups, neither spoke for a precise economic interest. Both included people from all economic levels, and both embraced business and agricultural elements. When economic legislation was considered in Congress, the votes usually followed sectional rather than party lines; Western Republicans and Southern Democrats, for example, were likely to unite behind a measure of benefit to the agricultural interests.

Although the Republicans usually dominated the presidency, they did not always control Congress. The Democrats, with the solid South behind them and with the support of highly organized machines in Northern cities and states, sometimes managed to secure a majority in one or both houses of the legislative branch and thereby block Republican programs. When a Democrat sat in the White House, the converse was often true: the Republicans ruled at least one house and voted down Democratic measures. The failure of either party to control consistently all branches of the government is, of course, another reason for the absence of firm issues and the relative paucity of positive legislation.

Of the three branches of government, Congress was predominant. Retaining most of the powers and prerogatives it had seized in the struggle with Andrew Johnson, it easily overshadowed the presidency and the judiciary. Nor did it encounter any serious challenge from its traditional rival, the executive arm. None of the Presidents elected between 1868 and 1888, with the possible exception of Grover Cleveland, was a strong political leader.

The Republicans Matt Quay in Pennsylvania and Roscoe Conkling in New York were outstanding examples of the boss type. Tall, handsome, and flamboyant, Conkling ruled the Republican party in New York and swayed its councils in the United States Senate. To him politics was a game for professionals, not for amateur "carpet knights," and it was a rough game: "Parties are not built by deportment, or by ladies' magazines, or gush."

When Benjamin Harrison won the presidency in 1888, he ascribed his victory to Providence. Matt Quay knew better. "Providence hadn't a damn thing to do with it," he announced. He wondered if the candidate knew how many men had approached the gates of the penitentiary to make him President. Harrison soon learned the facts of political life. "When I came into power," he said later, "I found that the party managers had taken it all to themselves. I could not name my own Cabinet. They had sold out every place to pay the election expenses." The machines sustained their position by various techniques: making alliances with business interests and securing campaign contributions and other subsidies, assessing officeholders a share of their salaries, and employing gangs of vote "repeaters" or "floaters" or using other fraudulent methods to carry elections.

HAYES AND THE PATRONAGE

Before the end of Rutherford B. Hayes' administration two groups—the Stalwarts, led by Conkling of New York, and the Half-Breeds, captained by James G. Blaine of Maine—were competing for control of the Republican party, and threatening to split it. Only a subtle difference separated the factions. The Stalwarts, consisting of state bosses like Conkling and Oliver P. Morton of Indiana and Zachariah Chandler of Michigan, stood for machine politics and the allocation of political and material spoils to the victor. They were professional operators who believed in politics for its own sake. The Half-Breeds had practically the same concept of the functions of parties, but circumstances—specifically, the fact that the Stalwarts at first were stronger—forced them to adopt a more circumspect and sanctimonious role. They rendered lip service to such issues as civil service and governmental efficiency, although most of them were no more interested in reform than the Stalwarts.

Although Hayes awarded some offices to the machine elements of his party, he consis-

tently held up merit as the primary standard of appointment. His cabinet, headed by William M. Evarts as secretary of state, John Sherman as secretary of the treasury, and Carl Schurz as secretary of the interior, was an exceptionally able one; but four of the members had bolted the party in the Liberal defection of 1872 and one was a Southern Democrat. Hayes' patronage policy horrified the Stalwarts and hardly pleased the Half-Breeds; at the same time, it was sufficiently political to raise doubts among the civil-service reformers. The President yielded much of his power to influence any faction of his party when he announced early in his administration that he would not be a candidate for reelection. To complete Hayes' handicaps, the Democrats controlled the House

President and Mrs. Hayes
This photograph catches the dignity and sincerity that were the hallmarks of Hayes' character. His wife was strongly opposed to the drinking of intoxicating liquors and did not permit any to be served at White House functions. Critics dubbed her "Lemonade Lucy." (Library of Congress)

when he entered office, and two years later they captured the Senate too.

After settling the Reconstruction issue to his satisfaction, Hayes turned to the problem of governmental reform. Long an advocate of civil service, he instructed his executive deputies that he wished appointments awarded on the basis of merit, that assessments of salaries of employees for political purposes must stop, and that the party activities of officials should be limited. Schurz placed the Interior Department on a merit basis, and Treasury Secretary Sherman and a few other department heads also made some effort to comply with their chief's wishes. Others ignored or evaded them. The strength of the spoils system was so great that Hayes could not force the executive branch to accept his policy. He had even less luck with Congress. Despite repeated appeals by the President, the legislators refused to appropriate money to renew the civil-service commission created under Grant.

Hayes' persistent advocacy of civil service precipitated his biggest fight with Congress. As part of his campaign to reform the spoils-ridden Treasury bureaucracy, he removed from office two prominent officials in the New York custom house, Chester A. Arthur and Alonzo B. Cornell. Both men were leaders in Roscoe Conkling's organization, and the senator interpreted their removal as an attempt to undermine his machine. Striking back with the arrogance of a great state boss, he persuaded the Senate to deny confirmation of the men Hayes had named to replace Arthur and Cornell. Stubbornly the President refused to retreat, and kept on transmitting new appointments until finally the Senate ratified his choices. Hayes was the first President since 1865 to resist successfully the constant attempts of Congress to encroach on executive prerogatives.

THE MARTYRDOM OF GARFIELD

Fortunately for the faction-rent Republicans, prosperity had returned by the time of the election of 1880. An increased export trade and an upward spurt in industrial and agricultural production signaled the end of the depression and the beginning of another boom period. But the Republican leaders knew that not even prosperity could guarantee victory: they had to

patch up their dissensions and settle on a nominee who could unite the party for another contest. Grant, backed by Conkling and the Stalwarts, was again a candidate, while the Half-Breeds were divided between Blaine and Sherman. At the Republican convention Grant led for thirty-five ballots but could not reach a majority. Then the anti-Grant forces united to nominate a "dark horse," James A. Garfield, a veteran member of the House of Representatives from Ohio. As Garfield was known as a Half-Breed, the convention, to conciliate the Stalwarts, gave the second place on the ticket to Chester A. Arthur, the Conkling henchman just dismissed from office by Hayes.

With the ancient and ill Tilden unavailable, the Democrats were without a leader. They acted as though they were also without hope of victory. As their candidate, they selected General Winfield Scott Hancock, who had won some fame as a corps commander in the Union army but was hardly a commanding national figure. Their apparent purpose was to refute the usual Republican charges of Democratic disloyalty in the Civil War. Also, having witnessed the success of the Republicans in running generals, they wanted to try their luck with a Democratic officer against Garfield, who had been a volunteer general. Although the platform called for a revenue tariff, it emphasized the "great fraud" of the election of 1876 as the paramount issue. As usual, the Democrats were harking back to the past instead of looking to the future.

During the bitter campaign, which revolved around such questions as Garfield's complicity in the Crédit Mobilier scandal and alleged errors committed by Hancock in the war, the Democratic candidate was pressed for a statement on the tariff. He replied that it was entirely a "local issue." As a description of how tariff schedules were arrived at in Congress, his phrase was reasonably accurate, but it constituted a virtual repudiation of the platform and removed the tariff as a campaign issue. In November Garfield piled up a decisive electoral majority of 214 to 155. But his popular vote was only about 10,000 more than his rival's: 4,454,000 to 4,444,000. The Republicans also captured both houses of Congress.

Up to the time of his accession to the presidency, the career of James A. Garfield had been a perfect example of the American success legend. Born in humble Ohio surroundings, in fact, in a log cabin, he worked from boyhood up, once laboring as a mule-driver on the Ohio Canal—"from the tow-path to the White House" was a theme the Republicans emphasized in the 1880 election. He worked his way through college, became a teacher, studied law and was admitted to the bar. In 1863 he was elected to the House of Representatives, where he served with increasing distinction until he became the Republican standard-bearer.

During his brief tenure of office, Garfield gave evidence that he intended to conduct a moderate Half-Breed administration. He appointed Blaine as secretary of state, and as postmaster general (the cabinet official having the most to do with patronage) Thomas L. James, a civil-service champion. Almost immediately James exposed a scandal in his department—the so-called star-route frauds. In many areas of the West mail was carried by stages or riders and assigned to contractors; on the postal list these routes were designated by stars. If a contractor could demonstrate that his costs had increased, his compensation could be raised without reopening the agreement. Investigation disclosed that collusive contracts had been awarded to certain Republican politicians, who then had secured increased payments for their services. Despite protests from some leading Republicans, Garfield backed up James in his inquiry. In dispensing patronage, Garfield gave the important jobs to Half-Breeds. He provoked a fight with Conkling by naming his own followers to federal positions in New York. When the President appointed a bitter Conkling foe as collector of the port of New York, the senator tried to prevent Senate confirmation. Failing this, he and his colleague, Platt, resigned and asked the New York legislature to reelect them. Their purpose was to awe Garfield into submission, but the legislators, in a fine display of perversity, chose two other men.

While the unseemly quarrel was dragging on, the evils of the spoils system were dramatically brought home to the American people. On July 2, 1881, after only four months in office, President Garfield was in the Washington railroad station, about to leave for a holiday trip, when a man in the crowd fired two pistol shots at him. As Garfield fell, the man with the gun shouted: "I am a Stalwart and Arthur is President now!" The assassin, Charles J. Guiteau, held a grudge because Garfield had refused to give him a government job (though evidently insane, Guiteau was hanged). Actually, Arthur was not yet President; Garfield lingered for nearly three months before dying. At his death, people concerned about the menace of machine politics were doubly grieved. Even some Republicans echoed the sentiment of the man who groaned: "Chet Arthur President of the United States! Good God!"

ARTHUR AND REFORM

For all of his political lifetime Chester A. Arthur had been a devoted, skilled, and open spoilsman. Before the assassination of Garfield, he had gone to Albany to lobby for the re-election of his benefactor and mentor, Conkling. But on becoming President, he pursued an independent course between the Republican factions, affiliating with neither and being dominated by neither, and he worked zealously and with partial success for the cause of reform. Undoubtedly he had been deeply affected by the grisly circumstances that brought him to the presidency. It may be that realizing he now stood in the spotlight of history, he guided his actions accordingly.

The revelation of the "new" Arthur dismayed most of the party bosses. Although the President reorganized the cabinet, he left the majority of Garfield's appointees in office. He vigorously pushed the prosecution of the star-route Republicans, who managed, however, to escape punishment. He vetoed a huge river and harbors bill on the grounds it was "pork-barrel" legislation, but Congress overrode him. In his first message to Congress he recommended a civil-service law, and he kept prodding the legislators to act. Although the spectacle of the great spoilsman championing reform seemed incongruous, Arthur was undoubtedly sincere, and his course was smart politics. With the public shocked by Garfield's assassination and disgusted by the postal frauds, sentiment for civil service was running high, and some kind of legislation would have been enacted whether Arthur had intervened or not.

Responding to popular as well as presidential pressure, Congress passed in 1883 the first national civil-service measure, the Pendleton

Act. By its terms a limited number of federal jobs were to be "classified": applicants for them were to be chosen on the basis of competitive written examinations. The law also forbade assessment of officeholders for political purposes. To administer the act, a bipartisan Civil Service Commission, headed by reformer Dorman B. Eaton, was established. At first only about 14,000 of some 100,000 offices were placed on the classified list. But the act provided that future Presidents might by executive order enlarge the number of positions subject to civil service. Every chief executive thereafter extended the list, primarily to "blanket" his appointees into office and prevent their removal by his successor. By this piecemeal and partisan process, the government finally achieved by the 1940s a system in which the majority of the people working for it were under the merit system.

RETURN OF THE DEMOCRATS

The election of 1884, with its absence of issues and its emphasis on the personal qualities of the candidates, epitomized the politics of the era of complacency. Arthur would have accepted the Republican nomination, but his independent course had pleased neither Half-Breeds nor Stalwarts. Ignoring him and other aspirants, the Republican convention nominated its most popular man and most vulnerable candidate, James G. Blaine, known to his adoring admirers as "the plumed knight" but to thousands of other Americans as "Old Mulligan Letters." His selection split the party badly. To the Stalwarts he was anathema; Conkling, asked if he intended to campaign for Blaine, snapped that he did not engage in criminal practice. The independent reform faction, now called the Mugwumps, announced they were prepared to bolt the party and support an honest Democrat. Rising to the bait, the Democrats nominated Grover Cleveland, the reform governor of New York. The platforms of the two parties were almost identical. Both endorsed revision of the tariff without endangering domestic industries, both approved and claimed credit for civil service, and both, taking account of popular rumblings against big business, spoke vaguely about subjecting corporations to some kind of national regulation.

With no real issues between the parties, the election was essentially a struggle for office, and the campaign developed into a mud-slinging contest involving the personal fitness, or more accurately, unfitness of the candidates. Eagerly the Democrats went to work on the plumed knight's unsavory record, reprinting the Mulligan correspondence and uncovering new damning letters. At torchlit rallies the Democrats chanted:

> *Blaine! Blaine! James G. Blaine!*
> *Continental liar from the state of Maine!*

Frantically the Republicans researched Cleveland's brief political career as mayor of Buffalo and governor of New York for evidence of corruption—a politician had to be corrupt, they seemed to assume—but found nothing. They did discover a juicy personal item. As a young man Cleveland had been accused of fathering an illegitimate child, and whether guilty or not, he had agreed to support the infant. He did not specifically deny the imputation when the Republicans brought it into the campaign. Thereafter at their rallies the Republicans roared out:

> *Ma! Ma! where's my Pa?*
> *Going to the White House. Ha! Ha! Ha!*

In addition to sex, the canvass featured the bloody shirt, waved vigorously by Blaine; freedom for Ireland from the British rule, held out to the Irish voters by Republican orators; and religion, a last-minute issue that may have decided the election. In the closing days of the campaign a delegation of Protestant ministers called on Blaine in New York City; their spokesman, Dr. Samuel Burchard, in the course of his remarks referred to the Democrats as the party of "Rum, Romanism, and Rebellion." Apparently Blaine, whose mother was a Catholic, did not catch the statement or notice its linking of elements. Soon the Democrats were spreading the news through New York and other Eastern cities that Blaine had countenanced a slander on the Catholic Church, and his denial came too late to counteract the charge. The so-called Burchard incident may have swung New York State to the Democrats, and New York was the pivotal state in what turned out to be an extremely close election. Cleveland had 219 electoral votes to Blaine's 182; the popular vote showed

James G. Blaine
*Blaine had an enthusiastic following among Republicans and was continually a
presidential hopeful from the 1870s to the 1890s, but he was handicapped by a
reputation for public dishonesty. This cartoon shows him as Narcissus—recalling
the Greek myth of the boy who fell in love with his own reflection and was
transformed into a flower. Blaine, covered with tattoos such as "corrupt lobby,"
here says to himself: "The remarkable resemblance to George Washington is what
strikes me!" (Culver Pictures)*

4,875,000 for Cleveland and 4,852,000 for
Blaine, a Democratic plurality of only 23,000.

Grover Cleveland was the ablest President
between Lincoln and Theodore Roosevelt.
Short and corpulent, brusque in manner, boldly beardless in a hirsute age, he was far from
being an appealing figure. He did possess character, courage, and integrity. In his brief career
in prominent offices—he had been elected
mayor of Buffalo in 1881 and governor of New
York in 1882—he had fought politicians, graft-
ers, pressure groups, and Tammany Hall. He
had become famous as the "veto mayor" and
the "veto governor," as an official who was not
afraid to say "No." This ability to be honestly
negative was the most positive feature of his

political personality; it was at once his greatest
strength and his most distressing weakness as a
political leader. It enabled him to withstand
pressure from any quarter, to oppose the
spoilsmen, and to uphold high standards of
official probity. It also rendered him tragically
incapable of understanding the problems of an
industrial society or the role of government in a
changing economic order.

CLEVELAND FINDS AN ISSUE

When Cleveland became President, he was
absorbed with plans to improve the administrative machinery of the government, to install

business standards in its operations, and to purify its processes. Issues such as the currency and the tariff did not greatly interest him, nor was he concerned with the problems of the farmer and the laborer. His knowledge of economics was slender and his economic philosophy almost primitively simple. He was sincerely opposed to a paternalistic and positive government that extended special favors to any group. Let all stand equal, the giant corporation and the worker, he proclaimed, never comprehending that there were vital power differences among contesting economic interests. He summed up his faith in a veto of an appropriation of $10,000 for drought-stricken farmers. The lesson must never be forgotten, he moralized, that "though the people support the Government, the Government should not support the people."

Although Cleveland was known as a civil-service reformer, in dealing with patronage he had to proceed with due partisan caution. After years of wandering in the political wilderness, the Democrats were hungry for offices, and they expected the President to throw the Republican "rascals" out — immediately and in wholesale lots. Instead, the President compromised in a manner that did not completely satisfy either his own party or his Mugwump followers. He added approximately 12,000 offices to the classified list, but of the jobs not under civil service he removed two-thirds of the incumbents and replaced them with deserving Democrats. Determined to check extravagance and congressional raids on the surplus, Cleveland vetoed a river and harbors bill, and attempted to introduce principles of economy and honesty into the awarding of soldier pensions.

On the pension issue, he stirred up a hornet's nest. For years real or alleged veterans of the Union army — who could not qualify under the existing general pension laws — had had no difficulty in getting Congress to enact private pension bills for their benefit. Many of the claims were fraudulent, but nobody ever examined them. Cleveland actually took the trouble to read them, and, outraged by what he found, vetoed over 200 such measures. When Congress, responding to pressure from the powerful Grand Army of the Republic (GAR), passed a Dependent Pension Bill to grant pensions to all veterans suffering from disabilities, no mat-

ter when or how contracted, he killed it with a veto. In reality, Cleveland was sympathetic to the claims of genuine veterans, and the total appropriation for pensions increased during his administration. But his vetoes enabled Republican and GAR orators to remind the voters of the peril of placing a Southern-dominated Democrat in the White House.

On another front of battle against corruption, Cleveland instructed his secretary of the interior to inspect past grants of public lands in the West to railroad, lumber, and cattle interests, and where the lands had been obtained on fraudulent or false ground to institute suits to recover them. Eventually some 81 million acres were restored to the government. Although businessmen bellowed that the President was acting like a radical, he was only being consistently conservative: no special favors to any group.

Cleveland himself precipitated one economic issue into the political arena. Always mildly dubious of the high tariff, he concluded after thorough study that the existing rates were responsible for the annual surplus that tempted Congress to reckless legislation. Once convinced, he acted with sudden and startling vigor. In December 1887 he devoted almost all of his annual message to the lawmakers to discussing the tariff and demanding its downward revision. Although he spoke bitingly of the great fortunes that had been built on protective duties and of the inflated living costs of the poor, he rested his case on immediate and practical considerations: the tariff was bringing in an unneeded surplus and the piling up of this surplus would eventually depress the economy. In a phrase that intrigued the public, he said: "It is a *condition* that confronts us, not a theory." Characteristically, he assured Congress that reductions could be made without endangering the interests of American manufacturers.

Immediately, the Southern and Western Democrats, who had been moving rapidly to a low-tariff position, responded to the President's leadership. They pushed the Mills Bill through the House, incorporating Cleveland's recommendations and providing for moderate reductions. Only four Democrats voted against it, and doubtless some of the Easterners went along in the knowledge that the Republican Senate would kill the measure. In the Senate

Grover Cleveland
Cleveland was the first Democrat to be elected President since the Civil War. Honest, courageous, and stubborn, he was extremely conservative and unable to understand some of the new economic problems emerging in his administration. A bachelor when elected, he married while in the White House. (Library of Congress)

preferred another candidate. The platform emphasized the tariff question and pledged support to the President's policy of moderate revision. The Republicans had in protection what they were certain was a winning issue, but they were hard put to find an acceptable and available nominee. They finally decided on Benjamin Harrison of Indiana, who was relatively obscure and formidably respectable, and in their platform endorsed protection for American producers and generous pensions for Union veterans.

The campaign of 1888 was the first since the Civil War that was fought out on a definite issue, the first that involved a question of economic difference between the parties. It was also one of the most corrupt campaigns in American political history. Both parties employed the usual fraudulent methods of the day, but the Republicans, with a campaign fund contributed by apprehensive business interests and amounting to several million dollars, were the worse offenders.

When the votes were counted, it was obvious that the people had not registered a clear decision or authorized a definite mandate. Harrison had an electoral majority of 233 to 168, but Cleveland's popular vote exceeded Harrison's, 5,540,000 to 5,440,000.

the Republican leaders, believing that they could sell the tariff to the voters, met the issue head-on. As an alternative to the Mills Bill they enacted a protective measure. Action was deadlocked for the moment, and the tariff was squarely before the people as an issue in the election of 1888.

As the tariff fight swirled to a climax, the Democrats again named Cleveland as their standard-bearer, although some machine bosses and some Easterners, disgusted by his stand on civil service and lower duties, would have

The Farmers Organize

GRANGERS AND RAILROADS

Most farmers had always been strong individualists. But many of them eventually concluded that they could solve their problems—high costs, increasing debts, falling prices, declining status—only by overcoming their traditional individualism. They would have to organize and act in politics as a group.

The first farm organization to appear after the Civil War was established in boom times as a social association and was turned into an agency of agrarian protest at the onset of the 1873 depression.

On a tour through the South, Oliver H. Kelley, a clerk in the Department of Agriculture at Washington, became impressed with the isolation and drabness of rural life. In 1867 he and other department employees founded the National Grange of the Patrons of Husbandry, to which Kelley devoted years of labor as secretary. Local lodges of the order were called granges, and the organization is commonly known as the Grange. Its announced purposes were social, cultural, and educational. By bringing farm men and women together in groups, it aimed to diffuse knowledge of scientific agriculture, machines, and markets, to furnish a community feeling hitherto absent in rural society, and to keep agriculture in "step with the music of the age." Recognizing that human nature is intrigued by secrecy and ceremony, the founders provided for an elaborate system of initiation and ritual.

At first the Grange grew slowly. It filled an obvious rural need, but farmers were not attracted to it in large numbers while times were good. Then the depression of 1873 struck, and suddenly the farmers saw benefits to be achieved through organization. By 1875 the Grange claimed over 800,000 members and 20,000 local lodges. These appeared in almost every state but were most numerous in the staple-producing sections of the Middle West and the South.

As membership increased, the lodges in the Middle West turned to economic issues. They stressed the necessity of collective action by farmers to eliminate the middleman — through the organization of cooperatives — and the urgency of political action to curb the monopolistic practices of the railroads and warehouses. All over the midlands on Independence Day 1873, the "Farmers' Fourth of July," embittered yeomen assembled to hear Granger orators read "The Farmers' Declaration of Independence." The resolutions proclaimed that the time had come for farmers, "suffering from long continued systems of oppression and abuse, to rouse themselves from an apathetic indifference to their own interests." The declaration also vowed that the farmers would use "all lawful and peaceful means to free [themselves] from the tyranny of monopoly."

The Grangers launched the first major cooperative movement in the United States, though successful collective societies had existed earlier in England and other countries. The Grangers set up cooperative stores, creameries, elevators, warehouses, insurance companies, and factories that turned out machines, stoves, and other items. Some 400 enterprises were in operation at the height of the movement, but eventually most of them failed because of the inexperience of the operators and the opposition of middleman interests. Not all business groups fought the cooperatives; some sought their trade, and one corporation was formed specifically in 1872 to meet the wants of the Grangers, Montgomery Ward and Company, which brought the mail-order business into existence.

In political action the Grangers labored to elect to state legislatures candidates pledged to their program. Usually they operated through the existing Republican and Democratic parties, only occasionally putting up nominees under such party labels as "Antimonopoly" or "Reform." Marshaling their votes in the local lodges, they were able to gain control of the legislatures in most of the Middle Western states. Their purpose, openly and angrily announced, was to subject the railroads to social controls.

Between 1870 and 1874 the legislatures of Illinois, Iowa, Minnesota, and Wisconsin enacted laws to regulate railroads and warehouse and elevator facilities. These "Granger laws" authorized maximum rates for passenger and freight traffic, provided rules and rates for the storing of grain, and prohibited a number of alleged discriminatory practices. They were to be administered and enforced by special state commissions.

The railroads contested the legality of the laws, and eventually fought them from the state courts up to the United States Supreme Court. In 1877 the highest tribunal handed down a decision in the first of the "Granger cases," the case of *Munn* v. *Illinois*, involving the right of a state to fix storage rates for warehouses. Other cases concerned state laws establishing maximum rates for railroads.

Chief Justice Morrison R. Waite spoke for the Court in the Munn case, and his opinion formed the basis for the decisions on the railroad laws. The complainants, the warehouses and railroads, had rested their cause on two points: (1) the laws infringed the power of Congress to regulate interstate commerce; and

(2) they violated the due-process clause of the Fourteenth Amendment, namely, that a state could not deprive a "person" of property without due process of law. The plaintiffs were contending not only that a corporation was a person within the meaning of the Fourteenth Amendment, but also that expected income was property and that any regulation reducing income was deprivation of property within the meaning of the amendment. The Court rejected their arguments and validated the Granger laws. It held that a state in the exercise of its police power could regulate private property devoted to public use and affecting the general community; it conceded the right of a state to regulate interstate commerce in the absence of national regulation; and it dismissed "due process" with the observation that it was not intended to restrict the police power.

The Grange soon lost its position as a major force in the agricultural scene. By 1880 its membership had shrunk to 100,000. The collapse of its cooperative experiments and the ineffectiveness of its railroad laws drove some members away. Above all, it was weakened by a return of prosperity in the late seventies. The embattled farmers, who once had shouted for collective action, soon left the fold and resumed their old and familiar individualistic ways.

THE FARMERS' ALLIANCES

In the 1880s the prices of the great staples again declined, hard times returned to the South and the West, and the farmers of those regions, more embittered and frustrated than the Grangers, turned to more militant forms of organization. From the Carolinas to the Dakotas a multitude of farm societies bearing a variety of names mushroomed into existence, but by the end of the decade they had been combined into two major organizations: the National Farmers' Alliance, centering in the prairie states west of the Mississippi, and the Farmers' Alliance and Industrial Union, largely restricted to the South and known as the Southern Alliance. Loosely affiliated with the Southern order was a Negro branch, the Colored Farmers' Alliance. Of the two main alliances, the Southern was the more tightly knit and the larger, numbering over a million members.

At their beginning both alliances toyed with the same kind of objectives that had intrigued the Grange: social and educational activities and cooperative enterprises. But almost immediately they shifted their emphasis to politics – and to a program designed to save the farmer by state and national legislation rather than improved business techniques. The Northern leaders decided that farmers could expect nothing from the Democrats or Republicans and would have to create their own political organization. In the elections of 1890 they ran candidates for national and state office under diverse party labels in all the prairie states. The Southern Alliance turned to politics more reluctantly, but by 1890 it too was ready for action, though not in the form of a third party. Fearful that a new party would split the solidity of the one-party South and endanger white supremacy, the Southerners, heeding the counsel of such farm leaders as Benjamin F. Tillman of South Carolina, set their sights on capturing control of the Democratic party from its conservative Bourbon rulers. In 1890 Alliance-backed candidates competed with Bourbon aristocrats in every corner of the former Confederacy.

The farmers startled conservatives and surprised themselves with their success in 1890. The farm forces won partial or complete control of the legislatures in twelve states, eight in the South and four in the West, and elected six governors, three senators, and approximately fifty congressmen. The magnitude of the agrarian sweep was not, however, as great as it seemed. In the South, where the triumph was most complete, the farmers had stuck fast to the Democratic party. Over forty of the farm congressmen were Southern Alliance-endorsed Democrats; the one Southern representative to admit a third-party affiliation was Georgia's Thomas E. Watson.

THE PEOPLE'S PARTY

After the elections of 1890, the leaders of the Northern Alliance were certain that the time was ripe for the formation of a national farmer-labor party. Some of the Southern leaders – the fiery Watson, consumed with an emotional hatred for monopoly, and Leonidas L. Polk of

The Meaning of Populism

The historical literature on Populism is of comparatively recent origin. The first scholarly study of the movement appeared in 1931, when J. D. Hicks published *The Populist Revolt*. It is still the only general treatment of Populism, and as a full and factual account it remains the standard work. Its viewpoint has, however, in recent years been subjected to question and possible modification.

That viewpoint is summarized in Hicks' statement that Populism represented "the last phase of a long and perhaps a losing struggle – the struggle to save agricultural America from the devouring jaws of industrial America." Hicks wrote at a time when scholars tended to see certain evils in American industrial society and definite virtues in the older agrarian America of the previous century; inherent in his pages was an assumption that the reforms proposed by the Populists were good. He seemed to lament the failure of the Populist dream, and yet he conceded that parts of the dream eventually became reality when, in later years, many Populist proposals were enacted into law.

This favorable view of the Populists prevailed for over twenty years. Then, in 1955, Richard Hofstadter put forth a different thesis and unleashed an attack on the Populists in *The Age of Reform*. Hofstadter represented a new school of history, one having its roots in an urban society and having certain doubts about the older rural order. He argued that important aspects of Populism had been overlooked by Hicks and previous writers. According to Hofstadter, Populism had a "soft side." It was essentially romantic and did not face up to the hard problems of a modern society. It proposed simple solutions and favored returning to an older and simpler America. Moreover, it had a dark side. Many Populists denounced international bankers, some of whom were Jewish, and therefore the movement displayed anti-Semitic tendencies. Other writers expanded this charge to say that Populism possibly reflected a fascist psychology.

While some historians adopted and elaborated on the Hofstadter view, others undertook to refute it. C. Vann Woodward, author of *Tom Watson, Agrarian Rebel* (1938), now reminded the anti-Populist historians that Watson and other Southern party leaders had encouraged political cooperation between whites and blacks. In *The Populist Response to Industrialism* (1962) Norman Pollack argued that the Populists had a sophisticated conception of society, accepted the modern world, and proposed sensible solutions to economic problems. In *The Tolerant Populists* (1963) W. T. K. Nugent maintained that, at least in Kansas, the Populists were the very reverse of what Hofstadter had called them. They welcomed Jews and other immigrants to the party, and they offered a practical, up-to-date program.

Nowadays some journalists and political scientists as well as historians apply the terms "populism" and "populist" to a great variety of recent movements and public figures – to men as different as, for example, the late Senator Joseph McCarthy of Wisconsin and Senator George McGovern of South Dakota. Such loose handling of the terms makes them practically meaningless.

North Carolina, perhaps the ablest mind in the agrarian movement – were coming to the same conclusion. Reluctantly the Southerners recognized that their local successes would have no weight whatsoever in determining the course of the national Democratic party.

Plans for a third party were laid at meetings in Cincinnati (May 1891) and in St. Louis (February 1892), attended by many representatives of the Northern Alliance, some Southerners, and spokesmen of the fading Knights of Labor. Then in July 1892, 1,300 excited and exultant delegates poured into Omaha, Ne-

braska, in the heart of the plains country, to proclaim the new party, approve an official set of principles, and nominate candidates for the presidency and vice presidency. By common consent the party already had a name, one first used by the Kansas agrarians – the People's party – from which, by way of Latin, were derived the terms Populist and Populism.

In a spirit of dedicated idealism reminiscent of the antislavery crusade, the delegates at Omaha adopted a platform. To achieve their ends, they were willing to invest government with powers that would horrify business con-

A Populist Orator
The outstanding Kansas Populist, "Sockless" Jerry Simpson, also known as the "Socrates of the Prairies," is photographed while engaging in an outdoor debate in a small Kansas town during the campaign of 1892. (Kansas State Historical Society, Topeka)

servatives: "We believe that the power of government—in other words, of the people—should be expanded . . . as rapidly and as far as the good sense of an intelligent people and the teachings of experience shall justify, to the end that oppression, injustice, and poverty shall eventually cease in the land."

The Populist platform demanded national government ownership and operation of the railroad, telephone, and telegraph systems (a significant advance on the state regulation urged by the Grangers); a flexible national currency issued by the government and not by the banks; the free and unlimited coinage of silver; government-operated postal savings banks; a graduated income tax; the subtreasury plan, an arrangement whereby farmers could deposit nonperishable produce in government warehouses and borrow in United States treasury notes up to 80 percent of the current value of their commodities (thus enabling farmers to withhold crops from sale until the price was right); prohibition of alien land ownership; and reclamation of lands held by railroads and other corporations "in excess of their actual needs." Bidding for the support of labor, the platform also demanded shorter hours for workers and restrictions on immigration, and denounced the employment of private detective agencies as strikebreakers in labor disputes. Other planks called for new political techniques to place government more directly under democratic control: the Australian, or secret, ballot; the popular election of United States senators; the initiative, a device whereby state legislation could be introduced or enacted by the voters; and the referendum, a method whereby the voters could veto actions of state legislatures.

"It is a struggle," cried one Populist orator, "between the robbers and the robbed."

Populism was strong in only three geographic centers: the South, the plains and prairie region (but chiefly Kansas, Nebraska, and North and South Dakota), and the Rocky Mountain states. The Populists evoked little response in the old Granger states of the Middle West. In this previous center of protest, diversified techniques, emphasizing dairying and a corn-hog complex, had brought a new prosperity and induced a new conservatism. Even in the South the hold of Populism was tenuous and temporary. Populist leaders, seeking to unite poor white and black people in politics, encountered the unyielding barriers of race. They could not, except for short periods and in a few states, persuade the white masses that class was paramount to color, and they could not overcome the traditional white loyalty to the Democractic party.

The Populists also failed to unite under their standard the forces of urban protest. Despite the brave platform talk about the common interests of rural and city workers, the Populists had no real interest in effecting such a combination. In any event, no realistic basis for an alliance between Populist farmers and urban dissenters existed. The Knights of Labor endorsed the new party, but the Knights were a dying organization.

Hardly any of the party leaders were dirt farmers. The great majority were of the rural middle class; they were professional men, editors and lawyers, or professional politicians and agitators. Only a handful had held office or exercised the responsibility of power. James B. Weaver, the party's presidential nominee in 1892, had run the political gamut. He had begun as a Democrat and deserted that party because it was controlled by the slavocracy, had joined the Republicans and left them because they were dominated by the business plutocracy, and had then become successively a Greenbacker and a Populist. Despite his seemingly erratic course, Weaver was a man with balance and ability and a fine sense of justice.

Many Populist leaders gave an impression of personal failure, of brilliant instability, of brooding communion with mystic forces. The matchless orator, Ignatius Donnelly of Minnesota, wrote one book locating the lost isle of Atlantis, another proving that Bacon wrote Shakespeare's plays, and a novel purporting to describe a Populist utopia. Georgia's Tom Watson, author of biographies of Jefferson and Napoleon (he referred curiously to the latter as a "great Democratic despot"), once championed political union across racial lines but ended his career baiting Negroes and Jews. Jerry Simpson of Kansas ridiculed a rival candidate for wearing silk socks and won the undying title of "Sockless Jerry, the Socrates of the prairies."

Despite the weaknesses of the People's party, its leaders and adherents looked forward enthusiastically to the election of 1892.

A Negative Response

At first the regular politicians gave a rather negative response to the demands of the organizing farmers. Although, yielding to pressure, Congress provided for the federal regulation of railroads, for the time being the government was given little real power to control rates. Then Congress passed an act to prohibit monopolies, but the government made no more than a half-hearted effort to enforce this law. And when Congress got around to acting on the tariff—that "mother of trusts"—it finally revised the rates, but it revised them in more an upward than a downward direction.

REGULATING THE RAILROADS

After the Supreme Court had upheld the Granger laws—by which some of the states were attempting to regulate railroad rates—the railroad companies continued to test the validity of these laws in the courts. Eventually the railroads won out. The undoing of the statutes came after new justices friendly to an expanded notion of property rights and willing to strike down state powers ascended to the Supreme Court.

The first step came in 1886 in the so-called Wabash case (Wabash, St. Louis, and Pacific Railway Co. v. Illinois). Involved was a statute prohibiting higher rates for a "short haul" than a "long haul" between points in Illinois and New York City. The Court held that the statute attempted to regulate interstate commerce and infringed on the exclusive power of Congress. Interstate rates were thus removed from state control, but within its own limits a state could still regulate railroads if the regulations did not directly affect interstate commerce. Later the roads eliminated even this regulatory power of the states by persuading the Court to accept the due-process clause as a "substantive" restriction on state authority. That is, due process, previously conceived of as guaranteeing the accused certain procedural rights, came to be defined as a limitation on the power of states to regulate private property or vested rights— with the judiciary acting as the guardian of property and reviewing the acts of legislatures. The Court arrived at this position gradually and with some indirection. It affirmed it in essence, although not explicitly, in Chicago, Milwaukee and St. Paul Railroad v. Minnesota (1890) and thereafter in starkly specific terms. Constant judicial review of state decrees meant, of course, that state regulation had become a mockery.

The only solution to the problem was national regulation. Since the 1870s demands had been voiced in and out of Congress for some kind of supervisory legislation, and revelations of such railroad practices as pooling, rebates, and other discriminatory devices stirred public support for action. Even some railway operators, alarmed by the fierce competition in their industry, were willing to accept regulation. Sentiment became so strong that Congress was finally forced to act. In 1887 it passed the Interstate Commerce Act, a measure described by its sponsor, Senator Shelby M. Cullom, as "conservative legislation."

The Interstate Commerce Act prohibited rebates, pools, long-short haul discriminations, and drawbacks. It required railroads to publish their rate schedules and file them with the government. It provided that all charges in interstate rail transportation should be "reasonable and just," but failed to furnish a standard or method to determine the justness of a rate. To administer the act, a five-man agency, the Interstate Commerce Commission, was created, with powers to hear complaints from shippers, examine witnesses, and inquire into the books and accounts of railroads. The law did not clearly authorize the commission to fix rates. After investigating a complaint, the commission could issue a cease-and-desist order to a carrier to lower its charges. If the road refused, the commission had to take its case to the courts and justify its decree, a cumbersome procedure that militated against effective regulation.

For almost twenty years after its passage, the Interstate Commerce Act was without practical effect; it did not accomplish widespread rate reduction or eliminate discrimination. No wonder an attorney general of the United States advised a railroad president not to ask for repeal of the act: "It satisfies the popular clamor for government supervision of the railroads at the same time that that supervision is almost entirely nominal."

DISPOSING OF THE TRUSTS

Benjamin Harrison, the victor in the close and corrupt election of 1888, assumed the presidency the following year in the nation's centennial inauguration. Just forty-eight years before, his grandfather, William Henry Harrison, had entered the same office and died almost immediately, leaving no trace of his influence on the presidency. Benjamin Harrison served out his term, but he left behind a record of negative accomplishment. Intelligent and honest, he was colorless in personality, cold in manner, and singularly aloof—from people, from the new currents of social change, and from the more sordid realities of politics. In White House annals his administration is notable for the wiring of the executive mansion for electricity.

Harrison's cabinet was, like himself, competent but drab. Secretary of State Blaine was the only member who rose above the level of average ability. Though known as a moderate civil-service supporter, Harrison extended the classified list but slightly. He permitted his Postmaster General, John Wanamaker, a hefty contributor to his campaign fund, to sweep 30,000 postmasters out of office in a year. One of his worst appointments was that of "Corporal" James Tanner as commissioner of pensions. While his actions wrung from some people the prayer, "God help the surplus," Tanner replaced Cleveland's policy of careful examination of pension claims with a reckless generosity that delighted politicians and veterans alike.

Harrison exerted little effort to influence legislation. With slender majorities in both houses, the Republicans could carry through a program only by submitting to rigid leadership and acting as a disciplined unit. The leadership came from Maine's Thomas B. Reed, Speaker of the House and a master of parliamentary law and savage wit. Some fruits of his control were a Dependent Pensions Act that almost doubled the number of pensioners and even stunned the GAR, and a flood of appropriations bills for internal improvements, subsidies to steamship lines, and naval expansion.

Public opinion forced the Reed Congress to consider legislation affecting broad areas of the economy, and in 1890 important measures dealing with big business and the tariff were enacted. Some fifteen Western and Southern states had adopted laws prohibiting combinations that restrained competition. But corpora-tions found it easy to escape limitations by incorporating in states that offered special privileges (New Jersey and Delaware were notorious examples). Acceptance by the Supreme Court of the argument that a corporation was a "person" before the law and entitled to the protection of the due-process clause of the Fourteenth Amendment in *Santa Clara County* v. *Southern Pacific Railroad* (1886) meant that any form of state control was subject to judicial negation. If antitrust legislation was to be effective, it would obviously have to come from the national government. In 1888 both parties promised to curb monopolies.

With little debate and by almost unanimous votes in both houses of Congress, the Sherman Antitrust Act became law in July 1890. Its provisions and phraseology were determined by the fact that the only basis for national action against trust derived from the power of Congress to regulate interstate commerce. The heart of the measure was in the first two sections: (1) "Every contract, combination in the form of trust or otherwise, or conspiracy, in restraint of trade or commerce among the several States, or with foreign nations, is hereby declared to be illegal"; (2) "Every person who shall monopolize, or attempt to monopolize . . . any part of the trade or commerce among the several States, or with foreign nations, shall be deemed guilty of a misdemeanor. . . ."

Even though the law on paper prohibited all combinations "in restraint of trade," Congress in passing it was making no very serious effort to break up monopolies. As one senator explained, his colleagues merely wanted to get up "some bill headed 'A bill to Punish Trusts' with which to go to the country" and get themselves reelected. Congress was making a gesture to appease popular discontent without changing the realities of contemporary economic life. The antitrust people now had their law, and business continued to have its trusts.

For over a decade after its passage there was little attempt to enforce the Sherman Act. Before 1901 the Justice Department instituted only fourteen suits under the law against business combinations, and failed to obtain convictions in almost every one. The courts, uniformly hostile to the law, proceeded to emasculate it. The crowning decision came in *United States* v. *E. C. Knight Co.* (1895), a case in which the government charged that the defendants controlled 98 percent of the manufacture of refined sugar in the country Chief Justice Melville W. Fuller, speaking for the Supreme Court, threw out the government's case with a curious distinction between manufacturing and commerce. He admitted that the present combination was a trust to monopolize the refining of sugar but denied that it was therefore illegal: the trust was not in interstate commerce but in manufacturing. The Knight decision created a "twilight zone" between state and national powers, an area of economic life outside the authority of any agency of government.

REVISING THE TARIFF

Having made an effort to dispose of the trust question, the Republicans turned with anticipation to the subject that most interested them and their business backers and that had been the paramount issue in the campaign of 1888, the tariff. William McKinley of Ohio, a rising party luminary and chairman of the House Ways and Means Committee, and Senator Nel-

son W. Aldrich of Rhode Island framed, with the assistance of the tariff lobbies, the highest protective measure yet offered to a Congress. It became law in October 1890 as the McKinley Tariff Act.

Seldom in American political history has a party in power suffered such a stunning reverse as befell the Republicans in the mid-term elections of 1890 Their majority in the Senate was slashed to 8, and in the House they could count only 88 seats to 235 for the Democrats and 9 for the Alliance-Populists. Popular revulsion against the McKinley duties, pictured by the Democrats as raising the living costs of the masses, was an undoubted factor in causing the Republican debacle; McKinley himself was among those going down to defeat. But the elections registered more than condemnation of a tariff. They reflected the deep anxieties of millions of Americans who were beginning to question the fundamental justice of the economic order.

In the presidential election of 1892 Benjamin Harrison was again the Republican nomi-

Populist Strength 1892

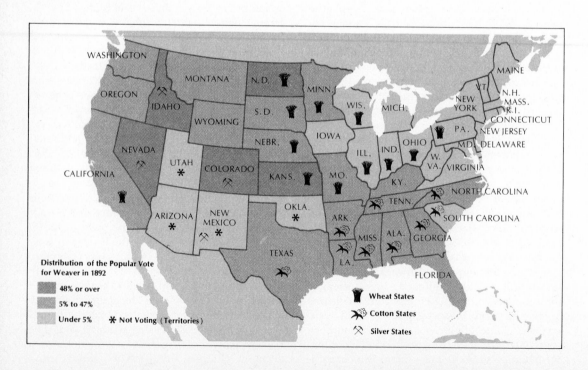

To Arms Against the Populists
*In no state did the Populists have greater support than in Kansas. In 1893,
however, the Republicans disputed the results of a state election and claimed
control of the legislature. For a time the Populists occupied and held the state
house. Finally the Republicans armed themselves, drove out the Populists, and took
control. (Kansas State Historical Society, Topeka)*

nee and Grover Cleveland the Democratic. Once more the platforms of the two parties were almost identical except for the tariff, with the Republicans upholding protection and the Democrats pledging reduction. Both parties in their official pronouncements ignored the pulsing currents of unrest in the country. Only the Populists, with James B. Weaver as their candidate, advocated economic reform. Cleveland amassed 277 electoral and 5,557,000 popular votes as compared to Harrison's 145 and 5,176,000 votes. For the first time since the Civil War the Democrats won a majority of both houses of Congress. Weaver polled 22 electoral votes from six mountain and plains states and over a million popular votes and the Populists elected at least a dozen senators and congressmen.

Despite Cleveland's negative record, a large proportion of the people who had voted for him expected him to devise some original approach to the new problems troubling America. His inaugural address rudely disillusioned them, as he reaffirmed his devotion to laissez faire: "The lessons of paternalism ought to be unlearned and the better lesson taught that while the people should . . . support their Government its functions do not include the support of the people."

Cleveland called on his party to redeem its pledge to lower the existing tariff rates. In the House William L. Wilson of West Virginia introduced a bill in 1894 designed to accomplish moderate downward revision and yet provide adequate protection for domestic producers. To get Populist support and to compensate for an anticipated loss in revenues, the bill provided for an income tax with a 2-percent levy on incomes over $4,000. When the Wilson bill reached the Senate, the customary lobbying

The Supreme Court Denounces Protest

When the Pollock case was argued before the Court, the lawyers appearing against the income tax passionately appealed to the Court to preserve the sanctity of property and halt the onward march of radicalism. Some of the justices responded with opinions more sociological than legal. One wrote:

The present assault upon capital is but the beginning. It will be but the stepping stone to others, larger and more sweeping, till our political contests will become a war of the poor against the rich; a war constantly growing in intensity and bitterness.

and logrolling began Eastern Democrats, directed by Maryland's Arthur P. Gorman and abetted by Republicans, added 634 amendments, most of them altering Wilson's duties upward. Strong pressure from the Democratic leadership induced the House to accept the Senate version. Cleveland denounced it as a violation of the party's platform but allowed it to become law without his signature.

The Wilson-Gorman Tariff reduced the general scale of duties only 10 percent, and its duties on raw and refined sugar and other items afforded ample protection to the sugar trust and every other trust. Far from the kind of tariff the Democrats had promised the country, the act seemed to confirm the Populist con-

tention that tariff-making was a sham battle between the major parties.

Even the one crust thrown to the Populists, the income tax, was shortly snatched away by the courts. In a case testing the right of the government to levy an income tax (*Pollock* v. *The Farmer's Loan and Trust Co.,* 1895), the Supreme Court declared in a 5-to-4 decision that a tax on incomes was a "direct" tax and hence had to be apportioned among the states according to population. Since an income tax, by its very nature, would be effective only if applied on a basis of individual wealth and would have no reality if reckoned on the distribution of population, the Court had made it impossible to levy such a tax.

"Battle of the Standards"

The Populists had done fairly well in 1892, and they were encouraged by the events that soon followed—the depression, the Pullman strike, and the growing bitterness of workers as well as farmers. In the state and local elections of 1894 the Populists added to their earlier victories. Then they looked hopefully toward the election of 1896.

But that year one of the major parties, the Democratic, adopted the most appealing of the Populist programs, free silver. Even so, the Democrats went down in defeat, and the People's party soon disappeared.

This short-lived party nevertheless left its mark on American history. One or both of the major parties sooner or later adopted other measures, besides free silver, that the Populists

had stood for. Some of these, in one form or another, became accepted features of American government—notably the income tax, a flexible (managed) currency, crop loans to farmers, the secret ballot, and the direct election of United States senators.

THE PANIC OF 1893

The Cleveland administration was hardly settled in office when the Panic of 1893 struck the country. There followed one of the most severe depressions up to that time. Its causes were various and complicated. The eighties had been a typical boom period, featuring overexpansion and overinvestment in railroads and industrial combinations. Depressed prices in agriculture since 1887 had weakened the purchasing power of a substantial section of the population. Depression conditions that had begun earlier in Europe were resulting in a loss of American markets abroad, a decline in the export trade, and a withdrawal by foreign investors of gold invested in this country. Whatever the causes of the depression, over 8,000 business concerns failed in a period of six months, 156 railroads went into receivership, and 400 banks suspended operations. Agricultural prices tumbled to new lows, and perhaps as many as a million workers, 20 percent of the laboring force, were thrown out of jobs.

Jacob S. Coxey, a Massillon, Ohio, businessman and Populist, proposed two lines of action: (1) Congress should issue $500 million in legal-tender notes to be used in the construction of roads throughout the country; and (2) local governments wishing to undertake public improvements should be authorized to issue noninterest-bearing bonds which could be exchanged at the federal Treasury for legal-tender notes. Coxey's ideas were hooted at in conservative circles. (But the notion of creating jobs by a building program would appeal to a later generation afflicted by depression. At the onset of the next great depression in the 1930s the government would inaugurate a public works program. Coxey, who lived until 1951, thus saw his scheme finally put into effect.)

Seeking to dramatize his program, Coxey organized a march of the unemployed on Washington to present a petition for work relief to Congress. Only 500 of "Coxey's army" were able to make their way to Washington, and they were barred from the Capitol by armed police. Coxey was arrested on a trumped-up charge of walking on the grass, and the marchers were herded into camps because their presence supposedly endangered public health.

THE SILVER QUESTION

The financial panic deranged the government's monetary system, and in the minds of people like Cleveland the silver policy became the primary cause of the depression. This money question had a long history.

Since the beginning of the republic the country had been on a bimetallic standard: the government purchased and coined all the gold and silver offered to it for sale. At first the relative value of the two metals had been set by commercial demand for them, but eventually the government fixed a legal ratio. Back in Andrew Jackson's period the ratio had been

---

The Currency Issue

The Republican Platform: *The Republican party is unreservedly for sound money. It caused the enactment of a law providing for the redemption [resumption] of specie payments in 1879. Since then every dollar has been as good as gold. We are unalterably opposed to every measure calculated to debase our currency or impair the credit of our country. We are therefore opposed to the free coinage of silver, except by international agreement with the leading commercial nations of the earth, which agreement we pledge ourselves to promote, and until such agreement can be obtained the existing gold standard must be maintained.*

The Democratic Platform: *We demand the free and unlimited coinage of both silver and gold at the present legal ratio of 16 to 1 without waiting for the aid or consent of any other nation. We demand that the standard silver dollar shall be a full legal tender, equally with gold, for all debts, public and private, and we favor such legislation as will prevent for the future the demonetization of any kind of legal-tender money by private contract.*

placed at sixteen to one, meaning that the silver dollar had sixteen times as much silver as the gold dollar did gold. For sound economic reasons, hardly any silver dollars were coined. Because of the relative scarcity of silver bullion, the price of gold in the open market was almost never sixteen times the price of silver, so that what silver was mined was sold for commercial purposes. Nobody objected when in 1873 Congress enacted a measure that, while keeping existing silver money in circulation, removed the silver dollar from the coinage list. Soon the inflationists, charging a banker conspiracy, would be calling this act the "Crime of '73."

Almost immediately there occurred a drastic change in the supply of silver. The discovery of huge new deposits of the metal in the Far West, notably in Nevada, increased the amount in the domestic market; at the same time, several European countries went on the gold standard, melting their silver coins and swelling the world supply. The inevitable result was that the price of silver plunged downward and fell far below the legal ratio. Silver-mine owners, pinched by the dropping price, joined the discontented farmers in demanding that the government return to the bimetallic system, that it purchase all the silver brought to the mint—"the free and unlimited coinage of silver."

In 1878 the inflationists, a coalition of Democrats and Republicans from the Middle West, South, and Far West, attempted to pass a free-silver measure through Congress. They were forced, however, to accept a compromise, the Bland-Allison Act, which provided that each month the government must purchase not less than $2 million and not more than $4 million worth of silver and convert it into dollars at the ratio of sixteen to one. The inflation forces had won only a partial victory.

Later, in 1890, the Sherman Silver Purchase Act directed the Treasury to buy 4.5 million ounces of silver each month, an amount estimated to be the maximum domestic production, and to pay for the purchased bullion in treasury notes. The purchased silver was not to be coined. The amount of money in circulation did not increase materially, and the price of silver continued to drop. Creditors and conservatives still argued for the adoption of a single metallic standard; debtors and inflationists still

agitated for the unlimited coinage of silver at the rate of sixteen to one.

The Populists at first did not emphasize silver. But as the party developed strength, the money question came to overshadow all other issues. Currency reform was already a popular issue with debtor farmers, who with some reason believed that inflation would ameliorate their ills. Besides, the Populists desperately needed money to finance their campaigns, and the only source of help was the silver-mine owners who insisted on an elevation of the money plank and the subordination of other proposals.

The influence of silver on the thinking of Populists, agrarian Democrats, and farmers was graphically illustrated by the enormous popularity of a small and not particularly profound book, *Coin's Financial School*, written by William H. Harvey and published in 1894. "Professor Coin" ran a school, an imaginary institution specializing in finance, and the book reproduced his lectures and his dialogues with his students. The professor clearly indicated the marvelous restorative qualities of free silver: "It means the reopening of closed factories, the relighting of fires in darkened furnaces; it means hope instead of despair; comfort in place of suffering; life instead of death."

Ever since the Resumption Act of 1875 the Treasury had aimed to maintain a minimum gold reserve of $100 million to redeem its paper and silver dollars. During the prosperous eighties the reserve increased, and it reached the figure of $190 million by 1890. But in the last two years of the Harrison administration it fell off sharply. The prohibitive duties of the McKinley Tariff reduced imports and hence revenue; the pension and internal improvements appropriations ate up the surplus; and the Sherman Silver Purchase Act forced the government to buy increased amounts of silver and issue new treasury notes that the Treasury insisted on redeeming in gold. Holders of greenbacks and silver certificates, jittery at rumors the government might be swept off the gold standard, demanded gold, and when Cleveland assumed office in 1893, the reserve had shrunk to a little over $100 million.

The panic intensified the rush for gold, and soon the reserve sank below the minimum deemed necessary to sustain the gold standard.

Cleveland had always disliked the Sherman Silver Purchase Act, and now he was convinced that it was the chief factor draining gold from the Treasury and that, if allowed to stand, it would force the country off the gold standard and impair the government's financial honor. In one of his rare moods of leadership, the President summoned Congress into special session and demanded the repeal of the Sherman Act. He worked his will, but only by swinging the patronage lash hard on recalcitrant Democrats and enlisting the support of Eastern Republicans. Western and Southern Democrats fought repeal to the last, and in defeat were incredibly bitter. A historic party split was in the making.

The President had his victory, but the financial crisis deepened. In 1895, Cleveland approached the big New York bankers for help. A banking syndicate headed by J. P. Morgan agreed to take up a $65 million bond issue and to use the influence of the financial community to check the flow of gold to Europe. As a result, public faith that the government would maintain the gold standard was strengthened. The stampede to redeem notes eased. To agrarian Democrats and Populists, however, it seemed that Cleveland had sold out to Wall Street and concluded a crooked deal with the money lenders. Actually, there had been no deal and no corruption, though the bankers undoubtedly turned an excessive profit.

The Cleveland administration ended amidst flaming portents of social unrest. The Democratic party was bitterly divided. The President's gold policy had aligned the Southern and Western Democrats in a solid phalanx against him and his Eastern followers.

"A CROSS OF GOLD"

As the election of 1896 approached, Republicans were confident of victory.

Marcus A. Hanna, boss of the Ohio machine and soon to be national boss of the party, was a wealthy industrialist who aspired to be a President maker. He represented a new type in politics, the businessman who held office and actively manipulated parties instead of remaining in the background and paying out money for services rendered. He had picked out his man and had been grooming him carefully

since 1890. The man was William McKinley, governor of Ohio, who as a congressman had been the author of the tariff act of 1890. Hanna's support of McKinley included providing him with generous campaign contributions, bailing him out of a threatened bankruptcy, and advertising his availability to Republican bosses in other states.

By the time the convention met, Hanna had lined up enough Middle Western and Southern delegations to nominate McKinley. Everywhere and on every occasion he presented his candidate as "Bill McKinley, the advance agent of prosperity" and the champion of protection for American producers.

The platform as finally framed endorsed the protective tariff, ignored completely such questions as the income tax, railroad and trust abuses, and labor injunctions, and opposed the free coinage of silver except by international agreement with the leading commercial nations. As other countries, and particularly Great Britain, were unlikely to abandon the gold standard, the Republicans were supporting gold. Thirty-four delegates from the mountain and plains states walked out when the currency plank was adopted. Their obvious destination was the Democratic party.

The Democrats met amid scenes of drama seldom equaled in American politics. The Southern and Western delegates came to the convention determined to seize control of the party from the Easterners. Alarmed by the rise of Populist strength in their sections, they intended to write free silver and other planks of the third party into the platform and to nominate a silver candidate.

The resolutions committee presented to the convention two reports. The majority platform demanded tariff reduction, endorsed the principle of the income tax, denounced the issue of currency notes by the national banks, condemned the use of injunctions in industrial disputes, pledged a "stricter control" of trusts and railroads, and—this was the issue that headlined the platform—called for free silver: "We demand the free and unlimited coinage of both silver and gold at the present legal ratio of 16 to 1, without waiting for the aid or consent of any other nation." The minority resolution opposed the free coinage of silver except by international agreement, a stand identical to that of the Republicans.

William Jennings Bryan
*The United States has produced many orators who could sway crowds with the
magic of their voice, but it is generally agreed that Bryan had no superior in
power and persuasiveness. Here he is speaking at a later date than 1896. The
poster on the platform, in the lower left-hand corner of the picture, shows him as
he appeared when he was the Boy Orator of the Platte engaged in the silver
crusade. (Library of Congress)*

Six speakers debated the resolution, three
for gold and three for silver. The defenders of
gold had the better of the oratorical tournament – up to the final address. Then from the
Nebraska delegation a strikingly handsome
young man walked to the platform to close the
debate. He was William Jennings Bryan, thirty-
six years of age. His political experience was
limited to two terms in the House of Representatives, but he was widely known in the plains
country as a magnetic orator, and he eagerly
hoped for the presidential nomination.
Through the farthest reaches of the vast hall
now rang his magnificent organ-like voice.

He ended with a peroration that brought
the delegates and the spectators to their feet in
a frenzied tumult of passion and that was declaimed by later generations of schoolboys all
over rural America: "If they dare to come out
in the open and defend the gold standard as a
good thing, we will fight them to the uttermost.
Having behind us the producing masses of this
nation and the world, supported by the commercial interests, the laboring interests and the
toilers everywhere, we will answer their demand for a gold standard by saying to them:
'You shall not press down upon the brow of
labor this crown of thorns; you shall not crucify
mankind upon a cross of gold.' "

The majority platform was adopted. The
agrarians had found their leader, and the following day Bryan was nominated on the fifth
ballot. It is doubtful if he understood the technical implications of the money problem that he
discussed so eloquently before the convention.
It is even more dubious if he realized the full
import of the protest movement or the Populist
program. He seized on one Populist plank, free

silver, the most superficial of the various protest proposals, and erected it into a personal
and political obsession.

One Republican (Joseph Foraker), when
asked if he thought Bryan's title, the Boy Orator of the Platte, was an accurate phrase, replied that it was, because the Platte River was
six inches deep and six miles wide at the
mouth. More descriptive was another designation applied to Bryan: the Great Commoner.
Born in Illinois of typical middle-class stock, he
had attended a small sectarian college, had
practiced law with only average success, and
then, repeating a normal American pattern,
had moved to Nebraska, a frontier area, to try
his fortunes. Almost completely he represented
the feelings and emotions of rural, middle-class
America.

The choice of Bryan and the nature of the
Democratic platform placed the Populists in a
cruel quandary. They had expected both of the
major parties to adopt conservative programs
and nominate conservative candidates, leaving
the Populists to represent the growing forces of
protest. But now the Democrats had stolen
much of the Populists' thunder. The Populists
faced the choice of naming their own candidate

and splitting the protest vote, or endorsing
Bryan and losing their identity as a party.
When the party assembled, the convention
voted to approve Bryan but nominated its own
vice-presidential candidate, Tom Watson,
whom the Democrats were expected to adopt
but whom they ignored.

BRYAN IS BEATEN

There has never been another campaign quite
like the one of 1896. It had unequaled drama,
intense excitement, a clean-cut issue, and a
David-and-Goliath theme: the boy orator
Bryan contending against the powerful boss
Hanna. The boss had the great advantage of
ample funds to spend on organization. The
business and financial community, frightened
beyond reason at the prospect of Bryan's sitting in the White House and taking advice from
John P. Altgeld and Ignatius Donnelly, pressed
contributions upon Hanna. Just how much
money Hanna had to dispense has been disputed, but the lowest estimate is $3.5 million
and the highest is $7 million. The Democrats,
by contrast, reported expenditures of only

Election of 1896

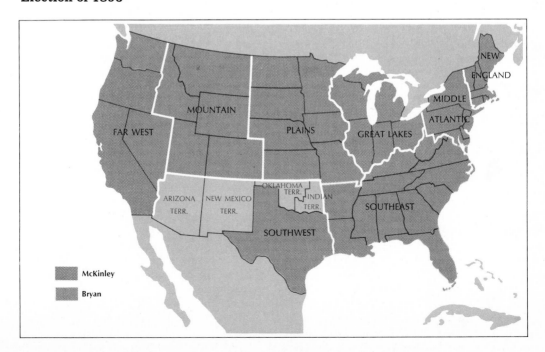

$300,000, a sum only slightly larger than the contribution of one firm, Standard Oil, to the Republican war chest. With his almost inexhaustible resources, Hanna organized the most lavish propaganda machine yet to operate in American politics.

Shrewdly, Hanna kept McKinley off the hustings, knowing better than to pit his solemn candidate against the matchless Bryan. From his home at Canton, Ohio, McKinley conducted a dignified "front-porch" campaign. To Canton came pilgrimages of the Republican faithful, organized and paid for by Hanna, to offer tribute to the standard-bearer. They came every day but McKinley always had a speech ready for them, and always he stressed one theme: the Republican party was the only agency that could bring prosperity to the country.

No such decorous restraint marked the campaigning of the young and vital Bryan. Joyously bearing the brunt of the battle for his party, he inaugurated techniques never before witnessed in American political contests. Previous candidates had addressed audiences in campaigns and had even toured the country to speak at a few selected points. But Bryan was the first to stump systematically every section, to appear in villages and hamlets, the first, really, to say frankly to the voters that he wanted to be President. He traveled 18,000 miles, speaking several times a day, and addressed an estimated 5 million people.

As Bryan's campaign mounted in intensity, cold fear gripped the East. Employers told their workers not to report for work in case of a Democratic victory: industry would have to close down in anticipation of being taken over by the government. Some employers threatened to dismiss workers who voted for Bryan. The banks let it be known that farmers supporting the Democratic candidate probably would have their mortgages foreclosed or at least not renewed.

Everything broke right for the Republicans in the closing weeks of the election. Crop failures abroad brought an increased demand for American products, and on the eve of the election the price of wheat almost doubled.

On Election Day, McKinley polled 271 electoral votes to Bryan's 176. The popular vote was 7,105,000 to 6,503,000. Bryan won the Confederate South plus Missouri, swept the plains and mountain states with the exception of North Dakota, but lost California and Oregon on the Pacific coast. In short, he carried only the mining regions and the areas where staple farming was predominant and agricultural prices were lowest. He went down to defeat in all the Granger states in the Middle West. The Democratic program, like that of the Populists, had been designed to serve the needs of one segment of one class, the most depressed fraction of agriculture, and this was too narrow an appeal to win a national election.

McKINLEY AND PROSPERITY

William McKinley, a shrewd political operator, was the last of a long list of officer veterans of the Union army (beginning with Grant) to sit in the White House. Friendly, kindly, and lovable, he was inclined to defer to stronger characters like Hanna and to act in harmony with his party's leaders. He and they realized the dangers inherent in the currency issue. Silver had many adherents, as evidenced by Bryan's huge popular vote, and the Republican party numbered many silverites in its Western wing. Impulsive action might divide the party in its hour of victory.

Postponing action on the money problem until a more propitious time, the administration turned to an issue on which Republicans were agreed, the necessity for higher tariff rates. Immediately after assuming office, McKinley summoned Congress into special session to consider tariff revision. With record brevity the Republican majority whipped into shape and passed the Dingley Tariff, raising the duties to an average of 57 percent, the highest in history.

On the currency question the administration proceeded in accordance with the party's platform pronouncement that bimetallism could not be established except by international action. McKinley sent a commission to Europe to explore the possibility of a silver agreement with Great Britain and France. As he and everyone else anticipated, Britain refused to abandon her gold standard, thus effectively ending any hopes for international bimetallism. The administration could now argue that if the United States embarked on a silver program alone it would be economically isolated from the rest of the world, and the argument was hard to refute. Believing that their position was unassailable, the Republicans finally moved to enact currency legislation. The Currency, or Gold Standard, Act of 1900 legalized the gold standard and enlarged the redemption fund, which was to be maintained as a separate and special charge to protect the supply of gold from depletion.

And so the "battle of the standards" ended in victory for the forces of conservatism. Economic developments seemed to prove that the conservatives had been right in the struggle. In 1898 prosperity returned to America. Foreign crop failures enlarged the farmer's market and sent farm prices surging upward. At the same time business entered another cycle of booming expansion. Prosperity and gold had come hand in hand — the lesson seemed obvious.

But it was not quite that simple. Bryan and the silverites were essentially right in demanding currency inflation. In the quarter century before 1900 the countries of Western civilization had experienced a spectacular augmentation of productive facilities and population. Yet the supply of money had not kept pace with economic progress, because the supply was tied to gold and the amount of gold remained practically constant. A committee of the British House of Lords, hardly a radical agency, reported after a careful investigation that the world's economy required a larger money supply.

It so happened that the supply was vastly increased soon after the Republicans took over the government in 1897. A new technique for extracting gold from low-content ores, the cyanide process, made it possible to work mines previously considered marginal or unprofitable. At the same time huge new gold deposits were discovered in Alaska, South Africa, and Australia. In 1898 two and a half times as much gold was produced as in 1890, and the currency supply soon was inflated far beyond anything proposed by Bryan. The price level, which had been declining since 1865, started on an upward swing.

With McKinley, then, there came a tariff increase, the gold standard, and prosperity. There also came a new departure in foreign policy, as the nation entered upon the path of overseas imperialism and took its place among the "great powers" of the world.

Selected Readings

Overviews

W. A. White, *Masks in a Pageant* (1928); Matthew Josephson, *The Politicos, 1865–1896** (1938); D. J. Rothman, *Politics and Power: The United States Senate, 1869–1901** (1966).

Republican Politics

Harry Barnard, *Rutherford B. Hayes and His America* (1954); R. G. Caldwell, *James A. Garfield, Party Chieftain* (1931); D. S. Muzzey, *James G. Blaine, a Political Idol of Other Days* (1934); D. B. Chidsey, *The Gentleman from New York: A Life of Roscoe Conkling* (1935); G. F. Howe, *Chester A. Arthur* (1934); A. B. Sageser, *The First Two Decades of the Pendleton Act* (1935); H. J. Sievers, *Benjamin Harrison, Hoosier Statesman* (1959).

Cleveland and the Democrats

Allan Nevins, *Grover Cleveland: A Study in Courage* (1932); H. S. Merrill, *Bourbon Leader: Grover Cleveland and the Democratic Party* (1957) and *Bourbon Democracy of the Middle West, 1865–1896* (1953); J. R. Hollingsworth, *The Whirligig of Politics: The Democracy of Cleveland and Bryan* (1963); G. H. Knowles, *The Presidential Campaign and Election of 1892* (1942); J. A. Barnes, *John G. Carlisle* (1931), Cleveland's Secretary of the Treasury.

Agrarian Protest

S. J. Buck, *The Granger Movement** (1913); J. D. Hicks, *The Populist Revolt** (1931); Norman Pollack, *The Populist Response to Industrial America** (1962); W. T. K. Nugent, *The Tolerant Populists* (1963); R. F. Durden, *The Climax of Populism** (1965); Theodore Saloutos, *Farmer Movements in the South, 1865–1933** (1960); R. B. Nye, *Midwestern Progressive Politics: A Historical Study of Its Origins and Development, 1870–1958** (1958); C. V. Woodward, *Tom Watson, Agrarian Radical** (1938); F. B. Simkins, *Pitchfork Ben Tillman* (1944); Stuart Noblin, *Leonidas Lafayette Polk* (1949); Martin Ridge, *Ignatius Donnelly* (1962).

Economic Policies

F. W. Taussig, *The Tariff History of the United States* (1931); Milton Friedman and A. J. Schwartz, *Monetary History of the United States, 1867–1900* (1963); D. R. Dewey, *Financial History of the United States* (1934); F. B. Webeg, *The Background of the Panic of 1893* (1929); D. L. McMurry, *Coxey's Army* (1929).

Bryan and McKinley

S. L. Jones, *The Presidential Election of 1896* (1964); P. W. Glad, *The Trumpet Soundeth* (1960) and *McKinley, Bryan, and the People** (1964); P. E. Coletta, *William Jennings Bryan, Political Evangelist, 1860–1908* (1964); H. W. Morgan, *William McKinley and His America* (1963); Margaret Leech, *In the Days of McKinley* (1959); Herbert Croly, *Marcus Alonzo Hanna* (1912).

*Titles available in paperback.

Emergence of a World Power

HOOP-'E-HOO-DOO

EXPA

PROSPERITY

Twenty

In the 1890s the United States took what seemed like a startling new departure in foreign affairs when it began to acquire possessions overseas. From the very beginning, however, the republic had been expansionist. As the American people moved relentlessly westward across the continent, their government from time to time acquired new lands for them to occupy: the trans-Appalachian region (in the treaty ending the Revolutionary War), the Louisiana Territory, Florida, Texas, a part of the Oregon country, California and New Mexico, Alaska.

Almost all these acquisitions—the fruits of what might be called the old Manifest Destiny—were contiguous with existing territories of the United States. Desired mainly as places for settlement by Americans seeking farms, these acquisitions represented a kind of agricultural imperialism. And they were expected to be organized as territories and ultimately as states, the equals of all the rest.

The expansionism of the 1890s, the new Manifest Destiny, was in some respects different. It meant acquiring island possessions—some of which were already thickly populated, were not suitable for settlement by migrants from the United States, and were expected to be held indefinitely as colonies—not as states or even territories. The new expansion was motivated largely (though not entirely) by considerations of trade. Thus it represented a kind of commercial imperialism.

Some Americans had begun to interest themselves in overseas acquisitions—Cuba, the Hawaiian Islands—as early as the 1850s, but the sectional controversy had intervened to frustrate that expansionist movement. In 1867 the United States annexed tiny Midway Island in the Pacific, and a few years later President Grant tried in vain to annex Santo Domingo in the Caribbean. The nation was not yet ready for the new imperialism.

The Expansion Rooster
As the twentieth century opened, the prevailing spirit of Americans was cockiness, as illustrated by this 1900 cartoon. At home, the country was prosperous; abroad, it was launching upon imperialism. The victorious Republicans were crowing. The anti-expansionist opposition, here labeled "Bryanism," was a dead bird. (The Bettmann Archive)

By 1900 the United States had finally become an empire. It was now recognized as a "world power," though in fact it had been one of the great nations of the world for some time. As such, it pursued three basic and long-standing foreign policies — one for each of three broad areas of the globe. With respect to Europe, the aim (often inaccurately called "isolation") was to promote commerce while avoiding diplomatic involvements. With respect to the Americas, the purpose was expressed in the Monroe Doctrine, as supplemented by the idea of Pan-Americanism. With respect to Asia, the slogan came to be the Open Door, signifying opportunity for American commercial interests in China. The Monroe Doctrine and the Open Door were reaffirmed and strengthened by events of the late nineteenth century. The policy of "isolation" began to be questioned, however, on the grounds that it was inconsistent with imperial obligations, with the responsibilities of "world leadership," and with the spirit of Anglo-American friendship which, by the end of the century, was about to prevail.

Imperialist Stirrings

In the two decades after 1870 the American people seemed to have forgotten the expansionist impulse of the prewar years. They were occupied with things closer to home — reconstructing the South, settling the last frontier, building a network of railroads, and expanding their great industrial system. By the 1890s they were ready — indeed, eager — to try imperialism, to resume the course of Manifest Destiny that had impelled their forebears to wrest an empire from Mexico in the expansionist forties.

THE NEW MANIFEST DESTINY

Various developments subtly played a part in shifting the attention of Americans from their own country to lands across the seas. The passing of the frontier gave rise to a feeling that resources would soon become scarce and that they must be sought abroad. The depression beginning in 1893 seemed to confirm the fear of certain businessmen that industry had been overbuilt and was producing more goods than customers at home could buy. The bitter class protests of the time — the Populist movement, the free-silver crusade, the bloody labor disputes — led many people to believe that the nation was threatened with internal collapse. Some politicians advocated a more aggressive foreign policy to divert the popular mind from dissensions at home.

The swelling volume of American exports to other countries altered the nature of our trade relations and directed the attention of political leaders to the importance of foreign markets — and to the possible necessity of securing foreign colonies. The value of American exports in 1870 was approximately $392 million; in 1890 the figure was $857 million, and by 1900 it had leaped to $1,394,000,000. "But today," Senator Albert J. Beveridge of Indiana cried in 1899, "we are raising more than we can consume. Today, we are making more than we can use. Therefore, we must find new markets for our produce, new occupation for our capital, new work for our labor."

In the century's closing years the powers of Europe partitioned most of Africa among themselves and then turned eager eyes on the Far East and the feeble Chinese empire. Imperialism was in the air, and a leading American expansionist, Senator Henry Cabot Lodge of Massachusetts, warned that the United States "must not fall out of the line of march."

A philosophic justification for expansionism was provided by historians, professors, clergymen, and other intellectuals, who found a basis for imperialism in Charles Darwin's theories. These thinkers contended that, among nations, or "races," as well as biological species, there was a struggle for existence and only the fittest could survive. If the strong dominated the weak, that was in accordance with the law of nature.

One of the first to argue this proposition was the popular writer John Fiske, who predicted in an article in *Harper's Magazine* (1885)

Defeat of the Anti-Imperialists
This 1899 lithograph, reproduced from Puck *magazine, pictures Bryan and other
members of the "Anti-Expansion Band" leaving Washington in defeat and
humiliation, while McKinley smilingly rides the "Expansion Train" toward
continued political success. (Culver Pictures)*

that the English-speaking peoples would eventually control every land that was not already the seat of an established civilization. Support for Fiske's position came from Josiah Strong, a Congregational clergyman and champion of overseas missionary work. In a book entitled *Our Country: Its Possible Future and Its Present Crisis* (1885), Strong declared that the Anglo-Saxon "race," and especially its American branch, represented the great ideas of civil liberty and pure Christianity and was "divinely commissioned" to spread its institutions over the earth. John W. Burgess, founder of Columbia University's School of Political Science, gave the stamp of scholarly approval to imperialism. In his *Political Science and Comparative Law* (1890), he flatly stated that the Anglo-Saxon and Teutonic nations possessed the highest political talents. It was the duty of these nations, he said, to uplift less fortunate peoples, even to force superior institutions upon them if necessary: "There is no human right to the status of barbarism."

The ablest and probably the most effective apostle of imperialism was Alfred Thayer Mahan, an officer in the navy. Mahan presented his philosophy in three major works: *The Influence of Sea Power upon History, 1660–1783* (1890); *The Influence of Sea Power upon the French Revolution and Empire, 1793–1812* (1892); and *The Interest of America in Sea Power* (1897). His thesis may be briefly stated. The sea-power nations were the great nations of history, and the United States, a huge island, had to build its greatness on sea power. The essential links in sea power were a productive domestic economy, foreign commerce, a merchant marine to monopolize national trade, a navy to defend the trade routes and national interests, and colonies to provide raw materials and markets and to serve as bases for the navy. Specifically, Mahan advocated that the United States construct a canal across the isthmus of Central America to join the oceans, acquire defensive bases on both sides of the canal in the Caribbean and the Pacific, and take possession of Hawaii and other Pacific islands. "Whether they will or no," he proclaimed, "Americans must now begin to look outward."

Mahan doubted that the United States would achieve its destiny, because its navy was not large enough to play the role he envisioned for it. But he did not accurately gauge the progress of the naval construction program launched in the Garfield-Arthur administration and continued by every succeeding administration. By 1898 the United States had advanced to fifth among the world's naval powers, and by 1900 to third.

HEMISPHERIC HEGEMONY

The most ardent practitioner of the new, assertive diplomacy was Harrison's Secretary of State, James G. Blaine, who in 1889 was beginning his second tour of duty in the foreign office. He believed that his country was destined to dominate the Caribbean and the Pacific. His expansionist policy was based largely on his conviction that the United States had to find enlarged foreign markets for its surplus goods. The most likely foreign outlet, he believed, was Latin America, with whose countries he wanted friendly commercial relations.

During his first term of office (1881), Blaine had invited the Latin nations to a Pan-American conference at Washington to discuss trade matters and arbitration of disputes. But after Garfield's death Blaine left office, and his cautious successor withdrew the invitations. Shortly before the Harrison administration took office, however, Congress authorized the convoking of a conference, and the State Department issued the invitations. With delegates from nineteen American nations in attendance, the first Pan-American Congress assembled in 1889. Blaine tried to persuade the conference to endorse his two principal objectives: (1) to draw the United States and Latin America into a customs union and (2) to create machinery to arbitrate controversies among the hemispheric nations. The Latin delegates rejected both proposals. They preferred to buy in the cheaper European market, and they feared the dominance of the United States in arbitration. Still, the meeting was not entirely a failure. Out of it arose the Pan-American Union, an agency in Washington that became a clearing house for

distributing information to the member nations, and other congresses would meet in the future to discuss common hemispheric matters.

When, after the election of 1892, the Democrats took over, the change in personnel meant no break in the new self-assertive diplomacy. Indeed, in 1895 President Cleveland and his Secretary of State, Richard Olney, in a dispute with Great Britain over the boundary of Venezuela, carried the country close to the brink of war.

For years Britain and Venezuela had argued about the boundary between Venezuela and British Guiana, the dispute assuming new importance when gold was discovered in the disputed area. Both Cleveland and Olney, as well as the American public, were disposed to sympathize with Venezuela as the little, underdog country confronting the great power. The President and Congress publicly expressed hopes that Britain would see fit to arbitrate the matter. When the English government took no action, Olney drafted a note to Lord Salisbury of the foreign office protesting that Britain was violating the Monroe Doctrine. Any European interference with hemispheric affairs – and a boundary dispute constituted interference – came within the scope of the famous doctrine, said the secretary. In bellicose language designed to make England sit up and listen, he declared: "Today the United States is practically sovereign on this continent, and its fiat is law upon the subjects to which it confines its interposition."

After months of delay Salisbury replied to Olney. With firm finality and a touch of condescension, he informed the secretary that the Monroe Doctrine did not apply to boundary disputes or the present situation and was not recognized as international law anyway. Britain was not going to arbitrate. Cleveland was enraged. In December 1895 he sent a special message to Congress reviewing the controversy. He asked for authority to create a special commission to determine the boundary line, and declared that if Britain resisted the commission's decision the United States should fight.

Enthusiastically Congress voted support for Cleveland's plan, and war talk flamed all over the country. Belatedly the British government realized that it had stumbled into a genuine diplomatic crisis. The last thing in the world that England wanted or could afford was a war with the United States. Suddenly the British backed down and agreed to arbitration.

However clumsy the Cleveland-Olney techniques had been, they had produced the desired results. The prestige of the United States was enhanced, the Monroe Doctrine was vitalized, and the bonds of friendship between the two great English-speaking nations were actually strengthened by strain.

HAWAII AND SAMOA

The first area into which the United States directed its expansionist impulse after the Civil War was the vast Pacific Ocean region.

The islands of Hawaii in the mid-Pacific had been an important stopover station for American ships in the China trade since the early 1800s. The first American settlers to reach Hawaii were New England missionaries, who, like their fellows in Oregon at approximately the same time, advertised the economic possibilities of the islands in the religious press. Soon other Americans arrived to become sugar planters and to found a profitable new industry. Eventually, officers of the growing navy looked longingly on the magnificent natural base of Pearl Harbor on the island of Oahu.

The American residents of Hawaii came to dominate the economic life of the islands and also the political policies of the native ruler. Commercial relations were inexorably pushing Hawaii into the American orbit and making it, as Blaine accurately contended, a part of the American system. A treaty signed in 1875 permitted Hawaiian sugar to enter the United States duty-free and bound the Hawaiian kingdom to make no territorial or economic concessions to other powers. The trade arrangement tied the islands to the American economy, and the political clauses meant that, in effect, the United States was guaranteeing Hawaii's independence, and hence was making the islands a protectorate. In 1887 a new treaty renewed the existing arrangements and granted the United States exclusive use of Pearl Harbor as a naval station. The course of events was rendering outright political union almost inevitable.

Sugar production in Hawaii boomed, and prosperity burgeoned for the American planters. Then the McKinley Tariff of 1890 dealt

the planters a bad blow; by removing the duty on foreign raw sugar and giving domestic producers a bounty, it deprived Hawaii of its privileged position in the American sugar market. Annexation seemed the only alternative to economic strangulation. At the same time there ascended to the throne a new ruler, Queen Liliuokalani, who was determined to eliminate American influence in the government.

The American residents decided to act at once. They started a revolution (1893) and called on the United States for protection. At a critical moment the American minister, John L. Stevens, an ardent annexationist and friend of Blaine, ordered 160 marines from a warship in Honolulu harbor to go ashore to aid the rebels. The Queen yielded her authority, and a delegation representing the triumphant provisional government set out for Washington to negotiate a treaty of annexation. They found President Harrison highly receptive, but before the resulting treaty could be acted on by the Senate he was succeeded by Cleveland.

However disposed Cleveland was to upholding American rights under the Monroe Doctrine, he had old-fashioned ideas about taking other people's property. Suspicious of what had happened in Hawaii, he withdrew the treaty and sent a special representative to the islands to investigate. When this agent reported that Americans had engineered the revolution, Cleveland endeavored to restore the Queen to her throne. But the Americans were in control of the kingdom and refused to budge. Reluctantly the President had to accord recognition to their government as representing the "republic" of Hawaii. Cleveland, actuated by honorable motives but opposing the course of history, had only delayed the inevitable. In 1898, with the Republicans again in power and with the United States, as we shall see, constructing a colonial empire in both oceans, Hawaii was annexed by joint resolution of both houses of Congress.

Three thousand miles to the south of Hawaii, the Samoan Islands dominated the sea lanes of the south Pacific and had long served as a way station for American ships in the Pacific trade. As American commerce with Asia increased after the completion of the first transcontinental railroad in 1869 and the extension of a steamship line from San Francisco to New Zealand, certain business groups regarded

Samoa with new interest, and the navy eyed the harbor of Pago Pago on the island of Tutuila. In 1872 a naval officer visited the islands and negotiated a treaty granting the United States the use of Pago Pago, but the Senate rejected it. President Grant nevertheless dispatched a special representative to Samoa to encourage American trading and business interests. The familiar chain of events leading to involvement was being set in motion. In 1878 a native prince was brought to Washington, where he signed a treaty, which was approved by the Senate, providing for an American naval station at Pago Pago and binding the United States to employ its "good offices" to adjust any differences between a foreign power and Samoa. This indicated that the American government meant to have a voice in Samoan affairs.

The opportunity for expressing that voice soon came. Great Britain and Germany were also interested in the islands, and they hastened to secure treaty rights from the native princes. For the next ten years the three powers scrambled and intrigued for dominance in Samoa, playing off one ruler against another

and coming dangerously close to war. In 1889 warships of the contending nations appeared in one Samoan harbor, and a clash seemed imminent. But a tropical hurricane dispersed the vessels, and the German government, not wishing to antagonize the United States, suggested a conference of the interested powers in Berlin to settle the dispute. Germany and Britain would have preferred a division of the islands, but Secretary Blaine insisted on preserving native Samoan rule. The result was that the conferees agreed on a tripartite protectorate over Samoa, with the native chiefs exercising only nominal authority.

The three-way arrangement proved unsatisfactory, failing altogether to halt the intrigues and rivalries of the signatory members. It was abrogated in 1899 when the United States and Germany divided the islands between them, with Britain being compensated elsewhere in the Pacific. Germany obtained the two largest islands, but the United States retained Tutuila with its incomparable harbor of Pago Pago. Everyone was satisfied — with the possible exception of the Samoans.

War with Spain

Though imperialist ambitions had begun to stir the United States, American imperialism did not flower until the coming of the war with Spain in 1898.

CONTROVERSY OVER CUBA

The immediate background of the Spanish-American War lay in the Caribbean island of Cuba, which with nearby Puerto Rico comprised nearly all that was left of Spain's once extensive Latin American empire. The Cubans had long resented Spanish rule, and they had engaged in a notable attempt to overthrow it between 1868 and 1878 (the Ten Years' War). During that revolt the American people were strongly sympathetic to the Cuban cause, but their feelings did not go beyond expressions of support. The government maintained a position of strict neutrality, despite the provocation offered by Spain. In 1873 the Spanish authori-

ties captured a Cuban-owned, arms-running ship, the *Virginius*, and executed fifty-three of her crew. Because the vessel had flown an American flag and some of her seamen were Americans, popular indignation was intense. But Secretary of State Hamilton Fish avoided a crisis by inducing the Spanish government to return the *Virginius* and pay an indemnity to the families of the executed men.

In 1895 the Cubans rose up again. Not only the continuing Spanish misrule but also the American tariff policy created conditions of misery that prepared the way for revolt. Cuba's principal export was sugar, and the bulk of the crop went to the United States. The Wilson-Gorman Tariff in 1894, with its high duties on raw sugar, shut off the island's chief source of wealth and prostrated its economy.

From the beginning the struggle took on aspects of ferocity that horrified Americans. The Cubans deliberately devastated the island to force the Spaniards to leave. To put down the insurrection, the Spanish resorted to methods equally extreme. General Valeriano Weyler — or "Butcher" Weyler, as he soon came to be known in the American press — confined the entire civilian population of certain areas to hastily prepared concentration camps, where they died by the thousands, victims of disease and malnutrition.

Many of the same savage techniques had been employed earlier in the Ten Years' War without shocking American sensibilities. But in the nineties a wave of anger ran through the American public. The revolt of 1895 was reported more fully and floridly by the American press than the former outbreak — and so reported as to give the impression that all the cruelties were being perpetrated by the Spaniards.

At this time Joseph Pulitzer with his New York *World* and William Randolph Hearst with his New York *Journal* were revolutionizing American journalism. The new "yellow press" specialized in lurid and sensational news; when such news did not exist, editors were not above creating it. To Hearst and Pulitzer, engaged in a ruthless circulation war, the struggle in Cuba was a journalist's dream. Both sent batteries of reporters and illustrators to Cuba with orders to provide accounts of Spanish atrocities. "You furnish the pictures," Hearst supposedly told a too scrupulous artist, "and I'll furnish the war."

The mounting storm of indignation against Spain left President Cleveland unmoved. Convinced that both sides in Cuba were guilty of atrocities and that the United States had no interests justifying involvement in the struggle, he issued a proclamation of neutrality and attempted to arrest the numerous filibustering expeditions being organized by a "junta" of Cuban refugees in New York City. When Congress, in a state of excitement, passed a resolution favoring recognition of Cuban belligerency, he ignored the action. His only concession to the demands for intervention was to offer America's good offices to mediate the conflict, a proposal that Spain declined.

When McKinley took over the presidency in 1897, he renewed the American mediation offer, which was again refused. Taking a stronger line than his predecessor, he protested to Spain against her "uncivilized and inhuman" conduct. The Spanish government,

alarmed that McKinley's course might forebode American intervention in Cuba, recalled Weyler, modified the concentration policy, and took steps to grant the island a qualified autonomy. At the end of 1897, with the insurrection losing ground, it seemed that war might be averted.

If there was any chance of a peaceful settlement, it was extinguished by two dramatic incidents in February 1898.

A Cuban agent in Havana stole a private letter written by Dupuy de Lôme, the Spanish minister in Washington, and thoughtfully turned it over to the American press. First published in Hearst's New York *Journal,* the minister's letter described McKinley as a weak man and "a bidder for the admiration of the crowd." This was no more than many Americans, including some Republicans, were saying about their President — Theodore Roosevelt described McKinley as having "no more backbone than a chocolate éclair" — but when a foreigner made such a remark it was a national insult. Popular anger was intense, and Dupuy de Lôme resigned before the outraged McKinley could demand his recall.

While the excitement was still at fever pitch, even more sensational news hit the front pages: the battleship *Maine* had been blown up in Havana harbor with a loss of over 260 lives. This vessel had been ordered to Cuban waters in January on a "friendly" visit, but the real reason for its presence was to protect American lives and property against possible attacks by Spanish loyalists. Many Americans jumped to the conclusion that the Spanish had sunk the ship — "an act of dirty treachery," Theodore Roosevelt announced — and the imperialists and the jingoists screamed for war. This opinion seemed confirmed when a naval court of inquiry reported that an external explosion by a submarine mine had caused the disaster. As war hysteria swept the country, Congress unanimously appropriated $50 million for military preparations. "Remember the *Maine*" became a national chant for revenge.

After the *Maine* incident there was little chance that the government could keep the people from war, although McKinley did not wish to resort to force. In March 1898, he asked Spain to agree to an armistice, with negotiations for a permanent peace to follow, and an immediate ending of the concentration system.

Wreck of the Maine
During the night after the explosion, the Maine settled down into the mud on the harbor bottom, so that only the wrecked superstructure remained visible, as shown here. Soon afterward, divers examined the hull. From their findings and from other evidence a naval court of inquiry concluded that an underwater mine had exploded, setting off explosions in the ship's powder magazines. Years later, in 1911, the wreck was raised so that it could be examined for a second court of inquiry. This court agreed with the first one on the essential point—that there had been both external and internal explosions—but disagreed on certain significant details. Finally, the hulk was towed out to sea and sunk in water too deep to permit another examination. (National Archives)

After a slight delay, Spain essentially accepted the American demands on April 9. Two days later McKinley asked Congress for authority to use military force to end the hostilities in Cuba—in short, for a declaration of war. After reviewing the reasons that impelled him to recommend war ("in the name of humanity, in the name of civilization, in behalf of endangered American interests"), he mentioned only casually, at the end of the message, that Spain was already capitulating to his requests.

By huge majorities Congress on April 19 passed a joint resolution declaring Cuba free and authorizing the President to employ force to expel the Spanish from the island. Added to the resolution was the Teller Amendment, disclaiming any intention on the part of the United States to annex Cuba.

"A SPLENDID LITTLE WAR"

The Spanish-American War was, in the words of Roosevelt's friend John Hay, "a splendid little war." Indeed, to all Americans, with the possible exception of the enlisted men who fought it, it was almost an ideal conflict. It was the last small, short, individualistic war before the huge, protracted, impersonal struggles of the twentieth century. Declared in April, it was over in August. Newspaper readers easily and eagerly followed the campaigns and the heroic exploits of American soldiers and sailors. Only 460 Americans were killed in battle or died of wounds, but some 5,200 perished of disease: malaria, dysentery, typhoid, and other ills.

Blithely and confidently the United States embarked on a war it was not prepared to fight. The regular army, numbering only 28,000 troops and officers scattered around the country at various posts, was a tough little force, skilled at quelling Indian outbreaks, but with no experience in large-scale warfare. Hastily Congress directed the President to increase the army to 62,000 and to call for 125,000 volunteers. It was expected that the National Guard, the state militia, would furnish the bulk of the volunteers, and in addition the President was authorized to accept directly into the national service three volunteer cavalry regiments. By far the most colorful of the cavalrymen were the Rough Riders, nominally commanded by Leonard Wood but actually by Theodore Roosevelt, who was about to burst onto the front pages as a war hero. The services of supply,

The Spanish-American War: Pacific Front

manned by elderly bureaucratic officers, proved incapable of meeting the modest wants of the forces raised during the war. On hand were enough Krag-Jorgensen repeating rifles, using smokeless powder, for the regulars, but the volunteers had to make do with the old black-powder, single-shot Springfields. American soldiers campaigning in tropical regions were clothed in the traditional heavy blue uniforms and fed canned rations that they called "embalmed beef."

The Spanish army numbered almost 130,000 troops, of whom 80,000 were already in Cuba at the beginning of the war. Despite its imposing size, it was not an efficient force; its commanders seemed to be paralyzed by a conviction of certain defeat. The American navy, fifth largest in the world, was far superior to the Spanish in ships, gunnery, and personnel.

The greatest weakness in the American military system was that no agency in it, either in the army or the navy, was charged with strategic planning. Only the navy had worked out an objective, and its objective had little to do with freeing Cuba.

The Assistant Secretary of the Navy in the McKinley administration was Theodore Roosevelt, ardent imperialist and proponent of war. In consultations with naval officers, Roosevelt prepared to seize Spain's Philippine Islands in the far Pacific. He strengthened the Asiatic squadron and instructed its commander, Commodore George Dewey, in event of war to attack the Philippines. Immediately after war was declared, Dewey left the China coast and headed for Manila, where a venerable Spanish fleet was stationed. On May 1 he steamed into Manila Bay, and as his ships prepared to pass down the line of anchored enemy vessels he uttered the first slogan of the war: "You may fire when ready, Gridley." When the firing was finished, the Spanish fleet was completely destroyed, one American sailor lay dead—of a heat stroke—and George Dewey, immediately promoted to admiral, had become the first hero of the war.

The Spaniards still held Manila city, and Dewey had no troops with which to attack them. While he waited nervously, the government assembled an expeditionary force to relieve him and take the city. Not until August 13 did the Americans receive the surrender of Manila.

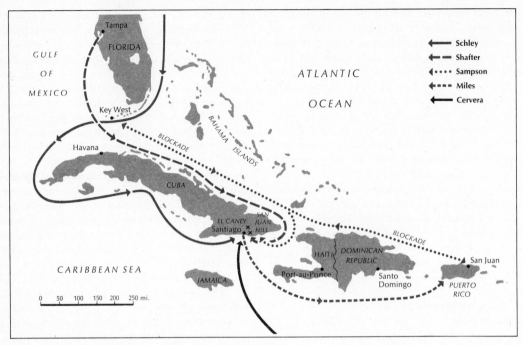

The Spanish-American War: Caribbean Front

In the rejoicing over Dewey's victory, few Americans paused to note that the character of the war was being subtly altered. What had begun as a war to free Cuba was becoming a war to acquire colonies.

But Cuba was not to be left out of the war picture. Late in April it was known in the United States that a Spanish fleet under Admiral Pascual Cervera had sailed for the west, presumably for a Cuban harbor. Cervera's antique armada was no match for the powerful American Atlantic squadron, as the Spanish government well knew. The Atlantic squadron, commanded by Admiral William T. Sampson, with Commodore W. S. Schley second in command, was expected to intercept and destroy Cervera before he reached his destination. (The squadron was "as strong as Sampson and as Schley as a fox," newspapers happily assured their readers.) But the Spaniard turned out to be the fox. Easily eluding his pursuers, he slipped into Santiago harbor on the southern coast of Cuba, where he was not discovered by the Americans until ten days after his arrival. Immediately the Atlantic fleet moved to bottle him up.

While the navy was monopolizing the first phases of the war, the War Department was trying to mobilize and train an army. The volunteer and National Guard units were collected near Chattanooga, Tennessee, while the regulars, plus the Rough Riders, were assembled at Tampa, Florida, under the command of General William R. Shafter. The entire mobilization process was conducted with remarkable inefficiency. There were appalling shortages of arms, ammunition, food, clothing, and medical supplies.

The army's commanding general, Nelson A. Miles, veteran of the Civil War, had planned to train the troops until autumn, then to occupy Puerto Rico and in conjunction with the Cuban rebels attack Havana. But with a Spanish naval force at Santiago, plans were hastily changed. It was decided to send Shafter with his force of 17,000 to take Santiago. So in June the expedition left Tampa, the Rough Riders, for want of transport space, having to leave their horses behind. The embarkation was accomplished amidst scenes of fantastic incompetence, but it was efficiency itself compared to the landing. Five days were required to put the army ashore, and this with the enemy offering no opposition.

Once landed, Shafter moved his army toward Santiago, planning to surround and capture it. On the way he fought and defeated the Spaniards at two battles, El Caney and San Juan Hill. In both engagements the Rough Riders were in the middle of the fighting and on the front pages of the newspapers. Colonel Roosevelt rapidly emerged as a hero of the war. Shafter was now before Santiago, but his army was so weakened by sickness that he feared he might have to abandon his position. When he besought Sampson to unite with him in a joint attack on the city, the admiral answered that mines in the harbor made it too dangerous to take his big ships in.

At this point disaster seemingly confronted the Americans, but unknown to them the Spanish government had decided that Santiago was lost. On July 3 Cervera, acting under orders from home, broke from the harbor to attempt an escape that he knew was hopeless. The waiting American squadron destroyed his entire fleet. Shafter then pressed the Spanish army commander to surrender, and that official, after bargaining for generous terms, including free transportation back to Spain for his troops, turned over Santiago on July 16. While the Santiago campaign was in its last stages, an American army landed in Puerto Rico and occupied it against virtually no opposition.

Spain was whipped and knew it. Through the medium of the French ambassador in Washington she asked for peace, and on August 12 an armistice ended the war.

DECISION FOR IMPERIALISM

In agreeing to a preliminary peace, the United States had laid down terms on which a permanent settlement must be based: Spain was to relinquish Cuba, cede Puerto Rico to the United States, cede also to the victor an island in the Ladrones, midway between Hawaii and the Philippines (this turned out to be Guam), and permit the Americans to hold Manila pending the final disposition of the Philippines. The last clause reflected the confusion in the McKinley administration as to what to do about the islands where its forces had won a foothold. The demands for Puerto Rico and Guam showed how quickly the war to free Cuba had assumed an imperialist character. Aroused by the excitement of military victory and a heady sense of mastery, the American government and people were disposed to keep what American arms had won.

In October 1898, commissioners from the United States and Spain met in Paris, to determine a permanent peace. With little protest Spain agreed to recognize Cuba's independence, to assume the Cuban debt, and to cede Puerto Rico and Guam to the victor. Then the American commissioners acting under instruction from McKinley, startled the conference by demanding the cession of all the Philippines. The President later said that he had arrived at his decision as a result of divine guidance. Probably such mundane factors as the swelling sentiment for annexation in the country and the pressure of the imperialist leaders of his party influenced his thinking more. Stubbornly the Spanish resisted the American demand, although they realized they could retain the islands only by resuming the war. They yielded to the inevitable when the United States offered a money payment of $20 million. The Treaty of Paris was signed on December 10, 1898, and sent to the United States for ratification by the Senate.

When the treaty was submitted to the Senate, it encountered immediate and fierce criticism and occasioned in that body and throughout the country one of those "great debates" that frequently precede a departure in American foreign policy. The chief point at issue was the acquisition of the Philippines, denounced by many, including prominent Republicans, as a repudiation of America's high moral position in the war and a shameful occupation of a land that wanted to be free. Favoring ratification were the imperialists, the big navy lobby, the Protestant clergy, who saw in a colonial empire enlarged fields for missionary enterprise, and most Republicans. Business, which had opposed the war, swung over to support the treaty, converted by the notion that possession of the Philippines would enable American interests to dominate the Oriental trade. In the forces opposing the treaty were old-fashioned Americans who objected to their country's annexing other people against their will, traditionalists who feared that a colonial empire would necessitate large armaments and foreign alliances, a majority of the intellectuals, eco-

An Argument Against Imperialism [1899]

The anti-imperialists included both Democrats and Republicans and men as different as Andrew Carnegie and William Jennings Bryan. Most of them had long supported various political and social reforms. They organized the American Anti-Imperialist League, which in October 1899, in the midst of the Philippine insurrection, drew up a platform. This denied the obligation of Americans to support an unjust, undeclared war such as the one the United States was carrying on against the Filipinos. The platform also included the following statements:

We hold that the policy known as imperialism is hostile to liberty and tends toward militarism, an evil from which it has been our glory to be free. We regret that it has become necessary in the land of Washington and Lincoln to reaffirm that all men, of whatever race or color, are entitled to life, liberty, and the pursuit of happiness. We maintain that governments derive their just powers from the consent of the governed. We insist that the subjugation of any people is "criminal aggression" and open disloyalty to the distinctive principles of our Government. . . .

We hold, with Abraham Lincoln, that "no man is good enough to govern another man without that man's consent. When the white man governs himself, that is self-government, but when he governs himself and also governs another man, that is more than self-government — that is despotism. . . . Our reliance is in the love of liberty which God has planted in us. Our defense is in the spirit which prizes liberty as the heritage of all men in all lands. Those who deny freedom to others deserve it not for themselves, and under a just God cannot long retain it."

---

nomic interests like the sugar growers who foresaw colonial competition, and most Democrats.

After weeks of bitter wrangling, the treaty was ratified, February 6, 1899, but only because it received an unexpected assist from William Jennings Bryan, who expected to be his party's candidate again in the election of 1900. Bryan persuaded a number of Democratic senators to vote for ratification. It has been charged that he was looking for a campaign issue, and in his defense it has been said that he thought the question of the Philippines should be decided by a national referendum: if the Democrats won in 1900, they would free the islands.

In 1900 Bryan ran against McKinley again, and this time Bryan went down to a crushing defeat. Although the Republicans claimed a popular mandate for imperialism, other factors had helped to determine the outcome. The victors had again exploited the money and tariff issues; they had harped on the continuing prosperity in the country under a Republican administration; and they had displayed to the voters the colorful personality of their vice-presidential candidate, the hero of San Juan Hill, Colonel Theodore Roosevelt.

The Republic as an Empire

The new colonial empire was extensive enough to warm the heart of the most ardent imperialist. Stretching from the Caribbean to the far reaches of the Pacific, it embraced Puerto Rico, Alaska, Hawaii, a part of Samoa, Guam, the Philippines, and a chain of minor Pacific islands.

With the empire came new problems. Many of the predictions of the anti-imperialists proved accurate. Ultimately, as a colonial

An Argument for Imperialism [1900]

Senator Albert J. Beveridge of Indiana addressed the Senate on January 9, 1900, after visiting the Philippines, where American troops were fighting to put down the struggle of the Filipinos for independence. He began by saying that the "hurtful" resolutions and speeches of the anti-imperialists were "costing the lives of American soldiers." He continued:

The Philippines are ours forever, "territory belonging to the United States," as the Constitution calls them. And just beyond the Philippines are China's illimitable markets. We will not retreat from either. We will not repudiate our duty in the archipelago. We will not abandon our opportunity in the Orient. We will not renounce our part in the mission of our race, trustee, under God, of the civilization of the world. . . .

Mr. President, this question is deeper than any question of party politics; deeper than any question of the isolated policy of our country even; deeper even than any question of constitutional power. It is elemental. It is racial. God has not been preparing the English-speaking and Teutonic peoples for a thousand years for nothing but vain and idle self-contemplation and self-admiration. No! He has made us the master organizers of the world to establish system where chaos reigns. He has given us the spirit of progress to overwhelm the forces of reaction throughout the earth. He has made us adepts in government that we may administer government among savage and senile peoples. Were it not for such a force as this the world would relapse into barbarism and night. And of all our race He has marked the American people as His chosen nation to finally lead in the regeneration of the world.

---

power, the United States had to maintain large armaments, concern itself with the complexities of Far Eastern international politics, and modify its traditional policy of holding aloof from alliances.

GOVERNING THE COLONIES

Immediately, the nation faced the problem of how it was to govern its dependencies, and here a host of perplexing questions arose. Did Congress have to administer the colonies in accordance with the Constitution? Did the inhabitants of the new possessions have the rights of American citizens? Could Congress levy tariff duties on colonial imports? Or, in a phrase that pleased the public fancy, did the Constitution follow the flag? The Supreme Court pointed to a solution in the Insular Cases (*De Lima* v. *Bidwell*, *Downes* v. *Bidwell*, and others, 1900–1904), involving duties on colonial trade. In a series of decisions the Court distinguished, in extremely technical language, between "incorporated" and "unincorporated"

territories. In legislating for the latter—the insular possessions—Congress was not bound by all the limitations in the Constitution applicable to incorporated territories, although some restrictions did apply. What the Court was saying was that the Constitution followed the flag only if Congress so decided and that the government could administer its colonies in almost any way it saw fit.

Three of the dependencies—Hawaii, Alaska, and Puerto Rico—were given territorial status as quickly as Congress considered them ready for it. For Hawaii, with its large American population and close economic ties with the United States, a basis for government was provided by an act of 1900. This measure granted American citizenship to all persons who were citizens of the Hawaiian republic, authorized an elective two-house legislature, and vested executive authority in a governor appointed from Washington.

Alaska was being governed by appointed civil officials. The discovery of gold there in 1896 caused the first substantial influx of Americans, and in 1912 Alaska received territorial status and a legislature, and its inhabitants were given the rights of citizenship. In Puerto Rico the people readily accepted American rule. Military occupation of the island was ended and civil government was established by the Foraker Act in 1900. The governor and upper house of the legislature were to be appointed from Washington, while only the lower house was to be elected. The act did not declare the Puerto Ricans to be American citizens, this privilege being deferred until 1917.

Smaller possessions in the empire were dealt with more arbitrarily. Such places as Guam and Tutuila were placed under control of naval officials, and many of the small islands, containing only a handful of inhabitants, experienced no form of American government at all.

American military forces, commanded by General Leonard Wood, remained in Cuba until 1902, the occupation being protracted to enable American administrators to prepare the island for the independence promised in the peace treaty of 1898. The vigorous occupiers built roads, schools, and hospitals, reorganized the legal, financial, and administrative systems, and introduced far-reaching sanitary reforms.

At Wood's urging a convention assembled to draft a constitution for independent Cuba. This document contained no provisions concerning relations with the nation responsible for Cuba's freedom. The United States, with its expanding interests in the Caribbean, expected to exercise some kind of control over the island republic. Therefore, in 1901, Congress passed the Platt Amendment, as a rider to an army appropriation bill, and pressured Cuba into incorporating the terms of the amendment into her constitution. The Platt Amendment stated that Cuba should never impair her independence by treaty with a foreign power (this was equivalent to giving the United States a veto over Cuba's diplomatic policy); that the United States had the right to intervene in Cuba to preserve its independence, life, and property; and that Cuba must sell or lease to the United States lands for naval stations. The amendment left Cuba only nominally independent. With American capital taking over the island's economy — investments jumped from $50 million in 1898 to $220 million by 1914 — Cuba was in fact, if not in name, an American appendage.

Among the possessions in the imperial system, only the Philippines offered resistance to American rule. The Filipinos, rebellious against Spain before 1898, had hailed Dewey and the expeditionary force sent to Manila as their deliverers from tyranny. When the hard fact sank in that the Americans had come to stay, the Filipinos resolved to expel the new invaders. In 1899 they resorted to war (rebellion, by the American definition) and, ably led by Emilio Aguinaldo, they fought the army of occupation from island to island until 1901. In the end the Americans repressed the uprising, but only after employing methods unpleasantly reminiscent of Weyler's tenure in Cuba, including the use of concentration camps, and at a cost of $170 million and 4,300 American lives. Civil government began taking over from the military in 1901, and the Filipinos, with great adaptability, began the process of adjusting to American culture. Thus they started on the long road that would lead, in 1946, to the independence they so ardently desired.

THE OPEN DOOR

The acquisition of the Philippines made the United States an Asian power. American interest in the Far East, already aroused by our growing trade with China, reached a new intensity immediately after 1898. Other nations more experienced in the ways of empire were casting covetous eyes on China, ancient, enfeebled, and seemingly open to exploitation by stronger countries. By the turn of the century the great European imperialistic powers — England, France, Germany, and Russia — and one Asian power, Japan, were beginning to partition China into "spheres of influence." One nation would force the Chinese government to grant it "concessions" to develop a particular area; another would use pressure to secure a long-term lease to a region. In some cases the outside powers even asserted ownership of territory. The process, if continued, threatened to destroy American hopes for a vast trade with China.

The situation posed a delicate problem for the men directing American foreign policy. Knowing that public opinion would not support any use of force, they had to find a way to protect American interests in China without risking war. McKinley's Secretary of State, John Hay, attempted an audacious solution. In September 1899 he addressed identical notes to

The Open Door in China
"Uncle Sam has distanced all competitors in gaining access to the Flowery Kingdom," says the caption of this cartoon. He holds the key to the door while the other powers look on. Obviously, Secretary of State John Hay has aroused much popular enthusiasm by his Open Door notes, though in fact they represented no great diplomatic triumph for the United States. From the Utica, New York, Saturday Globe, March 3, 1900. (Culver Pictures)

England, Germany, and Russia, and later to France, Japan, and Italy, asking them to approve a formula that became known as the "Open Door." It embodied three principles: (1) each nation with a sphere of influence was to respect the rights and privileges of other nations in its sphere; (2) Chinese officials were to continue to collect tariff duties in all spheres (the existing tariff favored the United States); and (3) each nation with a sphere was not to discriminate against other nations in levying port dues and railroad rates.

Hay could hardly have expected an enthusiastic response to his notes, and he got none. Russia declined to approve the Open Door, and the remaining powers gave evasive replies.

Each one stated in effect that it approved Hay's ideas in principle but could make no commitment until the others had acted. Apparently the United States had met a humiliating rebuff, but Hay boldly announced that since all the powers had accepted the principle of the Open Door, his government considered their assent to be "final and definitive." Although the American public applauded his diplomacy, Hay had won little more than a theoretical victory. The United States could not prevent any nation that wanted to violate the Open Door from doing so — unless it was willing to resort to war.

Almost immediately after the diplomatic maneuvering over the Open Door ended, a secret Chinese society known as the Boxers instigated an uprising against foreigners in China. The movement came to a blazing climax when the Boxers and their supporters besieged the entire foreign diplomatic corps in the British embassy in Peking. At this point the powers with interests in China decided to send an international expeditionary force to rescue the diplomats. The situation seemed to offer a perfect excuse to those nations with ambitions to dismember China.

The United States contributed 2,500 troops to the rescue force, which in August 1900 fought its way into Peking and broke the siege. McKinley and Hay had decided on American participation in order to secure a voice in the settlement of the uprising and to prevent the partition of China. Again Hay sent a note to the world powers. This time he called for the Open Door not only in the spheres of influence but in "all parts of the Chinese Empire." He also called for the maintenance of China's "territorial and administrative integrity." This—the integrity, or independence, of China—thus became a corollary of the Open Door policy. He persuaded England and Germany to approve his views, and then with their support he induced the participating powers to accept a money indemnity as satisfaction. The sum allotted to the United States amounted to almost $25 million, which greatly exceeded damages, but later the American government reduced the obligation and even remitted the unpaid balance. China gratefully used part of this money to educate Chinese students in the United States.

A MODERN MILITARY SYSTEM

The war with Spain had revealed glaring deficiencies in the military system. The greatest weakness had appeared in the army, but there had been an absence of coordination in the entire military organization that might have resulted in disaster had the United States been fighting a first-rate power. The army, now being called upon to police the new colonial possessions, obviously needed a thorough overhauling. To do the job McKinley appointed Elihu Root, an extremely able administrator, as secretary of war in 1899. Between 1900 and 1903 Root put into effect, by congressional authorization or by executive order, a series of reforms that gave the United States what amounted to a new military system.

The Root reforms may be conveniently listed in summary form:

1. An enlarged regular army, with a maximum size of 100,000.
2. Federal supervision of the National Guard, provided by the Dick Act of 1903.
3. The creation of a system of officer-training schools, crowned by the Army Staff College (later the Command and General Staff School) at Fort Leavenworth, Kansas, and the Army War College at Washington.
4. The establishment in 1903 of a General Staff headed by a Chief of Staff, who would replace the former commanding general of the army and act as military adviser to the Secretary of War.

While Root was intent on improving the professional quality and the efficiency of all segments of the army, his primary concern was to provide it with a central planning agency modeled on the example of European staffs. The General Staff was charged with many functions (it was to "supervise" and "coordinate" the entire army establishment), but one of its most important branches was to devote its whole work to planning for possible wars. To ensure interservice strategic cooperation, an Army and Navy Board, representing both services, was created.

Whatever the shortcomings of the Root reforms, they invested the army with a new and needed competence. The United States entered the twentieth century with something resembling a modern military system.

Life in the Imperial Republic

The acquisition of a far-flung empire did not noticeably affect the daily lives of the American people, who numbered nearly 76 million according to the census of 1900. But the lives of the people were being profoundly affected by other developments—in technology, culture, and economics—that went on contemporaneously with overseas expansion.

AUTOMOBILES AND AIRPLANES

As the twentieth century opened, great changes were under way in communication and transportation, changes that were to make the new century very different from the preceding one. The telephone was becoming a familiar feature of the home as well as the office. In 1900 the Bell system operated 677,000 telephones; by 1915 the number was nearly 6 million, and coast-to-coast lines were in operation. Radio was in its infancy. In 1901 the Italian inventor, Guglielmo Marconi, flying a kite aerial in Newfoundland, caught signals from Cornwall, England. The next year the Marconi Wireless Telegraph Company of America was established, and by 1910 all large ships were equipped with radios.

At the beginning of the new century, the day of the radio as a familiar part of American life still lay a few decades in the future, and so did the day of the airplane. But the day of the automobile was already arriving. Since the introduction of railroads, men had been intrigued with the idea of installing some kind of engine in carriages or cars that would run on roads. Throughout the nineteenth century, inventors had experimented with engines driven by steam or electric power, but the vehicles thus propelled all demonstrated impossible mechanical drawbacks. In the 1870s designers in France, Germany, and Austria began to develop the internal-combustion engine using the expanding power of burning gas to drive pistons, and the gasoline engine soon prevailed over all other types. France seized the lead in the early automotive industry, introducing such terms as "garage," "chassis," and the word "automobile" itself.

Meanwhile, in the United States, inventors — the Duryea brothers (Charles E. and J. Frank), Elwood Haynes, Ransom Olds, and Henry Ford — were busily designing their own models. In 1893 the Duryeas built and operated the first gasoline-driven motor vehicle in the United States. Three years later Ford produced the first of the famous cars that would bear his name, a two-cylinder, four-horsepower affair. Other "firsts" followed in rapid succession. In 1898 the first automobile ad in the country appeared in the *Scientific American;* its headline read: "Dispense with a horse." The first automobile salesroom was opened in New York in 1899, and the next year the first automobile show was held at Madison Square Garden. In 1901 Ransom Olds built 1,500 curved-dash Oldsmobiles, thus becoming the first mass-producer of automobiles.

The first automobiles were built in various Eastern cities, but gradually production came to center at Detroit, Michigan. Detroit offered several attractions: it had an established carriage industry that could construct automobile bodies, and it was close to supplies of iron ore and lumber. In 1900 the automobile companies turned out over 4,000 cars, but the big development of the industry had to wait more than a decade.

A number of factors held back production. For one thing, the country's roads were not adequate for automobile transportation. Only 150,000 miles, 7 percent of the total mileage, were improved with gravel, oil, shell, or other forms of surfacing; by contrast, there were over 2 million miles of dirt roads. The greatest deterring force was the expense involved in the manufacturing process, which resulted in a car priced too high for the mass market. The first builders had to order their parts from many sources, including sewing-machine and bicycle companies, and then begin the job of assembling; but soon they turned to assembly-line techniques and mass-production methods.

There had been only four automobiles on the American highways in 1895; by 1917 there were nearly 5 million, and the automobile was beginning to remake American life. Automobiles then had become commonplace among upper middle-class families, just as telephones were almost essential in middle-class homes.

In 1903 the Wright brothers made their first flight at Kitty Hawk, North Carolina. It lasted only twelve seconds and covered a distance less than the wing span of the largest airplanes of fifty years later. Soon the Wrights and other inventors and pilots, in the United States and Europe, were busy improving the airplane, making longer flights with it, and even putting it to a few practical uses. In 1909 the Wrights delivered the first military plane to the United States Army. World War I stimulated rapid developments in aircraft design, especially in Germany and France. As early as 1914 a plane had begun to carry passengers on daily flights in Florida, and in 1918 regular air-mail service was started between New York City and Washington, D.C. For the time being, however, flying remained in an essentially experimental stage.

Herald Square   1910
By the first decade of the century, both electric trolley cars and automobiles were beginning to take over from the horse-drawn vehicles. New York City had entered the electric age with arc lights and illuminated signs. (Museum of the City of New York)

The Wright Brothers Making Their First Flight

On December 17, 1903, on the side of Kill Devil Hill at Kitty Hawk, North Carolina, Orville and Wilbur Wright became the first men to fly in a motor-driven machine heavier than air. Their airplane had a wing span of 40 feet; its two propellers were driven by an engine producing about 12 horsepower. "After running the motor for a few minutes to heat it up," Orville Wright later wrote, "I released the wire that held the machine to the track, and the machine started forward into the wind. Wilbur ran at the side of the machine, holding the wing to balance it on the track. . . . Wilbur was able to stay with it till it lifted from the track after a forty-foot run. One of the Life Saving men snapped the camera for us, taking a picture just as the machine had reached the end of the track and had risen to a height of about two feet." It traveled a little over 120 feet. Later Wilbur Wright stayed aloft 59 seconds and flew 852 feet. Only three papers bothered to print the news the next morning. (Official U.S. Air Force photo)

MASS PRODUCTION

Middle-class Americans, as they self-consciously greeted the twentieth century, congratulated themselves upon the enormous technical achievements that had advanced the United States to a position of preeminence in the world. The steel furnaces of Pittsburgh outproduced those of England and Germany and functioned with such efficiency and low cost that Carnegie could have sold steel rails at a profit in Birmingham, England. New manufacturing marvels of every sort were giving Americans the highest average level of living in the world's history.

In the factories, the new era meant acceleration of the introduction of labor-saving machinery. There was, for example, a bottle-making machine patented in 1903 that virtually eliminated the hand blowing of glass bottles, and another that ended manual production of window glass. The invention of a rotating kiln in 1899 made possible the cheap, standardized production of Portland cement at about the time a demand for paved highways was gaining momentum. A shift toward electric power was already well advanced. The first 5,000-horsepower alternating-current generator had been installed at Niagara Falls in 1895; within a few years steam generators of 100,000 horsepower

The Ford Assembly Line
In August 1913, at the main Ford plant in the Detroit suburb of Highland Park, it took twelve and one-half man-hours of labor to assemble every Model T chassis. Then the world's first moving assembly line for automobiles was installed; instead of the workers moving to the stationary work, the moving work came to the workers. Within six months, each chassis was being assembled in only one hour and thirty-three minutes. This picture, taken in 1914, shows a portion of the final assembly line where the radiator and the wheels were placed on the Model T chassis. At this time the company employed about 12,000 men in making cars, and another 1,000 men in making better tools to use in making cars—a fact that shows how the technical revolution in modern industry had been institutionalized and made continuous. (Ford Motor Company)

were commonplace. Electricity was entering the home, but even more important, it was becoming a great new source of efficient industrial motive power. In 1899 it ran only 5 percent of the machinery; by 1919, 55 percent; by 1925, 73 percent. Large-scale electric power also made possible electrolytic processes in the rapidly developing heavy chemical industry.

In the automobile and other industries, new principles of scientific management found spectacular application. Scientific management began with the work of an engineer, Frederick Winslow Taylor, who helped revolutionize the machine-tool industry with carbon steel high-speed cutting edges. As soon as Taylor learned how to manufacture tools that could cut efficiently while running white hot, he began to insist that machinists operate their lathes at correspondingly fast speeds. Taylor was beginning to apply the same sort of scientific techniques to management as to machinery. At first he looked upon workmen much as he did at machines. Fewer and fewer men could perform simpler tasks at infinitely greater speed; if not, Taylor would discard them as unhesitatingly as he had discarded the poorer cutting steel.

The new system, "Taylorism," meant less need for skills among workmen and more monotonous tasks for them. At first organized labor rebelled, and won at least a minor victory when it persuaded Congress in 1915 to forbid the introduction of efficiency systems into government arsenals or navy yards. But Taylor and his followers regarded themselves as scientific seekers after higher production and thus a higher living standard. He talked of the greatest good for the greatest number, including the workers. Indeed, if Taylorism were used to eliminate the intolerable inefficiencies in many industries, it could mean not only lower prices for consumers but also higher wages for employees. By the 1920s some unions recognized this and were cooperative.

American industrialists, usually ready to try new techniques, increasingly undertook Taylor "scientific management" studies of workers' motions. They also brought scientists and engineers into their plants to engage in research for new tools and products. A few years earlier any industrialist who established a laboratory would have been looked upon as a crackpot. Now laboratories became accepted, partly because of the phenomenal success of some of the pioneering ones. There was, as every schoolboy could proudly cite, the industrial laboratory of Thomas A. Edison at Menlo Park, New Jersey, out of which had come the incandescent lamp, the phonograph, the motion picture, and scores of other devices. By 1913 Bell Telephone, Du Pont, General Electric, Eastman Kodak, and about fifty other companies had established laboratories with budgets totaling hundreds of thousands of dollars per year.

Out of these new methods and machines came mass production. It required the technology, raw materials, transportation, and markets that the United States could supply in the twentieth century. Precision manufacturing made possible interchangeability of parts even in assembling a machine as complicated as the automobile. Ford began with stationary assembly, earlier used in manufacturing guns, clocks, and the like, then gradually changed by 1914 to the moving assembly line. This revolutionary technique cut the time for assembling a chassis from twelve and a half hours to an hour and a half. While Ford raised the wages and lowered the hours of his workers, he cut the base price of his Model T car from $950 to $290. Other industrialists, following his example, soon took over the assembly line and mass production for their plants also.

By 1914 American manufacturers were producing 76 percent more goods than in 1899. They were doing so with only 36 percent more workers and 13 percent more establishments. The greater output of goods reflected the rising living standards and the growth of population at home as well as the growth of the foreign market.

SOCIAL AND CULTURAL ADVANCES

In other ways, too, the United States took giant strides into the twentieth century. Medical advances helped bring about marked improvement in public health. The Caribbean adventures of the United States led to great discoveries in tropical medicine. In 1900 Dr. Walter Reed and his associates proved conclusively the hypothesis of a Cuban doctor that a striped variety of mosquito transmitted yellow fever. During the digging of the Panama Canal (1904–1914), Major William C. Gorgas applied the new knowledge so thoroughly that not one case of yellow fever originated there, and malaria was virtually eradicated. In Puerto Rico, Major Bailey K. Ashford discovered that the cause of the widespread anemia was hookworm and developed an inexpensive cure.

All this knowledge was valuable in the southern United States. In 1909 Rockefeller gave $1 million for the eradication of hookworm in the South, where almost 60 percent of the schoolchildren had some infestation. With chemicals and vaccines, some of which were important European developments, the nation made encouraging progress in combating venereal diseases, typhus, typhoid, and diphtheria. Sanitariums and a national association successfully combated tuberculosis. Campaigns against mosquitoes and flies, improvements in sanitation, the inspection of milk, and, beginning in 1908, the chlorination of water supplies reflected the new vigor of the state and municipal boards of health. To cap the entire program, the old marine hospital service was expanded in 1902, and in 1912 became the United States Public Health Service. The death rate dropped from 17 per thousand in 1900 to 13.2 in 1920; life expectancy increased from 49 years in 1901 to 56 in 1920.

The number of public high schools nearly doubled between 1900 and 1914; the number of students increased two and a half times. In higher education, enrollment more than doubled (to 216,493), while professional and graduate schools were greatly strengthened. In many fields, American universities at last rivaled those of Europe. Nevertheless, much remained to be accomplished in education. In 1900 the average child in elementary school attended a one-room school about half the time during a 143-day school year, to be taught by rote by an untrained young woman who received $38 per month. By 1914, he might attend 86 days out of 158, and be taught rather better by a woman receiving $66. American children went to school an average of only 6.16 years.

In increasing numbers people purchased the new popular newspapers, sending their circulation soaring, making them also big business. Several newspaper chains developed; the most powerful, that of William Randolph Hearst, by 1914 already numbered nine newspapers and two magazines. Most of the papers used their new wealth for greatly improved reporting, sprightly features and cartoons, and increased pictures. As papers drew more of their news from the Associated Press and the new United Press, founded in 1907, they became more standardized.

Before 1898 few American novels had sold 100,000 copies; by 1901 a number were doing

The Duryea Car
J. Frank Duryea sits at the tiller of his automobile after winning the first motor vehicle race in America in 1895. With him is one of his umpires. (Motor Vehicle Manufacturers Association of the United States, Inc.)

so. Edwin Westcott's homespun *David Harum* (1898) eventually sold more than a million copies, and two historical novels by the American Winston Churchill, *Richard Carvel* and *The Crisis*, 420,000 and 320,000 respectively. By 1904 the craze for historical fiction gave way to a vogue for the adventure stories of Jack London and Rex Beach, the sentimentalism of Kate Douglas Wiggin and Alice Hegan Rice, and the shrewd portrayal of American life, whether middle class or genteel, of Booth Tarkington and Edith Wharton. Popular fiction was for the most part American in theme, and some of it became progressive in overtone. London lost much of his audience when he turned from adventure to socialism, but Churchill kept his when he attacked the railroads in *Mr. Crewe's Career* (1908). Tarkington's first best seller, *The Gentleman from Indiana* (1899) portrayed an idealistic small-town editor, almost the progressive prototype.

The literary pioneers of the period, the so-called naturalists, drew for inspiration upon the French writer Emile Zola and European literary movements, but presented American realities harshly, in the spirit of rural and urban revolt. Theodore Dreiser's blunt, powerful *Sister Carrie* (1900) dealt so frankly with sex that it was suppressed by its publisher; it was not until 1911 when the public attitude had changed that his next novel appeared. Then in *The Financier* (1912) and *The Titan* (1914) he portrayed a ruthless Chicagoan who destroyed his business competitors. Frank Norris also wrote of unscrupulous businessmen, California railroad barons in *The Octopus* (1901) and Chicago grain speculators in *The Pit* (1903).

The new poets either extolled the common man or wrote about him with realism. Carl Sandburg, in free verse, applied the themes of Whitman to Chicago; Vachel Lindsay wrote chants like *The Congo*, full of mysticism and rhythm. In Chicago, Harriet Monroe founded *Poetry* magazine in 1912. In New England, Edwin Arlington Robinson seemed to represent a fading afterglow of Puritanism and transcendentalism; his verses in the *Outlook* received the praises of President Roosevelt. Robert Frost, writing in a quiet, almost vernacular way about the rural folk and nature of New England, failed at first to find an audience. In 1915 he returned from England, where he had published two books, to take his place as an accepted poet. Closer to European movements than American, Ezra Pound, an expatriate from Idaho, proclaimed the techniques of the Imagists. Among them were Amy Lowell of Boston and later T. S. Eliot of St. Louis, who in 1914 moved permanently to London. The Imagists discarded rhyme from their work as an obstacle in the way of creating a pure image of everyday life.

A similar ferment stirred other branches of the arts. In 1908 a group of eight young American painters—including John Sloan, George Luks, and George W. Bellows—rebelled against conventional academicians and painted urban life as Dreiser wrote about it. Conservatives dismissed these realists as the "Ash Can School," but were even more shocked by the Armory Show of 1913 which exhibited the American moderns and brought French Post-Impressionism to America. Modernistic architecture began with the low-lying "prairie houses" of Frank Lloyd Wright, whose designs influenced Europe more than the United States until the late 1920s. Well-to-do Americans did not accept Wright but reverted to graceful colonial styles for their homes.

The expanding theatrical business was dominated by a syndicate which nationally booked romantic plays and popular vaudeville. It was the heyday of the matinee idol. Experimental realism began, but only in the realm of little-theater groups like the Provincetown Players and in the "47 Workshop" of Professor George P. Baker of Harvard. These could hardly appeal to wide audiences. The real threat to the great theatrical producers like David Belasco and the mediocre playwrights who served them came from the motion picture. At first the idea of movies competing with the stage was ludicrous. The first film telling a continuous story was a melodrama, *The Great Train Robbery*, produced in 1903. By 1905 stores were being converted into "nickelodeons," which still seemed no threat to the stage, but by 1915 the lengthy, impressive feature film had arrived with *The Birth of a Nation*. This motion picture was as significant in marking the coming of age of a new art form as it was deplorable in its glorification of the Ku Klux Klan. A motion-picture monopoly movement began in 1909 and was smashed by the government in 1914, but the cinema was becoming a multimillion-dollar industry, and movies were being shown in large and impressive theaters.

HIGH NOON OF MONOPOLY

Twentieth-century industrialism brought evil as well as good. Populists, socialists, and the relative few who had followed reform theoreticians like the single-taxer Henry George and the utopian Bellamy no longer were alone in proclaiming that the American economic system was in need of reform. Even the thoroughly conservative Judge Peter S. Grosscup, who had issued the injunction to help break the Pullman strike, proclaimed in 1905 that the modern corporation was destroying the opportunity for the individual to participate in the proprietorship of the country. This was the recurring complaint of the middle class.

Monopolies could lead to higher prices and higher profits, which were often the basic reasons for the creation of combinations. (Their promoters argued the reverse, that they led to greater efficiency, lower prices, and a higher living standard.) Furthermore, the monopolists could use their great economic strength to wield proportionately great political power.

Despite all the agitation against "trusts," American industry moved toward greater consolidation and monopoly. From 1887 to 1897 there had been only 86 industrial combinations, and the capitalization of all of these combined had been less than $1.5 billion. By 1904 there were 318 so-called trusts with a capitalization of over $7 billion. These combinations included basic industries like copper, oil, and steel, and industries directly affecting the consumer like sugar and tobacco. Six financial groups controlled 95 percent of the nation's railway mileage. In the highly competitive steel industry, twenty-one significant mergers between 1898 and 1901 prepared the way for a large-scale struggle between Carnegie and Morgan. When Carnegie announced plans for plants that might be ruinous to Morgan and his associates, they chose to buy him out at his own inflated figure of $447 million and they then established the nation's first billion-dollar corporation, United States Steel. It was able to set standard prices for steel everywhere in the United States—prices from which none of the smaller steel companies dared to deviate.

Whatever pride Americans might have felt over the emergence of these industrial giants was mingled with serious misgivings. The United States Industrial Commission reported in 1902: "In most cases the combination has exerted an appreciable power over prices, and in practically all cases it has increased the margin between raw materials and finished products. Since there is reason to believe that the cost of production over a period of years has lessened, the conclusion is inevitable that the combinations have been able to increase their profits." Whether or not monopolies were to blame, prices were rising so rapidly between 1897 and 1913 that the cost of living went up about 35 percent.

THE RICH AND THE POOR

For millions of Americans the economic system meant personal poverty and misery. There was a vast disparity between the incomes of the wealthy few and those of the poor multitudes. One percent of the families owned nearly seven-eighths of the wealth; seven-eighths of the families owned only one-eighth of the wealth. While a fifth of the families were comfortable or even rich, four-fifths lived precariously. A careful estimate in 1904 indicated that about one-eighth of the people, or a total of 10 million, lived in poverty.

At the top, Carnegie had earned an estimated $23 million from his steel company alone in the one year 1900. It had paid him an average of $10 million a year during the previous five years. On none of this did he have to pay a cent of income tax. Carnegie lived comparatively modestly and devoted his millions to worthy causes, but many of the very rich created sensational headlines through their ostentatious living. The Vanderbilts, like a clan of feudal barons, maintained, in addition to their many country estates, seven mansions in seven blocks on Fifth Avenue in New York City.

These wealthy few often spent incredible sums on parties, accounts of which fascinated but also angered readers of yellow journals. The most notorious was the ball upon which Mrs. Martin Bradley spent $250,000; it created such a furor that she and her husband fled to exile in England. A less exceptional dinner, served on gold plates at the old Waldorf-Astoria in 1899, cost $10,000 for forty people, or $250 apiece. At this time, $250 was six months' wages for the average workingman. In part the millionaires were able to get their huge in-

Child Labor and Child Luxury

In the early 1900s, "breaker boys" worked long hours picking slate from coal at Pennsylvania mines. Often the coal dust was so thick that the boys could hardly be seen. (Photograph by Lewis Hine, International Museum of Photography, George Eastman House, Rochester, N. Y.) At the same time, the children of the rich enjoyed everything that money could buy. Here the children of the American multimillionaire George Jay Gould ride the streets of Paris in "voiturettes," French-made miniature electric automobiles. (Culver Pictures)

comes because of the low cost of labor in their factories, and to afford their huge estates and townhouses because of the low cost of servants. Middle-class families also benefited from cheap labor. While they did not enjoy the great variety of household appliances of later generations, they were able with the aid of servants to maintain large homes.

Servants at least were entitled to meals and garret rooms. Working girls could not count upon even these. One woman in five worked, and often for wages as low as $6 or $8 per week. Unless a girl lived at home, it was almost impossible for her to exist upon these wages. The popular magazine writer O. Henry (William Sidney Porter) was reflecting the widespread indignation of contemporary Americans when he described in his short stories how strong the temptation was for these nearly starving girls to succumb to predatory men. Advocates of a minimum wage law to protect women created a sensation in Chicago by bringing several women to a hearing to testify that low pay and poverty had driven them to prostitution. Nevertheless, the Illinois legislature failed to enact the desired law.

Child labor, which had always existed in the United States, was becoming an increasingly serious problem by the early 1900s. At least 1.7 million children under sixteen were employed in factories and fields. Ten percent of the girls between ten and fifteen, and 20 percent of the boys, were gainfully employed. At least thirty-eight states had laws to protect chil-

dren, but these typically applied only to children employed in factories, and set a minimum age of twelve years and a maximum workday of ten hours. Sixty percent of the child workers were employed in agriculture, which could mean a twelve-hour day picking or hoeing in the fields. In the cotton mills of the South, children working at the looms all night were kept awake by having cold water thrown in their faces. In canneries, little girls cut fruits and vegetables sixteen hours a day. Some children worked at dangerous machines without safety devices. As these young workers became exhausted at the end of a long day, or night, they might become careless as they leaned over a loom to retie broken threads, have their hair caught in machinery, and be scalped as it suddenly started up again.

Industrial accidents were commonplace. For most laborers, whether children, women, or men, working conditions were far from ideal. Many women labored in dark, cold, dirty factories or sweatshops without restrooms or fire escapes. For men, working conditions were even worse. As early as 1877 Massachusetts had required safety devices on elevators and machinery; some states also required mine inspection. But there was little effective enforcement of the laws, if indeed personnel for enforcement existed. In American factories and mines, and on the railroads, the accident rate was higher than in any other industrial nation in the world. As late as 1907 an average of twelve railroad men a week were killed. In fac-

---

"The Steerage" by Alfred Stieglitz
When Stieglitz (1864–1946), crossing the Atlantic in 1907, took this photograph of immigrants crowded in the cheapest quarters, his intent was not documentary, nor was his object to publicize the misery of these passengers. Rather, he was trying to utilize photography as a form of creative expression—an art in itself rather than an imitation of other arts. Picasso remarked of "The Steerage," "This is exactly what I have been trying to say in paint."

Stieglitz demonstrated the way in which an art form could take advantage of technical advances (in this instance, photographic emulsions) by taking unparalleled night photographs and capturing the feeling of rainstorms and snow. He also helped change American taste in painting. Between 1905 and 1917 at his New York gallery he displayed, in addition to photographic art, the paintings of French impressionists and their successors, at that time unknown in the United States, from Cézanne through Picasso. He became associated with an equally advanced group of American artists, including John Marin, Max Weber—and Georgia O'Keeffe, whom he married. (Collection Museum of Modern Art)

tories, not much had been done to prevent occupational diseases such as phosphorus and lead poisoning.

Nor was there economic incentive for employers to improve working conditions. Under the common law, if an accident was due, even in part, to the negligence of an employee himself or a fellow employee, the employer bore no responsibility. Even if the employer was liable under the common law, the courts were slow, and often too expensive for the maimed worker or his widow. Until 1911 there were almost no state workmen's compensation laws.

Cheap labor was one of the reasons for high profits; unrestricted immigration was one of the reasons for cheap labor. At the same time that the big industrialists fought against a lowering of the tariff bars, they welcomed and even recruited the low-paid workers of Europe. While the flow of the "old immigrants" from northern and western Europe continued, a new flood, comprising about 72 percent of the total immigration between 1900 and 1910, poured in from southern and eastern Europe. For the most part they were Italians, Slavs, and Jews. In the single year 1905, over 1.2 million arrived. In most big cities of the North, immigrants and their children outnumbered the native-born. Bewildered at being thrust into an alien culture, living under conditions far below the level of native Americans (except Negroes), they filled most of the backbreaking unskilled jobs in the new heavy industries, on the railroads, and around the cities. The Jews, many of whom brought their skill with the needle, went into the garment trade, but under just as wretched circumstances.

The American Federation of Labor (whose president, Samuel Gompers, was himself an immigrant) fought to cut off this flood of cheap, unskilled foreign labor, which was said to keep wages down and hamper unionization. Many Americans, both conservative and progressive, were susceptible to the popular dogma of Anglo-Saxon superiority and joined in the anti-immigration movement. They feared the high birth rate among immigrants as compared with the low birth rate among natives in the higher income groups; Theodore Roosevelt warned darkly against "race suicide." They blamed the squalor of the slums and the power of the political bosses largely upon the immigrants, and felt that through restriction could come improvement. In 1907 they succeeded in stopping the immigration of Japanese to the agricultural lands of the Pacific Coast through the "gentleman's agreement" that Roosevelt negotiated with the Japanese government. A series of restrictive laws prohibited various undesirables, ranging from ex-convicts to alcoholics, from entering the United States. In 1917, over the veto of President Wilson, Congress passed a law setting up a literacy test as a means of reducing the number of immigrants.

For all those, immigrants or natives, who were crowded into city tenements, life was far from enviable. Jacob Riis, the crusading journalist, thought that by 1900 the worst of the New York slums were gone. In their place were a scattering of parks and playgrounds; in some of the worst remaining areas there were privately financed settlement houses to aid the poor. Nevertheless, for millions of city dwellers, housing was barely tolerable. In New York City, two-thirds of the 3.5 million people lived in tenement houses. A typical tenement had direct light and air in only four rooms of the fourteen on each floor.

Selected Readings

The New Great Power

E. R. May, *Imperial Democracy: The Emergence of America as a Great Power* (1961); Walter LaFeber, *The New Empire: An Interpretation of American Expansion, 1860–1898** (1963); J. A. S. Grenville and G. B. Young, *Politics, Strategy, and American Diplomacy: Studies in Foreign Policy, 1873–1917* (1966); Dexter Perkins, *The Monroe Doctrine, 1867–1907* (1937).

Imperialist Stirrings

A. F. Tyler, *The Foreign Policy of James G. Blaine* (1927); D. M. Pletcher, *The Awkward Years: American Foreign Relations Under Garfield and Arthur* (1962); G. R. Dulebohn, *Principles of Foreign Policy Under the Cleveland Administration* (1941); S. K. Stevens, *American Expansion in Hawaii, 1842–1898* (1945); W. E. Russ, Jr., *The Hawaiian Revolution* (1959) and *The Hawaiian Republic* (1961); G. H. Ryden, *Foreign Policy of the United States in Relation to Samoa* (1933).

War with Spain
J. W. Pratt, *Expansionists of 1898** (1936); Walter Millis, *The Martial Spirit** (1931); Frank Freidel, *The Splendid Little War* (1958), a pictorial history; F. E. Chadwick, *The Relations of the United States and Spain: The Spanish-American War* (2 vols., 1911); Orestes Ferrara, *The Last Spanish War* (1937), a Spanish view; Theodore Roosevelt, *The Rough Riders* (1899).

The Colonies
J. W. Pratt, *America's Colonial Experiment* (1950); G. A. Grunder and W. E. Livezey, *The Philippines and the United States* (1951); J. F. Guggenheim, *The United States and Cuba* (1934).

The Open Door
Tyler Dennett, *John Hay, from Poetry to Politics* (1933); C. S. Campbell, Jr., *Special Business Interests and the Open Door Policy* (1951) and *Anglo-American Understanding, 1898–1903* (1957); L. M. Gelber, *The Rise of Anglo-American Friendship* (1938).

The Army and the Navy
P. C. Jessup, *Elihu Root* (2 vols., 1938); J. D. Hittle, *The Military Staff* (1949); Harold and Margaret Sprout, *The Rise of American Naval Power, 1776–1918** (1939); R. S. West, Jr., *Admirals of the American Empire* (1948); W. R. Herrick, *The American Naval Revolution* (1966); G. A. Cosmas, *An Army for Empire: The United States Army in the Spanish-American War* (1972).

Automobiles and Airplanes
J. B. Rae, *The American Automobile* (1965); D. L. Cohn, *Combustion on Wheels* (1944); Allan Nevins and F. E. Hill, *Ford: The Times, the Man, the Company* (1954); Douglas Rolfe, *Airplanes of the World from Pusher to Jet, 1490–1954* (1955); C. H. Gibbs-Smith, *The Aeroplane: An Historical Survey* (1960) and *The Invention of the Aeroplane* (1965).

Technology
Siegfried Giedion, *Mechanization Takes Command* (1948); Samuel Haber, *Efficiency and Uplift: Scientific Management in the Progressive Era, 1890–1920* (1964); M. J. Nadworny, *Scientific Management and the Unions, 1900–1932* (1955); H. G. J. Aitken, *Taylorism at Watertown Arsenal* (1960); Kendall Birr, *Pioneering in Industrial Research: The Story of the General Electric Research Laboratory* (1957).

Society and Culture
Mark Sullivan, *Our Times* (6 vols., 1926–1935); F. L. Allen, *The Big Change** (1952); H. F. May, *The End of American Innocence* (1959); Van Wyck Brooks, *The Confident Years: 1885–1915* (1952); W. L. O'Neill, *Divorce in the Progressive Era* (1968); Albert Rees, *Real Wages in Manufacturing, 1890–1914* (1961).

*Titles available in paperback.

The Progressive Movement

Twenty-one

In the opening years of the twentieth century a new political impulse — which came to be known as "progressivism" — aroused a large number of Americans. Those who thought of themselves as "progressives" saw with great concern the nation's rapid technological development and growing involvement in international affairs. They wanted to make sure that the United States, as an industrial giant and a world power, held on to the democratic ideals that it had inherited from the past.

There were many wrongs to be righted, and the progressives differed among themselves in both their aims and their methods. To some, the main evil was monopoly; to others, corruption in city government; to still others, the unequal status of women. And so it went. Various groups combined and cooperated, or they divided and worked against one another, on certain issues. For example, some favored and others opposed imperialism. Thus progressivism may be considered as an aggregate of causes rather than a single movement. Still, most progressives had in common the following convictions: (1) "the people" ought to have much more influence in government, and the "special interests" much less, and (2) government ought to be stronger, more active, and more efficient in serving the public welfare.

In certain respects, progressivism was a continuation of Populism. Progressives advocated some (though not all) of the reforms that the Populists had proposed, and some of the former Populists joined the progressive movement. But progressivism and Populism differed in important respects. The People's party members had been mostly distressed farmers of the Southern and the Great Plains and Rocky Mountain states. The progressive ranks included men and women from all parts of the country, but especially from the Northeast and the Midwest, and prominent among the progressives were persons of the urban middle class. The progressives had a broader concept of both "the people" and the public welfare than the Populists had had.

Suffragettes in Action
In the early 1900s, many young women became political activists seeking the right to vote, but their efforts were not realized until 1920 when the Nineteenth Amendment was passed. (Culver Pictures)

A third party took the name "Progressive," but the movement was too broad to be confined by party lines. Active in it were both Republicans and Democrats, though the Republicans were the more numerous. For most of them, regardless of party, the path of reform led from the city hall to the state capitol to the chambers of Congress and the White House. Many conspicuous evils of the time, incapable of cure by local or state authorities, required action by the federal government. Prominent figures of both major parties brought progressivism into national politics. Among the leading Republicans were Robert M. La Follette, Theodore Roosevelt, and William Howard Taft; among the Democrats, William Jennings Bryan and Woodrow Wilson. From 1901 to 1916, politics and government largely reflected the opinions and ambitions of these men—especially Roosevelt and Wilson—and their respective followings.

Local and State Beginnings

Progressivism in some of its phases got its start in the cities. Here it took two main forms: a movement for "social justice" and another for governmental reform. The proponents of governmental reform soon directed their attention also to the evils of statewide politics.

THE URBAN PROGRESSIVE

Progressive leaders were largely members of the urban middle class and were to a remarkable extent college-educated and self-employed professional men or small businessmen, of native-born Protestant background. For the most part they were about forty years old, financially secure civic leaders who had earlier been McKinley Republicans.

Following these leaders was a middle class, like them still clinging to the traditional agrarian values, but caught up in the social whirlpool of the new industrial age. The older segment of the middle class—the independent professional men and businessmen from which such a high proportion of progressive leaders came—somewhat more than doubled between 1870 and 1910. This meant it grew as rapidly as the population as a whole, which increased about two and a third times. The working class (including farm laborers) trebled; farmers and farm tenants doubled. But there was another group, a new middle class of white-collar workers—the clerks, sales people, and technicians who worked for corporations or service enterprises. This group increased almost eight times, from 756,000 to 5,609,000 people, thus reaching a number almost double the size of the older middle class.

While members of this new white-collar class did not provide leadership for the progressive movement, they did help to provide it with voting strength. Political action was their only outlet for economic protest, since they did not belong to unions or trade associations. Often it was they, on their fixed salaries, who were worst caught by rising prices. And basically, like the older middle class, they were urbanites who still expressed the emotions of their rural backgrounds. These two groups, the white-collar class and the older middle class, combined to form the respectable element of the towns and cities who, along with many of the more successful farmers and some of the laborers, were ready to accept the new progressive creed.

Middle-class people were frightened by urban political bosses, not only because of their corrupt ties with the industrial moguls but also because of their hold over the ignorant laboring masses (often largely immigrants) of the cities. Moreover, these middle-class people had some fear of the new rising labor unions. Populist farmers had shared these suspicions of the moguls and the masses. One of the Populist papers had said the purpose of the party was to serve as a "bulwark against the anarchy of the upper and lower scums of society." Progressives continued the same prejudices.

Theodore Roosevelt in his *Autobiography* has stated clearly the reasoning that led him, a conservative young plutocrat of the upper middle-class gentry, to enter politics. The men

Roosevelt knew best, cultivated clubmen, warned him that politics was a cheap affair of saloon keepers and horsecar conductors, which gentlemen should shun. "I answered," Roosevelt wrote, "that if this were so it merely meant that the people I knew did not belong to the governing class, and that the other people did—and that I intended to be one of the governing class."

Many progressives were converted to the cause by the writings of the so-called muckrakers. The muckrakers were the many journalists who dramatized the need for reform by writing exposés of the unsavory in business and government. They began to attract attention toward the end of 1902 and were at their peak of popularity in 1906. There long had been a literature of exposure, from the *Harper's Weekly* crusade against the Tweed Ring through Henry Demarest Lloyd's denunciation of Standard Oil in *Wealth Against Commonwealth* (1894). What was new was the scale of the revelations and the rapid attraction of a wide audience. Muckraking began almost by accident in about ten of the new popular magazines, selling for 10 or 15 cents, which were then building mass circulation. *McClure's*, already a magazine of broad appeal, began publishing Ida Tarbell's series on Standard Oil. The publisher, S. S. McClure, sent a new editor, Lincoln Steffens, out to see the country first-hand; this experience led Steffens to begin a series on municipal corruption. At the same time, Ray Stannard Baker contributed an article denouncing a union for wrongdoing during a coal strike.

At the height of the muckraking movement, ten journals with a combined circulation of about 3 million were devoting considerable space to the literature of exposure. In addition, some books like Upton Sinclair's *Jungle* (1906), an exposure of the meat-packing industry, sold over 100,000 copies. Many newspapers, most notably the New York *World* and the Kansas City *Star,* printed articles by muckrakers. It was exciting for a while, but by 1912 it was over. This was due partly to the hostility of business, which at times withheld credit and advertising from the muckraking magazines.

SOCIAL JUSTICE

The social-justice movement was already well advanced by the turn of the century. It had its roots in European, especially English, reform movements. Almost every prominent English reformer visited the United States, and conversely almost every American progressive leader fell under the influence of the British. Young Jane Addams had worked at the newly established Toynbee Hall in the Limehouse section of London; in 1889 she returned to the United States to establish Hull House, a slum relief center, in Chicago. Settlement houses, slum clearance agitation, and a great variety of other English reforms quickly had their counterpart in the United States.

The Salvation Army, which had recently come to the United States from England, by 1900 boasted a corps of 3,000 officers and 20,000 privates. It offered aid as well as religion to the dregs of the cities. So did ministers, priests, and rabbis who by the nineties were working in the slums. These men were united in their determination to improve the existence of the miserable people around them in addition to saving their souls. "One could hear human virtue cracking and crushing all around," Walter Rauschenbusch wrote of Hell's Kitchen (a slum section) in New York City. To him the way of salvation for these human souls seemed to be a Christian reform of the social and economic system. Thus many an American Protestant minister arrived at the "social gospel." Catholics like Father John Augustine Ryan joined in the fight for social justice under the authority they found in Pope Leo XIII's encyclical *Rerum Novarum.* This declared that "a smaller number of very rich men have been able to lay upon the masses of the poor a yoke little better than slavery itself. . . . No practical solution of this question will ever be found without the assistance of religion and the church."

Close behind the ministry were middle-class and upper-class women. In the 1890s many of them had seemed restless and discontented, reading more widely than their husbands or brothers, joining literary circles and women's clubs. By the early 1900s these clubs were beginning to display a remarkable growth. The General Federation of Women's clubs, from a membership of 50,000 in 1898, grew to over 1 million by 1914. In the new era, the members of the clubs were quick to take up the fight for the ballot and legal equality for themselves, and for a wide array of reforms on behalf of children and working women.

Another small but mighty social-justice group consisted of those who gathered careful

Chicago's "Ghetto": Jefferson and 12th Streets   1906
*Typical of the residents in this area were a Russian man and his wife who earned
$2 a day finishing coats. Their household was thus described: "Three small
children and the grandmother constitute the family, the latter dying of a cancer
without medical attendance or nursing. Man has been 18 years in this country and
owns a populous frame tenement house. He also owns the wretched rear cottage, on
the second floor of which his family lives. His work room contains a bed, an
upright piano, dining table, sewing machine and the couch on which his mother
lies dying. The filth and smell are intolerable. He does only the finest custom work
and was making a valuable coat. Most of the year he has been making police
uniforms." (Top left, Courtesy Chicago Historical Society)*

Life in an Immigrant Slum
*An Italian mother holds her baby in what appears to be a basement room in a New
York City tenement. This photograph was taken around 1900 by the Danish
immigrant, newspaperman, and crusader for housing reform, Jacob A. Riis.
(Bottom left, The Jacob A. Riis Collection, Museum of the City of New York)*

---

data and statistics on the need for reform. They
were often social-welfare workers who prepared articles for *Survey* magazine, or they
were frustrated crusaders working for federal
or state agencies. In many states before 1900
there were bureaus of labor which compiled
great quantities of data on deplorable working
and living conditions.

MUNICIPAL REFORM

The Shame of the Cities was the title Lincoln
Steffens gave to his notable series of exposés
which first appeared in *McClure's*, and shame
was what civic-minded progressives felt. They
tried to wrest control of their city governments
away from the machines, reorganize the governments scientifically, and use them as instruments of economic and social reform.

Arrayed in opposition were the bosses,
and behind them those interests so abhorrent
to the progressives, the saloons, brothels, and
various businesses that could gain more from
the bosses than from clean government. Allied
with the bosses were some newspapers, which
ridiculed the progressives as either kill-joys or
scoundrels. Finally, there was the great constituency of city working people, mostly of immigrant origins. To them the bosses were friends
who could be counted upon to help them when
they violated the law in some minor way, or
were in need of jobs or food. Progressives, on
the other hand, seemed to be do-gooders who
were trying to take away the saloon—the poor
man's club—and to deprive him of his amusements from prize fighting to Sunday baseball.

Many progressives, finding it difficult to
grasp the relationship between the bosses and
their constituents, saw the problem in simple
moral and legal terms. Bad government, they
thought, came from bad charters. Reformers
should seize the municipal governments and,
by remaking the charters, usher in the urban
millennium.

Municipal reform began in response to a
tragedy in Galveston, Texas, where the old,
ineffective government broke down in the
wake of a tidal wave. The citizens replaced it
with a commission of five, whose members
were jointly enacting ordinances and singly
running the main city departments by 1908. In
1907 Des Moines adopted the commission plan
with modifications to make it more democratic,
and other cities followed. Another variation
was the city-manager plan which placed a
trained expert, similar to the manager of a business, in charge of the city, and made him responsible to the commission or the mayor and
council. Staunton, Virginia, hired a city manager in 1908, and the new device attracted national attention when Dayton, Ohio, adopted it
in 1913 to speed rehabilitation from a serious
flood. By the end of the progressive era approximately 400 cities were operating under
commissions, and another 45 under city managers.

Whether through old or new city machinery, progressives fought to destroy economic
privilege on the municipal level. This meant
primarily trying to prevent the sale of streetcar
franchises, or to force exorbitantly high fares
downward. The most notable of the reform

mayors was Tom Johnson of Cleveland, who had invented the streetcar fare box. He was a "traction magnate" (a street-railway entrepreneur) converted to the ideas of Henry George. As mayor, Johnson fought to raise the ridiculously low assessments upon railroad and utility property, introduce city planning, and above all, lower streetcar fares to 3 cents. After his defeat and death, his brilliant aide, Newton D. Baker, was elected mayor and helped maintain Cleveland's position as the best-governed American city.

Many of the urban gains of progressivism were permanent, but in some cities, as soon as progressives relaxed, the old forces recaptured the city hall. In other municipalities, state control over city government made reform almost impossible. Cities derived all of their powers from the state, and many state legislatures granted new charters only reluctantly or controlled a large city within the state through special legislation. In the state of New York, which functioned this way, the reform mayor of Schenectady complained: "Whenever we try to do anything, we run up against the charter. It is an oak charter, fixed and immovable." Consequently, a municipal home-rule movement spread, to try to obtain state laws allowing cities to write their own charters. Much of the difficulty with state legislatures was even more serious. Many a reformer, like Johnson in Cleveland, or Joseph W. Folk in St. Louis, found himself helpless in the cities because the trail of corruption led back to the legislature.

IN THE STATEHOUSE

Hiram Johnson in California, Folk in Missouri, and other progressives moved on from cities, where they had been crusading district attorneys, to become progressive governors. Only by taking this step could Folk, for example, break the bosses. Johnson's avowed purpose as governor of California was to end the political hold of the Southern Pacific Railroad upon the state.

At the state level, progressives enacted a wide array of legislation to increase the power of crusading governors, give the people more direct control over the government, and decrease the functions of legislators. These ill-paid, relatively inconspicuous men were being exposed by muckrakers as the villains in many

states. William Allen White in *McClure's*, December 1905, wrote of Missouri: "The legislature met biennially, and enacted such laws as the corporations paid for, and such others as were necessary to fool the people, and only such laws were enforced as party expediency demanded." This view of the legislatures led progressives to circumscribe and circumvent them in almost every conceivable way. The most important of the devices, the initiative and the referendum, were first enacted in Oregon in 1902 as a result of the quiet but persistent advocacy of the secretary of several voters' organizations, William S. U'Ren. The initiative enabled voters to short-circuit the legislature and vote upon measures at general elections; the referendum forced the return of laws from the legislature to the electorate. By 1918 twenty states had adopted these schemes.

Progressives also tried to obtain better officials. They tried to eliminate machine choice of candidates through the direct primary, first instituted in Mississippi in 1902 and adopted in some form by every state by 1915. Unfortunately, machines often dominated the primaries.

One device for improving officials was the recall, which made possible their removal at a special election to be called after sufficient numbers of the electorate had signed petitions. This became a national issue when President Taft vetoed a bill admitting Arizona as a state because its constitution authorized recall of judges. Horrified conservatives approved of the veto, but soon after Arizona entered the Union without the offensive provision, the state's voters restored it.

Undoubtedly all these devices did bring about a greater degree of democratization. Progressives used them to obtain control of states, and then eradicated corruption and passed reform legislation. Robert M. La Follette in Wisconsin obtained firm regulation of railroads, compensation for workmen injured in industrial accidents, and graduated taxation of inheritances. Charles Evans Hughes in New York obtained a commission to regulate public utilities. In New Jersey, when Woodrow Wilson, fresh from the presidency of Princeton University, became governor in 1911, he obtained from the legislature a substantial array of measures to transform the state from the backward "mother of trusts" into a model of progressivism.

Until the 1940s, historians generally took progressives at their word and treated progressivism as a protest of "the people" against "special interests," as a broadly based campaign against abuses in both business and government, as a great popular surge toward the fuller realization of political, economic, and social democracy.

Then, in *The California Progressives* (1951), George Mowry described the California participants in the movement not as the mass of the people but as a comparatively small group of business- and professional men. According to Mowry, these men found themselves caught between big corporations and labor unions. They wanted to restore individual enterprise and their own social importance and self-esteem. Richard Hofstadter expanded this idea and applied it to progressives throughout the country in *The Age of Reform* (1955). Hofstadter saw them as middle-class people who, in the prosperous years of the progressive period, were suffering from "status anxiety" and responding to psychological rather than economic discontent.

Most historians accepted the Mowry-Hofstadter thesis, but some questioned it. Samuel P. Hays, in *The Response to Industrialism, 1885–1914* (1957) and in other writings, contended that the progressives were upper-class businessmen who desired to bring efficiency to government and order to economic life. J. Joseph Huthmacher disagreed, pointing out in an article (1962) that members of the working class, especially immigrants, pressed for a number of progressive reforms, such as workmen's compensation and wage and hour laws. The New Left historian Gabriel Kolko, however, went so far as to say, in *The Triumph of Conservatism* (1963), that the "progressive era" was really an "era of conservatism." True, a major aim was the regulation of business. "But the regulation itself was invariably controlled by the leaders of the regulated industry, and directed toward ends they deemed acceptable or desirable."

Dissenting from both the "status anxiety" and the "age of conservatism" views, David P. Thelen showed that, at least in Wisconsin, the progressive movement actually corresponded quite closely to the progressive rhetoric of the time. In *The New Citizenship: Origins of Progressivism in Wisconsin, 1885–1900* (1972) Thelen found a real clash between the "public interest" and "corporate privilege" in that state. The depression of the 1890s, he indicated, brought people of widely varying backgrounds together, as citizens and consumers, to try and make both business and government more responsible.

The foregoing and other writers used the term "progressive" to describe leaders as different as Theodore Roosevelt and Robert M. La Follette and to designate a great variety of demands for reform or change. Perhaps the phrase "progressive movement" (like "Jacksonian Democracy") was more confusing than helpful. "It is time to tear off the familiar label," Peter G. Filene suggested in 1970, "and, thus liberated from its prejudice, see the history between 1890 and 1920 for what it was—ambiguous, inconsistent, moved by agents and forces more complex than a [single, uniform] progressive movement."

Much of the sorely needed legislation came only late and after a hard struggle. New York, for example, adopted factory safety laws only when shocked into action by the Triangle Shirtwaist Factory fire (1911), which trapped and killed 148 persons, most of them young women, in New York City.

Progressive legislators in the states ran the risk that the Supreme Court would invalidate their handiwork. The Court made one great, although temporary, shift toward progressivism. This came in 1908 when Louis D. Brandeis argued in support of an Oregon law to limit women workers to a ten-hour day. He presented a brief in which he devoted only 2 of 104 pages to the legal precedents and the remainder to proofs that Oregon's police power was necessary to protect the health and general welfare of the mothers, and thus of all mankind. The Supreme Court accepted this argument and thus moved toward the "sociological jurisprudence" which Dean Roscoe Pound of the Harvard Law School had been developing. This, Pound explained, was intended to adjust "principles and doctrines to human conditions they are to govern rather than to assumed first principles."

Progressives seeking state reforms looked not only to the Supreme Court but also to Congress and the White House. Here obviously rested the ultimate power for the control of the many problems that crossed state lines. Reformers obtained from Congress in 1910 several laws to reinforce state legislation. The Webb-Kenyon Act, passed over Taft's veto, prohibited the interstate shipment of liquor into dry areas. The Mann Act outlawed the interstate transportation of "white slaves" and thus helped in the fight to break up prostitution syndicates, one of the main sources of underworld income.

At the state level, progressives fought to liberalize the United States Senate through the direct election of senators. State legislatures were occasionally open to bribery, and much too often they elected conservatives who did not represent the public choice. David Graham Phillips in his senatorial articles, "The Treason of the Senate," scourged the body as a rich men's club; a California senator replied that there were only ten millionaires in the Senate.

By 1902 the House of Representatives had already passed resolutions five times for a constitutional amendment for direct election of senators; each time the Senate blocked the amendment. Impatient progressives in various states provided in effect for direct election by means of preferential votes for senators; the legislatures were obligated to choose the candidate whom the voters preferred. By 1912 twenty-nine states had adopted these devices. In 1911 Governor Wilson of New Jersey gained renown by blocking the legislative election of a party boss. At the same time, in New York, Franklin D. Roosevelt, just twenty-nine, won his political spurs by leading legislative insurgents against Tammany's hand-picked candidate, a Buffalo traction magnate. That same year, the Senate ousted one of its members, Boss William E. Lorimer of Chicago, for vote-buying. In the wake of the public indignation that followed, the Senate in 1912 passed the Seventeenth Amendment, for the direct election of senators, and by 1913 the requisite number of states had ratified it. The new amendment did not startlingly modify the nature of the Senate, since most progressive states had already elected senators of a new mettle.

Neither did another progressive reform measure, the preferential presidential primary, have much consequence. This was begun in Oregon in 1910 and spread to twenty states by 1920, but it by no means eliminated the maneuvering in conventions. Its main effect was to provide a series of statewide popularity contests among leading candidates in the months before the convention.

WOMEN'S CAUSES

Women took an active part in many of the progressive reforms, such as those for the protection of female employees, who by 1910 included approximately 25 percent of all women over the age of fifteen. Women were especially important in the furthering of two causes that long antedated the progressive period but received new impetus from the reform spirit of the time. These two were temperance and woman suffrage.

Since 1874 the Woman's Christian Temperance Union, whose greatest leader was Frances E. Willard, had worked through schools and churches to arouse public opinion against strong drink. The Anti-Saloon League, containing both men and women, joined the crusade in 1893. For many years the cause

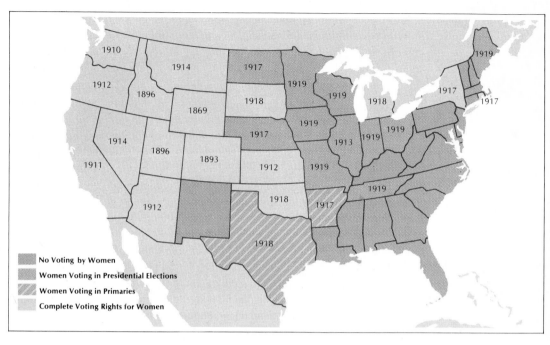

Woman Suffrage Before the Nineteenth Amendment

gained publicity from the one-woman campaign of Carry Nation, who took out after the saloons in her home state of Kansas with a hatchet.

Since 1880 Kansas had had an antiliquor law, but it was poorly enforced. The temperance crusaders undertook to get antiliquor legislation in other states and also to obtain a national prohibition amendment. By 1917 more than half of the states had banned liquor sales, and several others had permitted counties or municipalities to do so (through "local option"). In 1917 Congress approved an amendment prohibiting the manufacture, sale, or transportation of intoxicating beverages throughout the country. This, the Eighteenth Amendment, went into effect in 1920.

Of all the rights that women sought, the most important was the right to vote, for this would enable them to secure their other rights. So it seemed, at least, to feminist leaders of the late nineteenth and early twentieth centuries. A great many women contributed to the suffrage movement, but the two who had the most to do with its ultimate success were Susan B. Anthony (born in North Adams, Massachu-

setts, in 1820) and Carrie Chapman Catt (born in Ripon, Wisconsin, in 1859).

As early as 1868, Miss Anthony and her friend Elizabeth Cady Stanton had persuaded a congressman to introduce an amendment to enfranchise women, but nothing came of it. At that time the demand for woman suffrage was a response to the proposal of Negro suffrage. Miss Anthony and like-minded feminists called for "educated suffrage irrespective of sex and color." They objected to the Fifteenth Amendment, since it removed only race and not sex as a bar to voting. When black men began to vote, Miss Anthony voted and was arrested for doing so. In 1878 the suffragists got another amendment introduced in Congress, and they got it reintroduced in every session after that.

While urging the federal government to act, Miss Anthony also carried her campaign to the state legislatures. After taking over the leadership of the movement in the 1890s, Mrs. Catt decided to concentrate on state action, so as to produce enough "suffrage states" to compel the federal government to go along. When Wyoming entered the Union, in 1890, it was the only state with equal suffrage, having adopted

Are Women Human Beings? [1912]

Charlotte Perkins Gilman was probably the greatest intellect among the American feminists of her time. She gained international fame from her book *Women and Economics* (1898), in which she analyzed the effects of industrialization on women and argued for their economic independence. In a subsequent magazine article (1912) she raised the question "Are Women Human Beings?" She answered in part:

As social evolution has never waited for the complete enlightenment of mankind, we find the enfranchisement of women going on in all civilized countries; but since the opposition to it is strong enough to cause years of delay and a continuous outlay of organized effort, it seems worthwhile to point out the main error actuating that opposition. . . .

This error is due to a certain arrested development of thought. It consists in seeing in women only feminine characteristics; and, conversely, seeing in all the complex functions of civilization only masculine characteristics.

Under this conception it is held, quite naturally, that women need do nothing more than fulfill their "womanly duties," i.e., to be wives, mothers, and houseworkers; that for them to desire any other activities in life is to be unwomanly, unnatural, to become some sort of pervert or monster. They are spoken of as "denatured women," as "epicene," as "unsexed," as "seeking to become men." Miss Ida Tarbell in a recent magazine article describes women's professional and industrial advance as "making a Man of Herself. . . ."

As animals, we share in the universal distinction of sex; but as human beings, we alone possess a whole new range of faculties, vitally essential and common to both sexes. . . .

This universal, glaring fact is what these sex-obsessed opponents of the normal progress of women cannot see. They see only the feminine characteristics of women, and fail to see the human ones. . . .

The women of our age in most countries of the same degree of development are outgrowing the artificial restrictions so long placed upon them, and following natural lines of human advance. They are specializing, because they are human. They are organizing, because they are human. They are seeking economic and political independence, because they are human. They are demanding the vote, because they are human.

---

it as a territory in 1869. During the 1890s the neighboring states of Colorado, Utah, and Idaho followed the example of Wyoming. By 1914 a total of eleven states, all but one of them west of the Mississippi River, allowed women the same voting privileges as men. In 1916 the women voters of Montana helped to elect the first woman ever to serve as a member of Congress, Jeannette Rankin.

Progress with state action was so slow that, in the meantime, Mrs. Catt and most of the feminists had returned to the earlier emphasis on federal action. They disagreed, however, on the methods they should use. One leader, Alice Paul, favored imitating the "nuisance tactics" of radical English suffragettes who smashed windows, destroyed mailboxes, and disrupted public meetings to get attention for the cause. American suffragettes did march in parades and picket the White House, but Mrs. Catt and the majority of the leaders in the United States preferred the more conventional methods of persuasion and political pressure.

Resistance was strong. Antifeminists formed the Association Opposed to Woman Suffrage and chose a woman to head it. They had the support of the "liquor interests," who feared that women with the vote would hasten the day of national prohibition. The opponents also had the support of "preparedness" advocates, who argued that woman suffrage would weaken the nation in the face of possible war.

One male opponent (Henry L. Stimson) declared: "Participation in the decision of such questions by woman, who is not only wholly ignorant of the methods of force, but whose very nature shrinks from the thought of it, cannot but be a source of peril to the government which permits it."

Congresswoman Rankin did, indeed, oppose the declaration of war in 1917 (and she was to be the only member of Congress to vote against it in 1941). But Mrs. Catt, though herself a pacifist, believed that the cooperation of women in the war effort would help them to gain the vote. She was right. Women, suffragettes among them, contributed to victory in World War I by working on farms and in factories, assisting in the sale of war bonds, and joining in other patriotic activities on the home front. In 1919, more than half a century after the introduction of the first woman suffrage proposal, Congress finally endorsed the Nineteenth Amendment, which made it unconstitutional to deny or abridge "on account of sex" the right to vote. This was ratified in time for the election of 1920.

THE NEGLECTED NEGRO

The Negro was the forgotten man of the progressive era. He made few gains except in literacy—between 1900 and 1910 the percentage of Negroes who could read and write increased from about 65 to 70. In the South, despite the "separate but equal" theory, Negro schools were far inferior to those of the whites. In the nation as a whole there were, as late as 1910, only 8,251 Negroes attending high school.

In some respects the plight of black Americans worsened, and progressives themselves

---

**The Souls
of Black Folk
[1903]**

William E. Burghardt Du Bois, born in Great Barrington, Massachusetts (1868), was teaching at Atlanta University when he wrote *The Souls of Black Folk* (1903). At that time the problem of race relationships was largely, though by no means entirely, a regional one, since the vast majority of Negro Americans were still concentrated in the South. Of their position, Du Bois observed:

The dangerously clear logic of the Negro's position will more and more loudly assert itself in that day when increasing wealth and more intricate social organization preclude the South from being, as it so largely is, simply an armed camp for intimidating black folk. Such waste of energy cannot be spared if the South is to catch up with civilization. And as the black third of the land grows in thrift and skill, unless skilfully guided in its larger philosophy, it must more and more brood over the red past and the creeping, crooked present, until it grasps a gospel of revolt and revenge and throws its new-found energies athwart the current of advance. Even to-day the masses of the Negroes see all too clearly the anomalies of their position and the moral crookedness of yours. You may marshal strong indictments against them, but their counter-cries, lacking though they may be in formal logic, have burning truths within them which you may not wholly ignore, O Southern Gentlemen! If you deplore their presence here, they ask, Who brought us? When you cry, Deliver us from the vision of intermarriage, they answer that legal marriage is infinitely better than systematic concubinage and prostitution. And if in just fury you accuse their vagabonds of violating women, they also in fury quite as just may reply: The wrong which your gentlemen have done against helpless black women in defiance of your own laws is written on the foreheads of two millions of mulattoes, and written in ineffaceable blood. And finally, when you fasten crime upon this race as its peculiar trait, they answer that slavery was the arch-crime, and lynching and lawlessness its twin abortion; that color and race are not crimes, and yet they it is which in this land receive most unceasing condemnation, North, East, South, and West.

were largely to blame for this in the Southern states. Progressive leaders there concluded that political reform was hopeless so long as the Negro remained a potential voter, for their opponents could argue that the progressive movement, by dividing the whites and disrupting the solid South, would lead to "Negro domination." Hence progressives joined in the popular demand to remove the Negro, finally and completely, from politics.

Meanwhile Negroes suffered more and more at the hands of lynching mobs in the South and rioters in both the South and the North. In 1908, while the city's leaders were planning a 1909 celebration of the centennial of Abraham Lincoln's birth, a bloody race riot broke out in Springfield, Illinois, Lincoln's hometown. This event led directly to the rise of the first effective nationwide organization for Negro rights.

The emerging leader in the cause was William E. Burghardt Du Bois, a Negro historian and sociologist with a Harvard Ph.D. Du Bois openly challenged Booker T. Washington as the spokesman for their race. Washington taught Negroes that they must be patient and submissive until they had proved their worth, and thus he "tended to make the whites, North and South, shift the burden of the Negro problem to the Negro's shoulders and stand aside as critical and rather pessimistic spectators," Du Bois charged; "when in fact the burden belongs to the nation, and the hands of none of us are clean if we bend not our energies to righting these great wrongs."

At first Du Bois and a group of like-minded reformers, black and white, met from time to time in a fellowship known as the Niagara Movement. Then, on Lincoln's Birthday in 1909, they organized the National Association for the Advancement of Colored People. White men were named to most of the offices of the NAACP, but Du Bois as its director of publicity and research remained the guiding spirit. From 1909 on, the NAACP worked slowly but steadily for equal rights, mainly through legal strategy, through filing and winning one lawsuit after another in the federal courts.

The Square Deal

After intervening on behalf of striking coal miners (in 1902), President Roosevelt said he had tried to give them a "square deal." He also used this expression in reference to other reforms he sponsored, and it came to be a catch phrase for the domestic policies of his administration.

THE FIRST ROOSEVELT

Theodore Roosevelt gave the muckraking movement its name. At a banquet shortly after the appearance of David Graham Phillip's shocking articles on "The Treason of the Senate," Roosevelt arose to liken the writer to the man in *Pilgrim's Progress* who was so busy raking the muck at his feet that he could not see the heavenly crown that was offered him from above. The cynical, conservative Speaker of the House, "Uncle Joe" Cannon, is supposed to have replied to Roosevelt: "Yes, you're the chief muckraker." This was true. The great role of the muckraker was to publicize the need for reform. No one succeeded better than Roosevelt in dramatically arousing the indignation of the progressives and leading them toward political action on a national scale.

Roosevelt was an "accidental" occupant of the White House. As Vice President, he had taken over the presidency after McKinley's assassination in September 1901. The assassin, who shot McKinley at an exposition in Buffalo, New York, was a young drifter named Leon F. Czolgosz, who proclaimed himself an anarchist and said he had had an urge to kill a "great leader." He was electrocuted.

At the news of McKinley's death, his friend and mentor Mark Hanna exclaimed: "Now look, that damned cowboy is President of the United States!" Actually, as a rather uncertain fledgling President, only forty-two years old when he took office, Roosevelt had little inclination to put a vigorous progressive program into operation. He later admitted: "I cannot say that I entered the presidency with any deliber-

President Theodore Roosevelt in Yosemite Valley

Seen here with John Muir, the naturalist, Roosevelt dramatized his interest in conservation when he visited Yosemite and later succeeded in bringing it under federal administration. It became a national park in 1906. (The Bettmann Archive)

ately planned and far reaching scheme of social betterment." His greatest ambition obviously was to be elected President in his own right.

Even had Roosevelt possessed a detailed plan of legislation, he could have done little to forward it in the fall of 1901. Congress, like most of the governmental machinery in the United States from the municipalities up, was under the control of old-style politicians. "Uncle Joe" Cannon, as Speaker of the House, operated under the autocratic powers "Czar" Reed had seized in 1890. Though genial, Cannon so firmly controlled appointments to committees and debates on legislation that the few progressives beginning to appear in the House were obliged either to cooperate or to sit as impotent witnesses to Cannon's dictatorship. The Senate was under the domination of an intelligent and competent oligarchy of conservatives. The most commanding of them was tall, austere Nelson Wilmarth Aldrich, a wealthy banker of Rhode Island.

Roosevelt realized how futile it would be to thrust his spear single-handedly against the conservatives in Congress. For the time being, therefore, he was cautious and conciliatory toward their leaders. As he planned his first annual message to Congress, his strategy obviously was to try to attract a wide following without alienating these powerful men. "Before I write my message," he wrote Aldrich in 1901, "I should like to have a chance to go over certain subjects with you." Roosevelt wrote to Senator Chauncey Depew of the New York Central Railroad: "*How* I wish I *wasn't* a reformer, oh, Senator! But I suppose I must live up to my part, like the Negro minstrel who blacked himself all over!"

Roosevelt dispensed patronage throughout the Middle West in a manner calculated to break Hanna's control over the party, although the policies of the two men were in reality basically similar. It made little difference whether these appointments took Roosevelt to the left or right. In Kansas he backed a former Populist against Hanna's GAR supporter. From Wisconsin, to the chagrin of La Follette, he chose Henry Clay Payne of the Old Guard to be postmaster general. Payne, through his wide distribution of spoils, helped rally right-wing Republicans and Democrats behind Roosevelt. Finally, Roosevelt cemented alliances with businessmen in the North and reshuffled the unstable Republican organizations in the South. In the South, he reversed Hanna's "lily-white" policy, to appoint some qualified Negroes to office. Indeed, it was to discuss appointments that Roosevelt took the sensational step of inviting Booker T. Washington to the White House in the fall of 1901.

While playing the game of political patronage, Roosevelt markedly improved the quality of officeholders. Gradually he was able to pull into public service a group of distinguished men, both old and young, of a sort that previously had shunned government work. Henry L. Stimson, who had been earning enormous fees as a corporation lawyer, became United States attorney for the New York City area and brought into his office a group of brilliant and idealistic young lawyers, including Felix Frankfurter.

Partly because Roosevelt had attracted into the government progressives of stature, bound to him by strong ties of personal loyalty, and even more because he had won over or neutralized the Republican machines, he was in firm control of the party by 1904. He had not made it progressive, but he had made it answerable to him. Hanna died early in the year; had he lived and felt the inclination, he could have mustered little strength against Roosevelt at the convention.

In 1904 the Democrats abandoned Bryan to nominate Cleveland's former law partner, Alton B. Parker. When Roosevelt, fearing that Wall Street was putting $5 million behind Parker, allowed his campaign manager to tap the trusts, the money came pouring in. Businessmen might call Roosevelt the "mad messiah," but they were not really afraid of him. E. H. Harriman personally contributed $50,000 and J. P. Morgan, $150,000; far more came from their associates. The steel, beef, oil, and insurance trusts, and the railroads all aided. Roosevelt was not aware of the source of all the donations, nor did he feel he was putting himself under obligation.

After a dull campaign, he won by a popular majority of 2.5 million votes. While businessmen were convinced he was safe, progressives were confident he would lead in reform. In state elections throughout the nation, progressives were generally victorious. As a sidelight, the Socialists under Eugene V. Debs (often regarded as a left-wing offshoot of the progressives), received 400,000 votes, four times as many as in 1900. The growth of Socialist feeling gave Roosevelt a convincing argument that sane and slow reform was essential to forestall a violent upheaval.

TRUST BUSTING

While Roosevelt was quietly taking over the Republican machinery, he was spectacularly building an excited national following. He launched a series of attacks upon the corporate plutocracy—attacks that were vigorous but at the same time moderate.

In his first annual message to Congress, December 3, 1901, he set forth his basic policy toward trusts: "There is a widespread conviction in the minds of the American people that . . . trusts are in certain of their features and tendencies hurtful to the general welfare. This . . . is based upon sincere conviction that combination and concentration should be, not prohibited, but supervised and within reasonable limits controlled; and in my judgment this conviction is right." Roosevelt's position on trusts was ready-made for burlesque by Finley Peter Dunne's character, Mr. Dooley: "Th' trusts, says he, are heejoous monsthers built up be th' enlightened intherprise iv th' men that have done so much to advance progress in our beloved country, he says. On wan hand I wud stamp thim undher fut; on th' other hand not so fast."

Specifically, Roosevelt asked for legislation to give the government the right to inspect and examine the workings of great corporations, and subsequently to supervise them in a mild fashion. What he desired first was the power to investigate them and publicize their activities; on the basis of these data, Congress could later frame legislation to regulate or tax the trusts. Consequently he requested the establishment of a Department of Commerce and Labor, containing a Bureau of Corporations to carry on investigations. Congress set up such a department in 1903.

The establishment of a great railroad monopoly in the Northwest, after a bitter and spectacular stock-market battle in 1901, gave Roosevelt an opportunity to begin prosecution under the Sherman Antitrust Act. And so he did, even though his avowed purpose had been to regulate, not destroy, and to stamp underfoot only "malefactors of great wealth," while sparing large corporations that were benign. The new Northern Securities Company had emerged out of the struggle for control of the Northern Pacific between E. H. Harriman of the Union Pacific on the one side and James J. Hill of the Great Northern and J. P. Morgan on the other. In the eyes of progressives, these men were malefactors.

Morgan, feeling his position challenged, hastened to the White House, accompanied by Senators Hanna and Depew. According to Roosevelt, Morgan declared: "If we have done anything wrong, send your man to my man and they can fix it up." Morgan, Roosevelt later remarked, "could not help regarding me as a big rival operator, who either intended to ruin all his interests or else could be induced to come to an agreement to ruin none." Roosevelt was not set upon ruining Morgan, but to the joy of progressives, he was using his power as President to discipline industry.

When, in 1904, Roosevelt won the case and the Supreme Court dissolved the Northern

Securities combine, it in no material way injured Harriman, Hill, or Morgan. But it convinced progressives that Roosevelt, however cautious his avowed policies might be, was a heroic "trust buster."

Trust busting was popular and proceeded rapidly. Roosevelt's attorneys obtained twenty-five indictments altogether and instituted suits against the beef, oil, and tobacco combinations. In these, the government was ultimately successful, but the Supreme Court instituted a "rule of reason," declaring in effect that the Sherman Act prohibited only unreasonable restraints upon trade. Even though President Taft initiated ninety more suits and obtained forty-three additional indictments, the results of trust busting were disappointing.

Although Roosevelt's followers believed he was leading them into the millennium, the panic of 1907 illustrated the serious flaws still present in the American economic structure—and the President's unwillingness to go very far in trying to remedy them. Speculation and mismanagement during the boom years since the Spanish-American War led to a sharp break in prosperity in 1907. Roosevelt was quick to conciliate Wall Street. Judge Elbert H. Gary and Henry C. Frick called upon him one morning to tell him that unless United States Steel took over shares of the Tennessee Coal and Iron Company, this company would fail and its failure would threaten a widespread industrial smash-up. Gary and Frick desired assurance that the government would not consider the purchase a violation of the Sherman Act. Roosevelt tacitly agreed. United States Steel was thus able to buy out a vigorous competitor at a bargain price, thus reducing competition and holding back the development of the iron and steel industry in the South.

GOVERNMENT AND LABOR

Presidential intervention in labor disputes was nothing new—there had been, for example, the Pullman strike—but the government had usually acted as a strikebreaker for the employers. Now Roosevelt was ready to make the government an impartial arbiter instead. Here again, as in dealing with capitalists, he wished the government to be paramount over the conflicting economic forces and neutral in dealing with them. Organized labor, as long as it was well

Strikers Confront Militia   1912
*In January 1912, mill workers in Lawrence, Massachusetts, struck in protest
against a wage cut. Organizers from the radical IWW arrived to assist the
strikers and win recruits to the union. The mayor called in state militia, who
threatened the workers with guns. Before the strike ended, a woman was killed in
a clash between strikers and policemen. (Library of Congress)*

behaved, did not frighten the progressives nearly as much as did organized capital. The unions were comparatively weak; despite the great upsurge of the American Federation of Labor in the 1890s, by 1900 only about 4 percent of the working force, even excluding agricultural laborers, was organized.

Injustice toward workers was most extreme in anthracite coal mining. Eight coal railroads under Morgan's domination held a virtual monopoly over the industry. Wages were substandard, hours long, and the accident rate shockingly high. The workers, under John Mitchell, struck in May 1902, for an eight-hour day, a 20-percent wage increase, and recognition of the union. Mitchell so effectively presented the miners' claims, and George F. Baer, spokesman for the operators, was so truculent,

that public sympathy was aligned with the strikers. Baer foolishly asserted the divine right of the operators to deal with miners as they saw best. He remained adamant when Roosevelt called operators and miners to the White House early in October to ask them to accept arbitration. In contrast, Mitchell was quite willing to accept. Roosevelt eventually persuaded Morgan to force arbitration upon the operators. Even so, the miners after their long strike failed to gain union recognition and obtained only a 10-percent wage increase.

The coal strike and its settlement were evidence of "a honeymoon period of capital and labor," stretching from McKinley's inauguration through Roosevelt's first term. Union membership jumped from less than a half million to over 2 million. Monopolistic companies could well afford to deal liberally with unions, since the companies could thus avoid work stoppages in prosperous periods and pass on increased labor costs to the consumers. It was altogether fitting that Hanna, the high priest of modern big business, should assume the presidency of the National Civic Federation, which was founded in 1901 to bring about friendly relations between capital and labor, and that Samuel Gompers should become vice president.

Not all laborers were ready to accept the assumption of leaders like Gompers and Mitchell that differences with capitalists could easily be adjusted around a conference table. The Socialist minority within the American Federation of Labor succeeded in capturing unions of machinists and miners. Socialists won municipal elections in Milwaukee, Schenectady, and Berkeley. Militant western miners in 1905 founded the Industrial Workers of the World, which tried to organize the great masses of unskilled workers, mostly immigrants, whom the AFL ignored. The IWW, a syndicalist organization, aimed ultimately to form "one big union" including all workers, hold one big strike, and thus paralyze and then take over the government. Its members, popularly known as "Wobblies," were accused of responsibility for acts of violence. Employers and state and local authorities certainly did not hesitate to use violence against the Wobblies. Two episodes, neither the work of the IWW, especially outraged orderly progressives. These were the murder of a former governor of Idaho and the dynamiting of the plant of the Los Angeles *Times*, which was militantly antiunion.

Such episodes prompted many progressives to listen to the antiunion slogans of the National Association of Manufacturers and kindred organizations. The NAM, which proclaimed itself against union recognition in 1903, was predominantly made up of men who ran small plants and were dependent upon low labor costs to survive in highly competitive markets. It called the open shop the "American Plan," and the independent workman (strikebreaker) the "American hero." President Charles W. Eliot of Harvard gave formidable support by asserting that nothing was "more essential to the preservation of individual liberty" than protection of the independent workman.

The manufacturers had the backing of federal judges. The most spectacular court blow against collective bargaining grew out of the Danbury Hatters' strike of 1902. The courts held that the union's efforts to obtain a nationwide boycott of Loewe hats was a violation of the Sherman Act and assessed triple damages of $240,000 against the union. In another boycott case, involving the Buck's Stove and Range Company of St. Louis, a federal court issued a sweeping injunction that forbade the AFL to carry on the boycott, to include the company in a "We Don't Patronize" list in its newspaper, or even to mention the dispute orally or in writing. When Gompers and other AFL officials defied the injunction by mentioning the dispute, they were sentenced to prison for contempt of court. The sentences were never served, but the principle of the injunction stood. Union officials began a concerted and vigorous campaign to exempt labor organizations from the Antitrust Act and to outlaw antilabor injunctions.

Gompers and his followers demanded an end to governmental discrimination against them; they were not asking for welfare laws. To some extent Roosevelt sympathized with them. He denounced the Buck's Stove decision and inveighed against court abuse of injunctions. But he was more interested in paternalistic legislation for labor, similar to that being proposed in many state legislatures. He asked Congress for laws to regulate the hours and working conditions of women and children, establish employers' liability for accident compensation, and improve railroad safety measures. For the moment he made no headway.

REGULATION AND CONSERVATION

Roosevelt accepted his 1904 victory as a mandate for progressive reform. He was now free from his earlier preoccupation with winning reelection, having announced that he would not seek another term. He continued to operate from the political center, offending big businessmen who had contributed to his campaign, and at the same time offending Midwestern progressives who took up what he called "the La Follette type of fool radicalism."

While leaving the tariff alone, Roosevelt now exercised his presidential leadership to obtain more effective railroad-rate regulation. The courts had practically nullified the Interstate Commerce Act of 1887. By a series of intricate maneuvers, Roosevelt managed to force a new regulatory law through Congress. At one point he seemed to join Senator Robert M. La Follette, the recent reform governor of Wisconsin, in demands for really drastic regulation of railroads. La Follette wished to give the ICC power to evaluate railroad property as a base

Robert M. La Follette Campaigning in Wisconsin
*"Battling Bob" La Follette (1855–1925) in the 1880s was a Republican congressman sufficiently regular to help prepare the McKinley tariff. Although he remained in the party during the 1890s, he began to champion reforms of a Populist nature. In 1901, pledged to fight for a direct primary, tax reform, and railroad control, he was elected governor of Wisconsin. His advice came from experts at the University of Wisconsin, his votes largely from a rural constituency. In 1905, he finally obtained a legislature that would enact his program. Although he had already been elected United States Senator, he remained governor until the end of the year when his proposals had become law. In Washington he advocated a similar national program, especially rigorous regulation of railroads. It brought him into conflict with both the Old Guard and President Roosevelt; he entitled a chapter of his autobiography "Alone in the Senate." Roosevelt, La Follette wrote, "acted upon the maxim that half a loaf is better than no bread. I believe that half a loaf is fatal whenever it is accepted at the sacrifice of the basic principle sought to be attained." Although nationally La Follette was at times isolated in his advanced agrarian progressive position, in Wisconsin he and his sons commanded so loyal a following that they dominated the state politically for nearly forty years.
(State Historical Society of Wisconsin)*

The Sausages [1906]

There was never the least attention paid to what was cut up for sausage; there would come all the way back from Europe old sausage that had been rejected, and that was mouldy and white—it would be dosed with borax and glycerine, and dumped into the hoppers, and made over again for home consumption. There would be meat that had tumbled out on the floor, in the dirt and sawdust, where the workers had tramped and spit uncounted billions of [tuberculosis] germs. There would be meat stored in great piles in rooms; and the water from leaky roofs would drip over it, and thousands of rats would race about on it. It was too dark in these storage places to see well, but a man could run his hand over these piles of meat and sweep off handfuls of the dried dung of rats. These rats were nuisances, and the packers would put poisoned bread out for them; they would die, and then rats, bread, and meat would go into the hoppers together.—Upton Sinclair, The Jungle *(Garden City, N.Y.: Doubleday, 1906).*

---

for determining rates. He felt betrayed when Roosevelt abandoned him. Although the Hepburn Act of June 1906 was in La Follette's eyes only half a loaf, it was at least the beginning of effective railroad regulation. It empowered the ICC to put into effect reasonable rates, subject to later court review; extended its jurisdiction to cover express, sleeping-car, and pipeline companies; separated railroad management from other enterprises such as mining; prescribed uniform bookkeeping; and forbade passes and rebates.

It was a large half-loaf, and La Follette and his supporters in Congress soon were able to obtain the remaining part. In 1910 insurgent Republicans and Democrats passed the Mann-Elkins Act, prohibiting discriminatory freight rates, further extending the jurisdiction of the ICC, and strengthening other features of the Hepburn Act. The ICC could now suspend proposed new rates up to ten months, and could demand proof from the railroads that they would be reasonable. Finally, in 1913, La Follette's long agitation resulted in passage of a law authorizing the ICC to evaluate railroads and to set rates that would give a fair return of profit.

One of the many reasons for the clamor for lower freight rates had been to lower the rising cost of lumber. The forests of the Great Lakes area were depleted, and the increasing amounts of lumber coming from the Pacific Northwest had to bear the heavy cost of transportation eastward. Furthermore, trees were being felled faster than they were being grown. At this point, conflict developed between pro-

gressives in the West and those in the East. Westerners wanted the government to aid in the rapid development of their resources. Easterners were more interested in preserving the remaining wilderness; their concern was aesthetic and recreational.

Roosevelt, ardent sportsman and naturalist that he was, along with his Chief Forester, Gifford Pinchot, and most Eastern progressives, felt that the United States must develop great national forests like those of the European countries. For years Major John Wesley Powell, explorer of the Grand Canyon, and other experts had been advocating new policies for husbanding the public domain.

A beginning had come with the passage of the Forest Reserve Act of 1891; under its provisions 47 million acres had been set aside as national forests. Roosevelt, clothing his actions with the terminology of the progressive struggle against the vested interests, rapidly extended the government reserves. In 1907 Western congressmen succeeded in attaching a rider (unrelated amendment) to an appropriation bill, prohibiting him from withdrawing further lands. Roosevelt could not veto the appropriations bill without calamitous effects. So he quickly withdrew practically all remaining forests in the public domain and then signed the bill. Altogether he added about 125 million acres to the national forests, and reserved 4.7 million acres of phosphate beds and 68 million acres of coal lands—all the known coal deposits in the public domain.

At the same time, Roosevelt prepared the way for a new government policy on electric power by reserving 2,565 water-power sites, which expanding private utility companies were interested in obtaining. Further, he vetoed a bill to permit private exploitation of the power at Muscle Shoals on the Tennessee River, which a generation later became the heart of the Tennessee Valley Authority (TVA). The way was open for government development of huge power projects, a program as popular in the West as the withdrawal of other land was unpopular.

It was not the President but a Democratic senator from Nevada, Francis G. Newlands, who proposed an extensive federal reclamation program for the West. Roosevelt endorsed it and was able to win much of the credit for the Newlands Reclamation Act of 1902. This provided that money from the sale of Western lands should go into a revolving fund to undertake irrigation projects too large for private capital or state resources. Eventually, the government built huge dams for the development of power and storage of water, and extensive systems of canals to carry the water to arid lands. By 1915 the government had invested $80 million in twenty-five projects, of which the largest was the Roosevelt Dam on the Salt River of Arizona. The principle of government aid in irrigation and power development in the West had become firmly established.

Progressives undertook to legislate the nation into better health after muckrakers had made the public aware of the disgusting and dangerous substances that were being sold and eaten as food. None created a more shocked reaction than Upton Sinclair, who wrote a powerful novel of protest against exploitation of immigrant labor in the stockyards, and incidentally included nauseating descriptions of the preparation of meats. When *The Jungle* appeared in 1906, it hit Americans' stomachs as much as their consciences.

Roosevelt himself was horrified, and when a commission verified the descriptions in *The Jungle,* he sought reform. Two pieces of legislation were passed in June 1906. One was the Meat Inspection Act, which eventually did much to bring about the eradication of some animal diseases, especially tuberculosis. The other was the Pure Food and Drug Act, which bore the impressive descriptive title: "An Act for preventing the manufacture, sale, or transportation of adulterated or misbranded or poisonous or deleterious foods, drugs, medicines, and liquors, and for regulating traffic therein, and for other purposes."

A Rift in Republican Ranks

As early as 1904 Roosevelt had tentatively decided that his good friend William Howard Taft, then secretary of war, would make an excellent successor as President. But after Taft's election the two were to fall out and, in doing so, were to split the Republican party.

TAFT AND THE TARIFF

Taft was known for his achievements as one of the first viceroys of the new American empire. Between 1900 and 1908, he traveled over 100,000 miles on assignment to Manila, Rome, Panama, Cuba, and within the United States. His achievements were almost all in the realm of colonial or foreign policy; he had little to do with Roosevelt's domestic policies, although privately he subscribed to almost every one of them. If he was to the right of Roosevelt, it was only by a hairline. The great distinction was that while he regarded Roosevelt's objectives as justifiable, he felt, as he commented in 1910, that Roosevelt "ought more often to have admitted the legal way of reaching the same ends." This colorless way of saying things marked another contrast between Taft and Roosevelt.

In 1908 Roosevelt had no difficulty in securing the nomination of Taft. The smooth-running Republican machinery followed Roosevelt's bidding and gathered the votes of the delegates: organization men, officeholders, and Southern Republicans.

Business moguls preferred the gingerly progressive Republican candidate to the more forthright William Jennings Bryan, running forlornly for a third time. Rockefeller wired Taft congratulations on the nomination; Morgan remarked, "Good! good!" Carnegie sent a campaign contribution of $20,000. This did not mean that Taft had capitulated to Wall Street; indeed he was more careful about accepting corporate campaign contributions than Roosevelt had been in 1904.

Taft campaigned as the champion of smaller business interests. In his acceptance address he promised that he would perfect the machinery for restraining lawbreakers and at the same time interfere with legitimate business as little as possible. Most important, he appealed to small-business and middle-class concern over the rising cost of living by firmly promising a reduction in the tariff.

The election result was a foregone conclusion, a sweep for Taft. The electoral vote was 321 to 162, but there were portents of national unrest in the victory. Taft's lead over Bryan was only half the size of Roosevelt's plurality in 1904; several Western states shifted to Bryan, and several others in the Middle West elected Democratic governors even though they gave their electoral votes to Taft. Republican progressives, pleased at the outcome, proclaimed: "Roosevelt has cut enough hay; Taft is the man to put it into the barn." Republican conservatives rejoiced that they were rid of the "mad messiah."

Certainly Taft's intention was to load Roosevelt's hay into the barn, but the hay soon was drenched by violent political storms. Taft seemed incapable of negotiating with the Old Guard, as Roosevelt had done, without giving the impression that he had joined them. To the progressives Taft seemed guilty of betrayal.

The first of his betrayals in the eyes of progressives was the fiasco that occurred when Taft called Congress into special session to

"The Easy Umpire"
"He slugs me every chance he gets, and you can't or won't see it," the tiny player labeled "The Plain People" protests to the umpire, President Taft, while pointing at the bully, Senator Aldrich. For years the dominant figure in the Senate, Aldrich furthered the interests of big business. From Puck, *November 10, 1909. (Culver Pictures)*

enact a lower tariff. "I believe the people are with me," he had written, "and before I get through I think I will have downed Cannon and Aldrich too." But having proclaimed a tariff crusade, he remained behind while Middle Westerners carried their lances into battle. They were not "free traders" like some Southern Democrats, but they did want to weaken trusts by exposing them to foreign competition. The way to do this, they thought, was to lower tariff rates substantially. They thought the President was behind them, but he failed to send Congress a fighting message or to intervene with his patronage powers when congressmen began to succumb to the blandishments of lobbyists and logrollers.

The Payne-Aldrich tariff passed Congress over the votes of Midwest Republicans and was signed by Taft on August 5, 1909. He said it was not a perfect bill but represented "a sincere effort on the part of the Republican party to make a downward revision." Also it provided for a Tariff Commission which was to make scientific studies of rates—an appealing idea to some progressives, who felt that the tariff, like most problems, should be determined scientifically and taken out of politics.

Nevertheless, the Payne-Aldrich tariff seemed to favor Senator Aldrich's New England at the expense of the rest of the country. On a tour around the country in the fall of 1909, Taft tried to defend the new tariff in a hastily prepared speech delivered in the heart of the area of resentment, Winona, Minnesota. One line from that speech made damaging headlines against the President. He said: "On the whole . . . the Payne bill is the best bill that the Republican party ever passed." The remainder of the trip through the Midwest, wrote a reporter, was "a polar dash through a world of ice."

In 1911 Taft further alienated Middle Westerners when he submitted to the Senate a reciprocal trade agreement with Canada, an agreement that would have lowered tariffs on both sides and in effect would have brought the two countries into an economic union. Many Eastern manufacturers, seeing larger Canadian markets for their goods, were enthusiastic, but the Middle Westerners, fearing a flood of competing Canadian farm products and raw materials, were bitterly hostile. La Follette complained: "It singles out the farmer and

forces free trade upon him, but it confers even greater benefits upon a few of the great combinations sheltered behind the high rates found in the Payne-Aldrich tariff." He and his cohorts formed a strange alliance with die-hard members of the Old Guard but were defeated by Eastern Republicans and Southern free-trade Democrats. The Senate approved the reciprocity arrangement, 55 to 27. But the Canadian parliament refused to act, for many Canadians feared that tariff reductions might somehow lead to Canada's being annexed by the United States.

T. R. AGAINST TAFT

The progressive Republicans of the Midwest had cut loose from Taft. They blamed him, unjustly, for their failure to oust Speaker Cannon in 1909. By 1910, without the presidential blessing, they were strong enough to resume the effort. Under the leadership of George W. Norris they breached Cannon's formidable parliamentary defenses and opened a fierce debate that raged for nearly thirty hours. It ended with Cannon's removal from the Rules Committee, which henceforth was to be elected by the House. He remained as House Speaker, but he was no longer the obstacle he had been to progressive legislation.

Meanwhile, through the sensational Ballinger-Pinchot controversy, Taft lost the sympathy of most of Theodore Roosevelt's following in the urban East and the Far West. Taft had replaced Roosevelt's secretary of the interior with a man who wished to distribute to private interests the natural resources in the public domain. The viewpoint of the new secretary, Richard Ballinger, was dominant among businessmen of the West, who wished themselves to prosper and to see their region grow. But Taft had left in charge of the Forestry Service in the Department of Agriculture Roosevelt's ardent admirer, Gifford Pinchot of Pennsylvania, who, like most Eastern nature lovers and sportsmen, was zealous to preserve the public domain unspoiled, as a part of the nation's heritage. A violent clash between these two men was almost inevitable.

The occasion was the spectacular charge that Ballinger was conniving to turn over valu-

"Revising the Tariff Downward (?)"
(J. N. "Ding" Darling in the Des Moines Register)

able coal lands in Alaska to a Morgan-Guggen-heim syndicate. Taft, accepting Ballinger's rebuttal, publicly exonerated him. Immediately Roosevelt progressives throughout the country championed Pinchot as the defender of the national domain against the corrupt onslaught of big business. Pinchot, by going over the President's head directly to Congress, provoked Taft to discharge him for insubordination. A congressional committee investigated and, since the Old Guard dominated it, reported in favor of Ballinger. To the end, Taft stood by his Secretary of the Interior, whom he correctly considered to be an honorable man. But in refusing to dismiss Ballinger as an anticonservationist, Taft opened a rift between himself and the Roosevelt following that was as wide and deep as the one separating him from the La Follette supporters.

As early as the tariff fiasco in 1909, progressives had begun to look to the African jungle for their next presidential candidate. In the middle of June 1910, loaded with trophies from Africa and fresh impressions of reform from Europe, Roosevelt returned. Observers noted that his first hello was to Pinchot and that he

turned down Taft's invitation to the White House. Indeed, he had already met Pinchot in Europe, bearing messages from progressives, and had come to the conclusion that Taft had "completely twisted around the policies I advocated and acted upon."

Furious with Taft for helping bring about the split in the party, Roosevelt determined to do all he could to reunify it. He told reporters he was seeing all Republicans — "regulars and insurgents, party men and independents." But at Osawatomie, Kansas, on September 1, he delivered a speech that returned him to command of the progressives. At Osawatomie, he proclaimed the doctrines of the New Nationalism, emphasizing that social justice could be attained in the nation only through strengthening the power of the federal government so that the executive could be the "steward of public welfare." Men thinking primarily of property rights and personal profits "must now give way to the advocate of human welfare, who rightly maintains that every man holds his property subject to the general right of·the community to regulate its use to whatever degree the public welfare may require it." Going beyond these generalizations, frightening enough to the Old Guard, Roosevelt listed some specific proposals: graduated income and inheritance taxes, workmen's accident compensation, regulation of the labor of women and children, tariff revision, and firm regulation of corporations through a more powerful Bureau of Corporations and Interstate Commerce Commission. From the Mississippi westward, progressives were ready to acclaim him as the next presidential candidate, but among his right-wing enemies, Lodge warned him, he was regarded as "little short of a revolutionist."

Progressive Republicans of the Middle West hoped they could wrest the presidential nomination from Taft in 1912. In January 1911, a group of them formed the National Progressive Republican League to work for the nomination of La Follette. But a great majority of the progressive Republicans continued to hope that Roosevelt could be persuaded to run.

With Roosevelt receptive, many of La Follette's supporters switched to him with indecent haste after La Follette on February 2, 1912, exhausted and worried, delivered a rambling, repetitious talk. Roosevelt thus acquired new recruits, but he also won the undying hatred of La Follette and his loyal Middle Western progressive following. Nevertheless, in the primaries Roosevelt demonstrated that he was overwhelmingly the presidential choice of Republican voters.

The nomination at the Republican convention would depend upon the seating of the delegates; more than a third of the seats were contested. The Republican National Committee, made up almost entirely of loyal Taft supporters, allowed Roosevelt only 19 out of 254 contested seats, and thus in advance counted him out of the nomination.

Roosevelt had come in person to the convention to direct his forces, and the night before it opened, he told a hysterically cheering throng of 5,000 that he would not be bound by the convention if it failed to seat his contested delegates. He concluded thunderously: "We stand at Armageddon, and we battle for the Lord." As good as his word, he bolted, leaving the conservatives in complete command at the Republican convention. With Roosevelt's onetime friend Elihu Root presiding, Warren G. Harding, one of the most regular of the regulars, mellifluously nominated Taft, who was chosen on the first ballot.

During the Republican convention, Roosevelt had agreed to the formation of a new, Progressive party when Frank Munsey, the newspaper magnate, and George W. Perkins, of United States Steel and International Harvester, promised him financing. Announcing his willingness to run, Roosevelt said he was as fit as a bull moose, giving the party a symbol as well as a name. When the Progressives met at Chicago in August to nominate Roosevelt formally, the conclave was far more symbolic of progressivism than of ordinary American politics. Missing were La Follette and his following, five of seven governors who had signed a call for Roosevelt in January, and such notable Republican insurgents as Norris of Nebraska and William E. Borah of Idaho.

The convention was more like a camp meeting than the gatherings to which Roosevelt was accustomed. The delegates sang "Onward Christian Soldiers" and closed the convention with the "Doxology." Roosevelt seemed bewildered as he acknowledged their almost fanatical, hymn-singing welcome, for "they were crusaders; he was not."

Roosevelt's program would accept big business but would regulate it through a national industrial commission. And a Federal Securities Commission would police stocks and bonds. In the program there was much to appeal to the progressives of the cities, whether reformers or businessmen, but little of interest to farmers, and much paternalism but no guarantee of collective bargaining for organized labor. In an effort to win disgruntled Southern businessmen away from the Democratic party, Roosevelt endorsed a lily-white (excluding Negroes) Progressive party for the South.

The New Freedom

Between the time Roosevelt bolted the Republican convention and the time he received the Progressive nomination, the Democrats met in Baltimore and exulted in the knowledge that, though theirs was a minority party, they were almost certainly choosing the next President.

Woodrow Wilson and Champ Clark
*Speaker Clark seemed an almost certain nominee at the 1912 Democratic
convention, at one point receiving well over a majority of the delegates' votes,
556 to 350½, but it took two-thirds to nominate. When finally he lost to Wilson
he went to Sea Girt, New Jersey, where Wilson was spending the summer, to
demonstrate his party support. (Culver Pictures)*

WOODROW WILSON WINS

In Baltimore, Bryan, who long had dominated the party, stood aside while four contenders battled for the nomination. These were Governor Woodrow Wilson of New Jersey, Speaker Champ Clark of Missouri, the right-wing Governor Judson Harmon of Ohio, and Representative Oscar W. Underwood of Alabama, the champion of Southern conservatives and a low tariff. Wilson's spectacular reform achievements in New Jersey had made him the favorite of Democratic progressives in Eastern cities, and he took a quick lead for the nomination as he crisscrossed the nation to make hundreds of inspiring speeches denouncing special privilege and heralding the new progressive order. Yet, in 1912, he emerged from the primaries and state conventions with only 248 delegates to Clark's 436. Underwood swept most of the South.

It was little short of a miracle that Clark, who had the rural Democrats and most of the bosses behind him, and who obtained more than a majority of the votes on ballot after ballot, nevertheless failed to win the nomination. The main reason for the miracle was that the Wilson and Underwood forces stood firm, blocking Clark's nomination, while Wilson's managers negotiated deals with the machines and with Underwood's following. To some extent Clark's defeat may have been due to Bryan, who threw his support to Wilson at a critical moment in the convention struggle.

A crusade requires a crusader, and the Democrats obtained one at last on the forty-sixth ballot when they nominated Wilson. This lean, lantern-jawed son of a Southern Presbyterian preacher looked as well as acted the part. His aspiration had always been to become a political leader, but when he found the road rough as a beginning lawyer in Atlanta, he took a Ph.D. degree at Johns Hopkins, became a professor of political economy, and then served as president of Princeton University.

Both as president of Princeton and as governor of New Jersey, Wilson demonstrated the courageous strength and alarming weaknesses that would characterize his presidency. He had the vision to inspire multitudes but was dogmatic and distant with individuals. He could lecture an opponent in high moral terms, but his sense that he and he alone was absolutely right prevented him from stooping to necessary political negotiations.

Wilson had won the nomination without badly splitting the party. Backed by a progres-

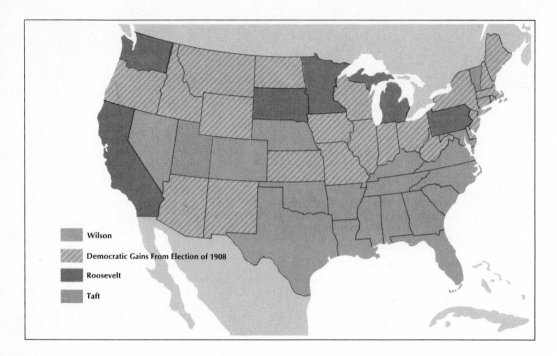

Wilson

Democratic Gains From Election of 1908

Roosevelt

Taft

Election of 1912

sive platform, he appeared before the electorate in armor at least as brightly shining as Roosevelt's. The distance between the positions of the Democratic party and the new Progressive party was not as great as campaign oratory made it out to be, just as personality more than principles separated Wilson from Roosevelt. Nevertheless, the differences in platform were significant in the campaign and in Wilson's future program as President.

Wilson's program, called the New Freedom, emerged as the campaign unfolded. His conversion to progressivism had come only two or three years before, and he had continued to cling to the state-rights position that the task of the federal government was the purely negative one of destroying privilege. Thus Wilson hoped to restore the good old days, which in reality had never existed, by recreating full opportunity for the small enterpriser. Roosevelt's New Nationalism, Wilson charged, would mean the federal licensing of the juggernauts of big business to crush the American people. In contrast, Wilson proclaimed his New Freedom as the fight for emancipation of the small businessman, the "man on the make." He pro-

claimed: "If America is not to have free enterprise, then she can have freedom of no sort whatever."

Wilson was able to win over Bryan's rural and small-town following with the same religious appeal, the same denunciation of the Wall Street money trust, that the "Great Commoner" had always used. Some well-educated people who had always scorned Bryan as a fool came to worship Wilson as a saint.

Thus Wilson was able to hold Democratic progressives, while Roosevelt was able only to pull progressives out of the Republican party. As for Taft, after several sad speeches, so conservative that they might have been written by Aldrich, he lapsed into silence. The Socialists, at the peak of their strength under Eugene V. Debs, criticized all three major candidates as defenders of capitalism. The main effect of the Socialists was to serve as a bugaboo for progressive leaders, who could warn that the only alternative to their own safe, moderate programs would be the drastic remedies of Socialism. Even in 1912, their heyday, the Socialists attracted only 901,000 votes, 6 percent of the total votes cast.

Because of the three-cornered contest, Wilson carried the electoral college overwhelmingly, with 435 votes to 88 for Roosevelt and only 8 for Taft. Wilson had received less than 42 percent of the popular vote, fewer votes than Bryan in any of his three campaigns. Yet, considering the combined Democratic and Bull Moose totals, the newly elected President had an overwhelming progressive mandate.

PRESIDENTIAL LEADERSHIP

Few Presidents have taken more seriously their electoral mandate or worked more effectively to transform it into law than did Wilson. He brought back into the White House a strong belief in firm, positive presidential leadership.

The closest of Wilson's advisers was the shrewd and ubiquitous Colonel Edward M. House, who virtually shared presidential powers as Wilson's alter ego until 1919. House served as an agent for Wilson in negotiations first with the men of economic power in America, and later with those of political power in Europe. His discretion and anonymity were so consumate that one contemporary remarked: "He can walk on dead leaves and make no more noise than a tiger."

Wilson's official advisers, the members of his cabinet, were less influential. Bryan had to be offered the post of Secretary of State in recognition of his long leadership of the party. Representative William B. Wilson, former secretary-treasurer of the United Mine Workers, became the first Secretary of Labor, establishing a twenty-year precedent that the office should be filled by a labor leader. It was the most Southern cabinet since the Civil War; half of its members were Southerners, at least by birth.

Wilson promptly undertook what Roosevelt had avoided and Taft had failed to achieve – a substantial lowering of the tariff. On the day he took office he called a special session of Congress. When it met, he did what no other President since Jefferson had done: he appeared before Congress in person. His short graphic message was aimed less at congressmen than at their constituents. It brought to a blaze the sentiment for real tariff reform. With the President's active support, Underwood introduced a bill in the House providing for tariff cuts substantial enough to bring European manufacturers into competition with Americans.

To make up for the loss of revenue under the new tariff, Representative Cordell Hull drafted a section for the bill, providing for a graduated income tax under the Sixteenth Amendment. Hull cautiously set the rates exceedingly low. Then, to his delight, progressive Republican and Democratic senators forced substantially higher rates upon the conservatives and the administration. This first modern income tax imposed a 1-percent tax upon individuals and corporations earning over $4,000, and an additional 1-percent tax on income over $20,000, ranging up to a maximum of 6 percent on income over $500,000. This income tax was the beginning of a great change in the American tax structure. Although more slowly than England and some other nations, the United States was beginning to place a proportionately greater share of the cost of government upon the rich. In so doing, it was beginning to chip away at the enormous disparity in incomes in the United States.

THE TRUSTS AGAIN

Rather than lose momentum, President Wilson held Congress in session through the sweltering summer to begin work on banking reform. In 1911 he had declared: "The great monopoly in this country is the money monopoly. So long as that exists, our old variety and freedom and individual energy of development are out of the question." Early in 1913, a House investigating committee headed by a Democrat, Arsene Pujo, published frightening statistics to back Wilson's accusation. These figures, to which Louis D. Brandeis gave wide circulation in a series of articles entitled "Other People's Money," indicated that small banks were depositing their surpluses with larger ones, which in turn deposited with a few great investment bankers concentrated on Wall Street. These bankers with their enormous capital, representing the aggregate savings of millions of people, were able to demand control over corporations in return for granting them financing, "the life blood of business." The Morgan-Rockefeller empire held "in all, 341 directorships in 112 corporations having aggregate

The Credit Monopoly [1913]

Far more dangerous than all that has happened to us in the past in the way of elimination of competition in industry is the control of credit through the domination of these groups over our banks and industries. . . .

Whether under a different currency system the resources in our banks would be greater or less is comparatively immaterial if they continued to be controlled by a small group. . . .

If the arteries of credit now clogged well-nigh to choking by the obstructions created through the control of these groups are opened so that they may be permitted freely to play their important part in the financial system, competition in large enterprises will become possible and business can be conducted on its merits instead of being subject to the tribute and the good will of this handful of self-constituted trustees of the national prosperity. — Report of the Pujo Committee, *February 28, 1913.*

---

resources or capitalization of $22,245,000,000." This was in 1913, when the entire national wealth was less than ten times this figure.

To Wilson, there was clearly a need to break the money trust. At the same time, paradoxically, one of the serious ills of the American banking system was its decentralization and independence, except for the loose tie of urban clearing houses. This, and the defective functioning of the national banking system, meant that in time of financial crisis and deflation it was hard for banks to draw upon their reserves or to expand their currency. With Wilson's encouragement, Congress responded to the need for banking reform.

The Federal Reserve Act (1913) created twelve regional banks. Each was to serve and be owned by the banks of its district. The Federal Reserve Bank would rediscount their notes, issue a new type of paper currency—Federal Reserve notes—and fulfill other banking functions for member banks and for the government. The act required national banks to become members and encouraged other banks to do so. Nearly half the nation's banking resources were represented in the system within its first year of operation, and four-fifths by the late 1920s. Bankers had no cause to fear the Federal Reserve Board, which governed the system, and to which Wilson appointed conservative, sympathetic men. The system was a notable advance in banking regulation, providing as it did for a more elastic currency, though it did not destroy the "money trust."

There remained the problem of the great business combinations. As several antitrust bills began to move through Congress in 1914, Wilson gave his support to one bill prohibiting unfair trade practices and establishing a Federal Trade Commission to watch out for them. He accepted the Clayton Antitrust Act, though it was not quite as strong a measure as he had desired. Conservatives in Congress put qualifying clauses around the sections outlawing interlocking directorates or stockholdings and exclusive selling contracts, so that the clauses, as a progressive Republican senator complained, did not have enough teeth to masticate milk toast. Labor gained nothing of practical importance from the bill, which did, however, contain a platitude that labor was not a commodity and declared that unions were not conspiracies in restraint of trade. President Gompers of the AFL chose to hail the Clayton Act as "Labor's Magna Carta" and to insist that organized labor was now exempted from antitrust prosecution. This assumption served merely to make bitterness and resentment greater when courts continued in the twenties to follow their earlier inclinations. The Sherman and Clayton acts, though ineffective for breaking up business monopolies, were stout clubs for disciplining boycotters and strikers.

The debate over antitrust legislation during the first half of 1914 coincided with a decline in prosperity. This came because the United States, still a debtor nation easily affected by European money markets, suffered from credit restrictions growing out of European pessimism over the Balkan wars and the likelihood of a bigger war. Within this country, businessmen blamed the recession upon the Underwood tariff, and the other legislation of the New Freedom. Wilson tried to placate business titans through friendly conferences and mild administration of his new reform legislation. He assured the leaders that he only opposed businesses that expanded "by methods which unrighteously crushed those who were smaller."

RETREAT AND ADVANCE

Through 1914 and 1915, to the disappointment of many advanced progressives, Wilson again and again applied the brakes to reforms. With a state-rights answer he turned aside the plea for female suffrage. He condoned the actions of his Southern cabinet members when they introduced Jim Crow practices (discriminating against Negroes) into the administration to an unprecedented degree. Only the angry protests of Northern liberals brought some reversal. He opposed a bill to establish federally backed land banks to ease credit to farmers, declaring it went beyond the proper scope of the government. He gave no aid to a child-labor bill because he thought it unconstitutional. Only with reluctance did he sign the La Follette Seamen's bill of 1915, the work of the eloquent president of the Seamen's Union, Andrew Furuseth, which improved safety regulations and working conditions for men in the merchant marine.

For Wilson, the New Freedom might be complete, but not for the progressive Democrats in Congress. At times they expressed their sharp dismay, though they did not have to engage in warfare with him as the Republican insurgents had done with Taft. When the election year 1916 opened, two things were apparent. The Progressive party, which had never been much more than a Roosevelt vehicle, was disintegrating. Unless the Democrats, who were normally a minority, presented a new, strong progressive program, they would be swamped at the polls by the reunited Republicans. Wilson saw this danger and again became an enthusiastic reformer, going beyond the New Freedom and allying himself with the progressives, farmers, and laborers to accept a series of laws that in many respects enacted the Progressive party program of 1912. From a negative policy of restriction he moved to a positive one of vigorous federal economic and social intervention. Curiously, this came at a time when Roosevelt had moved to the far right and no longer supported his 1912 proposals.

In January 1916, Wilson named Louis D. Brandeis to the Supreme Court and weathered the conservative storm in order to obtain Senate confirmation. Brandeis was both liberal and Jewish, the first man of his faith to serve on the highest bench.

In May the President accepted a farm-loan bank system in the Federal Farm Loan Act. At the urging of progressives, he applied pressure upon the Democratic leaders in the Senate to obtain a workmen's compensation system for federal employees and the first federal child-labor law. The child-labor law, the Keating-Owen Act of 1916, prohibited the shipment in interstate commerce of products manufactured by children. It marked not only a significant reversal on the part of Wilson but also a new assumption of federal control over manufacturing through the commerce clause. When the Supreme Court invalidated the law by a 5-to-4 decision in 1918, Congress passed an act levying a heavy tax on the products of child labor. This too President Wilson signed, and the Supreme Court ultimately invalidated, with Chief Justice Taft writing the decision.

Despite the setback in regard to child labor, this second wave of legislation of the Wilson administration significantly restored and enlarged the regulatory function of the federal government. After Wilson had failed to mediate a dispute between the railroad brotherhoods and the railroads, he signed an emergency measure, the Adamson Act, to prevent a nationwide railroad strike that would have paralyzed commerce. The measure provided for an eight-hour day at the previous ten-hours' pay for all railroad workers.

Other lesser-known pieces of legislation brought about even greater changes. Without attracting much attention, they undermined state rights by granting subsidies on a dollar-matching basis for states to undertake various types of programs. These laws, in combination with the new income tax, took money out of the wealthier Northeastern areas and redistributed it in the South and West. The first such law was the Smith-Lever Act of 1914, which provided money for states to establish extension work in agricultural education. This formalized and nationalized the new system of county agents to advise farmers, and facilitated the rise of the powerful American Farm Bureau Federation. It was followed by the Smith-Hughes Act of 1917 which subsidized vocational courses in secondary schools. Most important of all, the Federal Highway Act of 1916 appropriated $75 million to be spent for road-building over a period of five years.

Wilson was justified in his boast that the Democrats had come close to carrying out the Progressive party's platform as well as their own.

Selected Readings

Synthesis and Interpretations
Richard Hofstadter, *The Age of Reform** (1955); Eric Goldman, *Rendezvous with Destiny: A History of Modern American Reform** (1952); R. H. Wiebe, *Businessmen and Reform* (1962) and *The Search for Order, 1877–1920** (1967); Christopher Lasch, *The New Radicalism in America, 1889–1963* (1965); Gabriel Kolko, *The Triumph of Conservatism* (1963); J. R. Chamberlain, *Farewell to Reform** (1932).

Progressive Journalism
C. C. Regier, *The Era of the Muckrakers* (1932); Walter Johnson, *William Allen White's America* (1947); Charles Forcey, *The Crossroads of Liberalism: Croly, Weyl, Lippmann, and the Progressive Era, 1900–1925** (1961); Herbert Croly, *The Promise of American Life** (1909); Lincoln Steffens, *Autobiography* (2 vols., 1931).

States and Cities
G. E. Mowry, *California Progressives** (1951); R. S. Maxwell, *La Follette and the Rise of Progressivism in Wisconsin* (1944); D. P. Thelen, *The New Citizenship: Origins of Progressivism in Wisconsin, 1885–1900* (1972); H. L. Warner, *Progressivism in Ohio, 1897–1917* (1964); R. M. Abrams, *Conservatism in a Progressive Era: Massachusetts Politics, 1900–1912* (1946); Jane Addams, *Forty Years at Hull House** (1935); A. F. Davis, *Spearheads of Reform: The Social Settlements and the Progressive Movement, 1890–1914* (1968); Ray Lubove, *The Progressives and the Slums: Tenement House Reform in New York City, 1890–1917* (1962); J. D. Buenker, *Urban Liberalism and Progressive Reform* (1973).

Roosevelt
G. E. Mowry, *The Era of Theodore Roosevelt** (1958) and *Theodore Roosevelt and the Progressive Movement** (1946); H. F. Pringle, *Theodore Roosevelt* (1931); W. H. Harbaugh, *Power and Responsibility** (1961); J. M. Blum, *The Republican Roosevelt** (1954); J. A. Garraty, *Right Hand Man: The Life of George W. Perkins* (1960), a leading Bull Mooser.

Taft and the Insurgents
H. F. Pringle, *The Life and Times of William Howard Taft* (2 vols., 1939); Kenneth Hechler, *Insurgency: Personalities and Policies of the Taft Era* (1940); James Holt, *Congressional Insurgents and the Party System, 1909–1916* (1967); D. F. Anderson, *William Howard Taft: A Conservative's Conception of the Presidency* (1973).

Wilson
A. S. Link, *Wilson: The Road to the White House* (1947), *Wilson: The New Freedom* (1956), and *Woodrow Wilson and the Progressive Era, 1910–1917** (1954); A. C. Walworth, *Woodrow Wilson* (2 vols., 1958); J. M. Blum, *Woodrow Wilson and the Politics of Morality** (1956) and *Joe Tumulty and the Wilson Era* (1951); W. E. Leuchtenberg, ed., *Wilson: The New Freedom** (1961), containing selections from Wilson's writings.

Progressives and Conservatives
Belle and Fola La Follette, *Robert M. La Follette* (2 vols., 1953); R. M. La Follette, *Autobiography** (1913); Richard Lowitt, *George W. Norris: The Making of a Progressive, 1861–1912* (1963) and *The Persistence of a Progressive, 1913–1933* (1971); C. G. Bowers, *Beveridge and the Progressive Era* (1932); A. T. Mason, *Brandeis: A Free Man's Life* (1946); F. L. Allen, *The Great Pierpont Morgan* (1949); N. W. Stephenson, *Nelson W. Aldrich* (1920); Richard Leopold, *Elihu Root and the Conservative Tradition** (1954).

Progressive Policies
S. P. Hays, *The Gospel of Efficiency: The Progressive Conservation Movement, 1890–1920** (1959); E. R. Richardson, *The Politics of Conservation: Crusade and Controversies, 1897–1913** (1962); O. E. Anderson, *The Health of a Nation: Harvey W. Wiley and the Fight for Pure Food* (1958); A. Martin, *Enterprise Denied: Origins of the Decline of the American Railroads, 1897–1917* (1971).

Socialists and Unions

Ray Ginger, *The Bending Cross: A Biography of Eugene Victor Debs* (1949); Ira Kipnis, *The American Socialist Movement, 1897–1912* (1952); D. A. Shannon, *The Socialist Party of America* (1955); J. R. Conlin, *Bread and Roses Too: Studies of the Wobblies* (1971); Marc Karson, *American Labor Unions and Politics, 1900–1918* (1958); R. J. Cornell, *The Anthracite Coal Strike of 1902* (1957).

The Negro

I. A. Newby, *Jim Crow's Defense: Anti-Negro Thought in America, 1900–1930* (1965); E. M. Rudwick, *W. E. B. DuBois: A Study of Minority Group Leadership** (1960); R. S. Baker, *Following the Color Line** (1908); E. S. Redkey, *Black Exodus: Black Nationalism and Back-to-Africa Movements, 1890–1910** (1969).

*Titles available in paperback.

The War to End War

Twenty-two

While Americans clung to the old idea of keeping out of Europe's quarrels, the nation drifted toward the twentieth-century maelstrom of world conflict. The industrial developments in Europe had brought, along with increased material abundance, a heightened competition for markets, sources of raw materials, places for investment, and sheer national prestige. To the great powers came not only social gains but also military ambitions, with an arms race that grew more and more frightening as Europe divided into two hostile alliances.

As the foremost of all industrial nations, the United States could scarcely remain unaffected by world events for long. Its emergence from the Spanish-American War with Pacific and Caribbean colonies intensified the risks of involvement. So did certain phases of the progressive spirit itself, which stimulated increased activity in foreign affairs. Some progressives aspired not only to revitalize democracy at home but also to extend it abroad. Finally, World War I brought the greatest challenge in a hundred years to the time-honored policy of neutrality and diplomatic independence.

For three years, from 1914 to 1917, the United States remained at peace, and then it joined in the hostilities. Its entrance hardly meant that the traditional policy had failed, for strict neutrality had not been tried. The American people had closer ties of kinship and commerce with one set of European belligerents than with the other. The prosperity of this country had come to depend on swollen wartime trade with the one side, which needed supplies in order to continue the war. Both groups of warring countries attempted to cut off the other's imports, and both used methods that were contrary to international law as the United States had long interpreted it. But now the American government drew a sharp distinction between the violations of neutral rights on the one side and on the other. In the one case this government protested long-windedly and

Signing the Peace Treaty   1919
On June 28, 1919, in the resplendent Hall of Mirrors in the Versailles Palace, the Allies and Germany signed a treaty to end World War I. In this painting by Sir William Orpen, the Big Three among the Allied peacemakers—Wilson, Clemenceau, and Lloyd George—are sitting at the front, center. (Courtesy, Trustees of the Imperial War Museum)

perfunctorily; in the other, it took a stern and threatening stand, demanding a "strict accountability."

According to this country's constitutional system, one man has the ultimate responsibility for war or peace – the President. In 1917 President Wilson made the decision for war. He saw it as a war to end war, to bring about an international organization for keeping the future peace, and thus to "make the world safe for democracy." After the military victory had been won, however, the Senate refused to accept his plan for a League of Nations, despite his pleas that the United States must join the League if a second world war were to be prevented. At the height of his struggle for the League, he suffered a stroke that left him a partially paralyzed as well as a deeply embittered man.

Progressivism by the Sword

Progressive foreign policy, as practiced by Roosevelt, Taft, and Wilson, from 1901 to 1917, was rather aggressive, particularly in dealings with Latin America and the Far East.

T. R. AND WORLD POLITICS

As much as any other progressive, Theodore Roosevelt liked to engage in moralizing about the position of the United States in the world. His most often repeated theme was, as he once put it: "The just war is a war for the integrity of high ideals. The only safe motto for the individual citizen of a democracy fit to play a great part in the world is service – service by work and help in peace, service through the high gallantry of entire indifference to life, if war comes on land." This kind of talk rallied the support of many progressives, even those who were revolted by Roosevelt's blatant militarism – his equally incessant extolling of the soldierly virtues as "the most valuable of all qualities." Despite his bombast, he conducted foreign affairs with a sure hand.

Roosevelt's concept of the role of the United States in world politics emphasized sea power. Now that the United States had colonies, it needed to build a navy powerful enough to keep the sea lanes open to them. It also needed to build an Isthmian canal so that naval units could sail quickly from one ocean to another, and not have to make a long and difficult voyage around Cape Horn, as the *Oregon* had done during the Spanish-American War. In addition it needed to protect the Caribbean approaches to the canal from encroachment. All this predicated a strong naval policy at a time when the key to strength in the world was a powerful fleet. This meant a navy second only to that of Great Britain.

Such were the views of President Roosevelt at the time when Kaiser Wilhelm II was launching Germany upon a gigantic naval race with Great Britain. As Britain began construction of the first dreadnought (large modern battleship) in 1905, both Germany and the United States were building more and larger warships, amid growing alarums of war. Urged on by Roosevelt, the most effective of naval lobbyists, Congress voted appropriations for ten battleships and four armored cruisers between 1902 and 1904. These were more powerful and more widely ranging than the relatively light vessels of the nineties, which had been designed primarily to defend the American coast. By 1906 the American navy was second only to the British, but in the next few years was surpassed by the German navy.

Roosevelt liked to quote an African proverb: "Speak softly and carry a big stick." This certainly characterized his action in the Far East, as well as in the Caribbean. He hoped to make the Open Door policy effective against Russian expansion in Manchuria. For a moment in 1903 he expressed such indignation over the "treachery" and "mendacity" of Russia that he toyed with the idea of going to "extremes" with her. His practical policy, however, was to encourage Japanese efforts to check the Russian drive. When the Japanese made a surprise attack upon the Russian fleet

at Port Arthur, Manchuria, in 1904, he was inclined to cheer, as were most Americans. He
warned the French and Germans against aiding Russia, but he did not wish to see the Japanese totally victorious, since this might "possibly mean a struggle between them and us in
the future."

Roosevelt pursued this same policy in the
peace negotiations. Though the Japanese won
a series of spectacular victories, they faced
such serious financial difficulties that they
asked Roosevelt to mediate. He agreed and
called a peace conference at Portsmouth, New
Hampshire, in the summer of 1905. But he soon
offended the Japanese by opposing their demands for an enormous indemnity. He lost
their good will even though he approved their
territorial gains at the conference – control
over Korea and South Manchuria and annexation of the southern half of Sakhalin Island,
which had belonged to Russia.

Japanese-American relations, thus suddenly made worse, were not much improved
by a secret Japanese-American agreement
which was effected at the time of the Portsmouth conference. President Roosevelt had
dispatched Secretary of War Taft from Manila
to Tokyo to reach a Far Eastern understanding
with the Japanese. In the resulting Taft-Kat-
sura memorandum of July 1905, the Japanese
prime minister acknowledged American sovereignty in the Philippines, and the American
President recognized the suzerainty of Japan
over Korea.

Roosevelt's role in helping to negotiate the
1905 Treaty of Portsmouth won for him the
Nobel Peace Prize. His actions did indeed contribute to preservation of the peace by maintaining a power balance between Russia and
Japan on the Asian mainland. But in Asian
waters, Japan had risen to a new ascendancy
through its destruction of the Russian fleets.
Japan repaired and refloated many of the vessels and rapidly built new ships in the following
years. Japan undoubtedly had become powerful enough to seize the Philippines (which
Roosevelt came to regard as an Achilles heel)
because the American fleet would have had
trouble fighting effectively so far from home.
Unfortunately, at this same time, the people of
Japan and the United States became angry
with each other.

In October 1906, within a year after Japan's victory over a great European power, the
San Francisco school board ordered the segregation of Oriental schoolchildren. This step was
taken in response to the feelings of Californians
against the 500 to 1,000 Japanese immigrants
coming in each year, feelings which were intensified by lurid "Yellow Peril" articles in the
Hearst and other newspapers. Resentment in
Japan flared high, and jingoes in each country
fanned the flames still higher.

Roosevelt worked skillfully to douse the
flames. He persuaded San Francisco to desegregate its schools, and in return in 1907 he negotiated a "Gentlemen's Agreement" with
Japan to keep out agricultural laborers. Then,
lest the Japanese government think he had
acted through fear, he launched a spectacular
naval demonstration. He sent sixteen battleships of the new navy, "the Great White Fleet,"
on an unprecedented 45,000-mile voyage
around the world. It gave the navy invaluable
experience in sailing in formation while demonstrating the danger of dependence on for-
eign-owned coaling stations. The Japanese invited this formidable armada to visit Yokohama
and gave it a clamorous welcome. Thus Roosevelt came to feel that through brandishing the
big stick he had helped the cause of peace.

For the moment, the United States had
demonstrated sufficient naval strength to restore an unsteady balance in Asian waters. In
1908, before the fleet had returned home, Japan and the United States negotiated the comprehensive Root-Takahira Agreement. Both
countries agreed to support the Open Door in
China. The United States tacitly seemed to give
Japan a free hand in Manchuria (where rivalry
with Russia continued) in return for an explicit
guarantee of the status quo in the Pacific. This
precarious equilibrium might be destroyed by
any future upset in the naval ratios.

At the same time that he was directly engaged in balancing the powers in the Pacific,
Roosevelt was participating somewhat less directly in trying to maintain a balance in Europe. American relations with Great Britain
were increasingly cordial. In 1903, the British
agreed to refer a troublesome dispute over the
boundary between Alaska and Canada to a tribunal of three Americans, two Canadians, and
one Englishman. To cultivate the friendship of
the United States, the English member of the
tribunal voted against the Canadians and in
favor of the American claim. Then the British
government made another concession by pull-

ing its naval units out of the Caribbean and leaving it as virtually an American lake.

When Germany and France quarreled over Morocco, Roosevelt was reluctant to involve the United States. "We have other fish to fry," he told Taft in 1905. Nevertheless, he resolved to try "to keep matters on an even keel in Europe." Consequently he intervened on behalf of the German Kaiser to persuade France and England to attend an international conference for establishing the status of Morocco. Germany was protesting because the French had set up a protectorate there. At the conference, which met in Algeciras, Spain, in 1906, the American delegates sided with the British and the French to keep France dominant in Morocco while making some concessions to appease Germany. For the moment the United States had helped avert, or at least postpone, a war into which it might ultimately be dragged.

THE IRON-FISTED NEIGHBOR

Roosevelt's preoccupation with the American strategy of defense in the Caribbean—especially his almost obsessive fear of German penetration—betrayed him into acting like an iron-fisted neighbor toward small countries to the south. He first used his might impetuously to start work on a canal in Panama.

Before Roosevelt became President, the McKinley administration was negotiating with England to remove an old obstacle, the 1850 treaty agreeing that the two countries would jointly construct, operate, and defend any canal to be built in Central America. In 1901 the British, eager to court American friendship, consented in the Hay-Pauncefote treaty to exclusive American construction, operation, and fortification of a canal.

The next question was where to locate the canal. There were two possible routes. The

T. R. at the Panama Canal
Visiting Panama in 1906, while the canal was under construction, President Roosevelt posed at the controls of a gigantic steam shovel, which was being used for excavation at Culebra Cut. (Library of Congress)

Theodore Roosevelt's Latin American Policy [1905]

It cannot be too often and too emphatically asserted that the United States has not the slightest desire for territorial aggrandizement at the expense of any of its southern neighbors, and will not treat the Monroe Doctrine as an excuse for such aggrandizement on its part. . . . Moreover . . . we do not intend to permit the Monroe Doctrine to be used by any nation on this Continent as a shield to protect it from the consequences of its own misdeeds against foreign nations. . . . On the one hand, this country would certainly decline to go to war to prevent a foreign government from collecting a just debt; on the other hand, it is very inadvisable to permit any foreign power to take possession, even temporarily, of the custom houses of an American Republic in order to enforce the payment of its obligations; for such temporary occupation might turn into a permanent occupation. The only escape from these alternatives may at any time be that we must ourselves undertake to bring about some arrangement by which so much as possible of a just obligation shall be paid. . . . The justification for the United States taking this burden and incurring this responsibility is to be found in the fact that it is incompatible with international equity for the United States to refuse to allow other powers to take the only means at their disposal of satisfying the claims of their creditors and yet to refuse, itself, to take any such steps. — Annual Message to Congress, December 5, 1905.

---

shortest one would be across the Isthmus of Panama, but the rights there were owned by a French company, the successor of an earlier company that had tried and failed to dig a canal. For its franchise, the French company wanted $109 million, which would make a Panama canal more expensive than a Nicaraguan one. Consequently, both Congress and President Roosevelt favored the Nicaraguan route. But the French company had expert agents — Philippe Bunau-Varilla, its chief engineer, and William Nelson Cromwell, an attorney who had contributed heavily to the Republican campaign fund in 1900 — who hastily cut the price of their rights to $40 million. Unless sold to the United States and sold quickly, the rights would be worthless, for they would expire in 1904. This price cut and able lobbying caused Congress and the President to change their minds.

Impatient to begin construction, Roosevelt put pressure upon Colombia, which owned Panama, to conclude a treaty authorizing the United States to dig a canal there. In January 1903, Secretary of State Hay and the Colombian chargé d'affaires Tomas Herrán signed a treaty that was most unfavorable to Colombia. It authorized the United States to construct a canal in return for a payment of only $10 million and an annual rental of $250,000, as com-

pared with the $40 million the French company was to receive. The Colombian Senate, as it had every right to do, rejected the treaty.

Roosevelt was too furious to give thought to niceties or to the value of a friendly policy toward Latin America. Fuming that the Colombians were "inefficient bandits," he considered seizing Panama through twisting a technicality in an 1846 treaty with Colombia (then New Granada) guaranteeing the neutrality and free transit of the Isthmus. Roosevelt's intended seizure became unnecessary, because Bunau-Varilla helped organize a Panamanian revolution. There had been many previous revolts, all failures. But at the outset of this one, the United States landed troops from the U.S.S. *Nashville*, and, invoking the 1846 treaty obligation to maintain order, prevented Colombian forces from putting down the rebellion. Three days later the United States recognized the new republic of Panama and, soon after that, negotiated a treaty paying Panama the sum Colombia had rejected, in return for the grant of a zone ten miles wide. The minister from Panama who arranged the treaty was Bunau-Varilla.

Work on the canal proceeded smoothly and efficiently. The elimination of tropical diseases in the area, the digging of the tremendous cuts, and the installation of huge locks at a total cost $375 million filled Americans with patriotic enthusiasm, though some were ashamed of Roosevelt's ruthlessness. In 1911 he boasted: "I took the Canal Zone and let Congress debate; and while the debate goes on, the Canal does also." It opened in 1914.

Meanwhile Roosevelt was enlarging the Monroe Doctrine. In 1902 he had written to a German friend: "If any South American country misbehaves toward any European country, let the European country spank it." Germany, along with Italy and Great Britain, proceeded to spank Venezuela by blockading her coast. The object was to force the Venezuelan dictator to pay his country's debts to European bankers.

By 1903 Roosevelt had changed his mind. Americans were angered at the news of the German bombardment of a Venezuelan port, and he himself was beginning to fear that the Germans planned to establish a permanent base in Venezuela. He warned the Germans (according to his own later account) that Admiral Dewey had his fleet in the Caribbean and was ready to act in case they tried to acquire any territory. The Germans finally withdrew—as the British and Italians already had done—and agreed to submit the debt question to arbitration.

The Venezuela incident led to a new Caribbean policy usually called the "Roosevelt Corollary" of the Monroe Doctrine. The Hague Court declared that the powers that had threatened Venezuela had prior claim on payment of their debts; this increased the likelihood of future European intervention in the Western Hemisphere. For Roosevelt, who still believed that small nations must pay their just debts, the only way out seemed a drastic new device. If these little countries could not behave themselves, the United States reluctantly would police them and collect debt payments from them in order to forestall European intervention. Uncle Sam would act as a bill collector for European bankers. Roosevelt declared to Congress in 1904 that the United States might be forced, "however reluctantly, in flagrant cases of . . . wrongdoing or impotence, to the exercise of an international police power."

The occasion for putting the Roosevelt Corollary into operation was the defaulting of Santo Domingo on about $22 million of its debt to European nations. France and Italy threatened to intervene. In effect, the United States established a receivership, taking over Dominican customs, paying 45 percent of the receipts to the Dominican government, and paying the rest to foreign creditors.

As a part of an American strategy of Canal defense, Roosevelt's Caribbean policy was doubtless successful. As a means of securing the support and cooperation of nations to the south, it left much to be desired. Roosevelt's tactics inspired fear rather than friendship.

TAFT AND DOLLAR DIPLOMACY

President Taft was no readier in foreign affairs than at home to exert strong personal leadership as Roosevelt had done. For the most part he left the State Department to his Secretary of State, a former corporation lawyer, Philander C. Knox. Taft and Knox made no real effort to maintain a balance of power in either Europe or Asia. Instead, they concentrated upon promoting American banking and business interests overseas.

In Far Eastern relations, this policy brought to the forefront young Willard Straight, an agent of American bankers, formerly consul general at Mukden, Manchuria. He argued that dollar diplomacy was the financial expression of the Open Door policy, that it would make "a guaranty for the preservation, rather than the destruction of China's integrity." Taft, therefore, was ready to ignore Roosevelt's tacit arrangement with Japan that the United States would stay out of Manchuria, and to support the right of Americans to invest both there and in China. When British, French, and German bankers formed a consortium to finance railroads in China, Secretary Knox insisted that Americans should also participate. In 1911 they were admitted. Then Knox proposed that an international syndicate purchase the South Manchurian Railroad in order to neutralize it. This led the rivals Russia and Japan to sign a treaty of amity in 1910, thus closing the Manchurian door in Taft's face.

In the Caribbean there were no other great powers to block the amateurish American operations. As a result, a new pattern emerged there of interventions going far beyond Roosevelt's limited ones, to establish firm military, political, and, above all, economic control over several unstable republics to the south. Advocates of this program argued that

American investors must be invited in to replace European investors, who otherwise might eventually bring about European intervention. This was a logical step beyond the Roosevelt Corollary.

The new policy began in 1909 when Knox tried to arrange for American bankers to establish a financial receivership in Honduras. He persuaded New York bankers to invest in the National Bank of Haiti. Then he sent marines to Nicaragua to protect revolutionaries, sponsored by an American mining company, who were fighting to overthrow a hostile dictator. Knox negotiated a treaty with the new friendly government giving the United States financial control, but the United States Senate failed to approve it. American bankers, less reluctant, accepted Knox's invitation to move in. By 1912 the new pro-American government was so unpopular that a revolt broke out. Taft sent marines to crush the uprising, and some of them remained as late as 1925.

Even more than Roosevelt's policies, those of Taft alienated the neighboring countries to the south.

WILSONIAN INTERVENTION

President Wilson brought to the determination of foreign policy a flair for idealistic pronouncements. He was never unsure of his moral position but was often uncertain how to reach it. He and his Secretaries of State and the Navy, William Jennings Bryan and Josephus Daniels, were all devoutly religious, war-hating men of good will, who disapproved of the exorbitant moneymaking sometimes connected with dollar diplomacy. But the temptation to make use of the force at their disposal to uplift their brothers to the south was too great to resist. The need to do so seemed compelling to them, because like their predecessors they felt that they must maintain an American-sponsored stability in the Caribbean as a vital part of national defense.

Wilson expounded his new policies in a speech at Mobile, Alabama, in the fall of 1913. He disavowed imperialist intent. "The United States will never again seek one additional foot of territory by conquest," he declared. Rather, he sought "the development of constitutional liberty in the world."

The Wilson administration not only regularized through treaty the continuing occupation of Nicaragua, but also initiated new interventions in Santo Domingo and Haiti—to head off a supposed threat of German intervention. In spite of American customs control, revolution after revolution had swept through and impoverished Santo Domingo. The United States took over all Dominican finances and the police force, but the Dominicans would not agree to a treaty establishing a virtual protectorate. In 1916 Wilson established a military government. During the eight years that this government continued, the United States forcibly maintained order, trained a native constabulary, and promoted education, sanitation, and public works.

On the other end of the island of Hispaniola, the Negro republic of Haiti was even more revolution-wracked, the violence culminating in 1915 when a mob tore an unpopular president limb from limb. Wilson again sent in the marines, established another military government, and began the task of improving living conditions in Haiti. The marines demonstrated their efficiency in 1918 when they supervised an election to ratify a new American-sponsored constitution. The vote for it was 69,377 to 355. Nevertheless, that year they had to put down a serious revolt, killing some hundreds of Haitians in the process.

There was a persistent fear that the Germans might try to acquire the Danish West Indies. In 1902 the Senate ratified a treaty for their purchase, but the Danish parliament rejected it. Finally in 1917 the United States acquired the poverty-stricken islets, which were then renamed the Virgin Islands, for an exorbitant $25 million. Their value was negative: the United States wanted to make sure they were not in the possession of any potentially hostile power.

MAKING MEXICO BEHAVE

American business interests had invested about $1 billion in Mexico during the regime of a friendly dictator, Porfirio Díaz. They owned over half the oil, two-thirds of the railroads, and three-fourths of the mines and smelters. Popular though Díaz was in the United States, he came to be hated in Mexico because, while he encouraged foreigners to amass huge profits, he suppressed civil liberties and kept the masses in peonage. For the average Mexican, there was little of the progress toward democracy or economic security that President Wilson desired. In 1910 the aged Díaz was overthrown by a democratic reform leader, who in turn was murdered and succeeded by the reactionary Victoriano Huerta just before Wilson took office. Wilson turned a deaf ear to American investors who saw in Huerta's presidency an opportunity to return to the "good old days." Rather, he refused to recognize "the government of butchers."

Years of tedious complications followed. Wilson hoped that, by refusing recognition to Huerta's government, he could bring about its collapse and the development of constitutionalism in Mexico. He offered in June 1913 to mediate between Huerta and the opposing Constitutionalists of Venustiano Carranza. Both sides refused.

For several months Wilson pursued a policy of "watchful waiting," but when Huerta established a full military dictatorship in October 1913, Wilson began to bring increasing pressure against him. First he persuaded the British (who were obtaining most of their naval oil from Mexico) to stop supporting Huerta. Next he offered to send American troops to the aid of Carranza, but again he was rebuffed, since all Carranza wanted was the right to buy arms in the United States. Wilson granted this in February 1914 by lifting President Taft's arms embargo, but still the Carranzists did not win.

Wilson was in a dilemma: he might have to choose between recognizing Huerta, stronger than ever, or intervening with armed force, which could mean war against all the Mexican factions. Off the coast of Mexico, the commanders of American fleet units, engaged in watchful waiting, became increasingly restless. The precipitate action of one of them gave Wilson a way out. In April 1914 one of Huerta's officers arrested several sailors of the U.S.S. *Dolphin* who had gone ashore at Tampico; a superior officer quickly released them and apologized. But the American admiral demanded a twenty-one gun salute to the United States flag in addition. At this Huerta balked. Wilson, deciding to back the admiral, sent all available warships to Mexican waters and asked Congress for authority to take drastic action. Then, anxious to prevent a German ship loaded with munitions from reaching Huerta's forces, Wilson, without

The U.S. in Mexico   1914–1917

waiting for Congress to act, ordered the navy to seize Veracruz. It did so, on April 21 and 22, 1914, but not in the bloodless way that Wilson had anticipated. The Mexicans suffered 126 killed and 195 wounded; the Americans, 19 killed and 71 wounded.

At this difficult point, Argentina, Brazil, and Chile offered to mediate. With relief, Wilson accepted, and sent his delegates to confer with Huerta's at Niagara Falls, Canada, from May to July 1914. As the negotiations went on and on, the Carranzists advanced on Mexico City, finally bringing the result Wilson wished, the abdication of Huerta.

Under Carranza's presidency, the Mexican muddle did not clear up but got worse. By September 1914 civil war was again devastating Mexico, as a former general of Carranza's, Francisco ("Pancho") Villa, tried to overthrow him. In October 1915 the United States gave de facto recognition to Carranza's government.

This antagonized Villa, who was still roaming northern Mexico. He tried to bring about a war between the United States and Mexico by shooting sixteen Americans he seized from a train in January 1916. When that failed, in March he raided Columbus, New Mexico, just across the border, killing nineteen more Americans. Wilson retaliated by ordering a punitive expedition under Brigadier General John J.

The Course of American Art

IV. THE NEW CENTURY:
The Avant Garde and Isolationism

Plate 1: Cass Gilbert,
WOOLWORTH BUILDING, NEW YORK
(Photo by Sandak)

The beginning of the twentieth century was a turbulent time for the development of American art. The traditional flow of European influence continued to affect accepted taste, but, at the same time, energetic and inventive American artists, architects, and craftsmen began to challenge the artistic establishment and strive to create a truly American art.

The battle lines between progressive and conservative expression can best be observed in the evolution of that uniquely American structure, the skyscraper. Just as it seemed that Louis Sullivan and the Chicago school of architects had freed the tall building from the veneer of historical styles, a new wave of eclecticism spread across the country. The renewed interest in the Paris School of Beaux Arts gained impetus from the highly successful Chicago World's Fair of 1893, which emphasized historical and borrowed styles; and Sullivan's functionally inspired emphasis on the steel grid structure for the skyscraper gave way to a new variety of decorative shells.

The Woolworth Building *(Plate 1)*, erected in 1913 by Cass Gilbert, utilized a medieval vocabulary of gargoyles and intricate tracery to create a Gothic profile on the skyline of New York. The choice of historical style was influenced by a prevailing deification of business, reflected in the sentiments of the architect and his client, who called the building a "Cathedral of Commerce."

Not only the skyscraper but all forms of progressive architecture had been dealt a severe setback by the World's Fair of 1893. However, a new generation of designers in Chicago, led by Frank Lloyd Wright, arose to challenge the traditional approach. Wright, who was to become one of the century's most influential architects, began his long and creative career designing homes in suburban Chicago. As a young man Wright had worked

Plate 2: Frank Lloyd Wright, WARD WILLITS HOUSE, HIGHLAND PARK, ILLINOIS *(Photo by Sandak)*

as a draftsman for Sullivan, and he deeply respected the master's concern for functionalism. But Wright added to this a personal love of the natural environment. His domestic buildings of the period reflect in their low horizontal lines the flatness of the midwestern prairie on which they were built. In Wright's design for the Ward Willits house, built in Highland Park, Illinois, in 1902 *(Plate 2)*, the dominant feature is the roof, which spreads out over the structure and anchors it visually to its site. Wright's use of the massive roof, as well as the openness and freedom of the interior plan, were derived in part from Japanese architectural sources.

In painting as in architecture the traditional Beaux Arts approach was challenged by a new generation of young artists. They were led by Robert Henri, who, although he had studied in Paris, rejected the idealism and sentimentality associated with

academic painting in favor of an unflinching objectivity and an emphasis on momentary effects. This new school of American painters, known simply as "The Eight," derived their subjects from the teeming life of the cities and depicted them with vigor and immediacy.

Henri's portrait of a "Laughing Girl," ca. 1907 *(Plate 3)*, is boldly painted in a technique reminiscent of the seventeenth century Dutch master Franz Hals. The dynamic personality of the sitter is captured in the explosive brushwork.

Another of the painters of The Eight was John Sloan. Sloan's early training as a newspaper illustrator in Philadelphia was excellent preparation for his painting of the urban environment. His depiction of common, everyday people and events, as in his "Backyards, Greenwich Village," 1914 *(Plate 4)*, transformed the poor overcrowded immigrant section of New York into a vibrant

Plate 3: Robert Henri, LAUGHING GIRL
(The University of Kansas Museum of Art)

document of city life at the turn of the century.

The Eight — or the "Ashcan School" as they were derisively called by the establishment — had an immediate impact on American painting, and their exhibition at the Macbeth Galleries in 1908 focused attention on the innovative direction in American art. But just as these young painters were establishing a new American school another wave of European influence made itself felt. This time the imported style was that of the avant-garde Fauves and Cubists, whose work was first shown to the American public at the famous Armory Show of 1913 in New York.

This exhibition of the experimental European styles had a profound effect on many American painters. One of these was Joseph Stella, who, under the influence of the Italian Futurists, adopted the cubist technique of viewing an object simultaneously from a number of points of view. He utilized this technique in order to capture the dynamic rhythms of the new industrial age. In Stella's

Plate 4: John Sloan, BACKYARDS, GREENWICH VILLAGE *(Collection of the Whitney Museum of American Art)*

canvas of "The Bridge," 1922 *(Plate 5)*, the structural elements of the towers and cables frame the cubist fragments of the city skyline. Like the painters of The Eight, Stella's theme was the American city; but he attempted to recreate the abstract qualities of movement and dynamics rather than the visual facts of appearance.

Although the Armory Show represents one of the earliest appearances of abstract art in this country, some American artists learned about the new styles through their own travels in Europe. Edward Hopper, who at the turn of the century studied with Henri, went to Paris in 1906 where he saw the

experimental painting of Matisse and Picasso. Hopper, however, rejected the abstract subjectivity of contemporary European art, preferring an objectivity based on the reality he saw around him. He was fascinated by the theme of the city, but unlike his teacher Henri, whose interest was the outward drama of urban America, Hopper invests his painting with a mood of reflective introspection. In his canvas of 1939 entitled "New York Movie" *(Plate 6)*, the subject is the ornate interior of a motion picture theatre. In subdued light, the diffused image of the black-and-white screen is contrasted with the yellowish glow behind the usher. The power of Hopper's painting is

Plate 5: Joseph Stella, THE BRIDGE
(Collection of the Newark Museum)

Plate 6: Edward Hopper, NEW YORK MOVIE *(Collection, The Museum of Modern Art, New York)*

derived from its bold simplification of forms sensitively rendered in a haunting quality of light.

American sculpture in the first quarter of the twentieth century was largely unaffected by the avant-garde styles introduced by the Armory Show. Many Americans followed in the tradition of the French realist sculptor Auguste Rodin, working in a technique of roughly modeled surfaces. But in the nineteen-twenties an interest in primitive sculpture brought about a new style. One of the leaders of this new direction was Paul Manship, who was inspired by the archaic art of Greece and the simplified forms of oriental sculpture. His rhythmic compositions often depicted human figures with stylized anatomy and flowing decorative drapery. Manship's greatest success was in large-scale figures such as the statue of Prometheus for the Lower Plaza of Rockefeller Center, 1934 *(Plate 7)*. Here the

carefully balanced, streamlined figure floats elegantly above a dramatic fountain display. Although Manship's decorative treatment is sometimes overly refined, he was the most popular sculptor of the period.

The years between the World Wars produced a number of innovations in American architecture. Once again Frank Lloyd Wright led the way in inventive design. In his 1936 Administration Building for the S. C. Johnson & Son Co. in Racine, Wisconsin *(Plate 8)*, Wright introduced a new technological advance in the use of reinforced concrete columns. These cone-shaped supports widen from their narrow base into Wright's famous "lily pad" capitols which support the ceiling. The ceiling also represents an innovative design in its use of bands of glass tubing which provide an even and diffused light into the interior. In both his inventive approach to structural problems and his imaginative use of materials, Wright represents one of the major shapers of twentieth-century architecture.

In the 1930s, with the onset of the Great Depression, American painting, like American politics, moved away from European influence toward a greater isolationism. Many painters rejected avant-garde modernism, especially abstraction, in favor of a realistic narrative style. One such group of painters, known as Regionalists, took their subject matter from the folk legends of the Midwest. Their desire to create an American idiom was shared by writers and musicians of the period – among them William Faulkner and Aaron Copland – and supported by government-sponsored programs.

One of the artists associated with the

Plate 7: Paul Manship, PROMETHEUS *(Courtesy of Rockefeller Center, Inc.)*

Plate 8: Frank Lloyd Wright,
JOHNSON WAX ADMINISTRATION BUILDING:
LOBBY *(Photo Courtesy of Johnson Wax)*

Plate 9: John Steuart Curry, BAPTISM IN
KANSAS *(Collection of the Whitney Museum of
American Art)*

Plate 10: Jack Levine, WELCOME HOME *(The Brooklyn Museum, J. B. Woodward Memorial Fund)*

Regionalist movement was John Steuart Curry. In his 1928 painting "Baptism in Kansas" *(Plate 9),* Curry captures the image of the American "Bible Belt" heartland. The melodramatic event is realistically and vigorously rendered. At best Curry and the Regionalists were the expression of a search for a national style, but often their art degenerated into a narrow chauvinism, defensively rejecting urbanism and the new directions in modern art.

Whereas the Regionalists tried to rediscover America in picturesque depictions of grass-roots culture, another group of artists, more urban-oriented, derived their subjects from the social upheavals caused by the Great Depression. The style of the Social Commentators, as they were called, drew its inspiration from journalistic caricature, and their themes were often expressed as protests against inequality in American society. Whether depicting the conflict of racial exploitation, or dramatizing the plight of the dispossessed, these artists became propagandists in the struggle for social justice.

One of the leading figures of the movement was Jack Levine. Although his style was strongly influenced by such satiric painters as Goya and Daumier, his technique was extremely original. In his painting "Welcome Home" *(Plate 10),* executed in 1946 at the end of World War II, Levine caricatures through distortion and color intensity his feelings of disdain for those who profited from the war. His visual criticism, like that of his fellow Social Commentators, attacked corruption and used the painting medium to express his personal point of view.

Pershing to hunt down Villa. For this, Wilson had the permission of Carranza, but as Villa drew the American forces 300 miles into Mexico, two skirmishes with Carranza's army almost led to war. Again the peace forces outweighed the jingoes in the United States, and again Wilson accepted compromise. On July 4, 1916, Carranza suggested the appointment of a Joint High Commission to consider the problem. The commission debated into January 1917, when it broke up without establishing a basis for the withdrawal of American troops. By then the United States was so close to war with Germany that Wilson nevertheless withdrew the troops and in March 1917 gave recognition to Carranza's government.

Wilson had been elected President on a program of domestic reform, the New Freedom. Shortly before his inauguration he remarked: "It would be the irony of fate if my administration had to deal chiefly with foreign affairs." But so it was to be.

WAR IN EUROPE

Bryan, before he took office as secretary of state, suggested to Wilson a scheme for "cooling off" treaties with all the nations of the world. These would provide that disputes should go to permanent commissions for a one-year investigation before either party could strengthen its armaments or go to war. This proposal was in keeping with the progressive theory that war was unthinkable and that all disputes could be settled through reasonable discussion. Bryan negotiated thirty such treaties with large and small nations—but none with Germany.

The problem of the European balance gave Wilson at least slight concern in May 1914 when he authorized Colonel House to sail abroad to try to bring an end to the arms race. Within a few months, Europe became Wilson's greatest cause for anxiety, as fate directed his administration toward an overwhelming concern with foreign affairs.

Nothing but trouble had come out of Wilson's long and muddled intervention in Mexico. His bad tactics had aroused a hostility among the Mexican people which did not dissipate for years.

In other respects Wilson and his Secretary of State were slightly more successful in improving relations between the United States and Latin America. During 1913 and 1914 they negotiated a treaty with Colombia expressing "sincere regrets" for the Panama incident and paying an indemnity of $25 million. Roosevelt thundered that it was a "blackmail treaty," and his Republican friends in the Senate blocked it until after his death. In 1921 Congress voted to pay the indemnity but omit the apology.

Unneutral Neutrality

Americans paid little attention to the minor alarms that followed the assassination of the Austrian Archduke in Sarajevo, Bosnia, at the end of June. Balkan crises were familiar and boring news; events in Mexico where Carranza was driving out Huerta seemed more sensational. Even when Austria-Hungary declared war on Serbia on July 28, Americans were not shocked, but the week that followed left them stunned. The declaration of war against Serbia triggered a chain reaction of threats and counterthreats, commitments and countercommitments among the alliances. It detonated an explosion no one seemed really to want, but no one seemed able to avoid. By August 5, England, France, and Russia were at war with Germany and Austria-Hungary. The explosion had blown to bits the comfortable, optimistic Europe that had seemed so safe and stable.

Bewildered Americans congratulated themselves that at least the explosion could not extend to their shores; the New World was still secure. A sizable number, who were of German ancestry or had been educated in German universities, automatically saw the war as a valiant German struggle against the cruel despotism of Tsarist Russia. And most Irish-Americans sympathized with Germany as the foe of their ancient oppressor, England. But the vast majority of the people, with greater educational, economic, or sentimental ties to England

and France, were shocked by the German invasion of Belgium in defiance of a treaty. They were pro-Allied without being at all sure what the war was about. None of them in August 1914 envisaged American entrance into the war. There was no clear call for an American democratic crusade.

With the outbreak of war in Europe, Wilson feared that Japan would take advantage of the preoccupation of the Western powers to expand in the Orient. He reverted to a balance-of-power policy to try to stem the Japanese tide as much as possible. Japan declared war upon Germany and seized the German holdings on the Shantung peninsula of China; this the United States could not criticize. Next Japan tried to impose upon the Chinese a treaty embodying twenty-one demands that would have made China virtually a protectorate. At this point (in 1915), the American government with the aid of the British, exerted such strong pressure that Japan abandoned the treaty.

But the United States appeased Japan in the Lansing-Ishii Agreement of November 2, 1917. This recognized that Japan had "special interests in China, particularly in the part to which her possessions are contiguous." The Japanese were pleased, because in translating the ambiguous document into Chinese they could give the impression that the United States approved their policy. Secretary of State Lansing was satisfied because he felt he had protected China for at least the duration of the European war. For both nations, if they held to their policies, there was trouble ahead.

BLOCKADE AND SUBMARINES

In 1914 President Wilson had proclaimed neutrality and, going beyond that, had called upon the American people to remain impartial in thought as well as in action. Yet from the beginning he himself took one attitude toward the Allies and quite a different attitude toward Germany.

The immediate problem for Wilson was domestic: to bolster the economy, which was staggering under the impact of war. As European nations sought to liquidate their investments in the United States, Wilson closed the stock exchange to prevent panic and discouraged loans to belligerents in order to preserve the gold reserve. (Secretary Bryan asserted

that such loans by banks would be unneutral.) Then war orders began to turn the panic into a boom.

Americans soon learned that the nation in control of the seas would countenance no neutral trade with the enemy. President Wilson acquiesced, though not without protests, as the British developed and tightened their system of control. The United States could have retaliated with an embargo, but this would have created serious economic distress among American farmers and it would have hurt industry. Besides, the basically pro-Allied sympathies of the administration and a great majority of the people made so drastic a step unthinkable. Hence, the United States accepted the British blockade of the Central Powers but was not so ready to accept a German counterblockade.

Blockade warfare became essential to the strategy of both the British and the Germans. The development of rapid-firing cannons and of machine guns made frontal assault prohibitively expensive, so the war in Europe settled down into an exhausting trench warfare between the combatants. The counterpart on the high seas was the blockade. From the outset, Great Britain made use of her superior navy to wage economic warfare against Germany. Gradually she extended the "contraband" list. She even seized American vessels carrying foodstuffs to neutral countries, on the grounds that such shipments might release supplies that could go to Germany. Americans complained that the British were using the controls to benefit British firms at the expense of American business.

On the whole, the British blockade proved to be no economic handicap for the United States, since by early 1915 heavy war orders were arriving which more than filled the trade gap it had created. While trade with the Central Powers almost came to an end, that with the Allies between 1914 and 1916 jumped from $824 million to $3,214 million—a staggering figure for that time. In March 1915 the government relaxed its regulations to allow the Allies to float huge loans in the United States for financing their purchases. In effect the United States, embarking upon the greatest boom in its history, was becoming the great arsenal for the Allies.

This the Germans could not permit. During the first weeks of the war they imposed no blockades but concentrated upon trying to win

According to official propaganda, the United States went to war in 1917 to preserve the "freedom of the seas" and to "make the world safe for democracy." Afterward many Americans were disillusioned by the rise of dictatorships in Europe and by the findings of a Senate committee headed by Gerald P. Nye, which from 1934 to 1936 looked into the role of bankers and munitions makers in bringing about American involvement. The disillusionment found expression and further encouragement in a number of books, of which the most widely read was *Road to War, 1914–1917* (1935) by Walter Millis, a leading journalist. Millis thought that the decision to intervene was foolish, a result of sentimental ties with Great Britain and France, the effectiveness of British propaganda, American loans to the Allies, and the profit-seeking of manufacturers of war materials. The international lawyers Edwin M. Borchard and William P. Lage, hoping to keep this country out of a second world war, argued further, in *Neutrality for the United States* (1937), that neutrality had not failed in 1917; it had not even been seriously attempted, the Wilson administration having been partial to the Allies from the beginning.

After World War II the career diplomat George F. Kennan, author of *American Dipomacy, 1900–1950* (1950), and the political scientist Hans J. Morgenthau, author of *In Defense of the National Interest* (1951), criticized the Wilson policy on other grounds. These writers accused Wilson of pursuing unrealistic goals, of mouthing high-sounding "legalistic-moralistic" phrases instead of concentrating on the true national interest. But another political scientist, Edward H. Buehrig, disagreed. In *Woodrow Wilson and the Balance of Power* (1955) Buehrig contended that Wilson and his advisers were concerned not only with legal and moral issues but also with the problem of restoring the world balance (which had been upset by Germany) and thus maintaining the security of the United States.

All along, Wilson also had defenders among historians. Charles Seymour, in *American Neutrality, 1914–1917* (1935), insisted that Wilson sincerely desired to avoid war but had no alternative when Germany began her unrestricted submarine operations in 1917. Thus, according to Seymour, the cause of American entry could be summarized in one word, "submarine." Wilson's foremost biographer, Arthur Link, in *Wilson the Diplomatist* (1957) and in other writings, agreed with Seymour that, by 1917, Wilson had few or no alternatives. So did Ernest E. May, in *The World War and American Isolation* (1959). May believed that "in nearly every case requiring a decision by the President [from 1914 to 1917], there were present considerations of law, morality, power, national prestige, and domestic politics, all of which had to be taken into account." The ultimate responsibility for war, May implied, was the German government's, not Wilson's.

In recent years, historians have been less concerned about the rights and wrongs of American involvement than about the hows and whys. It has become a subject about which they can be reasonably objective – like the causes of the Trojan War.

a decision in France. The German armies drove deep but were halted short of Paris in the Battle of the Marne in September 1914. While on the Russian front great armies continued to move back and forth for several years, in the west the war turned into the grinding attrition of trench combat along lines extending from the North Sea to Switzerland. As a stalemate developed along the Western Front, Germany turned toward the submarine as a possible means of breaking the British blockade. Submarines had the advantage of surprise but were so vulnerable to attack by an armed ship that they could scarcely follow the accepted rules of international law. These rules called for visit and search of enemy merchantmen and allowed sinking only if provision were made for the safety of passengers and crew. The sinking of merchant vessels without warning seemed to Americans to add a new and frightful dimension to warfare.

Beginning on February 4, 1915, Germany announced that she would sink enemy vessels in a broad zone around the British Isles. This policy, the Germans explained, was in retaliation for the British food blockade, which they claimed would starve women and children in Germany. President Wilson declared on February 10 that he would hold Germany to "strict accountability" for unlawful acts.

A serious crisis came when, on May 7, 1915, a submarine fired a torpedo without warning into the Cunard liner *Lusitania*. The ship went down in eighteen minutes, drowning 1,198 people, among them 128 Americans. "An act of piracy," Theodore Roosevelt called it.

A few days earlier, April 22, the Germans had launched against the Allied lines at Ypres a new weapon of frightfulness, poison gas. On May 13 American newspapers carried lengthy excerpts from an official British report on almost unprintable alleged German atrocities in

The Lusitania Sailing From New York City
On May 1, 1915, newspapers carried both the Cunard advertisement that the Lusitania was sailing that day and an unusual German warning: "Vessels flying the flag of Great Britain, or any of her allies, are liable to destruction . . . and . . . travelers sailing in the war zone on ships of Great Britain or her allies do so at their own risk." Passengers and crew discussed the announcement, but the Lusitania sailed on time, and by May 6 was proceeding along the coast of Ireland much as in peacetime, at a slow pace and not zigzagging. The commander of the German submarine U-20, seeing a large ship, fired a torpedo. Almost immediately the ship listed so sharply that few lifeboats could be launched; then it sank. As its bow went high in the air, the U-boat commander for the first time read on the ship the name Lusitania. *(Brown Brothers)*

Belgium. Although it bore the respected name of the former ambassador to the United States, Lord Bryce, this report contained fabrications. Yet few Americans questioned its authenticity, for by this time most people were ready to believe almost anything against Germany. Even in their revulsion, however, they were not ready to fight.

Wilson came close to the point of coercion over the *Lusitania* incident, in the ensuing exchange of notes with Germany. In his first note he virtually demanded that Germany end its submarine blockade. When the Germans sent an argumentative reply, he drafted an even stronger second note—so strong that the peace-minded Secretary Bryan resigned rather than sign it. Wilson appointed the Counselor of the State Department, Robert Lansing, an expert in international law, to be the new secretary. Lansing was ready to take an adamant position. Wilson had said: "There is such a thing as a man being too proud to fight." Yet he was ready to risk war rather than surrender to Germany what he considered to be American maritime rights.

New trouble developed in the early months of 1916 when the Allies began arming merchantmen and ordering them to attack submarines. On February 10, 1916, Germany gave notice that she would sink them without warning. Wilson reiterated his doctrine of "strict accountability," and on March 24, when the channel steamer *Sussex* was torpedoed, he threatened to break off diplomatic relations if Germany did not abandon her unrestricted submarine campaign. He made the threat at a time when Germany still lacked sufficient submarines to maintain a tight blockade and did not wish to bring the United States into the war. Consequently, on May 4, the German foreign office pledged that submarine commanders would observe rules of visit and search. The President had won a diplomatic victory, and relations with Germany became less tense during the eight months that followed.

PREPAREDNESS—OR PACIFISM?

With the outbreak of war, generals and admirals, who in peacetime attracted little attention, began to gather followings as they raised a hue and cry for increased defenses. President Wilson through his pacifist Secretary of the Navy,

Josephus Daniels, was able to muzzle the navy rather effectively. Its demands for a huge fleet-building program and its warnings of the catastrophe that faced America if the British Grand Fleet collapsed appeared for the most part indirectly through friendly politicians and publicists. Roosevelt's close friend, Major General Leonard Wood, who had just finished a term as Chief of Staff, was not so easy to silence. The Secretary of War, Lindley M. Garrison, was a zealous advocate of preparedness, and several influential civilians like Roosevelt constantly made the headlines with their warnings.

The army was much less ready than the navy to fight a major war. The establishment of the General Staff and other administrative reforms had come into effect in the Roosevelt administration, but the older officers were still antagonistic toward such changes. The Quartermaster Corps in 1913 was thinking about using trucks, but as yet not seriously testing them. The air force, consisting of seventeen planes, was part of the Signal Corps; its 1913 appropriation was $125,000. The army numbered less than 80,000 men, a large part of whom were required to maintain the posts within the United States. The National Guard was somewhat larger, but was scarcely professional.

Wilson opposed new armaments, and so did public opinion, until the crisis over submarine sinkings frightened the nation into preparedness. In November 1915 the President proposed a long-range program which by 1925 would give the United States a navy second to none and would reorganize the army and provide a reserve force of 400,000 men. This proposal touched off a hot debate in Congress and throughout the country. Large numbers of those who had been agrarian progressives of the West and South rallied behind the House majority leader, Claude Kitchin of North Carolina, to block the army program. Throughout the country, the pleas of Bryan and peace organizations strongly appealed to farmers and workingmen. Wilson took the issue to the country in speeches in January and early February 1916, but the House would not budge.

Wilson had to compromise. He accepted the resignation of Secretary of War Garrison, and appointed in his place Newton D. Baker, an able Ohio progressive who had opposed preparedness only a few weeks earlier. Ultimately Congress passed legislation providing

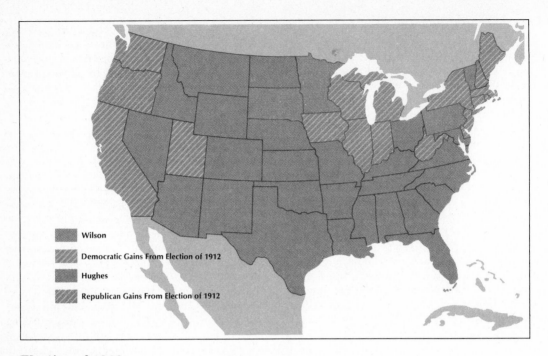

Election of 1916

for substantial increases in the army, the navy, and merchant shipping. The Merchant Marine Act of 1916 established the United States Shipping Board, which was empowered to own and operate vessels and regulate shipping.

Conservatives wished to finance the defense expenditures through bonds, but the administration proposed new, heavier taxes. Progressives denounced the tax proposals as falling too heavily upon the masses. In Congress the progressives fought through a tax measure frankly aimed at making the wealthy, whom they blamed for preparedness demands, pay the bill. The Revenue Act of 1916 levied income and inheritance taxes heavily upon the rich for the first time in American history.

In 1916 Democrats and Republicans fought the presidential campaign over the issue of foreign policy before a seriously divided people. At the Democratic convention, the keynoter began citing Wilson's interchanges with Germany, and the crowd whooped with enthusiasm. "What did we do? What did we do?" the

delegates chanted, and the keynoter responded: "We didn't go to war, we didn't go to war." Out of the convention came the slogan (which Wilson himself never used): "He kept us out of war." The Democrats went into the campaign far stronger than had been expected of a minority party battling against the reunited Republicans. Many of the former Bull Moosers, Republican farmers in the Midwest, and workers who had once voted for a full dinner pail now favored the Democrats. In part they did so because of Wilson's progressive domestic policy but still more because of their hope that the President could continue to keep the country out of the war.

As for the Republicans, they persuaded Charles Evans Hughes, who had an impeccable progressive record, to resign from the Supreme Court and accept the nomination. Primarily because of the whooping of Roosevelt and others on the sidelines, the Republicans gradually began to look like the war party. Hughes, under pressure from militant Republicans, wired Roosevelt congratulations on war-like speeches. This and Hughes' own remarks led voters to believe that he was more likely than Wilson to adopt a militant policy.

Wilson warned that a Republican victory would mean intervention in Mexico and war in Europe. The lure of progressivism and peace were still so irresistible in 1916 that the Democratic party, though normally a minority, squeezed through to victory. On election night returns from the East were almost solidly for Hughes; he appeared elected. Then, as returns from the West came in, the picture began to change, though it was not until Friday that Wilson's election was certain. The Democrats also retained a precarious control over both houses of Congress.

"A FEARFUL THING"

So far as elections can be regarded as national plebiscites, Wilson had received a narrow mandate to continue along the path of progressivism and peace. Undoubtedly he intended to follow such a course. Since the outbreak of the war he had repeatedly sought means to bring the warring nations into a peace conference. But both sides had invested too heavily in the conflict, and were still too hopeful of gaining from their investment, to talk of a negotiated peace.

Immediately after the election, in November 1916, Wilson renewed negotiations looking toward a settlement. The Germans, successful on the Russian front, for a while appeared to be willing. But the top German generals did not want any conference at all. Nevertheless, on January 22, 1917, Wilson spread his plan before the Senate, calling for a lasting peace that the American people would help maintain through a league of nations. It would be a peace with freedom of the seas, disarmament, national self-determination for subject peoples, and equality among nations. "Peace among equals" — a lasting peace — could come only through "peace without victory."

On January 9 the military leaders of Germany had decided upon one final cast of the iron dice. They had resolved to return to unrestricted submarine warfare even though it would bring the United States into the war. They hoped that they could crush France on land and starve Britain from the sea before America could make her weight felt. On January 31 the German ambassador announced that, beginning the following day, submarines would sink all ships, enemy or neutral, in a broad zone around the British Isles.

President Wilson now faced a dilemma of his own making. He had in effect during the previous eighteen months drawn a narrow line — the right of American citizens and vessels to travel on the high seas in time of war — and threatened Germany with war if she transgressed it. How could Wilson take the United States into a war against Germany for such a limited end, and still bring about the sort of peace he wanted, a just peace among equals, a peace without the victor dictating to the vanquished?

Gradually events carried Wilson toward war. On February 25 the British turned over to him an intercepted note from the German foreign secretary, Arthur Zimmerman, proposing that in the event of war, Mexico should attack the United States and receive in return her lost provinces north of the border. Americans were infuriated. At about the same time, the Russian revolution eliminated one of the moral problems in Wilson's mind by replacing a despotism among the Allies with a constitutional monarchy. (This government lasted only until November 1917, when Lenin and the Communists came into power.)

On March 18, 1917, news came that submarines had torpedoed three American ships. On March 20 the cabinet unanimously advised the President to ask Congress for a declaration of war. On the evening of April 2, 1917, President Wilson delivered his war message to Congress. After enumerating the German transgressions of American neutral rights, he declared: "It is a fearful thing to lead this great peaceful people into war, into the most terrible . . . of all wars. . . . But the right is more precious than peace, and we shall fight for the things which we have always carried nearest our hearts — for democracy, . . . for the rights and liberties of small nations, for a universal dominion of right by such a concert of free peoples as shall bring peace and safety to all nations and make the world itself at last free." Four days later, Congress passed the war declaration and the President signed it.

War Without Stint

President Wilson had called for war "without stint or limit." In this spirit the American government proceeded to mobilize economic resources on a grand scale, to launch massive campaigns against German submarines in the Atlantic and against German armies in France, and to indoctrinate the American people for enduring the burdens and the sacrifices of the total war.

CONTROLLING THE ECONOMY

Clumsily at first, but steadily and impressively, the unprepared nation built a gigantic war machine. Nearly 5,000 government agencies were set up to see that men, money, and materials were directed toward the war effort. These agencies brought an unprecedented degree of regulation and control to American economic life.

Troops had to be raised, the army enormously enlarged. Theodore Roosevelt, elderly and ill, still seemed to think in terms of the Spanish-American War; backed by a clique of Republican senators, he fought for permission to take a volunteer division to the Western Front. Speaker Champ Clark was so incensed at the prospect of a draft that he asserted from the floor of the House during debate: "In the estimation of Missourians there is precious little difference between a conscript and a convict." For weeks the debate went on, but in the end Roosevelt was turned down, and the Selective Service Act was passed.

During the debate it had become clear what a large figure in both money and men the President must write into the blank check that Congress (and the American people) had signed. In April British and French missions arrived and made clear for the first time their desperate need for money, men, and ships if they were to stave off imminent defeat. Congress soon authorized the Treasury Department to borrow $7 billion, of which $3 billion were to go as loans to the Allies.

In financing the war, Secretary of the Treasury William G. McAdoo raised about one-third of a $32 billion total through taxation. He felt that additional taxes would put too heavy a burden on low-income groups. The War Rev-

enue Act of 1917 imposed a great variety of excise taxes and income taxes steeper than any before — so steep as to take two-thirds of a $2 million income. Altogether, the taxes on individual and corporate incomes, excess profits, and inheritances provided 74 percent of the war tax revenues. There was one conspicuous loophole: many corporations distributed to their stockholders stock exempt from taxes, rather than giving them dividends.

In his borrowing policy, McAdoo tried, again, to keep the burden of the war from falling too heavily upon the poorer people. He sought to sell as many Liberty Bonds as possible to them so that they, not richer people, would reap the ultimate profit. Despite McAdoo's efforts, those with moderate incomes (under $2,000 a year) probably purchased no more than 30 percent of the $23 billion worth of bonds sold.

During the preparedness period, in August 1916, Congress had approved the establishment of a Council of National Defense, consisting of six cabinet members, and an Advisory Commission made up of representatives of industry, transportation, business, and labor. In July 1917 the council set up a centralized War Industries Board to coordinate government purchases. Wilson reorganized this board, conferred upon it sweeping powers over industry, and appointed as chairman a Wall Street broker, Bernard Baruch.

Food was almost as vital as munitions for the Allies. At the suggestion of the Council for National Defense, a Food Administration was set up by the President. After vigorous debate, it was later authorized by Congress, in the Lever Act of August 10, 1917. Its administrator was one of the most spectacular civilian heroes of the war, an American mining engineer, Herbert Hoover, who had supervised the relief feeding of Belgium. His task was to increase food production, cut waste, substitute plentiful for scarce foods, and protect consumers from speculators. Hoover, in keeping with his experience in Belgium, wished to be an administrator, not a dictator, and to run his program on a voluntary basis as far as possible. To a remarkable degree he was able to enlist the patriotic support of the public in conserving food and observing meatless and wheatless days. His slogan, seen on widely distributed posters, was "Food will win the war."

The shortage of wheat was especially critical because 1916 had been a bad crop year. Hoover encouraged wheat production by guaranteeing the purchase of the entire 1917 crop at $2.20 per bushel, a figure high enough to assure farmers a substantial profit. Wheat acreage jumped from 45 million in 1917 to 75 million in 1919, and the land produced bumper crops.

Hoover opposed retail price fixing, which he thought would lead to black markets, but he did protect consumers from speculation. Food prices went up gradually.

The Lever Act which established the Food Administration also authorized a Fuel Administration, which fixed the price of coal high enough to bring submarginal coal mines into operation and increase bituminous coal production by about 50 percent. In spite of this increase, the fuel shortage became so acute that

the Fuel Administration had to order a series of coal holidays for Eastern industries in the early months of 1918.

In order to guarantee war production in German-owned factories in this country, especially those producing chemicals, these and all other German assets came under the custody of an Alien Property Custodian, A. Mitchell Palmer. The Trading-with-the-Enemy Act of October 1917, provided for their seizure and administration. Palmer obtained additional authority to sell German property, which he utilized especially to license dye and chemical patents to American industry. This was punitive toward the Germans, immensely profitable for some American businessmen, and helpful for the development of a strong chemical industry in the United States.

The Aircraft Production Board failed to produce a promised 22,000 airplanes by July 1918 — a ridiculous figure, since neither side on

Fourth Liberty Loan Parade, New Orleans
Coming shortly before the armistice, in October 1918, the Fourth Liberty Loan drive set out to raise $6 billion. American heroes, celebrities, and volunteer workers all did their bit; the news from the Western Front was exciting. Again the loan was oversubscribed. (National Archives)

the Western Front ever had as many as 2,500 planes at one time. The failure to fulfill this overoptimistic promise led to harsh criticism. By the time the armistice was signed, the United States had delivered to France 1,185 De Haviland bombers and 5,460 Liberty motors.

In April 1918 President Wilson established the National War Labor Board to serve as a sort of supreme court for labor disputes. Labor and industry each provided five representatives for the board; the two chairmen represented the public. The War Labor Board would not countenance strikes or lockouts, but recognized the right of unions to organize and bargain collectively. It favored the eight-hour day, the establishment in any given area of the wages prevailing in it, the maintenance of a basic living standard for workers, and equal pay for women who did equal work. Like some other war agencies, it had to function through persuasion or use of the President's war powers.

President Gompers of the AFL did much during the war to enhance the prestige of organized labor. He sat with industrialists on the Council of National Defense and pledged to see that there would be no strikes, in return for recognition of unionism and wage increases. He also cooperated in the government onslaught against labor radicals, which meant the Industrial Workers of the World, who were engaging in sabotage in the West. The IWW almost disappeared, while membership in other unions jumped from 2,716,900 in 1914 to 3,104,600 in 1917 and 4,169,100 in 1919. Still, this was no more than one-eighth of all wage earners.

DELIVERING THE GOODS

Increased production and stringent economy within the United States would be of no avail unless supplies could be delivered to Europe. Into the winter of 1917–1918, transportation difficulties plagued the nation. Railroads could not get raw materials to Eastern factories or munitions to ports, even through cooperation with a voluntary Railroad War Board. On December 28, 1917, Wilson put the railroads under a Railroad Administration headed by Secretary of the Treasury McAdoo. He utilized expert railroad men to run the lines as one unified system. Railroads could draw upon a half-billion-dollar revolving fund for improvements, and received rent equivalent to their average earnings in 1914–1917. The transportation snarl was so effectively untangled that a freight-car shortage of 150,000 in 1917 was transformed into a surplus of 300,000 by the end of 1918.

Shipping was a still greater and more persistent problem. By the summer of 1917, submarines had sunk nearly a quarter of the British merchant fleet; that of the United States was relatively small, and mainly committed to coastal trade. The Emergency Fleet Corporation under the Shipping Board eventually began to make remarkable progress in building new shipyards to turn out 1,700 ships of steel and 1,000 of wood.

War vessels escorted fleets of transports and supply ships across the Atlantic to protect them from submarine attacks. At first, the British admiralty had opposed the use of such convoys and kept most of its destroyers as a curtain to protect the Grand Fleet and the channel ferries. Eventually, however, United States Admiral William S. Sims broke down the resistance of the admiralty, so that a convoying system was well established by August 1917.

Sinkings, which had totaled nearly 900,000 tons in April 1917, dropped to 350,000 tons by December 1917, and to only 112,000 tons by October 1918. This was primarily a British achievement, but the United States contributed to it substantially. The British provided 70 percent of the escorting ships, the French 3 percent, and the Americans 27 percent.

The American navy grew enormously in size and efficiency. By the time the armistice was signed, it had 200,000 men and 834 vessels convoying across the Atlantic or serving in European waters. It had grown in overall size to 533,000 men and 2,000 ships. It performed great feats in moving men and supplies across the Atlantic.

PEACE IDEALS AND WAR HATREDS

Ever since the hesitant entrance of the United States into the war, official agencies and private groups, from President Wilson and the Committee on Public Information to the yellow press, had sought to mold the minds of Americans. In conflicting ways they tried to explain the significance of the war, encourage Ameri-

The Sedition Act [1918]

Be it enacted. . . . Whoever, when the United States is at war, shall wilfully make or convey false reports or false statements with intent to interfere with the operation or success of the military or naval forces of the United States . . . or . . . obstruct the sale by the United States of bonds . . . or incite . . . insubordination, disloyalty, mutiny, or refusal of duty in the military or naval forces of the United States, or shall wilfully obstruct . . . the recruiting or enlistment service . . . [or] wilfully utter, print, write, or publish any disloyal, profane, scurrilous, or abusive language about the form of government of the United States, or the Constitution of the United States, or the military or naval forces of the United States, or the flag . . . or the uniform of the Army or Navy of the United States . . . or shall wilfully . . . urge, incite, or advocate any curtailment of production in this country of any thing or things . . . necessary or essential to the prosecution of the war . . . and whoever shall wilfully advocate, teach, defend, or suggest the doing of any of the acts or things . . . enumerated . . . shall be punished by a fine of not more than $10,000 or imprisonment for not more than twenty years, or both. . . .

cans in its vigorous pursuit, and prepare them for the peace to follow. As is all too easy in such circumstances, Americans learned readily to hate the Germans and German sympathizers but prepared themselves less well to assume a commanding role in maintaining a just peace in the postwar world. This in the end was to be the tragedy of President Wilson, of the American people, and consequently of all mankind.

Even before America entered the war, President Wilson had begun a series of idealistic addresses outlining the nature of the postwar world he wished to see emerge. He talked then of "peace without victory" and the right of the several submerged nationalities in Europe to organize governments of their own choosing. He asserted too that the American people would be willing to join a postwar association of nations. Many Americans of good will, like the members of the League to Enforce Peace, thrilled to Wilson's words. But his speeches remained merely words, since Wilson had not bound the Allies to his conditions as a basis for American intervention. And he seemed to reinforce the distinction between the United States and the Allies through the fiction that we were fighting Germany separately as an "associated power."

After American entrance Wilson had discovered that the Allies had made secret treaties among themselves. These treaties divided among the Allies the enemy's colonies as spoils of the war. The new Bolshevik government of

Russia publicized some of the treaties; their terms seemed to run counter to the idealism for which Wilson was exhorting Americans to fight. Wilson was sure that in time he could counteract the treaties and force the British and French to accept a just peace. On January 8, 1918, he expounded his own war aims, under fourteen headings, in a speech before a joint session of Congress.

His Fourteen Points, coming at a time when all the belligerent peoples were overwhelmingly weary of the war, met with an enthusiastic response among liberals and working people in the United States, in the Allied nations, and throughout the world. Even many Germans welcomed them and a later clarification of them, "the five particulars," as the promise of a democratic Germany that could assume a position of equality among nations. They were the most stirring and effective piece of propaganda the war produced.

It was not clear that Wilson had the American people behind him, even though his Committee on Public Information had been engaged in a large-scale effort to sell the war. George Creel, a progressive newspaperman who had worked in the 1916 presidential campaign, headed the committee. He persuaded newspapers to engage in voluntary self-censorship, an idea not entirely palatable to them. The committee disseminated countless tons of propaganda, and enlisted the services of 150,000 writers, lecturers, actors, and artists.

Throughout the country, 75,000 such volunteers arose to speak on almost every conceivable occasion. Throughout the United States and the world, 75 million pieces of printed matter carried the American view of the war. Much of what the Creel Committee disseminated was idealistic, in keeping with Wilson's speeches and the Fourteen Points, depicting the war as a great crusade for humanity. Much also, unfortunately, appealed more to fear and hate than to a spirit of altruistic sacrifice.

Throughout the country spread a hysterical hatred of all that seemed unpatriotic. Congress reflected and encouraged the hysteria by passing stern laws for the suppression of dissent. The Espionage Act of June 15, 1917, provided penalties running up to a $10,000 fine and twenty years' imprisonment, not only for those engaged in espionage, sabotage, and obstruction of the war effort, but even for those who should "willfully cause or attempt to cause insubordination, mutiny, or refusal of duty" or "willfully obstruct the recruiting or enlistment service." The law also empowered the postmaster general to ban from the mails any matter that in his opinion was seditious. The Trading-with-the-Enemy Act of October 1917 established censorship over international communications and the foreign-language press (in addition to authorizing various types of economic warfare against the Germans).

These measures were vigorously, and at times capriciously, enforced, but the administration sought still greater punitive powers to discipline the disloyal. Congress responded with the Sabotage Act of April 20, 1918, aimed primarily at the IWW, and the Sedition Act of May 16, 1918. The Sedition Act, modeled after a Montana statute for suppressing the IWW, was harsh beyond any previous legislation in American history. The enforcement of these laws was almost as stern as any lynch mob could desire. Over 1,500 were arrested for seditious utterances, though only 10 were taken into custody for sabotage. The force of the laws continued unabated after the armistice. In the fall of 1918, after a four-day trial, the Socialist leader, Eugene V. Debs, who had been pacifist, not pro-German, was sentenced to ten years in a federal penitentiary under the Espionage Act; in March 1919 the Supreme Court upheld his conviction.

Whatever pacifist or pro-German offenders escaped the federal net were likely to be caught in the meshes of state sedition laws, or to suffer the wrath of vigilantes. The furor was rather ludicrous in some ways, as sauerkraut became "liberty cabbage," and hamburger, "liberty sausage." It was a bit less funny to ban all German music, the teaching of the German language, or the keeping of German books in public libraries, as was done in many places. And it was frightening when a vigilance committee in Minnesota, having forbidden a pastor to speak German, caught him praying at the bedside of a dying woman who spoke only German, tarred and feathered him and rode him out of town on a rail.

THE AEF IN FRANCE

American strategic plans were drawn up after the country entered the war, and essentially these plans were developed in France at the headquarters of the commanding general of the American Expeditionary Force (AEF), John J. Pershing, a highly intelligent officer and a driving personality.

Pershing's goal was to build an American force in France numbering 1 million men by June 1, 1918. Many obstacles stood between him and his objective, as he came to realize after he arrived in Paris on June 14, 1917. The dispirited Allies stood on the defensive against the desperately aggressive enemy; they needed fresh American troops but wished to use them piecemeal as reinforcements along their own weary lines. They did not like Pershing's insistence that the Americans should operate as a separate army; they had no reason to trust the untried American soldiers or officers. In truth, there had been nothing in American military activities during the Spanish-American War and the Mexican intervention to warrant confidence. But General Pershing stood firm, with President Wilson behind him.

In the winter of 1917–1918 the Germans knocked the Russians out of the war. Lenin and his followers in Russia overthrew the constitutional government of Kerensky and opened peace negotiations. Meanwhile, the Germans along with the Austrians delivered a near fatal blow to the Italians at Caporetto. The stunned Allies organized a Supreme War Council and looked desperately to the United States for manpower. Pershing gradually had been building port facilities, running railroads

Captain Edward V. Rickenbacker and Other Pilots of the 94th Pursuit Squadron

The "hat-in-the-ring" squadron, as it was popularly known, was the first American-trained squadron to engage in combat. It began operations on April 3, 1918. The overall record of the Americans, who engaged for the most part in individual combat against German aviators flying the superior Fokker planes, was not impressive. At the armistice they constituted only 10 percent of the Allied air power. Individually they were brave to the point of foolhardiness—they refused to wear parachutes. The exploits of the seventy-one American aces (those who shot down five or more enemy airplanes) were followed eagerly at home by newspaper readers hungry for heroes. Captain Rickenbacker (center), who shot down at least twenty-six German planes, became more famous than most generals. (National Archives)

across France, and constructing training camps and supply dumps. As a trickle of troops began to arrive, he tried to give them three months' training before putting them into combat. While the number was small, he was willing to brigade his units temporarily among the Allies to give them experience and to meet emergencies. Thus the First Division went into action with the French in Lorraine in October 1917 and took over a quiet sector of its own near Toul in January 1918.

In the early months of 1918 Germany moved troops from the east and slammed them against the Allies in a series of great offensives designed to end the war before a significant number of Americans could arrive. The Ger-

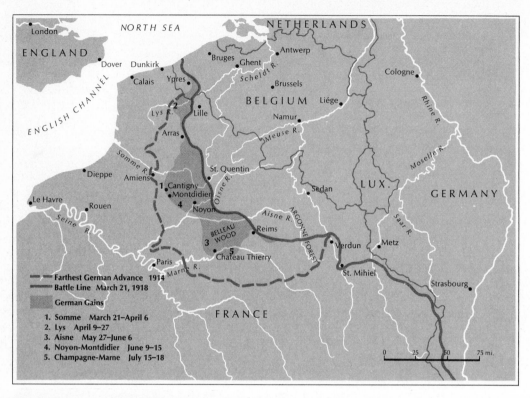

Major German Offensives   1918

The following labels appear on the map:

NORTH SEA · NETHERLANDS · ENGLAND · London · Dover · Dunkirk · Bruges · Ghent · Antwerp · Cologne · Calais · Ypres · Scheldt R. · Brussels · BELGIUM · Liége · Rhine R. · Lys R. · Lille · Namur · Meuse R. · Arras · Somme R. · St. Quentin · Oise R. · Sedan · LUX. · Moselle R. · GERMANY · Dieppe · Amiens · 1 Cantigny · Montdidier · 4 Noyon · Aisne R. · ARGONNE FOREST · Le Havre · Rouen · BELLEAU WOOD · Reims · Verdun · Metz · Seine R. · 3 · 5 · Saar R. · Paris · Château Thierry · St. Mihiel · Marne R. · Strasbourg · FRANCE · ENGLISH CHANNEL

Legend:
- - - Farthest German Advance 1914
— Battle Line March 21, 1918
German Gains

1. Somme   March 21–April 6
2. Lys   April 9–27
3. Aisne   May 27–June 6
4. Noyon-Montdidier   June 9–15
5. Champagne-Marne   July 15–18

0   25   50   75 mi.

mans had not succeeded by July 1, when Pershing had his million soldiers in France.

On May 30 the Germans had crossed the Marne River at Château-Thierry and threatened Paris fifty miles away. American and French troops, under the French command, fought to blunt the German drive. After a week of bitter counterattacking, the Americans recaptured Belleau Wood and thus helped stabilize the line. A little farther south at Reims, in the great bulge toward Paris, the Germans tried on July 15, the morning after Bastille Day, to crash through the French lines. Some 85,000 American troops helped repel the German thrust. By July 18 the German offensive was over; and the Allies began a counteroffensive, with American divisions participating, to liquidate the Marne salient (outward projection in the battle line). By August 6 it was gone.

In the months that followed, as American troops disembarked at a rate averaging 263,000 per month, the reinvigorated Allies pressed the exhausted Germans from Lorraine to the North Sea. On August 12 Pershing for the first time launched an offensive under his own command. He directed the First Army, consisting of 550,000 American troops, against the St. Mihiel salient protruding south of Verdun. Within thirty-six hours the drive had succeeded.

On September 26, 1918, the Americans began to advance along a 24-mile front in the Argonne Forest, as part of a grand, 200-mile-wide offensive, which was to continue for a total of forty-seven days. The American troops fought through what Pershing described as a "vast network of uncut barbwire, the deep ravines, dense woods, myriads of shell craters, and a heavy fog." The Allied high command had not imagined the Americans could make much progress against these obstacles, but after October 4 the regrouped army advanced. By the end of the month it had overrun almost all of the enemy's fixed positions, was beyond the Argonne Forest, and was driving toward vital German communications. On November 7 the Americans established bridgeheads across the

Meuse River, planted their guns looking down on the famous fortress of Sedan, and cut the railroad that carried German supplies to the front. It had been the greatest battle in which American troops had ever fought. The 1.2 million soldiers had used a greater weight of ammunition than had all of the Union forces through the four years of the Civil War.

During the Argonne fighting, other American divisions were deployed elsewhere along the front. All together, Americans participated in thirteen major operations, of which only two were under Pershing's command. By early November the weight of American troops was becoming irresistible; 2 million of them were serving in France.

All along the line, millions of Allied troops had pushed back the Germans, whose reserves were gone, regiments weakened, and communications threatened. They faced an invasion of their own country. They began to seek an armistice, a temporary cease-fire. Pershing, convinced that the Allies should demand a sur-render instead, would have liked to push on to Berlin, to make the Germans really feel the war. The day after the Americans reached Sedan, German envoys crossed the lines to meet the Allied Commander in Chief, the French General Ferdinand Foch, and receive armistice terms from him—terms so stiff that a resumption of hostilities would be impossible. The Germans accepted, and on November 11, 1918, the armistice went into effect.

Rejoicing Americans credited their armies with winning the decisive battles—"We won the war." Beyond question they had supplied the margin of victory. Still, the really crushing burden of the war had not fallen upon the American troops or the American people. The United States lost 112,000 men from enemy action or disease; 237,000 more were wounded. By comparison 1,385,000 French and 900,000 British died. Only 7 percent of the soldiers from the United States were casualties, compared with 73 percent of those from France and 36 percent of those from the British Empire.

U.S. Participation in Allied Offensives   1918

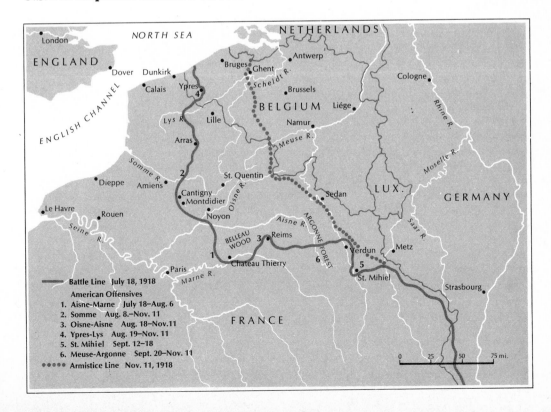

A Frustrated Peace

Wilson planned to attend the peace conference in person, and there he hoped to represent the masses of the world. Before the conference began, however, he had cause to wonder whether he would have even the people of the United States behind him.

REPUDIATION AT THE POLLS

Though the war had raised the income of millions of previously low-paid Americans, the Wilson administration failed to get the approval of a majority of the voters in the congressional elections of 1918. Throughout the war, Wilson had faced dissension within his own party as some of his congressional leaders of agrarian progressive background fought drastic war measures, helped impose heavy taxation on the more well-to-do, and hurried through wartime prohibition and a prohibition amendment to the Constitution. City Democrats were particularly unhappy over losing their beer. Southern Democrats prevented the limiting of the price of cotton while the price of wheat was controlled. The Midwestern grain belt, as a result, reacted angrily against all Democrats.

Even before the 1918 elections, it seemed likely that conditions at home would influence voters more than policies abroad. Nevertheless, with the war obviously almost over, the President put the election on the basis of high international policy. On October 24 he declared: "The return of a Republican majority to either house of the Congress would . . . be interpreted on the other side of the water as a repudiation of my leadership." This outraged those Republicans who had supported him in his foreign policy, since he had earlier declared "politics is adjourned" for the duration of the war. The fact that the Republicans captured both houses of Congress in 1918 would itself have a serious effect on foreign policy; the effect was exaggerated by Wilson's ill-considered appeal.

THE ARMISTICE

Repudiation at the polls created a sad atmosphere for Wilson's assumption of peace negotiations. The President, like the nation, was tense and tired, but he was ready to drive ahead. He strove to pull his own country and the reluctant Allies with him in his determination to make the Fourteen Points and especially the fourteenth—the League of Nations—a reality.

The pulling and hauling with the Allies went on through most of October 1918, during the negotiations that led to the armistice. The Germans sought through Wilson an armistice based on the Fourteen Points. The Allies denied even knowing what these points were, for the Allies were by no means ready to give up their claims for reparations and annexations. Only after Wilson had twice threatened to negotiate a separate peace were they willing to present a united façade. The Allies seemed to agree to the Fourteen Points in entirety, except for explicit reservations on reparations and freedom of the seas, and this apparent agreement led the Germans to expect generous treatment. Further misunderstanding developed because, while the Allies laid down military and naval terms that would make it impossible for the Germans to resume warfare, they used the term "armistice," which meant a negotiated pause in hostilities, rather than the word "surrender." What followed at Versailles was a conclave of victors dictating to a vanquished country, not a negotiated peace or the peace without victory that Wilson had once recommended.

The armistice that went into effect on November 11, 1918, provided that the Allies would negotiate peace on the basis of the Fourteen Points. The Germans agreed to withdraw their forces from France and Belgium and to surrender huge quantities of matériel. They accepted what was virtually the unconditional surrender of their fleet. While the peace was being drafted, the Allied blockade continued.

To the Allies as they assembled in Paris, there seemed no need to consult Germany on the nature of the peace. Indeed, the only obstacle to the kind of postwar world they had planned in their secret treaties was President Wilson. He made the unprecedented decision to leave the United States and attend the peace conference in person. Colonel House and other advisers urged him not to go.

Summary of the Fourteen Points [1918]

I. Open covenants of peace, openly arrived at. . . .

II. Absolute freedom of navigation upon the seas. . . .

III. The removal, so far as possible, of all economic barriers, and the establishment of an equality of trade conditions among all the nations consenting to the peace and associating themselves for its maintenance.

IV. Adequate guarantees given and taken that national armaments will be reduced to the lowest point consistent with domestic safety.

V. A free, open-minded, and absolutely impartial adjustment of all colonial claims. . . .

VI. The evacuation of all Russian territory. . . .

VII. Belgium, the whole world will agree, must be evacuated and restored. . . .

VIII. All French territory should be freed and the invaded portions . . . and . . . Alsace-Lorraine . . . [restored].

IX. A readjustment of the frontiers of Italy should be effected along clearly recognizable lines of nationality.

X. The peoples of Austria-Hungary . . . should be accorded the freest opportunity of autonomous development.

XI. Rumania, Serbia, and Montenegro should be evacuated . . . Serbia accorded free and secure access to the sea. . . .

XII. The Turkish portions of the present Ottoman Empire should be assured a secure sovereignty, but the other nationalities . . . should be assured . . . autonomous development, and the Dardanelles should be permanently opened. . . .

XIII. An independent Polish state should be erected . . . which should be assured free and secure access to the sea. . . .

XIV. A general association of nations must be formed. . . .

Wilson seriously miscalculated in refusing to take with him as one of the peace commissioners a leading Republican like Elihu Root or William Howard Taft. He would have done well, too, to include one of the powerful Republican senators, since it would take many Republican votes to muster the requisite two-thirds majority for the treaty in the Senate. Nevertheless, Wilson took only a nonpolitical Republican diplomat, Henry White, and relied neither upon him nor upon the other commissioners.

Arriving in Europe in December 1918, before the other European leaders were ready to confer, Wilson toured France, Italy, and England. Wherever he went hysterically cheering crowds greeted him; everywhere boulevards and plazas were renamed for him. The cheering millions reinforced his feeling that he was the spokesman for humanity. He was not aware that in each nation these masses looked to him to obtain for them much that ran contrary to the Fourteen Points. A little later, when he fought against some of their national claims, their adulation evaporated into disillusion.

WILSON AT VERSAILLES

The sessions at Paris began January 12, 1919, in an atmosphere of idealism tinctured with national aggrandizement, amidst glittering scenes reminiscent of the Congress of Vienna. To the east, however, there was an urgency born of imminent starvation and the threatening spread of Communism. Hoover, trying to get food into central Europe to fend off both threats, declared: "The wolf is at the door of the world." One of the greatest difficulties was that Russia, where Red Bolsheviks were still fighting White counterrevolutionaries, was entirely unrepresented.

At the outset Wilson had to struggle to prevent a division of spoils under the secret treaties. He tried to block the Japanese from obtaining permanently the German treaty rights in the Shantung peninsula of China and the former German islands north of the Equator in the Pacific, which could be Japanese strongholds. He had to give way, however, to the insistence of the British that they honor the treaty promises with which they had lured the

Japanese into the war. Wilson with more success persuaded the Allies to hold former German colonies and Turkish territories on a basis of trusteeship responsible to the League of Nations. This was the new and unprecedented "mandate" system.

Simultaneously, Wilson worked on the drafting of the League Covenant. He insisted that it form the first part of the treaty and be inseparable from it, and he labored long and hard to draft it in meticulous detail. In the League Covenant he saw the one possible way of overriding the vengeful selfishness that seemed dominant among the victorious nations. Whatever imperfections and inequities there were in the treaty he thought could be rectified through the League: through it and it alone, the world could avoid future wars. In the League he envisaged a potentially powerful (but not armed) international organization through which the nations of the world could share responsibility in maintaining the security of all against any aggressor.

At the end of February 1919, as Congress prepared to adjourn, Wilson came home to sign bills. He brought with him the League Covenant, determined that he would force the Senate to accept it without compromise. The acclaim with which Bostonians greeted him, the friendliness of editorials in most newspapers, and the energy with which large and influential organizations advocated the League, all encouraged him to think public sentiment was overwhelmingly behind him. When Colonel House warned him he must be prepared to compromise with the Senate, he retorted: "I have found that you get nothing in this world that is worth-while without fighting for it."

A stiff fight was taking form. In the Senate, on March 4, 1919, Henry Cabot Lodge produced a round robin signed by thirty-nine senators, a number sufficient to block the treaty, announcing that they would not accept the Covenant in its existing form. Wilson, about to reembark for Paris, retorted angrily. But back at the conference he did obtain some of the amendments upon which the Senate would obviously insist. These provided that a nation need not accept a mandate against its will, that a member could withdraw with two years' notice, that the League would not regulate immigration and other internal matters, and that it would not infringe upon the Monroe Doctrine. The Republican senators, however, were not

appeased. Many of them saw in the struggle over the Covenant a means of embarrassing Wilson, stripping him of some of his glory, and developing a winning issue for the campaign of 1920.

While Wilson was obtaining revisions to the Covenant, the conference was also grappling with the critical problem of Germany and the remaking of the European map. Together with the British prime minister, Lloyd George, Wilson resisted the French proposal to break up western Germany into buffer states. He did sanction the return of Alsace-Lorraine to France, and the establishment of a strong Poland and Czechoslovakia on Germany's borders, all in keeping with the national self-determination clauses of the Fourteen Points. He also supported German demilitarization, long-term Allied occupation of the west bank of the Rhine, and an Anglo-French-American mutual defense pact (which was never ratified). If maintained, these security provisions should have prevented the resurgence of Germany as a military menace to the West.

Elsewhere the remapping of Europe proceeded rather fitfully. Italy obtained the Brenner Pass area, in which 200,000 Austrians lived, then was outraged at not also receiving Fiume, which Wilson felt must be a port for the new nation of Yugoslavia. In this region and others, the economic needs of nations conflicted with the principle of national self-determination of peoples. Back in the United States, ethnic groups were ready to clamor for more for their native countries. The Irish in the United States insisted that Wilson should fight for national self-determination for Ireland, wracked by civil war. Wilson took up the matter privately with Lloyd George but did not make a public stand.

Wilson's most important departure from the Fourteen Points was his acceptance of British and French demands for heavy reparations from the Germans. Even before the armistice, he had partly accepted the demands that Germany pay for civilian damages. At the conference, he permitted these demands to cover even pensions for veterans; the astronomical sum was to be set later by a reparations commission. Meanwhile, though Wilson himself for years had taken an economic-determinism view of the origins of the war, the other powers insisted that Germany must accept sole responsibility for starting it. The "war-guilt" clause and the reparations bill embittered the German people. Even in the United States, the harsh peace meted out against Germany disillusioned many liberals and alienated them from Wilson. They regarded the treaty as a "hell's brew" which would ultimately lead to another war.

THE LEAGUE REJECTED

Wilson returned to the United States confident that the Senate, despite the difficulties Lodge was stirring up, would ratify the treaty. On July 10, 1919, when he presented it to the Senate, he asked rhetorically: "Dare we reject it and break the heart of the world?"

Through a combination of coercion and compromise he might have brought about ratification. But he was suffering from hardening of the arteries and, while in Paris, had been so ill that he may have been close to a stroke. His physical condition robbed him of political suppleness; instead of using patience and tact, he was more likely to shower his opponents with self-righteous anger.

Wilson's opponents in the Senate were moved by both principle and partisanship. The fourteen "irreconcilables" were men of conscience, of Middle Western or Far Western progressive tradition, like Republicans William E. Borah of Idaho, Hiram Johnson of California, and Robert M. La Follette of Wisconsin, and Democrat James Reed of Missouri. They acted from a deep conviction that their nation could best be served by staying out of the League. Other opponents with less conviction were more concerned with constructing a winning issue for the Republicans in the 1920 election than they were with assuring the future of the world. Senator Lodge, applying all his brilliant intellect to his loathing for Wilson, was ready, as chairman of the Senate Foreign Relations Committee, to use every possible tactic to obstruct, delay, and defeat the treaty. Public sentiment seemed to favor ratification, and Lodge needed time to marshal forces against it. Consequently, he spent the first two weeks after it reached the committee reading aloud every word on its nearly 300 pages. Next, he held a full six weeks of public hearings, listening to the complaints of every disgruntled minority.

From the White House, Wilson did some conferring with Republican senators. He explained to them that he considered the collec-

tive-security provision of Article X (according to which League members guaranteed one another's territorial integrity) to be more of a moral obligation upon the United States than a legal one—but to Wilson moral obligations were the more important. The senators were not impressed; it began to appear that Wilson would have to accept some of Lodge's reservations if he wished to obtain ratification. When one senator told him this, he retorted: "Never! Never! . . . I'll appeal to the country!"

So Wilson, at the end of his physical resources, against the stern warnings of his physician, undertook a cross-country speaking tour, writing his speeches as he went along, delivering them night after night. In twenty-two days he traveled over 8,000 miles, giving thirty-six addresses averaging an hour in length. At first the halls were not entirely filled nor were his speeches always well polished. As the tour proceeded, he gained larger and more enthusiastic audiences and grew more eloquent in his moral fervor. Had it been possible to sway the United States Senate through public opinion, the tour might have been a success. But Wilson became more and more frail. Finally after speaking at Pueblo, Colorado, September 25, he suffered such acute headaches that he had to cancel the tour and return to Washington.

Then he suffered an acute stroke which partially paralyzed his left side. For two weeks he was close to death, and for six more weeks so seriously ill that he could attend only to what little business his devoted wife and doctor thought would not unduly upset or fatigue him. When some officials tried to see the President on vital matters, Mrs. Wilson turned them away, saying: "I am not interested in the President of the United States. I am interested in my husband and his health."

At this critical juncture the Senate Foreign Relations Committee finally reported the treaty, recommending forty-five amendments and three reservations. Lodge managed to marshal the Republican senators so well that in November he obtained adoption of fourteen reservations. By this time Wilson had recovered sufficiently to give stern directions to the Democratic minority: they must vote only for the treaty without any reservations whatsoever. Although none of the Lodge reservations would have devitalized the League, Wilson preferred no ratification of the treaty to ratification with reservations. While he was by no means his old self, he was able to exert power enough to maintain discipline over the loyal Democrats. When the vote came on November 19, 1919, forty-two Democrats joined with the thirteen Republican irreconcilables to vote down the treaty with reservations. Next, the Senate voted on ratification of the treaty without reservations. There were thirty-eight sena-

tors, all but one of them a Democrat, who voted for it; fifty-five voted against it.

On the day of the final vote, March 19, 1920, when the Senate considered the treaty with fifteen reservations, it came within 7 votes of receiving the requisite two-thirds majority. By this time, President Wilson was looking to the election of 1920 as a "solemn referendum" on the League issue.

Selected Readings

T. R. and the Far East

H K. Beale, *Theodore Roosevelt and the Rise of America to World Power** (1956); C. E. Neu, *An Uncertain Friendship: Theodore Roosevelt and Japan, 1906–1909* (1967); R. A. Esthus, *Theodore Roosevelt and Japan* (1966); T. A. Bailey, *Theodore Roosevelt and the Japanese-American Crisis* (1934); Tyler Dennett, *Roosevelt and the Russo-Japanese War* (1924); P. J. Treat, *Diplomatic Relations Between the United States and Japan, 1895–1905* (1938); E. H. Zabriskie, *American-Russian Rivalry in the Far East, 1895–1914* (1946); W. R. Braisted, *The United States Navy in the Pacific, 1897–1909* (1958); M. H. Hunt, *Frontier Defense and the Open Door: Manchuria in Chinese-American Relations, 1895–1911* (1973).

Caribbean Policy

Dexter Perkins, *The United States and the Caribbean* (1947); D. G. Munro, *Intervention and Dollar Diplomacy in the Caribbean, 1900–1921* (1964); W. H. Callcott, *The Caribbean Policy of the United States, 1890–1920* (1942); Gerstle Mack, *The Land Divided: A History of the Panama Canal and Other Canal Projects* (1944); D. C. Miner, *The Fight for the Panama Route* (1940); D. F. Healy, *The United States in Cuba, 1898–1902* (1963); G. K. Lewis, *Puerto Rico: Freedom and Power in the Caribbean** (1967).

Mexican Relations

D. M. Pletcher, *Rails, Mines, and Progress: Seven American Promoters in Mexico, 1867–1911* (1959); C. C. Clendenen, *The United States and Pancho Villa: A Study in Unconventional Diplomacy* (1961); R. E. Quirk, *An Affair of Honor: Woodrow Wilson and the Occupation of Vera Cruz* (1962).

Wilsonian Diplomacy

Harley Notter, *The Origins of the Foreign Policy of Woodrow Wilson* (1937); A. S. Link, *Wilson the Diplomatist** (1957); N. G. Levin, Jr., *Woodrow Wilson and World Politics: America's Response to War and Revolution* (1968); R. E. Osgood, *Ideals and Self-Interest in America's Foreign Relations* (1953).

Going to War

E. R. May, *The World War and American Isolation, 1914–1917** (1959); E. H. Buehrig, *Woodrow Wilson and the Balance of Power* (1955); Charles Seymour, *American Diplomacy During the World War* (1934) and *American Neutrality, 1914–1917* (1935); Walter Millis, *Road to War: America, 1914–1917* (1935); E. M. Borchard and W. P. Lage, *Neutrality for the United States* (1937); C. C. Tansill, *America Goes to War* (1938); Armin Rappaport, *The Navy League of the United States* (1962); R. H. Heindel, *The American Impact on Great Britain, 1898–1914* (1940); Bradford Perkins, *The Great Rapprochement: England and the United States, 1895–1914* (1968).

Combat

E. M. Coffman, *The War to End All Wars: The American Military Experience in World War I* (1969); H. A. De Weerd, *President Wilson Fights His War: World War I and the American Intervention* (1968); D. F. Trask, *The United States in the Supreme War Council: American War Aims and Inter-Allied Strategy, 1917–1918* (1961); J. G. Harbord, *The American Army in France, 1917–1919* (1936); Frank Freidel, *Over There: The Story of America's First Great Overseas Crusade* (1964), a pictorial history; E. E. Morison, *Admiral Sims and the Modern American Navy* (1942); J. J. Hudson, *Hostile Skies: A Combat History of the American Air Service in World War I* (1968).

The Home Front

F. L. Paxson, *American Democracy and the World War* (3 vols., 1936–1948); S. W. Livermore, *Politics Is Adjourned: Woodrow Wilson and the War Congress, 1916–1918* (1966); D. R. Beaver, *Newton D. Baker and the American War Effort, 1917–1919* (1966); Margaret Coit, *Mr. Baruch* (1957); B. M. Baruch, *American Industry in the War* (1941); H. N. Scheiber, *The Wilson Administration and Civil Liberties, 1917–1921* (1960); H. C. Peterson and G. C. Fite, *Opponents of War, 1917–1918* (1957); J. R. Mock and Cedric Larson, *Words That Won the War* (1939); H. C. Peterson, *Propaganda for War* (1939).

Peacemaking
R. J. Bartlett, *The League to Enforce Peace* (1944);
H. R. Rudin, *Armistice, 1918* (1944); L. E. Gelfand, *The Inquiry: American Preparations for Peace, 1917–1919* (1963); T. A. Bailey, *Woodrow Wilson and the Lost Peace** (1944) and *Woodrow Wilson and the Great Betrayal** (1945); L W. Martin, *Peace Without Victory: Woodrow Wilson and the British Liberals* (1958);

D. F. Fleming, *The United States and the League of Nations, 1918–1920* (1932); J. M. Keynes, *Economic Consequences of the Peace* (1919); Herbert Hoover, *The Ordeal of Woodrow Wilson* (1958); J. A Garraty, *Henry Cabot Lodge* (1953).

*Titles available in paperback.

VOL. LXXVI....No. 25,319. NEW YORK, SATURDAY, MAY 21, 1927.

LINDBERGH SPEEDS ACROSS NOR
KEEPING TO SCHEDULE OF 100 M
SIGHTED PASSING ST. JOHN'S,

LOWMAN GETS POST AS ANDREWS QUITS IN BIG DRY SHIFT

Mellon, in Same Stroke, Names Chief Chemist Doran Commissioner in Place of Haynes.

STEP TO CHECK FRICTION

Andrews Will Retire Aug. 1 With Work Completed—Haynes Is Forced Out in Shake-Up.

MOVE SATISFIES ALL SIDES

Both Nominees Are on Record as Prohibition Advocates and Are Acceptable to Dry League.

Special to The New York Times.

WASHINGTON, May 20.—In the most drastic overturn in the history of dry enforcement, which is expected to lead to further changes in the Washington headquarters as well as in the field, Secretary Mellon at one stroke today accepted the resignation of General Lincoln C. Andrews of New York, as Assistant Secretary of the Treasury in charge of prohibition enforcement, and appointed a successor to Major Roy A. Haynes of Ohio, the Acting Commissioner of Prohibition.

Mr. Mellon designated Seymour W. Lowman, former Lieutenant Governor of New York, for Presidential appointment to the post of General Andrews and named Dr. James M. Doran of North Dakota, now Chief Chemist of the Prohibition Unit, to be Prohibition Commissioner in place of Major Haynes.

Mr. Lowman is expected to enter upon his duties as Assistant Secretary on Aug. 1, assuming jurisdiction over the Customs and Prohibition Bureaus and the Coast Guard. Dr. Doran will take charge of the Prohibition Bureau at once.

End of Factionalism Expected.

Hope was expressed today by Administration officials that the retirement of General Andrews and Major Haynes would end the factionalism in the Prohibition Bureau, which, in their opinion, has tended to lessen the efficiency of enforcement. Major Haynes, a former officer of the Anti-Saloon League, has been at swords' points with his Treasury superiors for years and the law enforcement work of General Andrews has been frequently criticized by Wayne B. Wheeler and others associated with the Anti-Saloon League.

Major Haynes's failure to land the Prohibition Commissionership is regarded here as a defeat for the Anti-Saloon League and a victory for dry leaders who do not train with the Wheeler organization. At the same time league officials take comfort from the prospective retirement of General Andrews, whom they have long regarded as "unfriendly" to their purposes.

Party Chiefs Sponsored Lowman.

Mr. Lowman was endorsed for the assistant secretaryship by National Committeeman Hilles and Ogden L. Mills, Under Secretary of the Treasury. He was the running mate of Mr. Mills on the Republican gubernatorial ticket in New York last year, and has a record as a dry that makes him acceptable to most of the dry leaders. He was originally considered for Commissioner of Prohibition, but a switch was made when General Andrews gave notice of his resignation.

It is assumed here that Secretary Mellon consulted with the President before he announced his designation of Mr. Lowman. Mr. Lowman will come to Washington on June 1 to familiarize himself with the duties of his new office, but he does not expect to be sworn in until General Andrews quits, on Aug. 1.

No provision has been made for Major Haynes to remain in the dry service and he is expected to resign forthwith. He is now functioning as "Acting Commissioner" under a temporary arrangement that became effective under the reorganization law on April 1.

Major Herbert D. White, special investigator, probably will be named Assistant Commissioner. James E. Jones and L. G. Nutt, who were appointed Deputy Commissioners in April, will remain in those positions at least for the present.

Mellon Stresses Promotion System.

In announcing the appointment of Dr. Doran, Secretary Mellon stated

'Too Old,' Says Hughes at 65, To Run for the Presidency

Declaring that he was "too old to run for President," Charles Evans Hughes, after reading in the morning papers yesterday of a movement to start a Hughes boom in the event that President Coolidge should decide not to become a candidate for re-election, issued a statement declaring he would not accept a nomination. He was 65 years old April 11.

"I know nothing of the movement to which reference is made," Mr. Hughes said. "There should be no doubt as to my own attitude. I am for President Coolidge, first, last and all the time, and I believe that he will be renominated and re-elected. I do not wish my name to be used in any contingency. I am too old to run for President and I would neither seek nor accept the nomination."

SINCLAIR SENTENCED TO 3 MONTHS IN JAIL

Oil Man Is Also Ordered to Pay $500 Fine for Refusing to Reply to Senators.

APPEALS AND GIVES BOND

Littleton Argues in Vain That His Client Exercised His Constitutional Rights.

Special to The New York Times.

WASHINGTON, May 20.—Harry F. Sinclair, oil operator, under indictment with former Secretary Fall for conspiracy to defraud the Government, was sentenced today to serve three months in jail and to pay a fine of $500 on a charge of contempt of the Senate committee which investigated the naval reserve oil leases. Immediately after Justice William Hitz pronounced the sentence in the District of Columbia Supreme Court, Sinclair gave bond in the sum of $5,000 pending appeal to the Appellate Court.

The penalty was imposed notwithstanding the plea by Martin W. Littleton, Sinclair's counsel, that the Court do nothing which would humiliate, shame, disgrace, mortify or worry his client, and despite Mr. Littleton's argument that the entire proceedings, beginning with Mr. Sinclair's appearance before the Senate committee March 22, 1924, and ending with the sentence, were "irregular."

Mr. Sinclair was originally charged with refusing to answer nine questions by the Senate committee regarding the lease of the Teapot Dome reserve in Wyoming by his Mammoth Oil Company. Sinclair's counsel filed a demurrer, and the number of questions was reduced to six.

A special appeal was then allowed, but the progress of this was blocked by the Walsh bill, initiated by Senator Walsh of Montana, "prosecutor" for the Senate committee, and designed to prevent appeals from interlocutory orders of the criminal courts. Following the passage by Congress of the Walsh bill, Sinclair was tried in April and was convicted. The number of questions involved was reduced at the trial to four.

No Crime, Says Littleton.

When Sinclair stood up for sentence, he declared that he had nothing to say. Mr. Littleton, however, related the history of similar cases, and stated that when he advised Mr. Sinclair to refuse to answer the Senate committee's questions he was not giving his client a "horseback opinion," but an opinion which was founded on substantial law.

"My client has done nothing to warrant this procedure," Mr. Littleton declared. "The question of the right of either house of Congress, acting separately or together, to compel a citizen to testify has never been definitely decided and, in fact, the United States Supreme Court in the case of Kilbourne versus Thompson deliberately refused to decide that question.

"The committee which summoned Mr. Sinclair was denied nothing, nor did he impose a single obstruction in the path of the committee. There is no crime committed here, no offense involving moral turpitude—merely a citizen of the United States who had and exercised a right which belongs to every American gentleman."

The Four Questions Asked.

The four questions which Mr. Sinclair declined to answer, on advice from Mr. Littleton, and which were

LINDBERGH LEAVES NEW YORK AT 7:52 A. M.

With Cool Determination He Braves Death to Get Off in the Misty Dawn, Winning Out by Luck and Skill.

PLANE FALTERS AND THEN RISES AND IS OFF

Hundreds Gasp as Unconquerable Youth by Sheer Wizardry Lifts Machine Carrying 5,200-Pound Load, With Failure a Few Yards Off.

By RUSSELL OWEN,

Staff Correspondent of The Times, Who Reported the Polar Flights of Byrd and Amundsen.

Copyright, 1927, by The New York Times Company.

A sluggish, gray monoplane lurched its way down Roosevelt Field yesterday morning, slowly gathering momentum. Inside sat a tall youngster, eyes glued to an instrument board or darting ahead for swift glances at the runway, his face drawn with the intensity of his purpose.

Death lay but a few seconds ahead of him if his skill failed or his courage faltered. For moments, as the heavy plane rose from the ground, dropped down, staggered again into the air and fell, he gambled for his life against a hazard which had already killed four men.

And then slowly, so slowly that those watching it stood fascinated, as if by his indomitable will alone, the young pilot lifted his plane. It dipped and then rose with renewed speed, climbing heavily but steadily toward the distant trees.

The spirit of unconquerable youth had won, and "Slim" Lindbergh was on his way to Paris.

All the romance which had surrounded this boy since his meteoric flight here from the Pacific Coast a week ago reached its climax in that take-off. The uncertainty of it, the frightful disaster which threatened him, the quick recoveries which showed a cool, keen mind fighting for mastery, made veteran pilots gaze in fascination.

"God be with him!" exclaimed Commander Byrd fervently, when at last it seemed that Lindbergh was safely on his way.

The boyish, smiling lad, with the quiet confidence of bravery and belief in his own ability, has won the hearts of every one who came near him. Until two weeks ago he was hardly considered a factor in the race to be first through the air to Paris, that long, treacherous flight of 3,600 miles. And then he came on with speed of the wind, making only one stop between the Pacific Coast and New York, and while rival camps squabbled over money or worked through long, tedious tests, Lindbergh rolled his plane out in the gray dawn and got away, all alone.

Youth Breaks All Barriers.

It may not have been the safest kind of flying; perhaps it was only a daring gesture, but it was magnificent. It was youth refusing to admit obstacles, breaking down barriers, and it brought him luck. For even as Lindbergh prepared his plane the fog that had choked his path to Newfoundland rolled back, and all the way from New York to Europe stretched a clear path of fair weather, with gentle favoring winds. Even the sun came out as he started, and it seemed that the fates which deal with brave men's lives were smiling at the youth who had defied them.

When Lindbergh made his decision to start just before midnight on Thursday, it seemed the height of folly. Heavy fog settled over Roosevelt Field under inky black skies which dripped slow drops of rain. It was dismal and threatening. But the young pilot, who has guided his temerity with a keen and thoughtful mind, saw in the late weather reports the possibility that the skies might clear to the north. All he needed was one look at Newfoundland before he left the land for his long, weary flight across the sea which had already claimed Nungesser and Coli.

The huge hangar in which his plane was housed was closed to every one except the mechanics, who went over the plane with zealous care and partly filled the gasoline tank. Lindbergh, after a parting word with them, went to the Garden City Hotel at midnight for a brief sleep. He lay down with orders that he be called at 2:15 o'clock in the morning, but before 2 o'clock he was downstairs.

While he had been resting weather reports indicated that the fog was lifting all along the coast, although it was depressingly wet at the field. The clouds had opened and poured down a short deluge, which left puddles in which shone the glare of many lights. Through a small opening in the hangar door the silver nose of Lindbergh's plane gleamed through the glancing rain drops.

CAPTAIN CHARLES A. LIN

The First American Flyer to Start on the York and Paris.

LINDBERGH'S STORY FOR

When next heard from, Lindbergh will wri exploit especially for readers of The Times and newspapers. It will appear in New York exc

BELLANCA FLIGHT HELD BACK BY WIND

Hop, Set for Dawn, Is Called Off After All Preparations—Bertaud Writ Thown Out.

With Captain Lindbergh well on his way to Paris last night, those connected with the Columbia Aircraft Company's Bellanca monoplane Columbia made arrangements for a hop-off from Roosevelt Field at 4 o'clock this morning. Before midnight Charles A. Levine, backer of the company, made a definite statement that the Bellanca plane would start at daylight.

At 1:30 A. M., however, Clarence Chamberlin, senior pilot of the monoplane, announced that there would be no start today.

"The weather report shows northwest winds, which would give us a head wind all the way to Newfoundland," he said. "We will not make the attempt today."

Levine's statement earlier in the evening was supplemented by additional information from a spokesman for him.

"After a conference at the Hotel Biltmore tonight between Charles A. Levine, Chairman of the Board of Directors of the Columbia Aircraft Corporation, and ex-Senator Charles Lockwood, representing Clarence D. Chamberlin, Mr. Levine decided that as a purely sporting proposition the flight should be made at once," the spokesman said.

He refused to reveal the name of the navigator who had been selected to replace Lloyd Bertaud and accompany Chamberlin on the flight.

"The navigator," he said, "will not be announced until just before the flight."

Lloyd Bertaud was definitely

LONE F FRENC

Lindbergh to Par Co

Copyright, 1927, Special Ca

PARIS, Lindbergh's the Atlanti New York the French have done. has tonigh prayers for

His calm and efficie panied by French mi real Ameri the doughb Mihiel and for sundry since.

To welco so huge a greeted C Coli in Ne too far out in the fortu all France ica's anxiety morrow for denied their which Capt. makes so g

As fully tions have Lindbergh's ly, the wea is not so en been for so is not unfa the predict clouds follo rising temp stay in th help to the

H ATLANTIC,
LES AN HOUR;
F., AT 7:15 P.M.

GETS HIS BEARINGS IN NEWFOUNDLAND

With the First Leg of His Flight to Paris Over, He Puts to Sea and Heads for Ireland

ALL OF THE "BREAKS" ARE IN HIS FAVOR

Fog Disperses, Weather Clears and Gentle Following Winds Help to Speed Him Along on His Hazardous Venture.

Copyright, 1927, by The New York Times Company.
Special Cable to THE NEW YORK TIMES.

ST. JOHN'S, N. F., May 20.—Captain Lindbergh's airplane passed over St. John's at 8:15 o'clock tonight [7:15 New York Daylight Saving Time]. It was seen by hundreds and disappeared seaward, heading for Ireland. It is assumed that it passed over Cape Race and places south of this in the dense fog which prevailed there all day.

It was flying quite low between the hills near St. John's and went east over the Signal Hill Station, following the track of Hawker and Greeve and also of Alcock and Brown on the first transatlantic flights eight years ago.

There was intense excitement during the passage of Lindbergh's plane, and citizens motoring in the suburbs or strolling on the country roads are coming back with tales of its transit. Many noted the fact that the flier seemed to be getting his bearing before setting out on the second leg of his flight.

Michael Sullivan, member of the Newfoundland Cabinet, saw the plane while motoring and followed its progress in his car on the road that leads to the signal station, keeping it in sight for several minutes, but when he reached the summit it had passed from sight, so great was its speed.

Robert Job, principal of the firm of Job Brothers, shipping merchants, also saw it and watched its course over the city. He could see it so distinctly as to notice that it had some letters on its side, though he could not make out words.

Strong Wind Is in His Favor.

By The Associated Press.

ST. JOHN'S N. F., Saturday, May 21.—Strong westerly breezes, approaching gale force, were blowing here early tonight and marine authorities declared that they should be of great assistance to Captain Lindbergh in his transatlantic crossing.

It was estimated here that he might reach the Irish coast by daylight.

Leaves American Continent.

Copyright, 1927, by The New York Times Company.
Special to The New York Times.

SYDNEY, N. S., May 20.—Captain Lindbergh got his last sight of the American continent at 5 o'clock [4 o'clock Eastern Daylight Saving Time] this afternoon when he passed out into the Atlantic over Main-a-dieu, Cape Breton. The plane was flying low and at great speed, and her number, 211, was plainly visible to watchers with powerful glasses.

Should Lindbergh succeed in navigating through a fairly dense curtain over the Newfoundland banks he will have fair weather across the North Atlantic, ships at sea reporting good visibility with no indications of a storm within the next twenty-four hours.

By The Associated Press.

HALIFAX, N. S., May 20.—Captain Lindbergh passed over Mulgrave on the Strait of Canso, which separates the mainland of Nova Scotia from Cape Breton Island, at 4:05 P. M. Atlantic Day Time [3:05 o'clock Eastern Daylight Saving Time]. He was flying high and the markings on his gray monoplane could not be seen.

Reaches Nova Scotia Coast.

Copyright, 1927, by The New York Times Company.
Special to The New York Times.

YARMOUTH, N. S., May 20.—Captain Lindbergh passed over New Tusket, about forty miles from here, at 12:45 o'clock this afternoon (11:45 Eastern Daylight Time). He was flying low, but traveling very fast.

By The Associated Press.

MIDDLEBORO, Mass., May 20.—A monoplane, believed to be that of Captain Lindbergh, was seen over West Middleboro about 9:15 this morning flying northeasterly.

Chester Rice, clerk at the Middleboro police station, could not make out the letters on the wings, but is sure the numbers were 211.

Twenty-three

"America's present need is not heroics, but healing; not nostrums, but normalcy." The year was 1920, and the speaker, with a fine sense of alliteration as well as a feeling for the spirit of the time, was Warren G. Harding, soon to be President of the United States. "The world needs to be reminded that all human ills are not curable by legislation."

Harding's remarks provided a catch phrase for the period following World War I. The American people, or at least the majority of them, were tired of legislation, tired of wartime restrictions, tired of progressive reforms. They wanted a return to "normalcy," to the good old days, to the days that never had existed except in nostalgic reverie.

The days that were to come in the 1920s were old in some respects but new in others. They were old—like those of the late nineteenth century—in respect to the position of big business, which again dominated both government and society. Indeed, business was more sanctified than ever. "The business of America is business," said Calvin Coolidge, who succeeded Harding in the presidency. In *The Man Nobody Knows* (1925), a best seller of the period, Bruce Barton described Jesus Christ as "a startling example of business success," the author of "the most powerful advertisements of all time," and "the founder of modern business."

But much was new in the decade of the twenties. This was the time when the automobile came into its own, with production increasing from 1.5 million cars in 1921 to 4.75 million in 1929, by which year the automotive industry was responsible, directly or indirectly, for the employment of more than 3 million persons. It was the time of the coming of numerous household gadgets: the radio, the refrigerator, the vacuum cleaner, and many others. It was an age when the federal government sought to impose a species of morality by prohibiting the manufacture, sale, or transportation of intoxicating

"Lindbergh Speeds Across North Atlantic"
On May 20, 1927, Charles Lindbergh began the first solo nonstop flight from New York to Paris. The trip, which took almost thirty-three and a half hours, made Lindbergh a national hero. (© 1927 by The New York Times Company. Reprinted by permission.)

beverages—and an age of what seemed to many like unprecedented license in speech and behavior, the age of "flaming youth" and of unrestrained dances like the "bunny hug" and the "Charleston."

From 1923 to 1929 it was also a time of remarkable prosperity (for most but by no means all Americans). The people generally assumed—and experts in business, economics, and government told them—that this was veritably a new era in human history. The country had reached a "permanent plateau" of prosperity and need never worry again about the possibility of a serious slump. But prosperity, like "normalcy," proved to be an illusion. Eventually the country fell into much the worst economic depression it had ever known.

The Postwar Reaction

In the immediate postwar years, prices rose and people complained of the "h. c. l.," the high cost of living. Suddenly, in 1921, prices dropped and a brief recession followed, giving way to full recovery by 1923. Meanwhile, fears of radicalism, heightened by the spread of Communism in Russia and elsewhere in Europe, provoked a hysterical spirit of reaction in America.

THE RED SCARE

Union workers tried to preserve their wartime economic gains by striking for higher wages as living costs went upward. In 1919 a great wave of strikes spread across the country, involving about 4 million workers. In many of these strikes—such as those conducted by longshoremen, printers, and laborers in the clothing, textile, telephone, and other industries—the strikers succeeded in raising their living standards. In the process they alienated much of the public, which was quick to accept the industrialists' explanations that higher wages were responsible for higher prices, and that the strike leaders were radicals.

The outbreak of a steel strike in September 1919 brought antilabor feelings to a boil. The grievances of the workers were serious. They were working an average of nearly sixty-nine hours per week for bare subsistence wages and were becoming so discontented that the AFL's organizing committee made rapid headway among them. United States Steel discharged all union men and refused to negotiate with Gompers or any other union official. Some 343,000 men struck in the Chicago area, and additional workers left their jobs in other areas. Despite the workers' valid claims, United States Steel was able to swing public sentiment away from the strikers by claiming that the leaders were Communists. The chief organizer, William Z. Foster, once a follower of Bryan, was to emerge in 1924 as the presidential candidate of the Communist party. The company brought in Negro strikebreakers, and state and federal troops prevented picketing. In rioting at Gary, Indiana, eighteen strikers were killed. Within a few weeks tens of thousands of strikebreakers under armed protection were operating the plants at three-quarters capacity, and by January the workers were starved out.

Public opinion turned even more firmly against organized labor when a police strike broke out in Boston. The policemen were working long hours on prewar salaries under unpleasant conditions. After their organization, the Boston Social Club, obtained an AFL charter and threatened to strike, a Mayor's Citizens Committee prepared to meet their demands except for recognition of their union. The police commissioner, responsible only to the governor, refused and dismissed nineteen leaders. In response, the police struck. As mischief-makers and rowdies took over, horrified citizens put on their military uniforms and, armed with rifles and shotguns, began patrolling the streets. The mayor mobilized state troops and restored order. The following day Governor Calvin Coolidge, who had done nothing to prevent the strike or preserve the peace, suddenly acted. He ordered in troops and backed the decision of the police commissioner never to reemploy any of the strikers. When President Gompers of the AFL appealed to Coolidge, the governor wired back: "There is no right to strike against the public safety, anywhere, anytime." This one telegram made Coolidge a formidable contender for the Republican presidential nomination in 1920.

In Washington Attorney General A. Mitchell Palmer was becoming prominent through his war on both labor and radicals. When the new president of the United Mine Workers, John L. Lewis, took the bituminous coal workers out on strike in November 1919, Palmer smashed the strike with federal court injunctions.

Sacco and Vanzetti Being Taken into Court   1927

When Sacco and Vanzetti were brought before Judge Webster Thayer on April 9, 1927, they were allowed to speak. Sacco said: "I never knew, never heard, even read in history anything so cruel as this Court. . . . I know the sentence will be between two classes, the oppressed class and the rich class, and there will always be collision between one and the other." Vanzetti said: "I am suffering because I am a radical and indeed I am a radical; I have suffered because I was an Italian, and indeed I am an Italian. . . . but I am so convinced to be right that you can only kill me once but if you could execute me two times, and if I could be reborn two other times, I would live again to do what I have done already." Judge Thayer then sentenced them to death. One of the counsel for the two men who did not "belong even remotely to [their] school of thoughts," warned after the execution of "minds that are closed by deep prejudice or transient passion." "If," he declared, "the local hostility was inflamed by foolish words of their sympathizers or wicked deeds of their exploiters, this also is a fact to be recollected." The publisher of the conservative Boston Herald, which had called for an impartial commission to review the case, asserted: "The momentum of the established order required the execution of Sacco and Vanzetti, and never in your life or mine, has that momentum acquired such tremendous force." (Brown Brothers)

Palmer attracted even more attention with his crusade against Reds. Throughout the country the violent suppression of alleged pro-German activities during the war had been continued in the persecution of the Industrial Workers of the World (IWW), the Socialists, and all other left-wingers. Both Congress and the New York state legislature denied seats to Socialists. By 1920 one-third of the states had enacted criminal syndicalist laws to punish radicals. The New York law prohibited "advocating, teaching, or aiding and abetting the commission of crime and sabotage, or unlawful acts of force and violence or unlawful methods of terrorism as a means of accomplishing a change in industrial ownership or control, or affecting any political change."

Bombings and attempted bombings captured the headlines. A bomb damaged the front of Palmer's home in June 1919; bombs addressed to a number of government leaders were discovered in the mails; a year later an explosion on Wall Street killed thirty-eight people. Four members of the newly founded American Legion were killed in an attack on IWW headquarters in Centralia, Washington, on Armistice Day 1919. These incidents furnished the material out of which the newspapers, with some aid from Palmer, built a great national panic. Within the country there were very few radicals to undertake a revolution: IWW membership was down to 35,000 and continued to decline; the Socialist party numbered 39,000 and was not revolutionary anyway; the Communist-Labor party (left-wing Socialists) had 10,000 to 30,000 members; and the Communist party, organized September 1, 1919, had 30,000 to 60,000.

Palmer's goal was to ferret out and eliminate the Communists. He proposed a sedition bill so drastic that Congress would not enact it, then he proceeded anyway without it. The Labor Department had already arrested and deported to Finland 249 Russian Communists. Nevertheless, Palmer, without advance notice to the Labor Department, conducted a great Red roundup on January 1, 1920, jailing some 6,000 suspects. Communists who were United States citizens he turned over to states for prosecution. The aliens came under the jurisdiction of the Labor Department, which gave them fair treatment. Only 556 proved Communists were deported.

In Massachusetts, a payroll robbery and murder in April 1920 led to the trial and conviction of two anarchists, Nicola Sacco and Bartolomeo Vanzetti. Many believers in civil liberties felt that the two men were being prosecuted more on the basis of their radicalism than on the criminal evidence. Ultimately throughout the country and even in western Europe, outraged liberals and radicals demanded the release of the two men, but in August 1927 they were executed. The Sacco and Vanzetti case was a *cause célèbre* of the 1920s.

XENOPHOBIA AND NEGROPHOBIA

War propaganda had stimulated a demand for "one hundred percent Americanism" and had aroused a feeling of hatred against the enemy, the "Hun." After the war, defeated Germany no longer served as an object of hate, yet the wartime emotion could not be immediately turned off. Much of it was redirected against radicals, racial and ethnic minorities, and other allegedly "un-American" groups within the United States.

On the part of rural Americans, especially native white Protestants, there had long been a suspicion of big cities, crowded as these were with immigrants, many of whom were Roman Catholics. Now, as the census of 1920 revealed, the urban population had come to outnumber the rural. This was seen as a menace to the traditional values of the small town and the farm.

The danger seemed likely to increase with the arrival of a new flood of immigrants, refugees from war-torn Europe. During the war, immigration had been cut off, but afterward it began to surge, rising from 111,000 in 1919 to 430,000 in 1920 and 805,000 in 1921. The Red scare, with the arrest of foreign-born radicals, led to fears that immigrants would bring a continuing infection of Communism from Europe to America. For a time it was thought that even returning American soldiers might carry the Communist germ. While still in Paris, in 1918, a group of army officers had founded the American Legion with the aim of organizing the veterans and instilling in them patriotism as an antidote to radicalism.

The Eighteenth Amendment, bringing nationwide prohibition in 1920, represented a victory for native Protestantism as well as for

The Ku Klux Klan Parading in Washington, D.C.
*In 1926 the Ku Klux Klan was still so powerful that it could march down
Pennsylvania Avenue with the Capitol in the background. It professed to be a
patriotic organization, but was openly anti-Negro, anti-Catholic, anti-Semitic,
anti-foreigner, and anti-Union. (Culver)*

women's rights. It got its strongest support from Methodists and Baptists, particularly in the rural areas of the South and West. It met its greatest opposition among Roman Catholics, especially in the cities of the Northeast.

The spirit of the time was also reflected in the postwar revival of the fundamentalist movement, which made its greatest headway within the Protestant churches of the South. Fundamentalists believed in the literal truth of every statement in the Bible. To them, the Darwinian theory of evolution was irreligious and wrong, since it conflicted with the account of Creation given in the book of Genesis. The fundamentalists campaigned for and succeeded in establishing state laws to prevent the teaching of evolution in public schools in Tennessee and a few other Southern states.

In 1925 a Tennessee schoolteacher, John T. Scopes, was brought to trial for violating the antievolution law. Defending him was the country's best-known criminal lawyer, Clarence Darrow, and assisting in the prosecution was the famous politician and orator William Jennings Bryan. The trial reached a spectacu-

lar climax when Bryan took the stand as a Bible expert and allowed Darrow to cross-examine him. At first, Bryan insisted that God had created the earth in exactly six days, just as the Bible said, but later he admitted that a "day" in Biblical terms might mean many thousands of years. Thus he gave away the main point of the fundamentalist argument, though the prosecution won the case. Scopes, after being convicted, was freed on a technicality.

Intolerance and nativism took their most extreme form in the new Ku Klux Klan. Revived in 1915 in Atlanta, Georgia, the Klan spread throughout the country, but it, too, drew its main strength from the rural areas of the South and West. At its height, in the mid-1920s, the Klan claimed 5 million members. They professed to stand for Christianity, morality, and Americanism. White-robed, hooded, often masked, Klansmen used fiery crosses, threats, torture, and even murder to intimidate people they considered immoral or un-American. The targets and victims were mostly members of minority groups, especially Roman Catholics and blacks.

The Klan became a political power in many states, most notably in Indiana, where a Klansman made himself governor and virtually dictator for a time. In national politics the Klan was strong enough to prevent the Democrats from nominating a Roman Catholic, Al Smith, for President in 1924 and to help defeat Smith after his nomination in 1928. Meanwhile, weakened by exposures of crime and vice among its leaders, the Klan had begun to decline in membership and influence.

No other group suffered so much from the postwar wave of intolerance as did the Negroes. For many of them the war had seemed to offer an opportunity to break out of the oppressive caste system of the South. Hundreds of thousands moved to the industrial centers of the North to get employment in the booming war industries and, they hoped, to find a less discriminatory society. In the North, however, they usually had to take jobs with the lowest pay, live in the worst slums, and contend with the animosity of unskilled white workers who feared black competition.

Some 400,000 blacks served in the army, half of them in Europe, where the local people usually drew no color line. Black veterans returned with a new-found sense of respect and dignity and with a determination to improve their status at home. They had fought in a war to "make the world safe for democracy," and some of them now applied the slogan to the United States. Speaking for the returning blacks, the NAACP magazine *The Crisis* proclaimed in 1919: "Make way for Democracy! We saved it in France, and by the Great Jehovah, we'll save it in the U.S.A., or know the reason why." They were soon disillusioned.

In both North and South, Negroes faced explosive resentment against them. In order to intimidate them back into their former subservience, Southerners resorted to the terrorism of the Klan and to lynchings, which increased from thirty-four in 1917 to more than seventy in 1919. Terrible race riots broke out, beginning in July 1919, in twenty-six towns and cities, mostly in the North. Hundreds of persons were killed or wounded, and millions of dollars' worth of property was destroyed. The worst of the outbursts began on a Chicago bathing beach and continued through thirteen days of pillaging and burning in the Negro district; 23 blacks and 15 whites were killed, 500 were injured, and 1,000 families, mostly Negro, were left homeless.

These terrors led millions of Negroes to follow a persuasive charlatan, Marcus Garvey, founder of the Universal Negro Improvement Association. In return for their contributions, he promised to take them home to an African empire. In 1923 Garvey was convicted of swindling and sentenced to federal prison, but Negro nationalism nevertheless persisted.

PERSISTING PROGRESSIVISM

Some Americans – not radicals but old progressives – would have liked to see the continuation of wartime government regulation or even ownership. At the close of the war the government owned most of the nation's commercial radio facilities (used as yet only for sending messages), commanded a vast merchant fleet, and controlled the railroads.

The call for nationalization, which frightened many Americans, went beyond the old progressive bounds. Congress was not willing to go so far but did pass the Esch-Cummins Transportation Act of 1920, establishing as tight federal control over railroad rates and securities as any progressive had ever visualized. Railroads suffered from the new rigorous competition of motor vehicles and other carriers and were seldom able to earn the 6-percent return the Interstate Commerce Commission allowed.

Shipping remained partly under direct government ownership, because private operation had to be heavily subsidized one way or another in order for American companies to compete successfully with those of other countries. These companies were subsidized by low prices and easy terms in buying government-owned ships and by generous mail contracts under the Merchant Marine Act of 1920. Congress refused to allow the navy to continue operating commercial radio communications, and so the navy reluctantly sold its stations to the newly established Radio Corporation of America.

Western progressives obtained two measures to stave off corporate onslaughts. One, the General Leasing Act, was intended to protect the naval oil reserves from oil companies that for some years had been trying to obtain them. It also authorized the leasing of other mineral and oil lands on terms favorable to the government. The other measure, the Water Power Act of 1920, was a first tentative step toward federal regulation of power. It established a Federal Power Commission (con-

sisting of the secretaries of war, the interior, and agriculture) to license the construction and operation of hydroelectric plants on public lands and to regulate rates on power from these plants when it passed across state boundaries.

Republican Prosperity

Though progressivism persisted, it had to yield to conservatism during the boom years of the 1920s. The wartime production miracles and the postwar writings of public relations experts and advertising men gave most Americans a renewed faith in business. The heroes of the time were the leaders of the great industries, and their interests were reflected by the dominant Republicans in politics.

THE HARDING TRAGEDY

In 1920 domestic politics made impossible a solemn referendum on a League of Nations; only an ill man sequestered from the flow of events, as President Wilson was, could have expected such a thing. A Democratic victory was so improbable that Republican leaders felt no compulsion to put forth any of their strong candidates.

The two leading contenders were Leonard Wood and Frank O. Lowden. General Wood, an ardent conservative nationalist, commanded most of Roosevelt's former following and collected a campaign chest of startling proportions ($1,773,000), with which he battled Lowden for delegates. Lowden, favorably known as an efficient governor of Illinois, also commanded large campaign funds, totaling $414,000. Progressive Republican charges that both contenders were deeply indebted to big business helped induce party managers to ignore them when the two deadlocked at the convention. Late one night in a smoke-filled hotel room a cabal of senators led by Henry Cabot Lodge turned to one of the most regular and pliable of their colleagues, Warren G. Harding of Ohio. The convention nominated Harding on the tenth ballot and chose as his running mate the Massachusetts governor,

Calvin Coolidge. These two were thoroughly conservative candidates running on a thoroughly conservative platform.

The Democrats, assembling at San Francisco, were rather confused because President Wilson, who could have easily designated a candidate, seemed to be waiting with pathetic coyness to be renominated for a third term. This was out of the question. For thirty-eight ballots, two of Wilson's cabinet members, his efficient son-in-law William G. McAdoo and his superpatriotic Attorney General, A. Mitchell Palmer, battled for the nomination. In the end the urban bosses stepped in and secured the nomination of an antiprohibition candidate who might salvage their city tickets for them. This was the former progressive governor of Ohio, James M. Cox. As a gesture toward the Wilsonians, Assistant Secretary of the Navy Franklin D. Roosevelt was nominated for Vice President.

Cox and Roosevelt campaigned arduously to make the election the League referendum that Wilson wished it to be. Harding, following the advice of his managers, made few speeches and took few positions on the issues of the day except to promise a return to what he earlier had called "normalcy." He displayed an ambivalence that was politically most successful. On the League he at first gave the impression that he favored adherence, then as city resentment against it flared, gave the impression he was against it. Lest Cox's crusade win away Republican votes, thirty-one distinguished Republicans signed a statement declaring that a vote for Harding was a vote for American entrance into the League with reservations.

The landslide exceeded even the expectations of the Republicans. Harding received 16,152,000 popular votes, 61 percent of the total, and carried every state outside of the solid

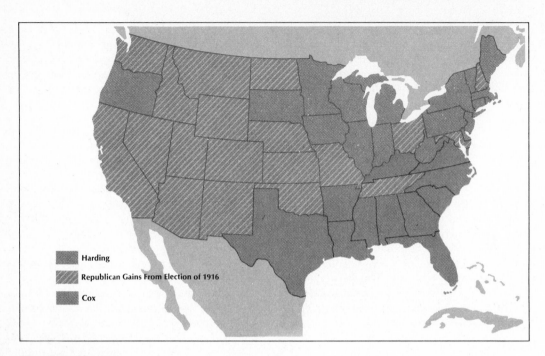

Harding

Republican Gains From Election of 1916

Cox

Election of 1920

South. He even won Tennessee. Cox received only 9,147,000 popular votes. Eugene V. Debs, running on the Socialist ticket while in the Atlanta penitentiary, received 920,000 votes. The sweep brought a Republican majority of 22 in the Senate and 167 in the House.

In voting against Wilsonianism, the electorate brought into power a weak, amiable conservative. Alice Roosevelt Longworth, daughter of a President and wife of the Speaker of the House, reared in the genteel tradition of Republican politics, could not forget the sight of a poker session in the President's study. "Harding was not a bad man," she reminisced. "He was just a slob."

President Harding wished to surround himself with the best-qualified men, and in part he succeeded. When he was persuaded that his friend Albert B. Fall was not of a caliber to be secretary of state, he placed Fall, a notorious anticonservationist, in charge of the Interior Department. He then appointed the brilliant and distinguished Charles Evans Hughes to be secretary of state. He placed Herbert Hoover, the friend of small enterprise and expert on efficiency, in charge of the Commerce Depart-

ment, and made Henry C. Wallace, spokesman for the Midwest farmers, secretary of agriculture. Andrew W. Mellon represented big business as secretary of the treasury. These able men, pulling in several directions, together with the congressional leaders, developed government policies.

The President seemed to be carrying out his campaign slogan: "Less government in business and more business in government." The Democrats made strong gains in the 1922 elections, reflecting the hard times that followed the war, but the return of prosperity soon afterward heightened Harding's popularity. He occasionally was even vigorous in his humanity. He took a step Wilson had curtly declined; on Christmas Day, 1921, he pardoned the Socialist Debs. At the urging of Hoover, he pressured the steel companies into granting an eight-hour day to their workers. The press of the country, overwhelmingly Republican, created the illusion that Harding was an exceptionally fine President.

Behind the façade, rot had set in. With singularly bad judgment, Harding had placed a number of his poker-playing and drinking companions into positions of trust, where they betrayed him and the American people. Probably Harding never knew in detail how shockingly they were looting the government, but he knew enough to be heartsick. One of the "Ohio Gang," Attorney General Harry Daugherty's friend Jesse Smith, had been engaging in large-scale "fixing" in the Department of Justice. After Harding ordered him out of Washington, Smith committed suicide. The director of the Veterans' Bureau, Charles R. Forbes, engaged in such colossal thievery that the total loss ran to nearly $250 million. When Harding received intimations of the corruption, he allowed Forbes to flee the country and resign. Ultimately Forbes served a two-year penitentiary sentence for defrauding the government.

The most spectacular fraud involved the rich naval oil reserves at Teapot Dome, Wyoming, and Elk Hills, California. Secretary of the Interior Fall persuaded Harding to transfer the oil reserves to his department, then secretly leased them to Harry F. Sinclair and Edward L. Doheny. Fall, who had been in financial straits, suddenly became affluent. An investigation headed by Senator Thomas J. Walsh of Montana during the fall and winter of 1923 and 1924 uncovered the reason. Sinclair had loaned Fall $308,000 in cash and government bonds and a herd of cattle for his ranch; Doheny had loaned him $100,000 more. In 1929 Fall was convicted of bribery, fined $100,000, and sentenced to a year in a federal penitentiary.

In the summer of 1923 Harding journeyed to Alaska. Tired and depressed, he responded wanly to the cheering throngs, who had no inkling of the mess in Washington. He never had to face the exposure of the mess because upon his return to Seattle he became ill. It was reported that he had been poisoned by seafood, but actually he had suffered a serious heart attack. He seemed to improve, so he continued to San Francisco. There he had a second attack and suddenly died. In the months that followed, as exposure after exposure crowded the headlines, his reputation collapsed.

KEEPING COOL WITH COOLIDGE

It was the singular good fortune of Calvin Coolidge to become President of the United States at a time when his largely negative custodial approach to the presidency could bring him popularity rather than disaster. He had reached the office through a curious mixture of luck, political regularity, and Yankee shrewdness. Unlike Harding, he had a clear-cut conservative philosophy. He always cooperated wholeheartedly with the big interests because he believed in them.

To the older circle in Washington, Coolidge's personality was not especially appealing. To the American public, however, there was an infinite appeal and security in his folksy virtues, so lavishly detailed and praised in the nation's press. Coolidge reinforced this appeal with little homilies drawn from his Vermont boyhood — exhortations (in which he fervently believed) to thrift, hard work, and respect for business.

Under this comforting moral leadership, the men of power in the United States could take a calm and even incredulous view of the Harding scandals as they came to light one by one in the winter of 1923–1924. Indeed, the respectable press showered indignation less upon the corrupt officials than upon those pressing the investigations. The two progressive Democratic senators, Thomas J. Walsh and Burton K. Wheeler, appeared to *The New York Times* to be "assassins of character."

Under Coolidge the Republicans seemed so patently incorruptible that the exposures appeared if anything to backfire against the exposing Democrats. Ultimately Coolidge forced Attorney General Daugherty to resign and helped clean up the scandals. As the election of 1924 approached, the revelations seemed to be doing no appreciable harm to the Republican party. The nation appeared ready to heed the party's campaign slogan: "Keep cool with Coolidge."

In 1924 the Democratic party was badly split between its rural and urban wings. Rural Democrats were backing as their candidate William Gibbs McAdoo, the competent heir to Wilsonianism. Strangely, the Teapot Dome scandal, which did no harm to the Republicans, tarnished McAdoo's reputation because he had served as a lawyer for Doheny, the California oil magnate. As for the urban wing of the party, it was advancing the candidacy of the equally competent liberal governor of New York, Alfred E. Smith, who was the son of Irish immigrants and had made his way upward from the Lower East Side of New York. Because of his background, and because he was a Catholic and a "wet" (an opponent of prohibition), he was the idol of many new Americans but an anathema to rural Democrats.

Finally both contenders withdrew, and on the 103rd ballot at the convention in Madison Square Garden the exhausted delegates nominated a compromise candidate, John W. Davis. Originally a West Virginian, Davis as solicitor general under Wilson had ably defended the legislation of the New Freedom before the Supreme Court. In the years since, he had become a lawyer for J. P. Morgan and some of the great corporations and had amassed a fortune.

While the Democratic convention dragged on, insurgent Republicans and allied representatives of labor held a third convention to organize a Progressive party and nominate Robert M. La Follette and Burton K. Wheeler. Their platform took an advanced progressive position, attacking monopoly and promising reforms for the farmers and workingmen. The party's support came from farmers, chiefly on the Great Plains, who had earlier formed the Nonpartisan League and the Farmer-Labor party, and from the Railroad Brotherhoods and the AFL.

This third party apparently was a real contrast to the Republican and Democratic tickets, and it served as a made-to-order target for the Republicans. They campaigned to frighten the electorate into choosing Coolidge as the only alternative to the "red radicalism" of La Follette. Before Election Day, labor became lukewarm toward La Follette; Republican farmers, as crop prices rose, decided to stay within the party. In its last thrust, the old Midwestern insurgency carried only Wisconsin and secured but 16.5 percent of the popular vote throughout the country. Coolidge polled 54 percent, and Davis only 28.8 percent.

In his inaugural, March 4, 1925, President Coolidge, declaring that the nation had achieved "a state of contentment seldom before seen," pledged himself to the maintenance of things as they were. During the prosperous years of the Coolidge era, as revenues came pouring in, the federal government did not greatly enlarge its services. It spent nothing in such areas as public housing, and little for farm relief or public works. Arms expenditures were a relative pittance. Consequently, the budget varied little between 1923 and 1929. Meanwhile, the national debt dropped by nearly a quarter.

FAVORED BUSINESS

Big business had a special friend in the government during the 1920s. Andrew Mellon, the Pittsburgh aluminum baron who served as secretary of the treasury from Harding's inauguration into the Hoover administration, was widely hailed as the greatest secretary of the treasury since Alexander Hamilton. His main function seemed to be to preside over tax cuts; cartoonists routinely pictured Mellon slicing a tax melon. So far as he could do so, as a matter of principle, he divided these cuts among the wealthy to give them the incentive to earn more money.

Smaller businessmen also had a strong champion in the government, Secretary of Commerce Hoover. In his own spectacular rise as an international mining engineer, Hoover epitomized the self-made businessman. Denouncing both the radicalism and reaction he had seen in Europe, Hoover set forth his own credo in 1922 in a small book entitled *American Individualism*. It extolled the equality of opportunity that enabled Americans to succeed on their own merits, and the "rising vision of service" that led them to develop community responsibility rather than merely to seek "the acquisition and preservation of private property." This had been Hoover's own way of life.

Hoover made Commerce the most active of the departments, as he sought to help small business become as efficient and profitable as big business. Through commercial attachés whom he sent to American embassies, he solicited foreign orders for American industry at the same time that he favored the tariff to protect it from overseas competition. Through the National Bureau of Standards, he performed innumerable other services for industry, such as standardizing products and eliminating waste.

The most significant of the ways to help small business was the sponsorship of voluntary trade associations similar to the committees of the War Industries Board. By 1921 some 2,000 were in operation. These associations, free from government regulation, could establish codes of ethics, standardize production, establish efficiency, and make substantial savings. They could serve even better than government prohibition of evil practices, Hoover had pointed out, to secure "cooperation in the business community to cure its own abuses." They could also arrive indirectly at higher standard prices which would bring them good profits. Their real value to highly competitive smaller businesses was to eliminate competition through setting up standardized schedules of quality and prices.

Voluntarism was at the heart of all of Hoover's projects. As the new field of commercial radio broadcasting began to develop, Hoover fostered voluntary self-regulation for it. When the efforts to keep stations off each other's wave lengths completely broke down, he moved toward compulsory government regulation through the Federal Radio Commission, established in 1927. In the same way, the Department of Commerce finally took over regulation of commercial aeronautics through the Air Commerce Act in 1926.

On the whole, business thrived from 1923 to 1929. In part this was due to benign governmental policies. Hoover's laudable efforts to bring about increased standardization and efficiency took the economy further away from free competition and contributed to the increased profits of business and consequently to the concentration of wealth. Secretary Mellon's tax policies helped the rich to become richer, while incomes of poorer people advanced little if at all. The tendency of the courts to frown upon trade-association price schedules helped stimulate mergers. And mergers helped to sustain the trend toward concentration of business which had begun after the Civil War. During the twenties, 8,000 mining and manufacturing companies disappeared into combinations, and 5,000 public utilities were swallowed, mostly by holding companies. By 1929 chain stores were selling more than a quarter of the nation's food, apparel, and general merchandise. The 200 largest nonfinancial corporations owned nearly half of all corporate wealth, and 22 percent of all national wealth. The 503 persons with the highest incomes received as much money as the total wages of 615,000 automobile workers.

THE DECLINE OF UNIONS

The onslaught against all Americans who did not conform, against any who might disturb the status quo, reacted strongly to the advantage of business leaders, who already basked in the public favor. These leaders were able to reestablish in the minds of many people the feeling that unionism was somehow un-American. In 1920 they began a great open-shop movement to break unions and reduce wages, under the alluring title, "The American Plan."

The paternalistic policies of welfare capitalism, together with the antiunion campaign, led to a decline in union membership during the 1920s. Many companies greatly improved working conditions by installing safety devices and improving sanitation. They raised their workers' morale by building attractive cafeterias and promoting athletic teams. Company welfare workers looked into the workers' family problems. By 1926 nearly 3 million workers could look forward to pensions upon retirement. In some companies they could buy stock below market value. Altogether they owned less than 1 percent, but even this did much to change some workers' attitudes. Further, they could voice their grievances through company unions or workers' councils, which were often effective safety valves for the employer. Through devices like these, companies helped fend off unionism from the new mass-production industries such as automobile manufacturing.

Within the skilled crafts, the AFL continued quietly and conservatively under the presidency of William Green. Its leaders seemed more interested in maintaining labor monopolies, especially in the building trades, than in organizing industrial workers. Membership in the United Mine Workers dwindled after unsuccessful strikes in 1922. Union membership declined from over 5 million in 1920 to around 4.3 million in 1929.

In some industries, like coal mining and textiles in the South, hours were long and wages were pitiful. At Elizabethton, Tennessee, in 1929, mill girls were working fifty-six hours a week for 16 to 18 cents an hour. Behind the harried workers was always the threat of legal action if they sought to help themselves through unions. Federal courts were granting injunctions to break boycotts or to enforce antiunion ("yellow dog") contracts. For most workingmen, however, conditions of labor had improved and living standards were up. Real wages increased about 26 percent between 1919 and 1929. They still were far from adequate. The average was less than $1,500 a year at a time when it was estimated that $1,800 was required to maintain a minimum decent living standard.

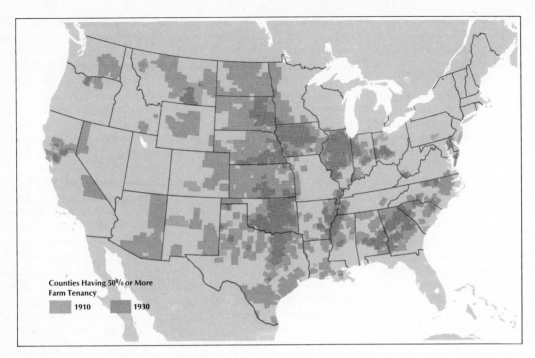

Farm Tenancy: 1910 and 1930

NO PARITY FOR FARMERS

While the income of most Americans advanced during the 1920s, that of the farmers drastically declined. In 1920 they lost their price supports at the same time that the bloated wartime European market contracted. At home, as machines released men from heavy manual labor, consumption of starches sharply dropped.

Within agriculture there were great variations. Truck gardening more than doubled, and dairying and citrus growing increased a third, reflecting the shifts in eating habits. Many such farmers enjoyed satisfactory incomes. At the same time, those on marginal or submarginal lands suffered so acutely that in the five years after 1919 13 million acres were abandoned. Poor farmers were unable to compete with large landowners using new, expensive machinery, which especially helped contribute to the glut of wheat. The number of tractors in use increased from 230,000 in 1920 to 920,000 in 1930, displacing 7,450,000 horses and releasing an additional 35 million acres of land for crops. On the Great Plains, speculators bought the lands of bankrupt farmers, and grew wheat on it with improved tractors and

combines. In the Texas Panhandle alone, nearly 3 million new acres were ploughed.

The success of the big operators made the desperation of small farmers even more acute. In the year ending June 30, 1927, the average income of all the 6.3 million farmers was only $548, and out of this farmers had to meet a variety of pressing obligations. Farm income in 1920 was 15 percent of the national total; by 1929 it was only 9 percent. The agricultural population dropped 3 million between 1921 and 1928. Many of those who remained on the farms ceased to own them and became tenants. Distressed farmers, both owners and renters, began to agitate militantly for relief.

Even during the bonanza years of the war, agrarian agitation had stirred the Great Plains. In 1915 wheat growers of North Dakota had organized the Nonpartisan League, pledged to strict regulation of railroads and banks, and state ownership of grain elevators and farm credit agencies. The league won control of the North Dakota government in 1916, then began to organize in adjacent states, and in 1920 joined with other radical groups to form the Farmer-Labor party. The new party had some success in the congressional election of 1922, but by 1924 even La Follette would not accept its support. It was too radical for farmers who were earning $1,000 to $4,000 a year.

These men, the middle 40 percent of the farmers in terms of income, produced 46 percent of the farm products, and were solid citizens in their communities. Often acting through the Farm Bureau Federation or the Grange, they sought government price supports. From the outset they had powerful strength in the Congress. During the special session of Congress in the spring of 1921, Midwestern congressional leaders from both parties, meeting in the offices of the Farm Bureau Federation, organized a farm bloc.

One price-raising scheme came to dominate the farmers' thinking. Behind the tariff barrier, the American-protected price for crops should be raised to a "fair exchange value" based on the price of the crop during ten prewar years as compared with the general average of all prices during the same period. This was the "parity" price. The means of obtaining parity for farmers would be for the government to buy up the surplus at the high American price and sell it abroad at whatever it would bring on the world market. In order to make up for the loss, an equalization fee or tax would be charged the farmers on their entire crop.

Between 1924 and 1928 Senator Charles L. McNary of Oregon and Representative Gilbert Haugen of Iowa promoted this scheme in Congress. In 1924 the McNary-Haugen bill covered only grain, and was defeated in the House, but in 1926 the addition of cotton, tobacco, and rice brought Southern support. In 1927 Congress passed it, but President Coolidge coldly vetoed it as being preferential legislation contrary to the principles of laissez faire. (On the same day he signed an order raising the tariff on pig iron 50 percent.) A year later Congress again passed the McNary-Haugen bill, and Coolidge again vetoed it.

The Resurgence of Isolationism

The task of developing Republican alternatives to Wilsonian foreign policy fell largely on the shoulders of Secretaries of State Charles Evans Hughes (1921–1925) and Frank B. Kellogg (1925–1929).

STEPS TOWARD PEACE

Hughes' policy involved first of all ending the war with Germany by an act of Congress, which was signed July 2, 1921. Hughes then negotiated separate peace treaties with the former Central Powers, to secure for the United States the benefits without the responsibilities of the Paris treaties. In time, Hughes permitted American delegations to participate in League conferences on minor matters as long as they did not make commitments. Throughout his years as secretary of state he was chilly toward every European proposal for collective security. He did, in February 1923, persuade President Harding to recommend that the United States join with reservations the World Court, an almost completely powerless body. But the World Court was an instrument of the League, and while internationally minded Americans ardently favored joining,

the irreconcilables in the Senate violently fought it. Each succeeding President through Franklin D. Roosevelt advocated American adherence to the League; each time, through 1935, the Senate blocked it.

Through the Washington Arms Conference, Republicans made it appear that they were taking positive steps to preserve the peace. This was in effect a Republican substitute for entrance into the League. In May 1921 Senator Borah had introduced a resolution calling for a conference to reduce armaments, but the basic impetus for the meeting came from the British, who feared a three-way naval race with the Americans and the Japanese. Japan had emerged from the war stronger than before in China and with troops still stationed in Siberia. She threatened to expand still further, to shut the "Open Door" in China, and to arm her new island possessions in the Pacific. American public opinion saw an even more serious threat in the Anglo-Japanese alliance. Hence the British, wishing to strengthen their amicable relations with the United States, proposed the conference. Hughes seized the initiative and President Harding issued invitations.

The arms conference opened on November 12, 1921, the day after burial rites for the Unknown Soldier at the Arlington Cemetery. Hughes in his opening speech startled the delegates and won enormous acclaim by dramatically presenting a concrete plan for the reduction in size of the fleets of the United States, Great Britain, and Japan. He proposed a ten-year moratorium on capital-ship construction (battleships, cruisers, and carriers) and the scrapping by the three powers of nearly 1.9 million tons of ships already built or under construction. A British observer declared: "Secretary Hughes sank in thirty-five minutes more ships than all the admirals of the world have sunk in a cycle of centuries."

In the negotiations that followed, Japan agreed to limit her capital ships to a total of approximately 300,000 tons compared with 500,000 tons each for the United States and Great Britain. In addition the United States pledged itself not to increase its fortifications in Guam and the Philippines. Japan and Great Britain made similar pledges. Thus the Five Power Pact of 1922 provided a ratio of 5:5:3 for the United States, Great Britain, and Japan, and 1.75:1.75 for France and Italy, stopping what otherwise could have become a disastrous armaments race. Two other treaties aimed at guaranteeing the status quo in the Far East. The Nine Power Pact pledged a continuation of the Open Door policy in China. Afterward Japan restored full sovereign rights to China in the Shantung peninsula and promised to withdraw the Japanese troops from Siberia. The Four Power Pact — among the United States, Great Britain, France, and Japan — represented a mutual recognition of insular rights in the Pacific. Upon its ratification, Japan relinquished her alliance with Great Britain.

These Washington treaties lowered the tension between the United States and Japan for nearly a decade. Their one unfortunate result was that the United States relinquished the physical force with which to impose its will in the Far East but retained its moral, economic, and political objectives in that area. The Senate came close to rejecting the Four Power Pact for fear it would commit the United States to some collective security arrangement in the Orient. On the other hand, the popularity of the Naval Limitation Treaty (Five Power Pact) is shown by the fact that only one senator voted against its ratification.

During the Coolidge administration millions of Americans signed petitions urging the United States to promote a multilateral treaty outlawing war. The French foreign minister, Aristide Briand, proposed a treaty of this sort between France and the United States. Secretary Kellogg responded by suggesting that other countries be invited to join. So, at Paris in 1928, most of the great nations, including the United States, signed a treaty solemnly renouncing war as an instrument of national policy, but providing no machinery whatever for enforcement. The treaty evoked much enthusiasm in the United States, for it seemed to offer collective security without any risks.

Hughes tried to extend the good will of the United States toward Latin America. During his first months in office, he was decidedly influenced by Sumner Welles, later one of the chief molders of the Good Neighbor policy. By 1924 Hughes had ended the marine occupation of Santo Domingo and prepared for its end in Nicaragua. He felt that the occupation was still necessary in Haiti.

Hughes moved away from the progressive policy of intervention and tried wherever possible to substitute the nonrecognition of undesirable governments for the landing of the marines. Neither he nor his successor in the Coolidge administration was ready to give up intervention entirely. For a time during the Coolidge administration, trouble with Mexico over the rights of American oil companies and renewed marine intervention in Nicaragua seemed to indicate a retreat to the old policies.

ECONOMIC NATIONALISM

In European affairs a persisting and troublesome issue was that of reparations and war debts. The failure of the United States to join the League of Nations had most serious repercussions on this problem, since the League's Reparations Commission, which was not under the chairmanship of an American as had been expected, set astronomically high sums for Germany to pay. Reparations payments depended to a considerable degree upon American private loans to Germany; war-debt payments from the Allies to the United States depended, in turn, almost entirely upon reparations. The American public insisted that the Allies should repay the $10 billion the

United States had loaned during the war. Coolidge later epitomized the popular view when he remarked simply: "They hired the money, didn't they?"

The United States pressured the former Allies, through a World War Foreign Debt Commission, to negotiate long-term schedules of debt payments. Between 1923 and 1926 the commission reached agreements with the Allies in regard to their debts (which the United States government insisted bore no relationship to German reparations payments). The administration did not worry as to how Germany, France, Italy, and the other debtors could make payments over the high tariff wall that the United States was raising against their exports.

What kept the payments going during the twenties was the huge total of private American loans pouring into German governmental units or corporations—about $2.5 billion between 1923 and 1930. Germany paid about $2 billion in reparations, and the former Allies about $2.6 billion in war-debt payments. Thus the Germans were paying the Allies, and the Allies paying the United States, with dollars that Americans were lending to the Germans.

As soon as the Republicans had come into power in 1921, they enacted an emergency tariff measure to raise the low Underwood rates. In 1922 they passed the Fordney-McCumber Act providing protection especially for agriculture, the chemical industry, and manufacturers threatened by Japanese and German competition. The tariff gave agriculture little real protection, but it provided industrialists with several benefits. It accepted the principle that, when foreign firms had costs of production lower than their American competitors, the tariff should be high enough to offset the differential. It prohibited most competing imports and led to higher prices at home. Other nations followed the American lead in economic nationalism; by 1928 some sixty countries had raised their tariffs.

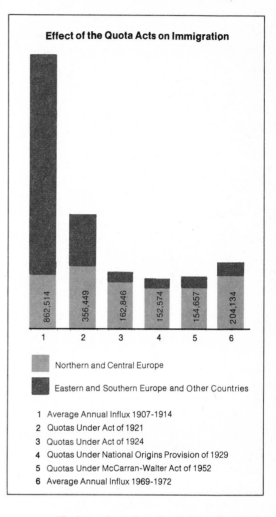

Effect of the Quota Acts on Immigration

862,514
356,449
162,846
152,574
154,657
204,134

1   2   3   4   5   6

Northern and Central Europe

Eastern and Southern Europe and Other Countries

1 Average Annual Influx 1907–1914
2 Quotas Under Act of 1921
3 Quotas Under Act of 1924
4 Quotas Under National Origins Provision of 1929
5 Quotas Under McCarran-Walter Act of 1952
6 Average Annual Influx 1969–1972

The bars above show the drastic effect of the laws of the 1920s in restricting immigration from Old World countries except those of Northern and Central Europe. The act of 1952 made little change, but the act of 1965 (taking effect in 1969) led to a considerable shift in Old World sources of immigration. The chart omits immigration from the Western Hemisphere. This was not restricted until the 1965 law put a ceiling of 120,000 a year on it.

IMMIGRATION RESTRICTION

Along with high walls against competing goods, Congress finally succeeded in erecting barriers against incoming foreigners. Racist objections to the "new immigrants," and the unionists' fear that the newcomers were perpetuating a

pool of cheap labor in the United States, were reinforced by the allegation that some of them were radicals. This led employers who had previously favored immigration to switch to the restrictive side.

In 1921 Congress passed an emergency

immigration act, setting up a quota system: immigrants from any country could not exceed 3 percent of the number of persons of their nationality who had been in the United States in 1910. This cut the number of immigrants from 800,000 in the year ending June 30, 1921, to about 300,000 in the following twelve months. Racists still were not satisfied, so Congress in 1924 enacted the National Origins Act. This measure not only banned the people of East Asia entirely, but set a quota of 2 percent for Europeans, and this on the basis of the 1890 census. It cut the yearly total to 164,000, heavily weighted in favor of those from northwestern Europe. On July 1, 1929, an overall limit of about 150,000 immigrants a year went into ef-

fect, but during the entire depression decade of the thirties the total net immigration was less than 70,000. The great flood of so many decades had been cut to a few drops.

Excluding all aliens ineligible to become citizens meant excluding the Japanese in particular. It was an unnecessary insult to the Japanese, since the Gentlemen's Agreement had worked well, and the application of a quota system to Japan would have allowed only a tiny trickle of immigrants. Indignation in Japan against the act of 1924 was so extreme that Hughes lamented privately: "It has undone the work of the Washington Conference and implanted the seeds of an antagonism which are sure to bear fruit in the future."

Life in the Twenties

For those who shared in the prosperity, the decade of the twenties was a wonderful era. The wealth of the United States, as newspapers never tired of reminding their readers, was almost as great as that of all Europe. "My God, how the money rolls in!" went the words of a popular song. And some of the money was spent in remarkable ways.

THE JAZZ AGE

It was the era when Florida real-estate salesmen hired the famous orator William Jennings Bryan to lecture on the climate. Even though only an infinitesimal portion of Americans bought real estate in Florida during the land boom of 1924–1925, the impression was that most people were dabbling in the speculation. So too with the stock market later in the decade. Millions shared in the national frenzies, but most of them did so only vicariously while living sober, quiet lives.

The average middle-class American family owned an automobile. There were 23 million cars in use by 1929, and on Sundays it seemed as though they were all out on the new concrete highways. At home, people listened to the radio. The first commercial station, KDKA, broadcast the news of Harding's election in November 1920. By 1924 the National Broadcasting Company had organized a nationwide

network of stations, and by 1930 over 12 million American families had radios. Millions also had electric vacuum cleaners and washing machines; many were beginning to buy electric refrigerators. Household appliances were supplanting the housemaid and the hired girl. Food and clothing accounted for only 44 percent of the family expenditures, compared with 58 percent in 1899 – a clear indication of the rising living standards.

The prosperity of the twenties spilled over into the educational system. The per-pupil expenditure jumped from $24 in 1910 to $90 in 1930. Free elementary education had become established throughout the nation; illiteracy dropped from 7.7 percent to 4.3 percent. Enrollment in high schools increased 400 percent, and enrollment in colleges and universities grew almost as fast.

Much money went to bootleggers, the dealers in illicit liquor, a new multimillion-dollar business. This was a response to the Eighteenth Amendment, which prohibited intoxicating beverages, and to the Volstead Act (1919), which defined them as all beverages containing more than one-half of 1 percent of alcohol, thus ruling out beer and light wines as well as hard liquor. The first prohibition commissioner had optimistically announced his determination to see that alcoholic beverages were "not manufactured, nor sold, nor given away, nor hauled in anything on the surface of the earth or under

Disposing of Illegal Booze

During the 1920s federal prohibition agents — like those emptying bottles down a sewer in this photograph — were assigned to confiscate and get rid of bootleg liquor. But the agents could not keep up with the bootleggers. The head of the Prohibition Bureau once estimated that law enforcement agencies were catching only one-twentieth of the liquor that was being smuggled in from Canada and other countries, to say nothing of the tremendous quantities that were being produced illegally in the United States. (Culver Pictures)

the earth or in the air." But with an insufficient budget and only a few thousand poorly paid agents — and with little or no cooperation from state and local authorities — the commissioner had an almost impossible task in patrolling 18,000 miles of coastline, guarding against the diversion of any of the 57 million gallons of industrial alcohol, overseeing hundreds of millions of medical prescriptions, and checking on 20 million homes to prevent the concoction of home brew, wine, or "bathtub gin."

Gangsters turned to the large-scale smuggling or manufacture and distribution of liquor. In Chicago, "Scarface" Al Capone built an underworld empire that was based on beer and extended out into slot machines, laundries, and labor unions; it grossed about $60 million per year. He guarded it against interlopers

with an army of 700 to 1,000 gunmen. Between 1920 and 1927 over 250 men were killed in Chicago gang warfare. Capone miraculously survived both his rivals and the forces of the law, until finally in 1931 he was convicted of federal income-tax evasion.

New ways of life, alarming to the older generation, swept America. Men wore wrist watches and smoked cigarettes, both of which had seemed rather effeminate before the war. Women seemed to have lost their modesty as they bobbed their hair, applied lipstick, donned short skirts and silk stockings, and unblushingly began using words previously reserved for males.

Young people talked openly and frankly about sex. Often their talk reflected the remote influence of Sigmund Freud, the Austrian founder of psychoanalysis, who had visited the United States before the war but had gotten little public attention at that time. During the 1920s, though few Americans read his works, many received a simplified and distorted version of his theories from popular magazines. The impression spread, erroneous though it was, that Freud had given a scientific justification for promiscuity. Mouthing Freudian terms such as "libido" and "inhibition," youthful Americans often were quite willing to believe that any repression of the sex urge was psychologically unhealthful.

The sex talk of the young, which frightened their elders, was made doubly frightening by the disappearance of chaperons and the availability of automobiles. Compounding the evil in the eyes of elders were the many new roadhouses and speakeasies, where young people flouted prohibition by drinking beer or cocktails. There too they listened to jazz and danced the new steps like the Charleston, which some preachers denounced to their flocks as lascivious. It seemed to many critics that Gertrude Stein had correctly labeled this the "lost generation"; these people could not believe that in time the "flaming youth" would mature into censorious middle age.

Motion pictures flamboyantly heralded the new moral code and together with tabloid papers helped fabricate false stereotypes of the period. An estimated 50 million people a week went to theaters to see the "it" girl, Clara Bow, the glamorous Rudolph Valentino, the comedian Charlie Chaplin, gangster pictures, Westerns, and great spectacles like the first film version of *The Ten Commandments*. These helped standardize American habits, and not always in the most edifying way. Further, since nine-tenths of the world's motion pictures were made in the United States, they brought curiously distorted notions of American culture to other countries. In 1927 a revolution struck the motion-picture industry when the first important all-talking picture, *The Jazz Singer,* starring Al Jolson, was a phenomenal success. Motion pictures also began to carry American speech around the world.

In journalism, the twenties brought an even greater sensationalism than the nineties in some mass-circulation city papers. From England came the idea of the half-sized tabloid, which led to the founding of the *News, Mirror,* and *Graphic* in New York City, and similar

papers throughout the country. Tabloid journalism came to mean what "yellow journalism" had meant earlier, with the addition of a strong emphasis upon serial comic strips and sensational photographs. Millions of readers followed the gang wars in Chicago and murder trials in New York and elsewhere. Even *The New York Times* had to capitulate its dignity to reader demands and lavish front-page space upon one spectacular murder trial, the Hall-Mills case, concerning the murder of a minister and a choir singer.

Among magazines, the *Saturday Evening Post*, with its conservative editorials and well-written stories, mirrored the era as faithfully as did President Coolidge. Close behind it in capturing the popular spirit was a reprint magazine founded in 1921, *Reader's Digest,* which filled its readers with inspiration and optimism, and guided them effortlessly through what they might consider difficult, serious subjects. It was the beginning of predigested reading. Much the same formula went into *Time,* the first of the news magazines, founded in 1925. In its cleverness, *Time* was one of the magazines tailored for the college graduates of the twenties. Another was the gay, sophisticated *New Yorker,* founded in 1925, which, with its clever cartoons and polished articles and stories, soon eclipsed the older *Life* and *Judge.* But the magazines that best typified the iconoclastic spirit of the intelligentsia and its rejection of middle-class values were *Smart Set* and the *American Mercury.* Their editors, Henry L. Mencken and George Jean Nathan, ridiculed the shibboleths of the decade, but more than that introduced to their readers many of the most vigorous writers of the era.

WRITERS, ARTISTS, MUSICIANS

Seldom before in American history has such a remarkable galaxy of new writers appeared at one time. There was as much negativism from the expatriates in Paris as there had been before the war from Greenwich Village; many took perverse delight in damning the United States as a dollar-grubbing philistine civilization. Despite this spirit, it was not a generation lost to letters, nor were the voices of protest ignored.

Sherwood Anderson, giving up his paint factory, wrote tart Freudian sketches of small-town America in *Winesburg, Ohio* (1919). Sin-

The Sinclair Lewises Go Camping

In 1916 Lewis bought a Model T Ford, and with his wife, Grace Hegger Lewis, embarked on a four-month trip from Sauk Center, Minnesota, to San Francisco. Lewis wanted to see firsthand more of the small-town life about which he wished to write a novel. This photograph was taken in Duluth. (Brown Brothers)

clair Lewis more spectacularly exploited the same vein in his satiric *Main Street* (1920) and *Babbitt* (1922). His onslaught against business philistinism, in a long series of novels, at times verged close to caricature, but in time brought Lewis a Nobel Prize. With far more pessimism, utilizing experimental episodic techniques, John Dos Passos dissected the life of the metropolis in *Manhattan Transfer* (1925). Theodore Dreiser came into his own in 1925 with *An American Tragedy,* which analyzed with compassion both the psychological and environmental factors that led a young man to consider drowning his mistress.

The novelist who best embodied the jazz age in both his personal life and his writing was F. Scott Fitzgerald, catapulted to success with *This Side of Paradise* (1920). Young novelists who helped set patterns for later decades were Ernest Hemingway and William Faulkner. Hemingway stated the reaction against war most vigorously in his novel of disillusion, *A Farewell to Arms* (1929), which also helped set a new literary style. Faulkner, analyzing the

South with morbid intensity in novels like *The Sound and the Fury* (1929) and *Sanctuary* (1931), developed an abstruse stream-of-consciousness technique which profoundly influenced other writers.

In drama these were the golden years of Eugene O'Neill, who drew from Ibsen, Strindberg, and Freud to develop American plays that were both critical and popular successes. *The Emperor Jones* (1920), *Anna Christie* (1922), *Strange Interlude* (1928), and other plays won O'Neill three Pulitzer Prizes in the decade, and helped maintain him in the forefront of American dramatists a decade later. A number of other young playwrights wrote for the experimental stage, which flourished at scores of colleges and cities, even while motion pictures were superseding the old legitimate theater circuits.

In poetry, two of the most significant writers were expatriates from the United States. These were T. S. Eliot in London, whose *The Waste Land* appeared in 1922, and Ezra Pound, who settled in Italy where he wrote *Cantos* and

T. S. Eliot on Expatriates of the Twenties

The situation is different for the young men of today compared with the earlier part of this century. I don't know what Prohibition had to do with it. Certainly it was easier then for youngsters to earn a living overseas. And the American literary scene didn't offer them much encouragement. That was a very dull period.

In Europe there was a desire to aid younger people. Pound introduced me to Yeats. I got to know Virginia Woolf. People were interested in my poetry. I had never experienced such interest at home. But now the trend seems to be in the other direction. Young Americans go back and find they can make a living teaching in colleges, that there is genuine interest in them. A young writer needs the society of other writers, both his contemporaries and benevolent older writers whom he can respect. There are more of these now in the United States. — The New York Times, *March 30, 1959.*

---

embraced Fascism. At home, Edna St. Vincent Millay typified the twenties with her hedonistic love poetry, while Robinson Jeffers turned to dark naturalistic themes. Older poets like Edwin Arlington Robinson and Robert Frost continued to write in established veins, and numerous young poets experimented with innovations in techniques and topics.

American artists continued to produce along lines that in many cases had been pioneered before the war. Architects filled the great cities with skyscrapers and were active in city planning. Some of the surplus wealth of the twenties poured into European painting; Mellon matched his ingenuity in keeping taxes down with his lavish purchases of old masters, some of them from the dollar-hungry Soviet Union. By 1930 American art galleries owned $2 billion worth of paintings. Along with this went a rapidly widening popular appreciation of fine art.

In music the twenties were notable for the rise of jazz, "the most important musical expression that America has achieved." It had originated among Negro musicians in the South, particularly in New Orleans, who drew upon their African heritage in composing and playing tunes with improvised harmonies and a syncopated beat. Among the outstanding black creators of jazz were the guitar-playing singer Huddie Ledbetter ("Leadbelly") and the band conductor William C. Handy, the "father of the blues," whose compositions include *St. Louis Blues* (1914). The new music first became widely known when jazzmen moved with the

general black migration northward during and after World War I. The great trumpet-player Louis ("Satchmo") Armstrong, for example, went from New Orleans to Chicago in 1922 to join a band that helped spread jazz through phonograph recordings. Meanwhile, white musicians had begun to take up the new form, modify it, and make it increasingly popular and even respectable by treating it as serious music. Prominent among them were the composer George Gershwin, who incorporated jazz elements in his *Rhapsody in Blue,* and the conductor Paul Whiteman, whose band presented a pioneering jazz concert in New York City in 1922.

"It was the period when the Negro was in vogue," Langston Hughes recalled of the 1920s. Certainly it was a time when Hughes and other black writers, as well as black musicians, gained recognition for contributing to American culture. So many excellent poets, novelists, and playwrights flourished in Harlem — Hughes, Claude McKay, and James Weldon Johnson outstanding among them — that the black literary revival came to be known as the Harlem Renaissance. It produced an eloquent and often bitter literature of protest. Though quite race-conscious, expressing a new pride in their blackness, the authors seldom repudiated the values of white society. They protested not so much against the country's democratic ideals as against its failure to live up to them. "In this approach," as John Hope Franklin has observed, "they proved to be as characteristically American as any writers of the period."

The Negro Artist [1926]

Born in Missouri in 1902, Langston Hughes traveled in Mexico, Africa, and Europe before settling in New York City, where he became the most prolific and versatile of the black writers, earning for himself the reputation of "Shakespeare in Harlem." In an article "The Negro Artist and the Racial Mountain," in *The Nation*, June 23, 1926, he wrote:

One of the most promising of the young Negro poets said to me once, "I want to be a poet—not a Negro poet," meaning, I believe, "I want to write like a white poet"; meaning subconsciously, "I would like to be a white poet"; meaning behind that, "I would like to be white." And I was sorry the young man said that, for no great poet has ever been afraid of being himself. And I doubted then that, with his desire to run away spiritually from his race, this boy would ever be a great poet. But this is the mountain standing in the way of any true Negro art in America—this urge within the race toward whiteness, the desire to pour racial individuality into the mold of American standardization, and to be as little Negro and as much American as possible.

. . . We younger Negro artists who create now intend to express our individual dark-skinned selves without fear or shame. If white people are pleased we are glad. If they are not, it doesn't matter. We know we are beautiful. And ugly too. The tom-tom cries and the tom-tom laughs. If colored people are pleased we are glad. If they are not, their dispeasure doesn't matter either. We build our temples for tomorrow, strong as we know how, and we stand on top of the mountain, free within ourselves.

A SEARCH FOR VALUES

In letters, the arts, and learning, there was a seeking for values that would be something more than the advertising man's paeans to mass-production cultures, as expressed in Bruce Barton's *The Man Nobody Knows*. This seeking is the reason so many of the younger writers were rejecting the popular values of the United States for those of Europe, which did not seem to them as yet caught in the new commercial maelstrom. Others were trying to interpret the new society with the psychoanalytical approach suggested by Sigmund Freud, or the economic determinism stemming from Karl Marx.

Among ministers, publicists, philosophers, and economists seeking to interpret the new order, there was some confusion. The fundamentalist ministers went on much as before, although in some quarters they were subjected to ridicule after 1925 when their champion, William Jennings Bryan, matched wits with the agnostic Clarence Darrow in the famous Scopes trial. Ministers to the middle class who earlier had so exuberantly preached the social gospel or the great crusade in Europe had been beaten down in 1919 when they took up the cause of the striking steelworkers. Many businessmen were ready to adopt paternalistic policies and label them "Christian industrialism," but they denounced the militant social gospel as Bolshevism. Ministers further lost their hold on their following as middle-class reaction spread against two of the causes in which they had been so deeply involved—the war in Europe and prohibition. Many ministers tended, consequently, to concentrate upon the building of fine churches and the development of a sophisticated theology embracing the new psychological concepts.

Many of the most popular publicists were negative in their view of government. Henry L. Mencken and Irving Babbitt launched some of their most scathing attacks against the American democratic system. Walter Lippmann, who had been deeply involved in the New Nationalism and the New Freedom, became aloof and brilliantly analytical in his observation of American society. The Socialist candidate for President in 1928, Norman Thomas, remarked: "The old reformer has become the Tired Radical and his sons and daughters drink at the fountain of the *American Mercury*."

H. L. Mencken
[1933]

As columnist for the Baltimore *Sun,* and especially as editor of the *Smart Set* and the *American Mercury,* Mencken exercised great influence for the fifteen years following World War I. Often regarded as an iconoclast whose value was purely negative, Mencken actually used the grace and taste of the eighteenth-century aristocracy as a standard to condemn the "booboisie" he saw around him. Outstanding for his pioneering studies of the American language, for his opposition to censorship and prohibition, and for his championing of such writers as Joseph Conrad, Theodore Dreiser, and Ring Lardner, he wrote a virile and sinewy prose. His wit (and his scorn for American politicians) shows in his obituary for Calvin Coolidge, published in April 1933:

In what manner he would have performed himself if the holy angels had shoved the Depression forward a couple of years—this we can only guess, and one man's hazard is as good as another's. My own is that he would have responded to bad times precisely as he responded to good ones—that is, by pulling down the blinds, stretching his legs upon his desk, and snoozing away the lazy afternoons. . . . He slept more than any other President, whether by day or by night. Nero fiddled, but Coolidge only snored. . . . Counting out Harding as a cipher only, Dr. Coolidge was preceded by one World Saver and followed by two more. What enlightened American, having to choose between any of them and another Coolidge, would hesitate for an instant? There were no thrills while he reigned, but neither were there any headaches. He had no ideas, and he was not a nuisance.

Nevertheless, some of the most influential philosophers and social scientists continued to write in modified progressive terms. John Dewey, at the peak of his influence, was expounding a socialized pragmatism: man through science and technology could develop an organized social intelligence which could plan a rational and fruitful future society. The aged Thorstein Veblen was placing a similar faith in science: the engineers in contrast to the businessmen could bring forth an economic utopia. This doctrine, carried to its ultimate conclusion, engendered the technocracy movement of the early thirties. Other economists would not go this far, but some of them accepted Veblen's emphasis upon craftsmen and technicians, who, unlike businessmen, would not raise prices and restrict markets. Around them could develop an economy of still greater abundance. Agricultural economists, who were thinking in opposite terms of restriction, also looked forward to an age of social and economic planning.

Charles A. Beard was disseminating some of these ideas among a wider group of readers. In his and Mary Beard's *Rise of American Civilization* (1927), expressing mild economic determinism and emphasizing social and cultural factors, he did much to perpetuate progressive thinking among the new generation of intellectuals. Vernon L. Parrington's *Main Currents of American Thought* (1927), tracing the same themes in literature, helped create a Jeffersonian cult. Writing on a popular level, Claude Bowers developed similar ideas. Franklin D. Roosevelt, reviewing Bowers' *Jefferson and Hamilton* in 1925, commented: "Hamiltons we have today. Is a Jefferson on the horizon?"

The Great Depression

"I do not choose to run in 1928," President Coolidge had announced. The way to perpetuate Coolidge prosperity, it seemed to Republicans, was to elect Herbert Hoover, the "Great Engineer," whose policies as secretary of commerce promised a continuation of businessmen's government. The Republicans nominated him on the first ballot. In accepting the nomination, he proclaimed: "Given a chance to go forward with the policies of the last eight years, we shall soon with the help of God be in sight of the day when poverty will be banished from the nation."

ELECTION OF 1928

Among Democrats, the experienced politicians were still almost as badly divided as in 1924, but they saw no reason to turn their convention into another brawl when their candidate had no chance of winning against Republican prosperity. Even those who were ardently dry and Protestant raised no barrier against the wet, Roman Catholic governor of New York, Alfred E. Smith. He was nominated to run on a platform not much more positive than that of the Republicans. It did, however, include a plank offering farmers the McNary-Haugen plan. More important, Smith promised to relax the Volstead Act for enforcing the Eighteenth Amendment. This brought prohibition to the forefront of the campaign. There was little except that and religion to campaign about.

Both Hoover and Smith were self-made men and proud of it. Hoover's path, from an Iowa farm through Stanford University, had been marked by a phenomenally successful rise as a business and government executive. Smith's path led from the East Side of New York through the Fulton Fish Market and the Tammany hierarchy to the governorship of New York. There he had demonstrated a consummate political and administrative skill. He had reorganized the state government, fought to build schools, parks, and parkways, and struggled for public development of the great power sites.

In the campaign, Hoover stressed prosperity, which was popularly translated into the notion of a chicken in every pot and two cars in every garage. Smith evoked more enthusiastic loyalty and venomous hatred than any candidate since Bryan. Millions of the urban masses, mostly of immigrant and Catholic background themselves, saw in Smith their spokesman, their great hero. Millions of Protestants in the rural South, where belief in prohibition was strong and the Ku Klux Klan boisterous in its anti-Catholicism, looked upon him as a threat

Election of 1928

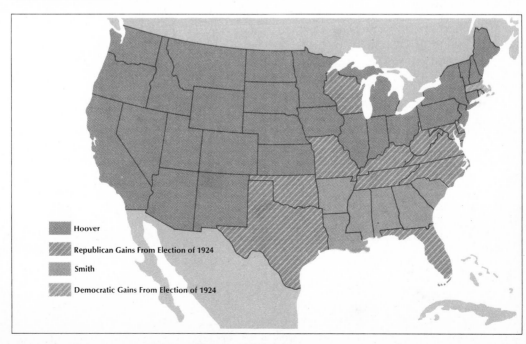

Hoover

Republican Gains From Election of 1924

Smith

Democratic Gains From Election of 1924

to their way of life. Fiery crosses greeted him near Oklahoma City, where he courageously denounced the Klan. But his cause was hopeless. The Republican landslide exceeded expectations, as Hoover received a popular vote of 21 million to 15 million for Smith.

THE WALL STREET CRASH

President Hoover, the prophet of permanent prosperity, had been in office scarcely six months when the Great Depression began. It was touched off by a collapse of the stock mar-

ket. For several years stock prices had been rising so rapidly that they ceased to have much relation to the actual earning power of corporations. The New York Stock Exchange had become for many speculators a great national gambling casino, where everyone won almost all the time. By the summer of 1929, however, there were many disquieting signs that the prosperity, so long gone for the farmers, was coming to an end for businessmen also Construction had passed its peak and was declining rapidly; automobiles were filling dealers' garages; business inventories of all sorts were three times larger than a year before; freight

The stock market crash marked only the beginning of the price decline. Stocks stayed low in 1930s and even relatively low in the 1940s. By the Korean War the great bull market was underway and continued with only brief interruption until the 1960s. The stock prices shown above are based on the Dow-Jones stock averages.

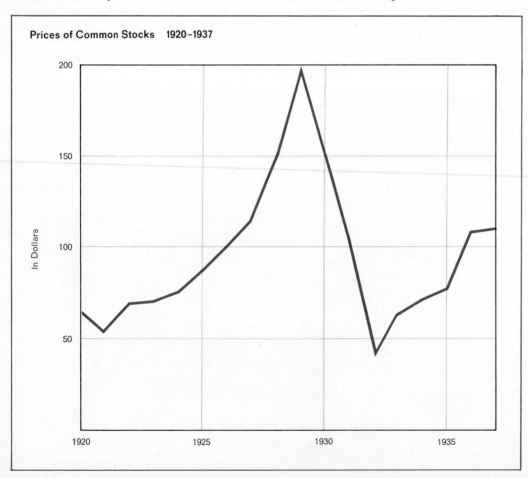

carloadings, industrial production, and whole-sale prices were all slipping downward.

On October 21, 1929, the stock market dropped sharply, and two days later the big crash began. Temporarily, J. P. Morgan and Company and other big bankers managed to stave off disaster, but on October 29 their efforts failed. That day 16 million shares were sold. Total losses for the month reached $16 billion. For two weeks more the market continued to drop, until stocks had lost over 40 percent in value.

The stock market collapse, though not the cause of the depression, precipitated it by replacing the inflationary spiral with a deflationary one even harder to stop. It brought to an end a decade of business optimism and opened one of almost unquenchable pessimism. Bewildered businessmen saw their only hope in retrenchment, and the more they retrenched, the worse conditions became.

For years afterward, economists, businessmen, and political leaders debated the causes of the depression. Certainly there had been serious defects in the economy of the 1920s. As production rose, too little of the profits went to farmers, other producers of raw materials, or workers. Too much went into the building of new industrial plants. So long as the expansion of capital facilities continued, new investments stimulated the economy, but the investments created more plant space than could be profitably used. By 1929, factories were pouring out more goods than consumers could purchase. This did not mean that Americans would not have consumed more had they had more income, for even in 1929 only one family in six had an automobile, only one in five a fixed bathtub or electricity, and only one in ten a telephone.

Government had played the wrong role in the economic system during the twenties. Taxes, by sparing the rich, had added to the inequality of incomes. High tariffs had discouraged foreign trade; large exports could have continued only so long as Americans kept on lending abroad. Failure to break up or regulate big business had encouraged concentration and resulted in rigidly high prices. Nothing had been done to check speculation or supervise the securities market, and nothing effective had been done to restore the buying power of farmers.

THE HOOVER PROGRAM

In the view of critics a generation later, the government continued to do the wrong things in facing the depression. It concentrated upon balancing the budget and maintaining the gold standard, both of which were deflationary, at a time when the country was already suffering from too much deflation. Blame for these policies should not fall solely upon President Hoover. They were the ancient formulas for the conduct of government during a depression; they were urged upon the President by leaders of both parties and of business and by experts in economics.

Actually, President Hoover was far more energetic and imaginative than any previous American President in trying to combat the depression. His Secretary of the Treasury, Mellon, was a "leave-it-alone liquidationist" who thought a thoroughgoing cycle of bankruptcy and deflation would be healthful. Hoover did not agree. He determined that the government should intervene positively but in a very limited way, seeking the voluntary cooperation of business and labor.

First, to restore confidence, Hoover declared: "The fundamental business of this country, that is, production and distribution of commodities, is on a sound and prosperous basis." Most of the business leaders echoed him. Next, he held a number of highly publicized meetings of business, farm, and labor leaders in an effort to rally the country to adopt a voluntary program. Businessmen pledged themselves not to cut payrolls or production; labor leaders, not to ask for better wages or hours. Hoover also announced a significant tax cut and arranged for the Federal Reserve to provide increased bank credit. He asked Congress for an increase of $423 million in public works — a huge sum for the period — and called upon mayors and governors to engage in the "energetic yet prudent pursuit" of public construction.

Already, in April 1929, Hoover had called Congress into special session to provide farm relief and raise the tariff. His farm program, embodied in the Agricultural Marketing Act of 1929, set up large-scale government machinery to aid the farmer. The program, as Hoover insisted, was voluntary and did not include any of the price-fixing schemes for which farm or-

Hoover Dam

Conservationists for years urged the construction of a huge dam on the Colorado River to utilize its large flow for irrigation and power production and to prevent disastrous flooding of the Imperial Valley in California. Only the federal government was large enough to provide sufficient funds for the project. Through the 1920s, Hoover worked as chairman of the Colorado River Commission to reconcile conflicting claims of the seven states in the Colorado basin and to obtain President Coolidge's reluctant approval of preliminary surveys. Hoover himself insisted that the power be sold as falling water to keep the government even out of the business of generating electricity. Work on the dam began in the Hoover administration. It was the first of the great self-liquidating public works to be constructed during the depression, directly employing 4,000 workers, and indirectly aiding thousands more. The dam and power houses cost $108 million; in addition, the cities of southern California constructed a $220 million aqueduct to carry part of the water 259 miles to the Pacific coast. The dam, 726 feet high, created an artificial lake stretching 115 miles up the river, holding enough water to cover the state of Connecticut to a depth of 10 feet. When the dam was finished in 1935, two years ahead of the contract date, it was dedicated by President Franklin D. Roosevelt. (National Archives)

ganizations were lobbying. It encouraged the voluntary combination of farmers to help themselves under government auspices. A Farm Board of eight members administered a revolving fund of $500 million, from which the board could make loans to national marketing cooperatives or establish corporations to buy surpluses and thus raise prices.

Within six months the depression precipitated farm prices toward new lows. Until the summer of 1931, the Wheat Stabilization Corporation and the Cotton Stabilization Corporation were able to keep prices a bit above world levels. By 1932 their funds were spent, their warehouses full, and grain prices at the lowest point since the founding of the American colonies. The Farm Board had operated on too small a scale, and it had lacked power to limit production. When President Hoover later called for voluntary reduction of the wheat crop, acreage dropped only 1 percent in Kansas. The Farm Board experiment thus underscored the futility of a voluntary crop-control program and prepared the way for a more drastic measure.

Congress, taking President Hoover's advice to raise agricultural tariffs, prepared an overall measure, the Hawley-Smoot bill, which contained 75 increases on farm products, and 925 on manufactured goods. It raised the average duty from the 26 percent of the Fordney-McCumber Act to a new high of 50 percent. By the time it was ready for the President's signature in the spring of 1930, a thousand members of the American Economic Association had signed a petition urging him to veto it as an unwise piece of economic nationalism. He ignored such warnings and signed the measure. Other nations in reprisal placed new restrictions on American goods. In a time of world depression, rampant economic nationalism was perhaps inevitable, but it was unfortunate that the United States led the way.

The worsening depression gave Democrats a political issue. In the fall of 1930 they won a bare majority in the House of Representatives and, with the aid of Republican progressives, took effective control of the Senate. From this point on, Congress began seriously to harass Hoover, demanding that he move from voluntary measures to large-scale federal relief and spending. He refused to budge. By the spring of 1931 conditions seemed to be improving, and Hoover and others thought the worst was over. But the American economy took another downturn in consequence of a European financial panic. By May 1931 the largest bank in Austria had collapsed, and the disaster threatened to wreck the banking and monetary systems of Germany and other nations of Europe.

To avert this, President Hoover proposed a one-year moratorium on reparations and war-debt payments, but France destroyed much of the good effect through her delay in accepting the plan. By September, England and most other nations of the world had gone off the gold standard. The crisis in western Europe caused European gold to be withdrawn from American banks, and European holdings of American securities to be dumped on the market. As other nations devalued their currency in going off the gold standard, American trade with them declined disastrously.

By December 1931, when Congress met, conditions were so frightening that President Hoover abandoned his reliance upon voluntary measures and proposed direct governmental action of an unprecedented sort to combat the depression. In January 1932 Congress created a giant loan agency, the Reconstruction Finance Corporation, which during 1932 loaned $1.5 billion, mostly to banks, railroads, and other businesses. Hoover, trying to parry criticism that he had set up a bread line for big business, asserted that his purpose was to stop deflation and thus increase employment, mainly by helping relatively small companies. Congress also provided for banks, together with further capital for existing loan banks, to help prevent mortgage foreclosures.

On the issues of very large-scale public works and direct relief for the unemployed, the President clashed bitterly with Republican progressives and Democrats in Congress. In July 1932 he vetoed their bill as being impractical and dangerous; he felt that direct relief was a state and local responsibility. Subsequently, he signed a bill he himself had recommended, authorizing the RFC to lend $300 million for relief, and another $1.5 billion for self-liquidating public works.

Hoover believed that, while people must not go cold and hungry, feeding them was a voluntary and local responsibility. "If we start appropriations of this character," he had declared, "we have not only impaired something infinitely valuable in the life of the American people but have struck at the roots of self-government." It was hard for desperate people to appreciate such niceties of thought. Hoover, who had been one of the most popular of American heroes, became the scapegoat for the depression.

To some observers the 1928 election had seemed to be a great national referendum in favor of prohibition, yet prohibition was not to last much longer than prosperity. Though Hoover had referred to it as a "noble experiment," enforcement was breaking down so badly that Congress stiffened the penalties for violating the Volstead Act and authorized the new President to appoint a National Law Enforcement Commission. This commission, headed by a former Attorney General, George Wickersham, ultimately reported in 1931 that prohibition was not only unenforced but virtually unenforceable.

Rampant gangsterism and the open flouting of the law by millions of otherwise respectable citizens convinced many thoughtful Americans that prohibition was not worth its price in lawlessness. With the coming of the depression, some well-to-do people, already banded into antiprohibition organizations, redoubled their efforts in the hope that repeal would bring lower income taxes and greater prosperity. In February 1933 Congress submitted to the states the Twenty-first Amendment, repealing prohibition; by December it had been ratified, and the experiment was at an end.

DEEPENING DESPAIR

As the depression deepened, there were surprisingly few signs of social disorder or outbursts of violence within the United States. Communists agitated, won a few converts among intellectual leaders, but made almost no impact upon the masses.

The chain reaction of unemployment slowly spread from 1930 into 1933. At first those in marginal or poorer jobs were hit hardest, as those who had been in better jobs moved downward. In time millions who had never been unemployed for any length of time were jobless and unable to find work of any sort. They were bewildered, for they had been brought up in the sturdy tradition of self-reliance and had accepted the doctrine of rugged individualism—that opportunities were limitless if only one had the ambition and energy to take advantage of them. Now these people were humiliated and baffled at not being able to provide for themselves and their families. As they remained idle for months and then years, they were in danger of losing their skills as well as their morale. Physical and moral erosion threatened.

Care of the unemployed had always been a responsibility primarily of private charity, and for several years the President and governors exhorted citizens to contribute to the Red Cross or to emergency funds. But the task soon became far too great for private charity to handle. By 1931, the Red Cross could provide only 75 cents a week to feed each hungry family in southern Illinois.

Although several European nations had maintained unemployment insurance programs for decades, not a single state in the United States enacted such a law until January 1932, when Wisconsin passed one. Even as the distress grew, many magazines and newspapers proclaimed that any permanent system of direct unemployment relief like the British dole would bankrupt the government and undermine the moral fiber of the recipients. Not until September 1931 did the New York legislature at the insistence of Governor Franklin D. Roosevelt establish the first relief organization of any state, the Temporary Emergency Relief Administration, which became the model for other states and the prototype of the later federal relief agency.

To some of the unemployed who had recently moved to cities, the solution seemed to be to return to the farm; the migration away

---

Shacks of the Unemployed, New York City   1932
Robert Bendiner has written: "To a New Yorker . . . the signs of collapse were aggressive. Along the Hudson, below Riverside Drive, I daily passed the tarpaper huts of a Hooverville, where scores of families lived the lives of reluctant gypsies, cooking whatever they had to cook over open fires within sight of passengers on the double-decker Fifth Avenue buses. Dozens of such colonies had sprung up in the city . . . but not nearly enough to accommodate the swelling army of the jobless and dispossessed." (Top right, Culver)

An Apple Seller in New York City
In the fall of 1931 and 1932, a number of unemployed tried to gain a pittance for themselves by selling apples. President Hoover later wrote: "One incident of these times has persisted as the eternal damnation of Hoover. Some Oregon or Washington apple growers' association shrewdly appraised the sympathy of the public for the unemployed. They set up a system of selling apples on the street corners in many cities, thus selling their crop and raising their prices. Many persons left their jobs for the more profitable one of selling apples. When any left-winger wishes to indulge in scathing oratory, he demands, 'Do you want to return to selling apples?' " (Bottom right, Culver)

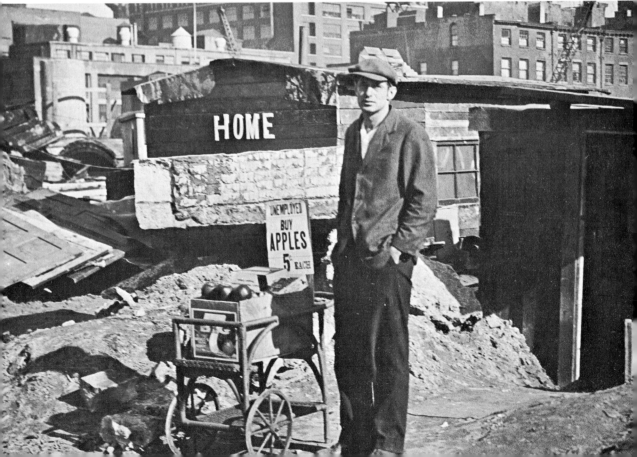

from farms was now reversed. But farm prices fell so low that once again, on parts of the plains, farmers burned corn to keep warm. A rancher sold seven lambs in the Denver livestock market and, after paying commissions and fees, received a check for 75 cents. In a railroad diner, two lamb chops cost the same amount. Prices of manufactured goods were relatively so high that it took ten bushels of wheat to buy a cheap pair of shoes. In drought areas farmers lacked even sufficient food.

Some bewildered farmers around Sioux City, Iowa, in 1932 embargoed milk bound for the city because they were receiving 2 cents a quart and it retailed for 8 cents. Many more Iowa farmers participated in Milo Reno's militant Farmers' Holiday Association to block all farm products from the market until prices rose.

Through the summer of 1932, some 12,000 to 14,000 unemployed veterans congregated in Washington to demonstrate for the immediate payments of their bonus for wartime service, not due until 1945. For weeks they lived in squalor in abandoned tenements and in shanties on the mud flats of the Anacostia River. After Congress failed to pass a bonus bill, about half of them, discouraged, went home. The continued presence of the rest alarmed Hoover and many Washingtonians. After a riot, the President called upon the army to oust the veterans. Under the personal command of General Douglas MacArthur, with tanks, gas masks, and fixed bayonets, the army did so. "That was a bad looking mob," MacArthur declared, expressing the alarm of conservatives. "It was animated by the essence of revolution."

Selected Readings

Surveys and Interpretations
J. D. Hicks, *Republican Ascendancy, 1921–1933** (1960); W. E. Leuchtenberg, *The Perils of Prosperity, 1914–32** (1958); George Soule, *Prosperity Decade: From War to Depression, 1917–1929* (1947); A. M. Schlesinger, Jr., *The Crisis of the Old Order** (1957).

Aspects of Life
G. H. Knoles, *The Jazz Age Revisited* (1955); F. L. Allen, *Only Yesterday** (1931); R. S. and H. M. Lind, *Middletown** (1929); N. F. Furniss, *The Fundamentalist Controversy, 1918–1931* (1954); Ray Ginger, *Six Days or Forever?** (1958), about the Scopes trial; Erik Barnouw, *A Tower in Babel: A History of Broadcasting in the United States*, vol. 1: to 1933 (1966); W. R. Ross, *The Last Hero: Charles A. Lindbergh* (1967).

Radicalism and Reaction
W. Preston, Jr., *Aliens and Dissenters: Federal Suppression of Radicals, 1903–1933* (1963); R. K. Murray, *The Red Scare** (1955); Zechariah Chafee, Jr., *Free Speech in the United States* (1941); S. Coben, *A. Mitchell Palmer, Politician* (1963); G. L. Joughin and E. M. Morgan, *The Legacy of Sacco and Vanzetti** (1948); David Brody, *Labor in Crisis: The Steel Strike of 1919** (1965); Irving Bernstein, *The Lean Years: A History of the American Worker, 1920–1933** (1960); David Chalmers, *Hooded Americanism** (1965), on the Klan; E. D. Cronon, *Black Moses: The Story of Marcus Garvey** (1955).

The Eighteenth and Nineteenth Amendments
J. H. Timberlake, *Prohibition and the Progressive Movement, 1900–1920* (1963); Andrew Sinclair, *Prohibition: The Era of Excess** (1962); Charles Merz, *Dry Decade* (1931); Virginius Dabney, *Dry Messiah: The Life of Bishop Cannon* (1949); A. S. Kraditor, *The Ideas of the Woman Suffrage Movement, 1890–1920* (1965); David Morgan, *Suffragists and Democrats: The Politics of Woman Suffrage in America* (1972); J. S. Lemons, *The Woman Citizen: Social Feminism in the 1920's* (1973); A. F. Scott, *The Southern Lady: From Pedestal to Politics, 1830–1930* (1970).

Literature
Alfred Kazin, *On Native Grounds: An Interpretation of Modern American Prose Literature** (1942); Edmund Wilson, *The Shores of Light** (1952) and *The American Earthquake** (1958); Frederick Hoffman, *Freudianism and the Literary Mind** (1947); Mark Schorer, *Sinclair Lewis** (1961); M. K. Singleton, *H. L. Mencken and the American Mercury Adventure* (1962).

Harding and Coolidge
S. H. Adams, *Incredible Era: The Life and Times of Warren G. Harding** (1939); Andrew Sinclair, *The Available Man* (1965), on Harding; Burl Noggle, *Teapot Dome: Oil and Politics in the 1920's* (1962); J. L. Bates, *The Origins of Teapot Dome: Progressives,*

Parties, and Petroleum, 1909–1921 (1963); W. A. White, *A Puritan in Babylon** (1938), on Coolidge; D. R. McCoy, *Calvin Coolidge, the Quiet President* (1967); H. H. Quint and R. H. Ferrell, eds., *The Talkative President: The Off-the-Record Press Conferences of Calvin Coolidge* (1964).

Foreign Affairs
J. C. Vinson, *The Parchment Peace* (1955); M. J. Pusey, *Charles Evans Hughes* (2 vols., 1951); Dexter Perkins, *Charles Evans Hughes and American Democratic Statesmanship* (1953); R. H. Ferrell, *Peace in Their Time* (1952); R. J. Maddox, *William E. Borah and American Foreign Policy* (1969).

Political Opposition
K. C. Mackay, *The Progressive Movement of 1924* (1947); J. J. Huthmacher, *Massachusetts People and Politics, 1919–1933** (1959); Frank Freidel, *Franklin D. Roosevelt: The Ordeal* (1954); Oscar Handlin, *Al Smith and His America** (1958); E. A. Moore, *A Catholic Runs for President* (1956); R. C. Silva, *Rum, Religion, and Votes: 1928 Re-examined* (1962).

Hoover and the Depression
A. U. Romasco, *The Poverty of Abundance: Hoover, the Nation, the Depression** (1965); H. G. Warren, *Herbert Hoover and the Great Depression* (1959); Herbert Hoover, *Memoirs: The Great Depression, 1929–1941* (1952); J. H. Shideler, *Farm Crisis, 1919–1923* (1957); Theodore Saloutos and J. D. Hicks, *Twentieth Century Populism: Agricultural Discontent in the Middle West, 1900–1939** (1951); J. K. Galbraith, *The Great Crash** (1955); Milton Friedman and A. J. Schwartz, *The Great Contraction, 1929–1933** (1965); R. Daniels, *The Bonus March: An Episode of the Great Depression* (1971).

*Titles available in paperback.

Experimenting with a New Deal

Twenty-four

During 1917 and 1918 the government of the United States, in order to win a war, had undertaken to control nearly all aspects of the economy. But never before the 1930s had the government intervened in so many ways in order to overcome a depression. Between 1933 and 1938, under the leadership of President Franklin D. Roosevelt, the government launched a bewildering variety of programs and set up a jumble of "alphabetical agencies" – AAA, NRA, TVA, and so on – to administer them. Some of these were intended to provide immediate relief for people facing a loss of income or property. Others were expected to stimulate economic activity and bring about recovery from the depression. Still others were designed to reform the economic system in order to reduce poverty and insecurity and avoid future depressions. Some of the programs served two or all three of these aims. All together, the series of measures constituted the New Deal.

The "three Rs" of the New Deal, then, were Relief, Recovery, and Reform. Its conservative critics, among them former President Hoover, contended that it involved also a "fourth R," namely, Revolution. Certainly the New Deal, which at first was rather cautious, emphasizing short-term measures of relief and recovery, gradually became somewhat more daring and placed greater emphasis on lasting reforms. All along, however, the programs were directed toward patching up and preserving, not destroying, the political and economic institutions that President Roosevelt and the American people had inherited. The programs were mostly improvisations that were drawn up to meet the needs of the moment. They were based on previous American experience. A precedent for practically every one of them can be found in something that had been proposed or tried out earlier. The New Deal was revolutionary only in the sense that it embodied a larger number of undertakings at one time and carried them to greater lengths than other

Rallying for the NRA   1933
The NRA emblem was a blue eagle clutching a cogwheel and a thunderbolt. To foster compliance with the NRA codes of fair competition, merchants and householders displayed the emblem on posters and communities staged rallies. Here, at a San Francisco rally, 8,000 children form a giant eagle on a baseball field. (UPI)

comparable movements, such as the New Freedom, had done.

The New Deal failed to bring about full recovery; not until after 1941 did war, the greatest of public works, take up the slack in the employment of human and other resources. But the relief measures enabled both the people and the economic system to survive the depression, and the reform measures made significant and enduring changes in the system itself. The role of government in economic life was vastly increased (and was to be increased still further by the ensuing war). The nation had become a welfare state. Henceforth the principle was to be generally accepted— though not always completely realized—that it was the government's duty to "provide for the general welfare" by controlling business and agriculture, maintaining full employment, and assuring at least a basic economic security to all members of society.

A Change of Leadership

In 1932 Republicans meeting in Chicago renominated Hoover in a spirit far from jubilant; they had little illusion about the outcome of the election. The Democrats, assembling later in an excited, expectant mood, saw almost certain victory after twelve years out of power. Almost anyone they nominated was sure to be elected.

THE INTERREGNUM OF 1932–1933

Well over a majority of the delegates came pledged to vote for Governor Franklin D. Roosevelt of New York. Roosevelt had been working astutely for the nomination for years. To a considerable degree he bridged the gulf between the urban and rural Democrats. He was ready to emphasize economic issues and ignore the earlier divisions over prohibition and religion.

Breaking precedent, Roosevelt flew immediately to Chicago to deliver his acceptance address before the convention. He endorsed the Democratic platform, which except for a promise of prohibition repeal was not much bolder than that of the Republicans. He declared: "I pledge you, I pledge myself, to a new deal for the American people." Thus the Roosevelt program acquired a name before the electorate had more than the haziest notion what it might embody.

Nor did the voters learn much during the campaign, for Roosevelt shrewdly confined himself to warm generalities which would offend few and yet would bring him the enormous vote of protest against Hoover. Through Roosevelt's speeches ran many of the old progressive themes, together with new suggestions of economic planning. An able team, largely of university professors under the leadership of Raymond Moley, helped devise policies and draft speeches for him. Newspapermen dubbed his group of advisers the "brain trust." At the Commonwealth Club in San Francisco, Roosevelt broke furthest from the past by insisting that the government must assist business in developing a well-regulated economic system. Everyone, he said, had a right to a comfortable living; the nation's industrial and agricultural mechanism could produce more than enough. If need be, to achieve this end, government must police irresponsible economic power. Roosevelt felt he was doing no more than restating the objectives of Jefferson and Wilson in terms of the complexities of the thirties when he proposed that the government should act as a regulator for the common good within the existing economic system. So far as Roosevelt explained the New Deal during the campaign, this was its essence.

President Hoover, tired and grim, took to the road in October to warn the populace that without his program things might be infinitely worse. His speeches, though earnest, were dull and dreary in both style and delivery compared with Roosevelt's breezy, optimistic performances. Hoover was the last of the Presidents to scorn the aid of speech writers.

Some voters, disappointed because they could detect little difference between Roosevelt's program and Hoover's, turned to Norman Thomas and the Socialists or to William Z. Foster and the Communists. Yet, even in this year

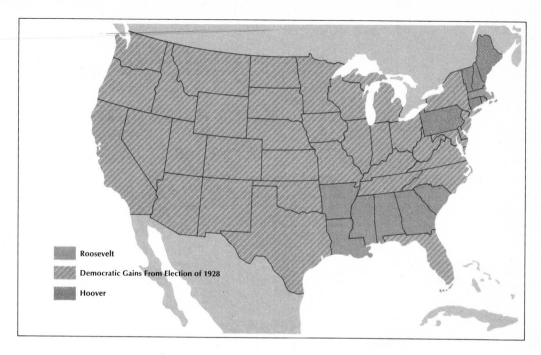

Legend:
- Roosevelt
- Democratic Gains From Election of 1928
- Hoover

Election of 1932

of despair, the Socialists polled only 882,000 votes, and the Communists only 103,000. Roosevelt received 22,822,000 popular votes (57.4 percent), Hoover 15,762,000 (39.7 percent). The Democrats carried both houses of Congress by top-heavy majorities. Roosevelt had won an overwhelming mandate — but for what?

Actually, there had been discernible differences between the two candidates and their programs — besides the obvious difference that Hoover was a worn, discredited President, and Roosevelt a buoyant candidate. Hoover had seen the depression as world-wide in origin and development; rather inconsistently he was ready to combat it internationally through currency stabilization, and nationally, through raising the tariff still higher if need be. Roosevelt chose to regard the depression as domestic, specifically Republican, in origin. During the campaign Hoover had forced him to equivocate on the old Democratic low-tariff position. Roosevelt was ready (as both his record as governor and his speeches indicated) to move toward economic nationalism. But he agreed with Hoover on the need for government thrift and a balanced budget.

President Hoover faced an agonizing four months before Roosevelt would take office on

March 4: the Twentieth ("lame duck") Amendment to end this long carry-over of a defeated President and Congress was not ratified until February 1933. There had been a brief economic upswing in the spring months of 1932, reaching a peak in July. (Economists later ascribed this to Hoover's own brief plunge into deficit financing through public works spending and Reconstruction Finance Corporation loans.) Hoover felt he was bringing an end to the depression and that only the threat of unsettling measures from Roosevelt was preventing continued recovery. Hence, in a series of interchanges with Roosevelt during the winter of 1932–1933, he tried to bind the President-elect to economic orthodoxy.

Hoover favored the reestablishment of an international gold standard. He hoped that the United States and other nations would agree to this at an economic and monetary conference that was scheduled to meet in London after Roosevelt's inauguration. But Roosevelt would make no commitment.

By February 1933 an acute banking crisis had developed. Bank resources and deposits had been declining at an alarming rate. In the previous three years, 5,000 banks had failed, and now one after another was collapsing as depositors lined up to withdraw their deposits. To stop the run on the banks, governors began proclaiming banking holidays in their states. By March 4 banking was at a halt or drastically restricted in all states but one.

President Hoover wrote a letter to Roosevelt, charging that the crisis was caused by "steadily degenerating confidence" in the President-elect, and calling upon him to give prompt public assurance that there would be no tinkering with the currency, no heavy borrowing, no unbalancing of the budget. Roosevelt had not the slightest intention of adopting Hoover's views.

F. D. R. TAKES COMMAND

When Roosevelt was inaugurated, on March 4, 1933, most of the nation's banks were closed. At least 13 million people were unemployed, some of them so close to starvation that they were scrabbling for food scraps in garbage dumps. Millions of farmers were on the brink of foreclosure; many others had fallen over the brink.

In his inaugural address, President Roosevelt spoke with vigor and confidence. "This great Nation will endure as it has endured, will revive and will prosper," he declared. "So, first of all, let me assert my firm belief that the only thing we have to fear is fear itself." Somehow these words, although they said nothing new, helped inspire the American people. From their depths of helplessness they were ready for the moment to be commanded, and in Roosevelt they saw someone ready to take strong leadership. Such leadership he promised. If Congress did not act, he announced, he would ask for "broad executive power to wage a war against the emergency, as great as the power that would be given to me if we were in fact invaded by a foreign foe."

Few Presidents have been better trained for the White House. Roosevelt had served in the New York state senate, been wartime assistant secretary of the navy, and had been twice elected governor of New York. He was skilled in both legislative and administrative techniques as well as in practical politics. As a youth he had spent much time in Europe, and maintained a continuing interest in foreign affairs. Roosevelt's ideology was progressive, influenced by his wife's uncle, Theodore Roosevelt, whom he admired, and his former chief, Woodrow Wilson, whom he revered.

Neither the new President nor his advisers were clear-cut in their thinking. What was important was that Roosevelt, while basically rooted in the older economics and the social-justice tradition of the progressives, was ready to experiment. His program would be flexible, not doctrinaire; the new economic theories would grow from it, not it from the theories. When one of the brain trusters warned of perils ahead, Roosevelt declared: "There is nothing to do but meet every day's troubles as they come." This was his political pragmatism, and out of it grew the New Deal economic policies.

With the banking crisis at its height, he might well have taken drastic steps such as nationalization of the banks. But he seemed bent above all upon restoring the confidence of businessmen. His initial program differed little from what they had been advocating. He met the banking crisis in a manner pleasing to the banking community. He issued a proclamation on March 6, 1933, closing all banks and stopping transactions or exports in gold for four days until Congress could meet in special session. On March 9 he sent in a conservative bill which would bolster the stronger banks. It authorized the Federal Reserve System to issue notes against their assets, and the Reconstruction Finance Corporation to make them loans. The bill dealt a death blow to weaker banks; inspectors would deny them licenses to reopen. It stopped the ebb of gold from the Treasury and the country through prohibiting hoarding and exportation. In effect, the country went off the gold standard (officially it did so April 19, 1933). Congress passed the bill within four hours of its introduction. In the House, a rolled-up newspaper substituted for it, since there had not been time to print copies.

On March 12, in the first of his "fireside chats" over the radio, the President, speaking in a warm, intimate manner, told the American people that the crisis was over. "I can assure you," he declared, "that it is safer to keep your money in a reopened bank than under the mattress." And so indeed it was; by his legislation and his confident leadership, Roosevelt had averted the threat to banks and the capitalist system. Three-fourths of the banks in the Federal Reserve System reopened within the next three days, and a billion dollars in hoarded currency and gold flowed back into them within a month. Practically all unsafe banks were now out of business; there were very few new failures in the years that followed.

On the morning after the passage of the Emergency Banking Act, Roosevelt further reassured business by sending Congress an economy bill, to balance the budget by cutting

**Roosevelt and Hoover en Route to Roosevelt's Inauguration
March 4, 1933**

Roosevelt never forgot the awkwardness of his ride to the Capitol with the grim, unresponsive Hoover, exhausted from grappling with the banking crisis. No one would have guessed in the black days before March 4, 1933, that the incoming President would set his mark on the age as have few Chief Executives. He alarmed even those closest to him with his amiability, his ready acceptance of suggestions, his quick "Fine, fine, fine." New Yorkers, fearful that his jaunty buoyancy, his facility at compromise, and his skill at political maneuver were a façade for weakness, had sometimes referred to him as "the Grin" or the "Boy Scout Governor." They did not as yet see the energy and persistence with which he applied himself, or the cold iron sometimes not far beneath the charm. His physical courage they realized, for after his polio attack in 1921 he had indomitably stayed in politics, refusing to surrender to his infirmity. He had subordinated it so thoroughly that most people regarded him only as somewhat lame and never thought of him as using a wheelchair. Again he demonstrated his self-possession at Miami in February 1933, by remaining astoundingly calm when an insane assassin missed him but mortally wounded the mayor of Chicago sitting beside him. Somehow Roosevelt was able to transmit some of his courage to the nation in March 1933. (United Press International)

salaries of government employees and pensions of veterans as much as 15 percent. This, Roosevelt declared, was the only way to avoid a billion-dollar deficit. This bill too passed almost instantly, although with such fierce opposition from veterans' organizations that it carried the House only with Republican votes. Pressure from veterans soon led Congress to rescind the pension cuts over Roosevelt's veto, but the President drastically slashed the regular expenditures of the government.

On March 13, 1933, Roosevelt proposed legalizing beer that had a 3.2 percent alcoholic content, pending repeal of the prohibition amendment. This, he felt, would stimulate recovery and bring in needed taxes. (It would also, as it turned out, rescue millions of law violators from the rigors of home brew and gangster-made beer.)

Thus far, except for the gold clause in the Emergency Banking Act, the program of the new administration might have been that of a Hoover with a smile. It restored the confidence of bankers and businessmen, the stock market going up 15 percent. But this was anticipatory of the real recovery to follow; for the moment nothing had been improved but the confidence of the American nation.

Tentative Beginnings

During his first hundred days in office, keeping Congress in special session, Roosevelt put through a series of laws and began to take steps that led him away from the "sound" position—so reassuring to bankers and other businessmen—that he originally had assumed.

EMERGENCY RELIEF

The first step was to feed the millions of hungry unemployed. While Roosevelt subscribed to his predecessor's maxim that relief was primarily the task of states and communities, he proposed that the federal government provide grants rather than loans to states. Congress established the Federal Emergency Relief Administration, and appropriated an initial half-billion dollars for it. Roosevelt appointed the director of the New York state relief agency, Harry Hopkins, whom he hardly knew as yet, to run the federal program. Hopkins was a dedicated social worker with a lively tongue and a keen sense of professional ethics. He ardently believed in work relief rather than direct relief, but in the spring of 1933 everyone hoped recovery was at hand so that relief would be needed only for a few months.

But recovery lagged, and some new way had to be found to care for the unemployed through the winter of 1933–1934. Relief administrator Hopkins persuaded the President to establish a temporary work relief program, the Civil Works Administration. Between November and April it put 4 million people to work at emergency projects. Sometimes it was made-work like leaf raking, to which critics applied an old Texas term, "boondoggling." Some of the projects, despite lack of funds for materials and tools, made substantial improvements. The output was of secondary importance; the work raised the morale of the unemployed and increased their buying power by $950 million. The purchasing power thus injected into the economy was probably responsible for the wavering recovery, as the index of production rose from 71 in November 1933 to 86 in May 1934. But soon Roosevelt capitulated to fierce conservative criticism and liquidated the program.

Congress also created an organization that reflected Roosevelt's keen interest in preserving natural as well as human resources, the Civilian Conservation Corps. It received a grant of $300 million to enroll 250,000 young men from relief families and 50,000 veterans and woodsmen, to work at reforestation and flood control. Ultimately the CCC enrolled 500,000 young men, but this was only a fraction of the unemployed youths in the nation.

Mortgage relief was a pressing need of millions of farm owners and home owners. Roosevelt quickly consolidated all farm credit organizations into a new Farm Credit Administration. Congress voted such large additional funds for it that within two years it had refinanced a fifth of all farm mortgages in the

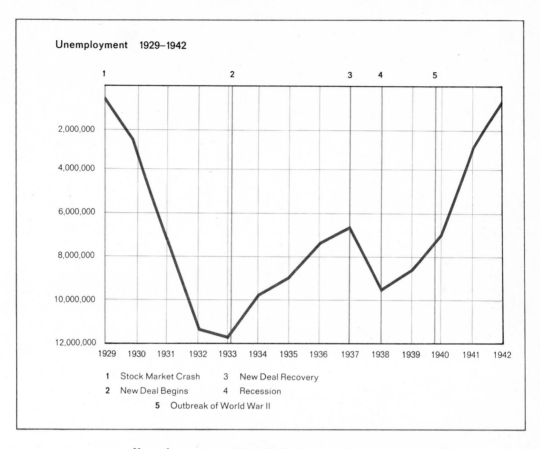

Unemployment   1929–1942

| | | | |
|1|2|3 4|5|

1 Stock Market Crash   3 New Deal Recovery
2 New Deal Begins   4 Recession
            5 Outbreak of World War II

Unemployment was especially high among young people, those who lived in areas where the textile mills and coal mines had been closed, and among the minority groups. The rate of unemployment changed drastically with the acute shortage of labor during the war years. Although the 1942 employment figures were up to the 1929 high, this chart does not reflect the proportionate population growth.

United States. The Frazier-Lemke Farm-Bankruptcy Act of 1933 enabled some farmers to regain their farms even after the foreclosure of mortgages. Unfortunately, these measures came too late to save all farmers; by 1934 a quarter of them for one reason or another had lost their property. A comparable Home Owners' Loan Corporation, established in June 1933, in a three-year period loaned $3 billion to refinance the mortgages of over a million distressed householders. Altogether it carried about a sixth of the nation's urban mortgage burden. A year later Congress established a Federal Housing Administration to insure mortgages for new construction and home repairs — more properly a recovery than a relief agency. All these mortgage agencies not only

rescued mortgage holders, but also eased the burden on banks and insurance companies, thus filling a recovery function.

Under the New Deal, the Reconstruction Finance Corporation continued to function as the key loan agency for relief to business. The Democratic Congress inveighed against the RFC policy of making large loans only to big businesses and not to individuals. Congress therefore broadened the RFC's lending power so that it could, and indeed did, also lend to small businessmen. Under the conservative management of a shrewd Texan, Jesse Jones, it continued to make most of its loans to large enterprises, including banks, and to governmental units, on sound security and with a high percentage of ultimate repayment.

THE FIRST AAA

The Agricultural Adjustment Administration, created in May 1933, marked the triumphant conclusion of the farmers' long struggle to get government aid for raising farm prices. Henceforth the farmers, who continued to be a declining fraction of the whole population, received preferential treatment from the government.

Roosevelt was mainly interested in the relatively substantial farmers, such as the 300,000 who even in 1933 were paying dues of $10 a year or more to the Farm Bureau Federation. These and the Grange members desired a program to limit crops. Poorer members of other farm organizations like the Farmers' Union and the National Farmers' Holiday Association opposed production cuts, seeking instead direct relief and, above all, inflation. Roosevelt hoped to develop a program that would fit the

Farm Bureau formula and yet would not drive poorer farmers into new revolt. He let the various farm organization leaders devise their own plan. Fifty of them met in Washington early in March 1933 and drafted an omnibus bill that contained scraps and reworkings of most of the old schemes. It provided for a "domestic-allotment" system. Producers of seven basic commodities (wheat, cotton, corn, hogs, rice, tobacco, and milk and other dairy products) were to receive benefit payments if they cut acreage or production. Funds for these payments would come from a tax upon the processing of commodities—for example, a tax on the milling of wheat. The tax would be added to the price of the flour or other product, and so it would be passed on to the consumer, who would thus indirectly pay the farmer for growing less. Farm prices were to be brought up to "parity," that is, a level that would provide the same

Drought Refugees Stalled on the Highway
Between 1935 and 1939, drought and depression impelled some 350,000 people to leave their farms in the Dust Bowl states, especially Oklahoma, and to seek precarious employment in the fields and orchards of California. In his novel The Grapes of Wrath *(1939) John Steinbeck gave a heart-rending account of an Oklahoma family's journey on Highway 66 across plains, deserts, and mountains. Breakdowns along the way were frequent—like this one photographed in New Mexico in 1937 by Dorothy Lange for the Farm Security Administration. (Library of Congress)*

Denouncing the New Dealers, former President Herbert Hoover once said they professed the "three Rs" of Relief, Recovery, and Reform but secretly espoused the "fourth R" of Revolution. How revolutionary was the New Deal in fact? To what extent did it break with the American past? Historians have given a wide variety of answers to these questions.

Some authors maintained that the New Deal was more evolutionary than revolutionary, that in essence it was an extension of the progressive movement. In *The History of the New Deal* (1944) Basil Rauch made a distinction between a "first" and a "second" New Deal. The first (1933–1935), rather conservative, concentrated on recovery as the chief aim and gave aid mostly to big business and big agriculture. The second (1935–1938), relatively liberal, paid more attention to reform and provided more benefits to industrial workers and small farmers. In *Rendezvous with Destiny* (1952) Eric F. Goldman saw the first phase as similar to Theodore Roosevelt's New Nationalism, the second as reminiscent of Woodrow Wilson's New Freedom, though Goldman thought "there was something more to New Deal liberalism," since it included such unprecedented measures as social security. But William E. Leuchtenburg, in *Franklin D. Roosevelt and the New Deal, 1932–1940* (1963), felt that the extent of the leftward shift had been exaggerated.

Other writers emphasized the elements of change rather than those of continuity. Richard Hofstadter, *The Age of Reform* (1955), conceded that there were continuities from progressivism but insisted that, as a whole, the Franklin D. Roosevelt program was a "drastic new departure" and was "different from anything that had yet happened in the United States." Hofstadter pointed out that many old progressives, still living in the 1930s, opposed the New Deal. Carl N. Degler, *Out of Our Past* (1959), called the New Deal the "Third American Revolution" (the first two being the Revolution of 1776 and the Civil War) and said it "marked the crossing of a divide from which, it would seem, there could be no turning back."

All the foregoing historians thought of themselves as liberals and, though in some respects critical, were basically sympathetic with Roosevelt and his program. A conservative, anti-Roosevelt historian, Edgar E. Robinson, considered the New Deal a sharp break with the past but deplored it. In *The Roosevelt Leadership, 1933–1945* (1955) Robinson complained that Roosevelt, "an eloquent proponent of revolutionary change," moved the country toward "many of the primary leveling objectives of communism."

Young radicals of the 1960s took just the opposite view. Concerned about the unsolved problems of their own generation, they criticized the New Deal for having preserved too many of the evils of capitalism. "Many millions — businessmen, professionals, unionized workingmen, commercial farmers — had been given substantial help," the New Left historian Howard Zinn wrote in his introduction to *New Deal Thought* (1966). "Many millions more — sharecroppers, slum-dwellers, Negroes of North and South, the unemployed — still awaited a genuine 'new deal.'"

price relationship of farm products to manufactured goods as during the period 1909–1914.

Because the 1933 farm season was well under way when the AAA began operations, large-scale destruction was necessary to cut surpluses. Six million pigs and 220,000 sows about to farrow were slaughtered. Nine-tenths of their weight was inedible and processed into fertilizer, but they nevertheless provided 100 million pounds of pork for needy families. Bad weather so drastically cut the wheat crop that the AAA did not have to intervene to reduce it. Cotton farmers ploughed under a quarter of their crop—but it was the poorest quarter and they so intensively cultivated the rest that 30 million acres produced more than 36 million had done the previous year.

Despite continued high cotton production, a short textile boom sent the price up from 5.5 cents per pound to 10.6 cents in the summer. Then the price began to sag again and was held to 9.6 cents only through another device. A subsidiary of the AAA, the Commodity Credit Corporation, loaned 10 cents per pound to cotton farmers who would agree to take additional land out of production the next year. Since the loan was in excess of the market value of cotton, the government in effect was buying the crop at a premium price in return for the promise of drastic cuts in production. In this way cotton farmers received double the cash in 1933 that they had in 1931.

Farmers in other crop-reduction programs did not fare as well, although corn producers too could obtain commodity loans in the fall of 1933. Drought more than crop limitations reduced the output of wheat, corn, and hogs. Rising prices of manufactured goods canceled out most of the farmer's gain in real income. Yet on the whole his relative position improved somewhat.

The AAA actually hurt many of the farmers on the least productive farms, especially in the cotton belt. At times the AAA indirectly dispossessed them because planters, in reducing their acreage, sometimes evicted tenants and fired field hands. Unintentionally the AAA stimulated the great migration away from sharecropper cabins, at a time when city jobs no longer awaited the migrants. Rapid mechanization of farms and destructive wind storms on the Great Plains gave the great migration its impetus.

THE NRA

Hard-pressed businessmen sought measures providing for government stabilization of business. Since 1931 leaders of the United States Chamber of Commerce and others had been urging an antideflation scheme that involved price fixing through trade associations. This plan would have necessitated suspension of the antitrust laws. President Hoover, who earlier had given strong support to the trade association movement, indignantly opposed price-fixing schemes. His attorney general forced five leading trade associations to dissolve, and the Federal Trade Commission compelled revision of the trade association codes for sixty-two industries.

In the spring of 1933, businessmen sought from Roosevelt what Hoover had refused them. Many of them also demanded government enforcement of their agreements in order to raise prices and stabilize production. The New Deal was ready to give them what they wanted if they would accept wages-and-hours regulation and other concessions for labor. As a consequence of such an arrangement, prices and wages would go up. Consumers' buying power might lag and thus defeat the scheme. Therefore the New Dealers drafting the great recovery bill added another ingredient for which there was much pressure: a large-scale public works spending program to prime the economic pump. This was the genesis of the National Industrial Recovery Act, which passed Congress in June 1933.

A new era of government alliance with business for the common good seemed to be opening. Roosevelt as he signed the act called it "the most important and far-reaching legislation ever enacted by the American Congress." On the same day, the President appointed as administrator the volatile, colorful General Hugh S. Johnson, who pictured himself as a sort of benign dictator presiding over the economy.

The President turned over the $3.3 billion for public works to Secretary of the Interior Harold L. Ickes, who slowly and methodically began to gather plans for projects, checking each carefully to make sure it would be really worthwhile. The need was for heavy spending in the next few months, but it was four years before Ickes' Public Works Administration pumped appreciable amounts of money into the economy.

President Roosevelt and NRA administrator Johnson called upon an excited nation to accept an interim blanket code, providing minimum wages of 30 cents or 40 cents an hour, maximum working hours of thirty-five or forty per week, and the abolition of child labor. Employers who agreed with the code were to display the NRA blue-eagle symbol; consumers who cooperated were to sign pledges that they would buy only from blue-eagle establishments. In much the spirit of 1917, the nation participated in NRA parades and rallies. As Johnson began negotiating codes with big industries, recovery seemed really imminent.

By the beginning of September 1933, specific codes for most of the big industries were in operation. In the drafting of the codes, Johnson had tried to serve as arbiter to balance the conflicting interests of business, labor, and the consumer. All three were represented at the bargaining table and received some degree of protection. Nevertheless, the real power in drawing up the regulations went to the businessmen themselves, to the leaders within each industry. They flocked to Washington and in the urgency of the moment rewrote their old trade association agreements into new NRA codes. These codes often contained provisions that were difficult for small units in the industry to maintain. Most of them provided for limiting production and, though often in disguised form, for price fixing.

Production, after a sharp rise, skidded downward during the fall of 1933, from an index figure of 101 in July to 71 in November, even as prices began to creep upward. The brave words and great NRA demonstrations of the spring and summer had not brought recovery. The New Deal honeymoon was over, and as General Johnson had predicted, the dead cats began to fly.

In the spring of 1934 a National Recovery Review Board under the famous iconoclastic lawyer, Clarence Darrow, reported that the NRA was dominated by big business; he hinted that what was needed was socialism. In the ensuing storm of vituperation between Johnson and Darrow, the NRA lost still more prestige.

A case involving the National Recovery Administration finally reached the Supreme Court. The Constitutional basis for the NRA was the power of Congress to regulate commerce among the states, but the test case involved alleged code violations by the Schechter brothers, who were operating a wholesale poultry business confined to one locality, Brooklyn. Among the charges against them were the selling of poultry in poor condition and the unfair treatment of employees. The Court (1935) unanimously held that the Schechters were not engaged in interstate commerce, and that Congress had unconstitutionally delegated legislative power to the President to draft the codes.

The "sick chicken" decision outraged Roosevelt. Seeing in it a threat to the whole New Deal, he lashed out at the judges for thinking in terms of the horse-and-buggy era. Actually, the decision proved to be more a blessing than a catastrophe for the New Deal, since it ended the decrepit NRA code system with its tacit suspension of the antitrust laws. "It has been an awful headache," Roosevelt confessed privately.

TVA AND CONSERVATION

Increasingly New Dealers turned their attention to measures that would remedy conditions they felt had helped bring on the depression. Their indignation burned expecially hot against the private power interests, which they felt had gulled investors and overcharged consumers. The spectacular collapse of the great Insull utility empire in the Middle West lent credence to their charges. Hence the first and most far-reaching of the New Deal reform measures was the creation of the Tennessee Valley Authority.

Through the twenties, millions of progressive Americans of both parties had shared the dream of Senator George Norris of Nebraska that the government might develop the nation's great water resources to provide cheap electric power. Millions of others accepted the educational program of the utilities companies, which spent $28 million to $35 million per year combating the idea of a national power program. The battle centered on the great dam that had been started at Muscle Shoals on the Tennessee River but had not been finished in time to provide nitrates during the war. Coolidge and

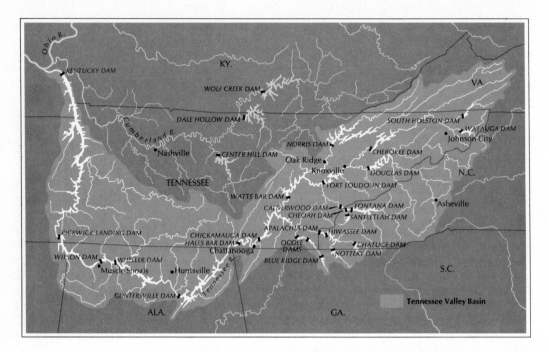

The Tennessee Valley Authority

the conservatives wished to sell it to Henry Ford for private development. Norris and his cohorts in Congress blocked them. Norris wished to make Muscle Shoals the center for developing the resources of the area and bringing abundance to millions of people living in poverty. His bill was vetoed by Coolidge and again by Hoover but was approved by Roosevelt in May 1933.

Basically, the TVA aimed to prevent the devastating floods that all too frequently had rolled down the rivers of the area, and to provide cheap, plentiful electricity as a yardstick for the measurement of private rates. More than this, the project became a great experiment in regional planning and rehabilitation.

Under a three-man board of directors with wide powers, the TVA in the next twenty years improved five existing dams and constructed twenty new ones. It stopped floods in the largest heavy-rainfall region in the nation and, by holding back the water, provided an inland waterway system with a nine-foot channel 652 miles long, soon heavy with traffic. From water power, and increasingly from steam plants, the TVA became the greatest producer of electricity in the United States. It also manufactured

low-cost phosphate fertilizers. It taught farmers how to use them, how to restore the fertility of their soil, and how to end erosion by means of contour plowing and reforestation. TVA worked no miracles, but it did bring a higher living standard to the farmers of the area. It brought new light industry and increased business. When World War II came, the new power plants provided indispensable electricity for the production of munitions, aluminum, and plutonium.

In its "yardstick" function, TVA drove down the price of power in the area from 10 cents a kilowatt hour to 3 cents. Throughout the country, because of TVA and other pressures, the average residential rate dropped from 5.52 cents in 1933 to 3.67 cents in 1942. To private power companies the "yardstick" seemed grossly unfair, and they claimed that the TVA did not set its rates on the basis of true costs, including taxes. Its officials replied that its payments to local and state governments were comparable to the taxes assessed against private power companies.

Other great public power and irrigation developments were under way in the West during the same years. On the Colorado River, the Hoover Dam (begun during the Hoover administration) was finished in 1936, and on the Columbia River the Bonneville Dam was constructed in 1937 and the Grand Coulee Dam in 1942. In 1937 Norris proposed the creation of six additional regional authorities like the TVA; Congress failed to act, and the debate over public versus private development of power continued.

To combat drought conditions in the West, Roosevelt in 1934 by executive order set aside $15 million to build a "shelter belt" of trees on the Great Plains, to break the wind, collect moisture, and harbor wildlife. Critics scoffed, but somehow the trees grew where no one had believed they would. A Soil Erosion Service (later Soil Conservation Service), using much Civilian Conservation Corps manpower, was active, especially in the West. Homesteading on the range, which meant dry farming under almost insuperable difficulties, came to an end with the passage of the Taylor Grazing Act of 1934, which withdrew overgrazed land and set regulations for the use of public rangeland. Spoliation of Indian lands came to at least a temporary halt with the passage of the Indian Reorganization Act of 1934, intended to preserve the tribal domain, customs, and civil liberties of the Indians.

MONEY AND BANKING

Much of the New Deal was aimed at raising prices as a means of stimulating recovery. One way was to cut down production, as the AAA tried to do for agriculture and the NRA for industry. Another way was to put money into circulation through government spending, as was done in the relief programs (though recovery was not the primary aim of these). Still another way — at least in theory — was to manipulate the currency so as to increase the money supply.

By the summer of 1933, Roosevelt was ready to follow the reasoning of two Cornell University agricultural economists, who contended that if the price of gold were raised, the prices of other commodities would rise in rough proportion. The government needed only to purchase quantities of gold and cut the gold content of the dollar (as authorized by Congress). When financially orthodox Treasury officials refused to make the purchases, Roosevelt turned to the head of the Farm Credit

Administration, Henry Morgenthau, Jr., who began buying gold every day along with wheat, corn, and oats. Soon Morgenthau was made secretary of the treasury.

The silver-purchase program had much the same object as the gold-purchase program. From the seven silver-producing states with their fourteen senators came strong pressure, reminiscent of that of the Populist era, culminating in the Silver Purchase Act of 1934. This measure nearly tripled the price of silver at home. It also sent up the world silver price and wrought havoc in nations whose currency was on a silver standard. It did little or nothing to raise prices in the United States.

Roosevelt explained to a critical congressman: "I have always favored sound money, and do now, but it is 'too darned sound' when it takes so much of farm products to buy a dollar." In January 1934 he fixed the gold content of the dollar at 59.06 percent of the former amount. The resort to managed currency created new precedents for government action and thus, like the income tax a generation earlier, helped bring about an important change in the relationship of government and the economy. But it had little immediate effect upon recovery.

Through other legislation the government acquired new powers over the banks, including the power to manage the supply of bank credit through increased control over the Federal Reserve System. In June 1933 Roosevelt signed the Glass-Steagall Act aimed at curbing speculation by banks. This also established the Federal Deposit Insurance Corporation, which he had not favored. The FDIC guaranteed small deposits up to $2,500 and functioned so successfully that the guarantee was raised by successive stages, eventually reaching $15,000. It was a longer task to work out a comprehensive overhauling and strengthening of the Federal Reserve System to remedy the defects that had appeared during the depression. This was accomplished through the Banking Act of 1935, which established a seven-man board of governors with direct power over interest rates. By lowering the rates, the board could encourage borrowing from banks, and this would ordinarily have an inflationary (price-raising) effect.

To protect investors further, Congress passed the so-called Truth in Securities Act of 1933, requiring corporations floating new securities to register them with the Federal

Trade Commission, and provide full and accurate information on them. In June 1934 Congress went further and established the Securities and Exchange Commission to police the stock markets. Wall Streeters protested, but their complaints lost some of their effect when a former head of the New York Stock Exchange was sentenced to Sing Sing for larceny.

A Shift to the Left

Though President Roosevelt originally wished to provide for the welfare of each of the main economic and political groups in the nation, realities forced him to become the champion of the new political coalition of farmers, laborers, and the underprivileged in general. Roosevelt shifted partly because he felt that large business had defected, that it had betrayed his recovery program and was fighting politically to destroy the New Deal. Aligned against him were about 70 percent of the newspaper publishers and most of the large contributors of campaign funds.

Far more important was the threat from the left; this was mainly responsible for the gradual change in emphasis of the New Deal. In undermining this threat, Roosevelt's political pragmatism combined with his humanitarian inclinations to carry him even further than the progressives had dared venture toward positive government action for the general welfare.

THE PRESSURE OF POLITICS

Through 1934 the President was still trying to hold the support of businessmen and bankers. As late as October he told the American Bankers' Association: "The time is ripe for an alliance of all forces intent upon the business of recovery. In such an alliance will be found business and banking, agriculture and industry, and labor and capital. What an all-American team that would be!" There was little chance of it. In August 1934 conservative businessmen and self-styled Jeffersonian Democrats founded the American Liberty League to fight for free enterprise, state rights, the open shop, and an end to New Deal bureaucracy.

As the congressional elections of 1934 approached, conservatives within the Liberty League and without campaigned against the New Deal on the grounds that it was destroying the Constitution and driving the country toward bankruptcy. All they succeeded in doing was to drive the dispossessed millions closer to the New Deal. Instead of losing ground to the Republican party—which would have been normal in a midterm election—the Democrats gained an additional ten seats in the Senate and also in the House.

Throughout the nation leaders arose who promised much to those despairing people whom the New Deal had not yet rescued. An elderly physician in California, Dr. Francis E. Townsend, attracted a following of 5 million destitute old people with his plan to obtain a federal pension of $200 per month for everyone over sixty. This would have cost nearly half the national income. The Townsendites claimed, however, that since the pensions would have had to be spent within the month, "the velocity of money" would have ended the depression. The immediate realities of the movement were that its promoters raised nearly a million dollars in two years and commanded a formidable bloc of votes.

Among restless people in Northern cities, Father Charles Coughlin's politico-religious broadcasts attracted a wide following. Starting with a mixture of papal encyclicals and Populism, he at first supported, then went far beyond, Roosevelt. Coughlin advocated silver inflation and nationalization of banks, utilities, and natural resources. Ultimately in 1938 he founded the antidemocratic, anti-Semitic Christian Front. In January 1935 he was able to demonstrate his power by inspiring an avalanche of letters and telegrams to senators protesting against the World Court. His program was vague, but the discontent he was able to tap was concrete.

From the South, Senator Huey P. Long of Louisiana succeeded in launching a far more telling assault upon the New Deal. A skillful politician, he built a powerful organization in Louisiana and a rapidly growing following that spilled out first into neighboring states, then by

1935 into the Middle West, the Pacific Coast, and indeed every part of the country. Within Louisiana, he had delighted his poverty-stricken supporters by immobilizing their traditional enemies through his strong-armed techniques. Within the state, he built bridges, roads, hospitals, and a modern educational system. It was an era of dictators in Europe, and it was easy to assail the self-styled Louisiana Kingfish with ambitions to be a Fuehrer, although his techniques were the time-honored ones of the American political boss. Ambitious to become President, he lured the masses by offering them more than Roosevelt. His "Share Our Wealth" program promised through confiscatory taxes on great fortunes to provide every family with what in those depression years seemed in itself a fortune: an income of $2,500 per year and a homestead worth $5,000. Even in Iowa, farmers guffawed when he called the Secretary of Agriculture "Lord Corn Wallace." The New Dealers' political tactician, Postmaster General James A. Farley, estimated in the spring of 1935 that Long could poll 3 or 4 million votes on a third-party ticket and possibly could throw the 1936 election to the Republicans.

The "thunder from the left" was so ominous early in 1935 that many despairing New Dealers, chafing at Roosevelt's apparent inertia, predicted defeat in 1936. Roosevelt, who never liked to explain his tactics, remarked confidentially that he had no intention of engaging in public debate with the leaders of the "lunatic fringe." Rather, he quietly went about stealing their thunder with the reform programs the New Dealers had long been planning.

THE WORKERS' WELFARE

Frances Perkins, the first woman cabinet member, had accepted the office of labor secretary only with Roosevelt's pledge that he would support a social-security program. For several years, she and a group of New Dealers sought to win converts in the cabinet, in Congress, and throughout the country to their view that social insurance would not only aid the unemployed but also help prevent future depressions.

The Social Security Act of 1935 provided two types of assistance for the aged. Those who were destitute could receive federal aid up to $15 per month, depending upon the matching sums that the states provided. Those who were working could receive upon retirement annuities provided from taxes upon their earnings and their employer's payroll. The 1935 law specified payments, to begin in 1942, ranging from $10 to $85 per month, and excluded wide categories of workers from the program — but it was a beginning. The act also provided for unemployment insurance, aid for the blind and crippled, and assistance for dependent mothers and children, all such funds to be administered by the states in keeping with minimum federal standards. A Social Security Board supervised the entire system.

Social security could not immediately help those already unemployed in 1935; to aid them, Congress in April voted $5 billion to supplant direct relief with the Works Progress Administration. Work relief was more expensive but was essential to prevent the moral erosion, and if possible to save the skills, of the unemployed.

The WPA under Harry Hopkins did much to "help men keep their chins up and their hands in." It enrolled an average of 2.1 million workers between 1935 and 1941 on a wide variety of projects. Since the WPA workers were, theoretically at least, the least employable segment of the working force, and since almost all WPA money went for wages rather than tools and materials, its undertakings could not compare in efficiency with private construction projects. Many people tended to forget this and regard WPA as a politically inspired paradise for loafers. Nevertheless, WPA built nearly 600 airports and built or rebuilt 110,000 public buildings, more than a half-million miles of roads and streets, over 100,000 bridges, a half-million sewers, and over a million privies. In the realm of art, music, and the theater it gave opportunities to a remarkable proportion of the nation's talented people: its writers, for example, produced a useful set of state guidebooks.

The National Youth Administration, established in June 1935, as a sort of "junior WPA," aided young people between sixteen and twenty-five, seven-eighths of whom received student aid in schools and colleges.

Meanwhile, improved living quarters were being provided for working-class families. From the outset in June 1933, the Public Works Administration (PWA—not the same as WPA), through an Emergency Housing Division, began federal sponsorship of public housing. It cleared some of the nation's most notorious slum blocks, replacing them with about fifty developments containing almost 22,000 family units. The rent was an average of $26 per month, too high during these years for many previous slum dwellers to meet. Congress in 1937 finally passed Senator Wagner's bill creating the United States Housing Authority, which with $500 million (later in 1941 increased to $1.6 billion) took over and expanded the housing program to 511 projects with 161,000 units intended for the truly poor. Almost one-third of the units went to Negroes—one of the largest pieces of federal aid they had ever received.

ENCOURAGING UNIONS

For those fortunate enough to be employed, Roosevelt preferred a paternalistic program of wages-and-hours guarantees and social security benefits. Union leaders wanted to use collective bargaining to gain these advantages for their workers, so they would look to the unions, not to the government.

Labor leaders had gained much of what they wanted just before the advent of the New Deal, with the passage in 1932 of the Norris-La Guardia Act. This prohibited the courts from issuing injunctions against most ordinary collective-bargaining practices, and it made unenforceable any "yellow-dog contracts"—pledges from employees that they would not join unions. The Norris-La Guardia Act stopped federal courts from interfering on behalf of employers in struggles with employees. It left management and the unions free to bring economic pressure upon each other as best they could in collective-bargaining procedures.

In the depression years, however, employers were usually stronger than unions. Besides, strikes could interfere with economic recovery. Hence in 1933 Section 7a of the National Industrial Recovery Act affirmed the right of labor to bargain collectively, and led to the establishment of a government agency—the National Labor Board—to settle disputes arising under Section 7a. The relatively weak board was at first favorable to employers.

While Roosevelt had always maintained cordial relations with labor leaders, he was little inclined to give them firm collective-bargaining guarantees in place of the weak Section 7a in the National Industrial Recovery Act. Congress, under the leadership of Senator Robert F. Wagner, felt differently. In May 1935 the Senate passed Wagner's bill providing strong government protection for the unions. Roosevelt, bowing to the inevitable, signed the measure. What he had reluctantly accepted became one of the mainstays of the New Deal. The Wagner Act, passed at a time when unions were relatively weak, outlawed a number of the "unfair practices" by which management had been bludgeoning them, and created a powerful National Labor Relations Board to police the employers. Militant labor thus obtained the governmental backing essential to a

---

The Wagner Act [1935] The National Labor Relations Act made it unlawful for employers to engage in the following unfair labor practices:

1. To interfere with employees in their right to self-organization, to form, join, or assist labor organizations, to bargain collectively through representatives of their own choosing, and to engage in concerted activities, for the purpose of collective bargaining or other mutual aid or protection.

2. To dominate or interfere with the formation or administration of any labor organization or contribute financial or other support to it.

3. By discrimination in regard to hire or tenure of employment or any term or condition of employment to encourage or discourage membership in any labor organization.

4. To discharge or otherwise discriminate against any employee because he has filed charges or given testimony under this Act.

5. To refuse to bargain collectively with the representatives of his employees duly chosen pursuant to other provisions in the Act.

Police Battling Strikers 1937
A newsreel photographer took pictures of the "Memorial Day Massacre," in which policemen wielding guns and billy clubs attacked strikers at the Republic Steel plant in South Chicago. The police killed ten C.I.O. pickets and seriously injured many other demonstrators. (Wide World)

drive to unionize the great mass-production industries.

Even before the adoption of the Wagner Act, union membership had risen from a depression low of less than 3 million to 4.2 million. A group of leaders of industrial unions (which offered membership to everyone within an industry) had chafed over the conservatism of the craft unions (which took in only those working at a given trade). In 1934 men like the head of the United Mine Workers, John L. Lewis, and the leaders of the two great garment unions, Sidney Hillman of the Amalgamated Clothing Workers and David Dubinsky of the International Ladies' Garment Workers, had forced President William Green of the AFL and the craft unionists to agree to charter new industrial unions in the big unorganized industries.

In 1935 organization of these industries began. It led to violent opposition not only from the corporations but also from the AFL craft unions, which feared they would be submerged by the new giant unions. Jurisdictional fights led to a schism between the AFL leadership and the industrial unionists, who formed a Committee for Industrial Organization (within the AFL) in November 1935. Industrial warfare followed, as both the AFL and the CIO mounted great rival organizational drives.

President Roosevelt and a few industrial leaders favored industrial unionism. Gerald Swope of General Electric told Roosevelt that his company could not conceivably negotiate with a large number of craft unions but might find advantages in contracting with a single industrial union. Generally, however, in the spring of 1936 the point was still far off when big business could see advantages in big labor. Vigorous young organizers had to battle it out, often by physical force, with "loyal" strong-arm squads, occasionally with the police, and sometimes with rival organizers. The great difference between this and earlier periods of labor warfare was the aid the federal government provided unions through the National Labor Relations Board.

Through 1936 the United Automobile Workers gained recruits despite vigorous company opposition. There was good reason, for in 1934, at about the time the organizing drive began, nearly half of the auto workers were receiving less than $1,000 per year. General Motors alone, in an effort to keep down union organization, spent almost $1 million on private detectives between 1934 and 1936. In the first two months of 1937, workers closed seventeen General Motors plants through the new device of the sit-down strike, the workers staying by their machinery inside the plants. General Motors soon recognized the UAW, and other automobile companies gradually did the same. Rubber and other industries were similarly organized. Newspapers saw in the sit-down strikes a menace to private property, and much of the public became thoroughly alarmed.

Bloody warfare in the steel industry heightened the alarm. In 1936 the CIO voted a $500,000 fund to organize the industry and began its great onslaught, winning tens of thousands of workers from company unions. United States Steel chose to capitulate rather than face a long strike just as prosperity seemed to be returning. In March 1937, to the amazement of the nation, one of the company's subsidiaries signed a contract with the Steel Workers' Organizing Committee. For the first time, "Big Steel" was unionized. But three of the "Little Steel" companies, under the leadership of Tom Girdler of Republic Steel, resisted furiously. At the Republic plant in South Chicago on Memorial Day 1937, the police killed ten strikers. Republic Steel, according to the prolabor La Follette committee, was the largest purchaser of tear gas and sickening gas in the United States; Youngstown Sheet and Tube Company owned an arsenal of over a thousand weapons. The Republic strikers lost completely, to the relief of middle-class Americans who, like the newspapers they read, blamed the strife upon the unions and the New Deal.

Yet organized labor continued to grow. By 1941 union membership totaled about 9.5 million.

MORE FOR FARMERS

In January 1936 the Supreme Court held that it was unconstitutional for the AAA to regulate farm production or to impose a tax for such a purpose. Congress hastily passed a law (the Soil Conservation and Domestic Allotment Act) to meet the Court's objections and yet continue the crop-reduction effort. Under the new law, Congress appropriated money to pay farmers for conserving the soil by leaving part of their land uncultivated. The law provided that landlords must share with their tenants and sharecroppers the payments for withdrawing land from production. Nevertheless, in 1937, while the average plantation operator was grossing $8,328, of which $833 came from the soil conservation program, the average tenant family received only $385, of which $27 came from the government.

Agricultural interests pressed for a new AAA to cope with an enormous threatened surplus. The end of the drought, increased mechanization, and other improvements like the rapid spread of hybrid corn in the Middle West outmoded the crop controls of the 1936 legislation. The Agricultural Adjustment Act of 1938 – the "second AAA" – provided a number of devices to cut back production: soil conservation payments, marketing quotas, export subsidies, and crop loans. Surpluses of five nonperishable commodities upon which farmers received federal loans would be stored under government seal until needed in lean years, thus creating what Secretary Wallace termed an "ever normal granary." The surpluses so stored were to be of vital aid in feeding allies during the war years. The 1938 act also established a Surplus Marketing Administration to channel surpluses to needy persons and provide food for school lunches.

To improve the condition of the poorer farmers, those on submarginal soil, the government undertook to resettle them on better land. The Resettlement Administration (1935) and its successor, the Farm Security Administration (1937), made short-term loans for rehabilitation and long-term loans for purchasing farms but

**Father and Sons Walking in the Face of a Dust Storm, Cimarron
County, Oklahoma**
*Beginning late in 1933, years of extreme drought and high winds further afflicted
the depression-plagued farmers of the Great Plains. The worst-hit area, centering
on the panhandles of Texas and Oklahoma, eastern Colorado and New Mexico, and
western Kansas, came to be known as the "Dust Bowl." "Only those who have
been caught out in a 'black blizzard' can have more than a faint conception of
its terrors," Lawrence Svobida, a Kansas wheat farmer, has written. "The dust
begins to blow with only a slight breeze. . . . The wind increases its velocity until
it is blowing at forty to fifty miles an hour. Soon everything is moving—the land
is blowing, both farm land and pasture alike. The fine dirt is sweeping along at
express-train speed, and when the very sun is blotted out, visibility is reduced
to some fifty feet; or perhaps you cannot see at all, because the dust has blinded
you and even goggles are useless to prevent the fine particles from sifting into your
eyes."—Lawrence Svobida,* An Empire of Dust *(Caldwell, Idaho: The Caxton
Printers, 1940). (Library of Congress)*

succeeded in moving only a few thousand farm
families.

The more fortunate farmers were benefited by the Rural Electrification Administration,
which was established in 1935 to extend power
lines to farms through cooperatives. Since its
activities also stimulated private power companies to extend into the country, it was effective
both directly and indirectly. Power lines had
reached only 4 percent of the farms in 1925;
they reached 25 percent by 1940.

LESS FOR BIG BUSINESS

After the NRA had been declared unconstitutional, parts of the law were reenacted piecemeal and with alterations to form a "little
NRA." As early as February 1935, in response
to the Supreme Court invalidation of legislation
to prevent the overproduction of oil, Congress
passed the Connally Act prohibiting the shipment of "hot oil" (oil produced in excess of
state limitations) in interstate commerce. The

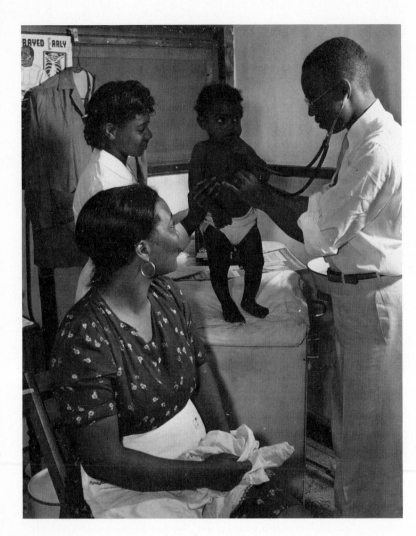

Caring for Farm Workers
The Farm Security Administration tried to relocate and rehabilitate displaced farmers and migrant workers. Here a camp doctor examines a patient at an FSA agricultural camp, Bridgeton, New Jersey, in 1942. From an FSA photograph. (Library of Congress)

Guffey Act of August 1935 virtually reenacted the NRA bituminous-coal code, fixing prices, limiting production, and protecting labor. When the Supreme Court threw out the new coal-control law in 1936, Congress passed the second Guffey Act of 1937. Roosevelt feared a wages-and-hours law would be unconstitutional, but he signed the Walsh-Healey Act of August 1936, setting minimum wages and maximum hours for work done on federal contracts. In order to protect small retailers, the Robinson-Patman Act of 1936 prohibited wholesalers or manufacturers from giving preferential discounts or rebates to chain stores or other large buyers; the Miller-Tydings Act of 1937 fortified state "fair trade" price-fixing laws.

As yet, Roosevelt did not resort to vigorous use of the antitrust laws, but he advocated tightening the regulation of big business. In March 1935 he recommended passage of an act to prohibit after five years the pyramiding of utility holding companies, which had led to flagrant abuses in the 1920s. In the 1930s thirteen companies still controlled three-fourths of the nation's electric power. They fought desperately through the summer of 1935 against what they viewed as a threatened "death sentence." One company alone spent $700,000 lobbying against the measure. In the Holding Company Act of 1935, the companies gained a partial victory; it permitted two strata of holding companies above the operating companies.

Between 1935 and 1940 Congress passed a series of other laws stiffening federal regulation. These strengthened the Federal Power Commission, brought trucks and carriers on inland waterways under the supervision of the Interstate Commerce Commission, created a new Maritime Commission to subsidize and regulate a merchant fleet, and set up a Civil Aeronautics Authority (later Board) to regulate airlines.

One of the most effective ways to regulate was to tax, and in 1935 Roosevelt proposed democratizing the federal tax structure by placing far higher levies upon big corporations and wealthy people. He pointed out that a person receiving $6,000 per year paid twice as high a tax as one receiving $4,000, yet the tax upon a $5 million income was only about five times as high as on $1 million. Conservative newspapers immediately attacked this proposal as a "soak the rich" tax scheme, but it passed Congress. It wiped away the last vestiges of Secretary Mellon's influence on tax policy, as it established the highest peacetime rates in history at the top: a maximum 75 percent income tax, 70 percent estate tax, and 15 percent corporate income tax. It was an important step toward the redistribution of American income.

Big business seemed to have grown bigger through New Deal inadvertence. The NRA relaxation of the antitrust laws had given it an opportunity to thrive at the expense of smaller business. In the two years after the end of the codes, the Attorney General initiated even

fewer antitrust suits than during the NRA period.

Then, in April 1938, the President sent Congress a message vehemently denouncing the unjustifiable concentration of economic power. Less than 5 percent of all corporations in 1935 owned 87 percent of all the assets, he declared. This was leading to such a serious maldistribution of income, he pointed out, that in 1935–1936 the upper 1.5 percent of the population had a share of the national income as great as the 47 percent at the bottom—and these had less than $1,000 per year per family. The remedy, Roosevelt proposed, was to study economic concentration and enact more modern antitrust laws to cope with the newer techniques of monopoly. In response, Congress established the Temporary National Economic Committee under the chairmanship of Senator O'Mahoney. It conducted lengthy public hearings and published thirty-nine volumes of reports and forty-three scientific monographs by the end of 1941. By that time the national attention was entirely engrossed elsewhere; legislation never followed.

Meanwhile, Roosevelt launched an immediate trust-busting program through Thurman Arnold, whom he appointed head of the Antitrust Division of the Department of Justice. Arnold, who felt there was nothing wrong with existing legislation, made new and sophisticated use of the Sherman and Clayton acts as he undertook 215 major investigations and 92 test cases.

The Limits of Reform

In 1936 Roosevelt was at the zenith of his popularity and power. But soon he was to run into stronger political opposition than ever, and by 1938 he was to turn his attention from domestic reform to foreign policy and military defense.

MANDATE FROM THE PEOPLE

Roosevelt's vigorous reform program, enacted in its main outlines by 1936, made him a sure winner in the election of that year. Many millions felt that their personal lot had been improved by the New Deal. The violent attacks upon it from the right, and the cries of anguish

over such measures as the "soak the rich" taxes, convinced them even more that Roosevelt was their friend. Despite the misgivings of many conservatives within the party, the Democratic convention in 1936 renominated him by acclamation. His control was so complete that he even obtained abrogation of the two-thirds rule through which minorities had often hamstrung conventions.

As for the Republicans, they nominated their strongest candidate. Ignoring former President Hoover and the right wing, which was crying calamity, they chose a one-time Bull Mooser who had never strayed far from the 1912 Progressive position. This was the compe-

President Roosevelt's Second Inaugural Address [January 20, 1937]

I see a great nation, upon a great continent, blessed with a great wealth of natural resources. . . . I see a United States which can demonstrate that, under democratic methods of government, national wealth can be translated into a spreading volume of human comforts hitherto unknown, and the lowest standard of living can be raised far above the level of mere subsistence.

But here is the challenge to our democracy: In this nation I see tens of millions of its citizens—a substantial part of its whole population—who at this very moment are denied the greater part of what the lowest standards of today call the necessities of life.

I see millions of families trying to live on incomes so meager that the pall of family disaster hangs over them day by day.

I see millions whose daily lives in city and on farm continue under conditions labeled indecent by a so-called polite society half a century ago.

I see millions denied education, recreation, and the opportunity to better their lot and the lot of their children.

I see millions lacking the means to buy the products of farm and factory and by their poverty denying work and productiveness to many other millions.

I see one-third of a nation ill-housed, ill-clad, ill-nourished.

---

tent governor of Kansas, Alf M. Landon. His running mate was another Bull Mooser who had moved well to the right, the Chicago publisher Frank Knox. The Republican platform promised to do most of what the New Deal was undertaking—but more competently, constitutionally, and without running a deficit. Landon's dry voice could not match Roosevelt's radio eloquence, and Landon was further handicapped because, though he was a moderate, he had to try to hold the militant Republican right.

The election demonstrated the extent to which the New Deal depended upon a coalition of farmers, union men, and the poor. The unions were the heaviest Democratic campaign contributors, providing $1 million. Negroes switched en masse from the party of Lincoln to that of Roosevelt. The "lunatic fringe" coalition against Roosevelt stirred hardly a ripple. Huey Long had been assassinated the year before; the Union party candidate was "Liberty Bell" William Lemke—who was "cracked," said wiseacres. His ticket polled only 890,000 votes; the Socialists, 190,000; the Communists, under 80,000.

A preelection postal card poll by the *Literary Digest* had indicated that Landon would win by a big margin. How could it be so wrong? The names and addresses of those polled were taken from old telephone directories. A majority of people who could afford telephones and had not been forced to move favored Landon. In the election he received 16,680,000 popular votes, compared with 27,477,000 for Roosevelt, and got the electoral votes of only Maine and Vermont.

In the campaign Roosevelt had challenged his right-wing opponents—"economic royalists," he called them—and now he had not only received an overwhelming endorsement for himself, but he had carried with him many congressmen pledged to his support. Nevertheless, those economic royalists would still have the upper hand so long as the Supreme Court continued to check New Deal laws. He felt he had a mandate from the people to do something about the obstructionist Court.

STORM OVER THE COURT

Foes of the Coal Act, the Holding Company Act, the National Labor Relations Act, and the Social Security Act were openly flouting these laws, confident that the Supreme Court would disallow them as it had already done the NRA and the first AAA. The Court, through its narrow interpretation of the federal power over commerce and taxation, and its broad interpretation of freedom of contract in the Fourteenth Amendment, seemed to have created an economic no man's land within which neither the federal nor the state governments could act.

Critics of the Court had been urging passage of some sort of constitutional amendment to provide the federal government with more extensive economic powers. Roosevelt's opinion (which subsequent Supreme Court decisions were to sustain) was that the Constitution granted adequate powers. All that was wrong was the Court's antiquated interpretation, he felt, but the four or five justices firmly opposed to the New Deal enjoyed excellent health and showed no signs of resigning. Consequently Roosevelt decided to propose adding to the Supreme Court — and to lower federal courts — new justices (presumably sharing his viewpoint) to match superannuated ones.

At this point Roosevelt's political sixth sense deserted him and, instead of presenting his proposal frankly and firmly in terms of its economic implications, he enclosed it in a larger scheme. Without informing congressional leaders in advance, in February 1937 he sent a surprise message proposing a needed general overhauling of the federal court system and the appointment of as many as six new Supreme Court justices. His nearest approach to frankness was a statement that the addition of younger blood would revitalize the courts and help them meet the needs and facts of an ever-changing world.

There was no real question about the constitutionality of Roosevelt's proposal, since Congress had from time to time changed the number of justices on the Supreme Court. Nevertheless, the plan aroused a great furor throughout the country. Many thoughtful people who had supported Roosevelt in 1936 heeded the warning of conservatives that, through such constitutional shortcuts, dictators came into power. Within Congress, the controversy cut across party lines. Some Democrats fought against the "packing" of the Court, while the Republican progressive Senator Robert M. La Follette, Jr., supported the President. La Follette declared that the Court had already been "packed" for years "in the cause of Reaction and Laissez-Faire."

Some of the old-line Democratic leaders, especially from the South, had gone along with the New Deal mainly because of party loyalty and pressure from their constituents. Now that

Election of 1936

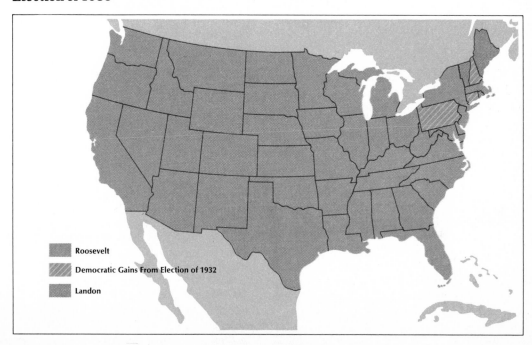

Roosevelt

Democratic Gains From Election of 1932

Landon

"Nine Old Men"
*President Roosevelt justified his plan to enlarge the Supreme Court on the ground
that too many of its members were old men who resisted progress and acted as if
they were still living in the "horse-and-buggy days." This cartoon endorsing
Roosevelt's view appeared in the radical magazine* New Masses *in March 1937.
(Brown Brothers)*

much of the electorate was turning against the administration, these conservatives broke loose. They joined with the bulk of the Republicans to form a new conservative coalition in Congress. Roosevelt fought back by using every device of party discipline to round up votes in Congress. He might have succeeded in obtaining at least a compromise measure, had not the Supreme Court itself eliminated the necessity for one.

The justices — including Louis D. Brandeis, the oldest and most liberal — had been indignant over charges that they were too old to handle the business of the Court. Chief Justice Charles Evans Hughes even wrote a letter insisting that they were not falling behind in their work. Four of them, far to the right, were of no disposition to take a broader view of the Constitution. Three of them took a more progressive if not a New Deal view. Chief Justice Hughes on occasion voted with them, while Justice Owen J. Roberts more often voted with the conservative four.

Just before the President sent his court plan to Congress, Roberts joined with Hughes

and the three more liberal justices in the case of *West Coast Hotel* v. *Parrish* to validate, by a 5-to-4 decision, a state minimum-wage law. This reversed a 5-to-4 decision of the previous year invalidating a similar law. "You may have saved the country," Hughes jubilantly told Roberts. The decision was announced on March 29, 1937. Two weeks later, the Court, again 5-to-4, upheld the Wagner Act, and in May, the Social Security Act. Since there no longer seemed to be any pressing need for judicial reform, the new conservative alliance in Congress easily dealt Roosevelt a personal defeat by voting down his court plan. At the same time, the shift of the Supreme Court's interpretation of the Constitution was a significant victory for Roosevelt and the New Deal.

Almost at once the older justices began retiring, and Roosevelt replaced them one by one with his appointees. In the next decade the Roosevelt Court rewrote large sections of constitutional law. The new justices sharply divided among themselves, but usually upon technical matters. In the main they interpreted the commerce and tax clauses so broadly and

The New Deal: Relief, Recovery, and Reform [1933–1938]

In their New Deal program, President Roosevelt and his advisers sought to achieve three objectives at once: to provide relief for those suffering from the depression, to bring about the recovery of business and agriculture, and to make reforms in the economic system. Not all the measures can be separated and put in neat categories according to the immediate objectives of relief and recovery and the long-range objective of reform; some measures were intended to accomplish more than one of these aims. Nevertheless, the following lists may facilitate an understanding of the complex and multifarious legislation of the period:

Relief and Recovery	Reform
Emergency Banking Act, 1933	Tennessee Valley Authority, 1933
Economy Act, 1933	Federal Securities Act, 1933
Civilian Conservation Corps, 1933	Glass-Steagall Act, 1933
Federal Emergency Relief Administration, 1933	Gold Reserve Act, 1934
Civil Works Administration, 1933	Reciprocal Trade Agreements Act, 1934
Public Works Administration, 1933	Public Utilities Holding Company Act, 1935
National Recovery Administration, 1933	Social Security Act, 1935
Agricultural Adjustment Administration, 1933	National Labor Relations Act, 1935
Farm Credit Administration, 1933	Soil Conservation and Domestic Allotment Act, 1936
Federal Housing Administration, 1934	National Housing Act, 1937
Works Progress Administration, 1935	Farm Security Administration, 1937
	Fair Labor Standards Act, 1938

the Fourteenth Amendment so narrowly that there remained few restrictions upon economic regulation by either the federal or the state governments. For several years the judges tended to restrict governments in their interference with organized labor, but by the end of a decade, labor too was subject to firm restraints. Thus almost all constitutional impediments to government regulation of the economic system were removed.

RECOVERY AND RECESSION

A sharp recession developed in the fall of 1937. It came just as many economists were fearing that an inflationary boom might get out of hand. There had been a remarkable recovery. The national income, which had dropped from $82 billion in 1929 to $40 billion in 1932, was back up to nearly $72 billion. Yet there were still 7.5 million unemployed and nearly 4.5 million families on relief. And there had been no upsurge of capital investment and business expansion as in the 1920s.

Recovery had come because of the enormous sums spent on work relief, the gradual momentum of the public works program, the loans to farmers, and the payment in 1936 (over Roosevelt's veto) of the veterans' bonus. All this government spending had powerfully stimulated the economy. Out of this experience emerged new economic theories, centering upon the concept that the government could help pull the nation out of a depression by liberal expenditures. As a corollary, the government could help curb inflationary booms by means of restrictive policies. These new economic theories came to be known as Keynesianism, after the famed British economist John Maynard Keynes.

In 1937 Roosevelt as much as his Republican opponents abhorred a deficit and worried about the mounting national debt, which had risen to $30 billion. He actually feared another disastrous crash like that of 1929. Acting in terms of the older economics, he had the Federal Reserve tighten credit even though the upswing had been sound rather than speculative. More important, he tried to balance the budget by drastically reducing government spending. Between January and August, 1937, he cut the WPA in half, sending 1.5 million workers on unpaid "vacation."

And since, with the ending of the drought, a huge farm surplus was again imminent, produce prices fell sharply. The fragile new boom collapsed and sent the economy plummeting. The index of production dropped from 117 in August 1937 to 76 in May 1938; 4 million additional workers were thrown out of employment. It seemed like 1932 all over again.

In October 1937 the President called Congress into special session to renew heavy public spending and to reform the "selfish interests" he blamed for the recession. Congress passed an emergency appropriation of $5 billion; the public works and work relief programs once again poured these large sums into the economy, and by June 1938 recovery was under way. The "spending school" had scored a point, and the government seemed to have assumed a new role in warding off threatened economic disaster.

Thus the New Deal entered into its final stage of reform, combining what was as new as Keynesianism with what was as old as progressivism. The trend had been toward big business, and now big government had come with the active intervention of the New Deal in so many aspects of the economy. The number of civilian government employees swelled from 588,000 in 1931 to 1,370,000 in 1941.

Since questions of constitutionality no longer seriously interfered after the changes in the Supreme Court, New Dealers fought the Fair Labor Standards Act through Congress in 1938. This established a minimum wage of 25 cents an hour (to be raised gradually to 40 cents by 1945) and a maximum work week of forty-

four hours (to be lowered to forty) for most laborers, excepting agricultural, domestic, and maritime workers. It also forbade employment of children under sixteen in most areas except agriculture. Low though these standards were, they raised the pay of 300,000 workers and shortened the work week for 1.3 million. In subsequent years the standards were raised repeatedly, and the scope of the law was broadened to include additional categories of workers.

Roosevelt worried about the strong negative power the conservative coalition was developing in Congress. In many states, the Democratic party was under the leadership of conservatives. Postmaster General Farley, in charge of patronage, had done little to aid New Dealers who tried to challenge this leadership. In 1938 Roosevelt intervened in several primaries, mostly in the South, to try to defeat powerful conservative Democrats who headed congressional committees. Since these men had strong organizations behind them, and the New Deal candidates were relatively unknown, the conservatives won in almost every contest. The 1938 elections reflected the degree to which the prestige of Roosevelt and the New Deal were waning. The Republicans gained eighty seats in the House and seven in the Senate. Together with the conservative Democrats, the Republicans could dominate Congress.

By the end of 1938 the New Deal was close to its limits. The threat of a second world war was beginning to overshadow even the most critical domestic problems. The President could drive Congress with its Southern committee chairmen in the direction of strong defense legislation and a vigorous foreign policy only if he conciliated them by abandoning reform.

Culture in the Depression

EXPRESSION AND ESCAPE

Both the depression and the government's efforts to combat it left a mark on the cultural life of the time. Unemployment left many people with unaccustomed leisure, which they used either to protest against or to escape from unpleasant realities. The federal government became a patron and promoter of culture on a scale it had never attempted before.

Even before the establishment of the Federal Art Project, which eventually enrolled 5,000 persons, the government had aided artists through an earlier relief project and the commissioning of extensive murals for new public buildings. Some of these artists expressed leftist themes comparable to those of the highly popular Mexican muralists. Many turned their attention, sometimes satirically, to the American scene. This was the heyday of Grant Wood, with his patterned Iowa landscapes and austere rural portraits, and of Thomas Hart Benton, who with dramatic sympathy portrayed sharecroppers and Negroes. In sculpture, responding to the new government aid and the resurgent nationalism, Gutzon Borglum finished the enormous heads of Washington, Jefferson, Lincoln, and Theodore Roosevelt which were carved on a rocky mountainside in the Black Hills. Altogether, thousands of artists and sculptors worked during the depression years; never before had America possessed so many who were competent and promising.

Appreciation of the arts took a strong upturn, partly through art classes sponsored by the Federal Art Project, partly through the opening of new art museums. In 1941, the National Art Gallery in Washington opened, displaying collections of European art valued at $35 million, the gift of Andrew W. Mellon. Samuel H. Kress added 400 Italian paintings. More people than ever before visited galleries and bought reproductions of the old masters and of the French impressionists, especially Vincent Van Gogh.

Although jazz more than held its own, interest in classical music increased. The Federal Music Project employed 15,000 persons. They brought concerts to 100 million people and gave free music lessons to over a half-million pupils, most of whom could have afforded neither concerts nor lessons. Much of the music they played was that of American composers, such as Roy Harris' Third Symphony, and Aaron Copland's *Music for the Theatre*. Through new high-quality radio receivers and recordings, many additional millions listened to fine music, especially the symphony broadcasts conducted by Arturo Toscanini and the Metropolitan Opera performances. In 1940 listeners contributed over $300,000 to help "save the Met." Many millions more mourned the death in 1937 of young George Gershwin, composer of *Porgy and Bess* and *Rhapsody in Blue*. To the great mass of Americans, music still meant either sweet popular songs played by bands like Guy Lombardo's, or jazz like Benny Goodman's which came surging back into favor in 1934.

After depression and competition from motion pictures had thrown most actors and old vaudeville performers out of employment, the Federal Theater Project found employment for 12,500 of them. It brought performances to millions who had never previously seen a stage production. Some of these were highly successful as entertainment, some were of an advanced experimental nature, and some were so far to the left that they kindled the wrath of Congress, which killed the project in 1939. Many of the Broadway playwrights, impervious to congressional hostility, also took a critical look at social problems, as did Lillian Hellman in *The Little Foxes*. Robert E. Sherwood, who illustrated another trend, stopped writing light comedies and dramatized the impotence of the intellectual (*The Petrified Forest*, 1936) and the menace of war (*Idiot's Delight*, 1936). Later, in the pressure of world events, he reversed themes, and glorified the intellectual fighting totalitarian aggression (*There Shall Be No Night*, 1940). Meanwhile, Thornton Wilder wrote *Our Town* (1938) and Eugene O'Neill, who in 1936 won a Nobel Prize, labored quietly on a long-continuing cycle of plays.

Novelists likewise divided into those who, like William Faulkner, seemed to be largely unaffected by the era, and others like Ernest Hemingway, who paralleled Sherwood's cycle from 1929 (*A Farewell to Arms*) to 1940 (*For Whom the Bell Tolls*). Thomas Wolfe richly and poetically portrayed the world swirling around him, in his *Of Time and the River* (1935) and his posthumous *You Can't Go Home Again* (1940). Many other novelists turned out proletarian themes from Marxist molds. John Steinbeck sentimentalized his suffering protagonists in his best-selling novel about the Oklahoman trek to California, *The Grapes of Wrath* (1939). The lure of romantic escape and the bargain of the sheer bulk helped make best sellers of Hervey Allen's *Anthony Adverse* (1933) and Margaret Mitchell's *Gone with the Wind* (1936).

Reading was one of the most inexpensive pursuits of the depression years, and although libraries suffered from slashed funds, book circulation increased considerably. Depression likewise cut the cost of radios and enlarged the size of audiences. In 1929 12 million families owned radios; by 1940 28 million families, comprising 86 percent of the population, owned them. This in part explains why Roosevelt, the master of the radio "fireside chat," campaigned so successfully with at least 70 percent of the metropolitan newspaper circulation opposing him. A radio serial, *Amos and Andy*, was so popular that Huey Long took the name of one of its characters, the Kingfish, as his so-briquet. Motion-picture audiences dropped one-third early in the depression, then by 1939 boomed to a yearly box-office average of $25 per family. Like radio serials, motion pictures dispensed mostly escapist themes—because of the vigor of the Catholic-led Legion of Decency, founded in 1934, it was a less sexy escape than in the twenties. Theaters also dispensed two movies rather than one and offered give-aways of a wide variety in order to bolster the box office. As yet, the coming threat to the movies, television, was still in the engineering labora-tory—a curiosity exhibited at the New York World's Fair of 1939. It was too expensive for commercial development during the depres-sion.

EDUCATION
AND THE PROFESSIONS

The two depression factors of lack of funds and excess of leisure also operated in education. It was estimated in 1935 that one-third of the unemployed were young people. Many went to school for lack of an alternative, and high school enrollment increased by one-third be-tween 1929 and 1935. In spite of this, economy-minded chambers of commerce and citizens' committees led a drive for cuts so deep that they carved out educational sinew along with the fat. Colleges and universities dropped in enrollment until 1935, then more than recuper-ated but continued to suffer budgetary crises. Vocational education was strongly emphasized on both the high school and the college levels. Serious students explored social and economic questions so energetically that frightened civic and patriotic organizations warned that "pinks" were taking over the educational sys-tems.

Alarmists feared pinks were taking over the churches also, for ministers responded as enthusiastically to the new demands for human welfare as they once had responded to the "so-cial gospel." Of 20,000 ministers polled in 1934, nearly one-third favored socialism, and three-fifths, a "drastically reformed capitalism." The main intellectual current among ministers was toward neoorthodoxy. Reinhold Niebuhr, with-out disavowing political and social liberalism, found powerful psychological pressures driv-ing man toward sin, from which man could be rescued only by faith, that is, submission to God.

Though the depression seriously cut funds for medical research, the thirties were another decade of advance in medical knowledge. Iron-ically, by 1935, when the American Medical Association was warning that 20 million people were suffering malnutrition or were close to it, highly publicized discoveries in vitamin re-search were leading the well-fed to consume a variety of vitamin-fortified foods and to swal-low vitamin pills in quantities second only to laxatives. Sulfa drugs, typhus vaccine, blood plasma, and the "artificial lung" all came into use. Life expectancy increased from fifty-six years in 1920 to sixty-four in 1940, but malnutri-tion, illness, and sometimes lack of good medi-cal care wrought a heavy toll during the de-pression. Army medical examiners rejected almost half of the first 2 million young men Selective Service called up in 1940–1941.

Yet doctors were ill-paid (even in 1929 half of them netted less than $3,000) and were idle much of the time. When some relief units and the Farm Security Administration offered med-ical aid to the destitute, the demand was over-whelming. Senator Wagner in 1938 introduced a national health bill, but it met stern opposition from the American Medical Association. Volun-tary group health and hospitalization plans spread rapidly in some sixty cities and gained 3 million or more subscribers.

While scientists suffered temporary cuts in research funds, university budgets and indus-trial resources for research were back at a peak level by 1936; federal expenditures, by 1940. Thus the decade was one of increasing scientific investigation. The need for reorgani-zation and reinvigoration of some of the gov-ernment's scientific agencies led to the creation in 1933 of a Science Advisory Board, which fu-tilely tried to obtain a New Deal for science. In 1935 the National Resources Committee (succeeding several similar planning agencies) took over the problem and prepared a study, *Research—A National Resource* (1940). The way was being prepared for centralized scien-tific planning in the future.

The thirties were years of marked scien-tific achievement in both basic and applied research in many fields. A series of discoveries by men of many nationalities opened the way to the possibility of nuclear fission. In 1931 Harold C. Urey of Columbia discovered a heavy isotope of hydrogen—deuterium—which, combined with oxygen atoms, formed heavy water. Bombardment of deuterium atoms by various types of atom smashers brought new knowledge about the nature of the atom, knowledge that could lead to revolutionary applications. Science, a neglected stepchild of the New Deal, was to become the nation's savior in time of war.

Selected Readings

Roosevelt and the New Deal
Basil Rauch, *History of the New Deal** (1944); A. M. Schlesinger, Jr., *The Age of Roosevelt: The Coming of the New Deal** (1959) and *The Politics of Upheaval** (1960); W. E. Leuchtenberg, *Franklin D. Roosevelt and the New Deal, 1932–1940** (1963); Frank Freidel, *Franklin D. Roosevelt: The Triumph* (1956); J. M. Burns, *Roosevelt: The Lion and the Fox** (1956); R. G. Tugwell, *The Democratic Roosevelt* (1957); Frances Perkins, *The Roosevelt I Knew** (1946).

Some New Dealers
J. R. Kearney, *Anna Eleanor Roosevelt: The Evolution of a Reformer* (1968); H. L. Ickes, *The New Democracy* (1934); Thurman Arnold, *The Folklore of Capitalism** (1937); Raymond Moley, *After Seven Years* (1939); J. M. Blum, *From the Morgenthau Diaries: Years of Crisis, 1928–1938* (1959); J. J. Huthmacher, *Senator Robert F. Wagner and the Rise of Urban Liberalism* (1968); O. L. Graham, *An Encore for Reform** (1967).

Relief, Recovery, Reform
S. F. Charles, *Minister of Relief: Harry Hopkins and the Depression* (1963); J. A. Salmond, *The Civilian Conservation Corps, 1933–1942* (1967); Roy Lubove, *The Struggle for Social Security, 1900–1935* (1968); Jesse Jones, *Fifty Billion Dollars* (1951), on the RFC; M. L. Eccles, *Economic Balance and a Balanced Budget* (1940), on spending for recovery; H. S. Johnson, *The Blue Eagle from Egg to Earth* (1935); E. W. Hawley, *The New Deal and the Problem of Monopoly* (1966); D. E. Lilienthal, *TVA: Democracy on the March** (1953); T. K. McGraw, *TVA and the Power Fight, 1933–1939* (1971); R. F. de Bedts, *The New Deal's SEC: The Formative Years* (1964); P. K. Conkin, *Tomorrow a New World: The New Deal Community Program* (1959); Richard Polenberg, *Reorganizing Roosevelt's Government* (1966).

The Farmers
H. A. Wallace, *New Frontiers* (1934); J. L. Shover, *Cornbelt Rebellion: The Farmers' Holiday Association* (1965); C. M. Campbell, *The Farm Bureau and the New Deal* (1962); R. S. Kirkendall, *Social Scientists and Farm Politics in the Age of Roosevelt* (1966); D. E. Conrad, *The Forgotten Farmers: The Story of Sharecroppers in the New Deal* (1965); Sidney Baldwin, *Poverty and Politics: The Rise and Decline of the Farm Security Administration* (1968).

The Unions
Irving Bernstein, *New Deal Collective Bargaining Policy* (1950); H. A. Millis and E. C. Brown, *From the Wagner Act to Taft-Hartley* (1950); Herbert Harris, *Labor's Civil War* (1940); Walter Galenson, *The CIO Challenge to the AFL* (1960); J. S. Auerbach, *Labor and Liberty: The La Follette Committee and the New Deal* (1966).

Opposition from Left and Right
D. R. McCoy, *Angry Voices: Left-of-Center Politics in the New Deal Era* (1958) and *Landon of Kansas* (1966); T. H. Williams, *Huey Long* (1969); C. J. Tull, *Father Coughlin and the New Deal* (1965); Abraham Holtzman, *The Townsend Movement* (1963); F. A. Warren, *Liberals and Communism: The "Red Decade" Revisited* (1966); George Wolfskill, *Revolt of the Conservatives* (1962), on the Liberty League; J. T. Patterson, *Congressional Conservatism and the New Deal: The Growth of the Conservative Coalition in Congress, 1933–1939* (1967).

The Supreme Court
E. S. Corwin, *Court over Constitution* (1938); R. H. Jackson, *The Struggle for Judicial Supremacy* (1941); C. H. Pritchett, *The Roosevelt Court* (1948).

Aspects of Life
F. L. Allen, *Since Yesterday* (1940); R. S. and H. M. Lind, *Middletown in Transition* (1935); Leo Gurko, *Angry Decade* (1947); Dorothea Lange and P. S. Taylor, *An American Exodus: A Record of Human Erosion in the Thirties* (1969); G. B. Tindall, *The Emergence of the New South, 1913–1945* (1967); D. T. Carter, *Scottsboro: A Tragedy of the American South* (1969).

Cultural Expression
Harvey Swados, ed., *The American Writer and the Great Depression** (1966); Daniel Aaron, *Writers on the Left** (1961); J. D. Mathew, *The Federal Theatre, 1935–1939* (1967); R. D. McKinzie, *The New Deal for Artists* (1972).

*Titles available in paperback.

The Abandonment of Isolation

PEACE
WITHOUT
VICTORY

VERSAILLES

Twenty-five

Having fought a war to end war and make the world safe for democracy, Americans of the 1920s were generally optimistic about the prospects whenever they gave thought to international affairs. True, the United States had failed to join the League of Nations, the organization that was intended to keep the peace. But this country took the lead in bringing the nations of the world to renounce war in the Kellogg Pact (1928), which many people hailed as the sign of a warless future. Henceforth, said admirers of the pact, aggressive war was illegal.

Optimism faded after the great depression struck. During the 1930s, Japan under fanatical militarists, Germany under Hitler and the Nazis, and Italy under Mussolini and the Fascists each launched programs of domestic tyranny and foreign conquest. Opposed to these aggressive nations were the contented powers of Europe—Great Britain, France, and the Soviet Union—which disagreed on many things but had a common interest in maintaining the status quo.

The American government faced a choice between two broad lines of policy. On the one hand, the United States might back Great Britain, France, and the Soviet Union (if they could manage to get together themselves) in the hope that all somehow could and would provide for their "collective security," enforce the Kellogg Pact, prevent aggression, and maintain peace—though in this there was the real risk of hastening a general war. On the other hand, the United States might follow a policy of so-called isolation. That is, this country might strengthen its position in the Western Hemisphere and concentrate on keeping out of war instead of preventing it.

Most of the American people favored the second of these alternatives. They were preoccupied with the depression and were determined to set their own country to rights, regardless of what might go on in the rest of the world. They were disillusioned about their

"Lest We Forget———"
As Americans faced the question of involvement in World War II, they were reminded of their disillusionment with World War I, which they had joined in order, supposedly, to "end war" and "make the world safe for democracy." This cartoon by Daniel R. Fitzpatrick of the St. Louis Post-Dispatch *was published on August 25, 1940.*

earlier effort to bring peace through war—
more than 70 percent of them, according to
an opinion poll in 1937, thought it had been
a mistake to go to war in 1917—and they
were in no mood to go on a second crusade.
Ever regardful of public opinion, President
Roosevelt hesitated to come out openly and
clearly in favor of collective security even
after the long-expected war had broken out

in Europe in 1939. He continued to talk the
language of isolationism, representing his
policy as one of keeping out of war, while he
committed the country to greater and greater
support of Great Britain and her allies. The
issues became more and more confused as
the debate between "interventionists" and
"isolationists" grew hotter. Suddenly, on
December 7, 1941, the debate was stilled.

Depression Diplomacy

Herbert Hoover—a Quaker, an engineer, and a
man of wide experience in international affairs—was impressed by the wastefulness of
war as a human enterprise. As President, he
held the United States to a rather modest and
cautious role in world politics. Franklin D.
Roosevelt, an admirer of his cousin Theodore
Roosevelt's bold and vigorous approach, favored an active role for the United States, but
during his first term he was restrained by his
preoccupation with the New Deal as well as by
his concern for public opinion.

HOOVER-STIMSON POLICIES

With regard to Latin America, Hoover continued the movement that under his successor
became the Good Neighbor policy. Before his
inauguration he toured much of the hemisphere, promoting good will; during his administration he prepared for the removal of marines from Haiti and finally withdrew them
from Nicaragua. He refused to intervene in
Cuba, which was restless under a dictatorship.
Throughout Latin America, as depression top-
pled about half the regimes, he recognized de
facto rulers without questioning the means by
which they had come into power. Even when
several countries defaulted on their obligations
in October 1931, he did not press them to pay or
threaten to seize their customs houses.

With reference to Europe, policy became
increasingly concerned with economic conditions as the depression deepened. The moratorium on war-debt and reparations payments,
begun in June 1931, aided Europe temporarily.
Secretary of State Henry L. Stimson wished it

to lead to a general cancellation of these obligations but could not convince the President, who
considered them sacred. Soon Germany
ceased reparations payments, and nations
owing money to the United States, except for
Finland, began to default or make mere token
payments.

With regard to the Far East, policies were
aimed at safeguarding American rights while
preserving peace. As unstable conditions in
China continued throughout the 1920s, the
United States could do little to protect China
from the encroachments of strong nations. As
Russia became stronger, she built up her forces
in eastern Siberia, and in 1929, when China
tried to oust her from northern Manchuria,
Russia fought an undeclared war to retain her
foothold. Stimson tried to invoke the Kellogg-
Briand Pact, which outlawed war, and to bring
about mediation; he failed, demonstrating the
weakness of the pact.

Japanese military leaders, feeling that
their treaty rights in southern Manchuria were
being threatened both by the Russians and by
the Chinese Nationalists under Chiang Kai-
shek, wrested the initiative from the Japanese
foreign office in a manner little short of mutiny. In September 1931 they launched a large-
scale military campaign in Manchuria at a
time when the United States and Great Britain
were preoccupied with the monetary crisis.
For several weeks Stimson was moderate, in
the hope that the civilians in the Japanese
cabinet could regain control; the British were
even less disposed to pursue a strong policy.
The Japanese foreign office engaged in conciliatory talk but was unable to alter events as the
army plunged deeper into Manchuria. By
January 2, 1932, the conquest was complete.

The Stimson Doctrine [1932]

The American Government . . . can not admit the legality of any situation de facto nor does it intend to recognize any treaty or agreement entered into between those governments, or agents thereof, which may impair the treaty rights of the United States or its citizens in China, including those which relate to the sovereignty, the independence, or the territorial and administrative integrity of the Republic of China, or to the international policy relative to China, commonly known as the open-door policy; and . . . it does not intend to recognize any situation, treaty, or agreement which may be brought about by means contrary to the covenants and obligations of the pact of Paris of August 27, 1928, to which treaty both China and Japan as well as the United States, are parties.

Identical notes were sent to Japan and China, January 7, 1932.

As early as October 1931, Stimson had felt the United States might have to cooperate with the League of Nations in imposing economic sanctions against Japan even though these might lead to war. Hoover strongly opposed such action and, in cabinet meetings, discouraged Stimson by referring to the Washington treaties and the Kellogg-Briand Pact as scraps of paper. He learned from the British that they too opposed sanctions. Hoover was willing to allow Stimson to exert moral suasion against the Japanese, and suggested that he apply the doctrine of nonrecognition against territorial changes brought by force of arms. Stimson did so on January 7, 1932.

The American people were eager to see the United States assume moral leadership — and nothing more — against aggression. Their ideal was international disarmament, not policing. Hoover himself took the same view.

After the Geneva Conference of 1927 had failed to extend quotas to destroyers, cruisers, and submarines, the United States had threatened to begin a substantial building program. Hoover, fearing a naval race, called a conference which opened in London in January 1930. There the United States, Great Britain, and Japan agreed not to build the capital ships authorized under the Washington treaty, and even to scrap some existing ships. They also agreed to ratios on smaller ships, to continue until 1936.

The United States participated vigorously in the World Disarmament Conference that opened under League sponsorship at Geneva in February 1932. With the Japanese attacking Shanghai, and Hitler daily winning new converts to his militaristic Nazi movement in Ger-many, the French firmly demanded an international army and compulsory arbitration rather than disarmament. In June 1932 Hoover tried to break the deadlock with a proposal to abolish immediately all offensive weapons, such as bombing planes and tanks, and to cut all land and naval forces approximately 30 percent. Despite much enthusiasm for the proposal, nothing came of it.

SEEKING FRIENDS AND CUSTOMERS

President Roosevelt inherited from the Hoover administration the questions of war-debt settlements, disarmament, and currency stabilization. He did not share Hoover's view that the proper settlement of these was a key to recovery. In April 1934 he signed an act sponsored by Senator Hiram Johnson, forbidding private loans to any defaulting nations; from then on all war-debt payments, except those from Finland, stopped altogether. Meanwhile, the United States continued to assert a strong moral position to try to bring about substantial disarmament. But Hitler was bent upon rearming, not disarming, and in October he withdrew from both the Geneva Conference and the League of Nations. A new arms race was under way.

In the same months that hopes for an arms settlement collapsed, so did those for international economic stabilization, and the blame this time was assessed against Roosevelt. He had agreed to cooperate in the World Economic Conference which President Hoover had called to meet in London in June 1933. He

Secretary of State Cordell Hull
*Secretary Hull (1871–1955), born in a log
cabin in backwoods Tennessee, was first
elected to Congress in 1907. Except for two
years as chairman of the Democratic
National Committee, he served in one or the
other house of Congress until 1933, strongly
advocating lower tariffs. William L. Langer
and S. Everett Gleason in* The Challenge to
Isolation *have analyzed his policies this
way: "Even earlier than Mr. Roosevelt, he
had sensed the dangers in the world
situation and had warned the country of
them. As a man of great integrity and high
principle he was especially disturbed by the
rapidly progressing breakdown of
international law and morality. His
prescription against this menace was
reaffirmation of traditional standards of
justice and fair dealing, insistence on the
value of peaceful methods to settle
international differences, and return to more
liberal trade relations as the only way to
alleviate the existing world tension. His was
a somewhat rigid, doctrinaire approach,
criticized by those who felt that his constant
harping on general principles revealed a
disinclination to come to grips with
concrete, practical problems. Mr. Hull was a
man of the people and as such easily moved
to that moral indignation characteristic of
the American people when confronted by
the iniquities of foreigners." (New York:
Harper & Row, 1952.) (Karsh, Ottawa)*

gave vague assurances to the representatives
of eleven countries who visited him in advance
that he favored currency stabilization, which
he announced on May 16 was essential to
"establish order in place of the present chaos."
This was the policy under which Secretary of
State Cordell Hull, a firm believer in international economic cooperation, and the American delegation went to London. After their
arrival, President Roosevelt changed his mind,
deciding that currency stabilization would be
disadvantageous until the dollar had fallen to a
competitive position on the world market.
Whatever chance of agreement there had been
disappeared when Roosevelt on July 3, 1933,
cabled Hull a "bombshell message" disavowing
currency stabilization.

The hope of stimulating foreign trade led
Roosevelt to recognize Soviet Russia in November 1933. Since the revolution of November 1917, the Russian government had gone
unrecognized while a number of irritating
questions between the two nations continued
to fester. Americans, hungry for what they
unrealistically dreamed would be a substantial
Russian trade, were eager for recognition.
The Russians had even stronger motives
for obtaining recognition, for they were
afraid of being attacked by Japan. Maxim Litvinov, the Russian foreign minister, after discussions with Roosevelt at the White House,
agreed that Russia would end its propaganda
activities in the United States, guarantee religious freedom and protection in the courts to
Americans resident in Russia, and negotiate a
settlement of debts and claims.

By January 1934 Roosevelt was ready to
listen seriously to Hull's homilies on the necessity of lowering tariff barriers in order to improve foreign trade. With Roosevelt's support,
Congress (in June 1934) passed Hull's cherished program, the Reciprocal Trade Agreements Act. It authorized the administration to
negotiate agreements, lowering tariffs by as
much as 50 percent on specified goods coming
in from individual nations in return for their
reducing tariffs on American goods.

The immediate effect of the reciprocal
trade agreements is difficult to estimate. During the depression years they were drafted
carefully to admit only products not competitive with American industry and agriculture.
By 1939 Hull had negotiated agreements with

twenty-one countries, ranging from Cuba to the United Kingdom. These lowered the tariff an estimated 29 percent, at the same time that they gained concessions for American export- ers, especially growers of cotton and tobacco. By the end of 1938 American exports to the six- teen nations with which it then had trade agreements had increased nearly 40 percent.

At the Inter-American Conference at Mon- tevideo in December 1933, Hull won such ac- claim with his proposals for reciprocity that President Roosevelt gave him full support upon his return home. To small nations like Cuba, dependent upon exports to the United States, reciprocity seemed a way out of the depression. While Hull offered economic suc- cor, he reiterated to the people of Latin Ameri- ca at Montevideo (and Roosevelt said the same thing in Washington), that the United States was opposed to armed intervention in Latin America. Hull even signed a convention declar- ing: "No state has the right to intervene in the internal or external affairs of another."

Thus Hull took the United States a step further than the Hoover administration, which had unofficially disavowed the Theodore Roo- sevelt Corollary to the Monroe Doctrine but had reserved the right to intervene in self- defense. This seemed to be the American policy, as late as the summer of 1933, when revolution exploded in Cuba. Sumner Welles, one of the chief draftsmen of the new Latin American policy, was sent into Cuba to offer the "good offices" of the United States. Welles helped bring pacification without calling in the marines. In 1934, when a more conservative government came into power in Cuba, the United States gave up its right of intervention under the Platt Amendment. It also withdrew the last marines from Haiti and negotiated a treaty (not ratified until 1939) relaxing the restrictions upon Panama.

The new Good Neighbor policy of nonin- tervention received a severe testing in 1938 when Mexico expropriated all foreign oil hold- ings, including property valued by its American owners at $200 million. The United States con- ceded the right of expropriation but at first con- tended that the price the Mexicans wished to pay was so trivial as to be confiscation. In 1942, after years of involved controversy, a commis- sion evaluated the property at $24 million, and the State Department then told the protesting

oil companies that they must accept the settle- ment or receive nothing. This renunciation of the right to intervene for the purpose of pro- tecting American property in Latin Ameri- ca was a reversal of dollar diplomacy. In encouraging trade, the new policy was of immediate benefit. It came to be even more valuable in promoting mutual defense, as the threat of war in Europe increased.

As for the Philippines, primarily the de- pression and secondarily isolationism brought them the long-sought but economically dubious blessing of independence. American producers of sugar, fats, and oils were determined to push their Filipino competitors outside the tariff wall. Isolationists were also eager to drop this dangerous Far Eastern military commitment. The Tydings-McDuffie Act of 1934 thrust upon the Philippines complete independence rather than the dominion status they sought. In 1935 the Philippines entered upon a transitional commonwealth period; on July 4, 1946, they became a fully independent republic. The United States was demonstrating that it was trying to rid itself of possessions rather than seize new ones.

At the London Naval Conference of 1935, the Japanese withdrew after they failed to ob- tain equality with the Americans and British in place of the 5:5:3 ratio, and thus the way was opened for competitive naval building. The United States soon turned to building the fleet with which it was later to fight the opening bat- tles of a Pacific war.

LEGISLATING NEUTRALITY

With the breakdown of the naval status quo and the threatened aggressions in both Asia and Europe, most Americans felt that at all costs they must stay out of impending wars. Many leaders of the peace movement – dedi- cated Wilsonians and advocates of the League – had become disgusted with the League's inability to stop Japanese aggression. They reasoned that internationalism had failed to maintain the peace. Others, taking an eco- nomic-determinist view of wars, concluded that Wall Streeters and munitions makers, along with Wilson's legalistic insistence upon out- moded neutral rights on the high seas, had trapped the nation into World War I. Senate investigators, under the progressive Republican Gerald P. Nye of North Dakota, revealed exorbitant wartime profits and tax evasion and claimed that bankers had sought war to rescue their loans to the Allies. President Roosevelt, himself impressed by the Nye investigation, privately wrote his regret that Bryan had left the State Department in 1915.

The Nye Committee findings and similar sensational popular writings convinced a large part of the public that entrance into World War I had been a frightful mistake. The way to avoid its repetition seemed to be to legislate against the supposed causes. As Mussolini openly prepared to conquer Ethiopia in 1935, Americans feared that a general European war might develop. They felt that the way to avoid involvement was not to participate in strong deterring pressure against Italy, since Mussolini might strike back. Rather it was to isolate the nation by means of neutrality laws.

President Roosevelt also favored legislation, but he desired, as Hull had proposed in 1933, a law that would enable the President to embargo war supplies to the aggressor and allow their sale to the victim. But Congress passed a neutrality act providing a mandatory embargo against both aggressor and victim and empowering the President to warn American citizens that they might travel on vessels of belligerents only at their own risk. This first Neutrality Act of 1935, a temporary measure, was renewed in 1936 and again, with even stronger provisions, in 1937.

When the attack upon Ethiopia came, in October 1935, the League branded Italy an aggressor and voted sanctions against her. England and France made gestures against Italy but showed no inclination toward determined action. Hull imposed a "moral embargo" upon oil. Mussolini easily conquered his African empire, and then withdrew from the League. In October 1936 he joined with Hitler to form a new Rome-Berlin axis.

All this seemed to strengthen the determination of the American people to stay out of war. The new public opinion polls (based on samplings of only 1,500 to 3,500 people, with a probable error of 4 to 6 percent) indicated top-heavy opinion against involvement. A typical poll in November 1935, after the attack on Ethiopia, queried: "If one foreign nation insists upon attacking another, should the United States join with other nations to compel it to stop?" The answer: yes, 28 percent; no, 67 percent; no opinion, 5 percent.

This anti-involvement sentiment continued to be the mood of the nation when a new danger arose in July 1936, as General Francisco Franco and the Falangists (modeled after the Fascists) revolted against the republican government in Spain. Hitler and Mussolini sided with Franco; Russia, France, and, to a lesser extent, Great Britain favored the Loyalists. To prevent the Spanish Civil War from spreading into a general European conflict, England and France agreed to send no aid to either side. Roosevelt, trying to cooperate with France and England, persuaded Congress to apply the existing Neutrality Act to civil as well as international wars. The result was that the United States and other Western nations denied assistance to republican Spain. The republican government came to depend increasingly upon Russia for what little help it received. As for Franco, he received massive aid from Mussolini and Hitler, and ultimately crushed the Loyalists.

American feelings became inflamed over the invasion of Ethiopia and the Spanish Civil War, but President Roosevelt voiced the majority attitude in August 1936, a month after the outbreak of the war in Spain, when he asserted: "We shun political commitments which might entangle us in foreign wars; we avoid connection with the political activities of the League of Nations. . . . We are not isolationists except in so far as we seek to isolate ourselves completely from war."

World War Again

A great Japanese drive into the five northern provinces of China began in the summer of 1937. At first the State Department pursued a middle-of-the-road policy, favoring neither country. Japan avoided declaring war, and President Roosevelt did not invoke the Neutrality Act. Private American ships at their own risk could carry arms and munitions to both belligerents. The administration's purpose was to help the Chinese, who needed American supplies more than the Japanese did.

FACING JAPAN AND GERMANY

By October 1937 the administration was ready to take a firm position against Japan. The British proposed a joint arms embargo, which seemed to involve no great risk. At this time and during the next four years, the consensus of the experts was that Japan was a mediocre military power. Hull persuaded Roosevelt to make a statement to counteract isolationism. The President, speaking in Chicago, declared: "The peace-loving nations must make a concerted effort in opposition to those violations of treaties and those ignorings of humane instincts which today are creating a state of international anarchy, international instability from which there is no escape through mere isolation or neutrality." War, he asserted, was a contagion which must be quarantined by the international community.

There is evidence that Roosevelt had in mind nothing more drastic than a collective breaking off of diplomatic relations, that he did not favor economic or military sanctions. Immediate press reaction and White House mail was favorable, but within a few days, as the Chicago *Tribune* and Hearst press continued to draw sinister implications from the "quarantine" speech, it plunged the nation, as the *Tribune* reported, into a "hurricane of war fright." This set back Roosevelt in his thinking. In November 1937 he sent a delegate to an international conference in Brussels to consider the Japanese aggression—but instructed him neither to take the lead nor to be a tail to the British kite.

Japan had no need to fear economic or military reprisals from the United States. On December 12, 1937, young Japanese aviators bombed and sank the United States gunboat *Panay* on the Yangtze River. The aviators claimed they bombed it in error, but visibility was excellent and an American flag was painted on the deck. As at the sinking of the *Maine* in 1898, a wave of excitement swept the country, but this time it was fear that the nation might become involved in war. The United States quickly accepted the profuse Japanese apologies and offers of indemnity.

At the end of 1938, as the Japanese supplanted the Open Door with their so-called New Order in East Asia, they were making conditions almost untenable for Americans in China. But the threat of war in Europe overshadowed the Asian impasse.

The traditional American isolationism, as exemplified by Hearst editorials and the speeches of several senators, implied strict nonintervention in Europe but a considerably more active role in Asia—no sanctions, but an insistence upon the Open Door in China. Within the Western Hemisphere, these isolationists were ready to give the President almost a free hand toward both Canada and Latin America. Indeed there were no more devout exponents of the Monroe Doctrine than they.

Roosevelt took full advantage of these feelings to inaugurate, within the hemisphere, policies that he could later apply across the Atlantic and the Pacific. In December 1936 he traveled all the way to Buenos Aires to put his personal prestige behind a pact to enlarge the Monroe Doctrine into a mutual security agreement. Henceforth, if any outside power threatened the American republics, instead of the United States acting unilaterally they would all consult together for their own protection. The understanding covered disputes among the republics themselves but was specifically aimed at meeting the threat of the Axis. It provided that the members would consult "in the event of an international war outside America which might menace the peace of the American Republics." In December 1938, with war in Europe imminent, the republics, at a meeting in Lima, Peru, established a means of consultation. Roosevelt also extended hemispheric security to the north when he issued a declaration of solidarity with Canada in August 1938.

By 1938 Hitler had rebuilt such a strong German army and air force that he was ready to embark upon a course of intimidation and conquest. In March he proclaimed union with Austria and paraded triumphantly through Vienna. This union put western Czechoslovakia into the jaws of a German vise. Hitler began tightening it with demands on behalf of the minority of 3.5 million Germans in Czechoslovakia. In September 1938 he brought Europe to the brink of war with his demands for the cession of the Sudeten area in which the minority lived. The Czechs, who had a strong army, were ready to fight rather than submit, but the people of other Western nations, appalled at the threat of another world conflict, were eager for a settlement on almost any terms. Roosevelt joined in the pleas to Hitler for a peaceful solution. At Munich on September 29 the French and the British signed a pact with Hitler granting his demands in Czechoslovakia. "This is the last territorial claim I have to make in Europe," he declared.

Within a few weeks, the once strong Czechoslovakia was whittled down to impotence. In March 1939 Hitler took over the remaining areas as German protectorates, thus demonstrating the worthlessness of his Munich pledge. In April, he began harassing Poland. The British and French, seeing clearly that appeasement had failed, gave firm pledges to Poland and to other threatened nations. They made half-hearted gestures toward Russia, which had been left out of the Munich settlement, but Stalin signed a nonaggression pact with Hitler in August. This freed Hitler to attack Poland if he could not frighten that country into submission. Poland stood firm, and Germany invaded her territory on September 1, 1939. Great Britain and France, true to their pledges, declared war on Germany on September 3. World War II had begun.

AIDING THE ALLIES

With the outbreak of war, Roosevelt issued a neutrality proclamation pointedly different from Wilson's 1914 plea for Americans to be impartial in thought as well as action. "This nation will remain a neutral nation," Roosevelt stated, "but I cannot ask that every American remain neutral in thought as well."

Promptly, Roosevelt called Congress into special session and, despite a heated debate, was able to muster the votes for a revision of the Neutrality Act. The 1939 measure still prohibited American ships from entering the war zones, but it allowed belligerents to purchase arms on a "cash-and-carry" basis. Had England and France been able to defeat Hitler with this limited assistance, Roosevelt probably would have been satisfied with it. Indeed, after the quick Nazi overrunning of Poland, over-optimistic American publicists during the quiet winter of 1939–1940 asserted that the Allies were calling Hitler's bluff and, after a long and

boring blockade on sea and land, would triumph. During these months of the "phony war," American indignation flared hottest over the Russian invasion of Finland. The administration applied a tight "moral embargo" on shipments of munitions to Russia but went no further.

Optimistic illusions about Hitler's weakness turned into panic in the spring of 1940 when the Nazis invaded Denmark and Norway, then swept across Holland and Belgium deep into France. On May 16 Roosevelt asked Congress for an additional billion for defense expenditures and obtained it quickly. On the premise that the United States must build great air armadas to hold off the Nazis, he set a goal of at least 50,000 airplanes a year.

On June 10, 1940, Mussolini joined the Germans by attacking France. Roosevelt that evening asserted: "The hand that held the dagger has struck it into the back of its neighbor." And, with France tottering from the German onslaught, he proclaimed that the United States would "extend to the opponents of force the material resources of this nation." He was taking the United States from a status of neutrality to one of nonbelligerency on the side of the democracies.

Twelve days later France fell, and in all western Europe only the shattered remnants of the British army that had been retrieved from Dunkirk opposed the Nazis. Already the new prime minister, Winston Churchill, was showering Roosevelt with requests for destroyers and arms of all kinds to help the British man their bastion. The odds against the British were heavy, but Roosevelt made the bold and dangerous decision to "scrape the bottom of the barrel" and make it possible for the British to buy all available war materials. As the Germans, preparing for an invasion, began to bomb Britain from the air, Roosevelt gave Britain fifty overage destroyers in return for ninety-nine-year leases on eight bases to be located on British possessions ranging from Newfoundland to British Guiana in the Western Hemisphere. The "destroyer deal" was, as Churchill later wrote, "a decidedly unneutral act." Roosevelt also turned back to the factories government-purchased war planes to be resold to Britain. In September 1940 he gave an indication that aid would not be confined indefinitely to materials alone when he pushed through Congress the Burke-Wadsworth bill, which inaugurated the first peacetime conscription of men in American history.

Roosevelt threw the resources of the United States behind the British as completely as Congress would let him. He did so with the feeling that an Axis victory would mean disaster to the nation. A large part of the public suddenly seemed to agree. In March 1940 only 43 percent of those polled thought a German victory would be a threat to the United States; by July, 69 percent did. In May 1940 only 35 percent favored aid to Britain at the risk of American involvement; four months later, 60 percent did. Yet as late as November 1941 only 20 percent of those polled favored a declaration of war against Germany. Roosevelt and the American public seemed to share incompatible aims. They wished to bring about the defeat of the Axis without involving the United States in a shooting war. Sometime in the next eighteen months, Roosevelt probably came to feel that complete entrance into the war was desirable; the public never did.

"INTERVENTION" OR "ISOLATION"?

The whole country was drawn into a great debate on the issue of neutrality as against all-out aid to the Allies. With a rather careless use of words on both sides, the advocates of neutrality called their opponents "interventionists," and the advocates of all-out aid responded with the term "isolationists."

William Allen White, the Kansas editor, headed the Committee to Defend America by Aiding the Allies, often called the White Committee. White himself (like a large percentage of Americans) favored merely aid, but a minority wanted to go further and declare war. In April 1941 this group founded the Fight for Freedom Committee. On the anti-involvement side, a Yale student, R. Douglas Stuart, Jr., organized an America First Committee under the chairmanship of a leading Chicago businessman, General Robert E. Wood. It drew upon the oratorical talent of the aviation hero Charles Lindbergh, General Hugh Johnson, and Senators Nye and Wheeler. It won the editorial support of the Hearst and other large newspapers. It appealed to a considerable

segment of patriotic Americans, and inevitably it also attracted a small fringe of pro-Nazi, anti-Semitic, and American Fascist fanatics. The debate was bitter, and through the summer and fall of 1940 it was complicated by a presidential election.

The Republicans met at Philadelphia in June, at the time of the collapse of France. National defense suddenly became the most important issue. Roosevelt underscored this and stole headlines from the Republican convention by appointing to his cabinet two of the most distinguished Republicans. He made the elder statesman Henry L. Stimson, secretary of war, and the 1936 vice-presidential candidate and sharp critic of the New Deal, Frank Knox, secretary of the navy.

The chagrined Republicans at Philadelphia promptly read Stimson and Knox out of the party but could not ignore the defense issue. They succumbed to the grassroots pressure, which had been built up through a careful advertising campaign, and nominated a young internationalist, Wendell Willkie. This was a startling blow to the isolationist majority among the Republican politicians, but it provided them with a tousle-haired, personable candidate who could win hysterical devotion from the amateur party workers. Both the platform and the candidate pledged that the nation would be kept out of war but would aid peoples fighting for liberty.

By the time the Democrats met in mid-July, it was a foregone conclusion that they would renominate Roosevelt. He was even able to force the Democratic politicians to swallow his choice for Vice President, Secretary of Agriculture Henry A. Wallace, who was considered an advanced New Dealer.

Willkie embarked upon an appealing but slightly amateurish campaign, whistle-stopping so vigorously that he nearly lost his voice, denouncing the bad management of the New Deal rather than its basic program, and always referring to his opponent as "the third-term candidate" (no President had ever run for a third term before). Numerous right-wing Democrats and even some early New Dealers like Moley and General Johnson supported him. John L. Lewis threatened to resign as president of the CIO if Willkie were not elected—a possibility that did not seem to frighten organized labor.

Lindbergh's Isolationist Argument [1941]

I know I will be severely criticized by the interventionists in America when I say we should not enter a war unless we have a reasonable chance of winning. . . . But I do not believe that our American ideals, and our way of life, will gain through an unsuccessful war. And I know that the United States is not prepared to wage war in Europe successfully at this time. . . .

There is a policy open to this nation that will lead to success—a policy that leaves us free to follow our own way of life, and to develop our own civilization. It is not a new and untried idea. . . .

It is based upon the belief that the security of a nation lies in the strength and character of its own people. It recommends the maintenance of armed forces sufficient to defend this hemisphere from attack by any combination of foreign powers. It demands faith in an independent American destiny. This is the policy of the America First Committee today. It is a policy not of isolation, but of independence; not of defeat, but of courage.—The New York Times, April 24, 1941.

Roosevelt, a wily old campaigner, tried to give the appearance of not campaigning at all. Defense problems were so acute, he insisted, that he had to spend his time touring army bases, munitions plants, and shipyards. He followed routes that somehow took him through innumerable cities, where he cheerily greeted quantities of voters.

Foreign policy was paramount. On this, both Willkie and Roosevelt had much the same views. Willkie approved of the destroyers-bases agreement. Both made fervent antiwar

---

Election of 1940

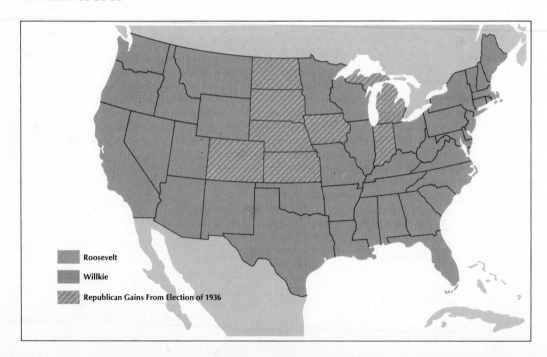

Roosevelt

Willkie

Republican Gains From Election of 1936

"Stop Hitler Now!" [1940]

We Americans have naturally wished to keep out of this war — to take no steps which might lead us in. But —

We now know that every step the French and British fall back brings war and world revolution closer to US — our country, our institutions, our homes, our hopes for peace.

Hitler is striking with all the terrible force at his command. His is a desperate gamble, and the stakes are nothing less than domination of the whole human race. . . .

WE CAN HELP — IF WE ACT NOW — before it is forever too late.

We can help by sending planes, guns, munitions, food. We can help to end the fear that American boys will fight and die in another Flanders, closer to home. . . .

The United States of America is still the most powerful nation on earth — and the United States of America is YOU!" — Advertisement written by Robert Sherwood for the Committee to Defend America by Aiding the Allies and widely published in June 1940.

---

statements to placate the isolationists. Willkie declared that if Roosevelt's promise to stay out of a foreign war was no better than his pledge to balance the budget, the boys were "already almost on the transports." This was an effective campaign issue which cut into Roosevelt's support. In Boston, Roosevelt (making the mental reservation that any attack upon the United States would not be a foreign war) picked up the challenge in words the isolationists were to mock incessantly: "I have said this before, but I shall say it again and again and again: Your boys are not going to be sent into any foreign wars."

A large part of the vote of those opposing aid to the Allies went to Willkie. Those favoring vigorous aid or even intervention (including many who fervently opposed New Deal domestic policies) voted for Roosevelt. They preferred Roosevelt's sure leadership to Willkie's inexperience. It was a relatively close vote: 27,244,000 for Roosevelt, and 22,305,000 for Willkie; 449 electoral votes to 82. The combined third-party vote was less than 200,000. Within a few weeks Willkie was on his way to England with a letter from Roosevelt to Churchill in his pocket.

ARSENAL OF DEMOCRACY

By mid-December, the British had so nearly exhausted their financial resources that they had practically stopped making new contracts, yet Churchill warned Roosevelt that their needs would increase tenfold in the future. The Neutrality Act of 1939 and the Johnson Act of 1934 forbade American loans; a request for repeal would have reawakened the old ill feelings about unpaid war debts. Roosevelt, cruising in the Caribbean after the election, thought of a formula. The United States, "to eliminate the dollar sign," should lend goods rather than money, while serving as an "arsenal of democracy."

A "Lend-Lease" bill went into the congressional hopper at the right moment to bear a significant number: it became House Resolution No. 1776. After fierce debate, the bill went through Congress by a wide margin and was signed by the President in March 1941. It empowered him to spend an initial $7 billion — a sum as large as all the controversial loans of World War I.

Lend-Lease formally committed the United States to the policy the President had been following since the fall of France, the policy of pouring aid into Great Britain to help her withstand the German onslaught. Since Lend-Lease shipments had to cross the Atlantic to be of aid, the United States acquired a vital interest in keeping the Atlantic sea lanes open against the formidable wolf packs of German submarines, which in the spring of 1941 were destroying a half-million tons of shipping a month, twice as much as could be replaced. The President did not dare to convoy vessels openly to England as Secretary Stimson urged; isolationists in Congress were too powerful. Instead he fell back upon the device of "hemispheric defense." The American republics had proclaimed an Atlantic neutrality zone in 1939; in 1941 Roosevelt extended it far to the east, almost to Iceland, and ordered the navy to patrol the area and give warning of aggressors. This meant radioing to the British naval and air forces the location of Nazi submarines. The United States occupied Greenland in April 1941 and began escorting convoys as far as Iceland in July.

In secret, the United States had gone even further, for in the spring of 1941 American and British officers in Washington reached agreement on the strategy to be followed if the United States should enter the war. President Roosevelt demonstrated publicly in August 1941 how close he had come to carrying the United States from nonbelligerency to cobelligerency with England when he met with Prime Minister Churchill off the coast of Newfoundland. Roosevelt refused to make military commitments but did join Churchill in signing a press release on mutual war aims—the Atlantic Charter. As Churchill later pointed out, Roosevelt, representing a nation not at war, subscribed to a document that referred to "the final destruction of the Nazi tyranny" as a war aim.

In June 1941 Hitler unleashed against Russia a surprise attack so powerful that American military leaders predicted that Russia would collapse in a few weeks or months. The Russians fell back before the deep Nazi invasion but continued to fight, and in September Roosevelt, again gambling, extended Lend-Lease to them. This made it even more imperative to patrol the seas effectively.

The German answer was to strike back with submarines. In May 1941 they sank the American ship *Robin Moor* off the coast of Brazil. The Nazis replied to protests by saying: "Germany will continue to sink every ship with contraband for Britain whatever its name." In September a submarine attacked but failed to hit the destroyer *Greer,* which was radioing the submarine's position to the British. President Roosevelt, who did not know or at least did not reveal what the *Greer* was doing, issued orders to the navy to "shoot on sight." In October another destroyer was hit, and the *Reuben James*

was sunk. Congress voted legislation to arm merchantmen and allow them to sail to belligerent ports. Naval war with the Nazis was under way.

The Chief of Naval Operations, Admiral Harold R. Stark, wrote in his diary that Hitler "has every excuse in the world to declare war on us now, if he were of a mind to." But Hitler was not, and war came from the Pacific, not the Atlantic.

PEARL HARBOR

The Japanese saw in the European crisis an unparalleled opportunity to extend their empire. In the summer of 1939 they forced from Great Britain concessions that demonstrated their intentions. The United States promptly took a most serious step and gave the requisite six months' notice to terminate its 1911 commercial treaty with Japan. Beginning in January 1940, the United States was free to cut off its shipments of oil, scrap iron, and other raw materials.

The United States was determined to restrain Japan, even at the risk of a war. More was at stake than tin, rubber, and other vital raw materials. In September 1940 Japan signed a defensive alliance with Germany and Italy (the Tripartite Pact); any further Japanese thrusts would damage the world status quo to which the State Department was committed. The administration policy toward Japan was inseparably interrelated with and subordinate to that policy toward Germany.

Under the Export Control Act, by the fall of 1940 the United States had placed an embargo upon aviation gasoline and almost all raw materials with military potential, including scrap iron and steel. Already war was close. The Japanese government of Prince Konoye wished to conciliate the United States if it could do so without serious concessions. Negotiations began in the spring of 1941 and dragged on into December. At first the Japanese informally suggested rather generous proposals, but by May they were making formal ones that were unacceptable: the United States should ask Chiang Kai-shek to make peace on Japan's terms, should restore normal trade with Japan, and should help Japan procure natural resources in Southeast Asia.

The Background of Pearl Harbor

After the end of World War II a number of critics charged that the Roosevelt administration had deliberately brought the United States into the war by provoking the Japanese to attack Pearl Harbor. Charles A. Beard, for one, presented the case against the administration in his *President Roosevelt and the Coming of the War, 1941* (1948). According to Beard, the American government refused to compromise with Japan and allow her to buy the raw materials she needed for her military adventure in China. Hence Japan had little choice but to strike out in the southwest Pacific and take the necessary supplies by force, even at the risk of war with the United States. From decoded Japanese radio messages, Roosevelt and his advisers must have known, by late November, that Japan was about to begin hostilities. Indeed, as War Secretary Henry L. Stimson recorded in his diary, Roosevelt at a cabinet meeting "brought up the event that we were likely to be attacked" in the near future, for the Japanese were "notorious for making an attack without warning." Stimson added, significantly: "The question was how we should maneuver them into the position of firing the first shot."

In *Roosevelt from Munich to Pearl Harbor* (1950) Basil Rauch undertook to refute Beard's argument, yet Rauch conceded that the administration had had in mind a "maneuver" of sorts. "The question," he explained, "was whether the President should ask Congress for a declaration of war *prior* to a Japanese attack on the Philippines or Guam, in order to avoid giving Japan the advantage of a surprise attack, or wait until Japan attacked American territory, that is, 'maneuver' Japan into firing the first shot."

Disagreeing with both Beard and Rauch, R. N. Current contended in *Secretary Stimson: A Study in Statecraft* (1954) that Roosevelt and his advisers intended neither to provoke an attack on Pearl Harbor nor to await one on Guam or the Philippines. Stimson and the others were expecting the Japanese to move against Dutch or British but *not* American possessions. When Stimson said "we were likely to be attacked," he meant "we" in the sense of "our side," including the British and the Dutch. If he and his colleagues had really been anticipating a blow at Pearl Harbor, they obviously would not have had to worry about how to provoke the Japanese to attack there. The real question, as Stimson saw it, was how to make the Japanese *appear* to be firing on the United States — in the sense of threatening vital American interests — if and when they aggressed upon Dutch or British territory in the southwest Pacific. He assumed that such a "maneuver" as this would be necessary in order to persuade Congress to pass a war declaration, which he believed to be in the best interests of the United States.

The most thorough and scholarly study of the subject is *Pearl Harbor: Warning and Decision* (1962), by Roberta Wohlsetter, who on the whole is favorable to the Roosevelt policy. Today few if any historical experts hold to the Beard provocation thesis, but they continue to disagree among themselves in regard to the appropriateness of various American diplomatic and military measures preceding the attack.

The Magazine of the U.S.S. Shaw Exploding During the Japanese Raid on Pearl Harbor

The destroyer Shaw, *in a new floating drydock, went through the first attack unscathed. One of the second wave of bombers at 9:12* A.M. *hit her badly, and fire spread to her forward magazine, which about 9:30 went up spectacularly, blowing off her bow and sinking the dock. From the bridge aft the damage was so slight that the* Shaw *was refloated and a month later put in the same repaired dock to be fitted with a temporary bow. She steamed to the mainland to be rebuilt and later rejoined the fleet. (Official U.S. Navy photo)*

The German attack upon Russia relieved the Japanese of one of their greatest worries, since they thought they no longer needed to fear interference from Siberia. They decided to move into southern Indochina and Thailand. The United States had broken the Japanese code and, through intercepted messages, knew this was probably a prelude to attacks upon Singapore and the Dutch East Indies. At the end of July 1941, when the Japanese occupied southern Indochina, the United States, acting firmly with the British and the Dutch, froze Japanese assets in their respective countries, so that the Japanese could not convert these assets into cash. This put the Japanese into such a desperate plight that they would either have to abandon their aggressions or attack British or Dutch East Indian possessions to get needed supplies.

Since the Japanese naval leaders wished to avoid a war they feared they might lose, the Japanese cabinet sought a compromise. Prince Konoye requested a personal meeting with Roosevelt at which Konoye was ready to make some concessions. (Simultaneously Japan prepared for war in case agreement could not be reached.) Roosevelt was enthusiastic, since Konoye was ready to promise that Japan would not expand farther southward and would not attack the United States in the event of war with Germany. Hull was becoming discouraged because he feared Konoye could not bind the Supreme Command. On Hull's advice, Roosevelt refused to meet Konoye without specific advance commitments about China, and these Konoye would not give.

Roosevelt and Hull seemed to make the foolish error of thinking Japan was bluffing when she was not. Instead of granting limited concessions that would have strengthened the Japanese moderates and postponed or avoided a war that the United States was in no position to fight in 1941, the American policy makers took an adamant moralistic position which played into the hands of the Japanese extremists. The Japanese made an even more grievous miscalculation by provoking a war that few of their leaders were sure they could win.

Each nation refused to budge on the question of China. On November 20, 1941, Japan offered a modus vivendi (temporary settlement) highly favorable to herself. Hull rejected it and replied in the basic American terms, insisting that Japan get out of China. He not only knew Japan would not accept these terms but knew also, through intercepted Japanese messages, that she had made her last offer and that after November 29 things would happen automatically. "I have washed my hands of the Japanese situation," Hull told Stimson on November 27, "and it is now in the hands of you and Knox, the Army and Navy."

The United States knew that Japan was on the move and that war was imminent. A large Japanese convoy was moving southward through the China Sea. The administration thought an attack upon American territory un-

likely. The commanders in Hawaii were routinely warned. Negligence there and in Washington, not diabolical plotting as was later charged, led to the disaster ahead. Meanwhile, on November 25, a Japanese naval task force had sailed eastward from the Kuriles.

At 7:55 on Sunday morning, December 7, 1941, the first wave of Japanese airplanes hit the United States naval base at Pearl Harbor, Hawaii; a second wave came an hour later. The attacks were successful beyond Japan's greatest expectations. Within two hours the planes destroyed or severely damaged 8 battleships, 3 light cruisers, 4 miscellaneous vessels, 188 airplanes, and important shore installations. There were 3,435 casualties. The Japanese task force withdrew without being detected, having lost 29 airplanes, 5 midget submarines, and fewer than 100 men. In the first strike, the United States was rendered almost impotent in the Pacific, but the bitterly wrangling nation was suddenly unified for the global war into which it had been precipitated.

The Battle for Production

"Yesterday, December 7, 1941 — a date which will live in infamy — the United States of America was suddenly and deliberately attacked by the naval and air forces of the Empire of Japan." Thus President Roosevelt addressed Congress on the Monday after the debacle at Pearl Harbor. Within four hours, the Senate unanimously, and the House 388 to 1, voted for a war resolution against Japan. Three days later Germany and Italy declared war against the United States, and on the same day, December 11, Congress reciprocated without a dissenting vote.

Total war made the planning of industrial production as vital as military strategy. "War is no longer simply a battle between armed forces in the field," the Industrial Mobilization Plan of 1939 had stated, " — it is a struggle in which each side strives to bring to bear against the enemy the coordinated power of every individual and of every material resource at its command. The conflict extends from the soldier in the front line to the citizen in the remotest hamlet in the rear."

MOBILIZING FOR DEFENSE

At the time of the Munich crisis in 1938, Roosevelt had ordered the armed forces to modernize their production plan. Just before the outbreak of war in Europe, he authorized the War and Navy departments to appoint a civilian advisory committee to survey the 1939 plan. This was the War Resources Board, made up of five leaders of big business together with the presidents of the Massachusetts Institute of Technology and the Brookings Institution, and an army colonel. At this point politics began. The unfortunate use of the word "war" rather than "defense" in the title frightened the public, especially after the invasion of Poland when even the existence of such a body seemed a move toward involvement. The firmly anti-New Deal attitude of the board pained Roosevelt. He speedily disbanded the War Resources Board and submitted to the pressures against substituting any new defense agencies.

With the collapse of France in the late spring of 1940, Roosevelt could delay no longer, even though he was embarking upon a new presidential campaign and wished to temper isolationist hostility. Rather than ask Congress to create defense agencies, he drew upon a 1916 statute for authority and reestablished the Advisory Commission of the Council of National Defense. This time he used the word "defense" rather than "war," and carefully balanced all of the major national interests. He headed it with William Knudsen, of General Motors.

Out of this prototype grew the many defense agencies with their shifting or nebulous lines of authority and often ill-defined powers. Out of it came many of the heads of subsequent war agencies. Out of it too came one clear fact amid the many uncertainties: whatever war agencies developed, Roosevelt was of no disposition to abdicate or share his presidential powers. At its first meeting, Chairman Knudsen asked Roosevelt: "Who's boss?" The President replied: "I am."

In January 1941, after the Advisory Commission had almost broken down and had lost its control over priorities to the military, Roosevelt set up a new Office of Production Management. After American entrance into the war, he replaced this with a War Production Board under Donald Nelson, of Sears, Roebuck and Company. Though personable and a good organizer, Nelson was not strong enough to force civilian control over priorities, or a more equitable distribution of contracts among smaller manufacturers, or a well-balanced production plan. He lost much of his power when President Roosevelt persuaded Justice James F. Byrnes to resign from the Supreme Court and act as a sort of assistant president in charge of war production. Brynes was at first head of the Office of Economic Stabilization, then (after May 1943) of the Office of War Mobilization, which developed into an effective agency.

MATERIALS FOR VICTORY

Meanwhile, with the awarding of the first large government contracts in the summer of 1940, industry began to boom.

Some manufacturers, still thinking in depression terms of an economy of scarcity, were at first reluctant to build new plants, which they feared would lead to overproduction after the war. Still others would not accept contracts until they were sure of an adequate profit. It was the initial task of Knudsen, the production genius of General Motors, to persuade manufacturers that it was their patriotic duty to take contracts. As for the new war plants, even if later they should prove to be excess capacity, manufacturers need not worry about paying for them; the Reconstruction Finance Corporation received authorization from Congress (June 1940) to finance the construction, expansion, and equipment of plants and to lease them to contractors. Or, if manufacturers put their own capital into defense construction, they would receive a fast five-year tax write-off. This meant that instead of deducting a normal 5 percent a year for depreciation from their taxes on wartime profits, they could deduct 20 percent of the cost of the plant. Manufacturers who turned to war production were not to suffer financially.

Neither were the war workers. The manufacturers, backed by the War and Navy departments, wished to abrogate New Deal restrictions on government contracts in order to lengthen the hours of workers without paying overtime. Labor leaders, wishing to increase employment, fought bitterly for double shifts. Ultimately the government decreed a forty-hour week with time-and-a-half for overtime. Contractors had to comply with New Deal labor legislation — the Walsh-Healey, Fair Labor Standards, and Wagner acts.

The Mushrooming of War Plants
These two pictures of a West Virginia valley taken from the same spot, the first in 1941 and the second in 1942, indicate the remarkable speed with which the Morgantown Ordnance Plant was built and went into production. This was typical of the mushrooming construction all over the nation. The plant was one of fifty-four built by Du Pont in thirty-two locations for the government at a total cost of $1,034,000,000. Du Pont received a total fee, after taxes and all applicable charges, of one-fifteenth of 1 per cent of the construction cost. (Du Pont)

At the time of Pearl Harbor, the United States still had little armament because so much had been shipped to Great Britain and because so many of the plants had only recently begun production. The new productive capacity was remarkably large. Despite errors and chaotic conditions, the United States was producing more combat munitions than any of the belligerents—indeed almost as much as Germany and Japan combined. Airplane production was up to a rate of almost 25,000 per year. The armed forces already had inducted and were training 2 million men. This mobilization was only a fraction of what was soon to come, for a large-scale construction of factories and training camps was under way. While the nation during the debate over neutrality had not built its defenses with the smoothness and speed that critics demanded, it had achieved a substantial degree of preparedness.

The Japanese attack on Pearl Harbor created almost as much chaos indirectly in American war production as it did directly in the fleet in the Pacific. The war agencies in Washington began ordering tremendous quantities—indeed far too much—of everything.

The problem of restoring some order to war production, then raising it to astronomical totals, was a joint one. The armed forces, the Maritime Commission, and other procurement agencies did the ordering. The War Production Board tried to control the size of the procurement program and to allocate materials between the armed forces and the civilians. The WPB was thus trying to control the entire economy and inevitably was coming into collision with the armed forces over the size and nature of war orders as opposed to what was to be reserved for civilians. Internecine conflict among the agencies and personality clashes among the administrators were unavoidable.

Out of the confusion a pattern gradually emerged. The first step, oddly enough, was to cut back the building of plants, although at times this created a furor throughout a region, as when the Higgins Shipyards in New Orleans were abandoned. After the middle of 1942, the amount of new construction being started declined sharply; in another six months, the larger part of the war plants and military facilities had been built.

The second step was to coordinate the various phases of the war-production program. As late as the summer of 1942, bottlenecks were halting some assembly lines. The vital shipbuilding program had to be cut back because of scarcities of raw materials like steel plate and glass, and of components like valves, turbines, and engines. The WPB eventually broke most of the bottlenecks through the Controlled Materials Plan, which established a balanced production of finished products and allocated precise quantities of raw materials to each manufacturer.

The shortage of rubber became so critical in 1942 that it required special attention. After the WPB failed to solve the problem, Roosevelt appointed a committee under Baruch to make a special report. This recommended sharp restrictions upon the use of motor vehicles, including a national speed limit of thirty-five miles per hour, and immediate construction of enormous synthetic rubber plants. Roosevelt ordered the restrictions, and appointed a Rubber Director in the WPB, William M. Jeffers, president of the Union Pacific Railroad, to construct the plants. By the end of 1943 the synthetic rubber industry was producing a third again as much rubber as the country had normally used before the war.

An indispensable adjunct of the war agencies was the Senate War Investigating Committee, headed by Harry S Truman, previously little known. The senators consciously patterned it after the Committee on the Conduct of the War of the Civil War period, but avoided the pitfalls of their predecessors by ruling out questions of military policy. Instead, they ferreted out incompetence and corruption in the war-production and military-construction programs: outrageous expense in building army camps, improper inspection of airplane engines, a quixotic scheme to build an Arctic pipeline, and the like. The Truman Committee uncovered and stopped hundreds of millions of dollars of waste. In the wartime expenditure of $400 billion there was amazingly little corruption.

By the beginning of 1944 factories had turned out what seemed to be needed to win the war. The output was double that of all Axis countries combined. Cutbacks began but were haphazard and ill-planned, and when the armed forces met reverses, some turned out to have been premature. With the cutbacks came pressure for a resumption of the manufacture of civilian durable goods. The military leaders staunchly opposed this.

War needs even at their peak took only about one-third of American production. While manufacture of such goods as automobiles, most electrical appliances, and nondefense housing had come to a halt in 1942, production of food, clothing, and repair and maintenance goods was continued or even slightly increased.

TRANSPORTING THE SUPPLIES

As war production grew, the problem of transporting the supplies within the country and overseas became acute. Inside the United States, the Office of Defense Transportation, established in December 1941, coordinated all forms of transport—railroads, trucking, airlines, inland waterways, and pipelines. In contrast to the system in World War I, railroads remained under private control, but functioned effectively, carrying double the traffic of 1939 with only 10 percent more locomotives and 20 percent more freight cars. Since they could not, however, transport sufficient oil to the East when German submarines began attacking coastal tankers in 1942, the government authorized construction of the Big Inch pipeline from Texas to eastern Pennsylvania.

Transporting troops and supplies overseas required one of the most spectacular construction programs of all. The Germans had sunk more than 12 million tons of shipping by 1942. To replace it, the United States Maritime Commission had to abandon its program of building fast, efficient ships requiring scarce turbines, valves, and electrical equipment. As early as July 1940, Admiral Emory S. Land, head of the commission, and Knudsen recommended to the President mass production of a freighter that, while slow (sailing only eleven knots), would be simple to construct and would not require scarce components. By using the existing designs for an old-fashioned British tramp steamer with a reciprocating engine and steam winches, they saved six months in starting production. This "ugly duckling" was the

Liberty ship. After a slow beginning, builders substituted welding for riveting and applied prefabrication and subassembly techniques in constructing it. In 1941 construction of a Liberty ship required an average of 355 days; by the end of 1942 the time had been cut to 56 days, and one of Henry J. Kaiser's companies completed one in 14 days. During 1942 alone 8 million tons of shipping were built; by 1945 the United States had over 36 million tons of ships afloat.

SCIENTISTS AGAINST THE AXIS

The most revolutionary changes for the future came out of laboratories, as scientists pooled their skill in a race against those of the Axis—above all the Germans—to turn the basic knowledge that was available to all into decisive weapons of war. Between the two wars, while the United States had neglected military research and development, Germany had sprinted far ahead, except in the field of radar. In the 1920s the Naval Research Laboratory in Washington had discovered the principle of radar by bouncing back a radio beam directed at a ship on the Potomac. The British had developed radar most highly, and it was their salvation during the air blitz of 1940–1941.

Other potential weapons were in the offing which, if the Germans developed them first, could mean Nazi victory in the war. (This was one of the reasons why the armed forces had decided to concentrate upon defeating Germany first.) The only way in which American scientists could catch up seemed to be through teamwork. The German threat brought the creation of a government scientific agency such as the New Deal had failed to produce. A leading scientist, Vannevar Bush, persuaded President Roosevelt to create a committee for scientific research in June 1940. A year later, under the direction of Bush, it became the Office of Scientific Research and Development, which mobilized scientists with such effectiveness that in some areas they outstripped their German opponents.

The Americans and the British developed superior radar, which not only detected enemy airplanes and ships but helped direct shells against them. In these shells, by 1943, were radio-directed proximity fuses that detonated the shells as they neared their targets. American rocket research produced weapons that enormously increased the fire power of airplanes, ships, and tanks. But the Americans still lagged behind the Germans, who before the end of the war were blasting London with enormous V-1 and V-2 rockets. The Germans also built the first jet airplanes and snorkel submarines, which would have been an even more serious menace if they had come into full production.

There was a danger, little publicized, that Germany might develop an atomic weapon. In the summer of 1939, a physicist, Enrico Fermi, and a mathematician, Albert Einstein, got word to President Roosevelt that German physicists had achieved atomic fission in uranium; what had long been theoretically possible had been accomplished. Next might come a bomb. The President authorized a small research project, and a race in the dark against the Nazis began.

In December 1942 physicists produced a controlled chain reaction in an atomic pile at the University of Chicago. The problem then became the enormous technical one of achieving this release of power in a bomb. Through the Manhattan District of the Army Engineer Corps, the government secretly poured nearly $2 billion into one project for producing fissionable plutonium and into another, under the supervision of J. Robert Oppenheimer, for building a bomb. This was an enormous and frightening gamble, against the hazards that the thing might not work and that the enemy might succeed first. Only after the war did the United States discover that the Germans were far from developing a usable atomic device. On July 16, 1945, after the end of the war in Europe, the first A-bomb was exploded, on a tower in New Mexico, producing the most blinding flash of light ever seen on earth, and then a huge billowing mushroom cloud.

The Impact on Civilians

No American could escape the impact of the war effort. Everybody was affected — and most people very deeply — by war jobs, wages, prices, rationing and other controls, taxes, and propaganda.

MANPOWER AND WOMANPOWER

The nation, after grappling for years with the problem of millions of unemployed, found itself hard pressed for sufficient people to swell the

---

The Home Front [1942]

That was the spring when women took to wearing slacks in the streets (a great blow to the human race), old toothpaste tubes had to be turned in for new ones, men's trousers were commanded to be cuffless, and a radio comedian named Bob Hope began to play soldiers' camps around the country. . . . That was the spring we first heard about sugar rationing, with gasoline rationing to come. Ice cream was reduced to ten flavors, and civilian suffering really hit its stride when the War Production Board banned the use of metals for asparagus tongs, beer mugs, spittoons, bird cages, cocktail shakers, hair curlers, corn poppers, and lobster forks. New York blacked out, and for days we talked about how beautiful the great city looked stark and naked, silhouetted against the moon and the stars. . . . Sex reared its pretty head in factories as an occupational hazard. Girls were requested to quit wearing sweaters, peekaboo waists, halters, and other revealing garments. The boys were rubbernecking themselves into too many accidents. — Paul Gallico in Jack Goodman, ed., *While You Were Gone* (New York: Simon and Schuster, 1946).

Women in War Work
*"Rosie the Riveter" was the subject of a popular song during World War II. Here
women riveters help with the production of planes for the army. (Library of
Congress)*

fighting forces, man the war plants, till the
fields, and keep the domestic economy functioning. There were periodic demands for national service legislation or a labor draft, but
unions were so vehemently opposed that no
such measure ever passed the Senate. The relatively weak War Manpower Commission tried
to coerce workers into remaining at defense
jobs at the risk of being drafted, but the war
came to an end without any tight allocation of
manpower comparable to that of materials.
The armed forces had first call upon men
through Selective Service, which had been in
operation since the fall of 1940. Altogether draft
boards registered 31 million men. Including
volunteers, over 15 million men and women
served in the armed forces during the war.
Nevertheless the working force jumped from
46.5 million to over 53 million as the 7 million
unemployed and many previously considered
unemployable, the very young and the elderly,

and several million women found jobs. The
number of civilian employees of the federal
government trebled.

This mobilization of manpower entailed
the greatest reshuffling of population within
such a short time in the entire history of the nation; altogether 27.3 million people moved during the war. It also meant a heavy weight of
wartime tension on American families. With the
return of prosperity and the impending departure of soldiers, both marriage and birth rates
rose. In 1942 and 1943 about 3 million children
were born each year, compared with 2 million
a year before the war. But young wives and
mothers fared badly in crowded housing near
defense plants or army bases, or, after husbands had been shipped overseas, back home
with parents. Draft boards deferred fathers as
long as possible, but more than 1 million were
ultimately inducted. More than 2.5 million
wives were separated from their husbands

because of the war. The divorce rate increased slowly. Because men in the armed forces could not be divorced without their consent, and many estranged wives stayed married in order to continue receiving allotment checks, a heavy backlog was built for postwar divorce courts.

When mothers were forced to work, children often suffered neglect, or were upset over the change. Court cases involving juvenile delinquency, especially among children from eight to fourteen, and among girls, the "bobby-soxers," increased 56 percent. Even among the nondelinquents, a serious price had to be paid at the time and later for the disruption of more American families for a longer period of time than ever before.

As adolescents found jobs, the percentage of those between fourteen and nineteen who attended school dropped from 62 in 1940 to 56 in 1944. Teachers also left for the armed forces or better-paying war jobs. Universities kept functioning through military research projects and training programs.

The great migration to war plants was stripping the agricultural South of underprivileged whites and blacks alike, as 5 million people moved within the South, and another 1.6 million left the area completely. In the South this exodus led to the false rumor among outraged white housewives that the departing Negro domestics had formed "Eleanor Clubs," named after Mrs. Roosevelt, to "get a white woman in every kitchen by 1943." In the North, it led to explosive tension when Negroes, enjoying their new freedom, were jostled in crowded streetcars against indignant whites newly migrated from the South. A serious riot, in which twenty-five blacks and nine whites were killed, shook Detroit in June 1943. New York narrowly averted a similar disaster. At the very time when the United States was fighting a war against the racist doctrines of Hitler, many whites became resentful over the rapid gains Negroes were making.

In June 1941, after the head of the Pullman porters' union, A. Philip Randolph, had threatened a march on Washington, President Roosevelt established the Fair Employment Practices Committee. It worked diligently throughout the war against discrimination in employment. By 1944 2 million Negroes were at work in war industry, and many previous barriers to economic opportunities for Negroes were permanently cracked.

Not everyone shared in the new prosperity. Government economists reported in 1943 that 10 million families still received less than the $1,675 per year requisite for a minimum standard of living. Most Americans, however, were relatively more affluent than they had been. The living standard of working people advanced rapidly. This was due less to wage increases than to payment of time-and-a-half for overtime beyond 40 hours. The average workweek lengthened from 40.6 hours in 1941 to 45.2 in 1944. As living costs rose (on a 1935–1939 base of 100) from 100.4 in 1940 to 128.4 in 1945, gross weekly wages went up from $25.20 to $43.39. Working women and children created social problems, but they also brought additional prosperity to millions of families.

RESTRAINING LABOR UNIONS

Labor unions rapidly grew in strength during the war, and their unpopularity among Americans of the middle and upper classes increased. Union membership rose with the rise in the working force, from about 10.5 million workers in 1941 to over 13 million in 1945. Keeping these workers satisfied was no easy matter. The administration was determined to prevent strikes and to restrain the formidable pressure of the labor unions from forcing wages, and thus all prices, upward. President Roosevelt followed the procedure of World War I by establishing a National Defense Mediation Board (March 1941) made up of representatives of management, labor, and the public. In November 1941 it broke down when the CIO members resigned over the refusal of the board to recommend a union shop (that is, one in which all new workers hired must join the union) in coal mines. In January 1942 Roosevelt replaced it with the National War Labor Board, similarly constituted but much stronger. This board could set wages, hours, and working conditions, and through the war powers of the President it could enforce these in a final extremity by government seizure and operation of plants.

On the union-shop question, which was creating much hostility between management and labor, the board arrived at a compromise, the "maintenance of membership" clause. Nonmembers hired into a war plant did not have to join a union, but members had to remain in it, and the union remained the bargaining agent for the duration of the contract. Pressure for wage increases, which might contribute to inflation, was more serious. The board hit upon a solution in ruling upon the Little Steel cases in July 1942. Taking January 1, 1941, as the base date when workers had received a standard wage, it recognized a 15-percent rise in the cost-of-living index since then. Consequently, it felt that a proportionate increase for steel workers would be equitable. The Little Steel formula, except for those receiving substandard wages (like some textile workers), served thereafter as a wage ceiling.

Despite the no-strike pledges of the major unions, there were nearly 15,000 work stoppages during the war, involving the loss of more than 36 million man-days. These stoppages involved only one-ninth of 1 percent of the working time (though they indirectly caused more damage than this). When John L. Lewis' United Mine Workers defied the government in their strike against the Little Steel formula in May 1943, Congress reacted by passing over Roosevelt's veto the Smith-Connally or War Labor Disputes Act (June 1943). This act required unions to wait thirty days before striking and empowered the President to seize a struck war plant.

PRICE CONTROLS, WAR FINANCE

At the beginning of the war, with a two-year supply of wheat, cotton, and corn stored in Secretary Wallace's ever-normal granary, there seemed no danger of food shortages in the United States. But within six months after Pearl Harbor, scarcities of many sorts began to develop. The United States felt the increased demand of the armed forces and its allies and the reduction of supplies due to the loss of fibers and oils from Southeast Asia. By 1942 meat production was half again that of depression years, but American consumers with their increased buying power were eager to buy even more. Consumer income in 1943 was 65 percent above depression levels, and much of it was in the pockets of people who had not eaten adequately for years.

A food administrator did exist, Chester Davis, but he resigned in protest when his views (and those of the American Farm Bureau Federation) did not prevail; his successor

was Marvin Jones. Neither man had the dictatorial powers to provide the scarce supplies and manpower that the dominant farm bloc in Congress would have liked to bestow upon agricultural producers. Rather, farmers had to depend upon whatever the War Production Board would allocate to them, and upon a generous draft-exemption program they obtained from Congress. They also received legislation raising the ceiling on commodity prices to 110 percent of parity. Since this came into conflict with the anti-inflation efforts of the administration, a dogged struggle developed between the President and the congressional farm bloc over farm prices. Neither side won entirely.

Pressures from business, farmers, and labor, combined with the scarcity of consumer goods and the burgeoning of buying power, created an almost irresistible trend toward inflation. During the defense period, the Office of Price Administration (OPA), under a vigorous New Dealer, Leon Henderson, lacked real coercive power and failed to halt inflation. Between the invasion of Poland and the attack on Pearl Harbor, prices of twenty-eight basic commodities rose by nearly one-fourth. Immediately thereafter, pressures became so acute that prices went up 2 percent per month. Soon Congress hastily passed a bill authorizing only selective price fixing and setting ceilings with a preferential trap door for agriculture.

In April 1942 the OPA issued a General Maximum Price Regulation that froze prices of consumer goods, and of rents in defense areas only, at their March 1942 level. But the rise of uncontrolled farm prices toward 110 percent of parity forced an upward revision of food prices. This gave ammunition to the labor unions' barrage against fixed wages. In October 1942 Congress grudgingly responding to the President's demand, passed the Anti-inflation Act. Under its authority, Roosevelt immediately froze agricultural prices, wages, salaries, and rents throughout the country.

In July 1943 Roosevelt appointed a former advertising executive with remarkable administrative talents, Chester Bowles, to head the OPA. With a small enforcement staff, Bowles braved general unpopularity to hold the increase in living costs during the next two years to 1.4 percent. Altogether, the price level went up less than 29 percent from 1939 to the end of the war, compared with 63 percent between 1914 and the armistice.

| FUEL OIL
25
GALLONS | R-1148B (ZONE B-1) SERIAL **J** 185456 | 1-PERIOD-1
ZONE B1
FUEL **5** OIL
UNITS
T-250 |
| | UNITED STATES OF AMERICA
OFFICE OF PRICE ADMINISTRATION
FUEL OIL RATION
Class 5B Consumer Coupons | 2-PERIOD-2
ZONE B1
FUEL **5** OIL
UNITS
T-300 |

Fuel Oil Ration Stamps
*During and immediately after World War
II, the Office of Price Administration not
only set price ceilings but also issued
rationing stamps, which entitled each
consumer to buy certain amounts of rationed
commodities. Rationing was intended to
insure an equitable distribution of scarce
goods and also to help hold prices down by
limiting the demand. (Courtesy of G. Litton)*

Consumers nonetheless suffered numerous irritations and discomforts. The OPA, through unpaid local volunteers manning 5,600 price and rationing boards, administered the rationing of canned goods, coffee, sugar, meat, butter and other fats, shoes, tires, gasoline, and fuel oil. The OPA could not, however, control deterioration of quality. Black-marketing and overcharging grew in proportions far beyond OPA policing capacity; in 1943 Congress slashed the funds of the enforcement division.

One of the most important inflationary controls was the sale of war bonds and stamps to channel off some of the excess purchasing power, which for the single year 1945 mounted to nearly $60 billion. Throughout most of the war, personal incomes were at least one-third greater than the available civilian goods and services. The Treasury Department, through eight war bond drives and its payroll deduction

plans, but with few of the lurid or coercive touches of World War I, sold $40 billion worth of series "E" bonds to small investors, and $60 billion more to individuals and corporate entities other than banks.

Had this been the total of government loans, the effect would have been to quell inflation, but the Treasury had to borrow $87.5 billion more from Federal Reserve and commercial banks. Since in effect the banks created new credits which the government then spent, the result was to inflate bank credits and money in circulation by over $100 billion.

Taxes did much more to drain off surplus purchasing power. The government raised 41 percent of its war costs through taxation, compared with 33 percent during World War I. The Revenue Act of 1942, which Roosevelt hailed as "the greatest tax bill in American history," levied a 94-percent tax on the highest incomes; the President had suggested that no one should net more than $25,000 per year during the war. Also, for the first time, the income tax fell upon those in lower income brackets. To simplify payment for these new millions, Congress enacted a withholding system of payroll deductions in 1943. Corporation taxes reached a maximum of 40 percent on the largest incomes. In addition, excess profits were subject to a 90-percent tax, reclaiming for the government a large part of the return from war contracts. However, these taxes could be rebated to companies to aid them in reconversion (changing back to peacetime production), a provision of future significance. In effect, the government taxed away a large part of the profits of corporations, then returned it later when it was needed. Heavy excise taxes on transportation, communication, luxuries, and amusements completed the levies.

Between 1941 and 1945 the government raised $138 billion through taxation—nearly a $100 billion of it from income and excess profits taxes. Those in the top 5 percent of the income scale suffered a serious relative economic loss, as their share of disposable income dropped from 26 percent in 1940 to 16 percent in 1944. Few persons or corporations were able to make fortunes out of the war, and a considerable amount of economic leveling—upward more than downward—had taken place. Despite the heavy taxation, by the end of the war consumers possessed an estimated $129 billion in liquid savings.

From 1941 to 1945 the federal government spent twice as much as the total appropriations from the creation of the government to 1941, and ten times as much as the cost of World War I—a total of $321 billion. The national debt rose from $49 billion in 1941 to $259 billion in 1945, yet the black warnings of national bankruptcy that had punctuated the New Deal years all but disappeared.

INFORMATION AND MISINFORMATION

As an incentive for winning the war, advertisers presented a vision of a postwar America in which every husband would have a chrome-trimmed car and every wife a gleaming kitchen filled with wonder-working gadgets. President Roosevelt promised even more. "In the future

days, which we seek to make secure," he told the people (January 1941), "we look forward to a world founded upon four essential freedoms." These were freedom of speech and worship, and freedom from want and fear. They were for the postwar future, not necessarily for the wartime present.

From Pearl Harbor on, there was the suspicion that through the Office of Censorship, almost immediately established under a competent Associated Press executive, Byron Price, the government was withholding information not because it was vital to the enemy but because it would be damaging to public opinion of the armed forces. Diligent newspapermen, aided by Price, exerted pressure on the armed forces to make censorship an instrument for security, rather than for the concealing of incompetence. Newspapers following

Taken by itself, the growth of the national debt since the 1930s appears to have been tremendous. It seems less disturbing in comparison with the even more rapid growth of the economy, as measured by the increase in the Gross National Product. The GNP for a given year represents the total value, at current prices, of all goods and services produced in the country during that year. The growth of the GNP reflects a rising price level as well as an increasing output of goods and services. The actual increase in output has been much less, therefore, than the graph seems to indicate.

The National Debt 1910-1972   The Gross National Product 1931-1972

In Billions of Dollars

1	U.S. Enters World War I	4	Japan Surrenders	7	Nixon Inauguration	▬▬ National Debt
2	Depression	5	Outbreak of Korean War			▬▬ Gross National Product
3	Outbreak of World War II	6	Vietnam War Escalation			(figures not available before 1931)

Office of Censorship rules censored themselves to withhold local news that might be of value to the enemy.

The overlapping and conflict among government information agencies led to the establishment in June 1942 of the Office of War Information under a shrewd news commentator, Elmer Davis. Although the OWI consolidated four previous organizations, it coordinated rather than assumed the information function of domestic war agencies.

The OWI aroused the misgivings of Congress, partly because of internal feuding and the mass resignation of the pamphlet writers, but mainly because conservatives objected to several of the OWI pamphlets: one on the dangers of inflation, another on Negroes in the war, and another on the need for high taxes. A fourth pamphlet, intended only for overseas distribution, a cartoon biography of Roosevelt, especially worried antiadministration congressmen. They feared that the OWI might promote New Dealish policies and the 1944 candidacy of Roosevelt. In 1943 Congress cut funds for the domestic branch of the OWI so drastically that it had to stop producing propaganda.

Overseas, the OWI carried on a program employing 8,400 persons by V-E Day. Through Voice of America broadcasts begun in 1941 and propaganda of many sorts, it presented an idealistic view of American war aims and aspi-rations for a peaceful postwar world. As the symbol of this idealism it dramatized President Roosevelt. By the end of the war, Roosevelt was more of a hero overseas than at home, and American aims appeared more idealistic abroad than in the United States.

The war produced less hatred and vindictiveness at home than had World War I. The energy that had gone into crude vigilantism in the earlier war now went into serving as air-raid wardens and doing similar duties for the Office of Civilian Defense. People continued to eat hamburgers and sauerkraut and listen to Wagner. They demonstrated little animosity toward Americans of German background and practically none toward Italians. A few Nazi agents and American Fascists were jailed, but the most ambitious effort to punish them, a sedition trial of twenty-eight, ended in a mistrial after the defendants' lawyers had engaged in long weeks of delaying tactics. A few papers like Father Coughlin's *Social Justice* were barred from the mails. But Socialists went unpunished, and religious conscientious objectors who were willing to register went to Civilian Public Service camps rather than to prison.

FATE OF JAPANESE-AMERICANS

In sad contrast to this moderation, the frenzy of public fury turned toward the Japanese. The fighting in the Pacific developed a fierce sav-

Relocation of Japanese-Americans
Americans of Japanese birth or ancestry living on the Pacific Coast were forced to leave their homes and move to camps in the interior of the country, where they were to stay for the duration of the war. The American Civil Liberties Union called the evacuation of these people "the worst single wholesale violation of civil liberties of American citizens in our history." In this news photo of September 21, 1942, members of the first group to depart from Los Angeles begin their trip to a camp in Arkansas. (ACM)

agery, reflected in the public anger within the United States. On the Pacific Coast, hatred of Americans of Japanese background became extreme. Wild stories circulated about sabotage at Pearl Harbor and plots to aid a Japanese landing on the California coast—later proved completely untrue. Under public pressure, Roosevelt, in February 1942, authorized the army to remove all people of Japanese ancestry from the West Coast. Some 117,000 people, two-thirds of them United States citizens, were abruptly herded behind barbed wire, and later shipped into ten relocation centers in wild and disagreeable areas. They suffered the financial loss of at least 40 percent of

their possessions and for several years were barred from lucrative employment. Yet Japanese-Americans in Hawaii were left unmolested without incident throughout the war. There were 17,600 Japanese-Americans in the armed forces. Their units, especially in Italy, established outstanding records for bravery under fire.

The Supreme Court in 1944 validated the evacuation and, in other decisions as well, upheld military control over civilians. In time of war or national emergency, United States citizens apparently could expect no court protection of their civil rights from military or executive authority.

Selected Readings

Biographical Studies
E. E. Morison, *Turmoil and Tradition: A Study of the Life and Times of Henry L. Stimson* (1960); R. N. Current, *Secretary Stimson: A Study in Statecraft* (1954); R. E. Sherwood, *Roosevelt and Hopkins** (1948); J. W. Pratt, *Cordell Hull, 1933–44* (1964); W. S. Cole, *Senator Gerald P. Nye and American Foreign Relations* (1962); E. D. Cronon, *Josephus Daniels in Mexico** (1960).

Depression Diplomacy
R. H. Ferrell, *American Diplomacy in the Great Depression* (1957); S. F. Bemis, *The Latin American Policy of the United States* (1943); Alexander De Conde, *Herbert Hoover's Latin American Policy* (1951); E. O. Guerrant, *Roosevelt's Good Neighbor Policy* (1950); Bryce Wood, *The Making of the Good Neighbor Policy** (1961); A. W. Griswold, *The Far Eastern Policy of the United States* (1938); Dorothy Borg, *The United States and the Far Eastern Crisis of 1933–1938* (1964); R. P. Browder, *The Origins of Soviet-American Diplomacy* (1953); W. A. Williams, *American-Russian Relations, 1781–1947* (1952); R. P. Traina, *American Diplomacy and the Spanish Civil War* (1968); A. Guttmann, *The Wound in the Heart: America and the Spanish Civil War* (1962).

Interventionists Versus Isolationists
Alexander De Conde, ed., *Isolation and Security: Ideas and Interests in Twentieth-Century American Foreign Policy* (1957); R. A. Devine, *The Illusion of Neutrality* (1962); M. L. Chadwin, *The Hawks of World War II* (1968); J. K. Nelson, *The Peace Prophets: American Pacifist Thought, 1919–1941* (1967); Manfred Jonas, *Isolationism in America, 1935–1941** (1966); W. S. Cole, *America First* (1953); Walter Johnson, *Battle Against Isolation* (1944); Warren Moscow, *Roosevelt and Willkie* (1968).

Steps Toward War
W. L. Langer and S. E. Gleason, *The Challenge to Isolation, 1937–1940* (1952) and *The Undeclared War,*

1940–1941 (1953), comprehensive accounts; C. A. Beard, *American Foreign Policy in the Making, 1932–1940* (1946) and *President Roosevelt and the Coming of the War, 1941* (1948), highly critical of F. D. R.; Basil Rauch, *Roosevelt from Munich to Pearl Harbor** (1950), an attempt to refute Beard; Herbert Feis, *The Road to Pearl Harbor** (1950); Roberta Wohlsetter, *Pearl Harbor: Warning and Decision* (1962); R. J. C. Butow, *Tojo and the Coming of the War* (1961); P. W. Schroeder, *The Axis Alliance and Japanese-American Relations, 1941* (1958); W. F. Kimball, *The Most Unsordid Act: Lend-Lease, 1939–1941* (1969).

War Production
Bureau of the Budget, *The United States at War* (1946); D. M. Nelson, *Arsenal of Democracy* (1946); Bruce Catton, *War Lords of Washington* (1946); Eliot Janeway, *The Struggle for Survival* (1951); H. M. Somers, *Presidential Agency: OWMR* (1950); L. R. Groves, *Now It Can Be Told* (1962), on development of the A-bomb; J. P. Baxter III, *Scientists Against Time* (1946); W. W. Willcox, *The Farmer in the Second World War* (1947); W. A. Nielander, *Wartime Food Rationing in the United States* (1947).

Wartime Life
Jack Goodman, ed., *While You Were Gone: A Report on Wartime Life in the United States* (1946); W. F. Ogburn, ed., *American Society in Wartime* (1943); R. Polenberg, *War and Society: The United States, 1941–1945* (1972); Reuben Hill, *Families Under Stress* (1949); E. S. Corwin, *Total War and the Constitution* (1947); Morton Grodzins, *Americans Betrayed: Politics and the Japanese Evacuation* (1949); R. Daniels, *Concentration Camps, USA: Japanese Americans and World War II* (1971); M. Q. Sibley and P. E. Jacob, *Conscription of Conscience: The Conscientious Objector, 1940–1947* (1952).

*Titles available in paperback.

Victory Without Peace

Twenty-six

President Woodrow Wilson had turned from progressive reform to a foreign crusade, with disillusioning results. Similarly, President Franklin D. Roosevelt turned from the New Deal to national defense and then war abroad, but he hoped to escape the frustrations that had befallen his predecessor. In trying to avoid the "mistakes" that Wilson had made, Roosevelt pursued essentially the same objectives by almost exactly the opposite means, so that at times his policies appeared to be the very reverse of Wilson's.

Thus, during World War II, Roosevelt did not hold the United States somewhat aloof from its allies and call it merely an "associated" power, as Wilson had done during World War I. To the contrary, under Roosevelt this country took the initiative in drafting and signing a Declaration of the United Nations (January 1, 1942). The document set forth the war aims of the Atlantic Charter, committed the country's entire military and economic resources to the prosecution of the war, and pledged unlimited cooperation with the other signatories to fight on and make no separate peace. In effect, the United States was taking the lead in forming a grand alliance among the twenty-six original partners and the twenty more that signed before the war was over.

In peacemaking as in warmaking, Roosevelt followed a course quite different from Wilson's. True, the war aims he presented in the Atlantic Charter, which he cosigned with Prime Minister Winston Churchill, were vaguely reminiscent of those that Wilson had announced, unilaterally, in his Fourteen Points. But Roosevelt, with his slogan of "unconditional surrender," was determined to allow no armistice short of the enemy's utter defeat. And he was careful to keep from repeating the steps that had led the United States to a fiasco in relation to the Versailles Treaty and the League of Nations. This time

Mushroom Cloud, Nagasaki
When the atomic bomb exploded over Nagasaki, Japan, August 9, 1945, people in the city saw an "intense flash," heard a "tremendous roaring sound," and felt a "crushing blast wave and intense heat," according to an official Japanese report. The "whole city suffered damage such as would have resulted from direct hits everywhere by ordinary bombs." (Official U.S. Air Force photo)

there was to be no general peace conference comparable to the one at Versailles, and the new peacekeeping arrangement was to be kept quite separate from the political settlements to be made. The wartime alliance itself was to be converted into a peacekeeping body—the United Nations organization.

When, at the war's conclusion, the Senate approved American membership in the U. N. organization, many liberal Americans rejoiced that their country now was righting the wrong it presumably had done in rejecting the League. They assumed that, with the United States as a member, the League would have prevented a second world war; surely the U. N. would prevent a third. This optimism soon passed. For Americans the consequences of the Second World War were to prove even more disillusioning than those of the First, as the people came to realize that the victory of the grand alliance had brought no real peace to the world.

Fighting a Global War

In December 1941 neither the army nor the navy seemed very well prepared for the enormous tasks ahead, and the disaster at Pearl Harbor did not improve confidence in their commands. Enormous industrial production alone could not win the war. The military leaders must know what to order, and where and how to use it, on a scale they had not envisaged in their prewar establishments.

THE AMERICAN WAR MACHINE

At the outset the navy possessed only 300 combat ships, but at the close of the war it had 1,167 and was employing only one of the prewar vessels in the final attacks on Japan.

The army in 1939 had in theory nine infantry divisions but actually only the equivalent of about three and a half at half strength. Nor could it organize tactical units larger than a division. By mid-1941 it had twenty-nine infantry and cavalry divisions at nearly full strength, organized into four field armies—still less than half a million men. The army air force, nominally under the army but in practice almost independent, had only 22,000 officers and men and 2,400 aircraft in 1939.

There was little hint of what was to come. The most important of the war plans, "Orange," devised to go into effect in case of conflict with Japan, had presumed primarily a naval war, with the army mobilizing over a million men. By 1940 the more comprehensive "Rainbow" plans superseded these; by December 1941 a substantial mobilization was under way, though it was still far short of wartime totals.

Vast increases in personnel and equipment forced rapid changes in planning and organization. General George C. Marshall, Chief of Staff of the Army, reorganized the army high command in March 1942. That same month, Admiral Ernest J. King, a clear-headed hard driver, became Chief of Naval Operations. Together with General H. H. Arnold of the army air force, these men met with a personal representative of the President, Admiral William D. Leahy, to constitute the Joint Chiefs of Staff. They functioned as the overall command and represented the United States in combined planning with the British or occasional negotiations with the Russians.

Over the Joint Chiefs of Staff was the Commander in Chief, President Roosevelt, who bore responsibility for the conduct of the war. Personally, and through assistants like Harry Hopkins and cabinet members, he coordinated the war planning of the Joint Chiefs with war production and manpower and with foreign policy. The War Plans Division of the Army General Staff had pointed out that civilians should decide the "what" of national policies, and the professional soldiers the "how." Roosevelt, who had always zealously guarded civilian control even in the Navy Department and the War Department, followed this course throughout the war. He depended heavily

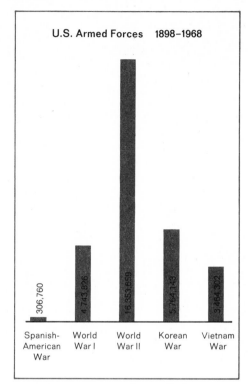

U.S. Armed Forces   1898–1968

Spanish-American War	306,760
World War I	4,743,826
World War II	16,353,659
Korean War	5,764,143
Vietnam War	3,464,302

In the seventy years opening with the Spanish-American War, the United States was engaged in five major confrontations, yet the total deaths during this period were less than those in the Civil War. Much of the difference was due to improvements in military medicine and handling of casualties.

while that against Japan was to be defensive. It was difficult to hold to this policy as the Japanese tide in the Pacific swelled far beyond the bounds that the most pessimistic planners had anticipated. For the President, furious over Japanese treachery, and the navy, primarily responsible in the Pacific, it was not an easy decision to maintain. General MacArthur, the panic-stricken public on the Pacific Coast, and most Americans elsewhere clamored for prompt and stern action against the Japanese.

During the first chaotic months of shocking reverses, the armed forces allotted their men and supplies piecemeal to try to meet each new Axis threat. Top strategists emphatically warned that such dissipation of effort might lead to defeat. No one was more insistent than Dwight D. Eisenhower, who had been brought to Washington after Pearl Harbor as a Far Eastern expert, and who by the spring of 1942 was head of the Operations Planning Division under General Marshall. In emphatic memoranda, Eisenhower hammered away at the need to build up men and supplies in Europe for the invasion of North Africa that Roosevelt and Churchill had decided upon in their December 1941 meeting. Because of his vigor and his important role in developing an invasion plan, Eisenhower became the logical man to send to England (in June 1942) as commanding general in the European theater.

upon the advice of the Joint Chiefs of Staff and, once major policy had been decided, seldom interfered with their strategy.

The first of the great policy decisions had come in 1940 when the Americans decided that, even if Japan entered the war, their primary goal would be to defeat Germany with its superior military force, war production, and weapons development. The United States confirmed this priority in the initial wartime conference with the British at the end of December 1941. This decision did not mean neglecting the war against Japan. By August 1941, when the build-up, especially of airplanes, was under way in the Philippines, and later when General Douglas MacArthur received orders to fight, the strategy was shifting to a two-front war. The war against Germany was to be offensive,

ON THE DEFENSIVE 1941–1942

While the United States was building and equipping its fighting forces, it had to depend upon the Russians and the British to hold back the Germans as best they could. During the discouraging first six months of American participation, the American forces had to stand perilously on the defensive in both the Atlantic and the Pacific. There even seemed danger of a breakthrough in Egypt and the Caucasus which might enable the Germans and Japanese to join forces in the Middle East or India.

Ten hours after the strike at Pearl Harbor, Japanese airplanes hit the airfields at Manila, destroying half the American bombers and two-thirds of the fighter planes. That same day the Japanese sank two British warships off Malaya, the only Allied warships in the Far

East. Three days later Guam fell; then, in the weeks that followed, Wake Island and Hong Kong. The great British fortress of Singapore in Malaya surrendered in February 1942, the Dutch East Indies in March, and Burma in April. In the Philippines on May 6 the exhausted Philippine and American troops, having made brave withdrawals to the Bataan peninsula and the Island of Corregidor in Manila Bay, ran down the last American flag in the Far East.

Only one weak outpost, Port Moresby in southern New Guinea, stood as a bulwark against the invasion of Australia. It seemed likely to fall, but there containment began through the efforts on land of Australian and American troops, and on the sea, of American aircraft carriers. In the Battle of Coral Sea on May 6–7, 1942, the Americans turned back Japanese invasion forces threatening Port Moresby. Under General MacArthur, who had escaped from the Philippines, American and Australian troops began clearing the Japanese from New Guinea.

After the Battle of Coral Sea, the navy, having intercepted Japanese messages, knew the next move and rushed every available plane and vessel into the central Pacific. Near Midway Island, June 3–6, 1942, these forces inflicted heavy damage on a Japanese invasion fleet and headed off a drive to capture the island and neutralize Hawaii. The United States had achieved its goal of containment in the Pacific, and as men and supplies could be spared from the operations against the Nazis, it could assume the offensive against Japan.

In the Atlantic during the early months of 1942, the Nazis tried by means of submarines to confine the Americans to the Western Hemisphere. By mid-January the Germans had moved so many submarines to the Atlantic coast, where at night they torpedoed tankers silhouetted against the lights of cities, that they created a critical oil shortage. Against convoys bound for Europe they made attacks with devastating success. In the first eleven months they sank over 8 million tons of shipping—1.2 million more than the Allies meanwhile built—and threatened to delay indefinitely the large-scale shipment of supplies and men to Europe. Gradually the United States countered by developing effective antisubmarine vessels, air patrols, detecting devices, and weapons.

The submarines made it difficult to send assistance to the British and Russians in the summer of 1942 when they needed it most. The German *Afrika Corps* raced to El Alamein, only seventy-five miles from Alexandria, Egypt, threatening the Suez Canal and the Middle East. At the same time, German armies in Russia were plunging toward the Caucasus. In May the Russian foreign minister, Vyacheslav Molotov, visited Washington to demand an immediate second front that would divert at least forty German divisions from Russia; the alternative might be Russian collapse. Roosevelt promised to do everything possible to divert the Germans by invading France. But Churchill arrived the next month, when the Gemans were threatening Egypt, and he strongly urged an invasion of North Africa instead.

THE MEDITERRANEAN OFFENSIVE

The overwhelming losses in the August 1942 raid on Dieppe, France, undertaken by experienced Canadian troops, indicated the wisdom of making the first American landing on a relatively unprotected flank. Through advance negotiations with officials of the Vichy government of defeated France, the Americans hoped to make a bloodless landing in French North Africa. At the end of October 1942 the British opened a counteroffensive at El Alamein which sent the *Afrika Corps* reeling back. On November 8, Anglo-American forces landed at Oran, Algiers, and Casablanca, Morocco, with some bungling and gratifyingly few losses. They met determined Vichy French resistance only at Casablanca.

Admiral Jean Darlan, earlier one of the most notorious collaborators with the Nazis, signed an armistice with the Allies on November 12. He ordered a cease-fire and promised the aid of 50,000 French colonial troops. Outraged American liberals protested against the deal with the Vichyites as opposed to the French resistance forces under General Charles de Gaulle. The critics quieted somewhat a few weeks later when Darlan was assassinated. Unsavory though it was to idealists, the Vichy gamble probably saved lives and speeded the liberation of North Africa.

The Germans tried to counter the invasion by ferrying troops from Sicily into Tunisia at

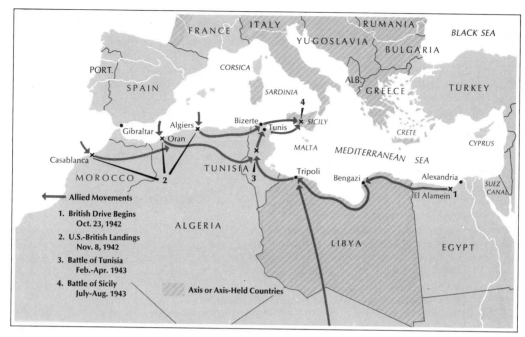

The North African and Sicilian Campaigns

the rate of a thousand a day. Early in 1943 the *Afrika Corps,* which had retreated westward across Tripoli, joined them and threw the full weight of its armor against the green American troops. The Americans lost heavily but with the aid of the British held onto their bases and gained in experience. Allied air power and the British navy so seriously harassed the Axis supply line from Sicily that Germany decided not to make a major stand in Tunisia. From March into May, the British army in the east and the armies in the west under Eisenhower gradually closed a vise on the German and Italian troops. On May 12, 1943, the last Axis troops in North Africa surrendered. The Mediterranean had been reopened, and the Americans had learned lessons that would be useful in the successful invasion of France.

That invasion, despite the continued clamoring of the Russians, was not to take place immediately. The fighting in Tunisia had tied up too large a part of the Allied combat resources for too long. Nazi submarines were still taking too heavy a toll of the Allies' inadequate shipping. Some of the ships and production had to be diverted to the antisubmarine war, and

others to the prosecution of the Pacific campaigns. Also, the planners in London had come to recognize that an enormous build-up was necessary for a successful cross-channel invasion. Fortunately for the Allies, the tide turned for the Russians also during the winter of 1942–1943, when they successfully held the Germans at Stalingrad in the Ukraine, eliminating an army of 250,000 men.

As early as mid-January 1943, Roosevelt and Churchill and their staffs, while conferring at Casablanca, looked ahead to the next move. This was to be an invasion of Sicily, even though General Marshall feared it might delay the invasion of France. Churchill argued persuasively that the operation in Sicily might knock Italy out of the war and lead the Germans to tie up many divisions in defense of Italy and the Balkans.

On the night of July 9, 1943, American and British armies landed in the extreme southeast of Sicily, where defenses were comparatively light. The Americans made grievous errors, the worst being to shoot down twenty-three planeloads of their own paratroops, but learned from their mistakes. In thirty-eight days the Allies conquered the island and looked toward the Italian mainland. Mussolini now fell from power, to be replaced by the pro-Allied Marshal Pietro Badoglio. At once Badoglio opened complicated negotiations to switch Italy to the side of the United Nations. As the negotiations went on, the Nazis moved eight strong divisions into northern Italy, concentrated other troops near Rome, and turned the country into an occupied defense bastion.

A limited but long and punishing campaign opened on the Italian peninsula on September 3, 1943. It started with the greatest optimism, for that same day the Italian government signed an armistice agreement, and the Allies quickly seized bases and airfields in southern Italy. But the Nazi defenders fought so fiercely from hillside fortifications that by early 1944 they had stopped the slow and deliberately moving Allies at Monte Cassino. When the Allies tried to break behind the line by landing at Anzio, south of Rome, they were almost thrown back into the sea. With relatively few divisions, the Nazis were tying down the Allies while concentrating their main effort upon Russia. Finally, in May 1944, the Allies captured Cassino, pressed on from the Anzio beachhead, and on June 4 captured Rome, just before the cross-channel invasion of France began.

THE LIBERATION OF EUROPE

In the fall of 1943 Germany was already reeling under the incessant blows from the growing Allied air power. Great Britain had begun its

The Invasion of Normandy
A coast guard combat photographer, climbing beyond the Nazi trench in the foreground to the top of the cliff, looked out at this panorama of channel waters crowded with ships while landing craft were putting ashore men and supplies. The barrage balloons floated overhead to protect the ships from low-flying enemy strafers. One of them is resting on the deck of an LST (landing barge). Long lines of trucks were heading inland, carrying reinforcements for the battle for the Cotentin peninsula. (Official U.S. Coast Guard photo)

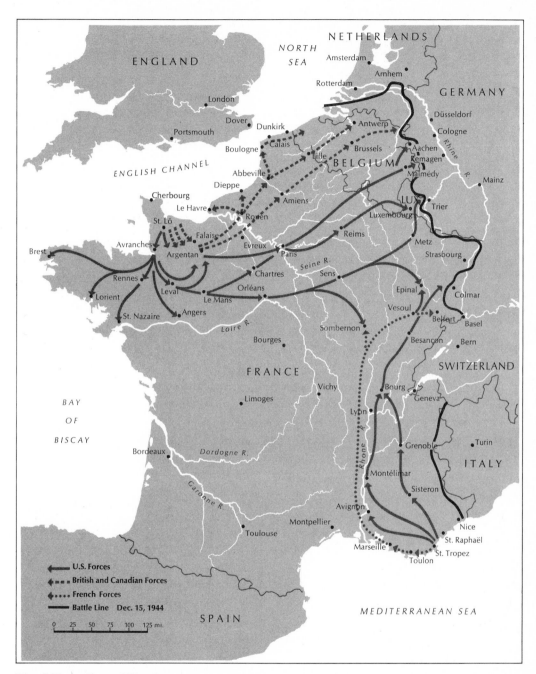

The Liberation of France

mass bombing of German industrial centers in the late spring of 1942 with a thousand-plane night raid on Cologne. In August the Americans made their first experimental daytime raids on the Continent. Bombing almost around-the-clock began on a gigantic scale in February 1944. One of the objects of these bombing raids was to draw German fighter planes into battle. By the end of the war the Americans were flying over 7,000 bombers and

6,000 fighters in Europe, had dropped nearly a million and a half tons of bombs, and had lost nearly 10,000 bombers. British figures were similar. Especially in the last year of the war, the bombing drastically cut production and impeded transportation. As early as the winter of 1944 it had so seriously demoralized the German people that 77 percent of them already regarded the war as lost.

The bombing attacks, first upon the aviation industry, then upon transportation, did much to clear the way for the invasion in the late spring. By May 1944 the *Luftwaffe* was incapable of beating off the Allied air cover for an invasion. As D-Day (invasion day) approached, the invasion was postponed from the beginning of May until early June despite the likelihood of worsening weather, in order to obtain an additional month's production of special landing craft. A sudden storm delayed the operation for a day, but on the morning of June 6, 1944, the invasion came, not at the narrowest part of the English Channel, where the Nazis expected it, but along sixty miles of the Cotentin peninsula on the Normandy coast. While airplanes and battleships offshore incessantly bombarded the Nazi defenses, 4,000 vessels, stretching as far as the eye could see, brought in troops and supplies.

Within two weeks after the initial landings, the Allies had put ashore a million men and the equipment for them. They also had captured Cherbourg, only to find that the Germans had blocked its harbor so skillfully that it could not be used until August.

Well into July, the Allies fought mile by mile through the Normandy hedgerows. The breakthrough came on July 25, 1944, when General Omar Bradley's First Army, using its armor as cavalry had been used in earlier wars, smashed the German lines in an enormous sweep southward, then eastward. The invasion on the Mediterranean coast, beginning on August 15, quickly seized new ports (also seriously blocked) and opened new supply lines for the Allies. On August 25 French forces rode into Paris, jammed with cheering throngs. By mid-September the Allied armies had driven the Germans from almost all of France and Belgium, including the port of Antwerp, and had come to a halt against a firm line of German defenses.

Cold weather, rain, and floods aided the Germans. In December they struck with desperate fury along fifty miles of front in the Ardennes Forest, driving fifty-five miles toward Antwerp before they were stopped (in the "Battle of the Bulge") at Bastogne.

While the Allies were fighting their way through France to the Westwall (German defense line) and up the Italian peninsula, the Russian armies had been sweeping westward into central Europe and the Balkans. The Russian armies advanced more rapidly than had been expected and, in late January 1945, launched an offensive of over 150 divisions toward the Oder River, far inside Germany.

After liquidating the German thrust into the Ardennes, which had almost exhausted the Nazi fighting capacity, the Allied armies pushed on to the Rhine. The Americans captured Cologne on the west bank March 6, 1945, and on the next day, through remarkable luck, captured a bridge across the Rhine at Remagen. Troops poured across it. By the end of March the last great drives were under way as the British commander Montgomery with a million troops pushed across the north while Bradley's army, sweeping through central Germany, completed the encirclement and trapping of 300,000 German soldiers in the Ruhr. Russian troops were about to mount a spring offensive only 35 miles from Berlin.

There were fears that the Nazis were preparing for a last stand in an Alpine redoubt centering on Berchtesgaden on the Austrian border. In fact, however, the German western front had been demolished. The only real questions were where the Americans would drive next and where they would join the Russians. The Americans, capable of moving much farther eastward than had been anticipated, could have beaten the Russians to Berlin and Prague. This would have cost American lives but would have reaped political gain in Europe. General Eisenhower decided, instead, to send American troops to capture the Alpine redoubt and then halt along the Elbe River in central Germany to meet the Russians.

On May 8, 1945, the remaining German forces surrendered unconditionally. V-E (Victory in Europe) Day arrived amidst monster celebrations in western Europe and in the United States. The rejoicing was tempered only by the knowledge of the continuing war against Japan.

THE PACIFIC OFFENSIVE

The offensive strategy against the Japanese involved amphibious warfare of a type that the marine corps had been developing since the early 1920s. In the Pacific these new tactics came to be so perfected that troops were able to cross and seize vigorously defended beaches when the United States could not by-pass them and immobilize advanced Japanese strong points. The American strategy was, whenever feasible, "Hit 'em where they ain't."

The southern Solomon Islands to the east of New Guinea were being developed as a Japanese base for air raids against American communications with Australia. In August 1942 the navy and marines opened an offensive against three of these islands, Gavutu, Tulagi, and Guadalcanal. Around and on Guadalcanal

a struggle of unprecedented ferocity developed as the United States and Japanese navies battled for control in a series of large-scale engagements. By the time the struggle was over, the United States and its allies had lost heavily in cruisers, carriers, and destroyers, but had sunk forty-seven Japanese vessels. The Japanese navy had lost its offensive strength and thereafter concentrated upon defensive operations.

During the months when the great naval battles had been going against the United States, the Americans had gained control of the air and thus were able to sustain the marines, and subsequently the army, in their precarious jungle onslaught. By February 1943 Guadalcanal had been won. Through the year the island-hopping continued all around the enormous Japanese-held perimeter: in the South

The War in the Pacific

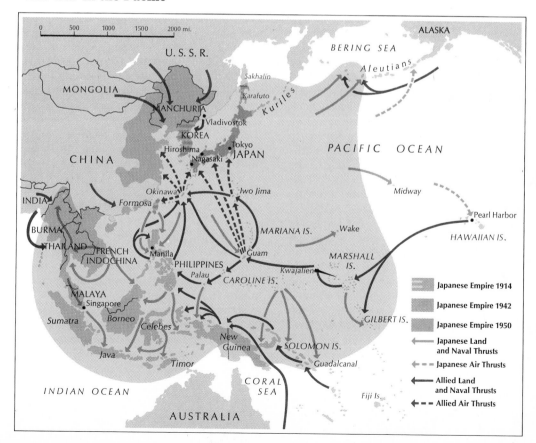

Pacific through the northern Solomons to New Georgia, and in November to Bougainville; in the central Pacific, also in November, the marine landing on Makin and the bloody assault on Tarawa in the Gilberts; in the northern Pacific, the inexpert reconquest of Kiska and Attu in the Aleutians.

Victories in the Marshall Islands in February 1944 cracked the Japanese outer perimeter, and before the month was out the navy had plunged far within it to wreck the bastion at Truk and raid Saipan in the Marianas. American submarines were increasingly harassing Japanese shipping, and thus hampering the economy. In 1943 the Americans sank 284 ships; in 1944 they sank 492 — necessitating by summer a cut of nearly a quarter in skimpy Japanese food rations and creating a crucial gasoline shortage. The inner empire of Japan was coming under relentless siege.

Meanwhile, in 1942, the Japanese forced General Joseph H. Stilwell out of Burma and brought their troops as far west as the mountains bordering on India. China was so isolated that the United States could send in meager supplies only through an aerial ferry over the "hump" of the Himalayas. On the return trip, the planes brought Chinese troops for Stilwell to train and arm. Through 1943, Stilwell with Chinese, Indian, and a few American troops fought back through northern Burma, constructing a road and parallel pipeline across the rugged mountains into Yunnan province, China. The Ledo or Stilwell road was not open until the fall of 1944, but meanwhile the Air Transport Command managed to fly in sufficient supplies to enable the Fourteenth Air Force (before Pearl Harbor, the "Flying Tigers") to harass the Japanese. The Command undertook a still larger task when B-29 bombers struck the Yawata steel mills in Japan from Chinese bases (June 1944). The Japanese retaliated in the next few months by overrunning the bases from which the bombers operated, and clearing the coastal area so they could bring supplies northward from Southeast Asia by rail or road. The drove so far into the interior that they threatened the Chinese terminus of the Ledo Road, and perhaps even the center of government at Chungking.

The great Japanese offensive precipitated a long-simmering crisis in Chinese-American affairs, centering upon the relations between General Stilwell and Chiang Kai-shek. Stilwell was indignant because Chiang was using many of his troops to maintain an armed frontier against the Chinese Communists and would not deploy them against the Japanese. In order to have bolstered Chiang adequately, the United States would have had to send such substantial immediate support that the campaigns against Germany and directly against Japan might have had to be slowed down or postponed.

During 1944 Japan came under heavy blockade from the sea and bombardment from the air. American submarines firing torpedoes and laying mines continued to make heavy inroads in the dwindling Japanese merchant marine.

In mid-June an enormous American armada struck the heavily fortified Mariana Islands, quickly but expensively capturing Tinian, Guam, and Saipan, 1,350 miles from Tokyo. These were among the bloodiest operations of the war. In September the Americans landed on the western Carolines. The way was being prepared for the return to the Philippines. For weeks in advance navy craft swept the central Pacific, and airplanes ranged over the Philippines and Formosa. Finally, on October 20 General MacArthur's troops landed on Leyte Island in the Philippines. The Japanese, threatened with being fatally cut off from their new empire in Southeast Asia, threw their remaining fleets against the invaders in three major encounters — together comprising the decisive Battle of Leyte Gulf, the largest naval engagement in history — and lost almost all their remaining sea power.

ATOMIC TRIUMPH OVER JAPAN

With remarkable speed but grievous losses the American forces cut still deeper into the Japanese empire during the early months of 1945. While fighting continued in the Philippines, the marines landed in February on the tiny volcanic island of Iwo Jima, only 750 miles from Tokyo. The Americans needed Iwo Jima to provide fighter cover for Japan-bound bombers and a landing place for crippled ones. The Japanese defended the island so grimly that the marines suffered over 20,000 casualties. It was the bloodiest battle in the history of the marine corps.

The battle for Okinawa, an island sixty-five miles long, beginning on April 1, 1945, was even

Hiroshima, Japan, Looking Northeast   October 1945
"A single atomic bomb, the first weapon of its type ever used against a target, exploded over the city of Hiroshima at 0815 on the morning of 6 August 1945. Most of the industrial workers had already reported to work, but many workers were en route and nearly all of the school children and some industrial employees were at work in the open on the program of building removal. . . . The explosion came as an almost complete surprise, and the people had not taken shelter. Many were caught in the open, and most of the rest in flimsily constructed homes or commercial establishments. The bomb exploded slightly northwest of the center of the city. Because of this accuracy and the flat terrain and circular shape of the city, Hiroshima was uniformly and extensively devastated. Practically the entire densely or moderately built-up portion of the city was leveled by blast and swept by fire. . . . The surprise, the collapse of many buildings, and the conflagration contributed to an unprecedented casualty rate. Seventy to eighty thousand people were killed, or missing and presumed dead, and an equal number were injured."
—Report, United States Strategic Bombing Survey. (National Archives)

bloodier. This island lies 370 miles south of Japan, and its conquest clearly would be a prelude to an invasion of the main islands. On land and from the air, the Japanese fought with literally a suicidal fury. Week after week they sent *kamikaze* suicide planes against the American and British ships, losing 3,500 of them but inflicting great damage. Ashore at night, Japanese troops launched equally desperate attacks on the American lines. The United States and its allies suffered nearly 50,000 casualties on land and afloat before the battle came to an end in late June 1945. The Japanese lost 110,000 killed and 7,800 prisoners.

This same sort of bitter fighting seemed to await the Americans when they invaded Ja-

pan—if indeed they should ever have to invade. There were signs that the Japanese might surrender, for they had almost no ships and few airplanes with which to fight. In July 1945 American warships stood offshore with impunity and shelled industrial targets, most of which were already in ruins from the heavy bombing attacks. Long since, moderate Japanese leaders had regarded the war as lost. Upon the invasion of Okinawa, the Emperor appointed a new premier and instructed him to sue for peace. The premier could not persuade the army leaders to lay down their arms, but nevertheless he, and in early summer the Emperor himself, tried to obtain mediation through Russia.

Apparently the Russians were determined, at their own time, to enter the war. But the atomic bomb rather than Russian intervention was to be decisive in bringing the war to an end. At a meeting of Allied leaders in Potsdam, Germany, in mid-July 1945, President Harry S Truman (who had succeeded Roosevelt) received word that the first atomic test was successful. He and Prime Minister Clement Attlee (who had succeeded Churchill) issued the Potsdam Declaration urging the Japanese to surrender or face utter devastation. The Japanese premier wished to accept the ultimatum, but the army leaders would not surrender. President Truman had set August 3 as the deadline; when it passed and the Japanese continued to fight, he ordered an atomic bomb to be dropped on one of four previously selected Japanese cities.

On August 6, 1945, a B-29 dropped an atomic bomb on Hiroshima, destroying most of the hitherto undamaged city, and killing 80,000 people (according to American estimates) or 200,000 (according to the Japanese). Even after the horror of Hiroshima, the Japanese army remained adamant. Russia declared war on Japan as of August 9. That same day, the air force dropped a second atomic bomb, on Nagasaki. This was the final blow. After frantic negotiations, on August 14 the Japanese government agreed to give up. On September 2, 1945, aboard the battleship *Missouri* in Tokyo Bay, the articles of surrender were signed.

World War II was at an end. All together, some 14 million men under arms had been killed, and countless millions of civilians had died. In comparison, about 322,000 Americans had been killed or were missing; total United States casualties were about 1,120,000. Despite this frightful expenditure in lives and an astronomical cost in material resources, the American people faced a future made uncertain and perilous by the tensions with the Russians and the threat of future atomic wars.

Frustrations of Peacemaking

Only the imminent threat of Axis victory had forced an uneasy and unsatisfactory form of cooperation between Russia and its Western allies, Great Britain and the United States. As the threat began to lift in 1943, it became increasingly difficult to keep the alliance cemented and to plan for a postwar world in which a decent peace could be maintained.

THE DANGEROUS ALLIANCE

The difference between British and American strategy — the British opposing a cross-channel invasion and preferring campaigns in southern and eastern Europe — affected the two nations' dealings with the Russians. To a certain extent the United States seemed nearer to the Russians in insisting with them upon an early invasion of France. Roosevelt seemed at times to take a middle position between Stalin and Churchill.

As the Nazi tide receded, the postwar patterns began to emerge throughout eastern Europe, as they were already doing in Italy. Firm political agreements were necessary if these areas were not to fall entirely under Russian hegemony, just as firm military plans were essential to the achievement of final victory.

At Casablanca, Morocco, in January 1943, after previous consultation with Churchill, Roosevelt announced the doctrine of unconditional surrender by the Axis. What Roosevelt seemed to desire was to avoid the sort of negotiations that had marred the 1918 armistice, causing bickerings among the Allies at the time and German misunderstandings afterward. As the war progressed, it became clear that "unconditional surrender" left the United Nations free to state to the Axis powers the peace terms the latter might expect. Roosevelt and Churchill both emphasized that the phrase did not mean, as the Nazi propagandists charged, that extremely severe terms would be imposed. Yet, after the war, some historians charged that the "unconditional surrender" doctrine seriously discouraged the anti-Nazi German underground movement, stiffened the Nazi will to fight, and thus lengthened the war.

In October 1943 Secretary Hull, although he was seventy-two and in precarious health, flew to Moscow to confer with the British and

Russian foreign ministers. His faith in Wilsonian idealism almost limitless, Hull returned from Moscow elated because the Russians had agreed to a Declaration of Four Nations on General Security. (China was the fourth nation.) This was a pledge to continue the united action of war "for the organization and maintenance of peace and security" and to create, as soon as practicable, a general international organization.

With an air of optimism Roosevelt and Churchill traveled eastward in November 1943 for a long-awaited meeting with Stalin at Teheran, Iran. On the way they stopped at Cairo to confer with Chiang Kai-shek and to prepare a statement (released after the Teheran conference) drawing a map for the postwar Far East. They proposed stripping Japan of her empire in order to restore Manchuria, the Pescadores, and Formosa to China, and to create in due course a free and independent Korea. Japan was to lose, in addition, all other territory she had acquired since 1914.

At Teheran, Roosevelt undertook to establish a friendly, intimate relationship with Stalin of the sort he enjoyed with Churchill. Stalin reaffirmed his intention to bring Russia into the Pacific war soon after hostilities had ended in

---

Stalin, Roosevelt, and Churchill at Teheran

"We — The President of the United States, the Prime Minister of Great Britain, and the Premier of the Soviet Union, have met these four days past, in this, the Capital of our Ally, Iran, and have shaped and confirmed our common policy.

"We express our determination that our nations shall work together in war and in the peace that will follow. . . .

"Emerging from these cordial conferences we look with confidence to the day when all peoples of the world may live free lives, untouched by tyranny, and according to their varying desires and their own consciences.

"We came here with hope and determination. We leave here, friends in fact, in spirit and in purpose." — From a joint statement issued December 1, 1943. (National Archives)

Europe, and expressed his satisfaction with the Cairo communiqué on Japan. In a cordial way the three leaders discussed the means, through an international organization, of keeping Germany from ever again becoming a menace. Stalin wished Russia to retain the areas she had seized in her period of collaboration with Germany, including eastern Poland as far as the so-called Curzon line proposed in 1919. Roosevelt and Churchill agreed to the Polish boundary.

Roosevelt and Churchill seem not to have recognized realistically the nature of the peace that was being foreshadowed at Teheran. In the general rejoicing over the apparent accord among the Big Three, and in their assumption that Russia would be content within its new boundaries, they overlooked the appraisal that one of the American participants at Teheran wrote a few days later: "The result would be that the Soviet Union would be the only important military and political force on the continent of Europe. The rest of Europe would be reduced to military and political impotence."

It was unrealistic to expect, as Roosevelt apparently did, that the Russians would forbear from exploiting the great European and Asian power vacuums that the defeat of Germany and Japan would create. This miscalculation led the United States into a tragic triumph — a victory without peace.

THE YALTA CONFERENCE

Churchill's mood fluctuated with the ebb and flow of Russian good will. Upon leaving Moscow, after a visit in the fall of 1944, he wrote Stalin: "This memorable meeting . . . has shown that there are no matters that cannot be adjusted between us when we meet together in frank and intimate discussion." By January 1945 he was so badly disillusioned that he wrote Roosevelt concerning the forthcoming Yalta meeting: "This may well be a fateful Conference, coming at a moment when the Great Allies are so divided and the shadow of the war lengthens out before us. At the present time I think the end of this war may well prove to be more disappointing than was the last." Such was the bleak and unpromising setting for the great conference at Yalta in the Crimea (February 1945).

At that time American forces were having to reduce Germany mile by mile; there seemed no reason to think Japan would be different. General MacArthur insisted on the necessity for Russian aid, taking the position that otherwise the United States would have to fight a series of difficult and expensive campaigns to overcome the Japanese in Manchuria. Consequently the Joint Chiefs did not revise their timetable calling for the defeat of Japan eighteen months after German surrender, and they continued to regard Russian aid as indispensable. Roosevelt expressed to Stalin his hope that Japan could be bombed into submission without invasion — but the Americans could not count upon it.

These were the limitations upon the Americans in their bargaining at Yalta. In return for Stalin's reiterated promise to enter the Far Eastern war two or three months after German surrender, Roosevelt and Churchill promised him the Kurile Islands north of Japan and the restoration of "the former rights of Russia" lost in the Russo-Japanese War. This meant the return of southern Sakhalin Island, the return of a lease on Port Arthur as a naval base and internationalizing of the port of Dairen, Manchuria (in both instances with recognition of Russia's preeminent interests), and joint operation with China of the Chinese Eastern and South Manchurian railroads feeding into the ports. China was to retain sovereignty over Manchuria, but Roosevelt did not clarify what "preeminent interests" meant. (For many months these clauses remained secret because Russia was still at peace with Japan.)

In its disposition of central European questions, the Yalta conference for the most part ratified previous decisions. Germany was to be divided into zones of occupation previously agreed upon. Since Berlin was to be deep in the Russian zone, the Americans and British proposed an accord providing freedom of transit into Berlin. The Russians held back, and in the general spirit of amity at Yalta, the matter was postponed. At the time, the Russian demands for heavy reparations in the form of German factories, goods, and labor seemed far more important. The British tried to scale down the Russian demand for $20 billion in such reparations, of which Russia was to obtain half. This would so strip and starve the Germans, Churchill pointed out, that the United States

Enlisting Russian Aid Against Japan at Yalta [1945]

I think there was the belief that Russia's entry into the war [against Japan] before we hit the islands would save hundreds of thousands of American casualties. . . . The disposition of Chinese territories, as you know, was subsequently embodied in the Soviet-Chinese Treaty of August 1945, which was almost universally hailed in this country, as well as, I believe, in China, as a great event, because this treaty involved the recognition by the Soviet Union of the sovereignty of the Chinese Nationalist Government over Manchuria. . . .

The first reaction from the Chinese was not one that they had been sold, as it were, down the river. Mr. T. V. Soong in his negotiations in Moscow found the Yalta agreement of considerable use to him as a backstop.

There are now, in retrospect, two valid criticisms of the agreement: First it was unnecessary, the war did not take the course predicted; and, secondly, it was done without the participation of the Chinese Government. — Testimony of Charles E. Bohlen (who had been an assistant to the Secretary of State and interpreter at Yalta), on his nomination as ambassador to Russia, before the Senate Committee on Foreign Relations, 1953.

---

and Great Britain would have to feed them. Consequently he and Roosevelt agreed to the Russian figure only as a basis for discussion by a reparations commission. Already, in the light of reality, the West had left far behind the Morgenthau plan (initialed by Roosevelt and Churchill at Quebec in October 1944) for the pastoralization of Germany.

One of the touchiest questions was what would constitute a democratic government for Poland, a matter over which Russia and the West had negotiated for months. The Russians did not wish to allow the Polish government in exile in London or the Polish underground to assume any substantial share of power with a government the Russians had established at Lublin. At the beginning of August 1944, as the Red army drove within ten miles of Warsaw, the underground in the city arose against the Germans. The Russians halted, ignored the revolt, and despite the strong pleas of the United States and Great Britain, stood by while the Polish patriots were annihilated in sixty-three days of fighting. The Russian explanation was military exigency, but the situation seemed to show the sort of government Stalin was determined to establish in Poland.

At Yalta the West managed to obtain Stalin's agreement that the Lublin (Communist) government should be broadened to include democratic leaders from Poland and abroad.

What the percentage should be was not specified. Subsequently the new government should hold "free and unfettered elections as soon as possible on the basis of universal suffrage and secret ballot." It would have been a satisfactory arrangement for the West if the terms had been interpreted in their Western meaning. As for the Polish boundary, it was to follow the Curzon line in the east, and the Poles were to receive territorial compensation in the north and west.

For the rest of liberated or defeated Europe, the Big Three agreed to establish interim governments "broadly representative of all democratic elements" and to provide for free elections that would create "governments responsible to the will of the people."

In years after the war, disappointed Americans harshly criticized the Yalta agreements, especially for their violations of the Atlantic Charter. The morality of the Far Eastern arrangements is open to challenge. Their purpose was to obtain Russian aid, which top military leaders thought would shorten the war against Japan and perhaps prevent a million American casualties. The terms promised nothing to Stalin that he could not have taken anyway. The morality of the European arrangements (except perhaps for the ethnic dislocations wrought by the new Polish boundaries) would have been defensible if the terms

had received their customary Western interpretation. Roosevelt may be most severely
criticized for not insisting at every point upon
absolutely clear, sharply defined agreements
that could receive only one interpretation in
Russia — the interpretation as understood by
the West. This was especially true of the question of entry into Berlin. Experience with the
Russians long before Yalta had pointed to the
need for precise understandings.

Roosevelt was careless in this respect
because he pinned his hopes upon the good
faith of the Russians and their willingness to
enter into and actively participate in an international organization for the preservation of
the peace.

THE U. N. ORGANIZATION

A few months before war broke out in Europe — and long before the attack at Pearl Harbor — Secretary Hull had taken the first step
toward proposing a new international organization in which the United States would participate. In January 1940 he appointed an
Advisory Committee on Problems of Foreign
Relations. Its membership was composed of
congressmen from both parties and distinguished experts from within and without the
State Department. Several private organizations like the Council on Foreign Relations also
prepared numerous studies for the State
Department.

Signing the U.N. Charter
*Delegates from fifty nations attended a conference that met in the
San Francisco Opera House, April 25, 1945, to prepare a charter
for the United Nations organization. The delegates signed the completed
charter on June 26. In this photograph President Truman shakes hands
with Secretary of State Edward R. Stettinius, Jr., chairman of the
American delegation, after the signing by the Americans. (United
Nations)*

President Roosevelt, firmly determined to avoid Wilson's failure, encouraged Hull to include Republicans in the planning for the peace. However, Roosevelt did not consult Congress before making his most famous statements of war aims; Senator Robert A. Taft asserted in 1943 that he did not believe "we went to war to establish the 'four freedoms' or any other freedom throughout the world," nor "for the purposes set forth in the Atlantic Charter." The administration, to counter this sort of resentment, included prominent Republicans in at least sketchy briefings on wartime diplomacy and let them participate more fully in postwar planning of many kinds. In this way it won their support. In 1943 four senators, two Republican and two Democratic, none of whom were serving on the Foreign Relations Committee, introduced a resolution calling for American leadership in establishing a United Nations organization. Public opinion polls indicated a general enthusiasm for the resolution; the Senate passed a similar declaration 85 to 5. Senator Arthur H. Vandenberg of Michigan, previously one of the most forthright isolationists, assumed Republican leadership in helping mold a "bipartisan" foreign policy. He thus gained for himself and the Republican party new power and stature.

The Big Four powers, conferring in the summer and fall of 1944 at Dumbarton Oaks, a Harvard-owned estate in Washington, drafted tentative outlines for a new international organization. These were the starting points for the drafting of a United Nations charter at a conference of fifty nations in San Francisco, opening April 25, 1945. President Roosevelt had appointed a bipartisan delegation headed by his new Secretary of State, Edward R. Stettinius, Jr. One of its most effective members was Senator Vandenberg, who helped to wrest concessions from the Russians at San Francisco and to win the votes of reluctant Republicans for ratification in the Senate.

Basically the charter of the United Nations was a refurbishing of the old Wilsonian League covenant with the former American objections removed through giving a veto to each of the five main powers. The Americans and British, as well as the Russians, had insisted upon the veto as a seemingly necessary protection of their sovereignty. The American delegates, led by Vandenberg, succeeded in obtaining for the small nations in the General Assembly freedom to discuss and make recommendations – in effect creating "a town meeting of the world."

The Senate quickly ratified the charter (July 1945) by a vote of 80 to 2, in remarkable contrast to the slow and painful defeat it had administered to American membership in the League of Nations. But the great and growing gulf between Russia and the West destined the United Nations to be, like its predecessor, the League, a town meeting for international discussion or a sounding board for national views, rather than the forerunner of a world government.

A FOURTH TERM FOR F. D. R.

With "bipartisanship" prevailing, there had been no serious disagreement between Democrats and Republicans on the issues of peace planning. But in regard to domestic questions there had been politics as usual. Indeed, despite all the platitudinous pleas to put aside politics in the interest of national unity, the struggles became even more virulent during war.

Conservatives saw in the war an opportunity to eradicate hated remnants of the New Deal; some liberals regarded it as an opportunity to bring Wilson's ideas to fruition, and even go beyond them to establish a global New Deal. Every one of the great pressure groups in the country fought to maintain or improve its relative position; spokesmen for large business and small, farmers and labor, jockeyed for position in Washington. The tenor of Congress continued to be conservative, and it was sensitive as always to the demands of organized constituents. Throughout the war, key committee chairmen who were leaders of the conservative coalition dominated Congress and forced their will upon President Roosevelt. Through the election of 1942, as the United States and its allies suffered unparalleled military disasters and the war administration in Washington seemed to compound confusion, the criticism rose to a crescendo. In the election, the Republicans gained forty-seven seats in the House and ten in the Senate. Within both parties the trend was to the right.

President Roosevelt, in order to get crucial congressional support in prosecuting the war and planning the peace, continued to accept the sacrifice of New Deal measures. At a press conference in 1943 he announced that "Dr. Win-the-War" had replaced "Dr. New Deal."

Dissatisfaction with wartime regimentation and smoldering resentments still glowing from the prewar debate over intervention seemed to give the Republicans an opportunity in 1944. They had seen auguries of a national shift toward the right in the congressional election of 1942. In their vigorous young candidate, Governor Thomas E. Dewey of New York, who ran with Governor John W. Bricker of Ohio, they seemed to have an answer to Roosevelt and the aging New Dealers.

As for President Roosevelt, it was a foregone conclusion that he would be nominated for a fourth term if he so desired. There was none of the suspense that had preceded the third-term nomination. Rather, since he was visibly aging, unwell, and thinning so that his clothes ill fit him, there was much speculation over his choice for the vice-presidential nominee. During the war, Vice President Wallace was the hero of most advanced New Dealers and much of the CIO membership. But he was sneered at by party bosses and some Southern Democrats as a visionary who wished to extend the New Deal to the entire globe, to bring "a quart of milk for every Hottentot." They rallied behind James M. Byrnes of South Carolina, who had been functioning ably as the unofficial assistant president — but Byrnes was unacceptable to organized labor. Out of the skirmishing among the rival factions within the Democratic party came Roosevelt's proposal of a compromise candidate acceptable to most of them, Senator Harry S Truman of Missouri. Truman had won newspaper approval as chairman of the Senate War Investigating Committee, was a consistent New Dealer in his voting record, and was from a border state. He was popular in the Senate.

In keeping with the bipartisan spirit, Republican and Democratic leaders had arranged for practically identical planks on foreign policy, thus eliminating it as an issue in the campaign. Dewey had a good chance to make it an issue when he got word that American intelligence had broken the Japanese code before Pearl Harbor. With this information, he could have charged that the Roosevelt administration knew — or should have known — of the coming Japanese attack. But an envoy from General Marshall dissuaded Dewey from using the information, which if made public would have caused the Japanese to change their code (American intelligence was still exploiting it) and thus would have disadvantaged United States forces fighting in the Pacific. Even without this issue, the election promised to be close — partly because the vote was likely to be small, and presumably a light vote would aid the Republicans.

The possibility was like an injection of adrenalin into Roosevelt. At the end of September 1944, addressing a raucously appreciative audience of Teamsters Union members, he was at his sardonic best. He followed this triumph with a strenuous campaign in Chicago and throughout the East. This he climaxed with a day-long drive in an open car through New York City in a soaking rain.

Roosevelt's seeming capacity to serve four more years, his international leadership, and his promise to return to the New Deal after the war were a winning combination. Organized labor, working through the CIO Political Action Committee, brought out the workers' votes. The President defeated Dewey by a margin of 432 electoral votes to 99, and a popular vote of 25,602,000 to 22,006,000. The Democrats lost one seat in the Senate, but gained twenty in the House. The Democratic victory seemed to mean a revival of the New Deal at home, and the campaign promises of both parties indicated that the United States would continue to take a lead in international affairs.

But President Roosevelt lived to see neither the triumph in war nor the tragedy of peace. Already his vigor was draining away, and he could ill afford the exertions of the campaign or those of the grueling trip to Yalta. Addressing Congress on his return, he was very tired and for the first time he made public reference to his paralyzed legs and his heavy steel braces as he remained seated and spoke optimistically of the Yalta agreement — which he said contained no secret provisions. Suddenly, on the afternoon of April 12, 1945, he died of a cerebral hemorrhage at his private retreat in Warm Springs, Georgia.

TRUMAN TAKES OVER

Through no fault of his own, President Harry S Truman was unbriefed and poorly prepared for the task of concluding the war and making the peace. No one doubted his sincerity when he remarked to reporters the day after he had suddenly taken his oath of office: "I felt like the moon, the stars, and all the planets had fallen on me. I've got the most terribly responsible job a man ever had."

During the first phase of his relations with the Russians, Truman was moderately firm but tried to give the Soviet government no cause for protest. He was chagrined when in May 1945 the Foreign Economic Administration enforced his order ending Lend-Lease so precipitately as to call back some ships at sea. The British were the most hard-hit, but Stalin complained most bitterly.

At the Potsdam conference (July 1945) Truman could secure few satisfactory agreements on questions involving occupied and liberated countries. Despite the failure at Potsdam, Truman's Secretary of State, James F. Byrnes, continued in a conciliatory fashion to seek accommodation with the Russians.

The Potsdam conferees provided for a Council of Foreign Ministers to draft treaties with Italy and the former Axis satellites. During a tedious and depressing round of meetings of the council in London, Moscow, Paris, and New York (between September 1945 and December 1946), relations between the West and Russia steadily deteriorated, though five treaties were concluded. The one with Italy reflected Western demands; those with Finland, Hungary, Rumania, and Bulgaria in effect incorporated Soviet armistice terms. By ratifying the three latter treaties, the United States acquiesced in the Russian domination of these nations.

In Berlin a four-power Allied Control Council began sessions marked by the same blocking and delaying tactics that made other joint conferences with the Russians so dismal. The Western nations had visualized unified controls for Germany to prevent its resurgence. But the Russians had no interest in a Germany reunified in a manner acceptable to the West. Germany was to remain split indefinitely.

Meanwhile in occupied Germany and Japan, the United States pursued firm but conflicting policies compounded of harshness and idealism. During the war the American people had come to hate the enemy leaders and were insistent that they be punished for their war crimes, especially those Nazis who were responsible for the maintenance of frightful concentration camps like Buchenwald and for the gas-chamber murder of millions of Jews. This led to the trials of thousands of Nazis and war criminals, capped by that of twenty-two key Nazi leaders before an International Military Tribunal at Nuremberg in 1945–1946. Eleven were sentenced to death.

There was also a sweeping purge of Japan, and a trial was held for twenty-five former top Japanese military and civil officials. Seven of them, including two premiers, were executed. The dangerous precedent seemed to be established, as Churchill pointed out, that "the leaders of a nation defeated in war shall be put to death by the victors."

At first the Americans seemed bent on the pastoralization as well as reform of conquered Germany. They banned all industry directly or indirectly contributing to German war potential, including even the construction of seagoing ships, drastically cut steel and chemical production, destroyed munition plants, and allowed the dismantling of some factories for shipment to the Russians. They disbanded cartels and encouraged only agriculture and peaceful domestic industries. Along with this, they wished to foster American-style democracy in place of the repudiated Nazism. These economic policies, coming at a time when so much of German housing and industry was rubble, and when several million exiles were making their way from eastern Germany and from Czechoslovakia, reduced western Germany to a living standard not much better than that of a giant relief camp. The army undertook to feed the German people between 1945 and 1948 at a subsistence level of 950–1,550 calories per day.

Even this near-starvation diet cost the British and Americans nearly half a billion dollars per year. The Russians were adding further to the economic burden by taking out of their zone (and from the western zones to the extent agreed at Potsdam) reparations totaling $1.5 to $3 billion dollars per year. They were siphoning out of Germany more than the Americans and British could pump in.

In Japan American occupation policy suffered fewer obstacles and profited from the initial errors in Germany. During the first critical weeks General MacArthur, the Supreme Commander for the Allied Powers (SCAP), set up an overwhelmingly American occupation, based on a directive radioed him from Washington on August 29, 1945. Truman refused Stalin's demand that Russians occupy part of the northern Japanese island, Hokkaido. The irritated Russians had a voice, but no real power, on an eleven-country Far Eastern Commission in Washington and on a four-power Allied Council to advise MacArthur in Tokyo.

The American occupation authorities in Japan acted rapidly to demilitarize and democratize the country. From the outset they recognized that Japan must be left with a healthy economy, but in practice — by limiting the nation's war potential — they reduced Japan like Germany to a relief state.

Postwar Readjustments

The glad new day that wartime propaganda had foretold was not to dawn when the fighting stopped. Somehow, Americans had to readjust to the troublesome realities of postwar life. The most serious political problems had to do with the adaptation of the military establishment and the economic system to the new conditions — which were themselves uncertain.

MILITARY REORGANIZATION

In the face of growing menaces in Europe and Asia, the United States speedily dismantled its army, air force, and navy. At the end of the war, there was a popular demand to "bring the boys back." In April 1946 President Truman announced that nearly 7 million men had been released from the army — "the most remarkable demobilization in the history of the world, or 'disintegration,' if you want to call it that." He proposed a system of universal military training, but Congress did no more between 1946 and 1948 than to pass limited Selective Service measures. The gradual whittling of the armed forces continued, until by the spring of 1950 the army was down to 600,000 men, and the ceiling on defense expenditures, to $13 billion. Lacking land armies, the United States sought to balance the Soviet power with atomic bombs and an air force that could deliver them.

Since September 1945 the administration had been ready to negotiate an agreement with Russia which would "control and limit the use of the atomic bomb as an instrument of war" and "direct and encourage the development of atomic power for peaceful and humanitarian purposes." Great Britain and Canada joined with the United States in proposing international control of atomic energy. The United Nations Assembly responded by creating the

United Nations Atomic Energy Commission (January 1946), to which the American member, Bernard Baruch, submitted a plan. This proposed a thoroughgoing system of control and inspection of atomic energy development through a United Nations agency. When the system became effective, the United States would liquidate its stockpile and join in an international ban on atomic bombs.

The Russians refused to accept the Baruch plan for international inspection and control of atomic development. They demanded that the United States first destroy its stockpile of atom bombs. Through their widespread propaganda the Russians tried to marshal world indignation against the United States while they rushed ahead with their own research on atomic weapons. American scientists and military leaders, not aware as yet of the successful Russian espionage, and underrating Russian scientific and technical proficiency, predicted that it would be many years before the Soviet Union could produce a successful bomb.

Meanwhile, Congress lengthily debated the domestic control of American atomic energy. Democrats wished to vest control in civilians; Senator Vandenberg and the Republicans urged giving it to the heads of the armed forces. A compromise was reached in the Atomic Energy Act of 1946. This created a five-man civilian Atomic Energy Commission with complete control over research and development of fissionable materials; linked to it was a Military Liaison Committee.

Under the protection of an atomic umbrella, military leaders indulged in the luxury of a vigorous and prolonged controversy over unification of the various armed forces. This measure, proposed to bring greater efficiency and effectiveness, led instead to heightened rivalry, as the generals pushed for it, and the admirals feared for the loss of the marine corps and the relative weakening of the navy. Both sides brought the utmost pressure upon Congress. Finally, the National Security Act (July 1947) provided for a secretary of defense to preside over separate Departments of the Army, Navy, and Air Force, with the Joint Chiefs of Staff serving as advisers to him and to the President. To coordinate diplomacy and military planning, the 1947 act also provided for a National Security Council to consist of the President, certain cabinet members, and other advisers on foreign and military policy. This control was to be served by two other new agencies, a National Security Resources Board and a Central Intelligence Agency.

Within the reorganized Pentagon Building the old rivalries continued. Indeed, through the creation of a separate air force there now appeared to be three separate services where there had been only two before. The first Secretary of Defense, James V. Forrestal, exhausted by the struggle to make unification effective, resigned in 1949 and committed suicide. His successor, Louis A. Johnson, became embroiled in a violent quarrel over cancellation of construction of a huge new aircraft carrier, a quarrel culminating in the resignation of the Secretary of the Navy and the replacement of the Chief of Naval Operations. This crisis led to amendments to the National Security Act, forcing greater unification, and formally establishing a Department of Defense.

RECONVERSION AND INFLATION

On September 6, 1945, only four days after the Japanese surrender ceremonies, the President sent to Congress a twenty-one-point domestic program outlining what he later termed the "Fair Deal." He called for the expansion of social security, the raising of the legal minimum wage from 40 to 65 cents an hour, a full employment bill, a permanent Fair Employment Practices Act, public housing and slum clearance, long-range planning for the protection of natural resources and building of public works (like TVA), and government promotion of scientific research. Within ten weeks he sent additional recommendations to Congress for federal aid to education, for health insurance and prepaid medical care, and for the St. Lawrence seaway project.

Congress acted upon several of the President's recommendations. The Maximum Employment Act became law in 1946. It established a three-man Council of Economic Advisers to aid the President and issue an annual economic report. Although the experts frequently disagreed, they became an integral part of the governmental machinery. They did much to accustom the public to the new economics that had been emerging during the New Deal and the war.

Congressional conservatives tried to steer Congress and the public away from the Fair Deal program by concentrating upon the reconversion of industry to peacetime production. Truman himself recommended, first, speedily removing all possible controls that would hamper reconversion and, second, preventing increases in prices, rents, and wages. The two aims could easily conflict.

Under the friendly Roosevelt administration, union membership soared during the New Deal and World War II. Note that CIO figures are not available for 1948–1950; from 1951 on, the chart indicates the combined AFL and CIO membership.

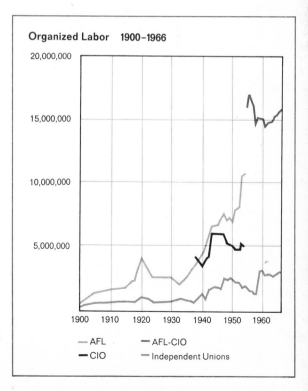

Organized Labor   1900–1966

After Germany surrendered, cutbacks in war orders began, and after Japan capitulated, $35 billion in contracts was suddenly cancelled. The War Production Board soon dropped controls, except on commodities that were still very scarce. Congress passed a new revenue bill cutting taxes nearly $6 billion. The War Assets Administration, established in January 1946, sold several hundred war plants, mostly to the corporations that had been operating them, and disposed of mountains of surplus, some of which enabled veterans with priorities to start small businesses. Members of the armed forces, who were being demobilized at an unparalleled pace, found their problems of readjustment to civilian life eased by the Servicemen's Readjustment Act of 1944 (the "G.I. Bill of Rights") which provided them with further education and training, or aid while unemployed or starting in business or farming.

Industry changed back to civilian production with more speed and less economic dislocation than had been expected. The gloomy forecasts of 8 million unemployed did not materialize. By the end of November 1945, peacetime employment was up to the end-of-the-war total, and 93 percent of the war plants had been reconverted.

The expected glut of surplus goods did not materialize either. Instead, acute problems of scarcity arose. Shortages ranged from automobiles and appliances to men's suits, nylon stockings, and beef. Consumers commanded some $129 billion or more in savings and billions more in credit with which to back their demands. Added to these were the needs of the rest of the world. Against such pressures, it was impossible for the Office of Price Administration to hold prices down to the 1941–1942 level.

If prices were to be checked, wages must be also, and if wages were to be held down, so must prices be. It was a vicious circle. By January 1946 workers had gone on strike in a number of the nation's critical industries — steel, automobiles, electrical manufacturing, and others. When Philip Murray demanded a 25-cents-an-hour increase for the United Steelworkers to bring them up to their wartime take-home pay, President Benjamin F. Fairless of United States Steel, acting as spokesman for the industry, refused unless the government would allow a $7-per-ton increase in the price of steel. President Truman announced that

labor was entitled to the 33 percent that living costs had gone up since January 1941. The Wage Stabilization Board must approve the increase; but if it cut profits below the prewar level, the companies might obtain corresponding price increases. Ultimately there was a steel settlement allowing raises of 18-1/2 cents an hour and $5 per ton. Throughout industry, the "bulge" led to a round of similar raises in wages and prices.

In April 1946 John L. Lewis precipitated a fresh crisis. He demanded that the bituminous coal workers receive, even before wage increases, drastic improvement in safety rules and substantial contributions to a health and welfare fund. Refusing White House suggestions of compromise, he led out 400,000 miners. Within six weeks, as coal supplies dwindled, much of the nation's industrial production had to be cut back. In mid-May Lewis allowed his workers back for twelve days' mining; in the interim a railroad strike threatened. The President, by broadcasting a warning that the army would run the railroads, managed to avert a new walkout. The government took over the coal mines and provided the workers with most of what Lewis had demanded.

While unions were going on strike for higher wages, businessmen and farmers were exerting almost equal pressure upon Congress to obtain higher prices. Controls, they argued, were preventing full production, encouraging a black market, and robbing producers of a fair profit. After long debate, Congress passed a circumscribed price-control bill on June 27, 1946, just three days before the existing act was to expire. President Truman unexpectedly vetoed the bill as "a sure formula for inflation," and most price controls expired.

During the first sixteen days of July 1946, the index of prices of twenty-eight basic commodities jumped 25 percent, compared with 13 percent during the previous three years. On the first day of free trade at the Chicago stockyards, prime beef jumped from $18 to $22 per hundred weight. As prices soared, stock raisers, who had been holding back their cattle, rushed them to market. Congress quickly passed a new price-control bill only slightly stronger than the vetoed one, and on July 25 President Truman signed it. The decontrol board it created studied meat prices, decided they were unreasonable, and ordered prices rolled back to the old levels. Stockmen once again held back cattle until they could force abandonment of controls; angry consumers chafed in near-empty butcher shops.

For several weeks President Truman stood firm, but as public discontent focused on the Democratic party, politicians already fearful of the worst in the congressional elections of 1946 persuaded him to relent. On October 14 he announced the immediate ending of meat controls. Meat came back, but like many other commodities, with new price tags so high that the old black-market price seemed to have become the new legal standard. Millions of consumers on small, inflexible salaries or pensions were hurt. Real earnings dropped 12 percent below those of July 1945.

"HAD ENOUGH?"

All that the Republicans needed in the fall of 1946 was the slogan, "Had Enough? Vote Republican." They captured both houses of Congress, controlling the House 246 to 188, and the Senate, 51 to 45.

President Truman, accepting the returns as a mandate to liquidate regulations, dropped almost all remaining controls on wages and prices and on the channeling of construction into low-cost homes. Congress continued rent control to March 1, 1948, but allowed rents to go up 15 percent. Retail prices moved upward 3 percent per month, canceling the gains organized labor had won in the spring of 1946. Unions fought for and obtained a second round of in-

creases in 1947, and in 1948 as prices still went upward, a third round. The spiral of inflation was creeping upward relentlessly. Workers and others in modest circumstances began to notice that it was taking place under a Republican Congress whose spokesmen had asserted that laissez faire would cure the nation's ills.

The Chairman of the House Appropriations Committee, John Taber, proclaimed that he would apply a "meat-axe to government frills." He did so. Congress refused to appropriate funds for public housing, even of the moderate sort championed by Taft. It would not aid education, or extend social security; it slashed budget allowances for reclamation and power projects in the West. It passed a tax bill that, as President Truman pointed out in vetoing it, reduced the taxes of families receiving $2,400 or less by only 3 percent, but those of families receiving $100,000 or more, from 48 to 65 percent.

One of the few noncontroversial domestic achievements of this Congress was authorization of a commission on reorganization of the executive departments. President Truman appointed former President Hoover chairman of the commission. Congress already had voted to improve its own procedures and to reorganize its committees, cutting those in the House from forty-eight to nineteen, and in the Senate from thirty-three to fifteen.

The principal positive handiwork of the Eightieth Congress was a new basic labor law to supplant the pro-labor Wagner Act of 1935. The Taft-Hartley Labor-Management Rela-

---

Restrictions on Unions in the Taft-Hartley Act [1947]

Outlawed "closed shop" (which required that one must be a union member to be hired), but permitted "union shop" (which meant that if the contract so provided, one had to join the union after being hired).

Provided "cooling off" periods and empowered the President to issue injunctions to prevent strikes imperiling national safety or health.

Prohibited as "unfair" union practices: jurisdictional strikes, refusal to bargain in good faith, secondary boycotts, exaction of pay for work not performed, and union contributions to political campaign funds.

Prohibited certification of unions as bargaining agents with employers until officers had filed affidavits that they were not Communists.

Required unions to register with the Secretary of Labor and submit annual financial reports to him.

Allowed employers to present their side during organizational campaigns, petition the National Labor Relations Board for elections to determine bargaining agents, and sue unions for breach of contract.

tions Act loosened some of the previous restrictions upon employers and added several prohibitions against the unions. It also provided for "cooling-off" periods before unions could strike. President Truman stingingly vetoed it on June 20, 1947. That same day Republicans and Southern Democrats in the House overrode his veto; the Senate followed three days later. In practice, the Taft-Hartley Act did not cripple organized labor, partly because of the skill of labor leaders and because of President Truman's appointment to the National Labor Relations Board of members sympathetic toward labor. But the law did emphatically turn most of organized labor against the Republicans and back to the support of President Truman.

TRUMAN BEATS DEWEY

When the Republicans met in Philadelphia (June 1948) to nominate a presidential candidate, they rejected Senator Robert A. Taft, the vigorous leader of the Eightieth Congress. Though the idol of many businessmen, Taft was hampered by his prewar isolationism and his lack of glamor as a campaigner. The Republicans again nominated Governor Thomas E. Dewey, who favored the new role of the United States in world affairs, and whose stand on domestic issues came closer to the Fair Deal than to the Republican record in Congress. His running mate was Governor Earl Warren of California, who was even more liberal. Their platform was a promise to continue all the things the Democrats had established, but to do them more efficiently and cheaply.

It seemed a winning ticket and program, especially since the Democratic party suffered from two schisms. A faction to the left followed Henry A. Wallace out of the party. Wallace ran on a "Progressive" ticket to fight for thoroughgoing reform at home and more friendly relations with Communists overseas. Around him rallied a sprinkling of Americans who felt that the Truman domestic policies were too slow and ineffective and who feared that the foreign policies would lead to a third world war. Around him also rallied the American Communists and fellow travelers.

Despairing Democratic liberals organized as Americans for Democratic Action, sought

Election of 1948

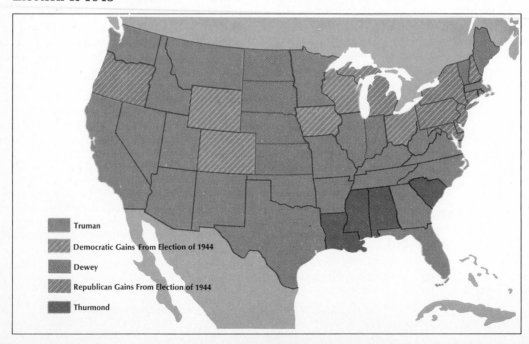

Truman

Democratic Gains From Election of 1944

Dewey

Republican Gains From Election of 1944

Thurmond

President Harry S Truman

*As a campaigner, President Truman apparently had no chance in 1948, but he was
remarkably successful in his extemporaneous speaking at whistle-stops, which
together with his policies had rallied behind him much of the farm and labor vote.
On the morning after the election, he gleefully displayed a newspaper that had
underestimated him—as indeed had much of the American public. (United Press
International)*

some more glamorous candidate than President Truman. The one candidate they could be sure would win votes by the million, General Eisenhower, rejected their overtures. At their convention (July 1948) the Democrats gloomily accepted the inevitable, the nomination of President Truman. Certain of defeat, the liberals salvaged what they could by fighting through a platform containing a strong civil-rights plank that proposed federal legislation to prevent discrimination in employment, penalize lynching, and outlaw poll taxes. This platform was expected to help Northern and city Democrats in their local and state elections.

But it drove Southern Democrats, already angered by President Truman's espousal of a strong civil-rights program, into open revolt. Waving Confederate flags, a number of them met at Birmingham, Alabama (July 1948), to form the States' Rights Democratic party and nominate Governor J. Strom Thurmond of South Carolina. They captured the party organization in Alabama, Louisiana, Mississippi, and South Carolina.

The defections on both the left and the right seemed to leave President Truman in a pathetically hopeless position; all the public opinion polls showed him trailing far behind. Governor Dewey, campaigning in a cold and

formal way, aroused as little animosity as possible, and seemed to be delivering previews of his inaugural. Instead of campaigning against the impeccable Dewey, who stood for much the same in domestic and foreign policy, Truman launched his attack at the Republican Congress. Because he felt the press was giving a hostile impression of his administration, Truman embarked upon a strenuous personal tour of the United States, traveling 31,700 miles to speak 356 times directly to the American people. In this "whistle stop" tour, he spoke only a few times from manuscripts, preferring his far more effective, rather blunt extemporaneous style. To all those groups who could be convinced they had a grievance against the Republican Congress, he appealed effectively, winning the strong support of organized labor, disgruntled farmers, and Northern Negroes.

On Election Day, to the amazement of everyone but himself, President Truman defeated Dewey, 24,106,000 to 21,969,000 in the popular vote, and 304 to 189 in the electoral vote. Thurmond's Dixiecrat ticket received 1,169,000 popular and 38 electoral votes. Wallace polled only 1,156,000. The Democrats also regained both houses of Congress by a margin of ninety-three seats in the House and twelve in the Senate.

Selected Readings

Military Operations
A. R. Buchanan, *The United States and World War II** (2 vols., 1962); Winston S. Churchill, *Second World War* (6 vols., 1948–1953); Fletcher Pratt, *War for the World* (1950), a brief account; K. R. Greenfield, *American Strategy in World War II* (1963); S. E. Morison, *Strategy and Compromise** (1958); M. S. Watson, *Chief of Staff: Prewar Plans and Preparations* (1950); R. S. Cline, *Washington Command Post* (1951); H. L. Stimson and McGeorge Bundy, *On Active Service in Peace and War* (1948); Forrest Pogue, *George C. Marshall* (2 vols., 1963–1966); D. D. Eisenhower, *Crusade in Europe** (1948); Chester Wilmot, *The Struggle for Europe** (1952), critical of Eisenhower; H. H. Arnold, *Global Mission* (1949); O. N. Bradley, *A Soldier's Story** (1951); S. E. Morison, *The Two Ocean War: A Short History of the United States Navy in the Second World War* (1963); E. J. King and W. M. Whitehill, *Fleet Admiral King* (1952).

Wartime Diplomacy
J. L. Snell, *Illusion and Necessity: The Diplomacy of Global War, 1939–1945* (1967); Gaddis Smith, *American Diplomacy During the Second World War, 1941–1945* (1965); W. L. Langer, *Our Vichy Gamble** (1947); W. R. Deane, *The Strange Alliance* (1947); H. W. Baldwin, *Great Mistakes of the War* (1950), critical of "unconditional surrender"; Anne Armstrong, *Unconditional Surrender* (1961); W. L. Neumann, *After Victory: Churchill, Roosevelt, Stalin, and the Making of the Peace* (1967); E. R. Stettinius, *Roosevelt and the Russians: The Yalta Conference* (1949); J. F. Byrnes, *Speaking Frankly* (1947); R. L. Walker and George Curry, *American Secretaries of State: E. R. Stettinius, Jr., James F. Byrnes* (1965); Herbert Feis, *Churchill, Roosevelt, Stalin** (1957), *Between War and Peace: The Potsdam Conference** (1960), *Japan Subdued* (1961), and *Contest over Japan* (1967); R. J. C. Butow, *Japan's Decision to Surrender** (1954); R. H.

Minear, *Victor's Justice: The Tokyo War Crimes Trial* (1973); John Hersey, *Hiroshima** (1946); Gar Alperovitz, *Atomic Diplomacy: Hiroshima and Potsdam* (1965); R. A. Divine, *Second Chance: The Triumph of Internationalism in America During World War II* (1967), on the U. N.; R. B. Russell, *A History of the United Nations Charter: The Role of the United States, 1940–1945* (1958).

Domestic Politics
A. H. Vandenberg, Jr., *The Private Papers of Senator Vandenberg* (1952); H. S Truman, *Memoirs** (2 vols., 1955–1956); Roland Young, *Congressional Politics in the Second World War* (1955); Jonathan Daniels, *Frontier on the Potomac* (1946); Joseph Gaer, *The First Round: The CIO Political Action Committee* (1944); R. A. Lee, *Truman and Taft-Hartley* (1967); E. C. Brown, *From the Wagner Act to Taft-Hartley* (1950); L. V. Chandler, *Inflation in the United States, 1940–1948* (1951); Jules Abels, *Out of the Jaws of Victory* (1959), on the 1948 election; Irwin Ross, *The Loneliest Campaign: The Truman Victory of 1948* (1968); K. M. Schmidt, *Wallace: Quixotic Crusade* (1960); C. W. Mills, *The New Men of Power* (1948); Samuel Lubell, *The Future of American Politics** (1952); E. F. Goldman, *The Crucial Decade: America, 1945–1955** (1956); John Gunther, *Inside U. S. A.* (1951); A. L. Hamby, *Beyond the New Deal: Harry S Truman and American Liberalism* (1973).

*Titles available in paperback.

Twenty-seven

In 1942 the American geopolitical expert Nicholas J. Spykman wrote that the United States had found itself in World War II because the balance of power on the opposite shores of both the Atlantic and the Pacific had been upset. So the American war aim should be to restore the balance, Spykman said. It should not be to annihilate either Germany or Japan, lest this leave Europe and the Far East exposed to Soviet domination. As for Europe: "A Russian state from the Urals to the North Sea can be no great improvement over a German state from the North Sea to the Urals." As for the Far East: "The danger of another Japanese conquest of Asia must be removed, but this does not inevitably mean the elimination of the military strength of Japan and the surrender of the Western Pacific to China or Russia."

In fact, however, the war was fought for "unconditional surrender," for total victory over the Axis, not for a restoration of the balance. The upshot was that Germany and Japan were eliminated as military powers for the time being. A "power vacuum" was left in Europe, and another in Asia. Only two really great powers remained in the world—the Soviet Union and the United States. Into the voids left by the war, the influence of the Russian Communists and later that of the Chinese Communists began to flow. The United States undertook to resist the spread of Communist power and thus came into collision with its recent allies, the Russians and the Chinese. It now sought new alliances not only with old associates like Great Britain and France but also with former foes, Germany (or a part of that country) and Japan, which it began to help revive and rebuild as strong nations. Such, in essence, was the "cold war" that commenced within two years after the end of World War II.

At first the United States appeared to hold the upper hand, for it had a monopoly of atomic weapons. But within a short time, in 1949, the Russians exploded an

Nuclear Disarmament?
Limitation and control of nuclear weapons seemed desperately urgent after the U.S.A. and the U.S.S.R. had acquired the ability to destroy one another, but disarmament talks in 1957 made no progress. As this 1957 cartoon by Reg Manning illustrates, neither country was willing to let its guard down without assurances that the other would do the same. (McNaught Syndicate, Inc.)

A-bomb of their own. The Americans got ahead again, in 1952, with the vastly more destructive hydrogen bomb, but the Russians produced an H-bomb, too, the following year. By 1957, when the Russians put into orbit the first artificial satellite, they seemed to have taken the lead in the capacity to deliver missiles with nuclear warheads. In any event, each of the great contestants now had the capability, quite literally, of destroying the other. A wholly new era had arrived, in which another world war could wipe out mankind itself. Nobody really knew whether the old rules of power politics had relevance any longer. If humanity was spared an all-out war, the reason was perhaps that the world had reached what *The New York Times* (in 1958) called a new "balance of terror."

Start of the Cold War

As early as January 1946 President Truman, concerned over Russian delay in withdrawing troops from Iran and Russian threats against Turkey, had written his secretary of state: "Unless Russia is faced with an iron fist and strong language another war is in the making."

CONTAINMENT OF COMMUNISM

Truman faced a peculiarly difficult task in trying to convince the American public that a truly deep and serious rift was developing between Russia and the West. During the war years they had listened to publicists ranging from the advanced New Dealer Henry Wallace to the Republican president of the United States Chamber of Commerce, Eric Johnston, praising the Russians and picturing Stalin as a sympathetic figure. Many had come to imagine him as a benign, pipe-smoking sage, "good old Uncle Joe." Not even the revered Winston Churchill could shift American opinion. In March 1946, speaking at Westminster College in Fulton, Missouri, Churchill proclaimed a grim warning: "From Stettin in the Baltic to Trieste in the Adriatic an iron curtain has descended across the Continent."

A new Truman policy for countering Communist aggression began to unfold in the spring of 1947. This policy followed the line laid down by State Department expert George F. Kennan, who proposed "a long-term, patient but firm and vigilant containment of Russian expansive tendencies." Russian pressure on Turkey and support of Communist guerrilla forces in Greece emphasized the immediacy of the Soviet threat. The British had been aiding the Greek government, but could no longer carry the burden. Unless Stalin were checked, he might achieve the centuries-old Russian prize of the straits leading from the Black Sea into the Mediterranean. Russia already controlled Albania on the Adriatic.

On March 12, 1947, President Truman appeared before Congress to request $400 million to bolster the armed forces of Greece and Turkey, and to enunciate the doctrine that came to bear his name: "I believe that it must be the policy of the United States to support free peoples who are resisting attempted subjugation by armed minorities or by outside pressures." Senator Vandenberg again backed the President, and the Republican Congress voted the Greek-Turkish Aid Act. The initial military aid and subsequent appropriations eased Russian pressure upon Turkey, and by the fall of 1949 brought to an end the long civil war against Communists in Greece.

Military aid was not enough. The Truman Doctrine logically led to a program of economic reconstruction to bolster the stability of Europe and help eradicate the misery out of which the Communist parties in western European countries were gaining recruits. In April 1947 Secretary of State George C. Marshall returned from the Conference of Foreign Ministers in Moscow convinced that the Russians were interested only in profiting from the economic plight of Europe, not in ameliorating it. The solution, he and President Truman agreed, lay in State Department plans to aid European nations that were willing to cooperate with each other in rebuilding their economies. Speaking at the Harvard University commencement in June 1947, Secretary Marshall offered aid to all those European nations (including Russia) who would join in drafting a program for recovery.

Kennan on Containment [1947]

The Soviet pressure against the free institutions of the Western world is something that can be contained by the adroit and vigilant application of counterforce at a series of constantly shifting geographical and political points, corresponding to the shifts and maneuvers of Soviet policy, but which cannot be charmed or talked out of existence. The Russians look forward to a duel of infinite duration, and they see that already they have scored great successes. . . .

But in actuality the possibilities for American policy are by no means limited to holding the line and hoping for the best. It is entirely possible for the United States to influence by its actions the internal developments, both within Russia and throughout the international Communist movement, by which Russian policy is largely determined. . . . It is . . . a question of the degree to which the United States can create among the peoples of the world generally the impression of a country which knows what it wants, which is coping successfully with the problems of its internal life and with the responsibilities of a World Power, and which has a spiritual vitality capable of holding its own among the major ideological currents of the time. — "X" [George F. Kennan], Foreign Affairs, July 1947.

Russia denounced the Marshall Plan as American imperialism and intimidated the satellites and Finland and Czechoslovakia into staying away from the planning conference. Germany had no government, and Spain was not invited. Sixteen other nations of Europe joined a Committee of European Economic Cooperation, which in September 1947 presented specifications for reconstruction to create a self-sufficient Europe by 1951. Opposition formed in Congress, but it was embarrassed from the start by possessing as unwelcome allies the American Communists, and in February 1948 it was overwhelmed by a shocked and aroused public opinion when Czech Communists seized power in Prague. Congress in April established the Economic Cooperation Administration and voted an initial $4 billion for it.

Altogether over a three-year period the United States spent $12 billion through the ECA. This helped to stimulate a remarkable recovery in Europe. By the end of 1950 industrial production was up 64 percent, economic activity was well above prewar levels, and Communist strength among voters in most areas was dwindling.

THE NORTH ATLANTIC ALLIANCE

In his inaugural address, January 20, 1949, President Truman challenged the nation to come to the aid of the "more than half the people of the world" who were "living in conditions approaching misery." Point Four of his foreign policy proposals was a plan for aiding them through technical assistance and the fostering of capital investment. The Point Four or Technical Cooperation program began in 1950 with an appropriation of only $35 million, but spent $400 million in the next three years.

Soviet leaders reacted vigorously against the American efforts for world economic recovery. They had organized their own Warsaw Alliance of nine satellite nations (September 1947) to combat "American imperialism." Through a new Cominform (Communist Information Bureau) they sought to eradicate traces of nonconformity throughout eastern Europe. Their successful coup in democratic Czechoslovakia in February 1948, as horrifying to western Europeans as to Americans, helped unify the Western world against the Communist countries. Later in the year, the pressure of Stalin and the Cominform on Marshal Tito provoked him to pull Communist Yugoslavia out of their orbit, and with American aid to embark upon an independent course between Russia and the West. In western Europe, Communist parties tried to thwart the Marshall Plan, especially by calling out on strike the unions they controlled in Italy and France. Despite the strikes, progress continued.

Meanwhile, the United States moved with the British and the rather reluctant French toward the creation of a self-governing, economically strong West Germany. The culmination came on June 7, 1948, when they announced plans for a new federal West German government with sovereignty over domestic matters and full membership in the European Recovery Program. They also reformed the currency to stop the inflationary flood of marks from the Soviet zone, which was hampering recovery.

The Russians retaliated. Taking advantage of a lack of a written guarantee of land transit across the Soviet zone, they clamped a tight blockade around the western sectors of Berlin. The object was to force the Western powers to abandon either Berlin or the proposed West German republic. President Truman, unwilling to risk war by sending in armed convoys by land, ordered the supplying of Berlin by air. Through the winter and into the spring of 1949, the airlift continued, carrying in more supplies than had previously been brought by train. Finally the Russians backed down and ended the blockade.

In October 1949 the German Federal Republic came into existence at Bonn in West Germany, and the Soviets established a German Democratic Republic for East Germany.

Meanwhile Russian intransigence was leading to the consolidation of the Western countries in a new grand alliance. The North Atlantic Treaty was signed April 4, 1949, by twelve nations, and subsequently also by Greece and Turkey. It declared that an armed attack against one would be considered an attack upon all, and provided for the creation of joint military forces. Under it, the signatory powers established the North Atlantic Treaty Organization to construct a defense force that, while not equal to that of the Russians, would be large enough to discourage an attack. The Mutual Defense Act of 1949 appropriated an initial billion dollars for armaments for the signatories.

The governing body of NATO, the North Atlantic Council, established military head-

Divided Germany and Austria

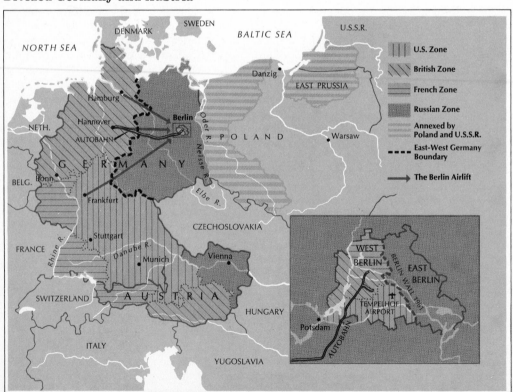

The Berlin Airlift
*"It was inspiring and somewhat heart-rending to witness the spontaneous visits of
the women and children of Berlin to Tempelhof airport to show their appreciation
of the airlift, bringing with them some precious last possession as a token of
gratitude to the members of the air crews," wrote General Lucius D. Clay,
military governor of the American zone. The pilots called the airlift "Operation
Vittles," and some of them informally instituted "Operation Little Vittles,"
dropping candy tied to handkerchief parachutes to the children. "Berlin had kept
its courage," Clay declared. Despite unemployment and an acute shortage of heat
and electricity through the winter, "the determination of the people did not falter.
They were proud to carry their burden as the price of their freedom." (United
Press International)*

quarters near Paris early in 1951 under the supreme command of General Dwight Eisenhower. This was SHAPE (Supreme Headquarters, Allied Powers in Europe). The number of divisions and airplanes under NATO command began gradually to grow, but while its power was still relatively feeble, its chief significance was the commitment that the United States had made with the nations of western Europe to stand firm against Russian threats.

That these threats were not to be taken lightly became even clearer on September 23, 1949, when President Truman issued a press statement: "We have evidence that within re-

cent weeks an atomic explosion occurred in the U.S.S.R." The years of relative safety for the American people were already at an end.

CHINA TURNS RED

While the United States was struggling to contain Russia in Europe between 1947 and 1949, the Chinese Communists were destroying the armies of Chiang Kai-shek. To prevent civil war and to effect a coalition government, the Truman administration in December 1945 had sent General George C. Marshall to China. At first he obtained a cease-fire and encouraging signs of accommodation, but irreconcilable differences kept apart the two Chinese governments—the *Kuomintang* (Nationalists) and the Communists.

Full-scale war broke out. Although the Nationalist armies were larger and better equipped, they soon began to fall back before the better-trained, more vigorous Communist forces. As the inept Chiang Kai-shek government failed both on the fighting front and at home, where inflation and inefficiency were rampant, it was plunging toward defeat.

President Truman now sent General Wedemeyer, who had been Chiang's chief of staff, to investigate. Wedemeyer warned that Communist control of China would imperil American interests, since the Communists were in fact closely tied to the Soviet Union. He believed that the United States could rescue Chiang only by sending 10,000 army officers and other advisers to introduce reforms, together with massive material support.

President Truman did not request such large-scale aid for Chiang, but did ask Congress to provide $570 million; in April 1948 it voted $400 million. The administration had decided, as Secretary Marshall made clear, that there was no feasible way the United States could make the Nationalist government "capable of reestablishing and then maintaining its control throughout all of China." The collapse was rapid, and it came through lack of morale rather than shortages of arms and supplies. At the end of 1949, Chiang and the Nationalists fled to Formosa. Though Great Britain and some of the western European nations recognized the new People's Republic of China, the United States refused to do so and blocked its entry into the United Nations.

Beginning in 1947, the American government had introduced new policies in Japan to strengthen that nation in a manner similar to the rebuilding of Germany. The American occupation in Japan was bringing a democratization of the government, extension of rights to women and underprivileged groups, expansion of the educational system (from a starting point as high as the goal of educational reform in China), land reform that was as drastic as that in China, a curbing of the power of the monopolistic *zaibatsu* industrial system, and an improvement in the status of labor. In Japan, more than anywhere else in Asia, the United States helped develop a dynamic alternative to Communism. In 1949, to stimulate Japanese recovery, the United States ended its reparations and stopped the dismantling of industrial combinations.

Negotiation of a Japanese peace treaty began in 1950 through the skilled offices of a Republican, John Foster Dulles, whom President Truman appointed to undertake the task. Aside from the fact that it stripped Japan of all her recent conquests, it was a generous treaty, a "peace of reconciliation," as Dulles called it. By recognizing the right of the sovereign Japanese nation to self-defense, it opened the way to rearmament. Thanks partly to its negotiation by a Republican, the treaty easily received Senate ratification and went into effect in 1952. A security treaty, signed at the same time, permitted the United States to maintain armed forces in Japan. Two years later, a mutual-defense-assistance pact provided for Japanese rearmament with American aid, but the building of armed forces proceeded slowly. Disarmament had been one of MacArthur's most cherished reforms, and the American-imposed Japanese constitution had banned war forever. This encouraged such a strong pacifist sentiment that as late as 1957 only 100,000 Japanese had joined the armed forces. The task of defending Japan continued to rest largely with the United States.

Several nations to the south that had suffered either invasion or the threat of invasion during the war viewed with some concern the rebuilding of Japan as a military power. To reassure them, the United States in 1951 signed a security treaty with the Philippines, and the ANZUS pact with Australia and New Zealand.

While rebuilding Japan, the Truman administration refused to capitulate to the demands of the so-called China Lobby for military and naval aid to Chiang on Formosa which might lead the nation into a war against Red China. In January 1950 Secretary of State Dean Acheson publicly outlined a Pacific defense perimeter which did not include Formosa or Korea. If these areas were attacked, he declared, the people invaded must rely upon themselves to resist, "and then upon the commitments of the entire civilized world under the charter of the United Nations."

Within a few months, East Asia became the focal point of American foreign policy as the cold war turned hot in Korea.

According to spokesmen for the American government, the Soviet Union was entirely to blame for the cold war. Stalin violated the Yalta agreement, imposed Russian control upon eastern Europe, and schemed to spread Communism throughout the world. The United States, reacting defensively, tried to contain Soviet expansion by means of the Truman Doctrine, the Marshall Plan, and the North Atlantic Treaty Organization. At first, American historians with few exceptions agreed substantially with the official view.

As time passed, and especially after the Vietnam War disillusioned many Americans about the containment policy, an increasing number of historians undertook to "revise" the interpretation of the cold war, as earlier historians had done with previous wars. Most of the cold war revisionists belonged to the New Left. The pioneer among them was William A. Williams, who anticipated most of the revisionist themes in his *American-Russian Relations, 1781–1947* (1952) and *The Tragedy of American Diplomacy* (1959).

According to the New Left writers, the United States was mainly if not solely responsible for the cold war. At the close of World War II, the Soviet Union was exhausted and in no position to threaten the United States. But this country, with a monopoly of nuclear weapons, was in a position to threaten the Soviet Union. In the opinion of some revisionists, Franklin D. Roosevelt would have continued the wartime Soviet-American cooperation, but Harry S Truman abandoned the Roosevelt policy and adopted a hard line toward the Russians. In the opinion of other revisionists, the line would have been the same regardless of any change in the presidency, since American foreign policy was simply a response to the needs of American capitalism, which sought American-controlled markets throughout the world.

As early as 1948 a British physicist, P. M. S. Blackett, in *Fear, War, and the Bomb,* had written that the dropping of the atomic bombs on Hiroshima and Nagasaki was "not so much the last military act of the second World War as the first major operation of the cold diplomatic war with Russia." Taking up the idea, a New Left political economist at the University of Cambridge, England, Gar Alperovitz, suggested in his *Atomic Diplomacy* (1965) that the United States dropped the bombs on an already defeated Japan in order to impress the Russians and make them more "manageable." In *The Atomic Bomb and the End of World War II* (1966) a former official in the Roosevelt and Truman administrations, Herbert Feis, argued (as Truman himself had done) that the United States used the bombs simply to assure a quick and complete victory over Japan with a minimum loss of lives.

Reviewing the work of Williams, Alperovitz, and five other revisionist authors, Robert J. Maddox in *The New Left and the Origins of the Cold War* (1973) charged them with misusing source materials and drawing conclusions at variance with their own evidence. "There is every reason to be sharply critical of recent American foreign policy," Maddox said, "but the criticisms should rest on more substantial foundations."

In *The United States and the Origins of the Cold War, 1941–1947* (1972), John L. Gaddis maintained that a variety of preconceptions had influenced the policy makers in both Washington and Moscow. He concluded that "neither side can bear sole responsibility for the onset of the Cold War."

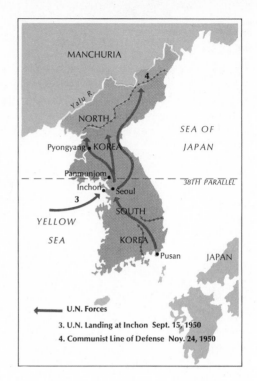

Communist Forces
1. North Korean Attack June 25, 1950
2. U.N. Line of Defense Sept. 10, 1950

U.N. Forces
3. U.N. Landing at Inchon Sept. 15, 1950
4. Communist Line of Defense Nov. 24, 1950

The Korean War   1950–1953

DEFENDING SOUTH KOREA

During the hectic days at the end of the war in the Pacific, the United States had hastily proposed that Americans accept the surrender of the Japanese in the lower half of Korea, up to the 38th parallel, and that the Russians do the same in the northern half. At the moment the arrangement was useful to the United States. Afterwards, however, the Russians were willing to accept a reunited Korea only if it were Communist-dominated.

The 38th parallel became more and more an impenetrable barrier. To the north of it, the Communists developed a "peoples' government" with a strong aggressive army. To the south, the United Nations held elections that led to a government under the ardently nationalistic Dr. Syngman Rhee, long an exile in the United States. Rhee would have liked to extend his government to the north, but the United States provided the South Korean army only with relatively light defensive weapons.

Consequently when the United States withdrew its forces from below the 38th parallel in June 1949, South Korea was left militarily weaker than its even more aggressive northern twin.

On June 24, 1950, the North Koreans acted swiftly, launching a full-scale invasion that caught the South Koreans and Americans completely by surprise. Almost immediately President Truman and Congress reversed the policy of withdrawal from the Asiatic mainland. The President brought the question of the invasion before the United Nations Security Council. It could act more quickly than the Assembly, and at the moment the Russians were boycotting it, and hence had no representative present to vote a paralyzing veto. The Council on June 25 passed an American resolution demanding that the North Koreans withdraw behind the 38th parallel, and two days later called upon members of the United Nations to "furnish such assistance to the Republic of Korea as may be necessary to repel

Communist Forces
5. Chinese-North Korean Attack Nov. 26, 1950
6. U.N. Line of Defense Jan. 12, 1951

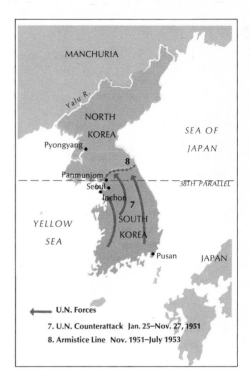

U.N. Forces
7. U.N. Counterattack Jan. 25–Nov. 27, 1951
8. Armistice Line Nov. 1951–July 1953

the armed attack." President Truman on June 27 sent United States air and sea forces to the aid of the South Koreans; on June 30 he ordered ground forces into Korea, and sent the Seventh Fleet to act as a barrier between the Chinese mainland and Formosa.

The Council of the United Nations on July 7, 1950, requested those nations providing troops to place them under a unified command headed by the United States. President Truman appointed General MacArthur commander in chief. Some fifteen nations besides the United States and the Republic of Korea provided troops, but these never comprised more than 9 percent of the total fighting force. The United States sent about 48 percent; South Korea mustered 43 percent. What was officially a United Nations "police action" came to most Americans to seem a war on the part of the United States.

General MacArthur, who at first could draw upon only four understrength divisions in Japan, rushed in troop units piecemeal to slow the rapidly advancing North Koreans as they pushed southward past Seoul, threatening to envelop the entire tip of the peninsula. By thus sacrificing themselves, these forces gave MacArthur an opportunity to build stable defenses around the port of Pusan in the extreme southeast. When the North Koreans struck there in force early in August, strong army and marine reinforcements fresh from the United States hurled them back at each point of assault. As men and supplies poured into Pusan, marine officers devised a bold plan of attack which General MacArthur reluctantly accepted. Rather than try to push the North Koreans back mile by mile, on September 15, 1950, while the United Nations troops around Pusan opened a sharp counteroffensive, he launched an amphibious assault far behind the North Korean lines at Inchon, near Seoul. It caught the Communists almost completely unprepared. The United Nations troops quickly recaptured Seoul; within two weeks the North Korean armies, disrupted and demoralized, were fleeing as best they could to north of the 38th parallel.

RETREAT FROM NORTH KOREA

Amid jubilation, the United States and the United Nations had to make new decisions. Should they capitalize upon their spectacular victory and move into North Korea? The premier of Red China on October 1 warned that the Chinese would "not allow seeing their neighbors being invaded by imperialists." A few days later, he announced the Chinese would send troops, and dispatched a warning to the United Nations through India. These threats worried American strategists, but there was a possibility that China was bluffing, and there was the probability that the North Koreans, unless pursued, would recoup their strength and strike new blows.

The Joint Chiefs of Staff on September 27, 1950, ordered MacArthur to destroy the North Korean armed forces, but under no circumstances to cross the borders of China or Russia. The United Nations Assembly gave its sanction to the project on October 7, reiterating its aim to create "a unified, independent and democratic Korea." Two days later, the United Nations forces poured across the 38th parallel toward the Yalu River, which marked the boundary with Manchuria.

For several weeks the advance into northern Korea went well. On October 19, the capital, Pyongyang, fell, and parachutists landed thirty miles beyond to trap much of the remaining North Korean army. Then, on October 26, a Chinese Communist soldier was captured; four days later, fourteen more were taken. By November 4, eight Chinese divisions had been identified, and Russian-made MIG fighter planes had briefly engaged the United Nations air force.

General MacArthur issued a special communiqué warning that "a new and fresh army now faces us," and he excoriated the Chinese for their international lawlessness in intervening without notice and "massing a great concentration of possible reinforcing divisions with adequate supply behind the privileged sanctuary of the adjacent Manchurian border." Both in his private communications to the Joint Chiefs of Staff and in the encouragement he gave to pressure groups in the United States, MacArthur engaged in a vigorous campaign for permission to bomb this "privileged sanctuary." President Truman refused to allow all-

out military action against China, because, he later explained, "if for no other reason . . . it was a gigantic booby trap."

When the Chinese suddenly appeared in overwhelming numbers, they stalled MacArthur's offensive and hurled back advance units. Through December 1950, in bitter weather, the outnumbered Eighth Army and X Corps fought a heroic withdrawal from North Korea. The United Nations tried to negotiate peace with the Chinese, but the Communists, as they swept below the 38th parallel and recaptured Seoul, set impossibly stiff terms. In March 1951 the Eighth Army counterattacked, for a second and final time capturing Seoul and recrossing the 38th parallel. President Truman was ready again to seek a negotiated peace.

General MacArthur, far from ready to accept the position of his commander in chief, repeatedly made public his eagerness to win total victory in Korea at the risk of full involvement in war with China. On March 20, 1951, he communicated his views to the Republican minority leader in the House of Representatives, Joseph W. Martin, concluding: "There is no substitute for victory."

President Truman clung to his thesis that, in the great struggle against Communism, western Europe with its concentration of heavy industry, not industrially weak Asia, was the main potential battlefield. He could not have won the support of western European partners in the United Nations for a more militant policy in Asia. He would not accept the arguments of the Asia-firsters that the United States should undertake unilateral action—"go it alone."

General MacArthur thus emerged as a major figure in American politics, trying to reverse the administration policies. Five days after Representative Martin released MacArthur's letter to the press, President Truman, on April 11, 1951, relieved General MacArthur of his commands. A groundswell of outrage swept the United States; a Gallup poll reported that 69 percent of those interviewed favored the General, only 29 percent the President. MacArthur upon his return was greeted hysterically wherever he appeared; millions watched their television sets as he addressed Congress.

Truman's policy of fighting a limited war of containment continued to baffle and exasperate a considerable part of the American people. It went against the American tradition of total victory. It was hard to explain to the public or to the soldiers fighting endlessly through the rice paddies and over the hilltops of Korea.

In June 1951 the Russian delegate to the United Nations hinted that settlement was possible. Armistice negotiations began on July 10, 1951, near the 38th parallel, and continued for many weary months at Panmunjom. They came to revolve around the difficult questions of locating the cease-fire line, enforcing the armistice, and repatriating prisoners of war. By the spring of 1952, agreements had been reached upon all but the last question. Finally, in October 1952, the negotiations were recessed. By then the nation was in the midst of a presidential campaign, and though there was no large-scale fighting in Korea, the interminable negotiations, endless skirmishing, and ever-growing casualties had worn out the patience of the American people.

The Politics of Fright

In the disappointing months and years that followed World War II, as warm friendship toward Russia turned into apprehension and alarm, the American public became increasingly afraid that traitors within the government were betraying it to the Communists.

HYSTERICAL LOYALTY

During the period of the New Deal and the war there had been some Communists and Communist sympathizers in the government. At a time when the Russians and the United States were allies this seemed of little consequence, but in 1942 and 1943 President Roosevelt established loyalty checks. By 1946 Russia seemed more a potential enemy than an ally. The Canadian government discovered that at least twenty-three of its employees in positions of trust had turned over secrets, some of them concerning nuclear fission, to Russian spies. Several of the spy rings had operated across the boundary in the United States.

The federal government began extensive efforts to ferret out Communists. President Truman established a Temporary Commission on Employee Loyalty (November 1946) to recommend loyalty investigation systems and safeguards of fair hearings. This led to the establishment of loyalty boards (March 1947) to undertake a sweeping investigation of all federal employees. In August 1950 the President authorized the dismissal in sensitive departments of even those deemed no more than "bad security risks." By 1951 more than 3 million government employees had been cleared, over 2,000 had resigned, and 212 had been dismissed.

Against the recommendations of the Departments of Defense and Justice and of the Central Intelligence Agency, Congress overrode the President's veto and passed the McCarran Internal Security Act (September 1950). This did not outlaw Communist organizations but required them to publish their records. It barred Communists from employment in defense plants and denied them passports.

Already, in 1948, the Attorney General had obtained indictments against eleven key Communist leaders for violation of the Smith Act of 1940, which prohibited conspiring to teach the violent overthrow of the government. During their nine-month trial in 1949, the Communists engaged in elaborate harassing tactics, which further aroused the public against them. They were convicted. In the 1951 case of *Dennis* v. *United States*, the Supreme Court in a 6-to-2 decision rejected their appeal. Chief Justice Fred Vinson held that advocating or teaching revolution in the existing state of the world, or even conspiring to do so, fell within Justice Holmes' earlier definition of what was punishable — that it constituted a "clear and present danger." In dissenting, Justice Hugo Black remarked: "There is hope that in calmer times, when the present pressures, passions, and fears subside, this or some later court will restore the First Amendment liberties to the high preferred place where they belong in a free society."

While the Supreme Court was solemnly deciding that civil liberties must be circumscribed to protect the modern state, some less careful politicians were capitalizing upon the growing public hysteria, among them Richard M. Nixon, of California. Nixon first gained national attention by helping to expose Alger Hiss. As a handsome and ambitious young man, Hiss had risen rapidly in the government during the 1930s to become a high-ranking official of the State Department. He was present as a clerk at the Yalta conference, but in no way influenced policy there. In 1947 he resigned to head the Carnegie Endowment for International Peace. Whittaker Chambers, a self-avowed former Communist agent, had denounced Hiss as early as 1939, but because he provided no details and no supporting evidence, Chambers was ignored. In 1948 he repeated his accusations before the House Un-American Activities Committee. When Hiss sued him for slander, Chambers produced microfilms of classified State Department documents that Hiss allegedly had given him in 1937 and 1938.

Hiss was brought to trial for perjury (the statute of limitations prevented indictment for espionage). He called upon a number of the nation's most distinguished liberals to bear witness to his character. The first trial ended with a hung jury (July 1949); the second ended with conviction (January 1950).

More important in convincing Americans that a real Communist menace existed was the revelation, in February 1950, that a young British scientist, Dr. Klaus Fuchs, had turned over to Russian agents full details on the manufacture of atomic bombs. His confession led to the trial and ultimate execution of Julius and Ethel Rosenberg, Americans who were alleged to have been his accomplices—and who were hailed as martyrs by Communists throughout the world.

A TROUBLED ELECTORATE

In 1950 the voters were disturbed by the charges of subversion, by the Communist victory in China, and by the Korean War. Many were led to believe that the events in China and Korea had resulted from a conspiracy in the State Department. Representative Nixon declared: "Traitors in the high councils of our own government have made sure that the deck is stacked on the Soviet side of the diplomatic tables." Bipartisanship in foreign policy disappeared as the Republicans pressed their issue. They did not capture Congress in November 1950, but they gained twenty-eight seats in the House and five in the Senate.

Meanwhile, President Truman made but little headway with his Fair Deal. Congress passed the Displaced Persons Act of 1950, liberalizing the 1948 legislation that the President had denounced as discriminatory against Catholics and Jews because its quotas were unfavorable to people from southern and eastern Europe. The new law increased the number of persons to be admitted from 205,000 to 415,000—but even this latter figure was a total for a three-year period, not a yearly number. Congress also implemented some of Truman's proposed reforms. The National Housing Act of 1949 provided for the construction over the succeeding six years of 810,000 housing units for lower-income families, together with a subsidy for forty years to bridge the gap between costs and the rents the tenants could afford to pay. It also provided grants for slum clearance and rural housing. Congress voted increased appropriations for power development and reclamation in the West, for TVA and for the Farmers' Home Administration (which carried on the rehabilitation work of the earlier Resettlement Administration and Farm Security Administration). In contrast, the Fair Deal health-insurance program went down to crashing defeat under the vigorous opposition of the American Medical Association, which raised a $3 million fund to combat it. Federal aid for education failed because of dissension over whether aid should go to parochial schools.

Republicans undermined the Truman administration with charges of favor-peddling and corruption, which implicated men in the White House though not the President himself. The President's military aide had received as a gift a $520 deep-freeze unit; the wife of an examiner of loans for the Reconstruction Finance Corporation had acquired a $9,540 mink coat. These became the symbols of a moral malaise in Washington. Apparently go-betweens, in return for a 5-percent fee, could obtain contracts, arrange RFC loans, and take care of tax difficulties in the Bureau of Internal Revenue. President Truman reorganized the RFC and reformed the Bureau of Internal Revenue and the Department of Justice, but much too slowly to satisfy his Republican critics.

As the election of 1952 approached, there was no indication that the majority of voters wished to reverse either Truman's foreign policy or his domestic program. They did want to "clean up the mess in Washington," and above all they wanted to see an end to the drawn-out, wearying Korean War.

EISENHOWER ELECTED

It was not surprising that in times so troubled the voters overwhelmingly turned to a successful and popular general who they felt could lead them to security in a frightening world. They turned not to MacArthur but to Dwight D. Eisenhower, who was closely linked to the military and foreign policies of the Roosevelt and Truman administrations.

The wing of the Republican party holding to the views of MacArthur was committed to Senator Robert A. Taft—but it was a minority with the party, even though it controlled the

Republican National Committee. The majority looked to General Eisenhower—whom some liberal Democrats had sought to draft in 1948. In a violent struggle on the floor of the convention, the Eisenhower forces won contested delegations and, with them, the nomination on the first ballot. Senator Richard M. Nixon, who was acceptable to conservative Republicans, was nominated for the vice presidency. The platform was ambiguous enough to cover disagreements between the two wings of the party.

As for the Democrats, President Truman had announced that he would not run again. So the Northern leaders drafted Governor Adlai E. Stevenson of Illinois, who had earlier declared he would not run. His running mate was the liberal Senator John J. Sparkman of Alabama. The platform stated the positions of the Northern Democrats: endorsement of the Truman foreign policies, civil rights, repeal of the Taft-Hartley Act, and high price supports for farmers.

Governor Stevenson began delivering speeches brilliant in their eloquence, clever in their wit, and startling in their candor. As he promised to "talk sense to the American peo-

Election of 1952

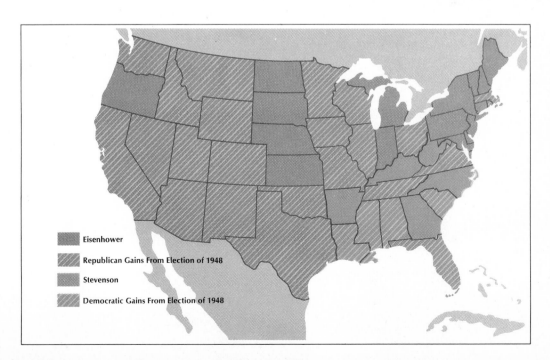

Eisenhower

Republican Gains From Election of 1948

Stevenson

Democratic Gains From Election of 1948

ple," he drew the hearty support of most intellectuals, whose critics derisively called them "eggheads." But General Eisenhower appealed much more effectively to businessmen and the masses by promising to end their various frustrations.

Republican campaigners played upon the triple theme of "Communism, corruption, and Korea." Speaking in Detroit on October 24, 1952, Eisenhower promised to bring the war to "an early and honorable end." To help do so, he promised he would make a personal trip to Korea. The response at the polls was overwhelming: Eisenhower getting 33,936,000 votes to 27,315,000 for Stevenson. Despite Eisenhower's victory, the Republicans failed to gain complete control of Congress. They won a majority of eight seats in the House and only an even split in the Senate. The Republican candidate was far more popular than his party.

New Hands at the Helm

John Foster Dulles, the Republican expert in foreign policy, had criticized the Democratic program of "containment" as a passive one that left the initiative to the Communist side. Dulles proposed, instead, a program of "liberation" that would lead to a "roll-back" of Communist expansion. As secretary of state in the Eisenhower administration, he continued to talk of new approaches. Yet the Eisenhower-Dulles policy was to be essentially a continuation of the Truman-Acheson policy.

A KOREAN ARMISTICE

Before his inauguration President-elect Eisenhower flew to Korea to talk to commanders about means of obtaining an honorable truce. In his inaugural he committed himself to a firm

Eisenhower in Korea
In the presidential campaign of 1952 General Eisenhower promised that, if elected, he would go to Korea, presumably to bring the war to an end. After his election and before his inauguration he did go to Korea. Here he is shown (left) at mess with American officers there. (U.S. Army photograph)

**Secretary of State John Foster Dulles Reporting
to President Eisenhower   May 17, 1955**
*The Eisenhower administration made extensive use of television
to dramatize its actions among the American people. For the first
time the President's press conferences were televised, and on several
occasions like this, Secretary Dulles reported to the President in
front of the television cameras. He had just returned from Europe,
where he had signed the treaty restoring sovereignty to Austria. (U.S.
Department of State)*

policy in Korea and elsewhere in the struggle against Communists.

Less than two months after President Eisenhower took office, Stalin died. This opened the possibility of an end to the Korean War and perhaps some moderation of the cold war. When the new Soviet Premier, Georgi Malenkov, seemed conciliatory, the President called upon the Russians to show their good faith by signing an Austrian peace treaty and supporting an armistice in Korea. On July 27, 1953, an agreement was finally signed at Panmunjom. It provided for a cease-fire and withdrawal of both armies about a mile and a half back of the existing battle line, which ran from coast to coast, from just below the 38th parallel in the west to thirty miles north of it in the east. A conference was to be held to seek peaceful reunification of Korea, but at the Geneva meeting

(1954) no agreement was reached. The armistice turned into an uneasy and indefinite armed truce.

The Korean War (officially only a "police action") had lasted more than three years and cost the United States alone 25,000 dead, 115,000 other casualties, and $22 billion. For Americans who liked to think in terms of total victory, it all seemed painfully inconclusive. The fighting had settled no problems in the Far East except to prevent the Communist conquest of South Korea.

"MASSIVE RETALIATION"

As secretary of state from 1953 to 1959, Dulles gave the impression of formulating policy decisions on his own. A sturdy moralist, a skilled and stubborn advocate, and a tireless worker, he seemed to feel that he must participate personally in innumerable top-level negotiations all over the globe. Since as secretary he flew 479,286 miles outside of the United States, his detractors liked to wisecrack that he was demonstrating an infinite capacity for taking planes. Assuming many of the normal functions of State Department officials, diplomats, and even the President, he dominated the making of foreign policy.

The Eisenhower administration had come into office firmly committed to existing collective-security arrangements and a Europe-first priority. Nevertheless, it maintained a tenuous compromise with the ardently nationalistic Asia-first wing of the party. This group was exploiting at home the thesis that setbacks in Asia were due to internal subversion in the Truman administration, that Communist aggression in Asia must be met with military force, and that economic aid to remove the grievances the Communists were exploiting was a waste of money. The hero of the Asia-firsters was Chiang Kai-shek, and their special villain, Red China, which they insisted must be curbed or destroyed at all costs. Concurring with this group at some points were the business leaders dominant in the Eisenhower administration, who were determined that defense expenditures must fit within a balanced budget.

The pressures of these groups helped lead to crucial decisions in 1953. Again, as before the Korean War, a movement began to reduce the military establishment. At the same time, the Eisenhower administration wished to meet the Communist challenge in Indochina and elsewhere. The solution seemed to lie in a "new look" in defense policy, equally pleasing to the secretaries of defense, the treasury, and state. This meant cutting the expensive army ground forces and basic scientific research. The United States would depend especially upon its thermonuclear weapons and their delivery by the air force. Popularized, this was the policy of "more bang for a buck."

A new diplomatic and strategic approach was necessary to make the "new look" in defense operate adequately. Secretary of the Treasury George M. Humphrey, looking at it from a standpoint of cost, asserted that the United States had "no business getting into little wars." If the nation had to intervene, he declared, "let's intervene decisively with all we have got or stay out." This was the economic basis for Secretary of State Dulles' proposal of "massive retaliation." The United States would depend less on local defense, he declared in an address on January 12, 1954, and depend more on "the deterrent of massive retaliatory power . . . a great capacity to retaliate instantly, by means and at times of our own choosing."

CHINA AND INDOCHINA

The Indochina crisis of 1954 offered the first test of the new approach. Under the leadership of Ho Chi Minh the people of Indochina, a French colony that had fallen to Japan in World War II, had been fighting for their independence—against the Japanese and then against the French. The end of the Korean War enabled the Chinese Reds to give indirect aid to the Indochinese nationalists, who were largely Communists, at a time when the French were tottering on the edge of military disaster. In 1954 the rebels besieged an army of 12,000 Frenchmen and friendly Indochinese in the frontier fortress of Dienbienphu. Already the United States was paying 70 percent of the French war costs, thus supporting colonialism as an alternative to Communism. Now, it appeared, the United States would also have to send direct military aid if Dienbienphu and all of Indochina were not to fall under Communist control.

At a press conference, President Eisenhower likened the nations in Southeast Asia to a row of dominoes. The moral was implicit; the first domino must not be allowed to fall. Many of the President's advisers favored at least bombing the besieging army with carrier-based planes, but Dulles failed to gain support among allied nations. Congressional leaders had no stomach for an intervention that might soon involve more ground troops than the Korean War, and in which the United States might have to fight alone. The United States did not intervene; there was no "massive retaliation." Dienbienphu fell on May 7, 1954. At a conference in Geneva, the United States, stripped of bargaining power (except for the threat of unilateral intervention), had to stand by, neither associating itself with negotiations with Red China, nor approving the agreements of July 1954, which provided for a cease-fire and the partitioning of Indochina into three independent nations.

After the Geneva conference, Secretary Dulles succeeded in building a Southeast Asia Treaty Organization (SEATO) to serve as a counterpart of NATO and help contain Communism. SEATO (established September 1954) was far less impressive, since the terms of the Geneva conference kept Nationalist China and nations of Indochina (Vietnam, Laos, and Cambodia) from participating. Several of the most important Asian states (India, Ceylon, Burma, and Indonesia) refused to join because they were committed to neutralism. This left only three nations of Southeast Asia—Pakistan, Thailand, and the Philippines—to join with the United States, Great Britain, France, Australia, and New Zealand. They drew up a pact, weaker than the North Atlantic Treaty, providing only that an attack upon one would be regarded as a threat to the others. SEATO opened the way for economic and military aid, but without the key nations of Southeast Asia participating, it remained a relatively ineffective organization.

The United States continued to function in Asia as best it could on a virtually unilateral basis. Trouble with Communist China developed over some offshore islands that Chiang continued to garrison—Quemoy and Matsu and Tachen Islands. Occasionally Chiang's air force attacked the Communists from them. Since the Mutual Defense Treaty with Chiang, signed at the end of 1954, did not include these islands, Red China in January 1955 began air attacks upon the Tachens and bombardment of Quemoy. Before invasion could follow, Congress granted President Eisenhower rather indefinite emergency powers to aid Chiang. These sufficed to maintain a precarious status quo.

Intermittently, the Chinese Communists renewed their pressure upon Quemoy and Matsu. In August 1958 they began another serious bombardment. Secretary Dulles, although not always clear in what he said, implied repeatedly that the United States would help Chiang defend the islands. But the United States could not count upon the support of other Western nations if a large-scale struggle with Red China developed. The militant Chinese Communists in 1959 pressed on other borders. After crushing a revolt in Tibet, they pushed troops across several ill-defined frontiers into areas claimed by India. Of much more

serious concern to the United States, they backed a Communist penetration deep into Laos, one of the nations of Indochina.

In the involved and unending struggle with Communist China, the American arsenal of atomic weapons was of relatively little effect even against a nation that as yet did not possess any. Against Russia, with its rapidly expanding nuclear strength, the threat of massive thermonuclear retaliation was still less effective.

OUR GERMAN ALLY

Fortunately, the United States and its allies did not depend upon nuclear power alone. The concept of the North Atlantic Treaty Organization was embodied in its emblem of a sword and a shield. The sword stood for atomic weapons, the striking force, and the shield for conventional ground forces, to deter or withstand attack. During the Korean War the United States began to rebuild its military establishment at home and gradually to pour funds into NATO, to strengthen its defenses in terms of ground forces as well as atomic weapons.

Europeans worried over the slowness of the United States to provide arms and men, its failure (partly because of constitutional limitations) to commit itself clearly in advance to resist any armed attack on western European nations, and its desire to rearm Germany.

While the French were still afraid of the Germans, the Germans themselves were so war-weary that it was difficult to persuade them to arm again. Between 1950 and 1954 they were able to win back step by step almost all their sovereignty in return for rearming.

To make the rearming of Germany acceptable to France, Great Britain promised in 1954 to keep four divisions and a tactical air force on the Continent as long as her allies wanted them. With this reassurance, France agreed to a treaty that same month restoring full sovereignty to Germany (except for the stationing of allied troops in West Berlin until Germany was reunified). The West German army was to be limited to twelve divisions, which would be supplied to NATO. Germany promised not to seek reunification or extension of her boundaries through force, and was prohibited from manufacturing nuclear, biological, or chemical weapons. Germany joined NATO and thus directly became a military ally of the United

States. In 1957 she contributed her first forces — five divisions totaling 120,000 men.

THE GENEVA SPIRIT

After the death of Stalin in 1953, there were increasing signs that new Russian policies might lead to some enlargement of freedom behind the Iron Curtain and some relaxation of tensions with the Western powers. Russia extended a peace overture to Tito of Yugoslavia, returned a key base to Finland, recognized the Federal Republic of West Germany, and signed a peace treaty with Japan. Above all, the Soviet Union joined with the Western powers in signing a peace treaty with Austria, making it a neutral state, and terminating the long military occupation.

The softening of Soviet policy and the increase in international exchanges led to demands from Europeans, Asians, and even Americans for a conference among the heads of state — a "summit conference" — to consider means of easing international tensions. But the greatest single motive for such a meeting was the knowledge that both the United States and Russia were manufacturing hydrogen bombs of staggering destructive power.

In August 1953 the Russians had set off a hydrogen explosive. President Eisenhower warned a few weeks later that the physical security of the United States had "almost totally disappeared before the long-range bomber and the destructive power of a single bomb." The meaning of this became dramatically clear in the spring of 1954 when the United States announced that it had exploded in the Pacific a bomb powerful enough to destroy or put out of commission all of New York City.

Against this background, the American people, after an initial wariness, became enthusiastic about the meeting of the heads of the United States, Great Britain, France, and Russia in Geneva (July 1955). President Eisenhower, hopeful that he could wage "a war for peace," proposed at the meetings that the Russians and the United States exchange blueprints of their armed forces and permit inspection of their military installations from the air. He declared to Premier Nicolai A. Bulganin: "The United States will never take part in an aggressive war." Bulganin replied: "Mr. President, we believe that statement."

The affability of the Russians at Geneva immensely relieved the American people, who were hopeful for the moment that a real change of policy had come about. This "Geneva spirit," as newspapermen called it, led to a general feeling on the part of most Western nations that a nuclear war between Russia and the United States would not develop. Secretary Dulles declared, however, that the conference had avoided "creating an illusion that all was now so well that we could safely relax our efforts to build individual and collective self-defense." All proposals from both sides had been referred to a future foreign ministers' conference. Even before it met, several nations began to scale down their NATO contributions.

President Eisenhower upon his return from Geneva warned: "We must never be deluded into believing that one week of friendly, even fruitful negotiations can wholly eliminate a problem arising out of the wide gulf that separates East and West." The American public, less inclined to caution, greeted the President with unrestrained acclaim.

The subsequent foreign ministers' conference failed dismally to agree upon German unification, disarmament, or lowering of trade barriers. Even before it adjourned, the "Geneva spirit" rapidly evaporated throughout the West.

MENACE IN THE MIDDLE EAST

Soon a new Russian drive was launched toward the Middle East, where the United States had long been deeply involved because of its conflicting interests in the people of the new state of Israel and in the oil of the Arab states.

During World War II, the British, in order not to offend the Arabs, had continued restrictions upon immigration to Palestine. Both political parties in the United States favored lifting these restrictions and creating a Jewish state. After the war, the British brought the problem to the United Nations, which recommended partitioning Palestine between Jews and Arabs. The Jews successfully fought off military attacks by the Arabs and, on the day the British mandate ended, May 14, 1948, proclaimed a new government. President Truman recognized it within a few minutes, thus ending United Nations proposals to put Palestine under a temporary trusteeship. The new nation, Israel, fought off armies from surrounding

Arab countries until the United Nations established an unstable truce in 1949. Although the United States tried to promote amity, relations between Israel and its neighbors continued close to the point of explosion, and other quarrels in the Middle East persisted.

Gradually the United States won over some of the Arab nations to the Western defense system. This country leased air bases from Saudi Arabia; and through the Baghdad Pact of 1955 Secretary Dulles managed to bring the northern bloc of Arab states — Iraq, Iran, and Pakistan — into the defense arrangement.

Dulles' diplomacy was less successful with Egypt, which for years had quarreled with the British over the Sudan and British bases along the Suez Canal. The United States tried to mediate; in 1954 the British agreed to remove their troops from the Suez area. After Gamal Abdel Nasser came to power, the State Department tried to woo him, although he proclaimed emphatic neutralist and Arab nationalist policies, and strove for leadership of the entire Arab world. Secretary Dulles tried to win him with offers of economic aid — even the sum needed to construct an enormous dam on the Nile. Meanwhile, the Russians concluded a deal, made public in September 1955, by which they gave Nasser large quantities of armaments in exchange for cotton.

With sufficient Communist arms Nasser might destroy Israel. He could also threaten the security system the United States was trying to build in the Middle East. With the arms that went to Nasser and his close ally, Syria, would also go Russian experts to show Egyptians how to use them. Secretary Dulles met the challenge. Instead of continuing to be conciliatory toward Egypt, in July 1956 he suddenly withdrew his promise to provide funds for a dam. A week later Nasser retaliated by seizing the Suez Canal, purportedly to obtain money for the Nile project. This action gave him a stranglehold on the main oil line to Europe, since two-thirds of the proved oil reserves of the world were in the Middle East, and four-fifths of the oil for western Europe flowed from there.

During the tedious months of negotiations with Nasser that followed, Great Britain, France, and Israel all came to feel that they were not obtaining as much support as they should from the United States. Meanwhile, the armed strength of Egypt was growing rapidly.

On October 29, 1956, Israeli forces struck a preventive blow at Egypt. The next day the British and French intervened to drive the Egyptian forces from the Suez Canal zone. They were militarily successful, but not before the Egyptians had thoroughly blocked the canal. The United States led the United Nations in denouncing the military intervention; the Western alliances seemed in danger of dissolving; Russia threatened to send "volunteers" to the aid of Egypt. Under these pressures, the British and French issued a cease-fire order on November 6. Another prolonged truce between Egypt and Israel began under the supervision of the United Nations.

The power vacuum in the Middle East in the weeks after the Suez cease-fire created new opportunities for the spread of Communism. Once again the American public was alarmed and incensed, since coincident with the Suez crisis came brutal Soviet suppression of an uprising in Hungary. Because of the nuclear stalemate, the United States could not intervene in Hungary. It limited itself to fostering United Nations resolutions of censure and to admitting tens of thousands of refugees.

In the Middle East more positive action afterward seemed possible. The public was receptive when the President appeared before Congress on January 5, 1957, to enunciate what came to be called the "Eisenhower Doctrine." He asked Congress to authorize military and economic aid "to secure and protect the territorial independence" of Middle Eastern nations "against overt armed aggression from any nation controlled by international communism." Congress authorized the President to use armed force as he deemed necessary, and to spend $200 million on economic aid in the area.

As an instrument of pressure upon Egypt, the Eisenhower Doctrine was of little effect. Nasser reopened the Suez Canal on his own terms. In April 1957 American policy seemed more successful when the United States rushed its Sixth Fleet to the eastern Mediterranean to bolster the government of Jordan. Three other states, Saudi Arabia, Iraq, and Lebanon, seemed to give at least tacit support to the Eisenhower Doctrine.

Soviet penetration in the next few months, both through feeding Arab nationalism and through providing arms to Egypt, Syria, and Yemen, effectively countered the American policy. In August 1957 the Russians negotiated a $500 million arms-and-aid pact with Syria. In its aftermath, a pro-Soviet army clique seized power. Since the clique of course did not ask for American aid, the Eisenhower Doctrine was inoperative in Syria, but the State Department, declaring that Syria's neighbors were alarmed, sent them weapons. The strong tone of the United States led to an unfavorable reaction among the Arab nations, and they reaffirmed their solidarity.

Egypt and Syria, combining to form the United Arab Republic, continued to exert pressure on their neighbors. When a pro-Nasser clique took over Iraq (July 1958), it appeared that Lebanon and Jordan might also come under Nasser's domination. The pro-Western government of Lebanon requested aid against rebels, and the United States rushed in troops. At the same time Great Britain sent forces into Jordan. In the fall of 1958, when conditions became stabilized in Lebanon, the United States withdrew its troops. Iraq, however, continued to be a serious problem. Secretary Dulles, in order to balance its loss from the Baghdad Pact mutual defense organization, announced that the United States would assume full partnership in the alliance. But the withdrawal of Iraq from the alliance did not lead that country into Nasser's United Arab Republic as expected. The elements favoring this course soon fell from power in Iraq, and the danger in 1959 and after seemed to be that the country would swing into the Communist bloc. Reacting against the Communist trend in Iraq, Nasser veered back toward the West, and the United States again began plying him with favors. Conditions were thus unstable and uncertain in much of the Middle East.

The Communists Gain

The Eisenhower administration was hard pressed to contain the expansion of Communist power in the world, even without attempting the "roll-back" of which Dulles once had spoken. Indeed, before the end of the administration, the Communists appeared to be making further gains.

THE ROCKET RACE

The onslaught of Communist ideology and power was especially frightening because of the apparent failure of the United States to keep pace with the Soviet Union in the development of intercontinental ballistic missiles, a failure that the Russians tried to exploit throughout the world. In early 1957 the United States had appeared to be abreast or ahead of Russia in the development of guided missiles with nuclear warheads. Because of the potential horror of these weapons, both nations seemed ready to reach disarmament agreements during seven months of discussions in 1957 at a meeting of the United Nations subcommittee in London. The United States insisted upon schemes of strict inspection, including proposals for aerial photography over strips of each other's territory. To this the Soviet Union would not agree.

Then, in August, Russia announced that she had successfully tested an intercontinental ballistic missile. In contrast, the United States had successfully tested only intermediate-range missiles that traveled from 1,500 to 3,000 miles. The Russian claims received sobering confirmation in October when Soviet scientists, using a rocket booster engine more powerful than any yet developed in the United States, launched the first successful satellite, the "sputnik."

Khrushchev, who in a series of bold moves had just consolidated his power in the Kremlin, now issued a series of strong statements. The intent of his "sputnik diplomacy" was clearly to shake the Western alliance and impress neutral nations. The reaction within the United States, especially when the first American attempt to launch a much smaller satellite failed, was more one of angry fear than of congratulations to the Russian scientists. Three months later the United States began launching its own, smaller satellites.

As an indication of his concern, President Eisenhower, although recuperating from a mild stroke, flew to Paris (December 1957) to lend strong moral support at a NATO conference. In January 1958 he devoted almost his entire annual message to Congress to the armaments crisis and to the need to surpass Russia

Launching the First American Satellite

*On January 31, 1958, four months after the Russians launched the first satellite —
three months after they sent up one so big that it contained a dog — the United
States, using a Jupiter-C launching vehicle, put into orbit the first American
satellite, called Explorer I. It was 80 inches long, 6 inches in diameter, and
weighed 30.8 pounds. In it were devices for measuring temperature, cosmic rays,
and the frequency of meteorite particles, and radios for transmitting the
measurements. (Official U.S. Army photo)*

in providing aid for underdeveloped countries. He called upon an acquiescent Congress for heavy additional expenditures to rush development and construction of long-range missiles and of submarines and cruisers that could launch missiles. The first task confronting the nation was "to ensure our safety through strength," he pointed out. "But we could make no more tragic mistake than merely to concentrate on military strength. For if we did only this, the future would hold nothing for the world but an age of terror."

Meanwhile, extensive nuclear testing after 1954 by both the United States and Russia, climaxed by the Russian explosion of several "dirty" bombs, greatly increased the fallout of radioactive isotopes. Throughout the world there was a fear of possible harmful effects. "Any dose, however small, produces some biological effect and . . . this effect is harmful," the Joint Congressional Committee on Atomic Energy granted in a 1959 report. If testing were to continue at the same rate over the next two generations, the report warned, the average concentration of radioactive strontium in the bones would be close to what scientists had estimated would be the maximum permissible body burden. This threat, well before 1959, was bringing popular pressure for the curtailing of nuclear tests.

In the spring of 1958 Khrushchev announced a unilateral abstention from nuclear tests by Russia. This left Eisenhower with the choice of two courses. He could follow the reasoning of most officials in the Defense Department, who held that nuclear weapons were the only way in which the United States could counter the enormous land armies of Russia and China—and continue tests. Or he could promise to stop tests on the condition that Russia would agree to adequate inspection.

He decided upon the latter course and announced that the United States and its allies would suspend tests for one year beginning October 31, 1958. The suspension would continue on a year-to-year basis, provided a proper system of control could be developed and substantial progress could be made on disarmament negotiations. Russia, proclaiming that this was a Western trick, announced that it would resume testing. Nevertheless, President Eisenhower declared that for the time being the United States would continue its suspension of

tests as it sought some workable agreement with the Soviet Union. Representatives of the United States, Great Britain, and Russia met in Geneva and slowly, laboriously, tried to construct a regulatory treaty.

In 1959 Khrushchev made much propaganda use of the failure of the United States to catch up with Russia in astronautical feats. These feats obscured the fact that the "missile gap" between the two nations was not as great as had been feared two years earlier. The United States was successfully producing and testing its own missiles and developing plans for hiding and spreading the launching sites so that it would require ten times as many Russian missiles to destroy them. The success of the navy in constructing atomic-powered submarines that could launch missiles, and in bringing the submarines up through the ice at the North Pole, was a dramatic example of American achievement. The naval development of "Project Tepee," a radio-monitoring system that could detect any missile launchings anywhere in the world, was an indication of the technical advance of American defense.

If the Russians were to attack the United States, they could not expect their own cities to remain unscathed. The reverse held equally true—that American nuclear power would be incapable of destroying all the sites from which the Russians could launch missiles. The Congressional Joint Committee on Atomic Energy reported in August 1959 that an attack upon the United States, if it came, might kill 50 million people, seriously injure 20 million more, and destroy or render unusable for months half of the dwellings in the country. Crops would be contaminated and swept by fire. The only hopeful note was the assurance that bomb shelters for the entire population could reduce casualties by 25 or 30 percent.

FRIENDLY OVERTURES FAIL

Suddenly, in November 1958, Khrushchev precipitated a new crisis over Berlin, where the West's position was, as always, vulnerable. He asserted that conditions had changed so markedly in Berlin since the end of the war that the occupation agreements no longer applied. In six months he proposed to sign a separate peace treaty with the government of East

President Eisenhower on Berlin [1961]

Berlin is not so much a beleaguered city or threatened city as it is a symbol — for the West, of principle, of good faith, of determination; for the Soviets, a thorn in their flesh, a wound to their pride, an impediment to their designs.

The Soviets want to banish the Allies from West Berlin because, first, it is to them an unwelcome show place of Western freedom and prosperity in a region otherwise completely regimented and impoverished; and, second, because the opportunity it creates for the unhappy East Germans to escape to freedom emphasizes to the outside world the emptiness of the phrase "people's democracies." In the meantime, they use it as a pretext to create and intensify tensions and to try to divide the West. — Saturday Evening Post, *December 9, 1961.*

Germany, turning over to it all the Russian occupation functions in Berlin including control over the access routes that stretched 110 miles to West Germany.

The United States insisted that its treaty rights still held and undertook the twofold task of trying to maintain unity among its Western allies and of getting from the Soviet government concessions that would correspond to any that the United States might make. Neither task was easy. Russia made alternate proposals that were as unacceptable as the first demand had been, and Khrushchev manipulated the issue to try to force a summit meeting. The United States was not willing to go further than a foreign ministers' conference unless the Russians became more conciliatory. The Geneva sessions beginning in May 1959 were discouragingly unfruitful.

Meanwhile, the burden of conducting American foreign policy had shifted to a new Secretary of State, Christian Herter, when Dulles, dying of cancer, resigned in April 1959. Herter was a strong successor. He had capped his foreign service record as a young man with a successful career in politics. But he did not continue the one-man determination of foreign policy that had distinguished Dulles. President Eisenhower now assumed a larger measure of responsibility, and this pointed toward new interchanges at the top with the Russians.

Exchanges at lower levels had been going on at an increasing rate since the Geneva thaw of 1955. One of its few positive effects had been personal and cultural interchanges of musicians, dancers, students, and delegations of all kinds, climaxed in the summer of 1959 by a visit to the United States of Anastas Mikoyan, a So-viet deputy premier, and to Russia of Vice President Nixon. The Russians demonstrated their wares at a fair in New York City, and the Americans at a corresponding fair in Moscow showed crowds of Russians the components of the high standard of living in the United States. While Nixon was at the fair, he engaged in informal debate with Khrushchev. The Russian press was for the most part hostile, but the crowds were friendly, and Khrushchev himself, while holding dogmatically to Soviet positions, seemed to demonstrate a keen interest in things American.

In August 1959 President Eisenhower announced that he would exchange visits with the Russian leader. The purpose in inviting Khrushchev, Eisenhower explained, was "to give him the opportunity to see what Americans are like" and "to give him, face to face, the basic convictions of our people on the major issues of the day." Khrushchev, during his travels in the United States, received on the whole a hearty welcome, despite the coldness of most American officials and the hostile demonstrations of certain groups, especially those sympathizing with the Hungarian rebels of 1956. He impressed Americans with his energy, toughness, and — except for a few petulant outbursts — good humor. Eisenhower, postponing nis return visit, made tours of western Europe, southern Asia, and Latin America, to the cheers of enthusiastic crowds at almost every stop.

A second "summit" conference, to meet in Paris, was scheduled for May 1960. On May 1 an unarmed American U-2 plane was downed inside the Soviet Union. The American government at first denied, then acknowledged and attempted to justify the fact that the plane had been engaged in aerial reconnaissance of a kind the United States had been carrying on, systematically but secretly, for some time. At the Paris meeting, unsatisfied by Eisenhower's belated promise to discontinue flights over Russian territory, Khrushchev made the U-2 incident an occasion for denouncing Eisenhower and breaking up the conference.

Khrushchev also took back his invitation for Eisenhower to go to the Soviet Union. Eisenhower, having planned to stop in Japan on the way home from Russia, went ahead with arrangements for a Far Eastern trip in June. A new security pact, authorizing continued American bases in Japan, awaited ratification. Communist agitators now played upon the pacifisim of the Japanese people, a pacifism that American occupation policies earlier had stimulated. In Tokyo mobs began wild demonstrations against the pact, against Premier Nobusuke Kishi, who sponsored it, and against the Eisenhower visit. At the last minute, after the President had reached as far as Manila, his Japan appearance was called off. The Kishi government managed to put the unpopular treaty into effect; but throughout the world the Eisenhower administration could scarcely avoid a serious loss to American prestige, which already had been weakened by the administration's handling of the spy-plane affair.

DISGRUNTLED NEIGHBORS

The incessant threats against areas close to the Communist perimeter so occupied the American government and people that they paid scant attention to an area of vital worth to the United States and of growing vulnerability to Communist influence — the area to the south. One of the minor ironies of this hectic age was the erosion of the Good Neighbor feeling between Latin American nations and the United States during the very years when this country was extending much of the Good Neighbor policy to Europe and Asia.

On paper there was no deterioration. Quite the contrary; the Latin American nations signed new pacts and received additional forms of aid. They all became members of the United Nations. In 1947, at a conference at Rio de Janeiro, they drafted an Inter-American Treaty of Reciprocal Assistance, and the following year established an Organization of American States. The United States had abandoned the old unilateral Monroe Doctrine by entering into pacts and organizations providing for mutual action whether in defense, settlement of disputes, or economic cooperation.

Yet the overwhelming military and economic power of the "colossus of the North" remained. Latin Americans were not pleased when the United States brought its prestige to bear against the totalitarian dictator of Argentina, Juan D. Perón, in 1946–1947, even though the pressure failed. They were not much more pleased when the United States successfully brought pressure against a pro-Communist regime in Guatemala in 1954. But in the late fifties, when many of the nations overthrew dictators, the more common complaint was that the United States had been too friendly toward despots, as in Venezuela, and not enthusiastic enough about rebels like Fidel Castro, who came into power in Cuba in 1959, and who thereafter devoted himself to denunciations of "Yankee imperialism."

Above all, the problems from which Latin American peoples were suffering were economic. After the close of World War II, they could no longer sell raw materials from their farms and mines to the United States in such large quantities or at such favorable prices as before. The soaring costs of the American manufactured goods they imported further hurt them. At home they were undergoing a rapid industrial revolution, an accompanying social evolution, and an explosive population increase at the highest rate in the world, as much as 2.5 percent per year. Already their combined population had passed that of the United States. All these factors helped create acute internal problems.

Inevitably the United States would have to be involved in the solution of economic questions because the hostility of neighbors to the south would be potentially ruinous, and because the two areas had become increasingly interdependent economically. Trade with Latin America exceeded $8 billion a year by the end of the fifties, and accounted for a third of the imports and a quarter of the exports of the United States. In Latin America 80 percent of the foreign capital was American; it had a book value of about $9.5 billion. (This figure was sec-

Peruvians Threaten Nixon

On his goodwill tour of South America in 1958, Vice President Nixon was the target of violent anti-American demonstrations. When, on May 8, he appeared at San Marcos University in Lima, Peru, local police had difficulty in restraining the mob. The demonstrators threw stones, one of which grazed the Vice President's neck. (UPI)

ond only to the $13 billion invested in Canada, which was also unhappy about its economic relations with the United States.)

It seemed to Latin Americans that, despite these close economic ties, the United States was doing little specifically to help them solve their problems — to provide adequate capital for large-scale development, to stabilize raw materials at a profitable level, and to conquer inflation. They felt neglected as the American government poured billions into Europe and Asia while giving Latin America only a comparative pittance. Secretary Dulles was occupied elsewhere, and the Eisenhower administration,

under the influence of two successive conservative secretaries of the Treasury, was cold to requests for government loans for development. The festering economic ills and other grievances that could easily be focused against the United States were ready-made for the Communists. Exercising an influence out of proportion to their small numbers, they were active from Cuba to Guatemala and Argentina.

Despite riots and disorders, the Latin American discontent received little notice in the United States until May 1958, when Vice President Nixon was mobbed in Lima and Caracas. In the aftermath of the national shock, the State Department speeded changes in policy which were already slowly under way. This country helped Latin American nations negotiate export quota pacts among themselves to raise the price of coffee and some metals, and it expedited negotiations toward the establishment of a regional common market among the republics. When, in June 1958, the President of Brazil called for an Operation Pan-America to speed economic development, the American government agreed to furnish nearly half the capital for a new billion-dollar Inter-American Bank to make development loans. It also tried to improve public relations in a way Nixon had suggested by giving no more than a correct handshake to dictators but offering a warm embrace to democratic leaders.

The administration was increasing its attention to Latin America none too soon, since it was obvious that the well-disciplined, widely pervasive Communist activities throughout the area were receiving direction from Russia. Early in 1959 Latin American Communist leaders returned from attending the twenty-first party congress in Moscow and began the systematic denunciation of every point of the new United States program.

The full import of the Communist challenge to the south became clear in 1960. Fidel Castro, whose revolutionary accession to power had been cheered by Americans at the beginning of 1959, turned his administration increasingly to the left and indulged in shrill tirades against the United States. The Eisenhower administration, acting with restraint, was slow to retaliate economically until, in the summer of 1960, Castro systematically confiscated a billion dollars' worth of American property. At this point the United States stopped importing Cuban sugar at a subsidized price. Castro complained to the United Nations Security Council that the United States was engaging in economic aggression.

The Soviet leader Nikita S. Khrushchev proclaimed that the Monroe Doctrine was dead and that, if the United States were to intervene militarily, Soviet artillerymen could "support Cuba with rocket fire." In the fall of 1960 tension heightened as Castro tried to spread his revolution to neighboring republics. President Eisenhower established a naval patrol to prevent an invasion of Guatemala or Nicaragua. At the same time, secretly, Americans were training an anti-Castro Cuban force at a camp in Guatemala. In January 1961 Castro ordered the staff of the United States embassy in Havana cut from eighty-seven to eleven. The United States then severed diplomatic relations with Cuba. Soviet influence clearly extended to within ninety miles of the United States.

Selected Readings

The Truman Administration
R. F. Haynes, *The Awesome Power: Harry S. Truman as Commander in Chief* (1973); R. M. Freeland, *The Truman Doctrine and the Origins of McCarthyism* (1972); W. C. Berman, *The Politics of Civil Rights in the Truman Administration* (1971).

The Eisenhower Administration
D. D. Eisenhower, *The White House Years** (2 vols., 1963–1965); E. J. Hughes, *The Ordeal of Power* (1963); Richard Nixon, *Six Crises** (1962); J. T. Patterson, *Mr. Republican: A Biography of Robert A. Taft* (1972); J. R. Beals, *John Foster Dulles* (1959); Richard Goold-Adams, *J. F. Dulles: A Reappraisal* (1962); Louis Gerson, *American Secretaries of State: John Foster Dulles* (1967); T. Hoopes, *The Devil and John Foster Dulles* (1973).

The Cold War
G. F. Kennan, *American Diplomacy, 1900–1950** (1951); J. W. Spanier, *American Foreign Policy Since World War II** (1962); W. G. Carleton, *The Revolution in American Foreign Policy: Its Global Range** (1963); Norman Graebner, *Cold War Diplomacy: American Foreign Policy, 1945–1960** (1962); M. F. Herz, *Beginnings of the Cold War* (1960); D. F. Fleming, *The Cold War and Its Origins, 1917–1960* (2 vols., 1961), critical of the U.S.; J. and G. Kolko, *The Limits of Power: The World and United States Foreign Policy, 1945–1954** (1972); J. L. Gaddis, *The United States and the Origins of the Cold War, 1941–1947* (1973); T. G. Paterson, *Soviet-American Confrontation: Postwar Reconstruction and the Origins of the Cold War* (1973); L. S. Wittner, *Rebels Against War: The American Peace Movement, 1941–1960* (1969); David Wise and Thomas Ross, *The U-2 Affair* (1962).

Nuclear Power and Military Policy
H. A. Kissinger, *Nuclear Weapons and Foreign Policy* (1957); L. L. Strauss, *Men and Decisions* (1962); R. G. Hewlett and O. E. Anderson, Jr., *The New World* (1962); Herman Kahn, *On Thermonuclear War* (1960); M. D. Taylor, *The Uncertain Trumpet* (1960); H. L. Nieburg, *Nuclear Secrecy and Foreign Policy* (1964).

Communism and Anti-Communism
E. L. Shils, *The Torment of Secrecy* (1956); J. A. Wechsler, *The Age of Suspicion* (1953); Whittaker Chambers, *Witness* (1952); Alger Hiss, *In the Court of Public Opinion* (1957); R. H. Rovere, *Senator Joe McCarthy** (1959); C. P. Curtis, *The Oppenheimer Case* (1955).

Germany
L. D. Clay, *Decision in Germany* (1950); Drew Middleton, *The Struggle for Germany* (1949); R. H. Jackson, *The Nürnberg Case* (1947); Eugene Davidson, *The Death and Life of Germany: An Account of the American Occupation* (1959); J. E. Smith, *The Defense of Berlin* (1963).

The Far East
E. O. Reischauer, *The United States and Japan** (1957); R. A. Fearey, *Occupation of Japan* (1950); F. S. Dunn, *Peace-Making and the Settlement with Japan* (1963); Herbert Feis, *The China Tangle** (1953);

Tang Tsou, *America's Failure in China, 1941–1950* (1963); David Rees, *Korea: The Limited War* (1964); Carl Berger, *The Korea Knot: A Military-Political History* (1957); G. D. Paige, *The Korea Decision, June 24–30, 1950** (1968); J. W. Spanier, *The Truman-MacArthur Controversy and the Korean War** (1959); A. D. Biderman, *March to Calumny* (1962), on "brainwashed" American prisoners; Melvin Gurtov, *The First Vietnam Crisis: Chinese Communist Strategy and United States Involvement, 1953–1954* (1967).

The Near East
Nadav Safran, *The United States and Israel* (1963); Hugh Thomas, *The Suez Affair* (1967); Herman Finer, *Dulles over Suez* (1964).

Latin America
M. S. Eisenhower, *The Wine Is Bitter: The United States and Latin America* (1963); B. F. Smith, *The United States and Cuba: Business and Diplomacy, 1917–1960* (1960).

*Titles available in paperback.

The Politics of Plenty

Twenty-eight

Though the peril of nuclear annihilation hung over them, the majority of the American people, in the phrase of the time, "never had it so good." They were riding a wave of prosperity much higher and longer-lasting than any previous one in the history of the country. The boom, beginning in the 1940s, continued through the 1950s and the 1960s, with an occasional recession or minor slump but with no real depression. A generation grew up that had never experienced such a calamity and could not believe it possible.

Yet there was much to be apprehensive about, at home as well as abroad. The prosperity was largely due to the foreign dangers, for it was stimulated by government spending for defense, and there was reason to wonder how long the good times would last if by some chance there should be a sudden "outbreak of peace." And even while the prosperity lasted, a large minority of the people, perhaps as many as 30 million of them, had little or no share in it.

A Swedish sociologist, Gunnar Myrdal, well acquainted with life in the United States, was moved to write: "I draw the conclusion that the common idea that America is an immensely rich and affluent country is very much an exaggeration. American affluence is heavily mortgaged. America carries a tremendous burden of debt to its poor people. That this debt must be paid is not only a wish of the do-gooders. Not paying it implies a risk for the social order and for democracy as we have known it."

Especially disadvantaged were the Americans of African descent. In a country that professed devotion to the creed of liberty and equality, they suffered from limitations on both. This contradiction between profession and practice was the theme of an elaborate study, *An American Dilemma* (2 vols., 1944), which Myrdal and a team of American scholars had made of the Negro's place in the United States. Myrdal had

---

Poverty in Appalachia
More white than black Americans of the 1960s and 1970s lived in poverty, though proportionately the number of black poor was greater. Many of the poorest whites were to be found in Appalachia, the Appalachian Mountain area of the Southeast. Here poor white children are playing near the entrance to a Kentucky coal mine. (Magnum)

warned that, after the war, Negro Americans could be expected to demand the rights that so long had been systematically denied them.

In the war black troops fought along with white for the declared object of creating an international order in which the "four freedoms" would be secure. Then, in the cold war, the United States sought the support of dark-skinned peoples throughout the world. These peoples, emerging from colonialism in their own lands of Asia and Africa, provided inspiration for blacks in America who began to insist upon the freedom they had not yet fully won a century after their emancipation had been officially proclaimed.

With his "Fair Deal," President Truman had made an abortive effort to solve some of the most pressing of the domestic problems. President Eisenhower announced no comparable program, but his successors John F. Kennedy and Lyndon B. Johnson proposed reforms going beyond Truman's.

The "Middle of the Road"

In the 1950s the majority of the voters seemed more interested in preserving their own economic gains than in remaking society. Viewing themselves as moderates, they gave whole-hearted support to the moderate President, Dwight D. Eisenhower. As early as 1949 Eisenhower had indicated his own approach when, as president of Columbia University, he addressed the American Bar Association. "The path to America's future," he then said, "lies down the middle of the road between the unfettered power of concentrated wealth . . . and the unbridled power of statism or partisan interests."

BUSINESSMEN IN GOVERNMENT

Once in office, President Eisenhower set up a businessmen's administration. To his cabinet he appointed one of the highest-paid corporation lawyers in the country (Secretary of State John Foster Dulles), the president of General Motors (Secretary of Defense Charles E. Wilson), the president of Mark Hanna's former firm M. A. Hanna and Company (Secretary of the Treasury George Humphrey), a New England manufacturer, two automobile distributors, a conservative specialist in farm marketing, and the wife of a wealthy Texas publisher (Mrs. Oveta Culp Hobby, who had been wartime commander of the WACs and who was named to head the Department of Health, Education, and Welfare when it came into existence in 1953). Something of an exception was the Secretary of Labor, Martin P. Durkin, the president of the plumbers' union, who had backed Adlai Stevenson in the 1952 campaign. "Eight millionaires and a plumber," the *New Republic* disrespectfully remarked. At the hearing on his appointment, Wilson played into the hands of Democratic critics by testifying that he had long assumed that "what was good for our country was good for General Motors, and vice versa." A few days later, Stevenson declared: "While the New Dealers have all left Washington to make way for the car dealers, I hasten to say that I, for one, do not believe the story that the general welfare has become a subsidiary of General Motors."

President Eisenhower's system of administering the government gave special importance to this cabinet made up preponderantly of businessmen. Borrowing from earlier army experience, he established his assistant, Sherman Adams, former governor of New Hampshire, as a sort of chief of staff, and from Adams down through the cabinet he extended a chain of command. Through the cabinet, and through numerous new committees, administrators arrived at important policy decisions that they referred to the President, who relied heavily upon these recommendations.

"EISENHOWER PROSPERITY"

At the beginning of the new administration, Secretary of the Treasury George Humphrey undertook to restrict bank credit and thus prevent inflation. By the fall of 1953 the threat was one of deflation instead. When the economy slackened, Secretary Humphrey and the Federal Reserve Board reversed the scarce-money policies and eased credit. The Republican administration's first venture with the expedients of Keynesian economics (manipulating money and credit to control the business cycle) was a success. By the summer of 1955 the American economy was again booming.

In order to avoid strikes that might unsettle economic conditions, several large industries, led by the automobile manufacturers, made new concessions to organized labor. As early as 1948 Walter Reuther, the president of the United Automobile Workers, had obtained from General Motors, and later from other manufacturers, an "escalator clause" in contracts, providing for automatic increases or decreases in wages every three months as the consumers' price index rose or fell. In 1955 he demanded from the Ford Motor Company a guaranteed annual wage. Ford compromised by agreeing that workers should receive 65 percent of their net weekly wages for the first four weeks they were unemployed, and 60 percent for the next twenty-two weeks. General Motors followed. A few months later, steelworkers received from the American Can Company and the Continental Can Company the first guarantee of an annual wage.

The round of wage raises continued through 1956. After a five-week strike, steelworkers won a substantial gain, and the United Mine Workers without a strike obtained a 30-cents-an-hour increase. Factory workers' wages went up to approximately $80 per week. These wage increases, together with other factors, led to widespread wholesale price rises and a renewed threat of inflation.

In December 1955 the American Federation of Labor and the Congress of Industrial Organizations merged at the top into a new giant federation, the AFL-CIO. The powerful Teamsters' Brotherhood in 1957 became the focal point of a congressional investigation into labor racketeering. A Senate committee charged the president of the Teamsters, David Beck, with the misappropriation of over $320,000 in union funds. When Beck appeared before the committee, he refused to answer questions, invoking the constitutional protection of the Fifth Amendment against self-incrimination. Ultimately the committee brought forth so much evidence against Beck that he declined to run for reelection as president of the Teamsters. But at their convention the Teamsters defiantly elected, as their new

president, James Hoffa, also under attack by the committee. His election resulted in the eviction of the Teamsters, the largest union in the United States, from the AFL-CIO. The congressional investigation led to the Labor Reform Act of 1959, which was intended to promote honest elections of union officials, safeguard union funds, ban Communist leaders, and restrict boycotting and picketing.

The great staples piled up in surplus, and from 1948 to 1956, farm prices dropped a third while the national income went up by half. In 1948 farmers received 8.9 percent of the national income; in 1956, only 4.1 percent. Farm population declined steadily, to 22,300,000 in 1956 — only a ninth of the nation. In that single year, one out of every eleven of the farm population either moved to a city or was absorbed in an expanding city. While farm produce prices fell, consumer food prices continued to rise. Mainly this was because distribution costs were steadily going up. The farmer was caught in a squeeze, as prices for his produce slipped while prices of what he bought gradually increased.

As surpluses of such agricultural staples as wheat and cotton piled up, the government sought to bolster the prices through $8 billion worth of purchases. In 1954 President Eisenhower and Secretary of Agriculture Benson proposed a shift away from rigid price supports to a flexible sliding-scale program. The purpose was to cut government losses and end artificiality in production and distribution. The 1955 harvest was the first to be grown under the new flexible system, but already Democratic politicians were denouncing flexible supports as ones that could only "flex" downward. Seeking to win the farm vote, in 1956 they wrote a bill providing for high price supports and a subsidy for farmers who let land lie fallow. They thought they had put President Eisenhower in an impossible position, and as they expected, he vetoed the bill. But in May 1956 he pulled out of the vetoed bill the provision for a "soil bank" of fallow land and threw it back at the congressional Democrats. In this form, Congress passed the bill and it became law. Under the 1956 program, farmers took 12.3 million acres out of production in return for payments of over $250 million.

In the realm of public power development, the administration demonstrated its friendliness toward private enterprise. The President in 1953 referred to expansion of the Tennessee Valley Authority as "creeping socialism." The administration sought to circumvent the TVA by contracting with the Dixon-Yates syndicate in 1954 to build a huge steam power plant on the banks of the Mississippi. The administration declared that the contract would save taxpayers an immediate $100 million in construction costs, but opponents pointed to the large profits that the syndicate would collect over many years. The power would cost the government $3.5 million per year more than TVA power. Ultimately in 1955, when the city of Memphis, Tennessee, offered to build the plant, the President retreated to the principle of decentralization and canceled the Dixon-Yates contract.

The Eisenhower administration proposed federal "partnership" with local public or private enterprise in power construction. Secretary of the Interior McKay thus permitted a private power company to plan three small power dams in Hell's Canyon on the Snake River, rather than obtain appropriations for one large federal multipurpose dam. In keeping with his feeling that development of resources should be decentralized, President Eisenhower signed a bill turning over to states offshore oil lands along the Gulf of Mexico and the Pacific coast.

While the Eisenhower administration moved toward the right, conciliating the Taft wing of the Republican party in Congress, the President retained the basic general welfare programs that had been enacted during the previous twenty years. He took a firm stand against so-called socialized medicine but proposed a public health-insurance program that would involve little more than limited underwriting of private insurance companies issuing health policies. Congress passed no health-insurance legislation, but in 1954 extended social security to 10 million more people, and unemployment compensation to an additional 4 million. In 1956 Congress authorized a ten-year highway building program for which it would allocate almost $25 billion.

This concept of the limited role of the federal government in providing for the general welfare was what Eisenhower referred to as "dynamic conservatism." It appealed to many members of Congress. During his first two years in office, when Congress was narrowly

Republican, the President was supported more often than not by a coalition of liberal Republicans and Democrats. Of eighty-three key issues brought to a vote in the 1953 session of Congress, the administration won seventy-four, but succeeded in fifty-eight of these only through Democratic support. After the elections of 1954 the Democrats controlled both the House and the Senate.

DECLINE OF McCARTHYISM

Among the politicians who, after the Communist victory in China, had encouraged and capitalized upon the American people's fear of Communism, none rose more sensationally than Senator Joseph R. McCarthy of Wisconsin. A Republican, McCarthy began in 1950 to charge that Communists and "fellow travelers" (sympathizers) dominated the State Department and shaped American foreign policy under the Truman administration. The Senate Foreign Relations Committee investigated and found not a single Communist or fellow traveler in the State Department. Nevertheless, millions were eager to believe McCarthy as he went on to make new and startling accusations more rapidly than they could be either substantiated or refuted. His followers applauded when he denounced as Communists or pro-Communists the "whole group of twisted-thinking New Dealers" who had "led America near to ruin at home and abroad." He got so much attention that "McCarthyism" became a synonym for hysterical anti-Communism. Only gradually after the Korean armistice was the nation relieved from the worst excesses of McCarthyism.

The hunt for subversives in the government, begun during the Truman years, was intensified early in the Eisenhower administration. Large numbers of employees resigned or were dismissed—a total of 2,200 according to an official report. But most of the serious security risks had already been removed in the Truman purge. A study of some 400 of the Eisenhower administration cases by the Fund for the Republic of the Ford Foundation indicated that in a majority of them the charges had been insupportable, and often reinstatement ultimately followed. In July 1955 the Congress established a bipartisan Commission on Government Security to reevaluate the security program.

COMMUNIST PARTY ORGANIZATION U.S.A-FEB. 9,1950

The Army-McCarthy Hearings

*During the 1954 televised hearings on alleged Communist influence in the Army,
Senator Joseph McCarthy of Wisconsin uses a map to show the supposed
distribution of Communists throughout the country, while the chief counsel for the
Army, Joseph Welch, and (at the extreme left) the assistant counsel, James
St. Clair, listen. Twenty years later St. Clair was to defend President Richard
M. Nixon against an impeachment move arising from the Watergate affair. (UPI)*

Senator McCarthy himself plummeted from the national limelight to relative obscurity. His downfall followed his serious blunder in obliquely attacking President Eisenhower and directly assailing Secretary of the Army Robert Stevens, in January 1954. The attacks led to congressional hearings, which turned into a great national spectacle viewed by millions over television. Many people for the first time saw McCarthy in action, as for thirteen days he bullied and harried Secretary Stevens, evading issues through irrelevant countercharges and insinuations, and interrupting to object at every point. As the public watched, McCarthy seemed to change from a national hero into something of a villain, then into a low buffoon. In December 1954 the Senate voted 67 to 22 to condemn him for conduct unbecoming a senator. He no longer had much of a following when he died in May 1957.

Remnants of the attitudes that had made possible the rise of McCarthy remained. There was, for example, the case of a consultant to the Atomic Energy Commission, J. Robert Oppenheimer, who had directed the wartime laboratory at Los Alamos that made the first atomic bomb. In 1950 he had opposed the development of a hydrogen bomb. The FBI in 1953 distributed to the White House and several government departments a report on Oppenheimer detailing his prewar associations with Communists. On order from President Eisenhower, a "blank wall" was placed between Oppenheimer and government secrets, pending hearings. A three-man board voted 2 to 1 against granting him security clearance; the AEC ratified the decision 4 to 1. Scientists were bitterly split over the wisdom of the decision.

The Supreme Court, as a result of the appointments of the Republican President, seemed to be moving toward a more liberal rather than conservative policy. In one case in 1957 it ruled that the government could not use secret FBI evidence against a defendant unless it was made available to his lawyers. Congress quickly passed legislation safeguarding FBI files. In four other cases the Court protected individuals who were suspected of being subversive against undue encroachment by federal or state power. In 1958 the Court ruled 5 to 4 that the State Department, in the absence of an act of Congress, was exceeding its authority in refusing passports to persons who failed to file affidavits "with respect to present or past membership in the Communist party." These decisions attracted relatively little attention compared with the Supreme Court rulings on desegregation.

DESEGREGATION BEGINS

A series of cases before the Supreme Court breaking down bit by bit racial segregation in public schools had been pressed by the National Association for the Advancement of Colored People since the late 1930s. Their target was a Supreme Court decision of 1896, *Plessy* v. *Ferguson*, which had interpreted the Fourteenth Amendment clause requiring that states give "equal protection of the laws" to mean that separate but equal facilities could be furnished to Negroes. Finally, the Supreme Court reversed this doctrine in the case of *Brown* v. *Board of Education of Topeka* in May 1954. Chief Justice Earl Warren (who had been appointed by President Eisenhower in 1953, after the death of Chief Justice Vinson) delivered the unanimous opinion of the Court: "We conclude that in the field of public education the doctrine of 'separate but equal' has no place. Separate educational facilities are inherently unequal." The Court called for the desegregation of schools "with all deliberate speed."

Some Southern and border states resorted to every possible legal device to avoid mixed schools. Each September mob action against integration in a few communities within the South attracted widespread attention throughout the world. By the fall of 1957, of some 3,000 biracial school districts in the South, a total of 684 had begun desegregation. Schools within these districts in large cities in the upper South

Brown et al. v. Board of Education of Topeka et al. [1954]

In approaching this problem, we cannot turn the clock back to 1868 when the [Fourteenth] Amendment was adopted, or even to 1896 when Plessy v. Ferguson was written. We must consider public education in the light of its full development and its present place in American life throughout the Nation. Only in this way can it be determined if segregation in public schools deprives these plaintiffs of the equal protection of the laws.

Today, education is perhaps the most important function of state and local governments. Compulsory school attendance laws and the great expenditures for education both demonstrate our recognition of the importance of education to our democratic society. It is required in the performance of our most basic public responsibilities, even service in the armed forces. It is the very foundation of good citizenship. Today it is a principal instrument in awakening the child to cultural values, in preparing him for later professional training, and in helping him to adjust normally to his environment. In these days it is doubtful that any child may reasonably be expected to succeed in life if he is denied the opportunity of an education. Such an opportunity where the state has undertaken to provide it, is a right which must be made available to all on equal terms.

We come then to the question presented: Does segregation of children in public schools solely on the basis of race, even though the physical facilities and other 'tangible' factors may be equal, deprive the children of the minority group of equal educational opportunities? We believe that it does. — Excerpt of opinion of the Supreme Court delivered by Chief Justice Earl Warren.

State of South Carolina, Resolution on Desegregation [1956]

For almost sixty years, beginning in 1896, an unbroken line of decisions of the [Supreme] Court interpreted the Fourteenth Amendment as recognizing the right of the States to maintain racially separate public facilities for their people. If the Court in the interpretation of the Constitution is to depart from the sanctity of past decisions and to rely on the current political and social philosophy of its members to unsettle the great constitutional principles so clearly established, the rights of individuals are not secure and government under a written Constitution has no stability. . . .

The educational opportunities of white and colored children in the public schools of South Carolina have been substantially improved during recent years and highly satisfactory results are being obtained in our segregated schools. If enforced, the decision of the Court will seriously impair and retard the education of the children of both races, will nullify these recent advances and will cause untold friction between the races. — Excerpt from Joint Resolution, February 14, 1956.

or the border area, like Washington, Baltimore, Louisville, and St. Louis, opened quietly on an integrated basis. But 2,300 districts, including all those in the deep South and in Virginia, remained racially separate. Some districts at-tempted desegregation on a very slow, "token" basis. One of these was Little Rock, Arkansas, where intervention by the governor and threats by a mob led President Eisenhower to send federal troops to maintain order.

Desegregation in Washington, D.C.
In the fall of 1954, following the Supreme Court decision against school segregation, McKinley Technical High School quietly opened on a basis of equality for all students regardless of color. Before this date, public schools in the nation's capital were segregated. (Wide World)

Pressure from growing blocs of Negro voters in the North, and from Negroes rising in economic status in the South, helped bring other changes. President Eisenhower completed the desegregation of the armed forces and tried to bring about greater integration in the government and the District of Columbia. "There must be no second-class citizens in this country," he wrote the Negro Representative Adam Clayton Powell. Representative Powell, ironically, was instrumental in killing President Eisenhower's school-aid program of 1956, which provided for grants of $250 million a year for five years to match state funds. Powell succeeded in amending the bill to ban racial segregation; Southern segregationists aligned themselves with Northern conservatives to defeat the bill.

Congress in August 1957, after debating sixty-three days, passed a new civil rights law—the first since Reconstruction—to give federal protection to Negroes wanting to vote. In eight Southern states with an adult Negro population of over 3,750,000, only 850,000 or 25 percent were registered and still fewer went to the polls. In a 1955 election in Mississippi, only about 1 percent of the adult Negroes had voted. The Civil Rights Act empowered the federal government to remove some of the obstacles that state and local officials were placing in the way of Negro registration and voting. Federal judges were authorized to enjoin state officials from refusing to register qualified persons. The judges could fine recalcitrant officials up to $300 and could sentence them to forty-five days in jail, without a jury trial.

With the Supreme Court ruling out school segregation and the Congress legislating for civil rights, it seemed that a "second Reconstruction" was beginning, one that would complete the task of emancipation left unfinished in 1877.

A SECOND TERM FOR IKE

In 1955 President Eisenhower was at the height of his popularity. Only the anti-third-term Twenty-second Amendment, ratified in 1951 as a belated slap at Roosevelt, seemed to bar him from staying in the White House as long as he chose. Apparently his health was excellent, but while vacationing in Colorado, on the morning of September 24, he suffered a heart attack.

The President began to make a promising recovery, but no one expected him to run for another term. In June, stricken a second time, he was operated upon for ileitis. Although the operation was serious, Eisenhower's advisers never let the question arise whether or not he would continue as a candidate—and except among some Democrats it seemed a matter above debate. At the Republican convention in San Francisco at the end of August, he and Vice President Nixon were renominated by acclamation. The proceedings seemed to some observers to reflect more the atmosphere of a coronation than a party convention. Regardless of Eisenhower's overwhelming popularity, Adlai Stevenson and Estes Kefauver fought vigorously for the Democratic nomination in state primary after primary. In the end, Stevenson triumphed at the Democratic convention and Kefauver became the vice-presidential nominee.

It was a rather dull campaign. Stevenson sought an issue by proposing that the United States agree to end hydrogen bomb tests. The average voter, relieved because the stalemate in nuclear weapons seemed to rule out a third world war, refused to worry about international affairs until actual shooting in the Suez area just before Election Day sent him to seek refuge with Eisenhower as commander in chief. Altogether, about 58 percent of the voters marked their ballots for Eisenhower, although he was sixty-six, the oldest man ever to be re-elected to the presidency, and had suffered two serious illnesses in little more than a year past. He received more than 35 million votes to only 26 million for Stevenson and carried forty-one states. It was not much of a triumph for the Republican party. The prestige of the President pulled some Republican congressmen to narrow victories, but the Democrats continued to control both houses of Congress.

During President Eisenhower's second administration, domestic policies were little changed. In 1957 Congress occupied itself largely with trying to slash the President's $71.8 billion budget, the largest in peacetime history. Even Secretary of the Treasury Humphrey (who resigned a few months later) joined in the onslaught against the "terrific" expenditures.

At the close of 1957 the nation skidded into the most serious recession since the war. By late spring of 1958 industrial production had dropped 14 percent below the level of a year earlier, and approximately 5 million workers were unemployed. Again the so-called built-in stabilizers of the economy, such as unemployment insurance payments to those out of work, somewhat softened the blow of the recession.

As Republicans prepared for the congressional campaign of 1958, they were handicapped by the persistence of economic trouble. Some of the more conservative Republican candidates, most notably Senate Minority Leader William Knowland, running for governor of California, centered their campaigns around attacks on organized labor. In some states they sought "right-to-work" laws to outlaw union shops (plants in which every employee hired must join the union). This onslaught, in most states, succeeded only in ensuring a large labor vote for Democratic candidates. The Republican party was also weakened by the revelation in the spring of 1958 that Sherman Adams, in effect the President's chief of staff, had received gifts from a New England textile manufacturer. Adams resigned in September, too late to benefit the party.

The result on November 4, 1958, was a Democratic landslide of impressive proportions. The Democrats won 13 additional seats in the Senate, giving them a 62 to 34 majority. They gained an added 47 seats in the House of Representatives, providing a majority of 282 to 153 — the largest margin since Roosevelt's 1936 victory.

The voter reaction in 1958 had slight effect upon the national administration in the two years that followed. President Eisenhower presented Congress in January 1959 with a $77 billion budget, which he promised would be in balance — a budget that northern Democrats decried as not sufficiently large in an expanding economy and not providing the services the nation needed. At first the Democrats in Congress gave promise of pushing far beyond the President's limited requests. As prosperity returned in the spring of 1959, however, public opinion began to react to the incessant warnings of the President and of conservative publicists that budget balancing was the only way to avoid another ruinous round of inflation. Eisenhower, acting more vigorously than in previous years, was able to marshal much public support and congressional voting strength for his conservative course, and Speaker Sam Rayburn and Senate Majority Leader Lyndon B. Johnson were more disposed to compromise than to throw their large Democratic majorities against him. As a result, Eisenhower succeeded in keeping down expenditures for inexpensive public housing for families displaced from slums and for other social services. He also succeeded in ending the 1960 fiscal year with a billion-dollar surplus. In the following year, he repeated the battle over the 1961 budget, which proposed expenditures of $70.8 billion and a surplus of $4.2 billion. But by the fall of 1960 the economy had again stalled into a recession; tax revenue declined, and the fiscal year ended with a serious deficit.

In his final State of the Union message, in January 1961, President Eisenhower granted that problems of recession and unemployment left little room for complacency. But he pointed out that during his eight years in office the inflationary spiral had all but ceased and that the nation's output of goods and services had increased 25 percent; the income of the average American family, 15 percent; and the real wages of workers, 20 percent. "In a united determination to keep this nation strong and free and to utilize our vast resources for the advancement of all mankind," he asserted, "we have carried America to unprecedented heights."

The "New Frontier"

KENNEDY OVER NIXON

The presidential election of 1960 was notable both for its remarkable closeness and for the relative sobriety with which the two major candidates addressed themselves to the issues.

"The world is very different now," said President John F. Kennedy in his inaugural address, January 20, 1961, "for man holds in his mortal hands the power to abolish all forms of human poverty and all forms of human life." To achieve the promise and avoid the peril was the twofold challenge of the time. This was what Kennedy called the "New Frontier" — a new challenge to the old pioneering instincts of Americans.

Kennedy won the Democratic nomination only after a vigorous struggle in the primaries. A forty-three-year-old senator from Massachusetts and a Roman Catholic, he was thought to

Two Presidential Candidates Debate on Television
*Before an estimated audience of 70 million viewers, the 1960 Republican nominee,
Vice President Richard M. Nixon, and the Democratic nominee, Senator John F.
Kennedy, participated in an unprecedented series of televised debates. Until then,
the lesser-known Kennedy had seemed the underdog. "It was the sight of the two
men side by side that carried the punch," Theodore H. White has written. "There
was, first and above all, the crude, overwhelming impression that side by side the
two seemed evenly matched—and this even matching in the popular imagination
was for Kennedy a major victory. Until the cameras opened on the Senator and the
Vice President, Kennedy had been the boy under assault and attack by the Vice
President as immature, young, inexperienced. Now, obviously, in flesh and
behavior he was the Vice President's equal."*—The Making of the President 1960
(New York: Atheneum, 1961), p. 288. (NBC)

be handicapped by his youth and his religion.
In the primaries he had to dispose of a fellow
senator, Hubert Humphrey of Minnesota, who
was considered more liberal than he. Then, at
the convention in Los Angeles, he had to overcome the powerful opposition of Lyndon B.
Johnson of Texas, the Senate majority leader.
In the 1930s, Johnson had been one of the cote-
rie of ardent New Dealers. By 1960, without
entirely abandoning his earlier allegiances, he
had become the most respected spokesman of
the industrialized and conservative South.
When Kennedy won the presidential nomination, he offered the vice-presidential nomina-

tion to Johnson, who accepted and campaigned
energetically.

The Republican nomination went almost
by default to Vice President Richard M. Nixon,
whom President Eisenhower favored. Nixon's
only rival, Governor Nelson Rockefeller of
New York, dropped out of the contest months
before the primaries. Henry Cabot Lodge,
ambassador to the United Nations, was nominated for Vice President.

Kennedy and Nixon represented the
broad moderate position within their respective parties, though Kennedy was slightly to the
left of center and Nixon slightly to the right. As

Vice President, Nixon had enjoyed eight years on the front pages and had even argued with Khrushchev in Moscow. Thus he was able to offer a continuation of President Eisenhower's "peace and prosperity," and—though he was only four years older than Kennedy—mature leadership.

When Kennedy challenged Nixon to a series of television debates, Nixon's advisers thought Kennedy would be no match for their man, and they agreed to four joint appearances. In the first debate, however, everything went wrong for Nixon. Not yet recovered from an illness, he appeared tired, haggard, and heavy-jowled, in contrast to Kennedy, who seemed relaxed, self-confident, and well informed—before an estimated 70 million television viewers. From then on, Kennedy seemed to take the lead from Nixon.

The business recession also hurt the Republicans. Nevertheless, in the closing days of the campaign, a vigorous Republican campaign drive, with the aid of President Eisenhower, brought a hairline decision at the polls. Out of 68,836,000 votes cast, Kennedy received 34,227,000 or 49.7 percent, and Nixon, 34,109,000 or 49.5 percent. (The remaining 502,000 votes were divided among thirteen minor candidates.)

Before the election, Kennedy had hoped that on taking office he could push through Congress a legislative program as sweeping as that of Franklin D. Roosevelt during the first hundred days of the New Deal. Kennedy did not abandon his reform plans, but the closeness of the decision led him to move with caution. Unlike the Eisenhower cabinet, which had predominantly represented business, the Kennedy cabinet balanced the economic and political as well as the regional interests in the nation. The most controversial of the appointments was that of Kennedy's thirty-five-year-old brother and campaign manager, Robert F. Kennedy, as attorney general.

Election of 1960

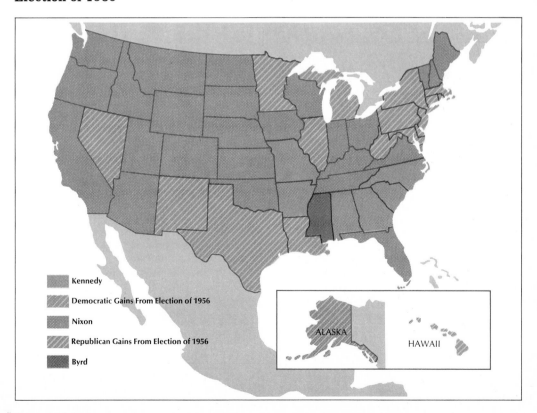

Kennedy

Democratic Gains From Election of 1956

Nixon

Republican Gains From Election of 1956

Byrd

ALASKA

HAWAII

THE KENNEDY PROGRAM

President Kennedy – the youngest man, except for Theodore Roosevelt, ever to occupy the White House – sent a record number of messages, twenty-five, to the first session of the Eighty-seventh Congress. Some called for long-range national undertakings: economic recovery and growth, health care for the aged, federal aid for schools, conservation and use of natural resources, highway construction, housing and community development.

The existence of a Democratic majority in each house did not mean that Kennedy could count upon an easy enactment of his program, since many Democrats were conservative and frequently voted with the Republicans.

By dint of persuasion and compromise he managed to obtain considerable legislation. An improvement in the minimum-wage law provided considerably less coverage than the President had wished, but it did bring an additional 3,624,000 workers under the law. It raised the minimum hourly pay rate, effective in several steps over two to four years, from $1.00 to $1.25. Another measure increased social security benefits substantially along the lines of the President's recommendations. The Housing Act of 1961 fully embodied his proposals, authorizing $4.9 billion in federal grants or loans over a four-year period for the preservation of open spaces in cities, the development of local mass transit systems, and the construction of middle-income housing. Congressional conservatives dealt the President two sharp setbacks when they defeated his bills to provide medical care for the aged and federal aid for school construction and teachers' salaries.

Kennedy obtained from Congress additional expenditures for unemployment compensation and aid to depressed areas – appropriations totaling $900 million. The only other large additions to the federal budget were $4 billion in defense spending to meet new challenges from Russia and large amounts of farm crop subsidies that had to be paid by virtue of earlier legislation. These expenditures were sufficient to bring about, well before the end of 1961, a substantial economic recovery.

But employment improved only slightly; in a time of record prosperity over 5 percent of the working force had no job. Out of a total of approximately 4.4 million unemployed (as of March 1962) between 1 and 2 million were formerly connected with eight industries in which the total number of jobs had declined from 7.5 million to 5 million in the years since World War II. Among these industries were textiles, coal, automobiles, and aircraft. The Kennedy administration tried to eliminate such unemployment through the retraining of dismissed workmen under the Manpower Training Bill and through the establishment of new industries in chronically depressed areas under the Area Redevelopment Act.

During his first two years in office, Kennedy emphasized that, because of the inflationary danger, the budget must be kept balanced. He also used his presidential power vigorously to try to prevent inflationary moves on the part of labor and industry. In the spring of 1962 he persuaded the United Steel Workers to accept a contract granting only small wage increases. When, almost immediately, United States Steel and most other companies unexpectedly announced 3.5-percent price increases, the President exploded with anger. During the three days that followed, he brought every variety of pressure he could muster, until the steel companies returned to their old prices. The cost to Kennedy was the hostility of the business community, which vented its anger upon him and blamed him for a stock-market drop a few weeks later. A year afterward, in the spring of 1963, when steel companies announced limited increases in prices, the President commented only that the companies had shown some restraint; he hoped the steel union and steel users would do likewise.

By January 1963 Kennedy had become convinced that the only way to stimulate economic growth and to reduce unemployment was a bold tax cut. He proposed to Congress a reduction of $13.5 billion in income taxes over a period of three years.

Kennedy was also becoming convinced that the government must do more than it had done for the Negroes – to whose votes he owed his narrow victory in the 1960 election. Nearly a decade after the Supreme Court's historic decision against segregation, the equal-rights movement was making little or no progress.

The National Association for the Advancement of Colored People (NAACP), which had led the cause, was still pressing lawsuits and seeking court orders, but more and more Negroes were growing impatient with its methods and were embittered by white obstruction of

**Martin Luther King Holding a Press Conference
at Birmingham, Alabama   1963**

*Throughout his years as head of the Southern Christian Leadership Conference,
King insisted that the civil rights movement must be nonviolent. He stated his
vision most vividly for America in August 1963 when during the "March on
Washington" he asserted from the steps of the Lincoln Memorial: "I have a dream
that one day this nation will rise up and live out the true meaning of its creed:
'We hold these truths to be self-evident, that all men are created equal.' . . . I have
a dream that my four little children will one day live in a nation where they will
not be judged by the color of their skin, but by the content of their character. This
is our hope. This is the faith that I go back to the South with—with this faith we
will be able to hew out of the mountain of despair a stone of hope." (Magnum)*

the cause. Blacks began to form more militant organizations. A desperate minority of perhaps 200,000 joined the Black Muslims and, in a spirit reminiscent of the Garvey black nationalism of the 1920s, proclaimed black supremacy and demanded a complete separation of the races. Others continued to struggle for integration but turned to direct action through new organizations such as the Congress of Racial Equality (CORE) and the Southern Christian Leadership Conference. The SCLC was led by an eloquent young Baptist minister, Dr. Martin Luther King, Jr., who had gained national and international fame as an advocate of passive resistance and, for his work, was to win the Nobel Peace Prize in 1964.

In the South, beginning in 1960, youthful blacks with some white sympathizers engaged in "sit-ins" to demand the right to eat in restaurants or at lunch counters or the right to use books in the main public libraries rather than in segregated branches. Negroes and whites went on "freedom rides" to desegregate inter-state buses and terminals. Thousands engaging in mass demonstrations accepted arrest; on several occasions the jails of Southern cities were filled to overflowing. Demonstrations spread to the North in mass attacks against de facto segregation in schools and housing and against the exclusion of all but a handful of Negroes from various kinds of employment. By the summer of 1963 the movement had reached such a peak that it was being proclaimed by news magazines as the "Negro revolution." More than 200,000 demonstrators (10 to 15 per-cent of them white) participated in a "March on Washington," converging on the Lincoln Me-morial.

In areas where federal power could be invoked, those protesting against segregation received the support of the Kennedy adminis-tration. Attorney General Robert F. Kennedy mustered federal force behind the integration of interstate transportation, and the President sent troops to the University of Mississippi to protect a Negro, James Meredith, who had been enrolled by order of a federal court. Throughout the South campaigns were under way to enroll Negro voters under the protec-tion of the civil rights legislation of 1957. As pressure intensified in 1963, President Kenne-dy threw the prestige of his administration be-hind the most comprehensive civil rights bill ever presented to Congress.

"LET US CONTINUE"

In the fall of 1963, though congressional con-servatives were blocking enactment of the two major bills in the New Frontier program, the civil rights and tax-cut measures, President Kennedy felt optimistic. He was looking ahead to the election of 1964, which most observers thought would result in his own reelection by a comfortable margin. He hoped that the election would bring to Washington a more liberal Con-gress.

To court Southern support, Kennedy visit-ed Florida and then Texas in November 1963. The Texas trip began well. On Friday, Novem-ber 22, as he drove through the streets of Dal-las, to the cheers of an enthusiastic crowd, the wife of Governor John Connally of Texas re-marked to him: "You can't say that Dallas isn't

friendly to you today." As Kennedy started to reply, he was hit in the neck by a bullet; anoth-er bullet struck the back of his head. His bleed-ing head cradled in the lap of his wife Jacque-line, he was rushed to a hospital.

An assassin, shooting three times in quick succession from a sixth-floor window, had killed President Kennedy and seriously wounded Governor Connally. Police arrested Lee Harvey Oswald, a self-styled Marxist who had once tried to expatriate himself in Russia, and charged him with the murder both of the President and a policeman. Piece after piece of circumstantial evidence seemed to tie Oswald to the murders, but through hours of question-ing he continued to protest his innocence. Two days after the shooting, while he was in the Dallas city jail, on his way to be transferred to the county jail, he was himself murdered by a Dallas night-club operator, before an incredu-lous national television audience. Inevitably rumors spread concerning the possibility that a ramifying plot lay behind President Kennedy's assassination. In an effort to eliminate uncer-tainties, a presidential commission headed by Chief Justice Warren sifted through the evidence and several months later reported to the American people that Oswald had been a lone assassin.

About two hours after the assassination, Vice President Lyndon B. Johnson was sworn in as the thirty-sixth President of the United States. When he addressed a joint session of Congress on November 27, President Johnson expressed his main theme in the words "let us continue." The most fitting memorial to Kenne-dy, he reminded Congress, would be the enact-ment of the civil rights and tax bills and, in-deed, the whole agenda of the New Frontier.

The Eighty-eighth Congress responded and, in its 1964 session, enacted not only sever-al vital measures of the New Frontier program but also one of President Johnson's own rec-ommendations, an antipoverty bill. In getting the program adopted, the new President uti-lized to the utmost the formidable political skills he had perfected earlier as Senate majority leader. Not only did he conciliate and persuade congressional majorities; he also built a great national following.

From the outset, Johnson assiduously courted businessmen. Most of them were Re-publicans, and the proposal of a tax cut deliber-

President Johnson Takes the Oath of Office

With Mrs. Johnson (left) and Mrs. Kennedy at his side, Lyndon Baines Johnson took his oath of office as President on the afternoon of November 22, 1963, before Judge Sarah T. Hughes aboard the presidential airplane at Dallas, Texas. Johnson, born on a cattle ranch near Stonewall, Texas, on August 27, 1908, was of Confederate forebears, but considered himself more a Westerner than a Southerner. He had to bear the handicap of being regarded as a Southerner in national politics, even though he pointed with pride to his grandfather, who had been a Populist member of the Texas legislature, and his father, who had also served in the legislature and had been a firm opponent of the Ku Klux Klan. Johnson taught elementary school for a year after graduating from Southwest Texas State Teachers College, then became secretary to a Texas congressman. An ardent New Dealer, he was Texas director of the National Youth Administration and, after his election to the House of Representatives in 1937, a protégé of President Roosevelt. When Roosevelt died, Johnson said: "He was just like a daddy to me always." After an initial defeat, Johnson won election to the United States Senate in 1948 by a primary margin of eighty-seven votes. As senator from a state in which new business and industrial interests were increasingly powerful, Johnson came to be known less for his liberalism (which he continued to avow) than for his moderation. He liked to quote, as had his father, the words of the prophet Isaiah: "Come, let us reason together." An unparalleled master of the arts of political persuasion, Johnson rose to the position of Senate majority leader. Again and again he managed to bring together and to compromise the differences among Democratic senators from South and North. As Vice President, Johnson lacked the opportunity to practice these arts: he spent much of his time on missions outside the United States. When he was suddenly elevated to the Presidency, he pointed out to the Congress that he had taken the leadership in obtaining the civil rights acts of 1957 and 1960. Once again he undertook to bridge divisions of opinion in order to obtain constructive legislation. (Wide World)

ately creating a deficit in the budget at a time of prosperity went diametrically against their economic thinking. Nevertheless, after Congress passed the legislation early in 1964, the reduction of taxes seemed to stimulate an unprecedented continuation of prosperity and economic growth. By the beginning of 1965, the United States had experienced four years of boom without recession, a peacetime record since 1945. The rate of unemployment had dropped to about 5 percent for the first time in years.

To the delight of many businessmen, Johnson accompanied the lowering of taxes with the presentation of a federal budget smaller than they had anticipated for the 1965 fiscal year. Despite the overall cutback, he was able to increase expenditures on health, education, and welfare, through sharp limitation of the defense budget. While courting business, the administration remained on cordial terms with labor leaders. Workingmen shared in the boom as take-home pay rose 4 percent in 1964.

To aid those who were not sharing in the national prosperity, the President in January 1964 called upon Congress to enact a thirteen-point program that would declare "unconditional war on poverty." In August 1964 the anti-poverty bill was passed. It called for the establishment of VISTA, a volunteer corps of social workers, and for remedial education, vocational training, part-time employment for teen-agers and students, and federal grants to states or communities for local attacks on poverty. The initial budget was almost a billion dollars.

COMMITMENT TO EQUAL RIGHTS

Throughout the nation the problem of civil rights was closely related to that of poverty. A large proportion of the very poor were Negroes, unable either South or North to obtain adequately paid, secure employment. In cities like New York, Negroes (together with Puerto Ricans) filled a large number of badly paid service positions and jobs not requiring skill. The average Harlem family received $2,000 a year less in income than its white neighbors. Of the Negroes (largely youths) 13 percent were unemployed, since the poorer jobs were the sort being most rapidly eliminated by automation. Either through discrimination or through lack of training, young people were barred from more highly skilled work. Many Northern Negroes were crowded into substandard housing, and their children were enrolled in poor schools integrated only in name.

A number of young Northerners went to Mississippi in the summer of 1964 to enroll several thousand young Negroes in "Freedom Schools" and to conduct drives registering Negroes to vote. Three of the first civil rights workers to arrive disappeared; after some weeks the FBI found their bodies buried deep beneath an earthen dam.

As the struggle intensified, President Johnson threw his weight behind the comprehensive civil rights bill that Kennedy had presented to Congress. Bipartisan leadership in the Senate finally overcame Southern opposition. In June 1964, for the first time in history, the Senate voted to end a filibuster, so that the bill could be passed. The Civil Rights Act of 1964 strengthened earlier legislation to protect the voting rights of Negroes and to expedite the desegregation of schools. It also prohibited discrimination in public accommodations and facilities and in private employment.

After the act went into effect, Negroes ate with whites for the first time in some restaurants in the deep South, stayed in some hotels and motels, sat in "white only" sections of motion-picture theaters, and swam in previously segregated swimming pools. Compliance was not universal, and several test cases challenging the constitutionality of the law were brought before federal courts.

In 1965 violence again erupted in the South, especially in Selma, Alabama, where masses of Negroes and a few white sympathizers demonstrated in protest against registration procedures which kept Negroes off the voting rolls. The state police brutally broke up a parade, and assassins (said to be Klansmen) murdered two white civil rights workers from the North. To protect the demonstrators, President Johnson called up the Alabama National Guard. He also persuaded Congress to pass a bill guaranteeing the right to vote in presidential, senatorial, and congressional elections. This law provided for federal registration of voters in those states where there were literacy or other special tests for registering and where fewer than half of the people of voting age actually went to the polls.

ONE MAN, ONE VOTE

Meanwhile, constitutional amendments and court decisions were affecting, actually or potentially, the political rights of many Americans, both Negro and white.

The Twenty-third Amendment (1961) gave the franchise in presidential elections to residents of the District of Columbia. Home rule for Washington, which had the highest percentage of Negroes of any city in the country, continued to be withheld by Congress.

The Twenty-fourth Amendment (1964) gave symbolic, if not much practical, aid to Negro voters by providing that the right to vote in any primary or other federal election should not be abridged for failing to pay a poll tax. Most states in the deep South were using methods other than the poll tax to try to disfranchise Negroes.

An issue involving the rights of representation of a large part of the American electorate came before the Supreme Court in 1962, in a case involving the apportionment of legislative districts in Tennessee. Although the state constitution called for reapportionment every ten years, none had taken place since 1901, with the result that rural dominance in the legislature was out of all proportion to population. Moore County, with a population of 3,454, sent one legislator; Shelby County (Memphis), with 627,019 residents, sent only three. A vote in Moore County was worth more than sixty times as much as one in Shelby County. By a 6-to-2 decision, the Supreme Court gave the federal district court a mandate to order reapportionment if it found a violation of the Constitution. Similar inequities existed in a surprising number of other states; in all but six states, fewer than 40 percent of the population could elect a majority of the legislature. As a result of the Tennessee decision, many states quickly made some reapportionment of their legislative districts, either as a result of court action or as a means of forestalling it.

An even more important Supreme Court decision (in *Reynold* v. *Sims,* 1964) held that congressional districts within a state also must be substantially equal in population. The case before the court involved the congressional district containing the city of Atlanta, Georgia, a district that had a population of 820,000 as compared with the population of 270,000 in another Georgia district. Several state legislatures quietly initiated a counteraction by endorsing a constitutional amendment (proposed by the National Legislative Conference) which would negate federally enforced reapportionment. Within a few years, thirty-three legislatures had approved it. If one more should act, Congress would be required, according to the Constitution, to call a national convention to consider submitting the proposal to the states for their ratification. The movement lost its chief congressional sponsor, however, when Senator Everett Dirksen of Illinois died in 1969.

The "Great Society"

As he took up and expanded the Kennedy program, President Johnson restated the objective as the creation of the "Great Society." "For half a century we called upon unbounded invention and untiring industry to create an order of plenty for all our people," he declared in May 1964. "The challenge of the next half century is whether we have the wisdom to use that wealth to enrich and elevate our national life — and to advance the quality of American civilization."

But President Johnson himself was to jeopardize the "Great Society" program when, in 1965, he committed the country to large-scale war in faraway Vietnam.

JOHNSON THRASHES GOLDWATER

In the presidential campaign of 1964 the moderate liberalism for which Johnson had spoken confronted extreme conservatism.

In the years following the collapse of McCarthyism, militant conservatives in the United States had organized a number of action groups. The best known was the John Birch Society, whose founder, Robert Welch, called for the impeachment of Chief Justice Earl Warren and seemed to suspect the loyalty of even President Eisenhower. Senator Barry Goldwater of Arizona, though not himself a member of the so-called radical right organiza-

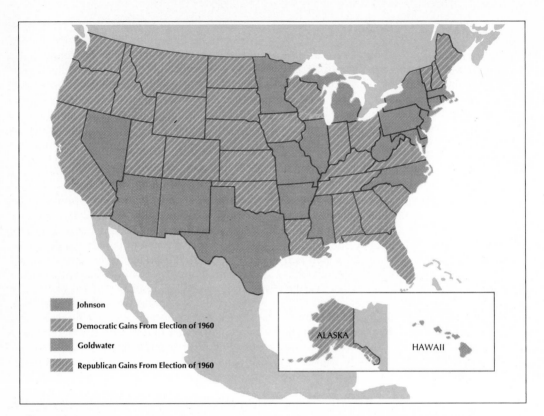

Johnson

Democratic Gains From Election of 1960

Goldwater

Republican Gains From Election of 1960

ALASKA

HAWAII

Election of 1964

tions, became the hero of most of these groups. In the Senate he had voted against tax reduction and against the antipoverty and civil rights bills.

At the Republican convention in San Francisco, the Goldwater forces were in complete command from the outset. They produced a platform conforming to their conservative philosophy and making no concessions to the moderate and liberal wings of the party. When Governor Nelson A. Rockefeller of New York tried to obtain a stronger civil rights plank, they hooted him down. Nor did Goldwater try to "balance the ticket" in his vice-presidential choice—Representative William E. Miller of New York stood staunchly to the right. Goldwater received tumultuous applause when, in his acceptance address, he declared: "I would remind you that extremism in the defense of liberty is no vice! And let me remind you also that moderation in the pursuit of justice is no virtue!"

As Senator Goldwater carried the Republican party far to the right, President Johnson tried to preempt not only the center of the road but also a wide strip to both the right and the left of it. Although he had been President for only nine months when the Democratic convention met at Atlantic City late in August 1964, he was firmly in control of his party. His main concern seemed to be to achieve as broad a consensus as possible in the platform. His supporters worked to minimize differences between the North and the South, especially over the seating of delegates. Delegates from Mississippi and Alabama were denied votes unless they pledged themselves to support the party's candidates in the November election, and most of them departed. Two votes were given to a Negro delegation representing the new Freedom Democratic party of Mississippi. In addition, the convention voted that in 1968 it would seat only those delegations that were chosen in a nondiscriminatory way.

The only drama in the convention concerned the question of whom President Johnson would ask the delegates to nominate for Vice President. Earlier he had eliminated one of the party's favorites, Attorney General Robert Kennedy, brother of the assassinated President. When Johnson, in person, revealed his choice to the convention, it was Senator Hubert Humphrey of Minnesota, identified with the liberal wing of the Democratic party.

Paradoxically, the campaign was one of the most hectic and yet one of the dullest ever to weary the electorate. In contrast to the comparatively precise debates of four years earlier, neither candidate ever went much beyond his acceptance speech. Yet each campaigned incessantly, often spanning the continent by jet in a day's appearances. Much of the Goldwater campaign centered upon charges of corruption and moral malaise in Washington. In mid-October, Johnson's chief White House aide was forced to resign because of personal scandal, but that same week the American people were even more startled by news of the precipitate removal of Nikita Khrushchev from the leadership of the U.S.S.R. New uncertainties abroad seemed to help drive the voters toward the President. Throughout the campaign President Johnson was as wary of making specific, detailed promises as Eisenhower had been in 1956 and Roosevelt in 1936; his best strategy seemed to be merely to gather the votes against Goldwater.

And gather them he did. He received more votes, over 42 million, and a larger plurality than any other candidate in history. On election night he told the American people that he regarded the overwhelming victory as a "mandate for unity." It gave him and the Democratic majority in Congress an opportunity to move on toward what he had been describing as the "Great Society," a society as free as it could be from poverty, prejudice, ignorance, and ugliness.

THE JOHNSON PROGRAM

When the Eighty-ninth Congress convened, President Johnson presented to it comprehensive proposals to make a beginning toward his long-range goals. With unprecedented speed, almost all of this far-ranging program became law. The overwhelmingly Democratic majorities in Congress, which had accompanied the landslide victory over Goldwater, were Johnson's to command.

A new immigration law, in response to the demands of urban and minority groups in America, abolished the inequities of the quota system established in the 1920s. The quota for England and Ireland of 83,000 persons per year had been seldom filled; that for Greece was only 308 persons. Gradually the government eliminated these quotas and began to allot visas not on a basis of national origins but giving preference on a basis of education and skills. Soon there were complaints that only an elite of professionals could enter the United States and that other nations, especially underdeveloped ones, were suffering a "brain drain" of their doctors, engineers, and highly educated specialists. In 1966 relatives of United States citizens began to receive preference, and a quota of 17,000 was set for professionals. Immigration from northwestern Europe declined and that from southern Europe and Asia increased.

Massive sustained federal aid to education at last began. President Johnson succeeded in circumventing the impasse in Congress over the question of whether parochial schools should receive a share of federal funds. He called for grants for text and library books for students in both public and parochial schools — and significantly the grants were to be made on the basis of the needs of individual students, not schools, a formula that the Supreme Court had approved when it applied to federal funds that were to provide milk or transportation to students. The Elementary and Secondary Education Act of 1965 and subsequent legislation gave aid to schools in both urban and rural areas in proportion to the number of poverty-stricken students in them. Federal funds purchased textbooks and library materials, financed special programs for adults and for the handicapped, and strengthened state educational agencies. Total federal expenditures in education and technical training rose from less than $5 billion in 1964 to more than $12 billion in 1967.

The establishment of Medicare for the 19 million Americans over sixty-five through the Medicare-Social Security Act of 1965 altered the lives of old people and had great impact upon American medicine. The debate over Medicare, which had been so bitter for twenty years, ended as the program went into effect. Expected resistance did not materialize. In the South, where hospitals had to accept desegregation in order to obtain funds, nearly nine-tenths of the hospitals complied. But numerous practical problems arose that made future adjustments likely. It was particularly difficult to institute the program in an era of rapidly rising costs. Objections to complicated paper work led more than half the nation's doctors to force patients to pay directly; patients were required to submit receipted bills for government reimbursement. The irritations were serious, but less important than the fact that large numbers of older people were receiving care that they could not previously have obtained or that would have exhausted their savings.

Rising costs also created problems for the Medicaid program, which was launched in 1968 to provide financial assistance to persons who were not old enough to qualify for Medicare but were too poor to pay their own medical bills. Under the Medicaid law each state was to set up its own plan, determining payments and standards of eligibility for them, and the federal government was to contribute from 50 to 80 percent of the expense. During the first year, however, the program cost the federal government more than ten times as much as had been expected. Congress and the state legislatures therefore changed their definition of the needy so as to make the benefits available to fewer people than had originally been covered.

Medicare and Medicaid were parts of the effort to eradicate the "pockets of poverty" within the prosperous nation. More than 9 mil-

By the 1960s, when President Johnson began his "war on poverty," the total family income of Americans had more than doubled since the depression decade of the 1930s. But shares of this income going to lower-income groups had increased only slightly. A great gap between the rich and the poor remained. In this chart the first "pie" shows the percentages of the total income for 1936 received by the poorest fifth of the people, the richest fifth, and the three fifths in between. The second pie reflects the same data for 1962. (Courtesy of W. E. Brownlee)

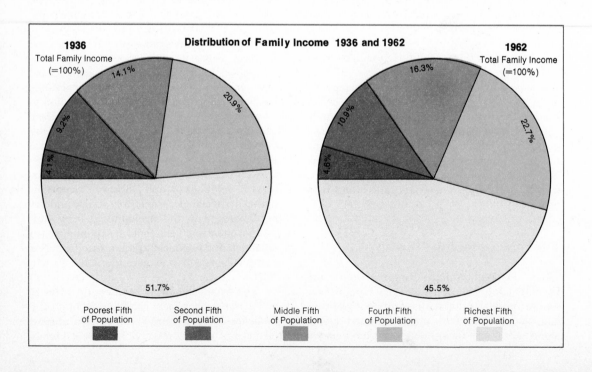

lion people classified as poor were receiving no aid from federal food programs, a Senate subcommittee learned. There was hunger in great cities, in Appalachia, the deep South, the Southwest, and on Indian reservations. Yet over 5 million people were receiving aid through federal food programs; either they were given food or could purchase it with reduced-cost stamps. Many millions were receiving other types of relief.

The poverty program of President Johnson, continuing and expanding that of Kennedy, approached the problem in numerous ways. By 1966 the Office of Economic Opportunity, established in 1964, had put about two-fifths of its budget into a variety of Community Action Programs. Another two-fifths went into youth programs — the Job Corps, Neighborhood Youth Corps, and College Work Study. Most of the remaining funds went into the Work Experience Program. VISTA (Volunteers in Service to America) served as a kind of Peace Corps at home.

While social security aided the considerable proportion of the poor who were aged, the Office of Economic Opportunity placed its emphasis upon helping the great numbers of poor among the young. The 1,000 core Community Action Programs were locally proposed and operated, in part by poor people themselves. Some of these programs not only gave poor people an opportunity to help themselves but gave them some feeling of political power. The job-training efforts, however, proved more expensive and less effective than had been predicted.

Especially among the urban Negro unemployed, the job-training programs were a disappointment. Although Negroes began to penetrate the ranks of the white-collar workers, the total numbers were small. Nominally, union restrictions against them no longer existed, yet few could gain employment as skilled, highly paid construction workers. Industries that might have hired Negroes were moving out of the cities, away from where they lived. The training programs could not easily provide the overall education and motivation that most of these unemployed Negroes lacked. A New York Negro woman declared in despair, "We are being trained for the unemployed."

While starting his "war on poverty," Johnson was escalating his war in Vietnam. The enormous costs of the latter made it more and more difficult to pay for the former.

BLACK POWER

The Negro population had been increasing more rapidly than the white population and had been shifting from the rural South to the cities throughout the nation, especially in the North. In 1910 only about a quarter of the Negroes lived in cities, and only a tenth outside the South; by 1966 69 percent were living in metropolitan areas; 45 percent were living outside the South. In several of the largest cities, the proportion of Negroes at least doubled between 1950 and 1968. Negroes constituted at least 30 percent of the population of seven of these cities and 66.6 percent of the population of Washington, D.C. A corresponding exodus of whites from the cities to the suburbs dramatically increased the areas of residential and school segregation in the "black ghettos."

While urban Negroes were sharing in the national prosperity, their proportional gains were decidedly less than those of the whites. Indeed, the gap between their incomes and those of whites was growing wider. Impatient urban Negroes, disappointed at the meager return that cooperation seemed to have brought them, began increasingly to turn toward other possible solutions: black power, separatism, or even violence.

With increasing rapidity after 1964, the United States moved into a double crisis, compounded of rioting in the poverty-stricken Negro areas in Northern cities and escalation of the intervention in Vietnam into a major — but stalemated — military confrontation. Each crisis interacted with the other. White college and university students and Northern liberals shifted their efforts from the civil rights drive in the South to concentrate on protest against the Vietnam War. Negroes in the rural South, and even more in the urban North, increasingly sought to take their destiny into their own hands through their own organizations, independent of aid or funds from whites.

The gradual shift from white participation and leadership to Negro domination of civil rights organizations was one indication of the new mood. The Congress of Racial Equality (CORE), founded in 1941–1942, had long been

Black Power: SNCC Paper

If we are to proceed toward true liberation, we must cut ourselves off from white people. We must form our own institutions, credit unions, co-ops, political parties, write our own histories, . . .

. . . on whatever level of contact . . . blacks and whites come together, that meeting or confrontation is not on the level of the blacks but always on the level of the whites. This only means that our everyday contact with whites is a reinforcement of the myth of white supremacy. Whites are the ones who must try to raise themselves to our humanistic level. We are not, after all, the ones who are responsible for a genocidal war in Vietnam; we are not the ones who are responsible for neocolonialism in Africa and Latin America; we are not the ones who held a people in animalistic bondage over 400 years. We reject the American dream as defined by white people and must work to construct an American reality defined by Afro-Americans. — Position paper by members of the Student Nonviolent Coordinating Committee, 1966.

---

the most interracial of the organizations, but by 1962 was predominantly Negro; after 1965 CORE allowed only Negro leadership in its chapters. At their height these organizations through direct action did succeed in obtaining some votes for Negroes and political participation, even in Alabama and Mississippi. In the North they helped force open new, desirable employment opportunities for adequately educated Negroes. But they could not change the inferior conditions under which most Negroes suffered. Their failure helped stimulate feelings of separateness and militancy among Negro youth in the large cities.

Out of James Meredith's march southward from Memphis, Tennessee, to Jackson, Mississippi, in June 1966 there grew the concept of black power. Politically it meant separate action through which blocs of Negro voters would win control in Northern ghettos or the Southern black belt. Economically it meant creating Negro business to serve Negroes. CORE and SNCC (the Student Nonviolent Coordinating Committee) became associated with the concept of black power—of Negro separateness. In some respects black power seemed to critics to be retrogressive, a harking back to the proposals of Booker T. Washington; it seemed to propose a withdrawal comparable to that which white racists had been demanding. Black militants replied that Negroes by themselves must attain economic and political parity with the white population before effective integration could take place.

On August 11, 1965, a Negro crowd had gathered in Watts, a Los Angeles suburb, to protest a traffic arrest; a policeman hit a bystander with his club, and several days of violence were touched off. Before the rioting was over, thirty-four people had been killed, hundreds wounded, and some $35 million in property destroyed. White Americans, hopeful that the civil rights movement was solving Negro problems, were shocked out of their optimism.

In the summer of 1966 there were forty-three outbreaks, with especially serious trouble in Chicago and Cleveland. In the summer of 1967 there were eight major riots. In the worst of these, at Detroit, forty-three persons (thirty-three Negroes, and ten whites) were killed. On their television screens, the people of the nation saw alarming scenes of arson, plunder, and military action. President Johnson, calling for law and order, warned also that the only genuine long-range solution must be an attack upon the conditions that were causing despair and violence. He appointed a group of distinguished citizens to a commission to investigate the disorders and recommend preventive measures for the future.

The report of the Commission on Civil Disorders, which appeared in the spring of 1968, deflated numerous wild stories: there had been few black snipers, and no organized conspiracy instigating and directing the riots. The report pointed to the complexities of the problems facing the occupants of the Negro ghettos, and it

Black Power: Commission's Report

What is new about "Black Power" is phraseology rather than substance. . . . The decade after World War I— which saw the militant, race-proud "new negro," the relatively widespread theory of retaliatory violence, and the high tide of the Negro-support-of-Negro-business ideology— exhibits striking parallels with the 1960's. . . .

Black Power rhetoric and ideology actually express a lack of power. The slogan emerged when the Negro protest movement was slowing down, when it was finding increasing resistance to its changing goals, when it discovered that nonviolent direct action was no more a panacea than legal action. . . . This combination of circumstances provoked anger deepened by impotence. Powerless to make any fundamental changes in the life of the masses—powerless, that is, to compel white America to make those changes—many advocates of Black Power have retreated into an unreal world, where they see an outnumbered and poverty-stricken minority organizing itself independently of whites and creating sufficient power to force white America to grant its demands. . . .

The Black Power advocates of today consciously feel that they are the most militant group in the Negro protest movement. Yet they have retreated from a direct confrontation with American society on the issue of integration and, by preaching separatism, unconsciously function as an accommodation to white racism.— Report of the National Advisory Commission on Civil Disorders, 1968.

---

recommended massive spending to erase these ghettos and the inequities their occupants suffered. "Only a commitment to national action on an unprecedented scale can shape a future compatible with the historic ideals of American society," the commission concluded. But Congress proceeded to cut rather than to increase spending for the alleviation of urban poverty.

In April 1968 the assassination of Dr. Martin Luther King, Jr., shocked the nation but did not alter the economizing mood of Congress. King, whose insistence upon Gandhi-like nonviolent techniques seemed old-fashioned to black militants, was preparing to lead a protest march on behalf of striking garbage workers in Memphis, Tennessee. While standing on a motel balcony, he was struck by a sniper's bullet and died within a few minutes. King's death touched off the most widespread rioting the nation had yet undergone in the Negro areas of cities from coast to coast. Looting and arson were endemic; forty persons were killed. Washington was the worst hit, as fires gutted buildings within sight of the Capitol and the White House. Yet within the Negro districts, innumerable residents worked doggedly to end the disorders. Simultaneously the nation mourned the assassinated leader, as King was given a funeral bringing together an assem-

blage of notables and receiving television coverage exceeded only by that of President Kennedy.

Within a week Congress responded by enacting the Civil Rights Act of 1968, which had been pending for two years. It outlawed racial discrimination in the sale and rental of four-fifths of all homes and apartments. But as poor people assembled in Washington a few weeks later in the campaign that King had been planning at the time of his death, Congress was still preoccupied with economy and little disposed to provide financial aid for them.

THE PAN-INDIAN MOVEMENT

The Indian population, growing much faster than the population as a whole, nearly doubled during the twenty years after 1950. By 1970 the total had reached about 800,000, of whom more than half lived on or near reservations and most of the rest in cities. The population increase had come in spite of a lower-than-average life expectancy. Indeed, the descendants of the aborigines were, as a group, much worse off than other Americans, even those of African descent. Annual family income for Indians was $1,000 less than for blacks, and the unemploy-

The Plight of the Indian	**American Indian**	**U.S.**
Suicides (1970)	32.0 per 100,000	16.0 per 100,000
Life expectancy (1970)	47 years	70.8 years
Unemployment rate (1972)	45% estimated	5.8%
Median family income (1971)	$4,000	$9,867
Infant mortality (1970)	30.9 per 1,000 live births	21.8 per 1,000 live births
Percent entering college (1971)	18%	50%

ment rate for Indians was ten times the national rate. Suicides among Indian youth were one hundred times as frequent as among white youth.

Despite the 1924 grant of citizenship to all Indians, those on the reservations continued to be treated as "wards of the nation," with little or no control over their own affairs. They had been promised a New Deal in the Indian Reorganization Act of 1934, which had been ex-

pected to reverse the policy laid down in the Dawes Severalty Act of 1887. Presumably the Bureau of Indian Affairs would no longer try to make white farmers out of Indians but, under the 1934 law, would encourage the revitalization of aboriginal culture and tribal government. Congress failed to provide sufficient funds, however, to help the Indians advance very far in the new direction. Then, in 1953, Congress reverted to the old policy of forcing

Indians at Alcatraz
Indians occupying Alcatraz Island, the site of an abandoned federal prison in San Francisco Bay, to demonstrate for Indian rights, raise clenched fists as they vote down a proposal that they allow the island to be converted into a national park. Photograph taken April 8, 1970. (Wide World)

V. AFTER WORLD WAR II:
A Period of Experimentation

Plate 1: Willem de Kooning, UNTITLED
Gift of Messrs. Julian J. & Joachim Jean Aberbach, New York; Brandeis University Art Col...

Since World War II, the American artist has no longer needed to look to European sources for his training and standards. For the last thirty years, not Paris but New York City has been the center of artistic innovation.

The first movement to focus attention on the United States as the artistic center was Abstract Expressionism, a uniquely American invention, based on abstraction and reflecting

the emotional intensity of th... movement can be traced to ... and first appeared in the w... Pollock in the years immedi... war. Pollock, whose earlier ... influenced by the Regionali... Benton, came in contact du... with a group of European p... fled Nazi Germany and emi...

Plate 2: George Tooker, THE SUBWAY
(Collection of the Whitney Museum of American Art, Juliana Force Purchase)

York. Many of these artists belonged to the school of Surrealism, which advocated the virtues of "automatic painting"—a technique in which the artist allows his subconscious mind to dictate the spontaneous execution of his painting. Utilizing this approach, Pollock and other members of the Abstract Expressionist group developed an explosively energetic style in which the act of painting, with its acceptance of the accidental and its fundamental expression of freedom, became the artist's primary objective.

Another leader of these "Action Painters," as they were called, was Willem de Kooning. De Kooning, like Pollock, emphasized the gestural approach in his large-scale compositions, but unlike Pollock, whose technique included the dripping and splashing of paint, de Kooning applied paint directly onto the canvas. In his painting "Untitled," 1962 *(Plate 1)*, the violent brush strokes seem in active conflict with each other. Although de Kooning gives no clue to a subject in this painting by way of a title, one senses the contours of a landscape in rhythms and movements of the painted surface.

The impact of Abstract Expressionism had international ramifications, and many European artists were deeply affected by the American experiment. But figurative art continued as a viable style for American painters in the postwar period, and although

they remained in the shadow of the more robust abstractionists, these painters maintained an active realist tradition. The subject matter of the realists varied greatly, from representational scenes to symbolic images. A major contributor to the realist school in the early 1950s was George Tooker. In a number of his paintings Tooker created enigmatic compositions of people trapped by the complications of modern society. In his meticulously painted work of 1950 entitled "Subway" *(Plate 2)*, Tooker depicts a dreamlike world of multiple-perspective and repetitive elements focusing on the monotonous and often frightening experience of the urban environment.

In architecture, as in painting, the dislocation of the onset of World War II brought to America a number of Europe's outstanding designers. Among these was the former director of the German Bauhaus school of design and a leading figure in the International Style of architecture, Ludwig Mies van der Rohe. Mies settled in the United States in 1937 and his influence was felt almost immediately. The International Style featured large geometric forms, large areas of untextured surfaces, and the use of glass, steel, and reinforced concrete. The Miesan aesthetic of structural clarity, which emphasized the form as a reflection of its function and downplayed the use of purely

Plate 3: Philip Johnson, GLASS HOUSE, NEW CANAAN, CONNECTICUT *(Courtesy of Philip Johnson; Photo by Sandak)*

Plate 4: Eero Saarinen, ARMCHAIR
(Collection, The Museum of Modern Art, New York. Gift of the manufacturer, Knoll Associates, Inc. U.S.A.)

decorative detail, was adopted by a whole generation of American architects. One of Mies's earliest disciples was Philip Johnson, who, for his own home in New Canaan, Connecticut, designed his famous "Glass House" in 1949 *(Plate 3)*. Although the industrial-like steel frame and large glass panes would appear not to be a proper solution for a country house, the transparent walls help to integrate the park-like setting with the unobstructed space within. Only the brick service core and fireplace create a vertical interruption in an otherwise crystalline flow of space. The furniture for Johnson's Glass House was designed by his mentor Mies.

Another American architect whose early work was influenced by the International Style was Eero Saarinen. Saarinen won a number of important commissions in the early 1950s, and like many other modern architects, he also experimented in furniture design. In 1958 he developed the innovative concept of his single-pedestal chair *(Plate 4)*. By using the technique developed for processing lightweight plastics, Saarinen conceived of a shell-like form poised on a single shaft flowing out of a pedestal base. The elegant lines of this free-form object were made possible by the use of contemporary materials and technology.

Throughout the 1940s and 1950s Abstract Expressionism dominated the American art scene, but in the early sixties a number of reactions to the extremely personal styles of the action-oriented painters took place. One of the most significant was that of the Pop Art movement, which sought to reintroduce everyday reality into art. Led by Andy Warhol, these artists based their style on popular images from the mass media, often finding their subject matter in the advertisements, comic books, and billboards of the affluent American society.

A sculptor whose work has been associated with the Pop Art movement is George Segal. In such works as "The Diner," 1964–1966 (Plate 5), Segal has narrowed the division between art and life. The white plaster figures of his composition are cast from live

Plate 5: George Segal, THE DINER
(Collection, Walker Art Center, Minneapolis, Photographer: Eric Sutherland)

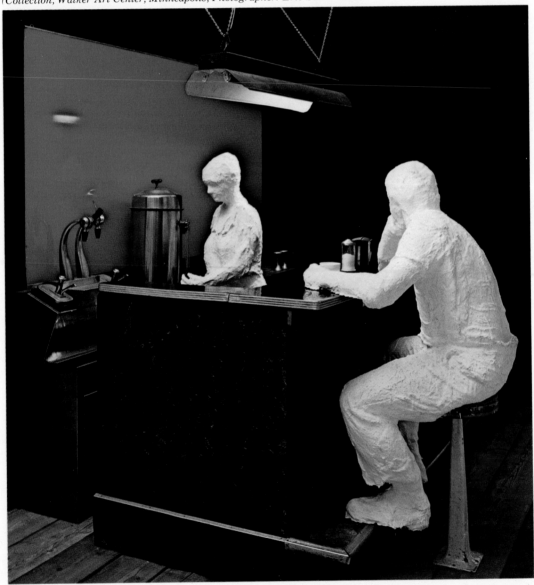

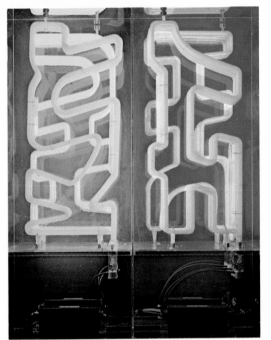

Plate 6: Chryssa, FRAGMENT FOR THE GATES
TO TIMES SQUARE *(Collection of the Whitney
Museum of American Art.
Gift of Howard and Jean Lipman)*

models and placed in an everyday setting. By showing his figures in their natural environment, Segal continues in the long tradition of American genre art.

In recent years contemporary sculptors have freed themselves from traditional sculptural materials in their search for new means of expression. The Greek-born American sculptor Chryssa was inspired by the technology of modern advertising in her use of plastics and electronic circuits. Her large piece "Fragment for the Gates to Times Square," 1966 *(Plate 6)*, is composed of plexiglass cubes into which are placed a series of curved neon tubes, and the result is a rhythmic multicolored effect. The variety of new materials used to create these light-boxes reflects the expanded visual vocabulary of modern sculpture.

The 1960s witnessed a number of important architectural innovations. Many of the former disciples of Mies van der Rohe, including Johnson and Saarinen, rejected the severity of the International Style in favor of more

Plate 7: Paul Rudolph,
ART AND ARCHITECTURE BUILDING,
NEW HAVEN, CONNECTICUT
(Courtesy of Yale University)

Plate 8: Kevin Roche, FORD FOUNDATION BUILDING, NEW YORK CITY (*ESTO for the Ford Foundation*)

sculptural and expressionistic designs. Although function continued to play a major role, new problems of mass and scale were explored in contemporary terms. The expressive power of architecture became a compelling concern of Paul Rudolph, who in his Art and Architecture Building at Yale University, 1962–1963 *(Plate 7)*, created an extremely dramatic structure. The vertical concrete piers of the exterior rise the full height of the building, contrasting in their massive form with the openness of the large plate glass windows. Rudolph's most imaginative innovation was his ability to create thirty-nine different levels in what appears from the exterior to be the space of seven stories. Although Rudolph's design has been severely criticized for its overly complicated maze-like interior plan, it has also received high praise for its relationship to its urban site and its concern for human scale.

Another architect of the sixties who attempted to redefine the traditional appearance of the multistoried building was Kevin Roche. In his Ford Foundation Building of 1967 in New York City *(Plate 8)*, Roche recognized the need to alleviate the density of the city block. His solution was to create a structure whose street façades are glass,

allowing sunlight to illuminate the interior offices. The offices surround an inner garden court on two sides. This unique design provides a buffer from the bustle of the city street, while at the same time creating an oasis of green in the midst of the urban environment.

Although, as has been noted, many artists of the last decade have reacted strongly to the lack of recognizable objects in Abstract Expressionist painting, the nonrepresentational style has continued as one of the most important idioms in contemporary painting. A direction pursued by one group known as "Chromatic Abstractionists" was the exploration of the subtle, emotive power of large areas of pure color. Strongly influenced by Mark Rothko's richly atmospheric paintings of floating rectangles, the painter Morris Louis developed a style which relied entirely on the sensation of color. In his work entitled "Blue Veil," 1958–1959 *(Plate 9)*, Louis allowed the acrylic pigment to saturate the fabric of his unsealed canvas. The diaphanous veils of color, flowing together, evoke a mood of mystery and quiet contemplation.

In the last few years American painting has shown a renewed interest in photographic-like

Plate 9: Morris Louis, BLUE VEIL *(Courtesy of the Fogg Art Museum, Harvard University, Gift of Mrs. Culver Orswell and Gifts for Special Uses Fund)*

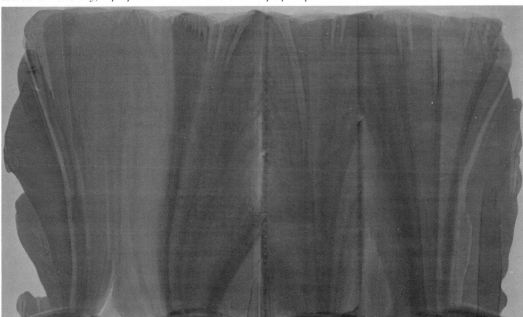

Plate 10: Jack Beal, STILL LIFE WITH PLANT AND MIRRORS
(Collection of the Whitney Museum of American Art. Neysa McMein Purchase Award)

realism. This trend has produced a variety of styles under such names as "Ultra-realism" or "Photo-realism," but the common denominator has been an intense fidelity to either photographic or real-life models. Many artists of this movement have utilized the commercial techniques of airbrush and enlargement grids as they translate to their canvas a sharply focused subject with every detail meticulously depicted.

Jack Beal's painting "Still Life with Plant and Mirrors," 1965 *(Plate 10)*, exemplifies the extreme complexity of these compositions. The subject is viewed from a slightly elevated position with the brightly colored pot and plant reflected in multiple mirrors at varying angles. The resulting effect is a dazzling pattern of shapes and forms.

American art in the last thirty years has been a succession of movements which has bordered on the chaotic. Experimentation in all the arts has presented the contemporary viewer with the persistent question of which of the various artistic movements has true historical significance and which will have enduring value. Only time and the opportunity for historical perspective will furnish the answers.

the Indians to adopt the white man's ways. A congressional resolution of that year declared the intention of terminating federal relations with the tribes and leaving them on their own. Thereafter relations with some tribes were terminated, among these the Menominee of Wisconsin, who saw their reservation converted into Menominee County. "Termination" led to further Indian impoverishment, both material and spiritual.

During the 1960s more Indians than ever before joined in a movement to bring all the tribes together and redress their common wrongs. In 1961 more than 400 members of 67 different tribes gathered in Chicago and drew up a Declaration of Indian Purpose, which stressed the "right to choose our own way of life" and the "responsibility of preserving our precious heritage." In 1964, while Congress was considering the Economic Opportunity Bill, hundreds of Indians and white sympathizers assembled in Washington to urge Congress to include Indians in the antipoverty program. After black militants had proclaimed black power as their aim, a number of young, college-educated Indians adapted the slogan to their own use and began to speak of red power. Some repudiated the name "Indian" — which, as they pointed out, whites had mistakenly given them — and insisted on being called "Native Americans" (a term that anti-immigrant whites had applied to themselves more than a century earlier).

Congress included Indians in the coverage of the Economic Opportunity Act, and for a time many of the reservation dwellers were allowed to plan and carry out their own antipoverty programs. Except for this, neither the Kennedy nor the Johnson administration did much more than the Eisenhower administration had done to meet the Indians' needs and demands. Johnson failed to give effect to his words of 1968: "I propose a new goal for our Indian programs: a goal that ends the old debate about 'termination' of Indian programs and stresses self-determination; a goal that erases old attitudes of paternalism and promotes partnership self-help."

Frustrated Indians turned more and more to direct action, to confrontations with whites, to defiance of state and federal authority. In 1968, Indian fishermen, seeking to exercise old treaty rights of fishing on the Columbia River and in Puget Sound, clashed with officials of the state of Washington. In 1969 a group of Indians of various tribes, to dramatize the plight of their people, landed on Alcatraz Island, the site of an abandoned federal prison in San Francisco Bay, and claimed the place "by right of discovery." The frustrations of many Indians found witty as well as angry expression in the writings of Vine Deloria, Jr., a Sioux, who titled one of his books *Custer Died for Your Sins* (1969).

THE SPANISH-SPEAKING MINORITY

Much more numerous than the descendants of North American tribes were the people of Latin American origin, most of whom also had Indian ancestors, and some of whom were at least partly of African descent. Numbering more than 9 million in 1970, the Spanish-speaking minority was, next to the American Negro minority, the largest in the country. The people of Puerto Rican background were concentrated mainly in New York, those of Cuban background mainly in Florida, and those of Mexican background mainly in California, Texas, and other states of the Southwest. The Mexican-Americans, totaling almost 7 million, included legal immigrants from Mexico, illegal immigrants ("mojados" or "wetbacks"), and temporary workers ("braceros") brought in under labor contracts, as well as descendants of families who had been living in Mexican territory at the time it was incorporated into the United States.

The Spanish-speaking peoples had suffered from various forms of discrimination, though they had not been consigned to separate schools. To advance their interests, many of them had joined organizations of one kind or another, but these were specialized or localized. During the 1960s, for the first time, large numbers of Mexican-Americans were brought together in a broad, inclusive "Chicano" (from "Mexicano") movement.

Its outstanding hero was César Chávez, an Arizona-born California farm worker. Its main focus, for the time being, was a farm workers' strike that Chávez called in 1965 and soon converted into a nonviolent crusade for social justice. He enlisted the cooperation of college students, churchmen and churchwomen, and civil rights groups, including CORE and SNCC. To bring pressure on employers, who brought in

Chicano Leader
*Evident in this picture is the magnetism of César Chávez, the labor organizer
who rose to be an outstanding hero of Mexican-Americans in the 1960s. He is
shown talking with grape workers at a California vineyard. (Paul Fusco from
Magnum)*

strikebreakers, he appealed for a nationwide
boycott of California table grapes. The boycott
gained the support of millions of sympathizers
throughout the country, but got no assistance
from the federal government, which increased
its purchases of grapes to be sent to American
troops in Vietnam. Chávez won a victory in
1970, when the growers of half of California's
table grapes signed contracts with his union.

WOMEN'S RIGHTS

American women in general could hardly be
called a minority, since 51 percent of the population was female; yet they suffered inequities
comparable to those imposed upon minority
groups, and women of these groups bore a
double burden of discrimination.

True, more and more job opportunities
were opening up for women, and an increasing
proportion of them, including wives and mothers, were working outside the home (fewer
than 25 percent of women over sixteen had
been counted as part of the labor force in 1940;
more than 43 percent were so counted in 1970).
But women were paid much less than men,
even for comparable work (in 1971, for men
employed full time, the median yearly pay was
$9,630; for women it was $5,700). Women had
fewer chances than men to make a professional
or managerial career. In the mid-1960s women
constituted only 7 percent of the nation's physicians and less than 4 percent of its lawyers, and
the proportion of women managers or owners
of businesses, already small, was actually declining. Women were being replaced by men in
top positions in schools, libraries, and social
work – which once had been considered wom-
en's fields.

In comparison with men, women were
receiving too little education, but in comparison
with their own career opportunities they were

receiving too much. They composed a smaller percentage of the college population in the 1950s than in the 1920s and were granted a smaller percentage of college degrees in 1960 than in 1930. During the 1960s they were earning only one in three of all B.A.s and M.A.s and only one in ten of the Ph.D.s. Yet the college graduates—like other, less well-educated women—often were handicapped in getting and holding outside employment because they had to carry the extra burden of bearing and rearing children and keeping house. Women with higher education seemed especially to resent the "double standard" that all women confronted in practically every aspect of life.

Educated women of the middle class took the lead (as they had done in earlier feminist crusades) in the dozens of "women's libera-

tion" movements that sprang forth in the 1960s. One of the most influential of the leaders was Betty Friedan, who in *The Feminine Mystique* (1963) denounced the American home as a "comfortable concentration camp" and called upon its inmates to free themselves. Friedan helped to found, in 1966, the most inclusive and effective of the new women's rights organizations, the National Organization for Women, or NOW. "There is no civil rights movement to speak for women, as there has been for Negroes and other victims of discrimination," the organizers of NOW declared, thus revealing that they, too, had been inspired, at least in part, by the example of the blacks. The organization's 1967 "bill of rights" demanded an Equal Rights Amendment to the Constitution— "Equality of Rights under the law shall not be

Abortion March
In the early 1900s, women's rights advocates demonstrated for the right to share in their own government by means of the vote. In the early 1970s some of them demanded the right to control their own bodies—through abortion. New York and a few other states responded with liberalized abortion laws. (Charles Gatewood)

denied or abridged by the United States on account of sex"—and Congress in 1970 approved the amendment and sent it to the states for ratification. NOW also called for enforcement of the 1964 Civil Rights Act, which prohibited discrimination in employment on account of sex as well as race, and "men wanted" and "women wanted" began to disappear from classified ads. Other NOW demands included the following: maternity leave for working women; public child-care centers, to enable mothers to compete more freely for jobs; absolute equality of educational opportunities at all levels; and the "right of women to control their own reproductive lives" through contraception and abortion.

NOW disclaimed any "enmity toward men" and advocated a "self-respecting partnership" with them, but some of the other liberation groups practically declared a war of the sexes. Some, resisting "male chauvinism," refused to let men open doors or light cigarettes for them. A few, protesting their treatment as mere "sex objects," publicly burned their brassieres or stripped off their clothes. Others forsook men and proclaimed themselves lesbians. The majority of American women, however, saw little need to support the feminist cause in any of its forms. A poll in 1970 put the question: "In your opinion, do women in the United States get as good a break as men?" Of the women replying, 65 percent said "Yes."

Selected Readings

Eisenhower
F. M. Shattuck, *The 1956 Presidential Campaign* (1960); Samuel Lubell, *The Revolt of the Moderates* (1956); R. H. Rovere, *Affairs of State: The Eisenhower Years* (1956); M. J. Pusey, *Eisenhower the President* (1956), very favorable; M. W. Childs, *Eisenhower, Captive Hero* (1956), rather critical; E. T. Benson, *Crossfire: The Eight Years with Eisenhower* (1962).

J. F. K. and L. B. J.
J. M. Burns, *John Kennedy: A Political Profile** (1959); T. H. White, *The Making of the President, 1960** (1961); A. M. Schlesinger, *A Thousand Days: John F. Kennedy in the White House** (1965); T. C. Sorensen, *Kennedy** (1965); William Manchester, *Death of a President** (1967); Tom Wicker, *JFK and LBJ: The Influence of Personality upon Politics* (1968); T. H. White, *The Making of the President, 1964** (1965); Rowland Evans and Robert Novak, *Lyndon B. Johnson: The Exercise of Power** (1966), critical; Robert Sherrill, *The Accidental President* (1967), critical.

Prosperity and Poverty
H. G. Vatter, *The U. S. Economy in the 1950's** (1963); Walter Heller, *New Dimensions of Political Economy* (1966); Gabriel Kolko, *Wealth and Power in America* (1962); Michael Harrington, *The Other America: Poverty in the United States* (1962); H. P. Miller, *Rich Man, Poor Man** (1964); Oscar Lewis, *La Vida: A Puerto Rican Family in the Culture of Poverty—San Juan and New York** (1966); H. M. Caudill, *Night Comes to the Cumberlands* (1963), on poverty in the Appalachians; J. D. Donovan, *The Politics of Poverty* (1967); Sar Levitan, *The Great Society's Poor Law: A New Approach to Poverty* (1969).

The Supreme Court
A. T. Mason, *The Supreme Court from Taft to Warren* (1958); J. D. Weaver, *Warren: The Man, the Court, the Era* (1967); W. F. Murphy, *Congress and the Court** (1962); R. G. Dixon, Jr., *Democratic Representation: Reapportionment in Law and Politics* (1968); R. B. McKay, *Reapportionment: The Law and Politics of Equal Representation* (1965); Loren Miller, *The Petitioners: The Story of the Supreme Court of the United States and the Negro* (1964); I. A. Newby, *Challenge to the Court: Social Scientists and the Defense of Segregation, 1954–1966* (1968).

Black Voices
M. L. King, Jr., *Stride Toward Freedom** (1958) and *Why We Can't Wait** (1964); James Baldwin, *The Fire Next Time* (1963); L. E. Lomax, *The Negro Revolt** (1963) and *When the Word Is Given: A Report on Elijah Muhammad, Malcolm X, and the Black Muslim World* (1963); *The Autobiography of Malcolm X** (1966); James Farmer, *Freedom—When?* (1966); Stokely Carmichael and C. V. Hamilton, *Black Power: The Politics of Liberation in America** (1967).

Civil Rights and Civil Disorders
Anthony Lewis, *Portrait of a Decade: The Second American Revolution* (1964); Louis Harlan, *Separate and Unequal** (1961), on segregated schools; A. P. Blaustein and C. C. Ferguson, *Desegregation and the Law** (1962); J. W. Silver, *Mississippi: The Closed Society** (1964); J. W. Anderson, *Eisenhower, Brownell, and the Congress: The Tangled Origins of the Civil Rights Bill of 1956–1957* (1964); D. M. Berman, *A Bill Becomes Law: The Civil Rights Act of 1960* (1962); A. I. Waskow, *From Race Riot to Sit-In: 1919 and the 1960's* (1966); James Peck, *Freedom Ride*

(1962); D. R. Matthews and J. W. Prothro, *Negroes and the New Southern Politics** (1966); N. V. Bartley, *The Rise of Massive Resistance: Race and Politics in the South During the 1950's* (1969); M. A. Schwartz, *Trends in White Attitudes Toward Negroes* (1967); Lee Rainwater and W. L. Yancey, *The Moynihan Report and the Politics of Controversy** (1967); *Report of the National Advisory Committee on Civil Disorders** (1968); A. Meier and E. Rudwick, *CORE: A Study in the Civil Rights Movement, 1942–1968* (1973); Richard Bardolph, *The Civil Rights Record* (1971).

Indians and Chicanos
Stan Steiner, *The New Indians** (1968); Vine Deloria, Jr., *Custer Died for Your Sins* (1969); H. W. Hertzberg, *The Search for an American Indian Identity: Modern Pan-Indian Movements* (1971); W. E. Washburn, *Red Man's Land / White Man's Law: A Study of the Past and Present Status of the American Indian* (1971); A. M. Josephy, ed., *Red Power** (1971); S. A. Levitan and B. Hetrick, *Big Brother's Indian Programs* (1972); Wayne Moquin, ed., *A Documentary History of the Mexican-Americans* (1971); Stan Steiner, *La Raza** (1970); M. S. Meier and F. Rivera, *The Chicanos: A History of Mexican Americans* (1972).

Woman's Place
W. H. Chafe, *The American Woman: Her Changing Social, Economic, and Political Roles, 1920–1970* (1972); Judith Hole and Ellen Levine, eds., *Rebirth of Feminism* (1972); Elizabeth Janeway, *Man's World, Woman's Place: A Study in Social Mythology* (1971); Juliet Mitchell, *Women's Estate* (1972).

*Titles available in paperback.

From Defiance to Détente?

Twenty-nine

"We face a hostile ideology—global in scope, atheistic in character, ruthless in purpose, and insidious in method. Unhappily the danger it poses promises to be of indefinite duration." So said President Eisenhower in the farewell address he directed to the American people shortly before leaving office in 1961. "A vital element in keeping the peace is our military establishment. Our arms must be mighty, ready for instant action, so that no potential aggressor may be tempted to risk his own destruction."

While warning of dangers from outside, President Eisenhower also drew attention to a possible threat arising within the nation. This was the threat of undue power accruing to the "military-industrial complex" that had developed to provide for the national defense. For the first time in their history, the American people had in their midst, on a permanent basis, the "conjunction of an immense military establishment and a large arms industry." Eisenhower did not fully describe the complex, but the military establishment consisted of the Armed Services, the Central Intelligence Agency, and other bodies provided for in the National Security Act of 1947. The arms industry included not only manufacturers of traditional armaments but also producers of a bewildering variety of new aviational, aerospace, electronic, chemical, and biological supplies. Supporting the industry and supported by it were certain labor unions and numerous scientific groups, many of these in universities that had government research contracts.

Under President Eisenhower's successors—Kennedy, Johnson, and Nixon—the United States continued to face a "hostile ideology" abroad. And the military-industrial complex continued to grow. It seemed to gain a greater and greater role in the determination of policy. Certainly it took a larger and larger share of the federal budget, leaving less and less for domestic needs, though these became increasingly serious. How

Peace March   1968
This peace march held in San Francisco in October 1968 was typical of the nationwide demonstrations against the Vietnam War. Students conducted frequent all-night teach-ins at their universities protesting the war; others went so far as to burn their draft cards. The varied backgrounds of the demonstrators were illustrated by the trial of several representative marchers ranging from a graduate student to one of the most prestigious physicians in the country, Dr. Benjamin Spock. (Photoreporters)

to provide for the national security while preserving and promoting individual freedom and opportunity—how to defend democracy without destroying it in the process—this was America's basic dilemma.

There was a ray of hope. Russia and China were ancient enemies, with differences of interest too profound to be patched over indefinitely by the shared ideology of Communism. By 1961, signs of serious conflict between the Soviet Union and the People's Republic had already begun to appear. If the conflict should worsen, one or both of the two Communist powers might be willing to seek or to accept improved relations with the United States. This prospect caused some Americans to look toward an eventual "détente," a relaxation of tensions in world politics. Actually, the most dangerous crisis between the United States and the Soviet Union was yet to come. By 1973, however, the achievement of some kind of détente seemed at last a real possibility.

Kennedy and Confrontation

In his inaugural address, President Kennedy had advised: "Let us never negotiate out of fear. But let us never fear to negotiate." During the next few years, as Russia and the United States faced one another over the issues of Berlin, Cuba, and nuclear testing, the spirit of negotiation was put to severe trials.

DIVERSIFIED DEFENSE

At the time Kennedy took office, the military establishment of the United States was spending half of the federal budget and nearly a tenth of the gross national product; it was directly employing 3.5 million people. The incoming President and his new Secretary of Defense, Robert McNamara, were as determined as President Eisenhower had been in his farewell address that this vast establishment should protect but not dominate the American nation. From the outset, McNamara established firm control over the enormous and complex Department of Defense. To the distress of some high-ranking officers and many congressmen, he brought in brilliant young civilians who, employing computers and cost-analysis techniques, plotted policy changes. He was accused of relying more upon civilian skills and problem-solving machines than upon military experience.

President Kennedy and Secretary Mc-Namara built their plans upon the theory that the strength of thermonuclear weapons on the part of both the United States and Russia was sufficiently great to constitute a "mutual deter-

rent" against war. During the campaign of 1960 Kennedy had warned that the United States lagged behind Russia; soon after he took office his secretary of defense reported that the missile gap, if there was one, favored the United States. This nation, possessing sufficient striking power to destroy the Soviet Union several times over, was committed to staying ahead of Russia in missile and nuclear development. The new administration speeded the placing of nuclear-armed missiles in underground sites and the building of nuclear-armed Polaris submarines to rove the seas. These retaliatory weapons would guarantee that, if the United States suffered destruction, so would the attacking nation.

There was the assumption, however, that under the umbrella of the mutual deterrence of countering nuclear forces, the Communists would seek to gain new territories by subversion or by conventional warfare. Experts pointed to areas like South Vietnam to illustrate what they meant; nuclear deterrents were of no value there. So the President wished to develop forces expert in guerrilla and jungle warfare and equipped with special arms. A million American men were thus trained in "counterinsurgency." In addition, United States military missions aided other countries in establishing their own programs. During its first two years the administration also committed more of its defense expenditures to increasing its conventional forces. It raised the number of army combat divisions from eleven to sixteen and air force tactical wings from sixteen to twenty-one.

Since the inception of the Truman Doctrine (1947) and the Marshall Plan (1948), the United States had depended on economic aid as well as military power to defend many areas of the world against Communism. For both strategic and humanitarian reasons, President Eisenhower year after year requested and received huge appropriations for the mutual security program.

Most of the new, emergent nations in Asia and Africa were suffering from poverty and ignorance and from a growth in population so explosive that it canceled out gains in living standards. Many of these nations were ready to accept aid from the United States at the same time that they were also receptive to both aid and propaganda from Communist Russia and Communist China. Even before the end of the Eisenhower administration, the United States no longer insisted that the countries receiving economic assistance align themselves on the Western side. Their right to be neutral in the cold war was conceded.

President Kennedy continued and in some ways elaborated upon the policy of financial assistance abroad. He established the Agency for International Development (AID) to coordinate various projects and to explore means of making them more effective. He sponsored the so-called Alliance for Progress, which was not really an alliance but a set of agreements between the United States and Latin American governments for cooperative undertakings in Latin America. He also brought about the establishment of the Peace Corps, which trained and sent abroad thousands of specialists, mostly young people, to work for two years in underdeveloped areas.

The returns from foreign aid were debatable. The most successful of the programs — and the least expensive — was probably the Peace Corps. The Alliance for Progress was criticized by businessmen in the United States on the grounds that the administration's demands for tax and land reforms, as prerequisites to aid, were frightening investors away from Latin America. The Alliance was opposed by businessmen and landowners in Latin America on the grounds that, by demanding reforms, the United States was encouraging Communism. Foreign aid appeared to help in counteracting Russian influence in the emerging nations of Africa. .

HEIGHTENING TENSION

The Cuban dictator Fidel Castro was drawing closer to Russia, heaping invective upon the United States, and exporting "Fidelismo" throughout Latin America. President Kennedy had declared: "Communist domination in this hemisphere can never be negotiated."

Once in office, Kennedy and his advisers faced the question of whether to go ahead with a project that the Eisenhower administration had begun. Under the direction of the Central Intelligence Agency, anti-Castro Cubans were secretly being trained and equipped in Central America for a landing in Cuba. They were intended to overthrow the Castro regime with the aid of discontented groups still on the island. Kennedy decided to authorize the invasion but refused to provide United States air support. On the morning of April 17, 1961, a force of about 2,000 rebels landed at the Bay of Pigs. No accompanying revolt, such as had been expected, took place in Cuba, and the invading rebels were left to the mercy of the Cuban army and air force. Within two days the beachhead was wiped out.

Throughout Latin America, and in many allied and neutral nations as well as Communist countries, the United States was the object of condemnation. This country reaped all the disadvantages and none of the potential advantages of the invasion attempt. President Kennedy retorted on April 20: "We do not intend to abandon [Cuba] to the Communists." But Castro moved rapidly toward aligning Cuba fully with the Soviet Union, proclaiming that it was a "socialist" state.

In the somber aftermath of the Bay of Pigs fiasco, President Kennedy in June 1961 met Premier Khrushchev in Vienna for a frank interchange of views. It was not encouraging. According to reports, Kennedy told Khrushchev that Russia wanted to trade an apple for an orchard, but the United States did not do business that way.

An ominous sequel to the conference was renewed Russian pressure upon Berlin, bringing with it the serious threat of nuclear war. On June 15, 1961, Khrushchev, who was then back in Russia, set a deadline for the settlement of the Berlin issue. "The conclusion of a peace treaty with Germany cannot be postponed any longer," he declared. "A peaceful settlement in

Europe must be attained this year." With or without the Western powers, he proposed to conclude a peace treaty with the East German government (the "German Democratic Republic"), which would then control access routes to West Berlin. As he well knew, the NATO powers did not possess conventional forces of sufficient strength to defend West Berlin and its access routes with any certainty of success. The defense of Berlin must rest upon the use of nuclear power, and Khrushchev acted as if he thought the United States would not risk the danger of world holocaust to defend Berlin.

What was pushing the Soviet Union toward this dangerous confrontation was the spectacular success of West Berlin as a "showcase of democracy" behind the Iron Curtain. East Germans could easily slip into West Berlin, though barbed wire and minefields prevented fugitives from crossing the rest of the border between Communist countries and western Europe. West Germany with its higher living standards and its demands for skilled workers and professional men was an irresistible lure to the poor, regimented East Germans.

Suddenly, before dawn on August 13, 1961, the East German government closed the border between East and West Berlin and in the next few days began erecting elaborate concrete block and barbed-wire barriers. East Germany was transformed into a vast concentration camp and West Berlin into a beleaguered island. Khrushchev had thus gained by a single act of force much that he had been seeking unsuccessfully at the conference table. The United States protested but was not ready to use armed force to destroy the new wall.

Fears of thermonuclear war ran so high throughout the United States that the nation faced seriously for the first time the problem of trying to construct fallout shelters sufficient to protect the entire population. There followed much controversy and some hysteria about shelters but little actual construction, despite the encouragement of the federal and state governments. Fears were intensified when the Soviet Union announced an extensive series of nuclear tests. During the autumn Russia exploded approximately fifty nuclear devices, one with an estimated force of sixty-five megatons – 3,000 times more powerful than the Hiroshima bomb. The series as a whole produced double the amount of fallout of all previous atomic tests. The United States, fearing it would fall behind in the nuclear competition, announced it would resume tests underground and in outer space.

CUBA: THE MISSILE CRISIS

The Berlin crisis slowly subsided during the autumn of 1961, to be succeeded a year later by a new, more frightening encounter, this time in regard to Cuba. In mid-July 1962, shiploads of Russian technicians and equipment began arriving on the island, and in August more than 30 Soviet ships unloaded 2,000 technicians and instructors, together with fighter planes, surface-to-air missiles, and patrol boats with missiles. Photographic reconnaissance, which the United States was carrying out secretly around the periphery of Cuba, indicated, as Kennedy announced on September 4, that the armaments were solely defensive. "Were it otherwise," he declared, "the gravest issues would arise."

Refugees from Cuba brought reports, however, that Russia was also introducing offensive missiles into the island. Kennedy authorized photographic reconnaissance of all Cuba to ascertain if this was true. On October 14, a U-2 plane brought back incontrovertible evidence – photographs of new missile sites being rushed to completion. Why were the Russians engaged in this dangerous and expensive gamble? This was the first question that President Kennedy's advisers pondered as they began deliberations on October 16. The Russian move would more than redress the missile balance that had favored the United States. According to the London *Observer* (October 28, 1962): "Seen from the Pentagon, the two most alarming features of the missile build-up [in Cuba] were proximity and speed. Radar would give 15 minutes' warning of a missile attack from Russia, but only two–three minutes from Cuba. Medium-range missile bases can be constructed in hours or days. Within a month, if the U.S. sat tight, Russia could get 200–300 missiles in position – enough, at least in theory, to knock out a large part of the U.S. retaliatory forces in a surprise 'preemptive' attack."

How could the United States counter the Russian move? One of the two main alterna-

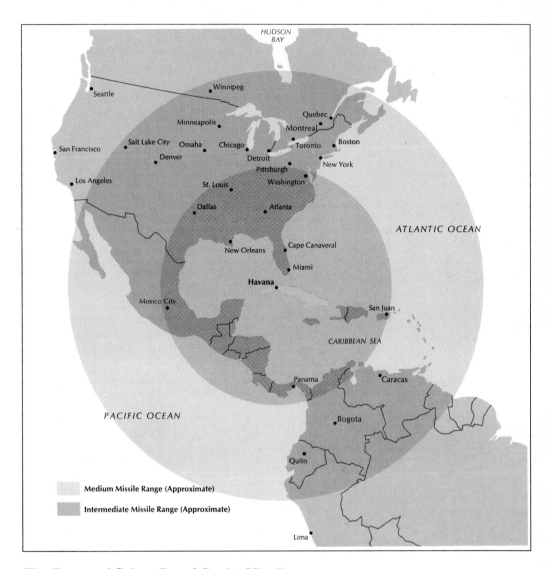

The Range of Cuban-Based Soviet Missiles

tives was to strike the bases from the air; the other was to blockade Cuba. The President and his advisers decided upon a "quarantine"—a blockade. Meanwhile, on October 18, Soviet Foreign Minister Gromyko called upon the President to assure him that Soviet assistance to Cuba was solely defensive.

On October 22, President Kennedy was ready to act. Appearing on television, he presented the photographic evidence of the missile sites and announced that the United States would establish a quarantine on all offensive weapons bound for Cuba. "This secret, swift and extraordinary build-up of Communist missiles—in an area well known to have a special and historical relationship to the United States and the nations of the Western hemisphere—is a deliberately provocative and unjustified change in the status quo which cannot be accepted by this country, if our courage and our commitments are ever again to be trusted by either friend or foe."

Several days of acute tension followed as the United States instituted its naval and air

A Cuban Medium-Range Ballistic Missile Launch Site
This photograph shows the site at San Cristobal, Cuba, on October 25, 1962, at the height of the crisis. Allen Dulles, former head of the Central Intelligence Agency, has hinted that the requisite skill in identifying Soviet missile sites from photographs had been acquired through data gathered by U-2 flights over Russia. (U.S. Department of Defense)

blockade, uncertain what would happen if a Soviet vessel among the twenty-five bound for Cuba should refuse to stop and should be sunk. Some of the Soviet ships changed course or stopped. But low-flying Navy P-8U planes brought back evidence that work on the Soviet bases continued at top speed.

This evidence made especially unacceptable to the United States a proposal issued by U Thant, acting secretary general of the United Nations, after strong urging by unaligned nations. U Thant requested Russia to suspend arms shipments, and he requested that the United States suspend the blockade for two or three weeks while negotiations took place. Khrushchev accepted U Thant's suggestion, but Kennedy declined.

All week long the United States negotiated with Russia, and behind the stand of each side was the threat of nuclear force. The United States left no doubt that it was in earnest. The navy established a 2,100-mile ring about Cuba,

employing 180 ships, including 8 aircraft carriers. The Strategic Air Command began "massive airborne" alerts on October 22, keeping quantities of its heavy nuclear-armed B-52 bombers in the air at all times. Behind these were 156 intercontinental ballistic missiles in combat readiness and a fleet of Polaris submarines. Soviet miscalculation could bring a holocaust.

Late on the evening of October 26, President Kennedy received a long, rambling letter from Khrushchev in which he compared the United States and the Soviet Union to two men tugging on a rope, pulling a knot tighter and tighter until it could be cut only by a sword. In effect, the letter said that if Kennedy would cease tugging on his end, Khrushchev would do likewise. The letter seemed to imply that Russia would remove the missile bases provided the United States would promise not to invade Cuba. The next morning Moscow radio broadcast quite a different proposal from

Khrushchev—that Russia would dismantle the bases in Cuba if the United States would withdraw its missile bases from Turkey.

Time was running out for the United States, and meanwhile in Cuba antiaircraft fire had downed one American plane and menaced others. Under these tense conditions, the President decided to accept Khrushchev's first offer and to ignore the second: if Khrushchev would remove the missiles, Kennedy proposed; the United States would end the blockade and not invade Cuba. The next day, October 27, Khrushchev accepted.

Though an armed clash had been avoided, trouble over Cuba by no means had been brought to an end. The Soviet Union did indeed remove the missiles and dismantle the bases, but Castro refused to allow on-the-spot inspection. Thousands of Soviet technicians remained, and although President Kennedy pressured Khrushchev to remove them, their return to Russia was slow. Cuban refugee groups, bewildered and angered by the no-invasion pledge, engaged in plots of their own against Castro and were resentful when the United States restrained them. In the immediate aftermath of the crisis, the national sentiment was one of profound relief, and President Kennedy's popularity rose.

LOOSENING OF ALLIANCES

While confronting one another over Cuba, the United States and the Soviet Union found themselves on the same side in a less serious and more remote crisis over India. The Chinese had launched surprise offensives along the Indian frontier. Already the Soviet Union was providing India with economic aid, and the United States now gave further assistance, ferrying weapons and other supplies in "flying boxcars" to the Himalayan front. Soon the Chinese agreed to negotiate their boundary dispute with India. The brief war had shown that, for the time being, Indo-American relations were close and cordial. It had also indicated that Russia and China were drawing further apart.

As relations between the Communist powers were being strained, so were those between the United States and one of its NATO allies—France. In western Europe the Marshall Plan had helped stimulate a recovery so

remarkable that by the 1960s some nations not only were more prosperous than ever before in their history but in percentage of annual growth were outstripping the United States. Their new economic power meant that, if they chose, they could either insist upon a more equal partnership or break loose to form a "third force" between the United States and Russia, such as some French leaders had long envisaged.

To strengthen western Europe against a possible Russian threat, the United States had encouraged the formation of the European Economic Community (or "Common Market"), in 1958. To give further encouragement, Kennedy in 1962 obtained from Congress authority to lower tariffs on trade with the Common Market countries. But President Charles de Gaulle of France jolted Kennedy's hopes for closer economic and political cooperation with Europe. In 1963, de Gaulle vetoed the British application to join the Common Market and did so because of the close British ties with the United States. He also proclaimed his opposition to American plans for creating a multination nuclear force within the North Atlantic Treaty Organization. He insisted upon creating a separate small nuclear force for France, in order to gain an independent voice in European policy. Later he recognized Red China, thus asserting an independent position in Asian affairs as well.

In the summer of 1963, perhaps in part because of growing trouble with China, the Soviet Union, after years of negotiation, agreed to a treaty banning atmospheric (but not underground) tests of nuclear weapons. The treaty, the first definite step in the direction of international arms reduction since the onset of the cold war, was ratified by almost every important country except Red China (who was preparing to test her own nuclear bomb), France, and Cuba. A notable thaw in the cold war followed. President Kennedy announced that the United States would be willing to sell large quantities of surplus wheat to the Russians, who were suffering from a shortage.

By 1964 many Americans were thinking hopefully of the prospect of a "détente" with the Soviet Union. But these prospects soon dimmed as the United States became more and more deeply involved in an anti-Communist crusade far from home in Southeast Asia.

Johnson's Dilemmas

During the presidential campaign of 1964 the Republican candidate, Senator Goldwater, urged that the United States take a much more active part in the war then going on between Communist North Vietnam and non-Communist South Vietnam. But President Johnson specifically repudiated the Goldwater policy. "There are those that say you ought to go north and drop bombs, and try to wipe out the supply lines, and they think that would escalate the war," Johnson declaimed in a campaign speech. "We don't want our American boys to do the fighting for Asian boys. We don't want to get involved in a nation [China] with 700 million people and get tied down in a land war in Asia."

In fact, Johnson himself was already preparing to enlarge the American role in Vietnam, and soon he was ordering bombs dropped on the north and was sending American boys by the hundreds of thousands to fight in that faraway land. As a consequence he lost all possibility of maintaining the "consensus" he had desired and of achieving the "Great Society" he had proclaimed. Never before had a President been elected by such a large popular majority, and never before had a President seen his popularity dwindle away so fast and so completely.

DOMINICAN INTERVENTION

While undertaking to prevent the spread of Communism in distant Asia, President Johnson faced what seemed like a new Communist threat much closer to home, in the Caribbean. There appeared to be a danger that a Castro-type government might be imposed upon the Dominican Republic, thus making that country a second Cuba. Johnson acted quickly to forestall the supposed Communist coup. In doing so, he laid himself open to charges of fostering imperialism and right-wing dictatorship.

After the assassination of the dictator General Rafael Trujillo in 1961, the Dominican Republic was slowly and painfully emerging from three decades of economic exploitation and political repression. The government of the democratically elected President, Juan Bosch, who was leftist though not Communist, floun-

dered. In 1963 a conservative military junta overthrew Bosch and, faring little better, became itself the target of unrest. There were rumors of Communist infiltration into the island. In the spring of 1965 when young military men sympathetic to Bosch rebelled against the junta, there was rioting, shooting, and looting in the streets of the capital, Santo Domingo.

Within the next few days, United States forces numbering 30,000 ashore and afloat helped restore order. In reply to criticisms that the United States had acted unilaterally, the President and Secretary of State Dean Rusk insisted that they had held preliminary consultations with other American states and that the need for sudden intervention to prevent loss of life arose too quickly for further reliance upon the Organization of American States.

The OAS did authorize the establishment of an Inter-American Peace Force. American troops, together with token forces from several other republics, donned blue and yellow OAS armbands, and served under the command of a Brazilian general. Bloody fighting continued for some days before order could be restored. More than a year later, on June 1, 1966, in a new presidential election, Bosch was defeated by a moderate candidate. The Peace Force was withdrawn in September 1966.

The United States achieved stabilization of the Dominican Republic only at the cost of much Latin American good will. In June 1965 a professor at the National University of Mexico wrote: "The way Juan Bosch has been treated and the clumsy invasion of the Dominican Republic have created more hatred toward the United States in Latin America than the combined anti-colonial propaganda of China and Russia."

INVOLVEMENT IN VIETNAM

The involvement of the United States in Vietnam had developed so slowly that when it began spectacularly to grow, in 1964 and 1965, few Americans could remember how it had originated.

After the close of World War II, Vietnamese nationalists, seeking independence from France, rallied around Ho Chi Minh, a Com-

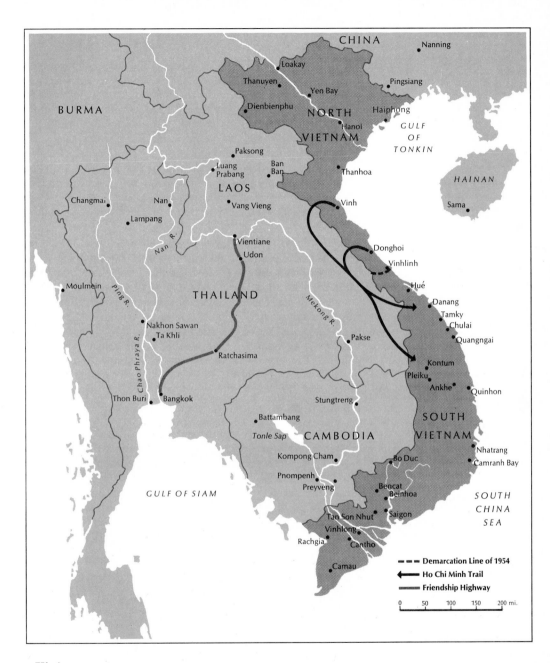

Vietnam

munist who during the war had led the anti-Japanese resistance and had cooperated with the Americans. Ho issued a declaration of independence echoing the American Declaration of 1776 and began negotiations with France. When negotiations broke down, Ho and his followers resorted to arms. The American government was little concerned until the fall of

Nationalist China and the outbreak of the Korean War. Then the Truman administration looked upon the French as manning a bastion to check the spread of Communism in Southeast Asia and began to send substantial aid. The Eisenhower administration increased the economic assistance and, when the French forces faced disaster in 1954, considered sending large-scale military aid as well. Eisenhower held back, however, because of the opposition of Congress and because of the refusal of Great Britain to cooperate.

There followed the 1954 settlements at Geneva, establishing Laos and Cambodia, and temporarily splitting Vietnam into a Communist north and non-Communist south until free elections could be held to unify the new nation. The United States did not participate in the negotiations or sign the agreements. It promised not to use force to upset them, but warned that "it would view any renewal of the aggression in violation of the . . . agreements with grave concern and as seriously threatening international peace and security." Subsequently, the State Department threw its influence against free elections, and they were never held.

The Eisenhower administration sought new arrangements to contain the Communists in Southeast Asia. Within two months of the Geneva agreements, Secretary Dulles succeeded in establishing the Southeast Asia Treaty Organization (SEATO), whose members agreed to consult one another regarding not only their own security but also the security of Laos, Cambodia, and South Vietnam. On October 23, 1954, President Eisenhower wrote the premier of South Vietnam, promising aid in return for certain reforms and offering to "assist the Government of Viet-Nam in developing and maintaining a strong, viable state, capable of resisting attempted subversion or aggression through military means." The SEATO treaty and President Eisenhower's letter were subsequently cited as the American commitments to assist South Vietnam—even though Dulles

---

Training Vietnamese Troops to Combat Communist Guerrillas
*One of the most vital of the programs to counter Communist nibbling tactics was
established in South Vietnam where a joint military assistance advisory group of the
United States armed forces intensively trained Vietnamese armed forces in the use
of American weapons and of limited warfare tactics against the Vietcong troops.
Army Chief Warrant Officer Richard Parsons (standing right) instructs Vietnamese
infantrymen on how to board an H-21C helicopter. (Official U.S. Army photo)*

The Tonkin Gulf Resolution [August 1964]

. . . The Congress approves and supports the determination of the President, as Commander in Chief, to take all necessary measures to repel any armed attack against the forces of the United States and to prevent further aggression.

The United States regards as vital to its national interest and to world peace the maintenance of international peace and security in Southeast Asia. Consonant with the Constitution and the Charter of the United Nations and in accordance with its obligations under the Southeast Asia Collective Defense Treaty, the United States is, therefore, prepared, as the President determines, to take all necessary steps, including the use of armed force, to assist any member or protocol state of the Southeast Asia Collective Defense Treaty requesting assistance in defense of its freedom. . . .

himself had told the Senate Foreign Relations Committee, when seeking its approval of SEATO, that if there should be a "revolutionary movement" in Vietnam, the SEATO members "would consult together as to what to do about it . . . but we have no undertaking to put it down; all we have is an undertaking to consult."

While the United States sought stabilization, it claimed that North Vietnam continued to seek through guerrilla activity the conquest of Laos and South Vietnam. Political turbulence and the economic dissatisfaction of many South Vietnamese made possible the successful growth of bands of Vietcong (short for Viet Communists), which by 1959 were receiving training and supplies from North Vietnam. At the end of 1960 the Vietcong established the "National Front for the Liberation of South Vietnam." Making its forays at night, murdering headmen and terrorizing villages, the Vietcong succeeded in controlling large parts of the countryside. The government of South Vietnam was confined to the cities and main lines of communication.

Gradually the United States sent increasing aid to South Vietnam. Between 1954 and 1959, of $2.3 billion in aid, only two-fifths was military. American military advisers helped train the South Vietnam army. President Kennedy, inheriting the problem, tried to build more effective resistance in Vietnam, not only through military counterinsurgency, but also through gaining the support of the peasants. Vice President Johnson, visiting Saigon in May 1961, recommended aid but warned against direct military involvement: "American combat troop involvement is not only not required, it is not desirable. . . . Possibly Americans fail to

appreciate fully the subtlety that recently colonial peoples would not look with favor upon governments which invited or accept the return this soon of Western troops."

As political and military conditions in Vietnam continued to deteriorate, President Kennedy, despite his misgivings, added to the number of military advisers. By the time of his assassination in November 1963, the American personnel in that country had reached a total of 15,500. Reports from American officials in Vietnam were optimistic, though internal troubles there caused newspapermen to cable home dark predictions. A new era of even greater instability began in the fall of 1963 when the South Vietnamese army seized control of the government from the aristocratic nationalist Ngo Dinh Diem.

ESCALATING THE WAR

Despite growing difficulties in Vietnam, in the summer of 1964 they were overshadowed by the political campaign in the United States. The number of military advisers was up to 20,000, and on its way to 25,000. Then, in August, there occurred an episode that was to give legal grounds for the reshaping of the war: American destroyers on patrol in international waters in the Gulf of Tonkin reported that they had been attacked by North Vietnamese torpedo boats. (In 1968 Senator Fulbright, chairman of the Foreign Relations Committee, held hearings and sharply inquired about what had happened in the Tonkin Gulf. He raised the question of whether there actually had been an attack.) In 1964 President Johnson and Congress were in a mood to take stern measures.

Congress at the request of the President passed by a vote of 88 to 2 in the Senate and 416 to 0 in the House, a joint resolution "To promote the maintenance of international peace and security in Southeast Asia." The resolution authorized the President to "take all necessary measures" to protect American forces and "prevent further aggression" in Southeast Asia. Senators Wayne Morse and Ernest Gruening, the only two men in Congress to vote against the resolution, opposed it as being a "predated declaration of war power." Subsequently it did serve as legal authorization for the escalation of the conflict.

By the beginning of 1965 the Vietcong, aided not only by supplies but also by military units coming from North Vietnam along the jungle "Ho Chi Minh trail" through Laos, were in the ascendancy. The American "advisers" had gradually become combatants and were already suffering serious casualties. At this point the United States began a rapid build-up of troops in South Vietnam and the launching of regular bombing attacks upon supply depots, army camps, and transportation lines in North Vietnam. In 1965 United States armed forces in Vietnam grew from 23,000 to over 180,000; in 1966, the number was doubled; by the end of 1967, it was approaching an authorized half-million. Air sorties were intensified until the tonnage of bombs being dropped exceeded that in Europe during World War II. Casualties mounted. By every statistic, the Vietnam War was becoming one of the most serious in United States history.

According to Johnson, the purpose of this enormous effort was to stop aggression and preserve the freedom of the South Vietnamese people. "We want nothing for ourselves," he declared in 1965, "—only that the people of South Vietnam be allowed to guide their own country in their own way." Yet the Johnson administration supported the military dictatorship of General Nguyen Van Thieu, who in 1965 seized control of the South Vietnamese government.

The Debate on Vietnam [1965]

A great debate on the Vietnamese conflict is now raging all over the United States. It goes from the White House, Congress and the Pentagon to every home, office, factory, and farm. It is unresolved because the Government has not yet decided on its policy or, if it has, President Johnson is not telling the American people. The debate's subject, in its simplest form, is whether to fight a big war in Vietnam or to seek a way out through a combination of continuing defense and diplomatic negotiation.

The case for a vastly stepped-up American military commitment—as set forth . . . by military analyst Hanson W. Baldwin—is that the "Communist strategy of creeping aggression" must be stopped in Vietnam before it swallows all of Asia and the world. Under this theory, the United States should undertake saturation bombing of North Vietnam and send as many as a million American soldiers, sailors and fliers into a "war to win."

Such an approach discards any pretense that our objective in Vietnam is to protect the Vietnamese people; it turns the conflict into a naked ideological struggle that ignores all the deep cleavages recent years have brought in both the Communist and free worlds. Not one of our major allies in the West could be expected to endorse, much less actively assist, an American involvement so massive it would amount to a military occupation of leaderless South Vietnam. America's efforts to demonstrate the superiority of its social system by abolishing poverty and building a Great Society would vanish under the necessity for pouring our youth and treasure into a limitless solo adventure.—The New York Times, February 21, 1965.

While the United States increased its economic and military aid to the Thieu regime, the Soviet Union and the People's Republic of China provided larger and larger shipments of arms and other supplies to the Ho Chi Minh government of North Vietnam, and the North Vietnamese stepped up their military action and their assistance to the Vietcong. The American intervention seemed to be bringing together the rival Communist superpowers, who had a mutual interest in preventing a Communist defeat in Vietnam. There appeared to be a danger that, if the United States should press its intervention to the point of victory for Thieu, the Chinese might intervene with their own troops in Vietnam as they had done earlier in Korea.

On occasions, the United States limited or halted its bombings and other offensive actions in efforts to persuade the North Vietnamese to begin negotiations. Each time North Vietnam refused, for the most part adhering to the position that the United States must unconditionally and permanently end all bombing. At times a further stipulation was attached to this condition: all American forces were to leave Vietnam.

President Johnson and his advisers refused to end the bombing unconditionally and permanently. They pointed out that during each bombing halt at the time of a holiday truce the North Vietnamese rushed men and supplies southward or prepared for new attacks. American military leaders, following a policy of seeking out and destroying enemy forces, were confident at the beginning of 1968 that given sufficient men and matériel they could eventually triumph.

DEESCALATION BEGINS

In the United States, where television brought pictures of the cruelty and destruction of the war into every living room, the war became more and more unpopular. Liberals and university students participated vigorously in demonstrations, "teach-ins," and "sit-ins." Some young men burned their draft cards. Senator Fulbright and a group of his colleagues became bitter critics of President Johnson and Secretary of State Rusk. Public opinion polls indicated that a majority of Americans still endorsed the war, but it had become the transcendent issue in the nation.

The drain of enthusiasm accelerated rapidly in the early months of 1968. During a truce in the fighting to observe Tet—the Chinese New Year—the Vietcong suddenly struck in

---

Why We Were in Vietnam [1965]

Speaking at the Johns Hopkins University on April 7, 1965, shortly after deciding to send combat troops to South Vietnam, President Johnson said that the "deepening shadow of Communist China" was falling over Asia and that the trouble in Vietnam was "part of a wider pattern of aggressive purpose." He continued:

Why are we in South Vietnam?

We are there because we have a promise to keep. Since 1954 every American President has offered to support the people of South Vietnam. We have helped to build and we have helped to defend. Thus, over many years, we have made a national pledge to help South Vietnam defend its independence.

I intend to keep our promise.

To dishonor that pledge, to abandon this small and brave nation to its enemy—and to the terror that must follow—would be an unforgivable wrong.

We are there to strengthen world order. Around the globe—from Berlin to Thailand—are people whose well-being rests, in part, on the belief they can count on us if they are attacked. To leave Vietnam to its fate would shake the confidence of all these people in the value of American commitment. The result would be increased unrest and instability, or even war.

almost every city of South Vietnam. They were dislodged only after days of bitter fighting, great devastation, and heavy casualties. The single blow destroyed the homes of a half-million South Vietnamese. The Tet offensive intensified the opposition to the war on the part of a growing segment of the American voters.

In the fall of 1967 Senator Eugene McCarthy of Minnesota had begun what seemed to be a futile protest campaign for the presidency. He had behind him only a handful of liberals and a growing group of enthusiastic students. In the first of the primary campaigns in New Hampshire, some of the young men cut their long hair and shaved their beards before ringing doorbells for McCarthy. In the voting, McCarthy was startlingly strong against Johnson, winning almost all of the delegates to the convention. The next day, Senator Robert Kennedy of New York, also a critic of the Vietnam War, announced his candidacy. There were indications that the challenge to President Johnson would be so strong that he might not be able to win renomination.

For months President Johnson had been considering a change in his course of action. On the evening of March 31, 1968, in a telecast to the nation, he suddenly announced that he was ordering a halt in the air attacks upon the populous areas of North Vietnam and was inviting the North Vietnamese to join him in a "series of mutual moves toward peace": "Tonight in the hope that this action will lead to early talks, I am taking the first step to de-escalate the conflict. We are reducing — substantially reducing — the present level of hostilities. And we are doing so unilaterally, and at once." At the close of his talk he made an announcement that removed any possibility that the deescalation could be looked upon as a political gesture: "I shall not seek and I will not accept the nomination of my party for another term."

The North Vietnamese government accepted President Johnson's invitation, and in May 1968 lengthy, fruitless negotiations began in Paris.

ELECTION OF 1968

During 1967 and 1968, the issues of the Vietnam War and urban violence became the focus of the preconvention presidential campaigns.

Significantly, the successful Republican contender, Richard Nixon, took no clear-cut stand on Vietnam. According to public opinion polls, he was running so far ahead in the first of the primary campaigns in New Hampshire that his principal opponent, Governor George Romney of Michigan, withdrew before the balloting. Nixon easily fended off last-minute threats from Governor Ronald Reagan of California on the right, and Governor Nelson Rockefeller of New York on the left, to win nomination on the first ballot. He chose Spiro Agnew, governor of Maryland, as his running mate.

The Vietnam debate, by contrast, wracked the Democratic party. After Johnson made his announcement not to run for another term, only Eugene McCarthy and Robert Kennedy (holding much the same views on Vietnam and domestic problems) were left to battle each other in the Democratic primaries. In late April, too late to become embroiled in the primaries, Vice President Humphrey entered the campaign. So many Democratic leaders in states without primaries backed Humphrey that he became an immediate favorite to win the nomination. Public attention focused on the primary contests. Kennedy won Indiana, lost Oregon to McCarthy, and then in the last primary in California, won again. At a Los Angeles hotel, on June 5, just after he had exhorted his cheering followers to seek victory with him at the Democratic convention, he was shot and killed by an assassin. National mourning for Kennedy brought a temporary cessation in the campaigning.

At the Democratic convention in Chicago, McCarthy (and some Kennedy followers backing Senator George McGovern of South Dakota) were unable to prevent the nomination of Humphrey on the first ballot. The critics of Humphrey, heir to administration policies, were bitter. Adding to their bitterness were the rough tactics of the Chicago police who shoved and harassed delegates and spectators to the convention, and before television cameras, clubbed and manhandled demonstrators in the streets of Chicago. An investigating committee subsequently referred to the violent police reactions to the taunts and attacks by the demonstrators as a "police riot." Through the campaign, Humphrey (although he had been distinguished for his liberalism throughout his political career) received little support from those who had followed McCarthy and Kennedy.

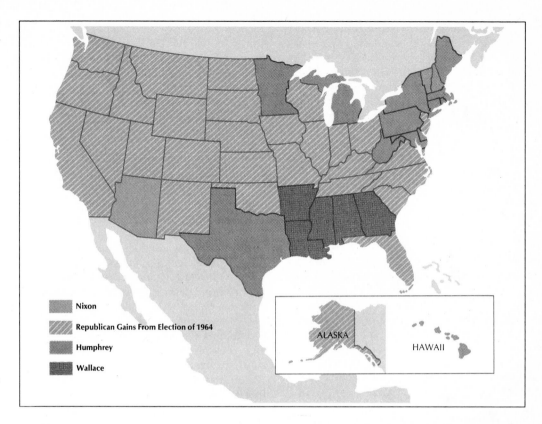

Nixon

Republican Gains From Election of 1964

Humphrey

Wallace

ALASKA

HAWAII

Election of 1968

The candidate who evoked the most enthusiastic responses and violent heckling wherever he spoke throughout the country was former Governor George Wallace of Alabama, running with General Curtis LeMay on the American Independent party ticket. "We are not talking about race," Wallace declared again and again, as he whipped up enthusiasm among audiences largely made up of white workers. General LeMay, who had been Chief of Staff of the Air Force, favored a hard line toward Vietnam. Public opinion polls showed Wallace at one point to be the favorite of a fifth of the voters; he hoped to throw the election into the House of Representatives. By Election Day his support had dropped substantially.

Neither of the major candidates evoked much enthusiasm. Nixon, campaigning methodically in almost computerized fashion, seemed far ahead from the outset. On the two main issues — law and order at home, and the Vietnam War — Nixon favored conciliation from a position of strength. He declared in his acceptance address that he would heed "the voice of the great majority of Americans, the forgotten Americans, the non-shouters, the non-demonstrators, that are not racists or sick, that are not guilty of the crime that plagues the land." Regarding the Vietnam War, he pointed out that at every point he had been a critic of the administration, and Humphrey its defender; beyond that comment he made little commitment.

In contrast to Nixon's campaign, Humphrey's seemed lacking in both planning and finance. On Vietnam, he and his opponent differed little, but on the problem of poverty he pledged federal aid for a massive "Marshall Plan for the cities" in contrast to Nixon's insistence that private capital must help the poor to help themselves. During the last weeks of the campaign, Humphrey's standing in the public opinion polls increased markedly, and the statements of both candidates became sharper.

Yet, as the front runner, Nixon refused to debate on television. Both candidates were occupying middle positions, with Nixon to the right and Humphrey to the left of center.

By a fairly narrow margin of some 500,000 votes, out of more than 73 million cast, Nixon defeated Humphrey. The electoral vote was far more decisive, 302 for Nixon to 191 for Humphrey and 45 for Wallace. In his victory statement, Nixon returned to a theme he had frequently touched upon during the campaign and asserted that "the great objective of this Administration at the outset" would be "to bring the American people together."

Nixon and a New Balance

Even more than Presidents Kennedy and Johnson, President Nixon preoccupied himself with foreign affairs. In doing so he failed to "bring the American people together" and, instead, aroused increasing bitterness and division among them when he frustrated the hope for an early withdrawal from Vietnam. Nevertheless, he won widespread approval by finally withdrawing and by redirecting basic policy in such a way as to improve the prospects for moderating the cold war and for realizing what he hailed as a "generation of peace."

THE NIXON-KISSINGER APPROACH

On the basis of his earlier experience as Vice President, Nixon considered himself something of an expert in diplomacy. During his first term as President, he depended on Secretary of State William P. Rogers, a New York corporation lawyer, to administer the State Department and to carry out certain diplomatic missions. He also turned frequently to Secretary of Defense Melvin R. Laird, a former Wisconsin congressman, for advice. But he relied mainly on his special assistant for national security affairs, Henry A. Kissinger, a Harvard professor of international politics, for aid in both the making and the execution of policy. For four years, Kissinger's White House office overshadowed the Department of State. Then, after the inauguration of Nixon for a second term, the President put Kissinger at the head of the department. A refugee from Nazi Germany, Kissinger was the first German-born and the first Jewish Secretary of State (though a foreign-born Jew, Judah P. Benjamin, had been Secretary of State in the Confederacy during the Civil War).

Before his appointment as Nixon's security adviser, Kissinger in books and articles had criticized the assumptions on which American policy was based. To him, as well as to some other observers, it seemed that the developments of the 1960s had made obsolete the containment policy of the 1950s. The signs of growing antagonism between Communist China and Communist Russia belied the concept of a single, combined program of Communist aggression. No longer were there only two power centers, the United States and the Soviet Union; there were now at least three, with China, and potentially more than that, if western Europe and Japan were to be included. For this new "multipolar" world, Kissinger proposed a flexible, many-sided balance-of-power system to take the place of the rigid, two-sided system that had prevailed since the start of the cold war. In the new arrangement the United States would deal with Russia and China on the basis of practical interests rather than anti-Communist feelings.

Early in his first administration Nixon implied a change in policy when he put forth what he termed the Nixon Doctrine. The United States, he declared, would "participate in the defense and development of allies and friends" but would leave the "basic responsibility" to those friends themselves, especially when it came to actual fighting. In 1971 he clearly announced the new aim of a complex equilibrium: "It will be a safer world and a better world if we have a strong healthy United States, Europe, Soviet Union, China, Japan—each balancing the other, not playing one against the other, an even balance."

When Nixon decided to open relations with the Chinese People's Republic and to improve relations with the Soviet Union, his decision was in keeping with the new diplomacy that he and Kissinger had proposed. Meanwhile Nixon continued the war in Vietnam, though Kissinger believed that American involvement had been based on "an outmoded foreign policy concept." Nixon undertook to "Vietnamize" the war—that is, to shift the burden of actual combat from Americans to the South Vietnamese, in accordance with the Nixon Doctrine—but the process was painfully slow.

VIETNAMIZATION   1969–1972

Regarding Vietnam, Nixon said in May 1969 that he hoped to achieve "a peace we can live with and a peace to be proud of." He did not specify the kind of peace he had in mind, but presumably it would be one that kept in power the Thieu regime in Saigon. Whatever the details, his kind of peace, like Lyndon B. Johnson's, remained unacceptable to the Ho Chi Minh government of Hanoi. In Paris the talks

Vietnamese Children Flee Napalm
Terrified children with napalm burns run from the village of Trang Ban, southwest of Saigon in South Vietnam, when South Vietnamese government planes mistakenly drop fire bombs on the village, June 8, 1972. (UPI)

went on—among the representatives of the United States, South Vietnam, North Vietnam, and the National Liberation Front—but rumors of progress toward a settlement proved disappointing again and again. The demise of Ho Chi Minh, late in the summer, had no visible effect on either the Paris negotiations or the Vietnam bloodshed.

As the months passed and no end to the fighting appeared in sight, "Johnson's war" began to be looked upon as "Nixon's war," and its critics in Congress and throughout the country grew in numbers and determination. By the summer's end an opinion poll showed a clear majority of the American people believed the involvement in Vietnam was a mistake. Youthful peace advocates were planning a series of nationwide demonstrations to occupy one day in October, two days in November, three in December, and so on, until the United States was out of the war. Nixon turned opinion in favor of his Vietnam policy, however, by a televised speech on November 3, 1969. He said the "silent majority" agreed with him that a "precipitate withdrawal" would be "disastrous for the future of peace" in the world. Vice President Agnew afterward denounced the peace demonstrators as an "effete corps of impudent snobs" and reprimanded newspaper and television commentators for daring to question the Nixon policy.

Making a concession to the war's critics, Nixon had announced earlier the beginning of partial troop withdrawals, the first of which would reduce by 60,000 the United States force of about 540,000 men in Vietnam. These withdrawals, he explained, were steps toward the "Vietnamization" of the war. That is, the South Vietnamese themselves would be trained and equipped to take over the defense of their country as the American fighting men were gradually pulled out.

Nixon also sought to lessen opposition by reforming the draft, which because of its uncertainties and inequities added to the difficulty of justifying the sacrifice of American lives in a small and distant country. To its critics, the draft seemed all the worse because of the highhanded way in which it was administered. Its director persisted in advising local draft boards to punish antiwar demonstrators by conscripting them, even after a federal court had held this to be illegal. Nixon recommended that the conscription law be changed so as to provide

for a "draft lottery" that would take only nineteen-year-olds and would take them at random. Such a lottery went into effect in 1970. Going still further, Nixon urged the formation of an all-volunteer army, with improved pay and other incentives for enlistment. By 1973, Americans were no longer being drafted.

The Vietnamization plan was going so well, Nixon announced in April 1970, that he would bring home 150,000 additional men within a year or so. Suddenly, before the end of April, he broke the startling news that he had ordered American troops to cross into neutral Cambodia and, with their South Vietnamese allies, to seize military bases that the enemy had been using for operations in South Vietnam. He explained that "increased military aggression" by the Communists in Cambodia had begun to jeopardize the continuing success of the Vietnamization program.

Up to this point, Nixon said, it had been American policy "to scrupulously respect the neutrality" of Cambodia. What he did not tell the people was that the United States was already deliberately and systematically violating Cambodian neutrality. For more than a year he had personally authorized the secret bombing of suspected North Vietnamese bases on the Cambodian side of the border. For several years American ground forces had been carrying on clandestine operations in Cambodia and in Laos as well. If these facts had been made public at the time, the popular protest in the United States might have gone to even greater extremes than it actually went.

At the news of the Cambodian incursion, the languishing peace movement came to life with a more determined spirit than ever. On campuses all over this country, during May, youthful protesters demanded that the universities close down in a "strike" against the government's war policy. A radical minority resorted to violence, smashing windows and fire-bombing buildings. Policemen and national guardsmen arrived to face rock-throwing mobs, which they tried to disperse with tear gas and, in a few instances, with gunfire. Four students (all white) were shot and killed at Kent State University in Ohio, and two (both black) at Jackson State University in Mississippi. A few months later a physicist died when antiwar protesters set off an explosion that wrecked several buildings at the University of Wisconsin in Madison.

Kent State Killings

*Students at Kent State University, Kent, Ohio, come to the aid of
a fellow student who was wounded when, on May 4, 1970, national
guardsmen fired tear gas and then bullets, killing four students
and injuring several others. The guardsmen were on the campus to
put down antiwar demonstrations, which had culminated in the burning
of a university building. (UPI)*

After ending the invasion of Cambodia, in June 1970, Nixon launched an invasion of Laos, in February 1971. This time he sent no American ground troops (Congress in the Defense Appropriations Act of 1970 had prohibited their use in Laos) but gave American air support to the invading South Vietnamese army. "The South Vietnamese by themselves can hack it," he declared. This was a test of his Vietnamization program, and it proved a failure. Within a few weeks the badly mauled army scrambled back to the relative safety of South Vietnam.

American critics of "Nixon's war," like those of "Johnson's war," were appalled by the horrible sufferings it brought upon civilians, both South Vietnamese and North Vietnamese. Millions of them were deprived of life, health, shelter, or livelihood as a result of American action—napalm bombing, population transfer, village destruction, crop burning, and forest defoliation. Hundreds were shot or bayoneted by American soldiers, as in the "My Lai massacre" (March 16, 1968), for which Lieutenant William L. Calley, Jr., was convicted of premeditated murder in 1971.

Nixon had said the Calley case should be vigorously prosecuted, so that the incident would not "smear the decent men" who had gone to war in Vietnam. Continuing his troop withdrawals, he announced in January 1972 that the total of American troops in Vietnam would shortly be reduced to 69,000, the lowest figure in nearly seven years. As troops were withdrawn, American casualties in the war decreased, and so did the outcry at home. Yet, while taking out ground forces, Nixon was sending in more and more air and naval forces. Eventually he authorized the dropping of a greater tonnage of bombs than Johnson had, and these bombs killed far more civilians than the 102 that Calley was charged with murdering at My Lai. Nixon ordered his greatest escalation of the war against the Vietnamese Communists after he had dramatically displayed his friendship with the Chinese and Russian Communists.

RAPPROCHEMENT WITH CHINA

Until 1949 the United States had sought to maintain the Open Door policy in China. Then, after the Communists under Mao Tse-tung and Chou En-lai got control of the Chinese mainland, the doors were closed on both sides. The Peking government taught hatred of Americans and excluded them from the country. The Washington government prohibited trade between the United States and the Chinese mainland, refused to recognize the Mao regime, and opposed its being represented in the United Nations. Washington continued to treat Chiang Kai-shek, after his flight to the island of Taiwan, as an ally and as the rightful head of all China.

From 1949 to 1971, no American in national politics had opposed the recognition of the Peking government more resolutely than had Richard M. Nixon. Eventually, making a complete turnabout, he reopened relations in a spectacular display of presidential diplomacy.

Recognition was long past due. China was the largest nation in the world, with about a quarter of all the world's people. It was one of the nuclear powers, having set off its first atomic bomb in 1964 and its first hydrogen bomb in 1967. By making friends with the Peking leaders, Nixon could hope to get their cooperation in ending the Vietnam War. He could also hope to use China as a counterbalance to the Soviet Union and thus as a means of inducing in the Russians a conciliatory mood and hastening a détente. The Chinese leaders, for their part, were eager to have the United States as a potentiality in their own balance-of-power arrangement against the Soviet Union. They feared that the Russians might attack China in an attempt to destroy the Chinese nuclear installations.

Early in 1971 Nixon hinted at a change in American policy when, in a public statement,

he used the legitimate name "People's Republic of China" for what he and other American officials always had called simply "Red China" or "Communist China." That spring the Peking government invited a team of American table-tennis players to visit China, and the Nixon administration gave them permission to go. Such "Ping-Pong diplomacy" led to speculation about higher-level contacts between the two countries but hardly prepared the American people for the startling announcement Nixon made in July. He said he himself had received an invitation to visit the People's Republic (an invitation that Kissinger had arranged on a secret trip to Peking) and would make the visit within the next several months.

To succeed in his new China policy, Nixon would have to approve the admission of the People's Republic to the United Nations. In the past the American delegates to the U.N. had repeatedly managed to prevent the seating of a Peking delegate, but the majorities on the American side had been growing smaller and smaller. Now the United States representative proposed giving a seat on the Security Council to the People's Republic while keeping a place for Nationalist China, that is, Taiwan. The Chinese Communists insisted, however, that the Chinese Nationalists must go. In October 1971 the United Nations admitted the People's Republic and expelled Nationalist China.

Nixon's China visit, when it finally came in February 1972, proved to be a theatrical success. For a whole week American television with Chinese cooperation followed the President and his entourage and explored various aspects of life in what had been to Americans a relatively unknown, mysterious land. Nixon was shown visiting the Great Wall and other tourist attractions, wining and dining with Communist dignitaries, exchanging pleasantries with party leader Mao Tse-tung and Premier Chou En-lai. Never before had a summit meeting been so elaborately staged or so extensively viewed. One effect was to reduce, if not to reverse, the anti-Chinese feelings that had been instilled in the American people for a generation.

The summit meeting was also something of a diplomatic success. In Peking the leaders of the two countries agreed to scientific, cultural, journalistic, and other exchanges and to the development of trade. They did not agree to the immediate establishment of formal rela-

Nixon in China
The first American President to visit China while in office, Nixon received a carefully staged welcome from the Chinese Communist leaders. On the day of his arrival, February 21, 1972, he was invited to review an honor guard of the Chinese army in company with Premier Chou En-lai. (UPI)

tions, with an exchange of ambassadors. The Communists, looking on Taiwan as part of their country, refused to accept an embassy from the United States so long as Taiwan had one. The United States must first break off diplomatic relations with Nationalist China. If the summit conferees arrived at any understanding in regard to the Vietnam War, they made no public announcement of the fact.

On subsequent journeys to Peking, Kissinger worked out details of trade arrangements and other matters and managed, as he put it, to "accelerate the normalization of relations." A year after the Nixon visit, the two countries agreed to set up "liaison offices" in each other's capitals. Except in name, these offices practically amounted to embassies. The United States was expected soon to remove some of the 9,000 American troops on Taiwan. By 1973, it appeared that relations with China were getting back to normal, after nearly a quarter century of nonrecognition and estrangement.

DÉTENTE WITH RUSSIA

Nixon had been the first American President to make a trip, while in office, to China; he was the second to travel to Russia. His Russian visit, in May 1972, provided less drama, for there was less mystery about the Soviet Union, less to be revealed to the American public. Yet the summit conference in Moscow was even more important than the one in Peking, since the Soviet Union, like the United States, was a true superpower, and China, as yet, was not.

From both the Russian and the American points of view, the time was ripe for a move toward a new understanding. The Soviet government, under the leadership of Communist party chief Leonid Brezhnev, looked to the United States for possible future support against China, for aid in overcoming Russia's technological lag, and for wheat and other foodstuffs to make up for her serious crop shortages. Having achieved something like nuclear parity with the United States, the Russians also were interested in the economies of slowing down the arms race. Nixon and his advisers shared the desire for a limitation of nuclear armaments, wished to promote American trade, and hoped for Soviet cooperation in ending the war in Vietnam and preventing war in other parts of the world, especially in the Middle East.

By 1972 the United States still led the Soviet Union in the number of long-range planes kept in readiness for delivering nuclear bombs. Moreover, this country had almost twice as many submarines equipped with nuclear mis-

An English View of Détente
With President Nixon visiting the Russian Communist leader Brezhnev in 1972, and Brezhnev returning the visit in 1973, America's NATO allies became distrustful of the summit diplomacy between the two. Fears grew that Nixon was sacrificing the interests of the United States as well as those of NATO. These feelings are reflected in this cartoon, which appeared in the Daily Express *of London on June 25, 1973. (Cummings/London* Daily Express*)*

"Which rumour is true, Mr. Agnew? Is Russia about to become the 52nd State of America, or Mr. Nixon to become Vice-President of Russia after he's fired from the White House?"

siles. But the Soviet Union had moved ahead in regard to land-based intercontinental ballistic missiles, or ICBMs, which could carry nuclear explosives all the way from the one country to the other.

The two superpowers were engaged in a "doomsday game" of competition in the development of more and more deadly weapons and delivery systems—a game that could conceivably lead to mutual annihilation. Each of the two was testing a multiple independently targeted reentry vehicle, or MIRV, a device that could be sent into orbit and then directed back into the earth's atmosphere above the enemy's territory, where it would drop separate nuclear warheads on widely scattered targets. Each nation was also planning an antiballistic-missile system, or ABM, which was intended to protect population centers or ICBM emplacements against missile attack. In the ABM system, nuclear "antimissile missiles" would be launched to intercept and explode approaching enemy missiles before these could reach their targets. The Nixon administration's ABM project aroused considerable opposition in the United States. Critics said the ABM would have little effect on ICBMs and still less on MIRVs but would endanger civilians in its vicinity and would intensify the arms race.

Already the United States and the Soviet Union had taken a small step toward the control of nuclear weapons, a step beyond the 1963 treaty banning atmospheric tests. In the "nonproliferation" treaty of 1968 the two powers agreed to discourage the spread of nuclear weapon technology to nations not yet possessing it. Great Britain was the only other nuclear power to sign the treaty, but France and China were producing their own hydrogen bombs, and Israel and India (among other countries) appeared to be capable of doing so. The treaty, then, did not prevent a widening of the arms race, nor did it lessen the competition between the two front runners.

The two took a step toward lessening this competition when, in 1969, American and Russian diplomats met in Helsinki to begin discussion of a strategic arms limitation treaty, or SALT. After continuing their talks, in Vienna, for two years and a half, the negotiators arrived at a temporary agreement. This first-phase treaty, or SALT I, would limit each country to only two ABMs and the existing number of

ICBMs. The compromise would leave the United States superior in numbers of warheads and the Soviet Union, with its warheads of greater size, superior in total megatonnage. The limitations were to last for five years. Applying only to quantity and not to quality, they would do nothing to prevent a continuing and even heightening contest for arms improvements in the meantime.

At their Moscow meeting in 1972, Nixon and Brezhnev signed SALT I and several other agreements. One of these promised a vast expansion of trade through American tariff reductions and credit extensions. A gigantic "wheat deal" led immediately to the sale of about a fourth of the total American wheat supply at a bargain price, one well below the market price, and the American government was to make up the difference by means of subsidies to the American wheat sellers. The prospect of a reduction in arms spending, however, did not last long. After Nixon's return from Moscow, the administration asked Congress to approve the largest military budget ever except during a declared war.

In June 1973 Nixon welcomed Brezhnev to Washington for a round of partying and further negotiating. A series of new agreements confirmed and extended those of the previous year. The two countries pledged to abstain from nuclear war, to speed up the conclusion of SALT II for a permanent "freeze" on offensive nuclear arms, and to cooperate in various economic, scientific, and cultural fields. Toasting his Russian guest at a dinner, Nixon said: "The question is: Shall the world's two strongest nations constantly confront one another in areas which might lead to war, or shall we work together for peace?" The question remained to be answered, despite all the talk of détente.

EXIT FROM INDOCHINA

Nixon's China and Russia diplomacy gave him added strength in his conduct of the Vietnam War. Neither China nor Russia stopped sending military supplies to North Vietnam, but both powers indicated that there were limits to their aid. Apparently each was somewhat reluctant to risk damaging its new relationship with the United States.

Vietnam Cease-Fire Agreement [1973]

Following are some of the key provisions of the "agreement on ending the war and restoring peace in Vietnam" that American and Vietnamese representatives signed on January 27, 1973:

Article 1. "The United States and all other countries respect the independence, sovereignty, unity, and territorial integrity of Vietnam as recognized by the 1954 Geneva Agreements on Vietnam."

Article 5. "Within 60 days of the signing of this agreement, there will be a total withdrawal from South Vietnam of troops, military advisers, and military personnel . . . of the United States. . . ."

Article 8. "The return of captured military personnel and foreign civilians of the parties shall be carried out simultaneously with and completed not later than the same day as the troop withdrawal. . . ."

Article 9. "The South Vietnamese people shall decide themselves the political future of South Vietnam through genuinely free and democratic general elections under international supervision."

Article 15. "The reunification of Vietnam shall be carried out step by step through peaceful means on the basis of discussion and agreements between North and South Vietnam, without coercion or annexation by either party, and without foreign interference. . . . Pending the reunification . . . The military demarcation line between the two zones at the 17th parallel is only provisional and not a political or territorial boundary, as provided for in paragraph 6 of the Final Declaration of the 1954 Geneva Conference."

Between Nixon's China visit and his Russia visit, the fighting in Vietnam actually intensified, going in some respects to greater lengths than ever before. In March 1972 the North Vietnamese launched their heaviest attack since the Tet offensive of 1968. Well equipped with tanks and artillery, they crossed into South Vietnam and proceeded to overrun much of its territory. In April Nixon responded by sending B-52 bombers to strike near Hanoi and Haiphong, thus reversing Johnson's 1968 decision to deescalate the air war in the north. On May 8—just before his scheduled trip to Peking—Nixon ordered the mining of Haiphong harbor and six other North Vietnamese ports, so as to prevent the delivery of war supplies by ship from China or the Soviet Union. Johnson had refrained from this extreme measure for fear it would provoke retaliation from one or both of those two countries. Now they confined themselves to comparatively mild protests.

In July 1972 the Paris peace negotiators (representing the two Vietnams, the Vietcong, and the United States) met for their 150th session, with no indication that, after four years, they were making any progress toward a settlement. It had recently come to light, however,

that Kissinger and North Vietnamese Foreign Secretary Le Duc Tho were meeting separately and secretly, and it was rumored that they were nearing a cease-fire agreement. "Peace is at hand," Kissinger finally announced on October 26, just before the American presidential election. The North Vietnamese government was ready and eager to accept the terms that Kissinger and Tho had arrived at, but President Thieu of South Vietnam raised objections, and Nixon refused to give his approval. On December 16, after Kissinger and Tho had broken off negotiations, Kissinger declared that the agreement was 99 percent complete, but he did not explain what the missing 1 percent consisted of.

The next day, December 17, without any announcement from the White House, American planes began to bomb North Vietnamese cities in the heaviest and most destructive raids of the entire war. The targets were docks, airfields, railyards, power plants, antiaircraft defenses, and the like, but these were located in or near residential areas, and homes, shops, schools, and even hospitals were hit. The destruction was achieved at considerable cost to the Americans. In the previous seven years of the Vietnam War, only one B-52 bomber had been lost in combat. Now, in two weeks of round-the-clock raiding, fifteen of the high-flying giant planes fell when struck by Russian-made surface-to-air missiles. On December 30 Nixon called off the bombing and announced that the North Vietnamese had consented to resuming the secret peace talks.

On January 27, 1973, representatives of the four parties (the United States and South Vietnam, North Vietnam and the "Provisional Revolutionary Government" of South Vietnam, that is, the Vietcong) signed an "agreement on ending the war and restoring peace in Vietnam." The main provisions of this agreement were the same as those of the October 1972 agreement, which Nixon had refused to approve. There was to be an immediate cease-fire, and within sixty days prisoners of war were to be returned and foreign military forces in South Vietnam were to be withdrawn. Contradictorily, both the South Vietnamese right of self-determination and the unity of all Vietnam, North and South, were recognized. Laos and Cambodia were to be evacuated, and their independence and neutrality were to be respected. An international commission was to supervise the cease-fire.

Nixon proclaimed that at last he had won a "peace with honor." In fact, he had gained two things in the peace arrangement. One was the return of several hundred American prisoners of war (whose numbers, incidentally, he had recently increased through the Christmas-season bombing and the exposure of downed B-52 crews to capture). The other gain for Nixon was to keep Thieu in power in South Vietnam for the time being. But Nixon had also yielded a lot in the truce terms. These included several references to the 1954 Geneva settlement, which the United States had never signed. They reconfirmed the Geneva principle of the ultimate reunification of Vietnam. That was what the North Vietnamese and the Vietcong had been fighting for, and at the time of the cease-fire they were in a strong position for achieving it, since they now occupied a large part of South Vietnam's territory.

Such were the inconclusive results of more than a decade of direct American military involvement in Vietnam, and they had been accomplished at a staggering cost. In money, this exceeded $100 billion for the United States

alone. In lives, it was approximately 1 million Vietnamese Communists, 200,000 South Vietnamese, and 55,000 Americans. Some 300,000 Americans were wounded, half of them seriously, and many of these permanently maimed. A total of about 3 million Americans served in the war, most of them unwillingly. Perhaps as many as 70,000 evaded service by dodging the draft or deserting after enlistment. Thousands of deserters and draft dodgers remained in hiding at home or in refuge abroad, particularly in Canada and Sweden, as Nixon with the backing of a public majority vowed to grant no amnesty. The psychological cost to Americans, both veterans and nonveterans, was incalculable. Never since the Civil War had the people been so badly divided. Understandably, the announcement of peace, after the longest war in American history, provoked no such demonstrations of popular rejoicing as had followed World War I and World War II.

There was no peace in Vietnam. The international commission, set up to supervise the cease-fire, was powerless to keep the Communists and the non-Communists apart. During the first year after the cease-fire the Vietnamese (both sides together) suffered more battle deaths than the Americans had suffered during the ten years before it. In Laos the fighting ended about a month after the cease-fire, when the Communists were left in control of more than half the country. In Cambodia the war continued, and American planes kept up and intensified their bombing in an effort to save the Lon Nol regime from its Communist enemies. Nixon refused to stop the bombing of Cambodia until Congress compelled him to do so.

Congress had been growing more and more critical of the President's assertion of warmaking powers without any congressional declaration of war, and both the Senate and the House had begun to consider proposals, mild at first, for holding him to constitutional limits. In 1969 the Senate advised the President that, in the future, he should get the approval of Congress before committing the United States to the use of armed forces abroad. In 1971 Congress repealed the 1964 Gulf of Tonkin resolution, which Johnson and Nixon had treated as the equivalent of a war declaration. Congress could have stopped the war by cutting off appropriations for it, but this would have been unpopular, since it would have looked like

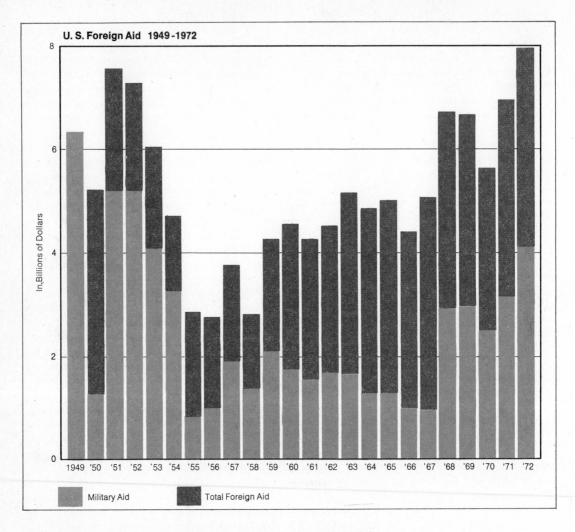

U. S. Foreign Aid 1949–1972

In Billions of Dollars

Military Aid   Total Foreign Aid

Since 1949 both the total amount expended to aid foreign countries and the proportion of this amount expended for military purposes have fluctuated from year to year. The nonmilitary expenditures have been intended chiefly to provide technical assistance, machinery, food, and capital loans. The growth in military aid after 1967 mainly reflects the increase in support for the government of South Vietnam.

abandoning American soldiers in the field. Nixon maintained that, as commander in chief, he had the power to use the armed forces as he saw fit in order to protect the troops while he was withdrawing them under his Vietnamization plan.

After the signing of the cease-fire and the withdrawal of the troops, Nixon no longer had that justification for waging war as he and his advisers saw fit. When he persisted in bombing Cambodia, despite congressional protests,

Congress set August 15, 1973, as a deadline for the cessation of all American military activity in Indochina, including the air warfare in Cambodia. Nixon discontinued the bombing only at the last minute.

Several months later Congress passed, over Nixon's veto, a measure intended to prevent a President from involving the country in future wars without congressional approval. Under this war-powers resolution of 1973, the President could order no troops into action without reporting to Congress, and he would have to halt the action immediately if Congress objected, or in ninety days if Congress failed to give its positive permission. The new law was a response to a growth in presidential power that Congresses as well as Presidents had been fostering for many years. Whether the measure was wise for the nuclear age, and whether it would work in any case, only time could tell.

OLD FRIENDSHIPS UNDER STRAIN

While relations with China and Russia were improving, relations with Japan, Western Germany, Great Britain, and other allies were getting worse.

The American conduct of the Vietnam War antagonized many Europeans. Some felt the United States was neglecting western Europe while preoccupying itself with Southeast Asia. Some were outraged by the warfare upon Vietnamese civilians, especially by the 1972 Christmas-season bombing of North Vietnamese cities.

The switch in American policy toward China and Russia disturbed the leaders of Japan and the western European countries. Japan, which had looked to the United States for security against China, now worried about the prospect of being abandoned. West Germany, under Chancellor Willy Brandt, approved of détente and was furthering it by making treaties with the Soviet Union and its Polish and East German satellites. To offset the risks of his new diplomacy, however, Brandt counted upon all-out American assistance in case of a Russian threat, and he wondered if he could be sure of such support after Nixon's negotiations with Brezhnev. British officials suspected that, in the negotiations, Nixon had gained less than he had given up. In general, the allies were uneasy at the thought of the United States going over their heads and dealing directly with the Communist powers.

Both American and European spokesmen pledged their respective governments' continued devotion to the North Atlantic Alliance as the alliance approached the twenty-fifth year of its existence. After the Vietnam cease-fire an American official said, "we have not been neglecting Europe. It is just a matter of Vietnam moving off the stage, and we now see that Europe is the center of the stage, as it normally is." Kissinger declared 1973 to be "the year of Europe" and proposed a "new Atlantic Charter" that would include Japan. Nixon was expected to offset his summit diplomacy with China and Russia by going to Japan and Europe to conclude new understandings with them. But his trips were repeatedly postponed.

The constant repetition of mutual reassurances, on the part of American and European leaders, was itself a sign that NATO was in serious trouble. American leaders had to pay some attention to the voice of the people, and more and more the American people were questioning the necessity of keeping United States troops in Europe (most of them, about 215,000, in West Germany). In response to popular demand, some of the Democrats in Congress were proposing to compel a reduction in the number of American troops abroad.

Nixon, along with Brandt and other western European leaders, opposed the withdrawal of American forces from western Europe unless there should be a corresponding withdrawal of Russian forces from Eastern Europe. Nixon and Brezhnev, at their 1972 Moscow meeting, had agreed to the calling of a European security conference for the discussion of "mutual balanced force reductions" on both sides, and MBFR talks were getting under way in Vienna. Meanwhile the American government disagreed with its European allies about the sharing of NATO costs. The Nixon administration insisted that the allies, now that they were financially strong, ought to make larger contributions than they had been making to the common defense.

Toward the European Economic Community (the Common Market), the American government's attitude had become ambivalent by 1973. On the one hand, the United States still officially favored the strengthening of the EEC and approved its enlargement when Great Britain was finally admitted, along with Ireland and Denmark. On the other hand, the United States seemed to fear the economic competition of the EEC and complained that it was discriminating against American exports.

Already there was a crisis in trade and monetary relations between the United States and both Japan and Europe. For years, the American government and American citizens had been spending larger and larger quantities of dollars abroad, for tourist travel, foreign goods, capital investments, and economic and military aid. The expenditures on the Vietnam War, after its escalation in 1964, added greatly to the dollar outflow. All together, Americans spent far more in foreign countries than foreigners spent in the United States. Hence the balance of payments was upset, and the dollar tended to lose value in relation to foreign currencies.

To keep the various currencies in a stable relationship with one another, the gold standard had been reestablished and the International Monetary Fund had been set up at the end of World War II. The price of gold was then fixed (as it had been since 1934) at $35 an ounce—which meant that the dollar was worth 1/35 of an ounce of gold. The International Monetary Fund was to buy currencies when necessary to stop their decline in value, but the surplus of dollars proved too much for the Fund's resources. Foreign holders of excess dollars began to exchange them for gold, and by 1968 the United States was suffering a serious depletion of its gold supply. At that time, President de Gaulle of France was glad to see the United States financially weakened, but six other European governments joined with the American government in agreeing not to sell their gold to private buyers but to use it only for transactions among themselves. For these transactions, the price was kept at $35 an ounce. On the regular gold market it was allowed to rise and fall in accordance with supply and demand.

This two-price arrangement seemed to work for a time, as the exchange rate remained constant between the dollar and the yen, mark, pound, franc, and lira. But the balance-of-payments gap persisted and, to make up for it, the American government had to transfer gold to other governments. By 1971 the Nixon administration felt compelled to take drastic steps. It put a temporary 10 percent surcharge on imports. Then it stopped giving up gold in return for the dollars that foreign governments held. This meant that the exchange rates were no longer controlled, and the dollar price of other currencies, especially the mark and the yen, began to rise. Finally Nixon did what no President since Franklin D. Roosevelt had done—he officially devalued the dollar. He raised the official price of gold from $35 to $38 an ounce and thus reduced the gold content of the dollar from 1/35 to 1/38 of an ounce. In 1973

he further devalued the dollar, raising the gold price to $42.

Devaluation was intended to overcome the balance-of-payments deficit by causing Americans to buy less of foreign goods and services, and foreigners to buy more of American goods and services. But the deficit kept growing, and the dollar kept falling. By the summer of 1973 it was worth only a little more than half as many German marks as it formerly had been. To cut down imports, the Nixon administration threatened to raise tariffs and to impose other trade controls, while the Japanese and the Europeans protested. By this time, exports had begun to increase, with large shipments abroad of American wheat and other crops. Now, to cut down on exports and prevent shortages at home, the administration put limits on the foreign sale of farm commodities and steel scrap, thus provoking new protests, especially on the part of Japan.

The international trade and monetary system of the preceding quarter century appeared to have broken down, and economic conflicts between the United States and its allies were putting a serious strain on the alliances.

TROUBLE IN NONPOWER REGIONS

The Nixon-Kissinger theory of five power centers left a subordinate place for the nonpower regions of the world, the distinctly weaker countries of Latin America, Asia, and Africa. Yet clashes arising in these areas could jeopardize relations among the powerful, as the Vietnam War at times had seemed likely to do.

During Nixon's presidency, the relations of the United States with many of the Latin American countries deteriorated. At the outset his personal representative, Governor Nelson Rockefeller of New York, on a fact-finding tour, ran into popular hostility like that which Nixon himself had experienced when, as Vice President, he made a similar trip in 1958. Capitalizing upon the popular sentiment, new military governments in Peru and Bolivia seized the property of American corporations. The constitutionally elected government of the radical Salvador Allende did the same in Chile. In retaliation, Nixon undertook to block financial aid, from either American or international sources, to Chile and other countries that failed to compensate American property owners satisfactorily. It was revealed that officials of the International Telephone and Telegraph Company, an American-based multinational corporation having extensive holdings in Chile, had consulted with officials of the Central Intelligence Agency about possible methods of preventing Allende's election to the Chilean presidency. This revelation lent some credence to the charge, in 1973, after Allende's overthrow and death in a military coup, that the American government had connived with his opponents.

In Asia the Nixon administration reversed American policy toward India while reversing it toward China. Previous administrations had tried to encourage the development of India, the largest democracy in the world, as an offset to China, the largest Communist nation. They had also given arms aid to Pakistan, a military dictatorship, for defense against the Chinese. Pakistan had used its American equipment in clashes with India, however, and had become more and more friendly with China.

In 1971 the Pakistani ruler, Yahya Khan, ordered his armed forces to put down discontent in East Pakistan, and they attempted to do so by killing hundreds of thousands of civilians. Millions of East Pakistanis took refuge in India, where they constituted a grave burden for India's economy. India's Prime Minister, Indira Gandhi, turned to the Soviet Union for support, signed a friendship treaty with Brezhnev, and launched a war to detach East Pakistan from the rule of Yahya Khan. During this Indo-Pakistani war, Nixon wanted the United States to "tilt in favor of Pakistan," and he ordered an American fleet to the Bay of Bengal, thus giving Indians the impression that he was trying to intimidate them. India quickly won the war and proclaimed the independence of East Pakistan under the name of Bangladesh. The Nixon policy accomplished nothing except to reinforce the India-Russia alignment and lessen American influence on the Indian subcontinent.

The Middle East, the scene of continual fighting between Arabs and Israelis, presented a dilemma for the Nixon administration, as it had done for previous administrations. Israel (whose prime minister, Golda Meir, was a former Milwaukee schoolteacher) had many sympathizers, both Jewish and non-Jewish, within the United States. They could exert considerable pressure in American politics. The Arab countries could count upon no such American constituency, but they possessed two-thirds of the world's known oil reserves, and they occupied areas that were of strategic importance to the United States in its global conflict with the Soviet Union. So long as the United States backed the Israelis, it antagonized the Arabs and tended to throw them into the Russian embrace. If, however, the United States should discontinue its support, Israel might face destruction as an independent country.

Violence in the Middle East had been renewed in 1967, after a United Nations peacekeeping force had been withdrawn at the demand of Egypt. Expecting an attack from Egypt, which was well equipped with Russian arms, Israel struck and in the Six-Day War defeated Egypt, Jordan, and Syria and occupied parts of their territory. A 1967 U.N. resolution called upon Israel to withdraw her armed forces from the occupied territories, but recognized the right of every nation in the area to "live in peace within secure and recognized boundaries." Israel refused to budge without guarantees of her security. After the 1967 war Israel rearmed with American aid, and Egypt and Syria with Russian aid. Intermittent shelling and raiding went on across the borders between Israel and her neighbors.

The Nixon administration, at first, attempted an "even-handed" policy in the Middle East. Nixon hoped for a compromise that would satisfy both sides and make it unnecessary for Egypt or Syria to depend on the Soviet Union. The Russians cooperated to the extent of agreeing to U.N. mediation, which resulted only in a brief truce, in 1970. Then Palestinian Arabs, living as refugees in Jordan, revolted against Jordan's King Hussein, who was trying to stay on good terms with Israel and the United States. While Hussein was putting down the rebellion, Nixon made a display of naval strength in the Mediterranean Sea, presumably as a warning to Russia against allowing Egypt to intervene in Jordan. Thereafter the Soviet Union rapidly increased its naval force in the Mediterranean, and Russian ships soon outnumbered American vessels there.

After 1972 the détente between the United States and the Soviet Union could have been expected to defuse the explosive Middle Eastern situation. In October 1973, however, war again erupted, when on the Jewish holy day of

Peacemaking in the Middle East

In the spring of 1974, after repeated visits to Egypt, Israel, and Syria, Secretary of State Kissinger succeeded in working out a cease-fire between Egypt and Israel and then between Syria and Israel. After accepting his plan for troop disengagements along the Syrian border, Israeli leaders gave him their thanks at a farewell party in Jerusalem on May 29. He was photographed at the party with Israeli Premier Golda Meir and Religious Affairs Minister Yitzhak Rafael. (Wide World Photos)

Yom Kippur the Egyptians and the Syrians suddenly attacked. Both they and the Israelis quickly lost huge quantities of tanks, aircraft, and other equipment, and both the Russians and the Americans resorted to airlifts to make up for the losses. Only after the Israelis had got the upper hand did the Russians show any interest in ending the war. Then Kissinger and Brezhnev worked out and the U.N. Security Council adopted resolutions calling for an immediate cease-fire and for the beginning of peace negotiations on the basis of the 1967 resolution — which would presumably require Israel to give up most if not all of her 1967 conquests in return for some guarantee of her continued existence.

As the shooting died down, the American-Russian détente seemed belatedly to be having an effect in the Middle East. All at once Nixon made the startling announcement that he was putting American forces throughout the world on a stand-by alert. He was doing so, administration spokesmen said, because the Russians were increasing their already large naval force in the Mediterranean and were preparing to fly troops to the Middle East to enforce the cease-fire. The Russians sent no troops, and a new U.N. peacekeeping force began to arrive. Relaxing the alert, Nixon declared that the United States had just passed through its most dangerous war crisis since the Cuban missile crisis of 1962. "Without détente," he said, "we might have had a major confrontation in the Mideast."

While Egypt and Israel disputed over the details of the cease-fire and threatened to resume hostilities, the Arab countries announced plans to reduce oil production and to cut off petroleum sales to the United States. The Arabs intended, by withholding oil from Israel's friends, to pressure them into supporting a Middle Eastern settlement that would force Israel to leave the Arab territories she had conquered in 1967. Japan and western Europe, which had been getting respectively 82 percent and 72 percent of their petroleum from Arab sources, were much more vulnerable than was the United States, which had depended on those sources for only 11 percent of its supply. Understandably, Japan and the leading powers of western Europe were careful not to offend the Arabs. The United States seemed likely to become careful, too, as the American people increasingly felt the pinch of the oil embargo during the winter of 1973–1974.

Meanwhile the "Yom Kippur war" intensified the strains within the North Atlantic Alliance. None of the principal NATO allies had backed the United States in its support of Israel. During the airlift several of them had forbidden American transport planes to refuel in their territories or even to fly over them. After the war the Nixon administration made its anger known to the allies. They, in turn, complained that the American government had disregarded their desperate need for Arab oil and had failed to consult them about its intentions, particularly about its intention to order a world-wide military alert. The alliance now appeared to be more badly shaken than at any time since 1956, when France and Great Britain had joined Israel in invading Egypt, and the United States had sided with the Soviet Union in bringing about U.N. action against the invaders.

Selected Readings

Diplomacy in General

Seyom Brown, *The Faces of Power: Constancy and Change in United States Foreign Policy from Truman to Johnson* (1968); Gabriel Kolko, *The Roots of American Foreign Policy: An Analysis of Power and Purpose* (1969), a radical view; Crane Brinton, *The Americans and the French* (1968); R. J. Walton, *Cold War and Counter-Revolution: The Foreign Policy of John F. Kennedy** (1972); Henry A. Kissinger, *American Foreign Policy* (1969); Henry Brandon, *Retreat of American Power* (1973); Adam Yarmolinsky, *The Military Establishment: Its Impact on American Society* (1971); C. W. Pursell, Jr., *The Military Industrial Complex** (1973).

Foreign Aid

E. S. Mason, *Foreign Aid and Foreign Policy* (1964); D. A. Baldwin, *Economic Development and American Foreign Policy, 1943–1962* (1966); M. K. O'Leary, *The Politics of American Foreign Aid* (1967); W. D. Rogers, *The Twilight Struggle: The Alliance for Progress and the Politics of Development in Latin America* (1967).

Cuba and Santo Domingo

H. B. Johnson, *The Bay of Pigs* (1964); Elie Abel, *The Missile Crisis* (1966); Henry Pachter, *Collision Course* (1963), on the missile crisis; J. B. Martin, *Overtaken by Events* (1966); on the Dominican intervention; Dan Kurzman, *Santo Domingo: Revolt of the Damned* (1966).

Vietnam

David Halberstam, *The Making of a Quagmire* (1956); M. G. Raskin and B. B. Fall, eds., *The Vietnam Reader** (1965); J. W. Fulbright, ed., *The Vietnam Hearings** (1966); R. N. Goodwin, *Triumph or Tragedy: Reflections on Vietnam* (1966); G. M. Kahin and J. W. Lewis, *The United States in Vietnam* (1967); A. M. Schlesinger, Jr., *The Bitter Heritage: Vietnam and American Democracy, 1941–1966* (1967); Robert Shaplen, *Time Out of Hand: Revolution and Reaction in Southeast Asia* (1969); Seymour Hersh, *My Lai Four* (1970) and *Cover Up* (1972); Townsend Hoopes, *The Limits of Intervention* (1970); Telford Taylor, *Nuremberg and Vietnam: An American Tragedy** (1971); Neil Sheehan and others, *The Pentagon Papers** (1971); David Halberstam, *The Best and the Brightest* (1972).

Election of 1968

Stewart Alsop, *The Center: People and Power in Political Washington* (1968); T. H. White, *The Making of a President, 1968* (1969); J. McGinniss, *The Selling of the President, 1968* (1970); E. Mazo and S. Hess, *Nixon: A Political Portrait* (1968), a campaign biography; Jules Witcover, *The Resurrection of Richard Nixon* (1970) and *White Knight: The Rise of Spiro Agnew* (1972).

*Titles available in paperback.

Toward the Twenty-first Century

Thirty

On Sunday, July 20, 1969, slowly, cautiously, a white-clad figure climbed down from his spacecraft and extended a heavy, well-insulated boot toward the surface of the moon, while hundreds of millions of people throughout the world followed his movements on television or radio. As the astronaut, Neil Armstrong, placed both feet on the strange, finely powdered lunar soil, he said: "That's one small step for a man, one giant leap for mankind." A human being was standing where none had ever stood before—on land beyond the earth. A new age of interplanetary exploration had begun.

Most Americans rejoiced in the event as a triumph for humanity in general and for the United States in particular. But there were voices of dissent. Some Americans, especially among those of African ancestry, argued that the billions of dollars spent on traveling to the moon might better have been used for eliminating poverty from the earth. A Black Panther leader, Eldridge Cleaver, from his exile in Algeria, dismissed the lunar voyage as "a circus to distract people's minds from the real problems, which are here on the ground."

Certainly the moon landing, the result of cooperative efforts by thousands of scientists and technicians, provided a spectacular illustration of what sociologists call "cultural lag," that is, the failure of social and political development to keep up with technological advances. Man was acquiring the ability to visit other worlds before he had the capacity to put his own in order, with peace and plenty for its inhabitants. Another example of cultural lag was the exploitation of nuclear energy with no adequate arrangement of human power to control it. Still other examples were to be found in new production techniques that brought the promise of greater abundance and leisure without assuring that these benefits would be well distributed

Cars and the City
From one end of the country to the other, cities were ripped up and paved over to provide freeways and parking lots, but traffic congestion and air pollution remained. During the early 1970s, some 350,000 motor vehicles a day were passing over this Los Angeles freeway with its spectacular four-level interchange. (UPI)

and without making sufficient provision for the protection of the natural environment. Improvements in communication — the spread of the "mass media," especially television — only made the masses of the people even more aware of the stark contrast between affluence and poverty. Humanity needed inventions and achievements in society and government that would match those in science and technology.

Technology itself seemed to be approaching a crisis. The technological achievements of the past, bringing such a marvelous increase in the production of material things, had depended on an abundance of natural resources for raw material and for fuel. As the twentieth century reached its final quarter, signs of the near exhaustion of many resources began to appear. Unless new resources or new ways to utilize existing ones were found, the rising generation would face a period of scarcity instead of plenty, even in such a relatively rich country as the United States.

Meanwhile, as the country neared the 200th anniversary of its independence, the American people were confronted with a constitutional crisis. The Constitution had provided for a balanced government, with three equal and coordinate branches, but in recent years the executive branch had greatly overbalanced the legislative. Both national security and domestic welfare demanded a strong presidency. Constitutional and democratic government, however, required a controlled and responsible one.

The "New Federalism"

President Nixon, though full of ideas about foreign affairs, took office in 1969 without having given much thought to a domestic program. He favored what he called "reform," which seemed to mean a reversal of the policies his immediate predecessors had sponsored under the slogans of "the New Frontier" and "the Great Society." He looked for a slogan of his own and came up with "the New Federalism." This implied that he would, in his words, "reverse the flow of power and resources from the states and communities to Washington and start power and resources flowing back . . . to the people all over America."

THE IMPERIAL PRESIDENCY

In fact, while reversing certain policies, Nixon did not stop the trend toward the centralization of power. Rather, he encouraged a development that had been accelerating since the presidency of Franklin D. Roosevelt. With respect to domestic as well as foreign affairs, Nixon undertook to concentrate more and more authority in the White House.

"I've always thought this country could run itself domestically without a President," Nixon had said in 1967. "All you need is a competent Cabinet to run the country at home."

Actually, the cabinet had been losing influence on policy making ever since World War II, and it continued to do so under Nixon. His own cabinet was distinguished by little competence and still less continuity. He appointed few outstanding public figures to it, and during his first five years he made more changes in its membership than any other President had made during any length of time. For the most part, the members merely administered their own departments, seldom if ever consulting with one another as a group or even individually with the President. An exception was John Mitchell, Nixon's former law partner, his 1968 campaign manager, and from 1969 to 1972 his attorney general and chief adviser on politics. Mitchell had direct access to the White House.

Few other department heads, government officials of lesser rank, or congressmen or senators could approach the President directly. Almost all of them had to deal with him through his top White House aide, the "keeper of the gates," H. R. Haldeman, or through the chief of his domestic policy staff, John Ehrlichman. These two, old friends and veteran Nixon campaigners, now subject only to the President himself, ran the executive office with respect to domestic affairs from 1969 to 1973. The executive office was a large and rapidly swelling bureaucracy, whose numbers during that four-year period grew from 2,000 to more than 4,200.

By 1969 the domestic programs of the federal government and the agencies to administer them had become so numerous that they were difficult if not impossible for the President to control. As far back as the Truman and Eisenhower administrations a commission under former President Herbert Hoover had made proposals for reorganizing and streamlining the executive branch, but few of the proposals had been carried out. Now, on the advice of Roy Ash, a prominent businessman, Nixon proposed a new plan for bringing together the widely scattered threads of administration. The plan was to reorganize and enlarge the powers of the Bureau of the Budget, which had been set up during Harding's presidency to coordinate the requests of the various bureaus for appropriations from Congress. A new Office of Management and Budget, responsible to the President, was to oversee the financing and directing of all administrative agencies, including the formerly quasi-independent regulatory ones such as the Federal Power Commission. Congress approved the plan even though it meant that Congress would no longer be able to supervise the departments and commissions by negotiating directly with them in regard to their budget requests. These requests had to go through the Office of Management and Budget after it went into operation, in 1970.

Again acting on the advice of businessman Ash, Nixon proposed to reorganize and reduce the number of executive departments. When Congress failed to approve, the President in 1973 went ahead on his own, with a revised plan. By executive order he raised three of the department heads to the level of "presidential councillors" and directed that the others report to one of the three, who in turn would report to a presidential aide (Erhlichman). With the three councillors constituting a "super cabinet," the authority and prestige of the traditional cabinet would be still further reduced.

Nixon presented his reorganization measures as long overdue reforms that would bring businesslike efficiency to the government. They would, of course, enable the White House to manage more effectively the executive branch as a whole. But Nixon also claimed unprecedented authority for the presidential office in relation to the legislative branch, especially after his reelection in 1972. Asserting "executive privilege" seemingly without limit, he took the position that congressional committees could not question administrative officials without the President's consent. Implying that the President, not Congress, should have the power of the purse, he ordered administrative agencies not to spend appropriated money after Congress had overridden his vetoes of appropriation bills.

By the beginning of his second term, Nixon faced a congressional revolt. His critics in Congress—including some members of the Republican minority as well as the Democratic majority—talked of a constitutional crisis. For many years Congress had been allowing Presidents more and more discretion, particularly in foreign affairs (as seemed unavoidable in a nuclear age). Now Nixon, while stretching to the utmost his powers as commander in chief in Southeast Asia, was thought to be doing the same with his powers as chief executive at home. Unless Congress acted soon to regain its lost authority, some of the critics believed, the checks and balances of the Constitution would become meaningless in actual practice.

LAW AND ORDER

From the beginning of his first term, President Nixon hoped to alter the direction of the Supreme Court, which under Chief Justice Earl Warren had been actively enlarging the sphere of both personal liberty and civil rights. The Warren Court's decisions on civil rights had antagonized conservatives, particularly in the South, and the decisions on personal liberty had aroused advocates of "law and order" (one of Nixon's themes in the 1968 campaign) all over the country. Especially resented were the *Escobedo* and *Miranda* cases (1964, 1966), in which the judges had limited the power of local police to extract confessions from persons accused of crimes.

As Chief Justice Warren approached retirement, President Johnson had tried to replace him with Abe Fortas, whom Johnson earlier had appointed as an associate justice. Fortas, a liberal, could have been expected to keep the Court on essentially the same track it had been following under Warren. The Republicans in the Senate blocked the Fortas appointment and thus gave Nixon an opportunity to choose his own chief justice. Nixon—who insisted that it was "the job of the courts to interpret the law, not make the law"—chose a conservative strict constructionist who agreed with him. This was Warren Burger, who had served for thirteen years on the United States Court of Appeals for the District of Columbia and who had spoken out against what he considered the Supreme Court's protection of the rights of criminals. Burger's appointment received the prompt approval of the Senate.

Nixon soon had a chance to put another man of his choice on the Supreme Court, but this time he ran into difficulty and embarrassment. The opening occurred when Justice Fortas resigned after the revelation that he had received a salary payment from a foundation whose donor was under indictment for fraud. To take Fortas' place, Nixon named a federal circuit court judge from South Carolina, C. F. Haynsworth, who had the endorsement of the American Bar Association, but whose past decisions showed that he lagged considerably behind the Warren Court in his devotion to civil rights. Spokesmen for black organizations and for labor unions vociferously opposed the confirmation of Haynsworth. They were joined by others, including prominent members of Nixon's own party, when it was revealed that Haynsworth had sat on cases involving corporations in which he himself had a financial interest. His critics now said he was even more insensitive to possible conflicts of interest than Fortas had been. Eventually the Senate rejected the Haynsworth nomination, and Nixon then named G. Harrold Carswell, a judge of the Florida federal appeals court, who lacked Haynsworth's legal eminence and who was shown to have made racist statements in the past. When the Senate turned down Carswell also, Nixon angrily charged the Senate majority with bias against the South. The Senate finally accepted the appointment of Harry A. Blackmun, who, like Chief Justice Burger, came from Minnesota and had a reputation as a conservative jurist.

Before Nixon had been in office three years, two more Supreme Court vacancies arose, and again he ran into trouble in trying to fill them. The American Bar Association refused to endorse his first two choices, one of whom was a woman. Nixon then nominated, and the Senate approved, Lewis F. Powell, Jr., a Virginian and a former head of the American Bar Association, and William H. Rehnquist, assistant attorney general in the Nixon administration and a Goldwater Republican from Arizona. "I shall continue to appoint judges," Nixon later said, "who share my philosophy that we must strengthen the peace forces against the criminal forces in America."

Through his four appointments to the Supreme Court, Nixon succeeded in changing its interpretations to some extent, at least in regard to criminal procedure. Usually his appointees voted together, and often Justice Byron White joined them to make a majority. With the cooperation of these five, the Court put new restrictions on the legal rights of defendants in criminal cases, even holding that a jury need no longer reach a unanimous verdict in order to convict. With White parting from the Nixon appointees, however, the Court in a five-to-four decision (*Furman* v. *Georgia*, 1972) banned capital punishment in states where juries could decide whether or not to impose it. With one or more of the new members concurring, the Court also diverged from Nixon's aims by giving some important decisions in favor of civil liberties and civil rights.

By 1969, a decade and a half after the Court's historic decision outlawing segregation, only about 20 percent of the black children in the South were attending mixed schools. Robert A. Finch—a civil-rights advocate whom Nixon had put in charge of the Department of Health, Education, and Welfare (HEW)—expressed determination to make the most of the government's power to withhold federal aid from schools whose authorities permitted no more than token integration. Finch indicated that he would not be satisfied with "freedom of choice" plans, which required the black child or his parents to take the initiative in seeking entrance to a school attended by whites. Then, in September 1969, the Nixon administration suddenly pulled back, ceased to insist on immediate steps toward integration, and granted Mississippi an additional delay in eliminating its dual school system. Several weeks later the Court overruled the administration and demanded that Mississippi integrate its schools "at once." But Nixon prevented the HEW Department from cutting off funds from noncomplying districts and continued to delay the carrying out of its desegregation plans. Finch and a number of other HEW officials soon left the department.

In many areas the achievement of racial balance in schools (so as to eliminate all racially identifiable ones) would require the transporting of children from one neighborhood to another. Busing to segregated schools was a common practice, but busing to integrated schools was quite another matter in the opinion of most whites (and some blacks). When federal courts began to order such busing, Nixon spoke out with the many who denounced it as unthinkable if not unconstitutional. Nevertheless, the Supreme Court unanimously upheld it in a 1971 case involving Charlotte, North Carolina. The next year Nixon tried, unsuccessfully, to induce Congress to pass an antibusing law. Meanwhile, opponents of busing in northern cities violently resisted court-ordered busing, those in Denver, Colorado, and Pontiac, Michigan, resorting to the fire-bombing of school buses. There was also resistance in the South,

but on the whole desegregation proceeded faster there than in the North. Before the end of Nixon's first term—thanks to the federal courts rather than the President—the proportion of Southern blacks in all-black schools had declined from about 80 to less than 20 percent.

Comparatively few blacks, North or South, approved of Nixon's policies in regard to schools or other matters. "For the first time since Woodrow Wilson," said an official of the National Association for the Advancement of Colored People, "we have a national administration that can be rightly characterized as anti-Negro." Nevertheless, during the first five years of Nixon's presidency, the country was spared the kind of racial violence that had been breaking out every summer for several years

Occupation of Wounded Knee
To draw attention to their demands for reform, members of the militant American Indian Movement (AIM) took over the tiny settlement of Wounded Knee on the Pine Ridge Reservation of the Sioux, in South Dakota. The AIM forces forbade federal agents to enter the place. In this picture, taken on March 11, 1973, an armed AIM guard holds four government officials and two farmers. The six were released after about an hour (UPI)

before 1969. The urban black communities had apparently come to the conclusion that rioting did them more harm than good.

The antiwar groups also calmed down after their campus eruptions at the time of the Cambodian invasion in 1970. Even the Christmas-season bombing of North Vietnam in 1972 provoked no riots. It was as if events had numbed the erstwhile protesters for peace.

But Indians resumed their demonstrations, sometimes with violence. At first, in 1969, the hopes of Indians had been raised when Nixon appointed a Mohawk-Sioux as Commissioner of Indian Affairs, and again in 1970 when Nixon promised Indians "self-determination without termination," that is, an increase in control over their own affairs and at the same time an increase in federal aid. The promises were not fulfilled, however, and among Indians anger and frustration took the place of hope. In November 1972 nearly a thousand protesters forcibly took over the Bureau of Indian Affairs building in Washington and, after six days, left it with damage to files and furniture that government officials estimated at $500,000 to $2 million. Later that winter members of the militant American Indian Movement occupied the hamlet of Wounded Knee on the Pine Ridge reservation in South Dakota, fortified the place (the site of a one-sided, bloody engagement between the United States cavalry and a group of Sioux in 1890), and held it for more than two months.

To deal with rioting and to put down "crime in the streets"—which were primarily state and local responsibilities—the Nixon administration gave millions of dollars to state and local law-enforcement agencies. Yet the number of crimes continued to go up, though at a decelerating rate. According to Federal Bureau of Investigation statistics, there were more than 6 million serious crimes committed in 1972, as compared with 4.5 million in 1968. That meant an increase of fully one-third in three years under Nixon. Though under the supervision of the federal government, the city of Washington itself remained unsafe, its downtown streets almost deserted at night.

THE GENERAL WELFARE

In dealing with the problem of poverty, Nixon appeared to follow a zigzag course. At first he saw himself as a conservative reformer who,

like Queen Victoria's great prime minister Benjamin Disraeli, would outdo his political opponents in his concern for the poor and thus would win broad popular support. Eventually he went to the opposite extreme. At the beginning of his second term he announced his determination to put an end to what he called "condescending policies of paternalism."

By 1969 the existing welfare system, which had remained essentially unchanged since the time of the New Deal, was in serious need of reform. During the 1960s the number of persons receiving aid had doubled, from 1 to 2 million, and federal expenditures had increased from about $2 billion to nearly $18 billion. The welfare rolls had lengthened to the point where they included 6 percent of the population as a whole and a much higher proportion of the urban population, as high as 25 percent of the people of Newark, New Jersey. Approximately half of the recipients were black. Very few were employable men. Almost all were women or children or old, blind, or otherwise disabled persons. Among the worst faults of the existing program were the following: it denied benefits to families with able-bodied men, and so it induced husbands and fathers to desert; it denied benefits to the poor who were employed, and so it discouraged welfare recipients from accepting jobs.

In 1969 Nixon proposed a new Family Assistance Plan, which his special adviser on urban and poverty problems, Daniel P. Moynihan, had devised. Under the Moynihan plan, every unemployed family of four would receive at least $1,600 a year. The working poor would get this minimum and would be allowed to keep part of their pay until their earned income reached $4,000, when the benefits would be discontinued. To be eligible for relief, the able-bodied (women as well as men) would be required to work. The plan would add about 6 million people to the welfare rolls, and it would increase federal spending by about $4 billion annually. In keeping with Nixon's principle of the New Federalism, the states would take over an increased share of the responsibility for administering the program.

The Moynihan plan had much to recommend it, but it provoked a bitter controversy, both in and out of Congress. Black militants, welfare recipients, and social workers opposed it as inadequate. Congress neither adopted it nor agreed on a substitute, and Nixon himself soon lost interest in the plan. He turned to recommending, instead, that welfare expenditures be cut and that payments to "ineligibles" be stopped.

Already Nixon had begun to undo the Johnson poverty program by closing more than half of the Job Corps training centers. He also reduced spending on other social-welfare agencies, including the National Institute of Health. In his budget for 1973–1974 he proposed to abolish more than a hundred federal grant programs that were giving aid to the unemployed, the mentally ill, veterans, college students, small businessmen, and other groups. He also proposed to discontinue spending for urban renewal, to end assistance for hospital construction, and to reduce expenditures on lunches for schoolchildren. In 1973 he proceeded, without congressional approval, to break up the Office of Economic Opportunity, which had been the main agency of Johnson's "war on poverty."

To replace many of the federal grants for specific purposes, Nixon had been urging that the federal government transfer funds to the states and cities, which would then be responsible for their own social programs. Such "revenue sharing" he viewed as the finest example of the New Federalism in practice. Congress approved, and revenue sharing began in 1973, when the federal government turned about $5 billion over to state and local governments. Big-city mayors soon lost their enthusiasm for revenue sharing, since it promised them less money for dealing with urban problems than the specific grants, now being reduced or eliminated, had provided.

Nixon favored individual as well as local responsibility in overcoming poverty. To help Negroes help themselves, he advocated the encouragement of "black capitalism" through both public and private assistance to Negro-owned business enterprises. Some progress was made along this line.

While economizing on aid to the poor, Nixon was generous to large corporations, especially those in the aircraft industry. He endorsed federal spending to subsidize an airplane manufacturer in the development of a supersonic transport (SST), a large plane that would carry passengers faster than the speed of sound and would compete with craft under construction by the Soviet Union and, cooperatively, by Great Britain and France. President

Kennedy had put the government into the SST project, and by 1969 some $300 million of federal funds had already been contributed to it. President Nixon persuaded Congress to appropriate another $96 million for 1969–1970. Objections arose, however, on the grounds that the transport would never pay for itself and would damage the environment. Nixon suffered a personal defeat in 1971 when Congress killed the project by refusing to appropriate more money for it.

Many Americans had hoped that, once the United States was finally out of the Vietnam War, the government could cut its military spending and could afford to increase its domestic expenditures. Yet in his first postwar budget, the one for 1973–1974, Nixon not only demanded a reduction in domestic expenditures but also asked for an increase in military spending, from $74.8 billion to $79 billion. The extra money was to go largely for the development of new weapons and for pay raises to attract recruits to the all-volunteer armed forces.

THE NIXON ECONOMY

When Nixon talked of reducing expenditures on social programs, he justified it as a necessary means of controlling inflation and keeping prices within reason. He had inherited the inflation problem from his predecessor, Johnson, who had built up a tremendous inflationary pressure by increasing expenditures for both the Great Society and the Vietnam War. Nixon faced a dilemma, since rising prices could mean booming business, while deflationary policies might bring on widespread unemployment. In handling the problem he proved to be neither consistent nor successful.

At the outset, in 1969, Nixon announced a deflationary "game plan." He was going to maintain a balanced budget by spending less and taxing more, yet he signed a tax bill that enlarged exemptions and thus reduced revenue. He was also going to tighten bank credit and raise interest rates through the operations of the Federal Reserve System, and he succeeded in doing so. Nevertheless, prices continued to rise. At the same time unemployment also rose. The country began to suffer from "stagflation," stagnation and inflation together.

The Economic Stabilization Act of 1970 authorized the President to impose direct controls on prices and also wages if and when he saw fit to do so. Nixon said: "I will not take this nation down the road of wage and price controls, however politically expedient that may seem." One year later he put into effect a two-phase control system. In Phase I, to last for ninety days, nearly all wages and prices were frozen at their existing levels. In Phase II, to last indefinitely, most wage and price increases were kept within strict limits. Inflation now slowed down temporarily, but the business recession continued, and the unemployment rate rose to more than 6 percent of the labor force for 1971, as compared with less than 4 percent for 1969.

If these economic conditions had persisted, they might have threatened the reelection of Nixon in 1972. So, in 1971, he suddenly reversed his original game plan of tight credit and a balanced budget. He got from Congress a bill further reducing taxes. The Federal Reserve Board lowered interest rates and encouraged borrowing from banks. Government agencies began to spend at a rate of $1 billion a month more than had previously been planned. The Department of Agriculture increased its crop subsidies to farmers (for taking land out of production) from $3.1 billion to $4.1 billion a year. Altogether, the government paid out so much more than it took in that the deficit for 1972 was by far the largest for any year since World War II. By Election Day, incomes were up and unemployment was down. Politically, the combination of easy credit and deficit spending proved a great success.

The consequences, however, were disastrous for consumers. Foods and other raw materials were already becoming scarce throughout the world. Nixon's wheat deal with the Soviet Union made the food shortage worse than it would otherwise have been in the United States. The Russians took a fourth of the entire American crop (at a price well below the market price, the difference being paid by American taxpayers through export subsidies to American grain dealers). Meanwhile, food production in the United States was declining as a result of Nixon's election-year farm policy. By pushing exports and restricting output, the administration was decreasing the available supply of foodstuffs within the country. By loosening credit and pouring out money, it was increasing the effective demand. Thus it was creating an explosive inflationary force. At this critical moment, early in 1973, Nixon chose to discontinue the strict wage-price controls of Phase II, which he replaced with the flexible, largely voluntary guidelines of what came to be called Phase III.

There followed the most rapid and extreme rise in the cost of living since the end of World War II. Prices of meat and grain products soared the highest. Housewives tried, with only partial and temporary success, to bring down prices by boycotting meat. Responding to consumer protests, the administration finally put a ceiling on the retail prices of meat and other foods but not on the prices of livestock or grain. This haphazard attempt at price fixing only worsened the food shortage. Squeezed

---

The End of American Independence [1973]

Throughout its two centuries of existence, the United States has enjoyed an uncommon degree of national independence, in part because two vast oceans have isolated it from political conflicts in Europe and elsewhere and in part because it has been an essentially self-sufficient continental storehouse of energy fuels and raw materials.

Suddenly, this is beginning to change, and very rapidly. As recently as 1970 we were importing only a small fraction of our petroleum and only a few of the important minerals. By 1985 we will be importing well over half of our petroleum and will be primarily dependent on imports for nine of the thirteen basic minerals required by a modern industrial economy. The import bill for energy fuels and minerals, which totaled $8 billion in 1970, is projected to multiply severalfold by 1985. Within a fifteen-year span, scarcely half a generation, we will make the transition from being an essentially self-sufficient country to—at least in terms of raw materials—a have-not country. We do not yet appreciate the economic, social, and political consequences of this historically abrupt transition.—Lester R. Brown in *Saturday Review/World*, December 18, 1973.

between rising costs and fixed prices, some poultrymen killed baby chicks, and some packers and bakers went out of business.

Belatedly the government took measures for stimulating instead of retarding farm output. The administration advised farmers to plant grain and soybeans on millions of acres they had left idle the previous year in order to qualify for subsidies, and it began to sell its own stocks of grain. It planned to abandon gradually the crop controls and price supports for wheat, feed grains, and cotton, and to discontinue the purchase and storage of "surplus" crops. Thus it intended to change the basic agricultural policy that had prevailed ever since the New Deal. Presumably the nation's farmers were to be left, for the most part, to make their own decisions about what and how much to produce, as they had done before the 1930s.

After his reelection in 1972, Nixon ended the government's spending spree and renewed his demands for economizing on social programs. He opposed a tax increase and argued that, if an increase should become necessary, Congress would be to blame because of its extravagance. In order to forestall a recession, he now wanted to moderate the business boom that had been under way in 1972 and that was to last through most of 1973.

The prospects for continued prosperity received a jolt in the fall of 1973, when the Arab nations cut back their oil production and put an embargo on petroleum shipments to the United States. There had already been, in this country, scattered shortages of fuel oil during the winter of 1972–1973 and gasoline during the summer of 1973. For the winter of 1973–1974, a much greater and more general shortage was anticipated, but experts differed as to how great it would actually prove to be. Natural gas and electric power (produced largely with petroleum) were also in short supply. To meet the "energy crisis," the federal and state governments took a variety of steps. These included an appeal to homeowners to lower their thermostats, allotments of fuel to airlines and a consequent elimination of many flights, allocation of fuel oil and gasoline to dealers, a reduction of highway speed limits to fifty-five miles an hour, a ban on Sunday sales of gasoline, and a contingency plan for gasoline rationing. Prices of gasoline and fuel oil started to take a steep rise. The shortage threatened to curtail production

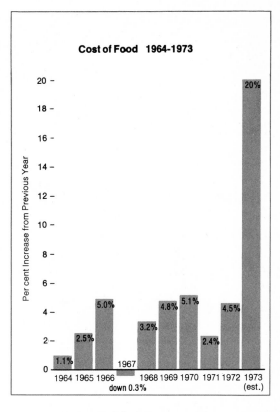

Cost of Food 1964-1973

Despite the escalation of the Vietnam War, food prices for American consumers rose only rather moderately until 1973. In that year, prices began to go up faster than at any time since immediately after the end of World War II. From a chart by J. Donovan. Time, August 27, 1973. (Reprinted by permission from TIME, The Weekly Newsmagazine; Copyright Time Inc.)

as well as transportation, since many industries depended directly or indirectly on petroleum for power, and others (such as those making or using plastics or synthetic fibers) depended on it also for raw material. By March 1974, the outlook was dim, with long lines of cars waiting for gas at filling stations in many parts of the country. The next month the prospect brightened, at least temporarily, when the Arab oil ban was lifted.

A TRIUMPHANT REELECTION

According to a 1970 book, the "real majority" in the United States was "unyoung, unblack, and unpoor." The mature, white, well-off citizens were most concerned about such things as

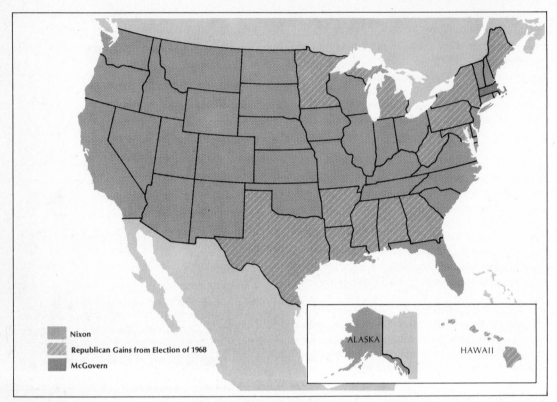

Nixon

Republican Gains from Election of 1968

McGovern

ALASKA

HAWAII

Election of 1972

campus protests, school integration, street crimes, and welfare costs. If these worried people could be induced to vote for Nixon, his reelection would be assured. This prospect formed the basis for the campaign strategy that Nixon's attorney general and political adviser, John Mitchell, adopted for 1972. In particular, Mitchell planned to attract to Nixon the voters who in 1968 had favored the American party candidate, George Wallace of Alabama. In addition to these Southern whites, the Republicans hoped to win over many Northern workers, especially the Catholics of immigrant background. Thus the Nixon forces might break up the already shaky Democratic coalition — which Franklin D. Roosevelt had put together in the 1930s — and replace it with a permanent Republican majority.

To Republican strategists it was hardly encouraging when, in 1970, Congress passed a bill to lower the voting age to eighteen. Nixon signed the bill, despite the widespread assumption that most of the young would vote Democratic. The Supreme Court ruled the new law

constitutional for federal but not for state or local elections. The Twenty-sixth Amendment, ratified in time for the elections of 1972, made eighteen the minimum age for voters in state and local as well as federal contests.

For the Republicans, the congressional elections of 1970 were also somewhat discouraging. Nixon put his own prestige at stake when he campaigned on behalf of Republican candidates, to denounce criminals and antiwar protesters, the "violent few." In San Jose, California, he taunted youthful demonstrators, who then threw stones and eggs at the presidential limousine. In Phoenix, Arizona, wildly gesticulating, he denounced the San Jose "terrorists." This performance was recorded and was nationally televised on election eve. It apparently did the Republicans little good. The next day they gained two seats in the Senate but lost nine in the House and also lost eleven state governorships.

Nixon's chances for reelection improved when, in May 1972, in a Maryland shopping center, a would-be assassin shot George Wallace, leaving him partially paralyzed and incapable of continuing his presidential campaign. Nixon's chances improved still further when, in July, the Democratic nominating convention met in Miami.

On the first ballot the convention chose George M. McGovern, an opponent of the Vietnam War and an advocate of a $1,000 yearly grant from the government to every citizen. While still a relatively unknown senator from South Dakota, McGovern had begun openly to seek the presidency far in advance, in January 1971. In the primaries he outdid the early favorite, Senator Edmund Muskie of Maine, and the previous candidate, Senator Hubert Humphrey of Minnesota. At the convention, McGovern benefited from reforms he himself had helped to bring about. The "McGovern rules"

were intended to make the convention broadly representative of the party by requiring certain proportions of women, blacks, and youths among the delegates. But the rules antagonized old-line politicians and had a very divisive effect on the party, especially when the convention unseated a powerful boss, Mayor Richard J. Daley of Chicago.

The very qualities that had brought McGovern the nomination—the qualities that appealed to liberals within the Democratic party—made him a weak candidate in the election. From the make-up of the convention, many voters got the impression that he was the candidate of hippies, aggressive women, and militant blacks. He offended many even among his adherents when—after the revelation that his vice-presidential choice, Senator Thomas Eag-

The Democratic Candidates 1972
In a jubilant mood, Senator George McGovern of South Dakota poses with his hand-picked running-mate, Senator Thomas Eagleton of Missouri, after their nomination in Miami. Their joy was not to last, as Eagleton soon withdrew from the ticket after the revelation that he had been treated for a nervous disorder, and McGovern went on, with Sargent Shriver as the vice-presidential candidate, to one of the most crushing defeats in American political history. (Wide World Photos)

leton of Missouri, had undergone treatments for an emotional disturbance – he at first said he stood "1,000 percent" behind Eagleton and then suddenly removed him from the ticket. During the campaign McGovern found it hard to maintain his credibility when he compared Nixon to Hitler and charged that the administration was the most corrupt in history. George Meany, head of the AFL-CIO, the nation's largest labor union, opposed McGovern, and so did all but a very few of the newspapers throughout the country.

While McGovern campaigned strenuously with limited financial resources, which came mainly from small contributors, Nixon (after a renomination, also in Miami, that was more a coronation than a contest) had an easy "non-campaign." He had the advantage of more money, most of it from large corporations, than any other presidential candidate had ever had at his disposal. Seldom appearing, Nixon was an "invisible candidate." His choice for a second time as Vice President, Spiro Agnew, together with other government officials, carried the campaign burden for Nixon, never mentioning him by name but always referring to him as "the President." The President now had only to reap the benefits of his recent policies. By virtue of his China and Russia visits and the Vietnam negotiations he appeared to be a bringer of peace. Since business was finally booming, he could be credited with prosperity. As a foe of busing for racial balance in schools, he had the gratitude of race-conscious whites. Through his "law and order" statements and his court appointments, he had made himself the apparent champion of peace at home as well as abroad.

Nixon won by one of the most decisive margins in history. He received the largest share of the popular vote (60.8 percent) of any candidate except Johnson (61.1 percent) in 1964. He received the largest proportion of the electoral vote (521 of 538) since Roosevelt (523 of 531) in 1936. McGovern carried only Massachusetts and the District of Columbia. He got little of the expected help from the newly enfranchised eighteen- to twenty-year-olds, as fewer than half of them bothered to go to the polls, and those who did divided their ballots almost evenly. He received a fairly solid black support, but scarcely more than half of the eligible blacks voted. He lost heavily among eth-

nic groups in the North and among whites generally in the South.

To judge by the presidential returns alone, it appeared that the Republicans had succeeded in their aim to replace the old Democratic coalition with a new one of their own. In the congressional elections, however, the Republicans had been deprived of two places in the Senate while gaining thirteen in the House, thus leaving the Democrats in control of the next Congress by margins of 57 to 43 and 243 to 192. So the returns as a whole hardly amounted to unqualified approval of the Republican party. Even the presidential victory, overwhelming though it was, probably meant less an endorsement of Nixon than a rejection of his opponent.

WATERGATE

As he began his second term, in January 1973, President Nixon stood at the height of his power and popularity. Soon his popularity, as measured by opinion polls, began to drop. It fell faster than that of any other President since such polls were first taken, in Franklin D. Roosevelt's time. Within a year, public confidence in Nixon was so low that serious doubts arose as to whether he should, or could, continue to lead the people. The reason for the sudden collapse of his prestige could be summed up in a word that became familiar to all newspaper readers and television viewers – "Watergate." That word designated a bewildering assortment of political scandals, the worst in American history.

The Watergate was a deluxe hotel-apartment-office complex in Washington. In it were located the headquarters of the Democratic National Committee. There, at about two o'clock in the morning of June 17, 1972, police arrested five men who had broken into the headquarters to "bug" them and to copy documents. Later two others were arrested, one of them the general counsel for Nixon's personal campaign organization, the Committee for the Re-election of the President (CREEP). Two months after the burglary, however, Nixon stated that "no one in the White House staff, no one in this Administration presently employed, was involved in this very bizarre incident." He added: "This kind of activity, as I have often

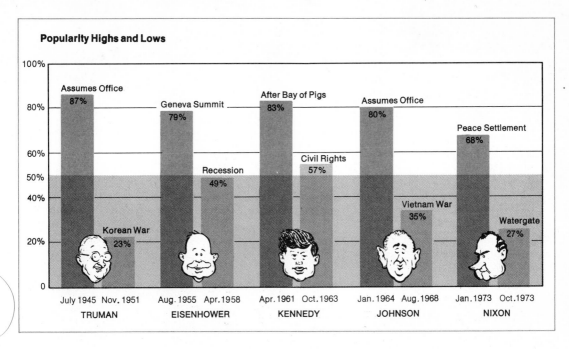

Popularity Highs and Lows

The bars indicate the percentage of people, as shown by Gallup opinion polls, who approved of the way the President was handling his job. Adapted from a chart prepared by J. Donovan and M. Witte and published in Time, July 30, 1973. (Reprinted by permission from TIME, The Weekly Newsmagazine; Copyright Time Inc.)

indicated, has no place whatsoever in our political process." His opponent, McGovern, tried in vain to make a campaign issue out of the crime.

When, after the election, the captured burglars went on trial, all but one of them pleaded guilty, and that one refused to talk. The Justice Department prosecutors failed to implicate anyone higher up than those arrested, but Federal District Judge John J. Sirica suspected that the whole truth had not been told. While sentencing the defendants to long terms in prison, Sirica intimated that if they would cooperate in getting at the truth, he would reduce the sentences. One of the defendants, James W. McCord, Jr., a former CIA agent and a "security coordinator" for CREEP, now agreed to testify before a federal grand jury and a Senate investigating committee, which was headed by Senator Sam J. Ervin of North Carolina. McCord led a long parade of witnesses who appeared, voluntarily or under subpoena, before the grand jury and the Ervin committee. The committee hearings, televised,

gave the public an opportunity to draw its own conclusions about the character and conduct of the men around the President. The testimony was so conflicting and confusing, however, that only with difficulty could the threads of the developing story be untangled.

Certain undisputed facts stood out. Nixon had been much concerned about the leaking of government secrets, especially the leaking of a Defense Department study of the Vietnam War, which The New York Times and other journals published as "The Pentagon Papers" in 1971. So, to plug the leaks, he set up and put Ehrlichman in charge of a special group of White House employees, who called themselves "the plumbers," and who tapped the telephones of newsmen and members of Kissinger's staff. Nixon ordered the plumbers to investigate the background of Daniel Ellsberg, the man responsible for leaking the Pentagon Papers. Using White House funds, two of the plumbers led a team of burglars who broke into the Los Angeles office of Ellsberg's psychiatrist

Watergate Hearings
*Of the many witnesses who appeared before the Senate committee on the Watergate
affair, as it held its televised hearings, John W. Dean III gave the fullest account of
the White House involvements. Dean, a former attorney on Nixon's staff, charged
that Nixon himself had taken part in the cover-up of the scandal. Here Dean begins
his testimony with a lengthy prepared statement, on June 26, 1973. Second from the
left at the table, his face partially hidden by a microphone, is Senator Sam J. Ervin
of North Carolina, chairman of the committee. (UPI)*

to search for Ellsberg's psychiatric files. Nixon
was eager to prosecute and convict Ellsberg.
While Ellsberg was on trial before a federal
court, Nixon told Ehrlichman to approach the
trial judge and find out if he would be interested in a promotion to the post of FBI director.
The judge dismissed the case.

Four of the psychiatrist's office burglars,
including the two leaders, took part, with
CREEP financing, in the Watergate break-in.
After the arrests, CREEP members and other
government officials hastily destroyed a tremendous quantity of their records. Nixon told
Haldeman and Ehrlichman to meet with top
CIA officials, and the CIA director concluded
that the White House was trying to "use" the
agency as a means of slowing down an FBI
probe and covering up CREEP activities. A

White House attorney suggested to one of the
Watergate defendants that he, the defendant,
would get a presidential pardon after a short
time in prison if he would keep silent about his
superiors' involvement in the affair. Nixon's
personal attorney and other White House staff-
ers covertly passed more than $400,000, mostly
from Nixon campaign contributions, to the defendants, their families, and their lawyers.

Besides the Watergate burglary, CREEP
agents had perpetrated a variety of "dirty
tricks" before and during the campaign, the
worst of them having been intended to destroy
the reputation of Nixon's strongest potential
rival, Senator Muskie, and thereby prevent his
getting the Democratic nomination. "I have
often thought we had too much money," one of
Nixon's campaign workers said afterward.

Part of the money came from corporations that were making unlawful contributions, part of it from persons or groups who were receiving specific government favors. The Justice Department compromised an antitrust suit against the International Telephone and Telegraph Company after the ITT had agreed to contribute. The President raised price supports for milk after dairymen's organizations promised large payments. Attorney General Mitchell and Secretary of Commerce Maurice Stans interceded with the Securities and Exchange Commission on behalf of a disreputable financier who made a contribution. Mitchell and Stans were indicted, but were eventually acquitted.

A PRESIDENT RESIGNS

Still others among Nixon's friends, advisers, and aides were indicted on, and some of them were convicted of, charges growing out of illegal campaign activities. The question became more and more insistent: Was Nixon himself guilty? Did he authorize any of the illegal activities or any of the attempts to cover them up? Did he have any knowledge of the misdeeds or the cover-up and fail to act on his knowledge, fail to stop what was going on and see that those responsible were punished? (Misprision of felony is itself a crime.) In a succession of statements Nixon altered and added to his original story, but he continued to maintain that he was innocent of any wrongdoing. "I am not a crook," he declared at one news conference. There was a possible way of testing, at certain points, his veracity as against that of his accusers. At his direction—as one of the very few who knew about it revealed in the midst of the Senate hearings—hidden tape recorders had been recording White House conversations. But Nixon refused to give up the relevant tapes until after Judge Sirica had ruled that he must, and then Nixon's spokesmen let it be known that two of the most important tapes were nonexistent and a third had a peculiar gap in it. A team of experts concluded that part of this tape had been deliberately erased.

To a growing number of Americans it seemed that, at the very least, Nixon had shown remarkably poor judgment in choosing some of his subordinates. It turned out that he had certainly been no judge of character when he twice endorsed Spiro Agnew for the vice presidency. Late in 1973 Agnew, the stern advocate of law and order, resigned as Vice President and pleaded nolo contendere (no contest) to a charge of income-tax evasion, the federal prosecutors agreeing in return to refrain from pressing charges of soliciting and accepting bribes. To replace Agnew, Nixon named the House Republican leader, Gerald Ford of Michigan. After a thorough investigation, Congress gave Ford its approval. He appeared to be, if not an imaginative or inspiring statesman, at least an honest politician.

With Ford as the prospective successor, old demands for the resignation or impeachment of Nixon were renewed. As 1974 began, Nixon still refused to resign. The Judiciary Committee of the House was busily gathering evidence for the decision whether or not to impeach. After requesting a number of the presidential tapes, the committee served the President with a subpoena when he refused to give them up. Finally, at the end of April, he responded, not by delivering the tapes, but by sending in and at the same time publishing 1200 pages of selected and edited transcripts. He and other Republican spokesmen claimed that these told the whole story of his relation to the Watergate scandal and completely exonerated him. Others, especially Democrats, drew a quite different conclusion. By a partisan vote, the committee ruled that Nixon had not made an adequate response to the subpoena.

By the summer of 1974, nine men—in addition to the "Watergate seven," the burglars and their accomplices—had confessed to or been convicted of Watergate-related offenses. These nine were former members of CREEP or of the White House staff, the highest ranking of them being Erlichman. Several others, including Haldeman and Mitchell, had been indicted and were awaiting trial. Nixon himself had been named as an "unindicted co-conspirator" by a federal grand jury.

For use as evidence in these cases the special prosecutor for the Justice Department, Leon Jaworski, asked for tape recordings of sixty-four White House conversations. Nixon refused to give them up, claiming that "executive privilege" justified him in thus protecting the confidentiality of his office. In the case of *United States* v. *Richard M. Nixon* the Supreme Court decided unanimously against the President in July 1974.

A few days later, after several months of thorough inquiry, the House Judiciary Committee voted to recommend three articles of impeachment. These charged that Nixon had (1) obstructed justice by helping to cover up the Watergate crimes, (2) misused federal agencies so as to violate the rights of citizens, and (3) interfered with congressional powers by refusing to turn over tapes and other materials that the committee had subpoenaed.

Though Nixon continued to assert his innocence, more and more signs of his complicity were coming to light. Newly released tapes proved what he had always denied—that he had been aware of and indeed had directed the Watergate cover-up from the beginning. With impeachment and conviction finally looming as unavoidable, he did what no President had ever done before. He resigned. Immediately, on August 9, 1974, Gerald Ford was sworn in as Nixon's successor. For the first time, there was a President who had not reached the office by going through a national election.

President Ford Addressing Congress
Gerald Rudolph Ford was sixty-one years old when he took office as President. Born in Omaha, Nebraska, he grew up in Grand Rapids, Michigan. After graduating from the University of Michigan, where he was a star football player, he earned a law degree at Yale. During World War II he served in the navy, rising to the rank of lieutenant commander. He was elected to the House of Representatives in 1948 and was reelected a dozen times after that. For nearly ten years, until he became Vice President, he was House minority leader. One of his first official acts after succeeding to the presidency was to name Nelson Rockefeller, a multimillionaire and former governor of New York, as Vice President. (Wide World Photos)

Articles of Impeachment [1974]

Article I. *In his conduct of the office of President of the United States, Richard M. Nixon, in violation of his constitutional oath faithfully to execute the office of President of the United States and, to the best of his ability, preserve, protect, and defend the Constitution of the United States, and in violation of his constitutional duty to take care that the laws be faithfully executed, has prevented, obstructed, and impeded the administration of justice. . . .*

Article II. *. . . has repeatedly engaged in conduct violating the constitutional rights of citizens, impairing the due and proper administration of justice and the conduct of lawful inquiries, or contravening the laws governing agencies of the executive branch and the purposes of these agencies. . . .*

Article III. *. . . has failed without lawful cause or excuse to produce papers and things as directed by duly authorized subpoenas issued by the Committee on the Judiciary of the House of Representatives. . . .*

In all of this, Richard M. Nixon has acted in a manner contrary to his trust as President and subversive of constitutional government, to the great prejudice of the cause of law and justice, and to the manifest injury of the people of the United States.

Wherefore, Richard M. Nixon, by such conduct, warrants impeachment and trial, and removal from office.

The Promise of Technology

Generation after generation, Americans had been preoccupied with material progress. Those of the late twentieth century saw technological achievements even more startling than those of earlier times. But people found it harder and harder to maintain the faith of their forefathers who had assumed that new inventions would almost automatically lead to a better life for everyone.

INNOVATIONS AND RESOURCES

A future of increasing abundance for the American people seemed to be promised by the continuing development of technical innovations summed up in the term "automation." Yet automation, like earlier phases of technical change dating back to the eighteenth century, threatened to create unemployment and social upheaval. Continuous automatic production was older than the term "automation," which a Ford Motor Company executive coined in 1946 to describe a system Ford was installing for the automatic handling of parts.

Essential to automation as it developed after World War II were electronic controls and the development of computer systems. The first electronic computer went into operation in 1946. Its name was descriptive: ENIAC, which stood for Electronic Numerical Integrator and Calculator. At first computers were large, cumbersome, and expensive, but the discovery that complicated electronic circuits, which had been assembled by hand, could be printed on cardboard or plastic and that compact durable transistors (invented in 1948) could replace fragile vacuum tubes made possible the rapid and spectacular advance in computer technology. By the end of the sixties, computers were a hundred times faster, ten times smaller in their electronic components, and provided information in a thousandth the time of earlier ones.

Computers, capable of answering in a few minutes problems that would require a thousand man-hours of calculation, were bringing a revolution in information processing. Jerome B. Wiesner, who had been President Kennedy's science adviser, described the change this way: "The computer, with its promise of a million-fold increase in man's capacity to handle information, will undoubtedly have the most far-reaching consequences of any contemporary technical development. The potential for good in the computer, and the danger inherent in its misuse, exceed our ability to imagine."

Computers could give answers to innumerable informational problems previously so complex as to be unmanageable. They were helping industry control inventories to eliminate the periodic scarcity or glut that had contributed to irregularities in the business cycle. They could fly jet planes, guide rockets to the moon, or control almost any sort of machinery. They could, critics feared, through data storage on every individual, destroy privacy; through the tasks they could guide, they might create serious unemployment.

The bituminous coal industry was a spectacular example of what automation could mean. By the end of the 1940s, coal, being mined with some machinery, was being priced out of the market by cheaper petroleum and natural gas. In 1948 the United Mine Workers gave the operators freedom to automate in exchange for a royalty of 40 cents per ton to be paid into UMW welfare funds. The companies, investing $500 million in new machinery, automated the mines and laid off far more than half the workers. A quarter-million miners had lost their jobs; only 150,000 were kept at work. Yet the alternative, the president of the Princess Coal Company, pointed out, would have been bankruptcy for the bituminous coal industry. "We've lost major markets and must compete with other fuels that have tax advantages," he declared. "The fact that the price of coal at the mine has not gone up in the past ten years—during a period of inflation—is a major accomplishment."

Whether in the long run automation would mean chronic unemployment was not entirely clear. In agriculture and industry as well as mining, automatic machinery was displacing labor rather than creating jobs. Its effects upon other groups of workers—those employed as clerks, for example—remained to be seen. Yet overall, the first seven decades of the twentieth century had brought an enormous increase in output per man-hour without any corresponding rise in unemployment.

As production grew, the United States began to change from a "have" to a "have-not" nation in natural resources, but innovations postponed the danger of disastrous shortages. Between 1900 and 1950, the production of bituminous coal rose two and a half times, of copper three times, of iron ore three and a half times, and of crude oil thirty times. Although Gifford Pinchot, writing in the Progressive era, had feared that bituminous coal would soon be exhausted, exhaustion was still far off. In fact, the Department of the Interior was still researching new uses—such as liquefication and gasification—for bituminous coal. In 1877 Secretary of the Interior Carl Schurz warned of a "timber famine" only twenty years away, but according to a 1962 estimate forests at that time were growing at a rate that exceeded by 60 percent the amount of timber cut. Synthetic substances, plastics, and metals had cut the demand for forest products. As the rich iron deposits began to dwindle, steel companies developed processes to make use of lower-grade ore. Once the huge investment had been made in plants that produced high-grade pellets from taconite ores, the steel companies reaped the advantage of higher productivity from furnaces into which they fed the pellets. New ore deposits were opened in Labrador. The United States became the largest importer of copper, lead, and zinc, leading to a flow of dollars overseas.

Already the United States was beginning to develop electric power from atomic energy. Two small power plants were completed in 1957. In the future nuclear reactors were likely to produce electric power at competitive rates. Already steam plants fueled by oil, gas, or coal could produce electric power more cheaply than could be expected at the few major hydroelectric sites remaining in the United States.

SCIENTIFIC RESEARCH

Applications of scientific knowledge, both civilian and military, were being developed at such a rapid pace that they created a sharp pressure for additional basic research. In 1957 a Department of Defense research officer declared: "We have been chewing up the findings of basic research since World War II at a speed faster than they are being produced in the laboratories and ivory towers."

The chief agency for promotion of basic scientific research was the National Science Foundation. In 1945 Dr. Vannevar Bush, who had been wartime director of the Office of Scientific Research and Development, proposed the establishment of a peacetime government agency to promote basic research. The United States could no longer depend upon Europe, Bush warned. In 1950 Congress established the National Science Foundation, but limited its annual appropriations to $15 million per year and appropriated less than that until the 1956 fiscal year. In the 1959 budget, after the sputnik crisis, President Eisenhower asked for $140 million for the National Science Foundation. Thereafter its budget, and its impact upon scientific research, increased significantly.

Overall federal expenditures on research and development—no more than a tenth of it for basic research—rose so spectacularly that by the end of the sixties they totaled more than the entire federal budget before Pearl Harbor. These sums were so large that many universities were dependent upon them for a considerable portion of their budgets. Concentration of expenditures in a few universities (68 percent of federal research funds were going to twenty-five institutions) had important side effects.

Scientific and engineering work at Harvard and the Massachusetts Institute of Technology had helped attract science-based industry, especially in electronics, to Highway 128 ringing Boston; the University of California and Stanford had brought similar industry to the San Francisco Bay region. Understandably, there developed considerable pressure to allocate more scientific grants to the Middle West and other areas in the United States. The House Appropriations Committee forbade the granting of more than 10 percent of the National Science Foundation fellowships to the residents of any one state.

The most comprehensive and spectacular of basic research enterprises, in which the United States cooperated with sixty-two other countries including Russia, was the International Geophysical Year, from July 1, 1957, to the end of 1958. It involved exploring the globe from pole to pole and from ionosphere to core, and included the launching of satellites and the establishment of an American base at the

South Pole. The research in Antarctica developed into a long-range scientific program, centering in a permanent base at McMurdo Sound, which supplied a number of outlying stations. By international treaty, national territorial holdings and armaments were barred from the continent; the United States, the Soviet Union, and a number of other nations carried on scientific work and shared information without friction.

In medical research, the most important advance was the development of an effective polio vaccine by Dr. Jonas Salk of the University of Pittsburgh. The vaccine was first used on a large scale in 1955, and within two years the polio rate in the United States dropped 80 percent. Many of the most spectacular innovations were made possible by electronic or atomic advances. The transplant of kidneys and even of a human heart were aided by chemical treatment and radiation to prevent rejection of the new organ. A number of mechanical and electronic inventions—among them artificial kidneys and miniature electronic generators to keep a heart beating at the right pace—helped to save lives. The laser beam, a ray of concentrated light, became a tool of eye surgery to repair damage to the retina.

Advances in medical research contributed to a lengthening life span. In 1900 life expectancy at birth had been forty-nine years; by 1955 it was seventy years. Most of the gain was in reducing the death rate among infants and children. Older people did not live much longer than before. In 1900 a sixty-four-year-old person had a remaining life span ahead of him that averaged about twelve years; in the 1960s it averaged fourteen years. Even if the two prime killers of the aged, heart disease and cancer, were to be eliminated, life expectancy would not be greatly increased.

THE SPACE RACE BEGINS

The American government had shown little interest in space exploration until October 1957, when the Soviet Union put its first satellite, Sputnik I, into orbit. Already the United States was carrying on a program of rocket research under the direction of Wernher von Braun, a German-born expert whose team had designed and built for the Hitler regime the V-2 rockets

that devastated London during the final stages of World War II. As the Russians advanced into Germany in 1945, they captured a few of the top men and hundreds of the technicians engaged in the V-2 project. Braun and others turned themselves over to the United States Army. In the early postwar years, however, the Americans were slower than the Russians in using German expertise to produce ballistic missiles, and still slower in using it to develop space rockets.

"Our satellite program has never been conducted as a race with other nations," President Eisenhower declared as he congratulated the Soviet Union on the launching of Sputnik I. But most Americans, including prominent public figures, assumed that a race was indeed on, and the United States appeared to be lagging far behind. Sputnik II carried a dog into space in November 1957 while Braun and his coworkers were still trying to launch a tiny, three-pound sphere, which they did not succeed in orbiting until January 1958. In October of that year, twelve months after the appearance of Sputnik I, the American government set up the National Aeronautics and Space Administration (NASA) to coordinate the nation's space efforts, but gave it only a small budget.

By 1961, when Kennedy took over the presidency from Eisenhower, the United States appeared to be making some gains. This country was ahead of the Soviet Union in the number of satellites put into orbit—thirty-three to nine. The total weight of the nine Soviet satellites, however, was more than twice as great as that of all thirty-three American ones, and the Russians were rumored to be testing a five-ton spaceship that could take a man into orbit. To the Russians, Kennedy said in his inaugural: "Let us explore the stars together." But the Russians showed little interest in that. In April 1961 they sent the world's first cosmonaut, Yuri Gagarin, once around the earth. After reentering the atmosphere and parachuting to safety, Gagarin issued the boastful challenge: "Now let the other countries try to catch us."

Eight days after Garagin's flight (and just one day after the Bay of Pigs fiasco in Cuba) President Kennedy directed a memorandum to Vice President Johnson, whom he had named as chairman of an advisory Space Council. "Do we have a chance of beating the Soviets," Kennedy asked, "by putting a laboratory in space, or by a trip around the moon, or by a rocket to land on the moon, or by a rocket to go to the moon and back with a man?" The best the United States could do for the time being was to propel Alan Shepard into a suborbital flight that went some 100 miles up to the edge of space and some 300 miles out into the Atlantic Ocean. Three weeks later, May 25, 1961, Kennedy appealed to Congress: "I believe this nation should commit itself to achieving the goal, before the decade is out, of landing a man on the moon and returning him safely to earth." Congress soon responded by making the first of the necessary appropriations.

The moon program, Project Apollo, was expected to cost $20 billion, ten times as much as the development of the atom bomb (but less than the Vietnam War was to cost for a single year). Advocates of the program maintained that it would be well worth the price on account of its scientific and economic benefits as well as its enhancement of national prestige. One space official declared: "Each improvement in our ability to fly unmanned and manned spacecraft results in a corresponding improvement in our ability to solve nature's mysteries."

TO THE MOON AND BEYOND

Until 1965 the United States continued to trail the Soviet Union in the launching of manned spacecraft, though not in the firing of unmanned satellites. A Russian cosmonaut circled the globe seventeen times (August 1961) before the first American, John Glenn, was put into space (February 1962), to return to earth after making only three orbits. Another and yet another American went around in one-man Mercury capsules similar to Glenn's, but the Russians kept the lead in flight endurance and took the lead in orbiting two vehicles close together, in launching two-man and then three-man craft, and in releasing a man from one of the ships to float in nothingness. But the United States was putting up, all together, more than twice as many satellites as was the Soviet Union. Some of these were intended for scientific purposes—to study solar radiation, the earth's magnetic field, and weather phenomena. Others, such as Telstar, facilitated around-the-world communication by telephone and television. Still others, such as the "eye in the sky" satellites Samos and Midas, gave the mili-

tary new means of observation or espionage. Meanwhile, from 1963 to 1965, the Americans discontinued manned flights and concentrated on the design and construction of improved space vehicles.

By 1965 the Americans were ready to achieve some firsts of their own with men in space. The new two-man Gemini, unlike the latest Soviet spaceships, was maneuverable; it was equipped with small rockets that could change its course in mid-orbit, as its pilots demonstrated on their first flight. On a second flight an astronaut stepped into space and, with a small oxygen-spitting gun, pulled the vehicle about on a tether. The third of the Geminis, orbiting for nearly 191 hours, broke the endurance record that the Russians had set. On a later launching, in 1966, a Gemini succeeded in overtaking an orbiting craft and joining up or "docking" with it—a maneuver essential for a moon trip. The United States now appeared to hold the lead in manned as well as unmanned flights.

The next stage involved the Apollo, a three-man spacecraft which, with over 2 million parts, was far more complicated than the Gemini or the Mercury. The project was set back and the nation was stunned when, early in 1967, a fire killed the three astronauts while they were rehearsing for the first Apollo take-off. While the craft was being redesigned and retested, a succession of Surveyors, unmanned, were being rocketed to the moon and were sending back tens of thousands of pictures of the lunar surface. One of the Surveyors landed on the moon and then took off from it, as a manned vehicle was scheduled to do eventually. In late 1968, after Apollo 7 had carried three men around the earth, Apollo 8 carried three others around the moon, the first men to leave the earth's gravitational field. During the next few months, Apollo 9 tested a lunar module (the landing craft that was to leave and rejoin the mother ship) in an earth orbit, and Apollo 10 tested one in a moon orbit.

". . . One Giant Leap for Mankind"
Astronaut Edwin "Buzz" Aldrin poses for a historic portrait photographed by the Apollo 11 Commander, Neil Armstrong. The surrealism of the fiction-like spacesuit and the starkness of the moon's landscape are brought to life by the astronauts' footprints and the reflection of the photographer and the lunar module as seen in Aldrin's visor. (NASA)

At last, in July 1969, Apollo 11 was blasted off on its epochal flight to land men on the moon. Ahead of them streaked a Russian spacecraft, Luna 15, heading for lunar orbit, but Luna carried no crew. Its launching seemed to show dramatically that, in space enterprises, the Soviet Union was still competing rather than cooperating—and now competing at a decided disadvantage. Not that sovereignty over the moon was at stake: by a treaty signed in 1966 the two superpowers had agreed that the moon should be a no man's land open to exploration and use by all nations. At issue were national prestige and (to the extent that the space programs yielded new techniques of warfare) military advantage.

The flight of Apollo 11 was a beginning, not an ending. During the next three years the United States launched a series of six additional Apollos, five of which succeeded in putting men on the moon, and all of which returned safely to the earth. Meanwhile both the United States and the Soviet Union sent space probes to Mars and Venus, and in 1973 the United States sent others to Jupiter and Mercury. Discontinuing lunar explorations for the time being, the Americans now concentrated their man-in-space efforts on experimental earth orbits. In 1973 they launched a two-story laboratory, Skylab, and three three-man crews in succession visited it to survey the earth's resources, test man's ability to live in space for long periods, and carry on other observations and experiments. At last, by an agreement of 1972, the Americans and the Russians were beginning to cooperate. They planned a joint earth-orbiting mission for 1975.

"There is no question but that we will go to Mars and colonize the moon, probably sooner than we now think," a NASA official said in 1972. "I think it will also become a reality that we'll pick up communications from other intelligence in the universe."

The Environment in Danger

"We have always assumed that progress and 'the good life' are connected with population growth," the President's Commission on Population Growth and the American Future reported in 1972. "If that were ever the case, it is not now. There is hardly any social problem confronting this nation whose solution would be easier if our population were larger."

THE CROWDING COUNTRY

In 1967 the demographic clock of the Census Bureau indicated that the population of the United States had passed the 200-million mark. In 1970 the census takers counted a total of 203,184,772. That was almost twice as large as it had been in 1920 and about 24 million larger than in 1960.

The rapid population growth after World War II belied the predictions of demographic experts who, on the basis of falling birth rates during the depression of the 1930s, had expected an early leveling-off. The baby boom of the 1950s caused pessimists to go to the opposite extreme. At the postwar rate of growth, some predicted, the population within 800 years would be so large that each American would have only one square foot of land to stand on. During the 1960s, however, the birth rate dropped even lower than it had been during the depression. By 1972 it was down to 2.11 per woman. This was a "zero population growth" rate, one that could mean eventually (after two more generations of childbearing women) just enough births to offset the number of deaths. Meanwhile the birth rate might rise again, and so population predicting remained as uncertain as ever.

Immigration accounted for less than a half million, or about 20 percent, of the population increase during the decade 1960–1970. The immigration act of 1965 eliminated the national-origins quota system, which had allowed only a certain percentage of each nationality to enter the country. The new law provided that, from 1969 on, there would be a ceiling of 120,000 on immigration from the Western Hemisphere and 170,000 from the rest of the world. The law allowed parents, spouses, and children of United States citizens to enter the country without regard to the overall limitations. There-

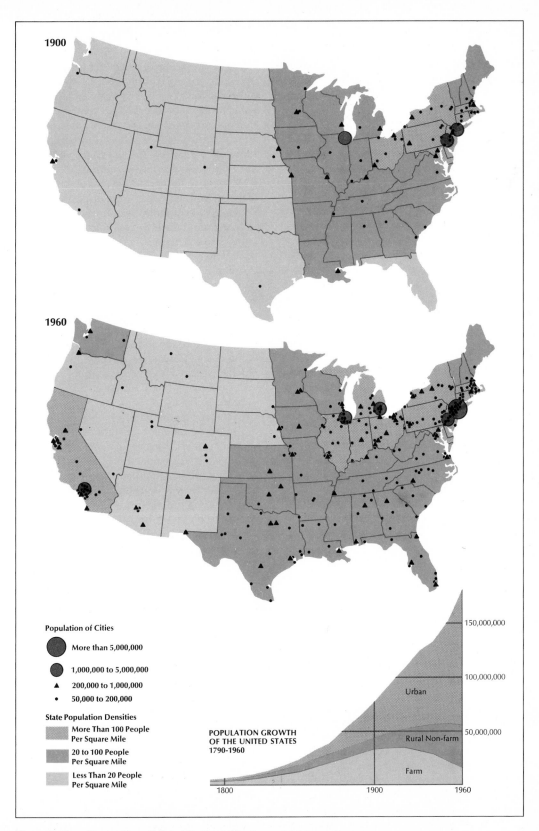

1900

1960

Population of Cities

⬤ More than 5,000,000

⬤ 1,000,000 to 5,000,000

▲ 200,000 to 1,000,000

• 50,000 to 200,000

State Population Densities

More Than 100 People
Per Square Mile

20 to 100 People
Per Square Mile

Less Than 20 People
Per Square Mile

**POPULATION GROWTH
OF THE UNITED STATES
1790-1960**

150,000,000

100,000,000

Urban

50,000,000

Rural Non-farm

Farm

1800   1900   1960

Population Density of the United States   1900 and 1960

after the largest numbers of immigrants no longer came from Canada and the United Kingdom but from Italy and the Philippines.

Mobility continued to characterize Americans, as it had always done. In 1970 more than one-fourth of the natives of the United States were living in a state other than the one they were born in (in 1850 the proportion had been about the same). During the 1960s, as during previous decades, the greatest interstate movement was to the Far West, especially to California, already the most populous state by 1960 and the home of nearly 20 million people in 1970. A reversal seemed under way in 1970 when, for the first time in a hundred years, as many people moved out of California as moved into it. From 1920 to 1960 so many blacks had left the South that the region lost more than it gained by migration, but during the 1960s it gained 1.8 million whites from the North while losing 1.4 million blacks to the North. As a whole, the black population grew 33 percent faster than the white during the decade and constituted about 11 percent of the nation's total population in 1970.

The flight from the farm continued, at an accelerating speed. In 1920 the people had been distributed about evenly between city and country. By 1970 the rural population had increased slightly, but the urban population had nearly tripled. The number of farms (and farmers) actually declined after 1935, from a peak of 6.8 million in that year to less than 3 million in 1970, and the figure was expected to be below 2 million by 1980. In 1970, some 63 million people were classified as rural (much the most of them nonfarm), about 62 million as strictly urban (living in cities proper), and 75 million as suburban.

RISE OF THE MEGALOPOLIS

During the decades after World War II, metropolitan areas expanded until they met and merged with one another. From north of Boston to south of Washington a single urban region—a megalopolis—was coming into being. From Raleigh to Greensboro and Charlotte, in a similar development on a smaller scale within North Carolina, an "urban crescent" or continuous series of thick settlements was developing. Elsewhere supercities of one kind or another were also taking form.

The proper governing of these areas was a problem. It was complicated by the escape of affluent whites from city jurisdictions and tax collectors to the suburbs, and by the concentration of poor blacks in the inner cities. While the city governments needed more and more financial resources, the tax basis was growing very slowly or actually shrinking.

Because individual metropolitan problems transcended city and sometimes state lines, special governmental authorities to deal with matters like harbor development or transit had come into existence. Together with traditional governments they led to a multiplicity of governmental agencies. Within the 212 standard metropolitan areas in the 1960s there were some 18,000 units of government, ranging from counties to school boards. There was little cooperation among them: most of these governments were ready to give little or no aid to the ailing cities. Many state, county, and suburban officials resisted the establishment of the federal Department of Housing and Urban Development, in 1965.

The problems with which metropolis and the merging megalopolis had to grapple were those long faced by city dwellers: improvement of housing, transportation, living conditions, educational and cultural opportunities, and above all the economic base for both the family and community; conversely, the elimination of pollution, blight, crime, and violence. The size of the new metropolitan areas made these problems far larger and sometimes more complex than in earlier generations.

Federally sponsored housing, which had originated three decades earlier in the New Deal era, together with the urban renewal programs developed after World War II, were good examples. Proponents of housing hoped through combining public and private funds to wipe out the blighted core of the metropolis; erect beautiful, modern structures; and in addition provide comfortable housing that families of varying incomes could afford. Much was achieved, but reality sometimes ran counter to the dream.

Federal aid in one form or another had helped make possible the vast growth of suburbia since 1945 – and then the white exodus from cities into suburbs. By 1963, 5 million families owned houses built with FHA aid; millions more lived in houses financed through the GI Bill of Rights. Federal guarantees had helped

Some Favorable Aspects of Metropolitan Development [1966]

The American urban pattern, in which cities merge in great metropolitan belts, developed as a consequence of the efforts of economically free agents to maximize profits and amenities. In North America, therefore, the city is especially an economic entity. The American city is free, in an economic if not a political sense, to push its boundaries outward. It can preserve a kind of density balance in which individuals' preferences for space are accommodated and technology is used both to concentrate a high intensity of activities and to disperse places of residence. Given the extraordinary heterogeneity of the American population, it is possible that the sprawling development of American cities has actually relieved tension and reduced intergroup conflict by substituting a stratified spatial order for a genuine social accommodation. — John W. Dyckman, "Some Conditions of Civic Order in an Urbanized World," *Daedalus*, Summer 1966, p. 800.

27 million home owners to borrow money for repairs. The government encouraged the deposit of money in savings and loan associations which issued millions of mortgages, by insuring the deposits.

Simultaneously with the growth of suburbs, attempts were made to rejuvenate decaying central cities through federal aid. Urban renewal projects were to transform slums into business and cultural areas and above all into attractive apartment complexes. The new buildings were expected to bring a fivefold increase in taxes, thus helping to solve urban financial problems.

A small beginning during the New Deal had involved federal clearing of slums and construction of public housing. From 1937 on, the federal government helped cities in the undertaking. The 1949 legislation provided for a bold departure. The federal government would help cities finance the purchase of slum land, which would then be sold to private entrepreneurs at reduced costs. Federal loans or mortgage insurance gave these builders a further profit incentive. Thus private enterprise would be persuaded to rebuild the cities.

For five years the program made little progress and thereafter seemed most effective in producing profits for the entrepreneurs. There were numerous complaints that it was the land where the poorest people (often Negroes) lived that was being taken over, and that these people seldom received adequate housing elsewhere at rents they could afford. Sometimes land was cleared and left idle for years while builders were sought. Sometimes the new construction was a complex of luxury apartments, as in the West End of Boston.

Beautification, cleanliness, and safety were also problems requiring community and even national action. Cities in an affluent society produced ever-increasing quantities of waste. Keeping streets and vacant lots clean was relatively simple compared with disposing of the innumerable tons of sewage, garbage, and trash. In 1920 the average person threw away less than 3 pounds of refuse per day; by the mid-sixties he was discarding 4.5 pounds. Household and industrial waste had turned many of the nation's rivers into huge sewers. Smoke and fumes from industries, automobiles, incinerators, and burning dumps created acute smog hazards in widespread areas.

Maintenance of safety was an old problem that each generation faced anew. In 1967 the President's Commission on Crime declared that there was far more crime than ever reported to the police — three times as many burglaries, half again as many robberies, double the number of assaults. The commission observed: "The existence of crime, the talk about crime, the reports of crime, and the fear of crime have eroded the basic quality of life of many Americans." Nevertheless, some specialists doubted whether per capita crime rates had really risen in the 1960s.

THE TRANSPORTATION HEADACHE

Increasingly, after World War II, older modes of conveyance deteriorated. Streetcars, which had taken over America in the early years of the twentieth century, almost completely disappeared, to be supplanted by buses or additional subways. Transit lines, unable to meet rising

Troubles of Rapid Transit
To serve San Francisco and neighboring cities on both sides of San Francisco Bay, the Bay Area Rapid Transit (BART) District was formed to build and operate an ultra-modern, computer-controlled system, with automated high-speed trains. After long delays and unanticipated costs, the partially completed system was opened on September 11, 1972. Less than two weeks later, it had its first wreck, when the automatic controls failed and a train smashed through a sand embankment at the end of the line. (UPI)

costs with revenues that failed to keep pace, faced bankruptcy. Municipally owned systems ran heavier and heavier deficits. Between 1955 and 1965 the number of riders on public transit lines declined 25 percent. Railroads, to cut losses, tried to drop commuter services. The number of passengers commuting by train declined 45 percent between 1929 and 1963 and continued to decline thereafter. City dwellers and suburbanites depended more and more upon automobiles, which were quicker and more convenient. But automobiles required six to forty-five times more space on highways per passenger than did buses, and multiple-unit rail cars were even more efficient.

While public transportation languished, the federal government helped subsidize the building of 6,000 miles of expressways. This forced the leveling of countless blocks of urban buildings (including a disproportionate amount of poor peoples' housing), and other buildings were leveled to provide parking lots. As a consequence, still more automobiles poured into the cities, compounding traffic problems and, during public transportation strikes, creating chaos. An opposite approach at both the local and federal level was to try to improve public transit or even to develop new systems as, most spectacularly, in the San Francisco Bay region. In 1966 Congress created a new Department of Transportation.

National transportation problems were interrelated, as railroad passenger service rapidly declined, and trucks became an increasingly important factor in carrying freight. The large-scale program of turnpike building that

Urban Transportation [1907–1966]

In 1907 it was found that the average speed of horse-drawn vehicles through the city's streets was 11.5 miles per hour. In 1966 the average speed of motor vehicles through the central business district was 8.5 miles per hour — and during the mid-day crushes slower still. — A. E. Palmer, Jr., New York City Transportation Administrator, before a Senate subcommittee, November 16, 1967.

marked the first decade after World War II came to an end as thousands of miles of toll-free superhighways were built, beginning with the Interstate Highway Act of 1956, which set standards for the roads (no grade crossings, for example) and provided federal funds for 90 percent of the cost. For public transportation, Americans had to depend either upon buses or airlines.

By the mid-fifties, airlines, which had been luxury transportation before World War II, were carrying over 30 million passengers per year. By the mid-sixties, the figure had nearly quadrupled and was expected to double again within a decade. Especially along the northeast coast, the air lanes were so crowded that at the height of the evening rush, about 100 planes would be landing or about to land at the three major New York area airports, while another 250 private planes were also taking off or landing at these and smaller fields. Despite an occasional collision, and numerous near collisions, the airlines were able to boast a remarkable safety record. But the congestion of people at the major airports worsened with the appearance, in 1970, of the "jumbo jet" carrying more than twice as many passengers as any previous airliner.

For the future, when airlines might not be able to meet the passenger demands along the northeast corridor between Washington and Boston, the federal government was fostering high-speed train service which it hoped ultimately would carry passengers at 160 miles an hour. The Metroliner, with a speed of 120 miles an hour, was operating between New York and Washington by 1969. There might be a future along a few congested routes for rail passenger service of this sort. In the early 1970s a government-owned corporation, Amtrak, was running passenger trains on a number of railroad lines and was attracting more and more riders, despite the handicap of poor roadbeds

and rolling stock. The principal railroad companies of the Northeast were bankrupt or facing bankruptcy, however, and only massive federal aid could keep them in business.

THE COSTS OF ABUNDANCE

For the American people as a whole, the quarter century following World War II was a time of unprecedented enjoyment of material things. But abundance had its costs in the pollution of the environment and the depletion of natural resources. By the 1970s it had begun to appear that the age of plenty was about over and a new age of scarcity was at hand.

In the 1960s most Americans were still enjoying a living standard far higher than any they had previously known. Though the population had been growing, the output of goods and services had been growing much faster. Even allowing for the rise in prices and in taxes, the average person was better off than ever before. True, income continued to be very unevenly distributed, the top 5 percent of the people receiving 20 percent of the income. Some 40 percent of the people lived in what was considered "either poverty or deprivation" (which meant, as of 1960, having a family income of less than $6,000 a year). Yet workers were getting more pay for less work than in the past. With a forty-hour instead of a forty-four-hour week, and with paid vacations, the average industrial employee enjoyed much more free time than his father or grandfather had in 1900. Workers could afford to spend a smaller proportion of their wages for food, clothing, and shelter and a larger proportion for automobiles, appliances, medical care, recreation, and other luxuries. Even among families classified as living in "poverty" (having an income of less than $4,000 a year), 60 percent owned automobiles in 1960. In 1964, 93 percent of the homes, including those of the poor as well as the rich, contained television sets.

The goods that came forth in such abundance were produced by industries the ownership and control of which were more and more highly concentrated. In 1960 the eighty-seven largest corporations held 26 percent of the total of corporate assets, and in 1970 they held 46 percent. During the 1960s companies merged at a faster rate than ever, usually to form conglomerates. Many of these became "multinational" firms by acquiring subsidiaries in foreign countries. Corporations, "agrobusinesses," took over a larger and larger share of agriculture in the United States, and the average size of farms increased as the number of farms declined.

While consumers enjoyed the bounty that industry provided, a growing number of them complained that too many of the products were useless, dangerous, falsely advertised, overpriced, defective, or lacking in durability. The complaints resulted in an accelerating movement for consumer protection. As early as the 1920s the Consumers Union had begun to test products and issue reports on them. In 1966 Ralph Nader emerged as a leading advocate of the new consumerism when he published a book, *Unsafe at Any Speed,* exposing the built-in hazards of many American cars. Nader started a number of consumer organizations to bring public pressure on both business and government. One of these organizations reported in *The Monopoly Makers* (1973) that federal regulatory agencies often conspired with the industries they were supposed to regulate.

Public services were less plentiful than commercial services and commodities. As population grew, the construction and maintenance of schools, hospitals, streets, sewers, public housing, and other community facilities fell behind the mounting needs. The times were characterized by private wealth and public poverty. That was the theme of John K. Galbraith's widely quoted book *The Affluent Society* (1958). "The line which divides our area of wealth from our area of poverty," Galbraith wrote, "is roughly that which divides privately produced and marketed goods and services from publicly rendered services." The contrast was symbolized by the picture he described of a prosperous middle-class family driving in an

air-conditioned car, over poorly paved and trash-littered streets and billboard-cluttered highways, to lunch on "exquisitely packaged food from a portable ice box" at a picnic spot beside a polluted stream.

There seemed to be, in some material respects, a lowering of the quality of American life, and for much of this the population growth itself was responsible. The results of growth, as the sociologist Dennis H. Wrong pointed out, included "traffic jams, spreading urban and suburban blight, the overcrowding and destruction of beaches, parks, and other outdoor recreational facilities, water shortages, air pollution," and "deterioration in professional and social services resulting from shortages of trained personnel."

The worsening pollution of the environment resulted not only from population growth but, much more, from the great increase in factory output and from the development of new industrial processes and products. The production of synthetic fibers, for example, used more energy and hence directly or indirectly yielded more pollutants than the production of cotton or wool. Synthetic detergents, plastic materials, and aluminum cans were not biodegradable as were the objects for which they were substituted.

One of the worst offenders, with regard to air pollution, was the automobile. Motor vehicle registrations, which had amounted to only 8,000 in 1900, rose from 31 million in 1945 to 109 million in 1970. Thus the number of vehicles grew by more than 300 percent while the number of people was growing by about 50 percent. Many of the newer cars and trucks had more powerful, higher-compression engines than earlier models and gave poorer mileage while using high-test gasoline that contained a lead compound, an additional pollutant.

The befouling of air and water posed an immediate threat to human well-being and an ultimate threat to human existence. Environmentalists raised a demand for government action, and Congress responded with the Clean Air Acts of 1963, 1965, and 1970. These encouraged states and municipalities to set up their own programs for controlling pollution from stationary sources and required car manufacturers to see that vehicle emissions were drastically cut by 1975. Pittsburgh had long since set an example for other municipalities by starting,

Air Pollution in New York
In any major American city the camera could underscore what gauges recorded: the serious pollution of the air, especially troublesome on windless days when an atmospheric inversion (a blanket of warmer air several hundred feet up) kept the pollutants from being dispersed. (New York Daily News*)*

in 1941, a smoke-abatement program which, by the 1950s, had changed the city from one of the smoggiest and grimiest to one of the cleanest. Most communities, however, were slow to act, though some of them experimented with methods of transforming waste into salable products—converting fly ash from incinerators into an ingredient for concrete, manufacturing fertilizer from garbage and sewage, and retrieving metal from dumps. Industrialists generally resisted the application of antipollution measures to their own industries, since such measures tended to raise production costs and lower profits.

The war effort of 1941–1945 had used up tremendous quantities of raw materials, and the ensuing production boom used up still larger quantities of resources, especially fossil fuel. After the war, Americans turned more and more away from coal to oil and natural gas for generating electrical energy as well as for heating houses and other buildings. Manufacturers of plastics, synthetic fibers, and petrochemicals demanded increasing quantities of petroleum as a raw material. Drivers of cars, trucks, and buses added greatly to the demand, and the air force added further with its fueling of bombers in Vietnam.

Signs of an approaching "energy crisis" appeared in the United States as early as the mid-1960s, with the sudden failures of the electrical supply and the temporary blackouts of New York City and other areas in the Northeast. The events of 1973–1974—the restrictions on oil exports by the Arabs and the fantastic price increases by the Arabs and other foreign producers—only made acute a condition that was already on the way to becoming chronic. For the indefinite future, Americans faced a recurring energy shortage. They could take little comfort in the probability that they would not be quite so bad off as the Europeans or the Japanese.

The United States still possessed considerable oil resources, already discovered or yet to be discovered, in addition to vast shale deposits

Strip Mining
Coal, lying just underground, remained abundant in various parts of the United States, but modern methods of removing the coal, though efficient, devastated the land. Here a mammoth strip shovel, as tall as a twenty-story building, is being operated in southeastern Ohio by the Hanna Coal Company. After viewing the scene from a plane—from which this photograph was taken, early in 1972—Governor John J. Gilligan said strip mines were making "Gobi Deserts" of Ohio. (Wide World Photos)

that eventually could be made to yield petroleum. The country had enough coal in the ground to last for centuries. It also had the capacity to build additional atomic-power plants. But the exploitation of petroleum, coal, or atomic fission endangered the environment in one way or another—through possible spills from drilling, damage to surroundings from oil transportation (as in the case of the Alaska pipeline to bring oil south from new Alaskan fields), destruction of mountains to get at shale, scarring of land by strip mining, pollution of air by the burning of low-grade coal, leakage of

radioactive wastes from an atomic reactor, or some even more deadly accident with an atomic-power plant.

In time the harnessing of the sun's rays might provide clean energy, but other resources would remain scarce in comparison with the abundant supplies of the past. Seemingly, as they advanced toward the twenty-first century, Americans would have to face the necessity of stabilizing their population, limiting their industrial growth, and changing their way of life so as to consume less of material goods.

Culture and Counterculture

After World War II the social and cultural life of Americans underwent noticeable changes. These, especially during the 1960s, seemed in some minds to portend the loss of moral values, the collapse of institutional authority, and the disintegration of society itself. Critics complained of a materialistic "consumer culture," a hedonistic "permissive society," and the "alienation" of children from parents and of individuals from the group. The changes, however, tended less in new and strange directions than in directions that already had long been set. Even the jeremiads were familiar. Complaints of the same tenor had been heard from time to time throughout the history of the American people and, indeed, the history of humankind.

THE "PERMISSIVE" SOCIETY

World War I had been followed, during the "roaring twenties," by deviations from traditional manners and morals, especially on the part of "flaming youth." World War II did not have so pronounced an immediate aftermath, but during the sixties, with the escalation of the Vietnam War, the deviations were even more spectacular. By the 1970s there were signs of a reaction away from some of the excesses.

"Togetherness" was a watchword of the 1950s, yet the family continued to lose its cohesion. By 1960, there was one annulment or divorce for every four marriages; by 1970, one for every three. Some attributed the rising divorce rate to the growing financial independence of women, more and more of whom were working outside the home. Yet the divorce rate, in 1970, was higher among the poor and the ill educated than among the better off and the better educated. It was higher for city dwellers than for rural folk, and much higher for non-whites than for whites.

There was talk of a "sexual revolution" in the 1960s as sex relations outside of marriage appeared to become much more widespread than ever before. Presumably the oral contraceptive—"the pill"—encouraged extramarital intercourse by practically eliminating the risk of pregnancy. But studies by Dr. Alfred C. Kinsey and his Institute for Sex Research, at Indi-

Memorandum on Youth

I would assume that adolescents today and tomorrow are struggling to define new modes of conduct which are relevant to their lives. . . . Yet, this is within the context of two culture factors which seem to be extraordinary in the history of moral temper. One is the scepticism of all authority, the refusal to define natural authority (perhaps even that of paternal authority) and a cast of mind which is essentially anti-institutional and even antinomian. . . . The second factor is an extraordinary hedonism—using the word in the broadest sense—in that there is a desacralization of life and an attitude that all experience is permissible and even desirable. . . . At the same time society imposes new forms of specialization, of extending training, of new hierarchies and organizations. Thus, one finds an unprecedented divorce between culture and the society. And, from all indications, such a separation will increase. . . . In this respect, assuming this hypothesis is true, the greatest strains will be on the youth. This particular generation, like its predecessors, may come back to some form of accommodation with the society as it grows older and accepts positions within the society. But the experiences also leave a "cultural deposit" which is cumulative consciousness and—to this extent I am a Hegelian—is irreversible, and the next generation therefore starts from a more advanced position of alienation and detachment.—Erik H. Erikson, *Daedalus*, Summer 1967, pp. 860–863.

ana University, cast doubt on the idea of a re-volution. Kinsey's *Sexual Behavior in the Human Male* (1948) showed that, among the preceding generation of Americans, sex activity had been much more varied than laws or morals would have led anyone to believe. "People talk more freely about sex nowadays, and young people are far more tolerant and permissive regarding sex," Kinsey's successor observed in the 1960s. Yet, though premarital intercourse had increased, it had not risen suddenly or dramatically; "it has been on the rise ever since the turn of the century."

For some women, sexual freedom meant freedom from unwanted children, not only through contraception but, when necessary, through abortion. Advocates of abortion-on-demand asserted the right of a woman to control her own body. Opponents insisted on the right of the unborn to the enjoyment of life. A few states liberalized their laws so as to permit abortion under a wide range of conditions, but most of the states retained laws that made it difficult if not impossible — except for illegal and often dangerous practitioners. In 1973 the Supreme Court struck down those state laws that prohibited abortion during the first three months of pregnancy.

Freedom of sexual expression in words and pictures raised another constitutional issue, that of freedom of speech and the press. In 1957 the Supreme Court narrowed the legal definition of obscenity to include only those works that were morally offensive by prevailing national standards and were "utterly without redeeming social value." This decision put the burden of proof on local authorities in obscenity cases. It opened the way for an unprecedented flood of pornography. Vivid representations of sexual activity in all imaginable forms appeared in movies, plays, and books and magazines which mushrooming "adult" bookstores purveyed along with a variety of sexual devices. President Johnson appointed a Commission on Obscenity and Pornography to study the effects. The commission finally reported, in 1970, that "exposure to explicit sexual materials" apparently had little or nothing to do with causing emotional disorders, delinquency, or crime. The commission recommended the repeal of all laws forbidding the dissemination of such materials to consenting adults. Instead of acting on that recommendation, President Nixon denounced the report as "morally bankrupt," and the Senate condemned it by a vote of 60 to 5. The Supreme Court, instead of further relaxing its stand, soon practically reversed itself. In 1973 it held that works were obscene if they lacked "serious literary, artistic, political, or scientific value" and if they were offensive by the standards of the local community. The burden of proof was now on the defendant, and local authorities here and there began successfully to prosecute.

Clothes may not make the man or woman, but changing styles of clothing seemed to reflect a changing relationship between women and men. In 1947 fashion designers decreed the "new look" of ankle-length skirts, and women meekly obeyed. Thereafter hemlines gradually rose until, in the late 1960s, they were much higher than they had been even during the 1920s. In 1971 the couturiers called for an end to "miniskirts" and to the even more abbreviated "hot pants" and for a return to long dresses, to mid-calf "midiskirts" or to full-length "maxiskirts." This time the women refused to heed. Instead, they turned to trousers and pant suits, or to blue jeans, which were already the uniform of the young, male and female alike. With young men and women wearing their hair to their shoulders, it was often hard to tell boy and girl apart — until, perhaps, one of them turned around and revealed a beard. The day of "unisex" seemed at hand, as distinctions of appearance if not also of role, became increasingly blurred. In the spirit of the time, homosexuals and lesbians came forth as never before to avow themselves openly and even proudly.

A great many middle-class young people, though by no means all of them, rejected the values as well as the clothes of adults. People spoke of the "generation gap" as if it were something entirely new. It did take new forms. Fringe groups, the "beatniks" of the 1950s and the "hippies" of the 1960s, went to extremes of unconventional dress and behavior. Drug use spread as growing numbers of youth retreated from a world they disliked. They were "turning on" (or, more accurately, turning off) by smoking marijuana, taking "mind-expanding" chemicals such as LSD, or injecting themselves with narcotics such as heroin. Blaring rock-and-roll music was a favorite with the young, along with ballads that, to a guitar accompaniment, protested against war, poverty, injustice, and the older generation, including everyone older than thirty. The youth movement reached a crescendo when, in August 1969, more than 300,000 gathered for a "rock festival" near Woodstock, New York, where most shed their inhibitions and many their clothing. The movement found a philosopher in Charles Reich, whose book *The Greening of America* (1970) praised "Consciousness III" as a new awareness, on the part of youth, of self as the only reality.

In the 1970s it appeared that young people were drawing away from their preoccupations of the previous decade. Some turned to religion of a traditional kind, the "Jesus freaks" singing, shouting, and clapping in the spirit of old-time revivalism. Others looked to even more unconventional cults. A sign of the changing times was the conversion of Rennie C. Davis. As a young radical, one of the "Chicago Seven," Davis had been charged (he was eventually acquitted) with inciting to riot at the Democratic national convention of 1968. Later he took up the mystical teachings of Maharaj Ji, a fifteen-year-old guru from India. In 1973 he proclaimed his love for the guru: "I would cross the planet on my hands and knees to touch his toe."

Leaders of the youth movement in the 1960s had rejected the past as "irrelevant." Now, in the 1970s, young people along with their elders acquired an enthusiasm for bygone decades, for the 1950s, the 1920s, or earlier periods. There developed a craze for reminders of what had come to seem like the good old days. This was reflected in art, dress, and the theater. It received a huge stimulus in 1974 from the promotion of a movie, *The Great Gatsby* (the third cinematic version of F. Scott Fitzgerald's 1925 novel), which drew large crowds eager to wallow in the sights and sounds of the 1920s. One might have concluded that, for many Americans of the 1970s, the past was more attractive than the present. Actually, such waves of nostalgia were not entirely new in American life. Previous generations, too, had looked back with longing beyond the immediate past to remoter and, in the haze of time, more glamorous eras.

The youth culture of the 1960s, in its various manifestations, had made so great an impression partly because young people were proportionally so numerous. With the aging of the population — with the disappearance of the youthful "bulge" in it — the influence of the young could be expected to decline.

EDUCATION AND RELIGION

After World War II, critics of public education charged that the schools were neglecting things of the mind in favor of athletics, band contests, vocational training, and "life adjustment." When the Soviet Union launched the first artificial satellite, sputnik, in 1957, many Americans assumed that the Russians had proved the superiority of their education in science and technology. A demand arose for fewer "frills" and more intellectual rigor, and school officials, teachers, and pupils responded. So did Congress. In 1958 it passed the National Defense Education Act, which provided for the spending of nearly a billion dollars over a four-year period to encourage the study of science, mathematics, and foreign languages.

Nevertheless, the schools continued to be criticized for their performance. At the end of the 1960s it appeared that 10 to 15 of every 100 pupils entering the fourth grade could not read (in ghetto schools, 35 to 50 of every 100). About 25 million adults in the nation as a whole were functionally illiterate, unable to comprehend a newspaper or magazine article or to fill out an application form. Most of these people were school dropouts.

With the gaining momentum of the civil rights movement, the emphasis of school reformers had shifted from academic excellence to equality of educational opportunity. This presumably would help the poor to rise out of poverty. But Christopher Jencks and seven associates at Harvard University's Center for Educational Policy Research questioned the assumption in a 1972 report. "If we want economic equality in our society," Jencks wrote, "we will have to get it by changing our economic institutions, not by changing the schools."

In fact, educational equality was yet to be tried. Annual expenditures per pupil ranged from a few hundred dollars in some schools to several thousand in others, even within the same state. Schools depended mainly on local property taxes, and resources therefore varied tremendously as between the poorest and the wealthiest districts. In the early 1970s, after the supreme court of California had declared the reliance on local school taxes unconstitutional in that state, suits were brought against similar financing arrangements in more than thirty other states.

The swelling enrollments of the 1950s and 1960s necessitated costly programs of school construction. At first the voters responded willingly by approving the issue of construction bonds, but eventually they grew more and more reluctant. In 1960 they approved nearly 90 percent of the bond issues put to referendums; in 1970, less than 47 percent. Undoubtedly the people were reacting against rising taxes, but they also seemed to be expressing a decline of confidence in the public schools.

During World War II, colleges and universities suffered from a loss of male students to the draft. The federal government helped many institutions by contracting with them to educate and train various kinds of specialists for the armed forces. After the war the government contributed to a sudden bulge in enrollments by paying the college expenses of veterans under the "GI Bill of Rights." During the 1950s and 1960s, attendance continued to swell, and at a faster rate than the college-age population, for a larger and larger proportion of young people were going on to secondary and higher education. Graduate and professional schools were especially thriving, as the demand for university teachers and other professional workers grew. The federal government heavily subsidized many programs that were directly or indirectly related to the national defense. State universities multiplied as teachers' colleges were converted into general colleges and these were raised, at least in name, to university status. Large campuses grew larger still—there were thirty-nine with more than 20,000 students in 1969 as compared with only two in 1941.

By the early 1970s the quarter-century-long academic boom appeared to be at an end. Federal support had been curtailed. Enrollments were leveling off and, in many institutions, even falling, while unemployment rose among holders of the Ph.D. and other advanced degrees. Private institutions, having had to raise tuition charges repeatedly in order to meet rising costs, had lagged far behind in the recruitment of students. Now many of the smaller and financially weaker private colleges faced the threat of extinction.

The first postwar generation of college students—especially the veterans, or GIs—seemed to be mainly interested in getting a degree in order to get ahead. A survey of members of the class of '49 concluded that they were "curiously old before their time" and were concentrating on the pursuit of economic security. Students of the 1950s also appeared to be looking ahead to jobs, especially corporation jobs. The prevailing campus spirit was quiet and conformist.

Then, in 1964, the campus of the University of California at Berkeley erupted, and during the next several years other large universities from coast to coast experienced a succession of student riots, with the rioters taking over and sometimes fire-bombing university buildings and "trashing" (vandalizing) business properties in the neighborhood. The rioters were giving expression to a variety of complaints—the impersonality of the gigantic and complex "multiversity," the irrelevance of its curriculum to their personal needs, its complicity in the Vietnam War (through war-related research and through the training of military officers in the ROTC), and its role as a bulwark of the socially unjust Establishment. Some of the rebels came from affluent families and were less preoccupied with upward striving than their successful fathers had been as college youths of the early postwar years. Other rebels, the blacks, were demanding the kind of college education that would enable them to rise in economic and social status and in self-esteem.

Colleges and universities responded to demands for "relevance" and personal involvement by relaxing requirements, adding courses in "black studies" and other contemporary concerns, and giving students some voice in administration. Some institutions, such as the City University of New York, adopted a policy of "open admissions," eliminating most entrance requirements.

During the postwar decade, church membership grew at about twice the rate of the population as a whole. This did not necessarily mean that Americans were becoming increasingly devout. When questioned, people generally identified themselves as Protestants, Catholics, or Jews, but relatively few expressed strong convictions. Many apparently referred to one faith or another as a means of indicating social background or of gaining, in an impersonal society, some sense of "belonging." Church attendance declined between 1958, when (according to a poll) 49 percent of the people were churchgoers, and 1972, when only 40 percent were. This, in turn, did not necessarily indicate a decline in religiosity. There were, indeed, signs of growing fervor on the part of groups who did not attend the traditional churches but who devoted themselves to Zen Buddhism, Hinduism, and other exotic faiths.

Churchmen, both Protestant and Catholic, were divided among themselves in regard to the mission of the church. Among Protestants, the most famous preacher, Norman Vincent Peale, wrote of religion as a force for success in the world (much as Bruce Barton formerly had done). The most popular revivalist, Billy Graham, offered a conventional message of individual salvation and, as a personal friend of Presidents Eisenhower and Nixon, associated with the politically powerful. But a spokesman for the World Council of Churches declared: "The Church must identify itself much more radically with the interests of the poor, the 'losers,' the outcasts and the alienated." While some Catholic priests revived the medieval practice of exorcising devils – and cooperated in the production of a 1973 movie on the theme, *The Exorcist*, a box-office hit – other priests, such as the brothers Philip and Daniel Berrigan, involved themselves in the antiwar movement and other social causes.

REFLECTIONS IN LITERATURE

The most prestigious figures in American writing, during the quarter century after World War II, were those who had made their reputations in earlier decades. Through the fifties, Ernest Hemingway and William Faulkner were two of the patriarchs of literature for the Western world as well as for the United States. Faulkner retained his master's touch in portraying the deep South he knew so well and through it viewing the world. Hemingway at times seemed to be parodying his earlier, virile, trenchant style, but produced one work in these years, *The Old Man and the Sea* (1952), that seemed destined to endure. It was the brief tale of an aged Cuban striving heroically, and unsuccessfully, to protect from the forays

of the sharks a huge fish he had caught. The poet Robert Frost seemed already a legendary figure before his death in 1963. After Eugene O'Neill's death in 1953, several of his previously unproduced plays ran for months on Broadway and on national tours.

By the sixties all these men of great reputation were gone. A large new generation of vigorous writers was attracting attention, but it was too soon to be sure which if any of them would win enduring top reputations. Among the novelists, their work ranged from the realism of John O'Hara and James Gould Cozzens, portrayers of the upper middle class, whose work seemed old-fashioned to younger critics, through a variety of newer styles and themes. The work of Robert Penn Warren, who won the Pulitzer Prize in both poetry and fiction, transcended Southern regionalism, but his most widely read novel, *All the King's Men* (1946), was a study of a political leader resembling Huey Long of Louisiana. In 1948 Norman Mailer produced the most acclaimed of the novels that came out of World War II, *The Naked and the Dead,* but in his subsequent work was more successful as a writer of nonfiction. J. D. Salinger through his account of the inward torture of an adolescent boy, *Catcher in the Rye* (1951), and subsequent stories about the precocious members of the Glass family (*Franny and Zooey,* 1962) became the spokesman for the generation of the 1950s.

Through the writings of several of the novelists ran a theme of alienation from, or at least serious questioning of, their culture. Saul Bellow began his work in this vein with *Dangling Man* (1944) and continued it in a number of successful novels, including *The Adventures of Augie March* (1953) and *Herzog* (1964). Nelson Algren, no admirer of middle-class values, wrote with blunt clarity about the flotsam of society, the men and women who had never had a chance, in his stories and novels, most notably, *The Man with the Golden Arm* (1949). Several Negro writers fell within this pattern. The most famous was James Baldwin, perhaps at his best in works of nonfiction like *The Fire Next Time* (1963); the most bitter, the poet and playwright, LeRoi Jones, especially effective in his one-act plays; and the most distinguished, Ralph Ellison, for a single novel, *Invisible Man* (1952). When the New York *Herald Tribune Book Week* in 1965 queried some 200 critics, authors, and editors, their consensus was that the work of fiction of the previous two decades most memorable and most likely to endure was *Invisible Man*. It is the sweeping, at times fantastic, drama of a young Negro's quest for identity. The novel that the critics listed second as most memorable was the polished social satire *Lolita* (1955) written by a Russian émigré, Vladimir Nabokov.

Among the novelists who emerged in the 1960s, perhaps the most notable were John Barth, Joseph Heller, Kurt Vonnegut, Jr., and Thomas Pynchon. Each dealt in his own way with what seemed to all of them like the cosmic absurdity of contemporary life. They were less interested in developing character or plot than in creating effects of intellectual ambiguity and emotional contradiction. In his mock-picaresque novel *The Sot-Weed Factor* (1961) Barth gave the impression that people could find no meaning in life except for the realization that they were merely acting their parts in a farce that had been written for them. In *Catch-22* (1964) Heller ridiculed the insanity and regimentation of war and, by implication, the insanity and regimentation of business society. In *Slaughterhouse-Five* (1969), his sixth novel, Vonnegut used his experience in World War II as a springboard for science fiction in which horror was mixed with humor. In his third novel, *Gravity's Rainbow* (1973), Pynchon made his central figure a German V-2 rocket of World War II. Baffling, jarring, full of complex symbolism, Pynchon's book gave an apocalyptic and paranoid vision of man's place in the universe. Some reviewers hailed it as the greatest American novel since *Moby Dick*.

Poetry, like painting, broke sharply with traditions after 1945. While poets like Frost and Carl Sandburg enjoyed fame in their old age, the liberal activism that moved poets like Archibald MacLeish during the depression and war years subsided after 1945. The newer poets moved away from public causes, toward the psychological and mythological, as did Randall Jarrell, or toward the autobiographical or confessional, as did Robert Lowell. Through much of this poetry ran a distaste for the established order. One critic, M. L. Rosenthal, suggests: "Behind it is the feeling, perhaps, that the humanistic way, which traditionally educated and romantic modern men still propose to protect, and indeed to project into a Utopian future, has already been defeated and is now no more than a ghost. It is that feeling which Robert Lowell in one of his poems calls, self-ironically, 'our universal *Angst*' – a heart-heavy realization that remorseless brutality is a condition not only of the physical universe but also of man himself."

CONSUMERS OF THE ARTS

Never had so many Americans shown so much interest in literature, art, and music as they did during the age of affluence that followed World War II. To some extent the federal and state governments encouraged cultural activity, the federal government establishing (1966) the Federal Arts and Humanities Endowments and a Federal Council on the Arts, and each of the states setting up its own arts council or commission. Some of the councils made financial grants, and private foundations provided more substantial sums. Most of the activity, however, was financed by individual spending.

The catering to cultural interests became a big business in itself, as statistics indicate. Between 1953 and 1960, expenditures on such interests rose by 130 percent, reaching an annual total of $3 billion. That was a larger sum than advertisers were spending on television commercials. In 1964, Americans paid the following amounts for certain cultural items: $1 billion for books, $600 million on musical instruments, $200 million on paintings or reproductions and art supplies, nearly $400 million to attend dramatic and musical performances, and $300 million to maintain art museums. By the end of the 1960s, total expenditures were approaching $7 billion a year. People were spending twice as much on the arts as on recreation in general and six times as much as on sports.

Nevertheless, the times were difficult for the performing arts, which suffered from rising costs, lagging attendance, and repeated deficits. A 1966 study showed that the nation was supporting only five full-time symphony orchestras, and the increase in attendance at concerts was somewhat slower than the increase in population. New York City accounted for nearly 40 percent of the receipts at musical performances and more than 50 percent of those at dramatic performances. The audiences represented only a very small and select portion of the people, consisting almost entirely of those with high incomes.

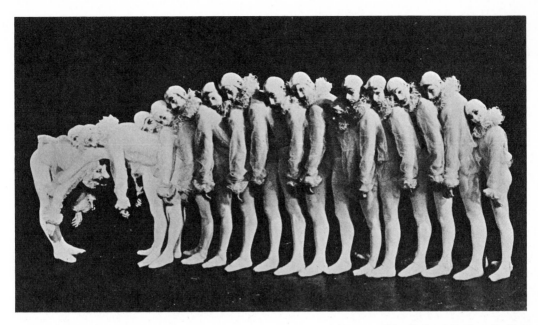

The Robert Joffrey Ballet
By the end of the 1960s a number of brilliant young companies were bringing both technical perfection and innovation to American ballets. (Herbert Migdoll)

Of all stage performances, musical comedies generally had the widest appeal. They constituted the American equivalent of a popular opera. Every few years an extremely successful one made its appearance: *Oklahoma!* in 1943, *My Fair Lady* in 1956, *West Side Story* in 1957, *Camelot* in 1960, *Hello Dolly* in 1963, and *Fiddler on the Roof* in 1964. *My Fair Lady* set a record for the longest Broadway run of a musical comedy. *Hello Dolly* broke that record and then was surpassed by *Fiddler on the Roof*, which in 1973 was still going strong.

Classical and popular music was available on improved, inexpensive phonograph records, the sales of which rose astronomically. In the 1940s, long-playing records of durable vinyl, turning at a speed of 45 or 33-1/3 revolutions per minute, began to replace the former short-playing, easily breakable 78 rpm disks. The quality of the reproduction was vastly improved, meanwhile, by the development of high-fidelity electronic recording and, during the 1950s, by the introduction of stereophonic sound. Together with television and both AM and FM radio, the improved phonographs provided good music to an audience vastly larger than that attending opera houses or concert halls.

THE ROLE OF TELEVISION

Television changed the leisure habits of the American people, made them better informed on the news and issues of the day, and even modified the patterns of American politics. In 1947 fewer than 10,000 people owned television sets with which they could view programs a few hours a day from a handful of stations. A decade later over 40 million sets in homes, hotels, and bars were tuned in to 467 stations. Motion-picture attendance dropped from a wartime high of 90 million a week to about 40 million. Not until the sixties did Hollywood begin to recuperate, by producing pictures that were better than before, or at least bolder. Professional sports, especially football and basketball, flourished as television brought them to millions of spectators at a time.

Television even more than radio meant mass communication to a nationwide audience. One musical show, telecast on 245 stations one night in March 1957 reached an estimated audience of 100 million—enough people to fill a Broadway theater every night for 165 years. Beginning with the 1952 campaign, television remade presidential elections as candidates began to make extensive and expensive use of the new medium. Radio was far from superseded, especially in the transistorized portable form that took over not only the United States but the entire world during these years.

Advertisers paid for the vast outpouring from commercial television and radio stations. They spent enormous sums to compete for the attention of the average television viewer who, surveys indicated, sat in front of his set as much as six hours a day. The manufacturers of one headache remedy, for example, spent nearly $750,000 in one month in 1958; their two nearest competitors spent a combined total of nearly $1 million that same month. In consequence, programs were patterned to draw the largest number of viewers, and when surveys indicated that the sets were tuned in elsewhere, the programs were ruthlessly pruned. Television lost one of its biggest sources of income when the federal government banned cigarette commercials after January 1, 1971.

One critic, Richard Schickel, commented that, to literate people, television was "an unparalleled purveyor of trash." Nevertheless, "we sit there, eyes glued to the set, watching this explication of the obvious in hateful fascination." A Canadian scholar, Marshall McLuhan, won a large following by extolling in confusing but thought-provoking prose the new era of mass media. He wrote, in *The Medium Is the Message* (1967): "The contained, the distinct, the separate – our western legacy – are being replaced by the flowing, the unified, the fused." The electronic medium of communication made its impressions all at once, he said, in contrast to the print medium, which made its impressions one after another. One reason for the generation gap and the youth revolt, he suggested, was the influence of the new medium on the young, who for the first time had been exposed to it in their formative years.

Foundations and the federal government tried to further the positive role of television. The Carnegie and Ford foundations proposed that educational stations be encouraged to take advantage of television's educational and cultural potentialities. The Public Broadcasting Act of 1967 authorized, though it provided no financing for, a noncommercial television network. Soon university-affiliated and other stations from coast to coast were providing high-quality theater, musical performances, and lecture courses with the cooperation of the Public Broadcasting System.

Commercial stations received and transmitted a large share of their programs from one or another of three great networks, the American Broadcasting Company, the National Broadcasting Company, and the Columbia Broadcasting System. These sources provided not only entertainment but also news and opinion for their affiliated stations. Bringing world events, or chosen segments of them, visibly into the home, the network programs had a much greater emotional impact (as in reporting the Vietnam War) than did newspaper accounts. A comparatively small number of prestigious commentators, outstanding among them Walter Cronkite of CBS, dominated the presentation of TV news. Hence questions arose regarding the breadth and balance of the coverage.

Vice President Agnew and other spokesmen for the Nixon administration, as well as Nixon himself, objected strongly to what they considered hostile treatment by the news media, especially television. Agnew demanded that commentators be "made more responsible to the views of the nation." The director of the White House Office of Telecommunications Policy attacked TV newsmen as "so-called professionals who confuse sensation with sense and who dispense elitist gossip in the guise of news analysis." He proposed a law that would put the responsibility on local stations for assuring "fairness," and the administration threatened to revoke the licenses of stations that failed to meet its standards.

An independent study (1973) by the Twentieth Century Fund concluded, however, that "presidential television" gave the President a great advantage over his critics. "Presidential television means the ability to appear simultaneously on all national radio and television networks at prime, large-audience evening hours, virtually whenever and however he wishes." Nixon exploited this advantage even more than his predecessors, taking as much TV time during his first eighteen months in office as Eisenhower, Kennedy, and Johnson together had taken during theirs. Congress, the courts, the opposition party could not keep up with the President in his ability to command free time on the air. Television appeared to be one of the factors that had increased the power of the executive as against that of the other branches of government.

Selected Readings

Nixon and Politics

Garry Wills, *Nixon Agonistes* (1970); Rowland Evans, Jr., and R. D. Novak, *Nixon in the White House: The Frustration of Power* (1971); R. J. Whalen, *Catch the Falling Flag* (1972); R. M. Scammon and B. J. Wattenberg, *The Real Majority* (1970); Samuel Lubell, *The Hidden Crisis in American Politics** (1970); L. K. Howe, ed., *The White Majority* (1970); Walter DeVries and V. L. Tarrance, *The Ticket-Splitters* (1972); T. H. White, *The Making of the President, 1972* (1973); R. S. Anson, *McGovern* (1972), a campaign biography; H. E. Alexander, *Money in Politics* (1972); L. Baritz, ed., *The American Left: Radical Political Thought in the Twentieth Century* (1972); J. P. Diggins, *The American Left in the Twentieth Century** (1973).

Economic Policies

R. L. Miller, *The New Economics of Richard Nixon* (1972); Leonard Silk, *Nixonomics* (1972); F. F. Piven and R. A. Cloward, *Regulating the Poor: The Functions of Public Welfare* (1971); D. P. Moynihan, *The Politics of a Guaranteed Income: The Nixon Administration and the Family Assistance Plan* (1973); Walter Hickel, *Who Owns America?* (1971); J. K. Galbraith, *The New Industrial State** (1971); R. F. Buckthorn, *Nader, The People's Lawyer* (1972).

Population

B. J. Wattenberg and R. M. Scammon, *The U.S.A. An Unexpected Family Portrait . . . Drawn from the Census* (1965); L. H. and A. T. Day, *Too Many Americans* (1965); Conrad and I. B. Taeuber, *The Changing Population of the United States* (1958).

Interpretations of Society

David Riesman, *The Lonely Crowd** (1950); D. M. Potter, *People of Plenty: Economic Abundance and the American Character** (1954); J. K. Galbraith, *The Affluent Society** (1958); C. W. Mills, *The Power Elite** (1956); D. T. Bazelon, *Power in America* (1967); W. H. Whyte, *Organization Man** (1956); Vance Packard, *The Hidden Persuaders** (1957); Marshall McLuhan, *Understanding Media: The Extension of Man** (1964) and *The Medium Is the Message* (1967); Alvin Toffler, *Future Shock** (1970); W. L. O'Neill, *Coming Apart: An Informal History of America in the 1960's* (1971).

The City

Jean Gottman, *Megalopolis: The Urbanized Northeastern Seaboard of the United States* (1961); Martin Anderson, *The Federal Bulldozer: A Critical Analysis of Urban Renewal, 1949–1962** (1965); Charles Abrams, *The City Is the Frontier** (1965); R. C. Wood, *Suburbia: Its People and Their Politics* (1959); Wilfred Owen, *The Metropolitan Transportation Problem** (1966); Claiborne Pell, *Megalopolis Unbound: The Supercity and the Transportation of Tomorrow* (1966); Frank Graham, *Disaster by Default: Politics and Water Pollution* (1966); J. R. Lowe, *Cities in a Race with Time: Progress and Poverty in America's Renewing Cities* (1967); F. R. Harris and J. V. Lindsay, *The State of the Cities* (1972).

Culture

Ronald Berman, *America in the Sixties: An Intellectual History* (1968); Bernard Rosenberg and D. M. White, eds., *Mass Culture* (1957); K. S. Lynn, ed., *The Professions in America** (1965); John Burchard and Albert Bush-Brown, *The Architecture of America** (1961); W. J. Baumol and W. G. Bowen, *Performing Arts: The Economic Dilemma* (1966); Richard Kostelanetz, ed., *The New American Arts** (1965) and *On Contemporary American Literature** (1964); Stephen Stepanchev, *American Poetry Since 1945** (1965); Charles Rembar, *The End of Obscenity** (1968).

Youth and Education

E. H. Erikson, *Identity: Youth and Crisis* (1968); Kenneth Keniston, *The Uncommitted: Alienated Youth in American Society* (1965); Christopher Jencks and David Riesman, *The Academic Revolution* (1968); S. M. Lipset and S. S. Wolin, eds., *The Berkeley Student Revolt: Facts and Interpretations** (1965); J. B. Conant, *The American High School Today** (1959) and *Slums and Suburbs* (1964).

Science and Technology

D. K. Price, *The Scientific Estate* (1965); Gerald Holton, ed., *Science and Culture** (1965); Herbert Simon, *The Shape of Automation* (1966); William Francois, *Automation: Industrialization Comes of Age** (1964); H. H. Goldstine, *The Computer from Pascal to von Neumann* (1972).

To the Moon

Walter Sullivan, ed., *America's Race for the Moon** (1962); Jay Holmes, *America on the Moon* (1962); Hugh Odishaw, ed., *The Challenges of Space* (1962); L. S. Swenson and others, *This New Ocean: A History of Project Mercury* (1966); R. L. Rosholt, *An Administrative History of NASA, 1958–1963* (1966).

*Titles available in paperback.

Appendices

The Declaration of Independence

In Congress, July 4, 1776,

THE UNANIMOUS DECLARATION OF THE THIRTEEN UNITED STATES OF AMERICA

When, in the course of human events, it becomes necessary for one people to dissolve the political bands which have connected them with another, and to assume, among the powers of the earth, the separate and equal station to which the laws of nature and of nature's God entitle them, a decent respect to the opinions of mankind requires that they should declare the causes which impel them to the separation.

We hold these truths to be self-evident, that all men are created equal; that they are endowed by their Creator with certain unalienable rights; that among these, are life, liberty, and the pursuit of happiness. That, to secure these rights, governments are instituted among men, deriving their just powers from the consent of the governed; that, whenever any form of government becomes destructive of these ends, it is the right of the people to alter or to abolish it, and to institute a new government, laying its foundation on such principles, and organizing its powers in such form, as to them shall seem most likely to effect their safety and happiness. Prudence, indeed, will dictate that governments long established, should not be changed for light and transient causes; and, accordingly, all experience hath shown, that mankind are more disposed to suffer, while evils are sufferable, than to right themselves by abolishing the forms to which they are accustomed. But, when a long train of abuses and usurpations, pursuing invariably the same object, evinces a design to reduce them under absolute despotism, it is their right, it is their duty, to throw off such government and to provide new guards for their future security. Such has been the patient sufferance of these colonies, and such is now the necessity which constrains them to alter their former systems of government. The history of the present King of Great Britain is a history of repeated injuries and usurpations, all having, in direct object, the establishment of an absolute tyranny over these States. To prove this, let facts be submitted to a candid world: —

He has refused his assent to laws the most wholesome and necessary for the public good.

He has forbidden his governors to pass laws of immediate and pressing importance, unless suspended in their operation till his assent should be obtained; and, when so suspended, he has utterly neglected to attend to them.

He has refused to pass other laws for the accommodation of large districts of people, unless those people would relinquish the right of representation in the legislature; a right inestimable to them, and formidable to tyrants only.

He has called together legislative bodies at places unusual, uncomfortable, and distant from the depository of their public records, for the sole purpose of fatiguing them into compliance with his measures.

He has dissolved representative houses repeatedly for opposing, with manly firmness, his invasions on the rights of the people.

He has refused, for a long time after such dissolutions, to cause others to be elected; whereby the legislative powers, incapable of annihilation, have returned to the people at large for their exercise; the state remaining, in the meantime, exposed to all the danger of invasion from without, and convulsions within.

He has endeavored to prevent the population of these States; for that purpose, obstructing the laws for naturalization of foreigners, refusing to pass others to encourage their migration hither, and raising the conditions of new appropriations of lands.

He has obstructed the administration of justice, by refusing his assent to laws for establishing judiciary powers.

He has made judges dependent on his will alone, for the tenure of their offices, and the amount and payment of their salaries.

He has erected a multitude of new offices, and sent hither swarms of officers to harass our people, and eat out their substance.

He has kept among us, in time of peace, standing armies, without the consent of our legislatures.

He has affected to render the military independent of, and superior to, the civil power.

He has combined, with others, to subject us to a jurisdiction foreign to our Constitution, and unacknowledged by our laws; giving his assent to their acts of pretended legislation:

For quartering large bodies of armed troops among us:

For protecting them by a mock trial, from punishment, for any murders which they should commit on the inhabitants of these States:

For cutting off our trade with all parts of the world:

For imposing taxes on us without our consent:

For depriving us, in many cases, of the benefit of trial by jury:

For transporting us beyond seas to be tried for pretended offences:

For abolishing the free system of English laws in a neighboring province, establishing therein an arbitrary government, and enlarging its boundaries, so as to render it at once an example and fit instrument for introducing the same absolute rule into these colonies:

For taking away our charters, abolishing our most valuable laws, and altering, fundamentally, the powers of our governments:

For suspending our own legislatures, and declaring themselves invested with power to legislate for us in all cases whatsoever.

He has abdicated government here, by declaring us out of his protection, and waging war against us.

He has plundered our seas, ravaged our coasts, burnt our towns, and destroyed the lives of our people.

He is, at this time, transporting large armies of foreign mercenaries to complete the works of death, desolation, and tyranny, already begun, with circumstances of cruelty and perfidy scarcely paralleled in the most barbarous ages, and totally unworthy the head of a civilized nation.

He has constrained our fellow citizens, taken captive on the high seas, to bear arms against their country, to become the executioners of their friends, and brethren, or to fall themselves by their hands.

He has excited domestic insurrections amongst us, and has endeavored to bring on the inhabitants of our frontiers, the merciless Indian savages, whose known rule of warfare is an undistinguished destruction of all ages, sexes, and conditions.

In every stage of these oppressions, we have petitioned for redress, in the most humble terms; our repeated petitions have been answered only by repeated injury. A prince, whose character is thus marked by every act which may define a tyrant, is unfit to be the ruler of a free people.

Nor have we been wanting in attention to our British brethren. We have warned them, from time to time, of attempts made by their legislature to extend an unwarrantable jurisdiction over us. We have reminded them of the circumstances of our emigration and settlement here. We have appealed to their native justice and magnanimity, and we have conjured them, by the ties of our common kindred, to disavow these usurpations, which would inevitably interrupt our connections and correspondence. They, too, have been deaf to the voice of justice and consanguinity. We must, therefore, acquiesce in the necessity which denounces our separation, and hold them as we hold the rest of mankind, enemies in war, in peace, friends.

We, therefore, the representatives of the United States of America, in general Congress assembled, appealing to the Supreme Judge of the world for the rectitude of our intentions, do, in the name, and by the authority of the good people of these colonies, solemnly publish and declare, that these united colonies are, and of right ought to be, free and independent states: that they are absolved from all allegiance to the British Crown, and that all political connection between them and the state of Great Britain is, and ought to be, totally dissolved; and that, as free and independent states, they have full power to levy war, conclude peace, contract alliances, establish commerce, and to do all other acts and things which independent states may of right do. And, for the support of this declaration, with a firm reliance on the protection of Divine Providence, we mutually pledge to each other our lives, our fortunes, and our sacred honor.

The foregoing Declaration was, by order of Congress, engrossed, and signed by the following members:

JOHN HANCOCK

New Hampshire

Josiah Bartlett
William Whipple
Matthew Thornton

Massachusetts Bay

Samuel Adams
John Adams
Robert Treat Paine
Elbridge Gerry

Rhode Island

Stephen Hopkins
William Ellery

Connecticut

Roger Sherman
Samuel Huntington
William Williams
Oliver Wolcott

New York

William Floyd
Philip Livingston
Francis Lewis
Lewis Morris

New Jersey

Richard Stockton
John Witherspoon
Francis Hopkinson
John Hart
Abraham Clark

Pennsylvania

Robert Morris
Benjamin Rush
Benjamin Franklin
John Morton
George Clymer
James Smith
George Taylor
James Wilson
George Ross

Delaware

Caesar Rodney
George Read
Thomas M'Kean

Maryland

Samuel Chase
William Paca
Thomas Stone
Charles Carroll,
   of Carrollton

Virginia

George Wythe
Richard Henry Lee
Thomas Jefferson
Benjamin Harrison
Thomas Nelson, Jr.
Francis Lightfoot Lee
Carter Braxton

North Carolina

William Hooper
Joseph Hewes
John Penn

South Carolina

Edward Rutledge
Thomas Heyward, Jr.
Thomas Lynch, Jr.
Arthur Middleton

Georgia

Button Gwinnett
Lyman Hall
George Walton

Resolved, That copies of the Declaration be sent to the several assemblies, conventions, and committees, or councils of safety, and to the several commanding officers of the continental troops; that it be proclaimed in each of the United States, at the head of the army.

The Constitution of the United States of America[1]

WE the People of the United States, in Order to form a more perfect Union, establish Justice, insure domestic Tranquility, provide for the common defence, promote the general Welfare, and secure the Blessings of Liberty to ourselves and our Posterity, do ordain and establish this CONSTITUTION for the United States of America.

Article I

SECTION 1.

All legislative Powers herein granted shall be vested in a Congress of the United States, which shall consist of a Senate and House of Representatives.

SECTION 2.

The House of Representatives shall be composed of Members chosen every second Year by the People of the several States, and the Electors in each State shall have the Qualifications requisite for Electors of the most numerous Branch of the State Legislature.

No Person shall be a Representative who shall not have attained to the Age of twenty-five Years, and been seven Years a Citizen of the United States, and who shall not, when elected, be an Inhabitant of that State in which he shall be chosen.

[Representatives and direct Taxes[2] shall be apportioned among the several States which may be included within this Union, according to their respective Numbers, which shall be determined by adding to the whole Number of free Persons, including those bound to Service for a Term of Years, and excluding Indians not taxed, three fifths of all other Persons.][3] The actual Enumeration shall be made within three Years after the first Meeting of the Congress of the United States, and within every subsequent Term of ten Years, in such Manner as they shall by Law direct. The Number of Representatives shall not exceed one for every thirty Thousand, but each State shall have at Least one Representative; and until such enumeration shall be made, the State of New Hampshire shall be entitled to chuse three, Massachusetts eight, Rhode-Island and Providence Plantations one, Connecticut five, New York six, New Jersey four, Pennsylvania eight, Delaware one, Maryland six, Virginia ten, North Carolina five, South Carolina five, and Georgia three.

When vacancies happen in the Representation from any State, the Executive Authority thereof shall issue Writs of Election to fill such Vacancies.

The House of Representatives shall chuse their Speaker and other Officers; and shall have the sole Power of Impeachment.

SECTION 3.

The Senate of the United States shall be composed of two Senators from each State, chosen by the Legislature thereof, for six Years; and each Senator shall have one Vote.

Immediately after they shall be assembled in Consequence of the first Election, they shall be divided as equally as may be into three Classes. The Seats of the Senators of the first Class shall be vacated at the Expiration of the second Year, of the second Class at the Expiration of the fourth Year, and of the third Class at the Expiration of the sixth Year, so that one-third may be chosen every second Year; and if Vacancies happen by Resignation, or otherwise, during the Recess of the Legislature of any State, the Executive thereof may make temporary Appointments until the next Meeting of the Legislature, which shall then fill such Vacancies.

No Person shall be a Senator who shall not have attained to the Age of thirty Years, and been nine Years a Citizen of the United States, and who shall not, when elected, be an Inhabitant of that State for which he shall be chosen.

[1]This version, which follows the original Constitution in capitalization and spelling, was published by the United States Department of the Interior, Office of Education, in 1935.
[2]Altered by the Sixteenth Amendment.
[3]Negated by the Fourteenth Amendment.

The Vice President of the United States shall be President of the Senate, but shall have no vote, unless they be equally divided.

The Senate shall chuse their other Officers, and also a President pro tempore, in the absence of the Vice President, or when he shall exercise the Office of President of the United States.

The Senate shall have the sole Power to try all Impeachments. When sitting for that purpose, they shall be on Oath or Affirmation. When the President of the United States is tried, the Chief Justice shall preside: And no person shall be convicted without the Concurrence of two thirds of the Members present.

Judgment in Cases of Impeachment shall not extend further than to removal from Office, and disqualification to hold and enjoy any Office of honor, Trust, or Profit under the United States: but the Party convicted shall nevertheless be liable and subject to Indictment, Trial, Judgment, and Punishment, according to Law.

SECTION 4.

The Times, Places and Manner of holding Elections for Senators and Representatives, shall be prescribed in each State by the Legislature thereof; but the Congress may at any time by Law make or alter such Regulations, except as to the Places of Chusing Senators.

The Congress shall assemble at least once in every Year, and such Meeting shall be on the first Monday in December, unless they shall by Law appoint a different Day.

SECTION 5.

Each House shall be the Judge of the Elections, Returns and Qualifications of its own Members, and a Majority of each shall constitute a Quorum to do Business; but a smaller number may adjourn from day to day, and may be authorized to compel the Attendance of absent Members, in such Manner, and under such Penalties, as each House may provide.

Each House may determine the Rules of its Proceedings, punish its Members for disorderly Behaviour, and, with the Concurrence of two thirds, expel a Member.

Each House shall keep a Journal of its Proceedings, and from time to time publish the same, excepting such Parts as may in their Judgment require Secrecy; and the Yeas and Nays of the Members of either House on any question shall, at the Desire of one fifth of those Present, be entered on the Journal.

Neither House, during the Session of Congress, shall, without the Consent of the other, adjourn for more than three days, nor to any other Place than that in which the two Houses shall be sitting.

SECTION 6.

The Senators and Representatives shall receive a Compensation for their Services, to be ascertained by Law, and paid out of the Treasury of the United States. They shall in all Cases, except Treason, Felony, and Breach of the Peace, be privileged from Arrest during their Attendance at the Session of their respective Houses, and in going to and returning from the same; and for any Speech or Debate in either House, they shall not be questioned in any other Place.

No Senator or Representative shall, during the Time for which he was elected, be appointed to any civil Office under the Authority of the United States, which shall have been created, or the Emoluments whereof shall have been increased, during such time; and no Person holding any Office under the United States shall be a Member of either House during his continuance in Office.

SECTION 7.

All Bills for raising Revenue shall originate in the House of Representatives; but the Senate may propose or concur with Amendments as on other bills.

Every Bill which shall have passed the House of Representatives and the Senate, shall, before it become a Law, be presented to the President of the United States; If he approve he shall sign it, but if not he shall return it, with his Objections, to that House in which it shall have originated, who shall enter the Objections at large on their Journal, and proceed to reconsider it. If after such Reconsideration two thirds of that House shall agree to pass the bill, it shall be sent, together with the objections, to the other House, by which it shall likewise be reconsidered, and if approved by two thirds of that House, it shall become a Law. But in all such Cases the Votes of both Houses shall be determined by Yeas and Nays, and the Names of the Persons voting for and against the Bill shall be entered on the Journal of each House respectively. If any Bill shall not be returned by the President within ten Days (Sundays excepted) after it shall have been presented to him, the Same shall be a Law, in like Manner as if he had signed it, unless the Congress by their Adjournment prevent its Return, in which Case it shall not be a Law.

Every Order, Resolution, or Vote to which the Concurrence of the Senate and House of Representatives may be necessary (except on a question of Adjournment) shall be presented to the President of the United States; and before the Same shall take Effect, shall be approved by him, or being disapproved by him, shall be repassed by two thirds of the Senate and House of Representatives, according to the Rules and Limitations prescribed in the Case of a Bill.

SECTION 8.

The Congress shall have Power To lay and collect Taxes, Duties, Imposts and Excises, to pay the Debts and provide for the common Defence and general Welfare of the United States; but all Duties, Imposts and Excises shall be uniform throughout the United States;

To borrow money on the credit of the United States;

To regulate Commerce with foreign Nations, and among the several States, and with the Indian Tribes;

To establish an uniform Rule of Naturalization, and uniform Laws on the subject of Bankruptcies throughout the United States;

To coin Money, regulate the Value thereof, and of foreign Coin, and fix the Standard of Weights and Measures;

To provide for the Punishment of counterfeiting the Securities and current Coin of the United States;

To establish Post Offices and post Roads;

To promote the Progress of Science and useful Arts, by securing for limited Times to Authors and Inventors the exclusive Right to their respective Writings and Discoveries;

To constitute Tribunals inferior to the Supreme Court;

To define and punish Piracies and Felonies committed on the high Seas, and Offenses against the Law of Nations;

To declare War, grant Letters of Marque and Reprisal, and make Rules concerning Captures on Land and Water;

To raise and support Armies, but no Appropriation of Money to that Use shall be for a longer Term than two Years;

To provide and maintain a Navy;

To make Rules for the Government and Regulation of the land and naval forces;

To provide for calling forth the Militia to execute the Laws of the Union, suppress Insurrections and repel Invasions;

To provide for organizing, arming, and disciplining the Militia, and for governing such Part of them as may be employed in the Service of the United States, reserving to the States respectively, the Appointment of the Officers, and the Authority of training the Militia according to the discipline prescribed by Congress;

To exercise exclusive Legislation in all Cases whatsoever, over such District (not exceeding ten Miles square) as may, by Cession of particular States, and the acceptance of Congress, become the Seat of the Government of the United States, and to exercise like Authority over all Places purchased by the Consent of the Legislature of the State in which the Same shall be, for the Erection of Forts, Magazines, Arsenals, Dock-yards, and other needful Buildings; — And

To make all Laws which shall be necessary and proper for carrying into Execution the foregoing Powers, and all other Powers vested by this Constitution in the Government of the United States, or in any Department or Officer thereof.

SECTION 9.

The Migration or Importation of such Persons as any of the States now existing shall think proper to admit, shall not be prohibited by the Congress prior to the Year one thousand eight hundred and eight, but a tax or duty may be imposed on such Importation, not exceeding ten dollars for each Person.

The privilege of the Writ of Habeas Corpus shall not be suspended, unless when in Cases of Rebellion or Invasion the public Safety may require it.

No bill of Attainder or ex post facto Law shall be passed.

No capitation, or other direct, Tax shall be laid unless in Proportion to the Census or Enumeration herein before directed to be taken.

No Tax or Duty shall be laid on Articles exported from any State.

No Preference shall be given by any Regulation of Commerce or Revenue to the Ports of one State over those of another: nor shall Vessels bound to, or from, one State, be obliged to enter, clear, or pay Duties in another.

No Money shall be drawn from the Treasury, but in Consequence of Appropriations made by Law; and a regular Statement and Account of the Receipts and Expenditures of all public Money shall be published from time to time.

No Title of Nobility shall be granted by the United States: And no Person holding any Office of Profit or Trust under them, shall, without the Consent of the Congress, accept of any present, Emolument, Office, or Title, of any kind whatever, from any King, Prince, or foreign State.

SECTION 10.

No State shall enter into any Treaty, Alliance, or Confederation; grant Letters of Marque and Reprisal; coin Money; emit Bills of Credit; make any Thing but gold and silver Coin a Tender in Payment of Debts; pass any Bill of Attainder, ex post facto Law, or Law impairing the Obligation of Contracts, or grant any Title of Nobility.

No State shall, without the Consent of the Congress, lay any Imposts or Duties on Imports or Exports, except what may be absolutely necessary for executing its inspection Laws: and the net Produce of all Duties and Imposts, laid by any State on Imports or Exports, shall be for the Use of the Treasury of the United States; and all such Laws shall be subject to the Revision and Control of the Congress.

No state shall, without the Consent of Congress, lay any duty of Tonnage, keep Troops, or Ships of War in time of Peace, enter into any Agreement or Compact with another State, or with a foreign Power, or engage in War, unless actually invaded, or in such imminent Danger as will not admit of delay.

Article II

SECTION 1.

The executive Power shall be vested in a President of the United States of America. He shall hold his Office during the Term of four years, and, together with the Vice President, chosen for the same Term, be elected, as follows:

Each State shall appoint, in such Manner as the Legislature thereof may direct, a Number of Electors, equal to the whole Number of Senators and Representatives to which the State may be entitled in the Congress: but no Senator or Representative, or Person holding an Office of Trust or Profit under the United States, shall be appointed an Elector.

[The Electors shall meet in their respective States, and vote by Ballot for two persons, of whom one at least shall not be an Inhabitant of the same State with themselves. And they shall make a List of all the Persons voted for, and of the Number of Votes for each; which List they shall sign and certify, and transmit sealed to the Seat of the Government of the United States, directed to the President of the Senate. The President of the Senate shall, in the Presence of the Senate and House of Representatives, open all the Certificates, and the Votes shall then be counted. The Person having the greatest Number of Votes shall be the President, if such Number be a Majority of the whole Number of Electors appointed; and if there be more than one who have such Majority, and have an equal Number of Votes, then the House of Representatives shall immediately chuse by Ballot one of them for President; and if no Person have a Majority, then from the five highest on the List the said House shall in the Manner chuse the President. But in chusing the President, the Votes shall be taken by States, the Representation from each State having one Vote; a quorum for this Purpose shall consist of a Member or Members from two-thirds of the States, and a Majority of all the States shall be necessary to a Choice. In every Case, after the Choice of the President, the Person having the greatest Number of Votes of the Electors shall be the Vice President. But if there should remain two or more who have equal votes, the Senate shall chuse from them by Ballot the Vice President.][4]

The Congress may determine the Time of chusing the Electors, and the Day on which they shall give their Votes; which Day shall be the same throughout the United States.

No person except a natural-born Citizen, or a Citizen of the United States, at the time of the Adoption of this Constitution, shall be eligible to the Office of President; neither shall any Person be eligible to that Office who shall not have attained to the Age of thirty-five years, and been fourteen Years a Resident within the United States.

[4]Revised by the Twelfth Amendment.

In Case of the Removal of the President from Office, or of his Death, Resignation, or Inability to discharge the Powers and Duties of the said Office, the same shall devolve on the Vice President, and the Congress may by Law provide for the Case of Removal, Death, Resignation, or Inability, both of the President and Vice President, declaring what Officer shall then act as President, and such Officer shall act accordingly, until the disability be removed, or a President shall be elected.

The President shall, at stated Times, receive for his Services a Compensation, which shall neither be increased nor diminished during the Period for which he shall have been elected, and he shall not receive within that Period any other Emolument from the United States, or any of them.

Before he enter on the execution of his Office, he shall take the following Oath or Affirmation: — "I do solemnly swear (or affirm) that I will faithfully execute the Office of President of the United States, and will, to the best of my Ability, preserve, protect, and defend the Constitution of the United States."

SECTION 2.
The President shall be Commander in Chief of the Army and Navy of the United States, and of the Militia of the several States, when called into the actual Service of the United States; he may require the Opinion, in writing, of the principal Officer in each of the executive Departments, upon any subject relating to the Duties of their respective Offices, and he shall have Power to Grant Reprieves and Pardons for Offenses against the United States, except in Cases of Impeachment.

He shall have Power, by and with the Advice and Consent of the Senate, to make Treaties, provided two-thirds of the Senators present concur; and he shall nominate, and by and with the Advice and Consent of the Senate, shall appoint Ambassadors, other public Ministers and Consuls, Judges of the supreme Court, and all other Officers of the United States, whose Appointments are not herein otherwise provided for, and which shall be established by Law: but the Congress may by Law vest the Appointment of such inferior Officers, as they think proper, in the President alone, in the Courts of Law, or in the Heads of Departments.

The President shall have Power to fill up all Vacancies that may happen during the Re-

cess of the Senate, by granting Commissions which shall expire at the End of their next Session.

SECTION 3.
He shall from time to time give to the Congress Information of the State of the Union, and recommend to their Consideration such Measures as he shall judge necessary and expedient; he may, on extraordinary occasions, convene both Houses, or either of them, and in Case of Disagreement between them, with respect to the Time of Adjournment, he may adjourn them to such Time as he shall think proper; he shall receive Ambassadors and other public Ministers; he shall take care that the Laws be faithfully executed, and shall Commission all the Officers of the United States.

SECTION 4.
The President, Vice President and all civil Officers of the United States, shall be removed from Office on Impeachment for, and Conviction of, Treason, Bribery, or other high Crimes and Misdemeanors.

Article III

SECTION 1.
The judicial Power of the United States, shall be vested in one supreme Court, and in such inferior Courts as the Congress may from time to time ordain and establish. The Judges, both of the supreme and inferior Courts, shall hold their Offices during good Behaviour, and shall, at stated Times, receive for their Services, a Compensation, which shall not be diminished during their Continuance in Office.

SECTION 2.
The judicial Power shall extend to all Cases, in Law and Equity, arising under this Constitution, the Laws of the United States, and Treaties made, or which shall be made, under their Authority; — to all Cases affecting ambassadors, other public ministers and consuls; — to all cases of admiralty and maritime Jurisdiction; — to Controversies to which the United States shall be a Party; — to Controversies between two or more States; — between a State and Citizens of another State;[5] — between Citizens of

---

[5]Qualified by the Eleventh Amendment.

different States,—between Citizens of the same State claiming Lands under Grants of different States, and between a State, or the Citizens thereof, and foreign States, Citizens or Subjects.

In all Cases affecting Ambassadors, other public Ministers and Consuls, and those in which a State shall be Party, the supreme Court shall have original Jurisdiction. In all the other Cases before mentioned, the supreme Court shall have appellate Jurisdiction, both as to Law and Fact, with such Exceptions, and under such Regulations as the Congress shall make.

The trial of all Crimes, except in Cases of Impeachment, shall be by Jury; and such Trial shall be held in the State where the said Crimes shall have been committed; but when not committed within any State, the Trial shall be at such Place or Places as the Congress may by Law have directed.

SECTION 3.

Treason against the United States, shall consist only in levying War against them, or in adhering to their Enemies, giving them Aid and Comfort. No Person shall be convicted of Treason unless on the Testimony of two Witnesses to the same overt Act, or on Confession in open Court.

The Congress shall have power to declare the Punishment of Treason, but no Attainder of Treason shall work Corruption of Blood, or Forfeiture except during the Life of the Person attainted.

Article IV

SECTION 1.

Full Faith and Credit shall be given in each State to the public Acts, Records, and judicial Proceedings of every other State. And the Congress may by general Laws prescribe the Manner in which such Acts, Records and Proceedings shall be proved, and the Effect thereof.

SECTION 2.

The Citizens of each State shall be entitled to all Privileges and Immunities of Citizens in the several States.

A Person charged in any State with Treason, Felony, or other Crime, who shall flee from Justice, and be found in another State, shall on demand of the executive Authority of the State from which he fled, be delivered up, to be removed to the State having Jurisdiction of the crime.

No Person held to Service or Labour in one State, under the Laws thereof, escaping into another, shall, in Consequence of any Law or Regulation therein, be discharged from such Service or Labour, but shall be delivered up on Claim of the Party to whom such Service or Labour may be due.

SECTION 3.

New States may be admitted by the Congress into this Union; but no new State shall be formed or erected within the Jurisdiction of any other State; nor any State be formed by the Junction of two or more States, or parts of States, without the Consent of the Legislatures of the States concerned as well as of the Congress.

The Congress shall have Power to dispose of and make all needful Rules and Regulations respecting the Territory or other Property belonging to the United States; and nothing in this Constitution shall be so construed as to Prejudice any Claims of the United States, or of any particular State.

SECTION 4.

The United States shall guarantee to every State in this Union a Republican Form of Government, and shall protect each of them against Invasion; and on Application of the Legislature, or of the Executive (when the Legislature cannot be convened) against domestic Violence.

Article V

The Congress, whenever two-thirds of both Houses shall deem it necessary, shall propose Amendments to this Constitution, or, on the Application of the Legislatures of two-thirds of the several States, shall call a Convention for proposing Amendments, which, in either Case, shall be valid to all Intents and Purposes, as part of this Constitution, when ratified by the Legislatures of three-fourths of the several States, or by Conventions in three-fourths thereof, as the one or the other Mode of Ratification may be proposed by the Congress; Provided that no Amendment which may be made prior to the Year One thousand eight hundred and eight shall in any Manner affect the first and fourth Clauses in the Ninth Section of the first Article; and that no State, without its Consent, shall be deprived of its equal Suffrage in the Senate.

Article VI

All Debts contracted and Engagements entered into, before the Adoption of this Constitution, shall be as valid against the United States under this Constitution, as under the Confederation.

This Constitution, and the Laws of the United States which shall be made in Pursuance thereof; and all Treaties made, or which shall be made, under the Authority of the United States, shall be the supreme Law of the Land; and the Judges in every State shall be bound thereby, any Thing in the Constitution or Laws of any State to the Contrary notwithstanding.

The Senators and Representatives before mentioned, and the Members of the several State Legislatures, and all executive and judicial Officers, both of the United States and of the several States, shall be bound by Oath or Affirmation to support this Constitution; but no religious Test shall ever be required as a qualification to any Office or public Trust under the United States.

Article VII

The Ratification of the Conventions of nine States shall be sufficient for the Establishment of this Constitution between the States so ratifying the same.

Done in Convention by the Unanimous Consent of the States present the Seventeenth Day of September in the Year of our Lord one thousand seven hundred and Eighty seven, and of the Independence of the United States of America the Twelfth. In Witness whereof We have hereunto subscribed our Names.[6]

George Washington
President and deputy from Virginia

New Hampshire

John Langdon
Nicholas Gilman

Massachusetts

Nathaniel Gorham
Rufus King

Connecticut

William Samuel Johnson
Roger Sherman

New York

Alexander Hamilton

New Jersey

William Livingston
David Brearley
William Paterson
Jonathan Dayton

Pennsylvania

Benjamin Franklin
Thomas Mifflin
Robert Morris
George Clymer
Thomas FitzSimons
Jared Ingersoll
James Wilson
Gouverneur Morris

Delaware

George Read
Gunning Bedford, Jr.
John Dickinson
Richard Bassett
Jacob Broom

Maryland

James McHenry
Daniel of
   St. Thomas Jenifer
Daniel Carroll

Virginia

John Blair
James Madison, Jr.

North Carolina

William Blount
Richard Dobbs Spaight
Hugh Williamson

South Carolina

John Rutledge
Charles Cotesworth Pinckney
Charles Pinckney
Pierce Butler

Georgia

William Few
Abraham Baldwin

[6]These are the full names of the signers, which in some cases are not the signatures on the document.

Articles in Addition to, and Amendment of, the Constitution of the United States of America, Proposed by Congress, and Ratified by the Legislatures of the Several States, Pursuant to the Fifth Article of the Original Constitution[7]

[Article I]

Congress shall make no law respecting an establishment of religion, or prohibiting the free exercise thereof; or abridging the freedom of speech, or of the press; or the right of the people peaceably to assemble, and to petition the Government for a redress of grievances.

[Article II]

A well regulated Militia, being necessary to the security of a free State, the right of the people to keep and bear Arms shall not be infringed.

[Article III]

No Soldier shall, in time of peace, be quartered in any house, without the consent of the Owner, nor in time of war, but in a manner to be prescribed by law.

[Article IV]

The right of the people to be secure in their persons, houses, papers, and effects, against unreasonable searches and seizures, shall not be violated, and no Warrants shall issue, but upon probable cause, supported by Oath or affirmation, and particularly describing the place to be searched, and the persons or things to be seized.

[Article V]

No person shall be held to answer for a capital or otherwise infamous crime, unless on a presentment or indictment of a Grand Jury, except in cases arising in the land or naval forces, or in the Militia, when in actual service in time of War or public danger; nor shall any person be subject for the same offence to be twice put in jeopardy of life or limb; nor shall be compelled in any criminal case to be a witness against himself, nor be deprived of life, liberty, or property, without due process of law; nor shall private property be taken for public use, without just compensation.

[Article VI]

In all criminal prosecutions, the accused shall enjoy the right to a speedy and public trial, by an impartial jury of the State and district wherein the crime shall have been committed, which district shall have been previously ascertained by law, and to be informed of the nature and cause of the accusation; to be confronted with the witnesses against him; to have compulsory process for obtaining witnesses in his favour, and to have the Assistance of Counsel for his defence.

[Article VII]

In suits at common law, where the value in controversy shall exceed twenty dollars, the right of trial by jury shall be preserved, and no fact tried by a jury, shall be otherwise reexamined in any Court of the United States, than according to the rules of the common law.

[Article VIII]

Excessive bail shall not be required, nor excessive fines imposed, nor cruel and unusual punishments inflicted.

[Article IX]

The enumeration in the Constitution, of certain rights, shall not be construed to deny or disparage others retained by the people.

[Article X]

The powers not delegated to the United States by the Constitution, nor prohibited by it to the

[7]This heading appears only in the joint resolution submitting the first ten amendments.

States, are reserved to the States respectively, or to the people.

[Amendments I–X, in force 1791.]

[Article XI][8]

The Judicial power of the United States shall not be construed to extend to any suit in law or equity, commenced or prosecuted against one of the United States by Citizens of another State, or by Citizens or Subjects of any Foreign State.

[Article XII][9]

The Electors shall meet in their respective States and vote by ballot for President and Vice-President, one of whom, at least, shall not be an inhabitant of the same State with themselves; they shall name in their ballots the person voted for as President, and in distinct ballots the person voted for as Vice-President, and they shall make distinct lists of all persons voted for as President, and of all persons voted for as Vice-President, and of the number of votes for each, which lists they shall sign and certify, and transmit sealed to the seat of the government of the United States, directed to the President of the Senate;—The President of the Senate shall, in the presence of the Senate and House of Representatives, open all the certificates and the votes shall then be counted;—The person having the greatest number of votes for President, shall be the President, if such number be a majority of the whole number of Electors appointed; and if no person have such majority, then from the persons having the highest numbers not exceeding three on the list of those voted for as President, the House of Representatives shall choose immediately, by ballot, the President. But in choosing the President, the votes shall be taken by states, the representation from each state having one vote; a quorum for this purpose shall consist of a member or members from two-thirds of the states, and a majority of all the

states shall be necessary to a choice. And if the House of Representatives shall not choose a President whenever the right of choice shall devolve upon them, before the fourth day of March next following, then the Vice-President shall act as President, as in the case of the death or other constitutional disability of the President.—The person having the greatest number of votes as Vice-President, shall be the Vice-President, if such number be a majority of the whole number of Electors appointed, and if no person have a majority, then from the two highest numbers on the list, the Senate shall choose the Vice-President: a quorum for the purpose shall consist of two-thirds of the whole number of Senators, and a majority of the whole number shall be necessary to a choice. But no person constitutionally ineligible to the office of President shall be eligible to that of Vice-President of the United States.

[Article XIII][10]

SECTION 1.
Neither slavery nor involuntary servitude, except as a punishment for crime whereof the party shall have been duly convicted, shall exist within the United States, or any place subject to their jurisdiction.

SECTION 2.
Congress shall have power to enforce this article by appropriate legislation.

[Article XIV][11]

SECTION 1.
All persons born or naturalized in the United States, and subject to the jurisdiction thereof, are citizens of the United States and of the State wherein they reside. No State shall abridge the privileges or immunities of citizens of the United States; nor shall any State deprive any person of life, liberty, or property, without due process of law; nor deny to any person within its jurisdiction the equal protection of the laws.

[8]Adopted in 1798.
[9]Adopted in 1804.

[10]Adopted in 1865.
[11]Adopted in 1868.

SECTION 2.

Representatives shall be apportioned among the several States according to their respective numbers, counting the whole number of persons in each State, excluding Indians not taxed. But when the right to vote at any election for the choice of electors for President and Vice-President of the United States, Representatives in Congress, the Executive and Judicial officers of a State, or the members of the Legislature thereof, is denied to any of the male inhabitants of such State, being twenty-one years of age, and citizens of the United States, or in any way abridged, except for participation in rebellion, or other crime, the basis of representation therein shall be reduced in the proportion which the number of such male citizens shall bear to the whole number of male citizens twenty-one years of age in such State.

SECTION 3.

No person shall be a Senator or Representative in Congress, or elector of President and Vice-President, or hold any office, civil or military, under the United States, or under any State, who, having previously taken an oath, as a member of Congress, or as an officer of the United States, or as a member of any State legislature, or as an executive or judicial officer of any State, to support the Constitution of the United States, shall have engaged in insurrection or rebellion against the same, or given aid or comfort to the enemies thereof. But Congress may by a vote of two-thirds of each House, remove such disability.

SECTION 4.

The validity of the public debt of the United States, authorized by law, including debts incurred for payment of pensions and bounties for services in suppressing insurrection or rebellion, shall not be questioned. But neither the United States nor any State shall assume or pay any debts or obligation incurred in aid of insurrection or rebellion against the United States, or any claim for the loss or emancipation of any slave; but all such debts, obligations, and claims shall be held illegal and void.

SECTION 5.

The Congress shall have the power to enforce, by appropriate legislation, the provisions of this article.

[Article XV][12]

SECTION 1.

The right of citizens of the United States to vote shall not be denied or abridged by the United States or by any State on account of race, color, or previous condition of servitude—

SECTION 2.

The Congress shall have power to enforce this article by appropriate legislation.

[Article XVI][13]

The Congress shall have power to lay and collect taxes on incomes, from whatever source derived, without apportionment among the several States, and without regard to any census or enumeration.

[Article XVII][14]

The Senate of the United States shall be composed of two Senators from each State, elected by the people thereof, for six years; and each Senator shall have one vote. The electors in each State shall have the qualifications requisite for electors of the most numerous branch of the State legislatures.

When vacancies happen in the representation of any State in the Senate, the executive authority of such State shall issue writs of election to fill such vacancies: *Provided,* That the legislature of any State may empower the executive thereof to make temporary appointments until the people fill the vacancies by election as the legislature may direct.

This amendment shall not be so construed as to affect the election or term of any Senator chosen before it becomes valid as part of the Constitution.

[Article XVIII][15]

SECTION 1.

After one year from the ratification of this article the manufacture, sale, or transportation of

---

[12]Adopted in 1870.
[13]Adopted in 1913.
[14]Adopted in 1913.
[15]Adopted in 1918.

intoxicating liquors within, the importation thereof into, or the exportation thereof from the United States and all territory subject to the jurisdiction thereof for beverage purposes is hereby prohibited.

SECTION 2.

The Congress and the several States shall have concurrent power to enforce this article by appropriate legislation.

SECTION 3.

This article shall be inoperative unless it shall have been ratified as an amendment to the Constitution by the legislatures of the several States, as provided in the Constitution, within seven years from the date of the submission hereof to the States by the Congress.

[Article XIX][16]

The right of citizens of the United States to vote shall not be denied or abridged by the United States or by any State on account of sex.

Congress shall have power to enforce this article by appropriate legislation.

[Article XX][17]

SECTION 1.

The terms of the President and Vice-President shall end at noon on the 20th day of January, and the terms of Senators and Representatives at noon on the 3d day of January, of the years in which such terms would have ended if this article had not been ratified; and the terms of their successors shall then begin.

SECTION 2.

The Congress shall assemble at least once in every year, and such meeting shall begin at noon on the 3d day of January, unless they shall by law appoint a different day.

SECTION 3.

If, at the time fixed for the beginning of the term of the President, the President elect shall have died, the Vice-President elect shall become President. If a President shall not have been chosen before the time fixed for the be-

ginning of his term, or if the President elect shall have failed to qualify, then the Vice-President elect shall act as President until a President shall have qualified; and the Congress may by law provide for the case wherein neither a President elect nor a Vice-President elect shall have qualified, declaring who shall then act as President, or the manner in which one who is to act shall be selected, and such person shall act accordingly until a President or Vice-President shall have qualified.

SECTION 4.

The Congress may by law provide for the case of the death of any of the persons from whom the House of Representatives may choose a President whenever the right of choice shall have devolved upon them, and for the case of the death of any of the persons from whom the Senate may choose a Vice-President whenever the right of choice shall have devolved upon them.

SECTION 5.

Sections 1 and 2 shall take effect on the 15th day of October following the ratification of this article.

SECTION 6.

This article shall be inoperative unless it shall have been ratified as an amendment to the Constitution by the legislatures of three-fourths of the several States within seven years from the date of its submission.

[Article XXI][18]

SECTION 1.

The eighteenth article of amendment to the Constitution of the United States is hereby repealed.

SECTION 2.

The transportation or importation into any State, Territory, or possession of the United States for delivery or use therein of intoxicating liquors, in violation of the laws thereof, is hereby prohibited.

SECTION 3.

This article shall be inoperative unless it shall have been ratified as an amendment to the

---

[16]Adopted in 1920.
[17]Adopted in 1933.

[18]Adopted in 1933.

Constitution by conventions in the several States, as provided in the Constitution, within seven years from the date of the submission hereof to the States by the Congress.

[Article XXII][19]

No person shall be elected to the office of the President more than twice, and no person who has held the office of President, or acted as President, for more than two years of a term to which some other person was elected President shall be elected to the office of the President more than once.

But this Article shall not apply to any person holding the office of President when this Article was proposed by the Congress, and shall not prevent any person who may be holding the office of President, or acting as President, during the term within which this Article becomes operative from holding the office of President or acting as President during the remainder of such term.

This article shall be inoperative unless it shall have been ratified as an amendment to the Constitution by the legislatures of three-fourths of the several states within seven years from the date of its submission to the states by the Congress.

[Article XXIII][20]

SECTION 1.
The District constituting the seat of Government of the United States shall appoint in such manner as the Congress may direct:

A number of electors of President and Vice-President equal to the whole number of Senators and Representatives in Congress to which the District would be entitled if it were a State, but in no event more than the least populous State; they shall be in addition to those appointed by the States, but they shall be considered, for the purposes of the election of President and Vice-President, to be electors appointed by a State; and they shall meet in the District and perform such duties as provided by the twelfth article of amendment.

SECTION 2.
The Congress shall have power to enforce this article by appropriate legislation.

[Article XXIV][21]

SECTION 1.
The right of citizens of the United States to vote in any primary or other election for President or Vice President, for electors for President or Vice President, or for Senator or Representative in Congress, shall not be denied or abridged by the United States or any state by reason of failure to pay any poll tax or other tax.

SECTION 2.
The Congress shall have the power to enforce this article by appropriate legislation.

[Article XXV][22]

SECTION 1.
In case of the removal of the President from office or of his death or resignation, the Vice President shall become President.

SECTION 2.
Whenever there is a vacancy in the office of the Vice President, the President shall nominate a Vice President who shall take office upon confirmation by a majority vote of both Houses of Congress.

SECTION 3.
Whenever the President transmits to the President Pro Tempore of the Senate and the Speaker of the House of Representatives his written declaration that he is unable to discharge the powers and duties of his office, and until he transmits to them a written declaration to the contrary, such powers and duties shall be discharged by the Vice President as Acting President.

SECTION 4.
Whenever the Vice President and a majority of either the principal officers of the executive departments or of such other body as Congress may by law provide, transmit to the President Pro Tempore of the Senate and the Speaker of

[19]Adopted in 1951.
[20]Adopted in 1961.

[21]Adopted in 1964.
[22]Adopted in 1967.

the House of Representatives their written declaration that the President is unable to discharge the powers and duties of his office, the
Vice President shall immediately assume the
powers and duties of the office as Acting President.

Thereafter, when the President transmits
to the President Pro Tempore of the Senate
and the Speaker of the House of Representatives his written declaration that no inability
exists, he shall resume the powers and duties of
his office unless the Vice President and a
majority of either the principal officers of the
executive departments or of such other body
as Congress may by law provide, transmit
within four days to the President Pro Tempore of the Senate and the Speaker of the
House of Representatives their written declaration that the President is unable to discharge the powers and duties of his office.
Thereupon Congress shall decide the issue,
assembling within forty-eight hours for that
purpose if not in session. If the Congress, within twenty-one days after receipt of the latter
written declaration, or, if Congress is not in session, within twenty-one days after Congress is
required to assemble, determines by two-thirds
vote of both Houses that the President is unable to discharge the powers and duties of his
office, the Vice President shall continue to discharge the same as Acting President; otherwise, the President shall resume the powers
and duties of his office.

[Article XXVI][23]

SECTION 1.
The right of citizens of the United States, who
are eighteen years of age or older, to vote shall
not be denied or abridged by the United States
or by any State on account of age.

SECTION 2.
The Congress shall have power to enforce this
article by appropriate legislation.

[23]Adopted in 1971.

Sovereigns of England and Great Britain, 1485–1820

The ruler was King (or Queen) of England until 1707, except for the interregnum of 1649–1660, during which Oliver Cromwell made himself Lord Protector. The ruler was King (or Queen) of Great Britain after the union of England and Scotland in 1707, and King (or Queen) of Great Britain and Ireland after 1800.

Henry VII   *1485–1509*

Henry VIII   *1509–1547*

Edward VI   *1547–1553*

Mary I   *1553–1558*

Elizabeth I   *1558–1603*

James I (VI of Scotland)   *1603–1625*

Charles I   *1625–1649*

  Oliver Cromwell   *1650–1658*

  Richard Cromwell   *1658–1659*

Charles II   *1660–1685*

James II   *1685–1688*

William III and Mary II   *1689–1694*

William III   *1694–1702*

Anne   *1702–1714*

George I   *1714–1727*

George II   *1727–1760*

George III   *1760–1820*

Admission of States to the Union*

1 Delaware	Dec. 7, 1787	26 Michigan	Jan. 26, 1837
2 Pennsylvania	Dec. 12, 1787	27 Florida	Mar. 3, 1845
3 New Jersey	Dec. 18, 1787	28 Texas	Dec. 29, 1845
4 Georgia	Jan. 2, 1788	29 Iowa	Dec. 28, 1846
5 Connecticut	Jan. 9, 1788	30 Wisconsin	May 29, 1848
6 Massachusetts	Feb. 6, 1788	31 California	Sept. 9, 1850
7 Maryland	Apr. 28, 1788	32 Minnesota	May 11, 1858
8 South Carolina	May 23, 1788	33 Oregon	Feb. 14, 1859
9 New Hampshire	June 21, 1788	34 Kansas	Jan. 29, 1861
10 Virginia	June 25, 1788	35 West Virginia	June 19, 1863
11 New York	July 26, 1788	36 Nevada	Oct. 31, 1864
12 North Carolina	Nov. 21, 1789	37 Nebraska	Mar. 1, 1867
13 Rhode Island	May 29, 1790	38 Colorado	Aug. 1, 1876
14 Vermont	Mar. 4, 1791	39 North Dakota	Nov. 2, 1889
15 Kentucky	June 1, 1792	40 South Dakota	Nov. 2, 1889
16 Tennessee	June 1, 1796	41 Montana	Nov. 8, 1889
17 Ohio	Mar. 1, 1803	42 Washington	Nov. 11, 1889
18 Louisiana	Apr. 30, 1812	43 Idaho	July 3, 1890
19 Indiana	Dec. 11, 1816	44 Wyoming	July 10, 1890
20 Mississippi	Dec. 10, 1817	45 Utah	Jan. 4, 1896
21 Illinois	Dec. 3, 1818	46 Oklahoma	Nov. 16, 1907
22 Alabama	Dec. 14, 1819	47 New Mexico	Jan. 6, 1912
23 Maine	Mar. 15, 1820	48 Arizona	Feb. 14, 1912
24 Missouri	Aug. 10, 1821	49 Alaska	Jan. 3, 1959
25 Arkansas	June 15, 1836	50 Hawaii	Aug. 21, 1959

*In the case of the first thirteen states, the date given is that of ratification of the Constitution.

Presidential Elections

Year	Candidates	Parties	Popular Vote	Electoral Vote
1789	**GEORGE WASHINGTON (Va.)***			69
	John Adams			34
	Others			35
1792	**GEORGE WASHINGTON (Va.)**			132
	John Adams			77
	George Clinton			50
	Others			5
1796	**JOHN ADAMS (Mass.)**	Federalist		71
	Thomas Jefferson	Democratic-Republican		68
	Thomas Pinckney	Federalist		59
	Aaron Burr	Dem.-Rep.		30
	Others			48
1800	**THOMAS JEFFERSON (Va.)**	Dem.-Rep.		73
	Aaron Burr	Dem.-Rep.		73
	John Adams	Federalist		65
	C. C. Pinckney	Federalist		64
	John Jay	Federalist		1
1804	**THOMAS JEFFERSON (Va.)**	Dem.-Rep.		162
	C. C. Pinckney	Federalist		14
1808	**JAMES MADISON (Va.)**	Dem.-Rep.		122
	C. C. Pinckney	Federalist		47
	George Clinton	Dem.-Rep.		6
1812	**JAMES MADISON (Va.)**	Dem.-Rep.		128
	De Witt Clinton	Federalist		89
1816	**JAMES MONROE (Va.)**	Dem.-Rep.		183
	Rufus King	Federalist		34
1820	**JAMES MONROE (Va.)**	Dem.-Rep.		231
	John Quincy Adams	Dem.-Rep.		1
1824	**JOHN Q. ADAMS (Mass.)**	Dem.-Rep.	108,740	84
	Andrew Jackson	Dem.-Rep.	153,544	99
	William H. Crawford	Dem.-Rep.	46,618	41
	Henry Clay	Dem.-Rep.	47,136	37
1828	**ANDREW JACKSON (Tenn.)**	Democrat	647,286	178
	John Quincy Adams	National Republican	508,064	83

*State of residence at time of election.

Year	Candidates	Parties	Popular Vote	Electoral Vote
1832	**ANDREW JACKSON (Tenn.)**	Democrat	687,502	219
	Henry Clay	National Republican	530,189	49
	John Floyd	Independent		11
	William Wirt	Anti-Mason	33,108	7
1836	**MARTIN VAN BUREN (N.Y.)**	Democrat	765,483	170
	W. H. Harrison	Whig		73
	Hugh L. White	Whig	739,795	26
	Daniel Webster	Whig		14
	W. P. Mangum	Independent		11
1840	**WILLIAM H. HARRISON (Ohio)**	Whig	1,274,624	234
	Martin Van Buren	Democrat	1,127,781	60
	J. G. Birney	Liberty	7,069	—
1844	**JAMES K. POLK (Tenn.)**	Democrat	1,338,464	170
	Henry Clay	Whig	1,300,097	105
	J. G. Birney	Liberty	62,300	—
1848	**ZACHARY TAYLOR (La.)**	Whig	1,360,967	163
	Lewis Cass	Democrat	1,222,342	127
	Martin Van Buren	Free-Soil	291,263	—
1852	**FRANKLIN PIERCE (N.H.)**	Democrat	1,601,117	254
	Winfield Scott	Whig	1,385,453	42
	John P. Hale	Free-Soil	155,825	—
1856	**JAMES BUCHANAN (Pa.)**	Democrat	1,832,955	174
	John C. Frémont	Republican	1,339,932	114
	Millard Fillmore	American	871,731	8
1860	**ABRAHAM LINCOLN (Ill.)**	Republican	1,865,593	180
	Stephen A. Douglas	Democrat	1,382,713	12
	John C. Breckinridge	Democrat	848,356	72
	John Bell	Union	592,906	39
1864	**ABRAHAM LINCOLN (Ill.)***	Republican	2,213,655	212
	George B. McClellan	Democrat	1,805,237	21
1868	**ULYSSES S. GRANT (Ill.)**	Republican	3,012,833	214
	Horatio Seymour	Democrat	2,703,249	80
1872	**ULYSSES S. GRANT (Ill.)**	Republican	3,597,132	286
	Horace Greeley	Democrat; Liberal Republican	2,834,125	66
1876	**RUTHERFORD B. HAYES (Ohio)**	Republican	4,036,298	185
	Samuel J. Tilden	Democrat	4,300,590	184
1880	**JAMES A. GARFIELD (Ohio)**	Republican	4,454,416	214
	Winfield S. Hancock	Democrat	4,444,952	155

*State of residence at time of election.

Year	Candidates	Parties	Popular Vote	Electoral Vote
1884	**GROVER CLEVELAND (N.Y.)**	Democrat	4,874,986	219
	James G. Blaine	Republican	4,851,981	182
1888	**BENJAMIN HARRISON (Ind.)**	Republican	5,439,853	233
	Grover Cleveland	Democrat	5,540,309	168
1892	**GROVER CLEVELAND (N.Y.)**	Democrat	5,556,918	277
	Benjamin Harrison	Republican	5,176,108	145
	James B. Weaver	People's	1,041,028	22
1896	**WILLIAM McKINLEY (Ohio)**	Republican	7,104,779	271
	William J. Bryan	Democrat-People's	6,502,925	176
1900	**WILLIAM McKINLEY (Ohio)**	Republican	7,207,923	292
	William J. Bryan	Dem.-Populist	6,358,133	155
1904	**THEODORE ROOSEVELT (N.Y.)**	Republican	7,623,486	336
	Alton B. Parker	Democrat	5,077,911	140
	Eugene V. Debs	Socialist	402,283	—
1908	**WILLIAM H. TAFT (Ohio)**	Republican	7,678,908	321
	William J. Bryan	Democrat	6,409,104	162
	Eugene V. Debs	Socialist	420,793	—
1912	**WOODROW WILSON (N.J.)**	Democrat	6,293,454	435
	Theodore Roosevelt	Progressive	4,119,538	88
	William H. Taft	Republican	3,484,980	8
	Eugene V. Debs	Socialist	900,672	—
1916	**WOODROW WILSON (N.J.)**	Democrat	9,129,606	277
	Charles E. Hughes	Republican	8,538,221	254
	A. L. Benson	Socialist	585,113	—
1920	**WARREN G. HARDING (Ohio)**	Republican	16,152,200	404
	James M. Cox	Democrat	9,147,353	127
	Eugene V. Debs	Socialist	919,799	—
1924	**CALVIN COOLIDGE (Mass.)**	Republican	15,725,016	382
	John W. Davis	Democrat	8,386,503	136
	Robert M. LaFollette	Progressive	4,822,856	13
1928	**HERBERT HOOVER (Calif.)**	Republican	21,391,381	444
	Alfred E. Smith	Democrat	15,016,443	87
	Norman Thomas	Socialist	267,835	—
1932	**FRANKLIN D. ROOSEVELT (N.Y.)**	Democrat	22,821,857	472
	Herbert Hoover	Republican	15,761,841	59
	Norman Thomas	Socialist	881,951	—
1936	**FRANKLIN D. ROOSEVELT (N.Y.)**	Democrat	27,751,597	523
	Alfred M. Landon	Republican	16,679,583	8
	William Lemke	Union and others	882,479	—
1940	**FRANKLIN D. ROOSEVELT (N.Y.)**	Democrat	27,244,160	449
	Wendell L. Willkie	Republican	22,305,198	82

Year	Candidates	Parties	Popular Vote	Electoral Vote
1944	FRANKLIN D. ROOSEVELT (N.Y.)	Democrat	25,602,504	432
	Thomas E. Dewey	Republican	22,006,285	99
1948	HARRY S TRUMAN (Mo.)	Democrat	24,105,695	304
	Thomas E. Dewey	Republican	21,969,170	189
	J. Strom Thurmond	State-Rights Democrat	1,169,021	38
	Henry A. Wallace	Progressive	1,156,103	—
1952	DWIGHT D. EISENHOWER (N.Y.)	Republican	33,936,252	442
	Adlai E. Stevenson	Democrat	27,314,992	89
1956	DWIGHT D. EISENHOWER (N.Y.)	Republican	35,575,420	457
	Adlai E. Stevenson	Democrat	26,033,066	73
	Other	—	—	1
1960	JOHN F. KENNEDY (Mass.)	Democrat	34,227,096	303
	Richard M. Nixon	Republican	34,108,546	219
	Other	—	—	15
1964	LYNDON B. JOHNSON (Tex.)	Democrat	43,126,506	486
	Barry M. Goldwater	Republican	27,176,799	52
1968	RICHARD M. NIXON (N.Y.)	Republican	31,770,237	301
	Hubert H. Humphrey	Democrat	31,270,533	191
	George Wallace	American Indep.	9,906,141	46
1972	RICHARD M. NIXON (N.Y.)	Republican	47,169,911	520
	George S. McGovern	Democrat	29,170,383	17
	Other	—	—	1

Chief Justices of the United States

John Jay, *N.Y.* 1789–1795
John Rutledge, *S.C.* 1795
Oliver Ellsworth, *Conn.* 1795–1799
John Marshall, *Va.* 1801–1835
Roger B. Taney, *Md.* 1836–1864
Salmon P. Chase, *Ohio* 1864–1873
Morrison R. Waite, *Ohio* 1874–1888
Melville W. Fuller, *Ill.* 1888–1910

Edward D. White, *La.* 1910–1921
William H. Taft, *Ohio* 1921–1930
Charles E. Hughes, *N.Y.* 1930–1941
Harlan F. Stone, *N.Y.* 1941–1946
Fred M. Vinson, *Ky.* 1946–1953
Earl Warren, *Calif.* 1953–1969
Warren E. Burger, *Minn.* 1969–

Speakers of the House of Representatives

F. A. C. Muhlenberg, *Pennsylvania* 1789–1791
Jonathan Trumbull, *Connecticut* 1791–1793
F. A. C. Muhlenberg, *Pennsylvania* 1793–1795
Jonathan Dayton, *New Jersey* 1795–1799
Theodore Sedgwick, *Massachusetts* 1799–1801
Nathaniel Macon, *North Carolina* 1801–1807
Joseph B. Varnum, *Massachusetts* 1807–1811
Henry Clay, *Kentucky* 1811–1814
Langdon Cheves, *South Carolina* 1814–1815
Henry Clay, *Kentucky* 1815–1820
John W. Taylor, *New York* 1820–1821
Philip P. Barbour, *Virginia* 1821–1823
Henry Clay, *Kentucky* 1823–1825
John W. Taylor, *New York* 1825–1827
Andrew Stevenson, *Virginia* 1827–1834
John Bell, *Tennessee* 1834–1835
James K. Polk, *Tennessee* 1835–1839
R. M. T. Hunter, *Virginia* 1839–1841
John White, *Kentucky* 1841–1843
John W. Jones, *Virginia* 1843–1845
John W. Davis, *Indiana* 1845–1847
R. C. Winthrop, *Massachusetts* 1847–1849
Howell Cobb, *Georgia* 1849–1851
Linn Boyd, *Kentucky* 1851–1855
N. P. Banks, *Massachusetts* 1856–1857
James L. Orr, *South Carolina* 1857–1859
William Pennington, *New Jersey* 1860–1861

Galusha A. Grow, *Pennsylvania* 1861–1863
Schuyler Colfax, *Indiana* 1863–1869
James G. Blaine, *Maine* 1869–1875
Michael C. Kerr, *Indiana* 1875–1876
Samuel J. Randall, *Pennsylvania* 1876–1881
Joseph W. Keifer, *Ohio* 1881–1883
John G. Carlisle, *Kentucky* 1883–1889
Thomas B. Reed, *Maine* 1889–1891
Charles F. Crisp, *Georgia* 1891–1895
Thomas B. Reed, *Maine* 1895–1899
David B. Henderson, *Iowa* 1899–1903
Joseph G. Cannon, *Illinois* 1903–1910
Champ Clark, *Missouri* 1911–1919
Frederick H. Gillett, *Massachusetts* 1919–1925
Nicholas Longworth, *Ohio* 1925–1931
John Nance Garner, *Texas* 1931–1933
Henry T. Rainey, *Illinois* 1933–1934
Joseph W. Byrns, *Tennessee* 1935–1936
William B. Bankhead, *Alabama* 1936–1940
Sam Rayburn, *Texas* 1940–1947
Joseph W. Martin, Jr., *Massachusetts* 1947–1949
Sam Rayburn, *Texas* 1949–1953
Joseph W. Martin, Jr., *Massachusetts* 1953–1955
Sam Rayburn, *Texas* 1955–1961
John W. McCormack, *Massachusetts* 1961–1970
Carl Albert, *Oklahoma* 1970–

Presidents, Vice Presidents, and Cabinet Members

President	Vice President	Secretary of State	Secretary of Treasury	Secretary of War
1. George Washington, Federalist 1789	John Adams, Federalist 1789	T. Jefferson 1789 E. Randolph 1794 T. Pickering 1795	Alex. Hamilton 1789 Oliver Wolcott 1795	Henry Knox 1789 T. Pickering 1795 Jas. McHenry 1796
2. John Adams, Federalist 1797	Thomas Jefferson, Dem.-Rep. 1797	T. Pickering 1797 John Marshall 1800	Oliver Wolcott 1797 Samuel Dexter 1801	Jas. McHenry 1797 John Marshall 1800 Samuel Dexter 1800 R. Griswold 1801
3. Thomas Jefferson, Dem.-Rep. 1801	Aaron Burr, Dem.-Rep. 1801 George Clinton, Dem.-Rep. 1805	James Madison 1801	Samuel Dexter 1801 Albert Gallatin 1801	H. Dearborn 1801
4. James Madison, Dem.-Rep. 1809	George Clinton, Dem.-Rep. 1809 Elbridge Gerry, Dem.-Rep. 1813	Robert Smith 1809 James Monroe 1811	Albert Gallatin 1809 G. W. Campbell 1814 A. J. Dallas 1814 W. H. Crawford 1816	Wm. Eustis 1809 J. Armstrong 1813 James Monroe 1814 W. H. Crawford 1815
5. James Monroe, Dem.-Rep. 1817	D. D. Tompkins, Dem.-Rep. 1817	J. Q. Adams 1817	W. H. Crawford 1817	Isaac Shelby 1817 George Graham 1817 J. C. Calhoun 1817
6. John Quincy Adams, Dem.-Rep. 1825	John C. Calhoun, Dem.-Rep. 1825	Henry Clay 1825	Richard Rush 1825	Jas. Barbour 1825 Peter B. Porter 1828
7. Andrew Jackson, Democratic 1829	John C. Calhoun, Democratic 1829 Martin Van Buren, Democratic 1833	M. Van Buren 1829 E. Livingston 1831 Louis McLane 1833 John Forsyth 1834	Sam. D. Ingham 1829 Louis McLane 1831 W. J. Duane 1833 Roger B. Taney 1833 Levi Woodbury 1834	John H. Eaton 1829 Lewis Cass 1831 B. F. Butler 1837
8. Martin Van Buren, Democratic 1837	Richard M. Johnson, Democratic 1837	John Forsyth 1837	Levi Woodbury 1837	Joel R. Poinsett 1837
9. William H. Harrison, Whig 1841	John Tyler, Whig 1841	Daniel Webster 1841	Thomas Ewing 1841	John Bell 1841
10. John Tyler, Whig and Democratic 1841		Daniel Webster 1841 Hugh S. Legaré 1843 Abel P. Upshur 1843 John C. Calhoun 1844	Thomas Ewing 1841 Walter Forward 1841 John C. Spencer 1843 Geo. M. Bibb 1844	John Bell 1841 John McLean 1841 J. C. Spencer 1841 Jas. M. Porter 1843 Wm. Wilkins 1844

President	Vice President			
11. James K. Polk, Democratic 1845	George M. Dallas, Democratic 1845	James Buchanan 1845	Robert J. Walker 1845	William L. Marcy 1845
12. Zachary Taylor, Whig 1849	Millard Fillmore, Whig 1849	John M. Clayton 1849	Wm. M. Meredith 1849	G. W. Crawford 1849
13. Millard Fillmore, Whig 1850		Daniel Webster 1850 Edward Everett 1852	Thomas Corwin 1850	C. M. Conrad 1850
14. Franklin Pierce, Democratic 1853	William R. D. King, Democratic 1853	W. L. Marcy 1853	James Guthrie 1853	Jefferson Davis 1853
15. James Buchanan, Democratic 1857	John C. Breckinridge, Democratic 1857	Lewis Cass 1857 J. S. Black 1860	Howell Cobb 1857 Philip F. Thomas 1860 John A. Dix 1861	John B. Floyd 1857 Joseph Holt 1861
16. Abraham Lincoln, Republican 1861	Hannibal Hamlin, Republican 1861 Andrew Johnson, Unionist 1865	W. H. Seward 1861	Salmon P. Chase 1861 W. P. Fessenden 1864 Hugh McCulloch 1865	S. Cameron 1861 E. M. Stanton 1862
17. Andrew Johnson, Unionist 1865		W. H. Seward 1865	H. McCulloch 1865	E. M. Stanton 1865 U. S. Grant 1867 L. Thomas 1868 J. M. Schofield 1868
18. Ulysses S. Grant, Republican 1869	Schuyler Colfax, Republican 1869 Henry Wilson, Republican 1873	E. B. Washburne 1869 H. Fish 1869	G. S. Boutwell 1869 W. A. Richardson 1873 B. H. Bristow 1874 L. M. Morrill 1876	J. A. Rawlins 1869 W. T. Sherman 1869 W. W. Belknap 1869 A. Taft 1876 J. D. Cameron 1876
19. Rutherford B. Hayes, Republican 1877	William A. Wheeler, Republican 1877	W. M. Evarts 1877	J. Sherman 1877	G. W. McCrary 1877 A. Ramsey 1879
20. James A. Garfield, Republican 1881	Chester A. Arthur, Republican 1881	J. G. Blaine 1881	W. Windom 1881	R. T. Lincoln 1881
21. Chester A. Arthur, Republican 1881		F. T. Frelinghuysen 1881	C. J. Folger 1881 W. Q. Gresham 1884 H. McCulloch 1884	R. T. Lincoln 1881
22. Grover Cleveland, Democratic 1885	T. A. Hendricks, Democratic 1885	T. F. Bayard 1885	D. Manning 1885 C. S. Fairchild 1887	W. C. Endicott 1885
23. Benjamin Harrison, Republican 1889	Levi P. Morton, Republican 1889	J. G. Blaine 1889 J. W. Foster 1892	W. Windom 1889 C. Foster 1891	R. Proctor 1889 S. B. Elkins 1891
24. Grover Cleveland, Democratic 1893	Adlai E. Stevenson, Democratic 1893	W. Q. Gresham 1893 R. Olney 1895	J. G. Carlisle 1893	D. S. Lamont 1893
25. William McKinley, Republican 1897	Garret A. Hobart 1897 Theodore Roosevelt, Republican 1901	J. Sherman 1897 W. R. Day 1897 J. Hay 1898	L. J. Gage 1897	R. A. Alger 1897 E. Root 1899

President	Vice President	Secretary of State	Secretary of Treasury	Secretary of War
26. Theodore Roosevelt, Republican 1901	Chas. W. Fairbanks, Republican 1905	J. Hay 1901 E. Root 1905 R. Bacon 1909	L. J. Gage 1901 L. M. Shaw 1902 G. B. Cortelyou 1907	E. Root 1901 W. H. Taft 1904 L. E. Wright 1908
27. William H. Taft, Republican 1909	James S. Sherman, Republican 1909	P. C. Knox 1909	F. MacVeagh 1909	J. M. Dickinson 1909 H. L. Stimson 1911
28. Woodrow Wilson, Democratic 1913	Thomas R. Marshall, Democratic 1913	W. J. Bryan 1913 R. Lansing 1915 B. Colby 1920	W. G. McAdoo 1913 C. Glass 1918 D. F. Houston 1920	L. M. Garrison 1913 N. D. Baker 1916
29. Warren G. Harding, Republican 1921	Calvin Coolidge, Republican 1921	C. E. Hughes 1921	A. W. Mellon 1921	J. W. Weeks 1921
30. Calvin Coolidge, Republican 1923	Charles G. Dawes, Republican 1925	C. E. Hughes 1923 F. B. Kellogg 1925	A. W. Mellon 1923	J. W. Weeks 1923 D. F. Davis 1925
31. Herbert Hoover, Republican 1929	Charles Curtis, Republican 1929	H. L. Stimson 1929	A. W. Mellon 1929 O. L. Mills 1932	J. W. Good 1929 P. J. Hurley 1929
32. Franklin D. Roosevelt, Democratic 1933	John Nance Garner, Democratic 1933 Henry A. Wallace, Democratic 1941 Harry S Truman, Democratic 1945	C. Hull 1933 E. R. Stettinius, Jr. 1944	W. H. Woodin 1933 H. Morgenthau, Jr. 1934	G. H. Dern 1933 H. A. Woodring 1936 H. L. Stimson 1940
33. Harry S Truman, Democratic 1945	Alben W. Barkley, Democratic 1949	J. F. Byrnes 1945 G. C. Marshall 1947 D. G. Acheson 1949	F. M. Vinson 1945 J. W. Snyder 1946	R. H. Patterson 1945 K. C. Royall 1947 **
34. Dwight D. Eisenhower, Republican 1953	Richard M. Nixon, Republican 1953	J. F. Dulles 1953 C. A. Herter 1959	G. C. Humphrey 1953 R. B. Anderson 1957	
35. John F. Kennedy, Democratic 1961	Lyndon B. Johnson, Democratic 1961	D. Rusk 1961	C. D. Dillon 1961	
36. Lyndon B. Johnson, Democratic 1963	Hubert H. Humphrey, Democratic 1965	D. Rusk 1961	C. D. Dillon 1961 H. H. Fowler 1965	
37. Richard M. Nixon, Republican 1969	Spiro T. Agnew, Republican 1969 Gerald R. Ford, Republican 1973	W. P. Rogers 1969 H. M. Kissinger 1973	D. M. Kennedy 1969 J. B. Connally 1970 G. P. Shultz 1972	
38. Gerald R. Ford, Republican 1974				

**Lost cabinet status in 1947.

	Attorney General	Postmaster General	Secretary of Navy	Secretary of Interior	Secretary of Agriculture	Other Members
(1.)*	E. Randolph 1789 Wm. Bradford 1794 Charles Lee 1795	Samuel Osgood 1789 Tim. Pickering 1791 Jos. Habersham 1795	Established April 30, 1798	Established March 3, 1849		
(2.)	Charles Lee 1797 Theo. Parsons 1801	Jos. Habersham 1797	Benj. Stoddert 1798			
(3.)	Levi Lincoln 1801 Robert Smith 1805 J. Breckenridge 1805 C. A. Rodney 1807	Jos. Habersham 1801 Gideon Granger 1801	Benj. Stoddert 1801 Robert Smith 1801 J. Crowninshield 1805			
(4.)	C. A. Rodney 1809 Wm. Pinkney 1811 Richard Rush 1814	Gideon Granger 1809 R. J. Meigs, Jr. 1814	Paul Hamilton 1809 William Jones 1813 B. W. Crowninshield 1814			
(5.)	Richard Rush 1817 William Wirt 1817	R. J. Meigs, Jr. 1817 John McLean 1823	B. W. Crowninshield 1817 Smith Thompson 1818 S. L. Southard 1823			
(6.)	William Wirt 1825	John McLean 1825	S. L. Southard 1825			
(7.)	John M. Berrien 1829 Roger B. Taney 1831 B. F. Butler 1833	Wm. T. Barry 1829** Amos Kendall 1835	John Branch 1829 Levi Woodbury 1831 Mahlon Dickerson 1834			
(8.)	B. F. Butler 1837 Felix Grundy 1838 H. D. Gilpin 1840	Amos Kendall 1837 John M. Niles 1840	Mahlon Dickerson 1837 Jas. K. Paulding 1838			
(9.)	J. J. Crittenden 1841	Francis Granger 1841	George E. Badger 1841			
(10.)	J. J. Crittenden 1841 Hugh S. Legare 1841 John Nelson 1843	Francis Granger 1841 C. A. Wickliffe 1841	George E. Badger 1841 Abel P. Upshur 1841 David Henshaw 1843 Thomas W. Gilmer 1844 John Y. Mason 1844			
(11.)	John Y. Mason 1845 Nathan Clifford 1846 Isaac Toucey 1848	Cave Johnson 1845	George Bancroft 1845 John Y. Mason 1846			
(12.)	Reverdy Johnson 1849	Jacob Collamer 1849	Wm. B. Preston 1849	Thomas Ewing 1849		*Secretary of Commerce and Labor* Established Feb. 14, 1903. G. B. Cortelyou 1903 V. H. Metcalf 1904 O. S. Straus 1907 C. Nagel 1909 (Department divided, 1913)
(13.)	J. J. Crittenden 1850	Nathan K. Hall 1850 Sam D. Hubbard 1852	Wm. A. Graham 1850 John P. Kennedy 1852	A. H. Stuart 1850		
(14.)	Caleb Cushing 1853	James Campbell 1853	James C. Dobbin 1853	Robert McClelland 1853		
(15.)	J. S. Black 1857 Edw. M. Stanton 1860	Aaron V. Brown 1857 Joseph Holt 1859	Isaac Toucey 1857	Jacob Thompson 1857		

Attorney General	Postmaster General	Secretary of Navy	Secretary of Interior	Secretary of Agriculture	Other Members
					Secretary of Commerce
(16.) Edward Bates 1861 Titian J. Coffey 1863 James Speed 1864	Horatio King 1861 Montgomery Blair 1861 William Dennison 1864	Gideon Welles 1861	Caleb B. Smith 1861 John P. Usher 1863		W. C. Redfield 1913 J. W. Alexander 1919 H. C. Hoover 1921 H. C. Hoover 1925 W. F. Whiting 1928
(17.) J. Speed 1865 H. Stanbery 1866 W. M. Evarts 1868	W. Dennison 1865 A. W. Randall 1866	G. Welles 1865	J. P. Usher 1865 J. Harlan 1865 O. H. Browning 1866	Cabinet status since 1889	R. P. Lamont 1929 R. D. Chapin 1932 D. C. Roper 1933 H. L. Hopkins 1939 J. Jones 1940
(18.) E. R. Hoar 1869 A. T. Ackerman 1870 G. H. Williams 1871 E. Pierrepont 1875 A. Taft 1876	J. A. J. Creswell 1869 J. W. Marshall 1874 M. Jewell 1874 J. N. Tyner 1876	A. E. Borie 1869 G. M. Robeson 1869	J. D. Cox 1869 C. Delano 1870 Z. Chandler 1875		H. A. Wallace 1945 W. A. Harriman 1946 C. W. Sawyer 1948 S. Weeks 1953
(19.) C. Devens 1877	D. M. Key 1877 H. Maynard 1880	R. W. Thompson 1877 N. Goff, Jr. 1881	C. Schurz 1877		L. L. Strauss 1958 F. H. Mueller 1959 L. H. Hodges 1961 J. T. Connor 1965
(20.) W. MacVeagh 1881	T. L. James 1881	W. H. Hunt 1881	S. J. Kirkwood 1881		A. B. Trowbridge 1967 M. H. Stans 1969 P. G. Peterson 1972 F. B. Dent 1973
(21.) B. H. Brewster 1881	T. O. Howe 1881 W. Q. Gresham 1883 F. Hatton 1884	W. E. Chandler 1881	H. M. Teller 1881		*Secretary of Labor* Established March 4, 1913.
(22.) A. H. Garland 1885	W. F. Vilas 1885 D. M. Dickinson 1888	W. C. Whitney 1885	L. Q. C. Lamar 1885 W. F. Vilas 1888	N. J. Colman 1889	W. B. Wilson 1913 J. J. Davis 1921 W. N. Doak 1930 F. Perkins 1933 L. B. Schwellenbach 1945
(23.) W. H. H. Miller 1889	J. Wanamaker 1889	B. F. Tracy 1889	J. W. Noble 1889	J. M. Rusk 1889	M. J. Tobin 1948 M. P. Durkin 1953 J. P. Mitchell 1953 A. J. Goldberg 1961
(24.) R. Olney 1893 J. Harmon 1895	W. S. Bissell 1893 W. L. Wilson 1895	H. A. Herbert 1893	H. Smith 1893 D. R. Francis 1896	J. S. Morton 1893	W. W. Wirtz 1962 G. P. Shultz 1969 J. D. Hodgson 1970 P. J. Brennan 1973
(25.) J. McKenna 1897 J. W. Griggs 1897 P. C. Knox 1901	J. A. Gary 1897 C. E. Smith 1898	J. D. Long 1897	C. N. Bliss 1897 E. A. Hitchcock 1899	J. Wilson 1897	*Secretary of Defense* Established July 26, 1947.
(26.) P. C. Knox 1901 W. H. Moody 1904 C. J. Bonaparte 1907	C. E. Smith 1901 H. C. Payne 1902 R. J. Wynne 1904 G. B. Cortelyou 1905 G. von L. Meyer 1907	J. D. Long 1901 W. H. Moody 1902 P. Morton 1904 C. J. Bonaparte 1905 V. H. Metcalf 1907 T. H. Newberry 1908	E. A. Hitchcock 1901 J. R. Garfield 1907	J. Wilson 1901	J. V. Forrestal 1947 L. A. Johnson 1949 G. C. Marshall 1950
(27.) G. W. Wickersham 1909	F. H. Hitchcock 1909	G. von L. Meyer 1909	R. A. Ballinger 1909 W. L. Fisher 1911	J. Wilson 1909	
(28.) J. C. McReynolds 1913 T. W. Gregory 1914 A. M. Palmer 1919	A. S. Burleson 1913	J. Daniels 1913	F. K. Lane 1913 J. B. Payne 1920	D. F. Houston 1913 E. T. Meredith 1920	
(29.) H. M. Daugherty 1921	W. H. Hays 1921 H. Work 1922 H. S. New 1923	E. Denby 1921	A. B. Fall 1921 H. Work 1923	H. C. Wallace 1921	

(30.) H. M. Daugherty 1923
H. F. Stone 1924
J. G. Sargent 1925

(31.) W. D. Mitchell 1929

(32.) H. S. Cummings 1933
F. Murphy 1939
R. H. Jackson 1940
F. Biddle 1941

(33.) T. C. Clark 1945
J. H. McGrath 1949
J. P. McGranery 1952

(34.) H. Brownell, Jr. 1953
W. P. Rogers 1957

(35.) R. F. Kennedy 1961

(36.) N. de Katzenbach 1965
W. R. Clark 1967

(37.) J. N. Mitchell 1969
R. G. Kleindienst 1972
E. L. Richardson 1973
W. B. Saxbe 1973

H. S. New 1923

W. F. Brown 1929

J. A. Farley 1933
F. C. Walker 1940

R. E. Hannegan 1945
J. L. Donaldson 1947

A. E. Summerfield 1953

J. E. Day 1961
J. Gronovski 1963

L. F. O'Brien 1965
W. M. Watson 1968

W. Blount 1969
†††

E. Denby 1923
Curtis D. Wilbur 1924

C. F. Adams 1929

C. A. Swanson 1933
C. Edison 1940
F. Knox 1940
J. V. Forrestal 1944

J. V. Forrestal 1945
††

H. Work 1923
R. O. West 1928

R. L. Wilbur 1929

H. L. Ickes 1933

H. L. Ickes 1945
J. A. Krug 1946
O. L. Chapman 1951

D. McKay 1953
F. Seaton 1956

S. L. Udall 1961

W. J. Hickel 1969
R. C. B. Morton 1971

H. C. Wallace 1923
H. M. Gore 1924
W. M. Jardine 1925

A. M. Hyde 1929

H. A. Wallace 1933
C. R. Wickard 1940

C. P. Anderson 1945
C. F. Brannan 1948

E. T. Benson 1953

O. L. Freeman 1961

C. M. Hardin 1969
E. L. Butz 1971

R. A. Lovett 1951
C. E. Wilson 1953
N. McElroy 1957
T. S. Gates, Jr. 1959
R. S. McNamara 1961
C. Clifford 1968
M. R. Laird 1969
E. L. Richardson 1973
J. R. Schlesinger 1973

Secretary of Health,
Education, and
Welfare
Established
April 1, 1953.
O. C. Hobby 1953
M. B. Folsom 1955
A. S. Flemming 1958
A. A. Ribicoff 1961
A. J. Celebrezze 1962
J. W. Gardner 1965
W. J. Cohen 1968
R. H. Finch 1969
E. L. Richardson 1970
C. W. Weinberger 1973

Secretary of Housing
and Urban
Development
Established
September 9, 1965.
R. C. Weaver 1966
G. Romney 1969
J. T. Lynn 1973

Secretary of
Transportation
Established October 15, 1966.
A. S. Boyd 1966
J. A. Volpe 1969
C. S. Brinegar 1973

---

*Numbers in parentheses indicate presidential administration.
**The postmaster general did not become a cabinet member until 1829.
††Lost cabinet status in 1947.
†††Discontinued in 1971.

Population of the United States

Division and State	1790	1800	1810	1820	1830	1840	1850	1860	1870
United States	3,929,214	5,308,483	7,239,881	9,638,453	12,866,020	17,069,453	23,191,876	31,443,321	39,818,449
GEOGRAPHIC DIVISIONS									
New England	1,009,408	1,233,011	1,471,973	1,660,071	1,954,717	2,234,822	2,728,116	3,135,283	3,487,924
Middle Atlantic	952,632	1,402,565	2,014,702	2,699,845	3,587,664	4,526,260	5,898,735	7,458,985	8,810,806
South Atlantic	1,851,806	2,286,494	2,674,891	3,061,063	3,645,752	3,925,299	4,679,090	5,364,703	5,853,610
East South Central	109,368	335,407	708,590	1,190,489	1,815,969	2,575,445	3,363,271	4,020,991	4,404,445
West South Central			77,618	167,680	246,127	449,985	940,251	1,747,667	2,029,965
East North Central		51,006	272,324	792,719	1,470,018	2,924,728	4,523,260	6,926,884	9,124,517
West North Central			19,783	66,586	140,455	426,814	880,335	2,169,832	3,856,594
Mountain							72,927	174,923	315,385
Pacific							105,871	444,053	675,125
NEW ENGLAND									
Maine	96,540	151,719	228,705	298,335	399,455	501,793	583,169	628,279	626,915
New Hampshire	141,885	183,858	214,460	244,161	269,328	284,574	317,976	326,073	318,300
Vermont	85,425	154,465	217,895	235,981	280,652	291,948	314,120	315,098	330,551
Massachusetts	378,787	422,845	472,040	523,287	610,408	737,699	994,514	1,231,066	1,457,351
Rhode Island	68,825	69,122	76,931	83,059	97,199	108,830	147,545	174,620	217,353
Connecticut	237,946	251,002	261,942	275,248	297,675	309,978	370,792	460,147	537,454
MIDDLE ATLANTIC									
New York	340,120	589,051	959,049	1,372,812	1,918,608	2,428,921	3,097,394	3,880,735	4,382,759
New Jersey	184,139	211,149	245,562	277,575	320,823	373,306	489,555	672,035	906,096
Pennsylvania	434,373	602,365	810,091	1,049,458	1,348,233	1,724,033	2,311,786	2,906,215	3,521,951
SOUTH ATLANTIC									
Delaware	59,096	64,273	72,674	72,749	76,748	78,085	91,532	112,216	125,015
Maryland	319,728	341,548	380,546	407,350	447,040	470,019	583,034	687,049	780,894
Dist. of Columbia		14,093	24,023	33,039	39,834	43,712	51,687	75,080	131,700
Virginia	747,610	880,200	974,600	1,065,366	1,211,405	1,239,797	1,421,661	1,596,318	1,225,163
West Virginia									442,014
North Carolina	393,751	478,103	555,500	638,829	737,987	753,419	869,039	992,622	1,071,361
South Carolina	249,073	345,591	415,115	502,741	581,185	594,398	668,507	703,708	705,606
Georgia	82,548	162,686	252,433	340,989	516,823	691,392	906,185	1,057,286	1,184,109
Florida					34,730	54,477	87,445	140,424	187,748
EAST SOUTH CENTRAL									
Kentucky	73,677	220,955	406,511	564,317	687,917	779,828	982,405	1,155,684	1,321,011
Tennessee	35,691	105,602	261,727	422,823	681,904	829,210	1,002,717	1,109,801	1,258,520
Alabama				127,901	309,527	590,756	771,623	964,201	996,992
Mississippi		8,850	40,352	75,448	136,621	375,651	606,526	791,305	827,922
WEST SOUTH CENTRAL									
Arkansas			1,062	14,273	30,388	97,574	209,897	435,450	484,471
Louisiana			76,556	153,407	215,739	352,411	517,762	708,002	726,915
Texas							212,592	604,215	818,579

EAST NORTH CENTRAL								
Ohio	45,365	230,760	581,434	937,903	1,519,467	1,980,329	2,339,511	2,665,260
Indiana	5,641	24,520	147,178	343,031	685,866	988,416	1,350,428	1,680,637
Illinois		12,282	55,211	157,445	476,183	851,470	1,711,951	2,539,981
Michigan		4,762	8,896	31,639	212,267	397,654	749,113	1,184,059
Wisconsin					30,945	305,391	775,881	1,054,670
WEST NORTH CENTRAL								
Minnesota						6,077	172,023	439,706
Iowa					43,112	192,214	674,913	1,194,020
Missouri		19,783	66,586	140,455	383,702	682,044	1,182,012	1,721,295
North Dakota								2,405
South Dakota								11,776
Nebraska							28,841	122,993
Kansas							107,206	364,399
MOUNTAIN								
Montana								20,595
Idaho								14,999
Wyoming								9,118
Colorado							34,277	39,864
New Mexico						61,547	93,516	91,874
Arizona								9,658
Utah						11,380	40,273	86,786
Nevada							6,857	42,491
PACIFIC								
Washington							11,594	23,955
Oregon						13,294	52,465	90,923
California						92,597	379,994	560,247

Division and State	1970	1960	1950	1940	1930	1920	1910	1900	1890	1880
UNITED STATES	203,211,926	179,323,175	150,697,361	131,669,275	122,775,046	105,710,620	91,972,266	75,994,575	62,947,714	50,155,783
GEOGRAPHIC DIVISIONS										
New England	11,841,663	10,509,367	9,314,453	8,437,290	8,166,341	7,400,909	6,552,681	5,592,017	4,700,749	4,010,529
Middle Atlantic	37,199,040	34,168,452	30,163,533	27,539,487	26,260,750	22,261,144	19,315,892	15,454,678	12,706,220	10,496,878
South Atlantic	30,671,337	25,971,732	21,182,335	17,823,151	15,793,589	13,990,272	12,194,895	10,443,480	8,857,922	7,597,197
East South Central	12,803,470	12,050,126	11,477,181	10,778,225	9,887,214	8,893,307	8,409,901	7,547,757	6,429,154	5,585,151
West South Central	19,320,560	16,951,255	14,537,572	13,064,525	12,176,830	10,242,224	8,784,534	6,532,290	4,740,983	3,334,220
East North Central	40,252,476	36,225,024	30,399,368	26,626,342	25,297,185	21,475,543	18,250,621	15,985,581	13,478,305	11,206,668
West North Central	16,319,187	15,394,115	14,061,394	13,516,990	13,296,915	12,544,249	11,637,921	10,347,423	8,932,112	6,157,443
Mountain	8,281,562	6,855,060	5,074,998	4,150,003	3,701,789	3,336,101	2,633,517	1,674,657	1,213,935	653,119
Pacific	25,453,688	20,339,105	14,486,527	9,733,262	8,194,433	5,566,871	4,192,304	2,416,692	1,888,334	1,114,578
Noncontiguous	1,068,943	858,939								
NEW ENGLAND										
Maine	992,048	969,265	913,774	847,226	797,423	768,014	742,371	694,466	661,086	648,936
New Hampshire	731,681	606,921	533,242	491,524	465,293	443,083	430,572	411,588	376,530	346,991
Vermont	444,330	389,881	377,747	359,231	359,611	352,428	355,956	343,641	332,422	332,286
Massachusetts	5,689,110	5,148,578	4,690,514	4,316,721	4,249,614	3,852,356	3,366,416	2,805,346	2,238,947	1,783,085
Rhode Island	946,725	859,488	791,896	713,346	687,497	604,397	542,610	428,556	345,506	276,531
Connecticut	3,031,709	2,535,234	2,007,280	1,709,242	1,606,903	1,380,631	1,114,756	908,420	746,258	622,700
MIDDLE ATLANTIC										
New York	18,236,967	16,782,304	14,830,192	13,479,142	12,588,066	10,385,227	9,113,614	7,268,894	6,003,174	5,082,871
New Jersey	7,168,164	6,066,782	4,835,329	4,160,165	4,041,334	3,155,900	2,537,167	1,883,669	1,444,933	1,131,116
Pennsylvania	11,793,909	11,319,366	10,498,012	9,900,180	9,631,350	8,720,017	7,665,111	6,302,115	5,258,113	4,282,891
SOUTH ATLANTIC										
Delaware	548,104	446,292	318,085	266,505	238,380	223,003	202,322	184,735	168,493	146,608
Maryland	3,922,399	3,100,689	2,343,001	1,821,244	1,631,526	1,449,661	1,295,346	1,188,044	1,042,390	934,943
Dist. of Columbia	756,510	763,956	802,178	663,091	486,869	437,571	331,069	278,718	230,392	177,624
Virginia	4,648,494	3,966,949	3,318,680	2,677,773	2,421,851	2,309,187	2,061,612	1,854,184	1,655,980	1,512,565
West Virginia	1,744,237	1,860,421	2,005,552	1,901,974	1,729,205	1,463,701	1,221,119	958,800	762,794	618,457
North Carolina	5,082,059	4,556,155	4,061,929	3,571,623	3,170,276	2,559,123	2,206,287	1,893,810	1,617,949	1,399,750
South Carolina	2,590,516	2,382,594	2,117,027	1,899,804	1,738,765	1,683,724	1,515,400	1,340,316	1,151,149	995,577
Georgia	4,589,575	3,943,116	3,444,578	3,123,723	2,908,506	2,895,832	2,609,121	2,216,331	1,837,353	1,542,180
Florida	6,789,443	4,951,560	2,771,305	1,897,414	1,468,211	968,470	752,619	528,542	391,422	269,493
EAST SOUTH CENTRAL										
Kentucky	3,218,706	3,038,156	2,944,806	2,845,627	2,614,589	2,416,630	2,289,905	2,147,174	1,858,635	1,648,690
Tennessee	3,923,687	3,567,089	3,291,718	2,915,841	2,616,556	2,337,885	2,184,789	2,020,616	1,767,518	1,542,359
Alabama	3,444,165	3,266,740	3,061,743	2,832,961	2,646,248	2,348,174	2,138,093	1,828,697	1,513,401	1,262,505
Mississippi	2,216,912	2,178,141	2,178,914	2,183,796	2,009,821	1,790,618	1,797,114	1,551,270	1,289,600	1,131,597
WEST SOUTH CENTRAL										
Arkansas	1,923,285	1,786,272	1,909,511	1,949,387	1,854,482	1,752,204	1,574,449	1,311,564	1,128,211	802,525
Louisiana	3,641,306	3,257,022	2,683,516	2,363,880	2,101,593	1,798,509	1,656,388	1,381,625	1,118,588	939,946
Oklahoma	2,559,229	2,328,284	2,233,351	2,336,434	2,396,040	2,028,283	1,657,155	790,391	258,657	
Texas	11,196,730	9,579,677	7,711,194	6,414,824	5,824,715	4,663,228	3,896,542	3,048,710	2,235,527	1,591,749
EAST NORTH CENTRAL										
Ohio	10,652,017	9,706,397	7,946,627	6,907,612	6,646,697	5,759,394	4,767,121	4,157,545	3,672,329	3,198,062
Indiana	5,193,669	4,662,498	3,934,224	3,427,796	3,238,503	2,930,390	2,700,876	2,516,462	2,192,404	1,978,301
Illinois	11,113,976	10,081,158	8,712,176	7,897,241	7,630,654	6,485,280	5,638,591	4,821,550	3,826,352	3,077,871
Michigan	8,875,083	7,823,194	6,371,766	5,256,106	4,842,325	3,668,412	2,810,173	2,420,982	2,093,890	1,636,937
Wisconsin	4,417,731	3,951,777	3,434,576	3,137,587	2,939,006	2,632,067	2,333,860	2,069,042	1,693,330	1,315,497

WEST NORTH CENTRAL										
Minnesota	780,773	1,310,283	1,751,394	2,075,708	2,387,125	2,563,953	2,792,300	2,982,483	3,413,864	3,804,971
Iowa	1,624,615	1,912,297	2,231,853	2,224,771	2,404,021	2,470,939	2,538,268	2,621,073	2,757,537	2,824,376
Missouri	2,168,380	2,679,185	3,106,665	3,293,335	3,404,055	3,629,367	3,784,664	3,954,653	4,319,813	4,676,501
North Dakota	36,909	190,983	319,146	577,056	646,872	680,845	641,935	619,636	632,446	617,761
South Dakota	98,268	348,600	401,570	583,888	636,547	692,849	642,961	652,740	680,514	665,507
Nebraska	452,402	1,062,656	1,066,300	1,192,214	1,296,372	1,377,963	1,315,834	1,325,510	1,411,330	1,483,493
Kansas	996,096	1,428,108	1,470,495	1,690,949	1,769,257	1,880,999	1,801,028	1,905,299	2,178,611	2,246,578
MOUNTAIN										
Montana	39,159	142,924	243,329	376,053	548,889	537,606	559,456	591,024	674,767	694,409
Idaho	32,610	88,548	161,772	325,594	431,866	445,032	524,873	588,637	667,191	712,567
Wyoming	20,789	62,555	92,531	145,965	194,402	225,565	250,742	290,529	330,066	332,416
Colorado	194,327	413,249	539,700	799,024	939,629	1,035,791	1,123,296	1,325,089	1,753,947	2,207,259
New Mexico	119,565	160,282	195,310	327,301	360,350	423,317	531,818	681,187	951,023	1,016,000
Arizona	40,440	88,243	122,931	204,354	334,162	435,573	499,261	749,587	1,302,161	1,770,900
Utah	143,963	210,779	276,749	373,351	449,396	507,847	550,310	688,862	890,627	1,059,273
Nevada	62,266	47,355	42,335	81,875	77,407	91,058	110,247	160,083	285,278	488,738
PACIFIC										
Washington	75,116	357,232	518,103	1,141,990	1,356,621	1,563,396	1,736,191	2,378,963	2,853,214	3,409,169
Oregon	174,768	317,704	413,536	672,765	783,389	953,786	1,089,684	1,521,341	1,768,687	2,091,385
California	864,694	1,213,398	1,485,053	2,377,549	3,426,861	5,677,251	6,907,387	10,586,223	15,717,204	19,953,134
NONCONTIGUOUS										
Alaska									226,167	300,382
Hawaii									632,772	786,561

About the Authors

RICHARD N. CURRENT is University Distinguished Professor of History at the University of North Carolina at Greensboro. He is co-author of the Bancroft Prize-winning *Lincoln the President*. His books include: *Three Carpetbag Governors; The Lincoln Nobody Knows; Daniel Webster and the Rise of National Conservatism;* and *Secretary Stimson*. Professor Current has lectured on U.S. history in Europe, Asia, South America, Australia, and Antarctica. He has been a Fulbright Lecturer at the University of Munich and the University of Chile at Santiago, and has served as Harmsworth Professor of American History at Oxford. He is President of the Southern Historical Association.

T. HARRY WILLIAMS is Boyd Professor of History at Louisiana State University. He was awarded both the 1969 Pulitzer Prize and National Book Award for his biography of *Huey Long*. His books include: *Lincoln and His Generals; Lincoln and the Radicals; P.G.T. Beauregard; Americans at War; Romance and Realism in Southern Politics; Hayes of the Twenty-Third; McClellan, Sherman, and Grant; The Union Sundered;* and *The Union Restored*. Professor Williams has been a Harmsworth Professor of American History at Oxford and President of both the Southern Historical Association and the Organization of American Historians.

FRANK FREIDEL is Charles Warren Professor of History at Harvard University. He is writing a six-volume biography of Franklin D. Roosevelt, four volumes of which have been published. Among his other books are: *Our Country's Presidents; F.D.R. and the South;* and *America in the Twentieth Century*. He is co-editor of the 1974 edition of the *Harvard Guide to American History,* and Vice President of the Organization of American Historians. He is also a former president of the New England Historical Society.

This book was set on the Linofilm in Textype, a typeface designed primarily for printing textbooks and related works requiring intensive study and prolonged reading. Its letter shapes and word patterns have been authenticated by modern scientific research in readability. Its features of design give it optimum characteristics of visibility and speed of reading with a minimum of fatigue. Originally designed and cut for Mergenthaler Linotype in 1929.

Composed by American Can Co., Printing Division, Clarinda, Iowa; printed and bound by the Kingsport Press, Kingsport, Tenn.

Color essays printed by New York City Press, New York, N.Y.